To Mm
Av   '87.

Jonathan, Victoria
Joe, Virginia +
Kieran.
xxx

D1587064

Cooking with
Robert Carrier

Cooking with
Robert Carrier

Hamlyn
London · New York · Sydney · Toronto

Photography in this book by Christian Delu, John Miller,
Jack Nisberg, Iain Reid, Pipe-Rich

Design by Martin Atcherley for The Nassington Press Ltd

Line drawings by Vana Haggarty, Sally Launder, Terri Lawler,
Ann Savage, Kate Simunek

Cover photography by Martin Brigdale

The material in this book has previously been published by
The Hamlyn Publishing Group in five volumes:
*Robert Carrier Great Starters, Great Main Dishes,
Great Casseroles, Great Salads and Vegetables,
Great Desserts and Pastries*
© Copyright Robert Carrier 1978
Some of the material also appeared in *The Robert Carrier Cookbook*
Published in 1965 by Thomas Nelson and Sons Ltd
© Copyright Robert Carrier 1965

This edition published by
The Hamlyn Publishing Group Limited
London · New York · Sydney · Toronto
Astronaut House, Feltham, Middlesex, England

© Copyright Robert Carrier 1982

Third impression 1984

ISBN 0 600 32301 3

Printed in Italy

Contents

Introduction

A comfortable chair, delicious food and witty, friendly conversation – these are the perfect components for a successful evening. And important above all is the food – nothing fussy, nothing contrived, just fresh, delicious ingredients presented as simply as possible by a hostess (or host) who is as relaxed and as unflustered as the guests.

I've planned this book so that even a beginner cook can successfully use the recipes simply by following the easy step-by-step instructions. So choose your menus carefully from this book so that there is no last-minute dash into the kitchen to stir a sauce or turn a spit. All this should be done in advance. And remember, the best results are achieved by choosing what *you* enjoy doing most, something with which *you* are most confident.

But don't be afraid to experiment: the excitement of food is in discovery. Only try out your new ideas first on your family or friends and not at a formal dinner party! You will find that just a touch of spice here – a sprinkling of fresh herbs there – can make a great deal of difference to the simplest dish. Then stir in a reduction of stock or wine to give your sauce or casserole depth of flavour and who knows what a world of difference you can bring to your favourite recipe?

And remember, however sophisticated your taste in food, I am convinced there is nothing to beat the flavour of fresh seasonal ingredients, especially in these days when we can have whatever we like at any time of the year. Are we in danger, I wonder, of losing one of the great delights of man? The excitement of the first tender tips of asparagus, the fresh sweet taste of picked strawberries, still warm from the sun, and the satisfaction of bringing your own crop of fresh herbs, garden peas, new potatoes, lettuce and tomatoes to the table.

The next time you are planning a memorable dinner, decide on an imaginative first course to set the mood for the meal to follow, choosing any of these tempting and delicious starters, from 'cooked appetisers from around the world', prepared with all the traditional spices and flavours which produce their characteristic aroma, to pancakes combined with rich sauces and seafood or with ham and cheese. Or try saffron rice with avocado with its delicate taste of wine and fascinating colour.

Dinner parties should be a pleasure, each course a gastronomic delight over which the host or hostess can relax and enjoy the company, so choose a main dish which you can prepare with confidence without spoiling your own enjoyment of the meal.

The fish recipes cover all manner of sea and fresh-water fish, from salmon to the humbler herring. There are succulent recipes for beef using a multitude of different cuts. Imagine thick tournedos, the juices captured in a light crust of flaky pastry with mushrooms and *pâté*, or a simple hamburger made with lean rump steak, spiked with fresh herbs. If you choose lamb, you will find all the classic favourites plus many more unusual ideas such as Bourbon barbecued lamb.

And for those to whom no meal is complete without a proper dessert, this collection of desserts and pastries will prove to be a treasury of 'meal-makers': home-made ice creams, sorbets, creams and custards, a selection of soufflés, both hot and cold, and dessert *crêpes* and fritters with fillings of fresh fruit with liqueur make exotic departures from the usual sweets and puddings. For a winter meal, what more mouth-watering a finale than a steamed pudding? Try some of these great hot desserts, moist with fruit and fragrant with spices. And last, but not least, are the cakes, and what cakes! Cheesecakes, devil's food cake, summer almond cake – all of them a paradise for the sweet-toothed.

In the following pages, I share with you some of my favourite recipes. I hope that you will find as much pleasure in their preparation as I have in their creation. The secret of presenting food at its best is that there *is* no 'art' to it . . . save that of being yourself. This simply means sticking to your own standards, not those you imagine are expected of you. And doing what you know you do best. In this way you can't fail to succeed.

Happy cooking!

Choosing Your Menu

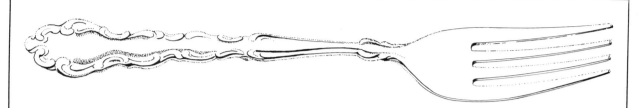

Choosing Your Menu

The conventional opening for a formal dinner has always been clear soup, followed by fish, an entrée and a pudding. But why be conventional? There are no longer any rules for this sort of thing. I much prefer a memorable dish such as **crêpes aux sardines,** a recipe brought back by the hostess from a holiday on the Basque coast – served with imagination and pride – to all the clear soups in the world. I shall always remember those *crêpes,* crisply golden, with their delicately blended filling of fresh sardines, pounded over ice and mixed (like *quenelles*) with whipped cream and egg white, and indeed, I have since served them (the sincerest form of flattery) at my own dinners. The *crêpes* were followed by **poulet à la basquaise,** chicken in a white wine sauce, served with baked green peppers stuffed with saffron rice.

So be adventurous and try new ways with old favourites – serve cold lamb with *mayonnaise comme au Pay des Landes*, creamy mayonnaise lightly flavoured with garlic; try the humble mussel, skewered *en brochette* with alternate slices of bacon, the whole rolled in flour, egg yolk and breadcrumbs, deep-fried in golden oil and served with sauce Béarnaise; or slit 'pockets' in thick lamb chops and stuff them with savoury garlic and herb butter. Delicious!

Serve a fillet of beef *en croûte*, but first cut your fillet into thick serving pieces; spread each slice with a paste of finely chopped mushrooms and onion which you have sautéed in butter until soft, and insert a slice of cooked ham or boiled bacon between each slice. This is skewered together and roasted in the usual way before being wrapped in its envelope of puff pastry and baked to golden perfection. It is as delicious cold as it is hot and makes an excellent buffet party dish as well. And for a gala party with no holds barred, precede this dish with salmon soufflé mousse with a prawn and lobster sauce. The mousse – a *quenelle*-like mixture – can be prepared in individual soufflé dishes or in one large ovenproof dish. Sometimes I turn it out just before serving and cover it with its sauce; at other times I serve it in the dish it was baked in, with the sauce passed separately. Either way it is a most attractive first course.

Your menu depends to some extent, of course, on the amount of time you have for preparation and on the time it takes to gather your guests to the table. I like to plan all dinner parties so that nothing, absolutely nothing, will spoil if kept waiting.

If guests are apt to be a little late, it is a good idea to copy the Russian *zakouski* table, set up in a room adjoining the drawing-room and wheeled in. I find this an easy and rather stimulating way to soften the cares of service, and often produce *hors-d'oeuvre*, both hot and cold in the Russian manner, in the drawing-room before going in to dinner, where a hot meat dish – or a hot fish dish followed by cold meats and salad – awaits the guests.

The meal can start in this way with, instead of soup, something which requires absolutely no preparation: the thinnest slices of smoked salmon served with fresh wedges of lemon on an oiled platter, or rolled (budget notwithstanding) around sombre cargoes of Russian caviar; smoked eels or sturgeon, served on beds of chopped ice; and firm pink slices of tongue and ham with olives. Perhaps greenhouse cucumbers, marinated in a soured cream and chives dressing, could bring a touch of early spring to your menu.

Useful Facts and Figures

Notes on metrication

When making any of the recipes in this book, only follow one set of measures as they are not interchangeable.

In this book quantities are given in metric and Imperial measures. Exact conversion from Imperial to metric measures does not usually give very convenient working quantities and so the metric measures have been rounded off into units of 25 grams. The table below shows the recommended equivalents.

Ounces	Approx gram to nearest whole figure	Recommended conversion to nearest unit of 25
1	28	25
2	57	50
3	85	75
4	113	100
5	142	150
6	170	175
7	198	200
8	227	225
9	255	250
10	283	275
11	312	300
12	340	350
13	368	375
14	396	400
15	425	425
16 (1 lb)	454	450
17	482	475
18	510	500
19	539	550
20 ($1\frac{1}{4}$ lb)	567	575

Note: When converting quantities over 20 oz first add the appropriate figures in the centre column, then adjust to the nearest unit of 25. As a general guide, 1 kg (1000 g) equals 2.2 lb or about 2 lb 3 oz. This method of conversion gives good results in nearly all cases, although in certain pastry and cake recipes a more accurate conversion is necessary to produce a balanced recipe.

Liquid measures

The millilitre has been used in this book and the following table gives a few examples.

Imperial	Approx ml to nearest whole figure	Recommended ml
$\frac{1}{4}$ pint	142	150 ml
$\frac{1}{2}$ pint	283	300 ml
$\frac{3}{4}$ pint	425	450 ml
1 pint	567	600 ml
$1\frac{1}{2}$ pints	851	900 ml
$1\frac{3}{4}$ pints	992	1000 ml (1 litre)

Can sizes

At present, cans are marked with the exact (usually to the nearest whole number) metric equivalent of the Imperial weight of the contents, so we have followed this practice when giving can sizes.

Oven temperatures

The table below gives recommended equivalents.

	°C	°F	Gas Mark
Very cool	110	225	$\frac{1}{4}$
	120	250	$\frac{1}{2}$
Cool	140	275	1
	150	300	2
Moderate	160	325	3
	180	350	4
Moderately hot	190	375	5
	200	400	6
Hot	220	425	7
	230	450	8
Very hot	240	475	9

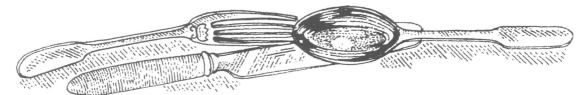

Notes for American and Australian users

In America the 8-oz measuring cup is used. In Australia metric measures are now used in conjunction with the standard 250-ml measuring cup. The Imperial pint, used in Britain and Australia, is 20 fl oz, while the American pint is 16 fl oz. It is important to remember that the Australian tablespoon differs from both the British and American tablespoons; the table below gives a comparison. The British standard tablespoon, which has been used throughout this book, holds 17.7 ml, the American 14.2 ml, and the Australian 20 ml. A teaspoon holds approximately 5 ml in all three countries.

British	American	Australian
1 teaspoon	1 teaspoon	1 teaspoon
1 tablespoon	1 tablespoon	1 tablespoon
2 tablespoons	3 tablespoons	2 tablespoons
$3\frac{1}{2}$ tablespoons	4 tablespoons	3 tablespoons
4 tablespoons	5 tablespoons	$3\frac{1}{2}$ tablespoons

An Imperial/American guide to solid and liquid measures

Solid measures

Imperial	American
1 lb butter or margarine	2 cups
1 lb flour	4 cups
1 lb granulated or castor sugar	2 cups
1 lb icing sugar	3 cups
8 oz rice	1 cup

Liquid measures

Imperial	American
$\frac{1}{4}$ pint liquid	$\frac{2}{3}$ cup liquid
$\frac{1}{2}$ pint	$1\frac{1}{4}$ cups
$\frac{3}{4}$ pint	2 cups
1 pint	$2\frac{1}{2}$ cups
$1\frac{1}{2}$ pints	$3\frac{3}{4}$ cups
2 pints	5 cups ($2\frac{1}{2}$ pints)

Starters

A glass of smoke-filled **pastis**, a dish of those perfect, hard, little green olives that are the natural fruit of Provence, and a parcel of bright blue sea stretching as far as the human eye can reach – and then some – is my idea of a summer meal of perfection. At least, the humble beginnings of a summer meal that might continue, if I were marooned in one of the little fishing ports along the coast of sunny Provence, with a Provençal anchovy salad, made with salted anchovies, wine and olive oil, and spiked with fresh herbs and thin lemon slices. The whole is marinated until the anchovies are tender and soft, and the essence of the lemon and herbs has permeated the flesh of these delicious fish.

In Britain we can get salted anchovies by the piece or the quarter pound from little speciality shops in Soho, or buy them in large cans and use them as the occasion warrants. It is an easy task to wash away the salt in which they are packed, snip off the heads and tails, and gently prise the rose-tinted fillets from their bones. It is simplicity itself to place these fillets carefully in a bowl and douse them in equal quantities of olive oil and red wine. They are then flavoured, as the spirit moves you, with finely chopped shallots, onions or garlic, or a hint of all three, and a judicious sprinkling of finely chopped fresh parsley, chives or basil and, of course, several thin rounds of lemon.

Another cool, summery-tasting appetiser that I enjoy preparing is the Greek fish pâté called **taramasalata**. My more sophisticated, softer tasting version uses cream cheese for its creamy emulsion instead of the more traditional boiled potato or white bread. Taramasalata is an eastern cousin of Provençal **poutargue** – salted and smoked roe of tuna or grey mullet, sliced thinly and served as an *hors-d'oeuvre* with freshly ground black pepper, olive oil and lemon juice. **Taramasalata** uses smoked cod's roe rather than tuna or grey mullet and is quite delicious.

Freshly caught fish from the Gulf of Pampelonne, just thirty feet across the sands from the open-air barbecues where they are cooked, is one of the great delights of St. Tropez in the summer. Some of the little restaurants along the beach are beginning to do barbecued fish and shellfish appetisers for lunch, and can be tempted to carry this on to late-night suppers under the stars. Everything here is of optimum freshness. The vegetables – and even the wines served at one or two of these restaurants – come from the farms and vineyards located in the flatlands just behind the beach. A recent meal I enjoyed there began with a sumptious **salade niçoise** – tiny whole artichokes sliced with celery, onions, radishes, small green peppers, tomatoes, cucumber and lettuce, and garnished with black olives, quarters of hard-boiled egg, tuna fish and anchovies, dressed with a wine vinegar and olive oil dressing. This was followed by fresh sardines from the Gulf, brushed with a sauce of olive oil, lemon juice and fresh herbs, grilled over charcoal, and served with a dressing of melted butter and finely chopped tarragon. Melon and black coffee provided the finale to a perfect open-air meal.

Barbecued lobster makes a delectable first course, too, when split, enfolded in fresh sprigs of tarragon, basil and chervil, and grilled to succulent, pink-shelled perfection over the coals. I like to dribble olive oil and lemon juice on them during cooking and serve them simply with melted butter to which finely chopped herbs and a little lemon juice impart their own special flavours.

Hot and Cold Appetisers

There are almost countless numbers of appetisers, but the preparation of a large number of them requires the skill of a professional chef, to say nothing of a great amount of time and expensive ingredients.

Heading the list of simpler ones are oysters on the half-shell, six or nine freshly opened natives of Colchester or Whitstable, served on ice with coarse black pepper, and a wedge or two of lemon. Surround them with tiny sausages, piping hot, as they do in Northern France; or remove the oysters from their shells, roll them in fresh breadcrumbs and fry them in oil and butter. Serve immediately with a Bérnaise sauce, or more simply, with wedges of lemon.

I like, too, great oiled platters of smoked fish – salmon, sturgeon, trout and eel – or small cups of dressed crab, prawns and lobster served on individual trays of crushed ice with a choice of subtle sauces. And here a word of warning: don't have seafood sauces too pungent and sharp if fine wines accompany the first course, or are to follow. Better serve your fresh shellfish very plain and very cold, with perhaps a dash of lemon juice or a touch of **Crème Marie Rose**, freshly made mayonnaise and whipped cream in equal parts, enlivened by a dash of Tabasco, a little tomato ketchup and a hint of cognac.

But all of the above – no matter how choice – can be prepared without thought or attention on the part of the host or hostess. I much prefer, when dining out, to be given something a little more personal. Hot and cold appetisers – the sort that one often meets with in France as the beginning of a country meal – are the perfect answer here. For the most part they can be prepared ahead of time; they are often made of left-overs; and they can be added to or subtracted from to balance the rest of the meal. Why not try a popular French dish from the Mediterranean? **Caviar d'aubergines** (a chilled 'poor man's caviar'), while quite unlike its namesake, is quite delicious.

To make caviar d'aubergines: bake 1 or 2 large aubergines in a moderately hot oven (200°C, 400°F, Gas Mark 6) until soft – about 1 hour. Peel and chop 1 Spanish onion, 1 small green pepper, 4 tomatoes, 1 clove garlic and sauté them until golden in 6 to 8 tablespoons olive oil. Peel baked aubergine, chop its flesh finely and add to other ingredients; simmer vegetables gently, stirring from time to time, until excess moisture has evaporated and the mixture is fairly thick. Season to taste with salt and freshly ground black pepper and allow to cool. Just before serving, stir in 1 or 2 tablespoons each of dry white wine, olive oil and finely chopped parsley. Chill and serve with lemon wedges and thin slices of French bread.

Again, from Provence, comes the well-known hot appetiser, **petits pâtes à la Proven-çale** (shortcrust pastry rounds filled with minced cooked ham or veal flavoured with finely chopped anchovy, onion and garlic). I often serve these piping hot with drinks or with an inexpensive dry *rosé* wine on-the-rocks at cocktail parties. Try them, too, with tuna fish instead of veal. Delicious and different.

Mushrooms à la Grecque is one of my favourite ways of starting a meal. Try vege-tables – cauliflower, carrots and beans – prepared in this way for a trio of vegetable appetisers that could lend freshness and flavour to a rustic meal. The secret here is to blanch the vege-tables slightly before cooking them in wine. Be sure not to overcook them or they will be tasteless and soggy.

Haricots blancs en salade – this highly decorative country salad of dried white beans, with its hearty sauce flavoured with finely chopped onion, garlic, parsley and mustard, is garnished with anchovy fillets, tomato wedges and black olives for a Mediterranean effect.

A favourite hot appetiser for September dinner parties is **brochette de moules** – mussels steamed open with dry white wine, finely chopped shallots and herbs, skewered alternately with fat cubes of bacon, brushed with butter and cooked under the grill. Serve with lemon wedges, or better still, a Béarnaise sauce.

Salade de boeuf is another appetiser-salad favourite of mine. This is a wonderful way of making good use of left-over roast beef, but do be sure it is rare. **Salade de boeuf** also makes a good light luncheon dish or can double as one of the star turns for a buffet party.

Two of France's most celebrated restaurants – the Pyramide at Vienne and the Bonne Auberge at Antibes – make a speciality of serving course after course of hot and cold appe-tisers with great *panache*. At Antibes some people make their whole meal of these delicious *hors-d'oeuvre*. You, too, can make this an easy entertaining pattern for your own parties.

Tomato Salad 'Fines Herbes' *Serves 4*
Cucumber-stuffed Tomatoes *Serves 4*
Raw Spinach Salad with Bacon and Beans *Serves 4*
Celeriac Salad *Serves 4*

13

Tomato Salad 'Fines Herbes'

8 large ripe tomatoes
8 level tablespoons finely chopped parsley
4 level tablespoons finely chopped onion
1 level tablespoon finely chopped garlic
2 level tablespoons finely chopped basil
2 level tablespoons finely chopped tarragon
6-8 tablespoons olive oil
2-3 tablespoons wine vinegar
salt and freshly ground black pepper
Vinaigrette Sauce (see page 415)

1. Place large, firm, ripe tomatoes in boiling water for a few minutes. Peel and cut each tomato in even-sized thick slices. Re-form tomatoes and place in a rectangular or oval *hors-d'oeuvre* dish.

2. Mix the next 8 ingredients to form a thick, green, well-flavoured dressing. Sandwich three-quarters of the dressing carefully between layers of each tomato. Chill.

3. Dilute remaining dressing with a well-flavoured Vinaigrette Sauce; spoon over herb-stuffed tomatoes and serve.

Cucumber-stuffed Tomatoes

8 large ripe tomatoes
salt and freshly ground black pepper
½ large cucumber

DRESSING
6 tablespoons olive oil
6 tablespoons wine vinegar
salt and freshly ground black pepper
sugar

1. Cut tops off tomatoes and scoop out pulp and seeds. Sprinkle with salt and freshly ground black pepper. Turn upside down on a plate and chill.

2. Cut unpeeled cucumber into very thin slices. Place slices on a plate and salt them generously; cover with another plate and place a weight on top. Leave them for 2 hours, then rinse cucumber with cold water. Place in a clean towel and press to rid cucumber slices of all liquids.

3. Make a salad dressing with equal parts of olive oil and wine vinegar; flavour to taste with salt, freshly ground black pepper and a little sugar, and fold sliced cucumber into dressing.

4. To serve: turn tomato cases right side up; fill with cucumber and serve as an appetiser, or as an accompaniment to poached salmon.

Raw Spinach Salad with Bacon and Beans

450 g/1 lb cooked kidney or broad beans
6-8 tablespoons olive oil
3 tablespoons wine vinegar or
    lemon juice
1 level tablespoon each finely chopped fresh
    tarragon, basil and parsley
1-2 cloves garlic, finely chopped
salt and freshly ground black pepper
450 g/1 lb young spinach leaves, raw
1 small onion, thinly sliced
2 rashers well-cooked bacon, crumbled

1. Mix cooked beans with dressing made of olive oil and wine vinegar or lemon juice, and finely chopped herbs and garlic. Add salt and freshly ground black pepper, to taste.

2. Serve on tender young spinach leaves and garnish with onion rings and crumbled bacon.

Celeriac Salad

1 celery root
salted water
300 ml/½ pint well-flavoured mayonnaise
    (see page 417)
freshly ground black pepper
mustard, curry powder or paprika

1. Trim and wash celery root. Cut into matchstick-sized strips and blanch until tender in boiling salted water. Drain; cool and dry.

2. Dress with mayonnaise seasoned to taste with freshly ground black pepper and mustard, curry powder or paprika.

14

Russian Tomato Salad

Illustrated on page 25

4-8 ripe tomatoes
150 ml/¼ pint double cream, whipped
4-8 level tablespoons well-flavoured
    mayonnaise (see page 417)
1 level tablespoon freshly grated horseradish
¼ level teaspoon paprika
salt and freshly ground black pepper
lettuce leaves
4 level tablespoons finely chopped parsley
    or chives

1. Peel tomatoes and chill until ready to serve.

2. Combine whipped cream with mayonnaise, grated horseradish and paprika, and season to taste with salt and freshly 'ground black pepper. Chill.

3. When ready to serve, place tomatoes on lettuce leaves on individual salad plates and top with dressing. Garnish with parsley or chives.

Vegetables with Aïoli Sauce

6 potatoes
6 baby marrows
450 g/1 lb new carrots
450 g/1 lb green beans
6 ripe tomatoes
salt and freshly ground black pepper
Aïoli Sauce (see page 417)

1. Peel potatoes and cut into 1-cm/½-inch cubes. Wash and cut baby marrows, new carrots and green beans into 1-cm/½-inch lengths.

2. Boil each vegetable separately until tender but still quite firm. Do not overcook. Chill.

3. Seed and cut large fresh tomatoes into 1-cm/½-inch cubes.

4. Arrange vegetables in colourful groups on a large shallow serving dish. Sprinkle with salt and freshly ground black pepper, to taste. Serve with Aïoli Sauce.

Salade de Tomates à la Crème

12 ripe tomatoes
1 Spanish onion, finely chopped
6 tablespoons olive oil
2 tablespoons wine vinegar
salt and freshly ground black pepper
6 level tablespoons mayonnaise (see
    page 417)
4 level tablespoons double cream
2 level tablespoons chopped parsley

1. Cut tomatoes in slices and place on a dish. Sprinkle with finely chopped onion.

2. Moisten with a simple dressing, made with olive oil and wine vinegar seasoned with salt and freshly ground black pepper.

3. Mix mayonnaise and cream, and cover tomatoes and onions. Sprinkle with parsley.

Sardine-stuffed Lemons

6 large fresh lemons
2 (120-g/4¼-oz) cans sardines or 1 (198-g/
    7-oz) can tuna fish
150 g/5 oz butter
prepared mustard
paprika
freshly ground black pepper
1 egg white, stiffly beaten
1 sprig fresh thyme, 1 bay leaf or small
    green leaf per lemon

1. Cut off tops of lemons; dig out pulp with a small spoon. Remove pips and reserve pulp and juice.

2. Mash sardines or tuna fish to a smooth paste with butter and mustard, and season to taste with paprika and freshly ground black pepper.

3. Stir in juice and pulp of lemons together with stiffly beaten egg white. Correct seasoning and stuff lemons with this mixture.

4. Chill. Top with a sprig of fresh thyme, a bay leaf or a small green leaf, and serve in eggcups.

Spanish Vegetable Salad

1 Spanish onion
iced water
1 large cucumber
12 ripe tomatoes
6 level tablespoons dry French breadcrumbs
150 ml/¼ pint garlic-flavoured French
    Dressing (see Seafood Salad, page 16)
2 level tablespoons chopped basil, or chives,
    or a combination of the two

1. Peel and slice Spanish onion thinly and soak in iced water for 1 hour. Drain well. Slice cucumber thinly, but do not peel. Peel and slice tomatoes. Grate dry French bread to fine crumbs.

2. Prepare French Dressing, flavouring it with finely chopped garlic.

3. Arrange cucumber, tomatoes, onion and breadcrumbs in alternate layers in a glass salad bowl. Pour over a well-flavoured French dressing. Chill. Just before serving, sprinkle with chopped herbs.

Italian Vegetable Salad
Illustrated on page 26

4 tomatoes
wine vinegar
olive oil
salt and freshly ground black pepper
1 small cucumber
2 small green peppers
100 g/4 oz button mushrooms
2 level tablespoons finely chopped parsley
    lettuce
2 hard-boiled eggs

ITALIAN DRESSING
150 ml/¼ pint olive oil
4 anchovy fillets, finely chopped
juice of 1 large lemon
salt and freshly ground black pepper
1 level tablespoon capers

1. Quarter tomatoes and toss lightly in a small bowl with a little wine vinegar, olive oil, salt and freshly ground black pepper.

2. Peel cucumber and slice thinly. Place in a small bowl with a little wine vinegar, olive oil, salt and freshly ground black pepper.

3. Remove seeds and pith from green peppers. Slice into thin strips and place in a small bowl with the same dressing as above.

4. Wash and slice raw mushrooms into thin slices. Dress with a little wine vinegar and olive oil and add 1 tablespoon finely chopped parsley.

5. To make Italian Dressing: slightly warm 150 ml/¼ pint olive oil and add finely chopped anchovy fillets, mashing them with a fork until they are well blended with the oil. Add lemon juice and salt, freshly ground black pepper and capers, to taste.

6. Just before serving, assemble salads on a bed of lettuce in a large wooden bowl. Garnish with quartered hard-boiled eggs and sprinkle liberally with Italian Dressing.

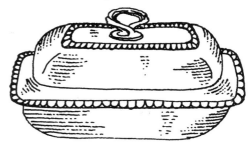

Haricots Verts 'en Aïoli'

450 g/1 lb green beans
6-8 level tablespoons Aïoli Sauce (see
    page 417)
freshly ground black pepper
3-4 level tablespoons finely chopped parsley

1. Cook beans in boiling salted water until tender – about 20 minutes. Drain well.

2. Mix while still warm with Aïoli Sauce. Toss well, season with salt and freshly ground black pepper, and chill.

3. Just before serving, toss well and sprinkle with finely chopped parsley.

Mushroom Salad with Chives *Serves 4 to 6*
Stuffed Tomatoes *Serves 4*
Seafood Salad *Serves 4*
Coeurs de Céléri en Salade *Serves 4*

16

Mushroom Salad with Chives
Illustrated on page 28

350 g/12 oz button mushrooms
juice of 1 lemon
8 tablespoons olive oil
salt and freshly ground black pepper
2 level tablespoons coarsely chopped chives
1 level tablespoon coarsely chopped parsley

1. Trim bottoms of mushroom stems; wash and dry mushrooms but do not peel.

2. Slice caps and arrange them in an *hors-d'oeuvre* dish or salad bowl. Pour well flavoured lemon and olive oil dressing over them.

3. Toss carefully, sprinkle with chopped chives and parsley, and chill in the refrigerator for 1 hour before serving.

Stuffed Tomatoes

8 large tomatoes
150 g/5 oz butter
6 level tablespoons chopped spring onions
2 cloves garlic, finely chopped
2 level tablespoons finely chopped parsley
225 g/8 oz cooked ham, finely chopped
8-12 level tablespoons shredded white bread
salt and freshly ground black pepper
dried breadcrumbs

1. Slice tops off tomatoes and scoop out interiors, being careful not to break cases. Chop pulp coarsely.

2. Melt 100 g/4 oz butter in a large thick-bottomed frying pan, and sauté onions, garlic, parsley, ham and tomato pulp until onions are soft. Add shredded white bread which you have soaked in water and squeezed relatively dry. Season with salt and freshly ground black pepper.

3. Stuff tomato cases with this mixture. Top with breadcrumbs, dot with remaining butter and bake in a moderate oven (180°C, 350°F, Gas Mark 4) for 20 minutes. Serve stuffed tomatoes either hot or cold.

Seafood Salad

1 soft-leaved lettuce, washed and chilled
1 Cos lettuce, washed and chilled
225 g/8 oz cooked prawns
225 g/8 oz cooked lobster meat
225 g/8 oz cooked white fish
225 g/8 oz cooked crabmeat
4 ripe tomatoes
8 large black olives

FRENCH DRESSING
1 tablespoon lemon juice
1-2 tablespoons wine vinegar
$\frac{1}{4}$ teaspoon dry mustard
coarse salt and freshly ground black pepper
6-8 tablespoons olive oil

1. Line salad bowl with lettuce and Cos leaves. Arrange prawns, lobster, white fish and crabmeat, cut in cubes, on bed of salad greens. Garnish with wedges of ripe tomato and black olives.

2. To make French Dressing: mix together lemon juice, wine vinegar and dry mustard, and season to taste with coarse salt and freshly ground black pepper. Add olive oil and beat with a fork until the mixture emulsifies.

Coeurs de Céléri en Salade

2 heads celery
1 chicken stock cube
1 level tablespoon salt
300 ml/$\frac{1}{2}$ pint well-flavoured Vinaigrette
    Sauce (see page 415)
$\frac{1}{2}$ level teaspoon paprika
cayenne
150 ml/$\frac{1}{4}$ pint double cream
4 hard-boiled eggs
4 level tablespoons finely chopped parsley

1. Trim heads of celery, cutting off top third of branches and outside stalks. Cut each head in half; put celery in a saucepan with trimmings, chicken stock cube and salt. Cover with cold water and bring slowly to the boil. Simmer for 10 minutes, remove from heat and leave in hot water for 5 minutes. Drain and cool.

17

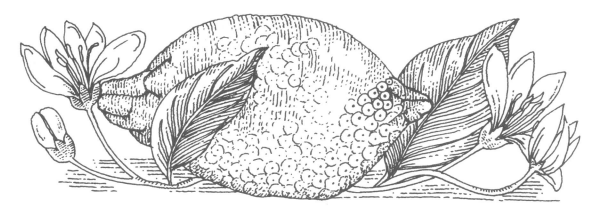

2. Arrange celery in a flat serving dish. Spoon over half of the Vinaigrette Sauce and allow celery to marinate in this mixture for at least 1 hour.

3. Combine remaining Vinaigrette Sauce with paprika, a pinch of cayenne and the double cream; mix well.

4. Separate yolks from whites of eggs and rub each separately through a wire sieve.

5. To serve: place blanched celery hearts on a serving dish. Cover each celery half with dressing; garnish one-third of each portion with sieved egg white, one-third with sieved egg yolk, and remaining third with finely chopped parsley. Serve immediately.

Appetiser Salad Marly

225 g/8 oz green asparagus tips, cooked
100 g/4 oz button mushrooms
4-6 tomatoes

SAUCE MARLY
1 level tablespoon Dijon mustard
175 ml/6 fl oz thick cream
juice of ½ lemon
salt and freshly ground black pepper
few drops of vinegar

1. Arrange cooked and drained asparagus tips on a long dish. Slice raw mushrooms thinly on top. Cut tomatoes into wedges and arrange around dish. Pour Sauce Marly over centre of dish.

2. To make Sauce Marly: combine mustard, cream and lemon juice, and season to taste with salt, freshly ground black pepper and vinegar.

Smoked Cod's Roe Mousse

1 jar smoked cod's roe (about 175 g/6 oz)
1½ (85-g/3-oz) packets cream cheese
¼ Spanish onion, grated
1-2 cloves garlic, mashed
olive oil
juice of 1 lemon
1 tablespoon finely chopped parsley
green olives
butter
hot toast

1. Place cod's roe in a mortar. Add cream cheese and pound mixture to a smooth paste.

2. Stir in onion and garlic. Then add enough olive oil and lemon juice (alternately a little at a time) stirring well until mixture acquires a smooth, uniform consistency. Strain through a fine sieve. (The above can be done in an electric blender, in which case the mixture does not need to be sieved.)

3. Serve in a salad bowl, sprinkled with finely chopped parsley and garnished with green olives. Serve with butter and hot toast.

18

Frozen Asparagus Tips with Prosciutto

1 (227-g/8-oz) packet frozen asparagus tips,

**thin slices of prosciutto poached
butter
4 level tablespoons double cream
4 level tablespoons freshly grated Parmesan
cheese**

1. Wrap 2 poached asparagus tips in each slice of *prosciutto*. Fasten with wooden cocktail sticks.

2. Arrange bundles in a well-buttered ovenproof dish, and sprinkle with double cream, freshly grated Parmesan and 50 g/2 oz butter, diced. Bake in a moderately hot oven (200°C, 400°F, Gas Mark 6) for 5 minutes.

3. Melt 50 g/2 oz butter; pour over asparagus bundles and serve immediately.

Fresh Asparagus Hollandaise

1 bunch fresh asparagus

HOLLANDAISE SAUCE
**lemon juice
1 tablespoon cold water
salt and white pepper
225 g/8 oz softened butter
4 egg yolks**

1. To boil asparagus: select a deep, narrow pan in which the asparagus stalks can stand upright, and pour in boiling water to just under the tips; in this way, the stalks can cook in water and the tender heads can cook in steam. Simmer gently – about 10 to 15 minutes from the time the water comes to the boil again after immersion is just about right. Slender stalks will take less time.

2. To steam asparagus: lay asparagus stalks flat in a *gratin* dish; add 4 tablespoons chicken stock or water, 4 tablespoons butter, and salt and freshly ground black pepper, to taste. Place *gratin* dish in the top of a double steamer over boiling water (or on a trivet or brick to hold *gratin* dish over water

in a large saucepan); cover pan and steam for 15 to 20 minutes, or until tender.

3. To make Hollandaise Sauce: combine 1 teaspoon of lemon juice, water and a pinch each of salt and white pepper in the top of a double saucepan or *bain-marie*. Divide butter into 4 equal pieces. Add the egg yolks and a quarter of the butter to the liquid in the saucepan, and stir the mixture rapidly and constantly with a wire whisk over hot, but not boiling, water until the butter is melted and the mixture begins to thicken. Add the second piece of butter and continue whisking. As the mixture thickens and the second piece of butter melts, add the third piece of butter, stirring from the bottom of the pan until it is melted. Be careful not to allow the water over which the sauce is cooking to boil at any time. Add rest of butter, beating until it melts and is incorporated in the sauce. Remove top part of saucepan from heat and continue to beat for 2 to 3 minutes. Replace saucepan over hot, but not boiling, water for 2 minutes more, beating constantly. By this time the emulsion should have formed and your sauce will be rich and creamy. 'Finish' sauce with a few drops of lemon juice. Strain and serve. If at any time in the operation the mixture should curdle, beat in 1 or 2 tablespoons cold water to rebind the emulsion.

4. Drain boiled or steamed asparagus and serve with Hollandaise Sauce.

Mushrooms in Mustard

**450 g/1 lb button mushrooms
juice of 1 lemon
8 tablespoons olive oil
6 black peppercorns
2 bay leaves
1–2 level tablespoons Dijon mustard
salt
2–3 level tablespoons finely chopped parsley**

1. Wash and drain mushrooms. Trim ends of stems with a sharp knife and cut mushrooms in halves or quarters.

2. Marinate in lemon juice and olive oil with

peppercorns and bay leaves for at least 8 hours. Drain mushrooms (reserving marinade juices) and arrange them in an *hors-d'oeuvre* dish.

3. To make mustard sauce: combine 4 to 6 tablespoons marinade juices with Dijon mustard in a small jar, and shake until well blended. Add salt and a little more lemon juice or olive oil if necessary.

4. Pour sauce over mushrooms. Sprinkle with finely chopped parsley.

Artichokes with Green Mayonnaise

4 artichokes
salt
juice of ½ lemon

GREEN MAYONNAISE
300 ml/½ pint well-flavoured mayonnaise (see page 417)
1 handful each sprigs of watercress, parsley and chervil
2 level tablespoons finely chopped watercress leaves
2 level tablespoons finely chopped chervil
4 level tablespoons finely chopped parsley
2 level tablespoons finely chopped tarragon leaves
lemon juice
freshly ground black pepper

1. Remove tough outer leaves of artichokes and trim tops of inner leaves. Trim the base and stem of each artichoke with a sharp knife.

2. Cook until tender – 30 to 40 minutes – in a large quantity of salted boiling water to which you have added the juice of ½ lemon. Artichokes are ready when a leaf pulls out easily. When cooked, turn artichokes upside down to drain.

3. To make Green Mayonnaise: wash sprigs of watercress, parsley and chervil. Pick them over carefully and put them in a saucepan with a little salted boiling water. Allow greens to boil for 6 to 7 minutes; drain and press as dry as possible. Pound greens in a mortar. Rub through a fine

sieve and add green purée to mayonnaise. Whirl green mayonnaise and finely chopped watercress leaves and herbs in an electric blender, or blend well with a whisk. Add lemon juice, salt and freshly ground black pepper, to taste.

4. Serve artichokes with Green Mayonnaise.

Italian Antipasto Platter
Illustrated on page 27

1 lettuce
4 tomatoes, cut in wedges
4 fennel, cut in wedges
1 (198-g/7-oz) can tuna fish or 2 (120-g/4¼-oz) cans sardines
1 (198-g/7-oz) can artichokes in oil or brine
8 slices Italian salami
4 slices mortadella or prosciutto
8 radishes
8 black olives
2 level tablespoons finely chopped parsley or capers

ITALIAN DRESSING
150 ml/¼ pint olive oil
2 anchovy fillets, finely chopped
lemon juice
salt and freshly ground black pepper
capers

1. To make Italian dressing: warm olive oil slightly and add anchovy fillets, finely chopped, mashing them with a fork until they are well blended with the oil. Add lemon juice and salt, pepper and capers, to taste.

2. Wash and trim lettuce. Dry leaves throughly. Cut tomatoes into wedges and toss lightly in Italian dressing. Clean and trim fennel and cut into thin wedges; toss lightly in dressing. Drain oil from tuna fish (or sardines); drain oil from artichokes. Chill vegetables.

3. Arrange lettuce leaves on a large serving dish. Place sliced meats, fish, vegetables, radishes and black olives in colourful groups on lettuce. Sprinkle with finely chopped parsley or capers. Serve with crusty bread and butter.

Leeks à la Vinaigrette *Serves 4*
Herbed Carrots Vinaigrette *Serves 4*
Brussels Sprouts à la Vinaigrette *Serves 4*
Italian Pepper Salad *Serves 6*

20

Leeks à la Vinaigrette

12 small or 8 large leeks
salt
6–8 tablespoons olive oil
2 tablespoons wine vinegar
freshly ground black pepper and
   mustard
finely chopped parsley

1. Trim roots and cut off the tops of leeks, leaving 2.5 cm/1 inch to 7.5 cm/3 inches of the green portion. Halve the leeks, leaving the halves attached at the root end. Wash thoroughly.

2. Simmer leeks in boiling salted water for 20 minutes, or until tender. Drain thoroughly.

3. Arrange leeks in an *hors-d'oeuvre* dish.

4. Combine olive oil and vinegar with salt, freshly ground black pepper and mustard, to taste. Pour over leeks and garnish with finely chopped parsley.

Herbed Carrots Vinaigrette

450 g/1 lb new carrots
4 level tablespoons butter
4 tablespoons chicken stock
sugar
salt and freshly ground black pepper
2 level tablespoons each chopped parsley
   and chervil
well-flavoured French Dressing (see Tossed
   Green Salad, page 263)

1. Wash carrots and cut diagonally into thin slices.

2. Place prepared carrots in a saucepan of cold water, bring to the boil and drain.

3. Simmer carrots for 15 to 20 minutes in butter and chicken stock, with sugar, salt and freshly ground black pepper, to taste. Cool.

4. Just before serving sprinkle with chopped parsley and chervil and toss in French dressing.

Brussels Sprouts à la Vinaigrette

450 g/1 lb small Brussels sprouts
salt and freshly ground black pepper
6 tablespoons olive oil
grated rind and juice of $\frac{1}{2}$ lemon
2 tablespoons finely chopped chives
2 tablespoons finely chopped parsley
2 tablespoons chopped hard-boiled egg

1. **To prepare Brussels sprouts:** cut off stem ends and remove any wilted or damaged outer leaves from small Brussels sprouts. (If Brussels sprouts are older, remove tough outer leaves entirely.) Soak sprouts in cold water with a little salt or lemon juice for 15 minutes.

2. **To cook Brussels sprouts:** add sprouts to boiling salted water and simmer, uncovered, for 5 minutes. Cover pan and continue to cook for 7 (if very young) to 15 minutes longer, until just tender. Drain well and season generously with salt and freshly ground black pepper.

3. Place sprouts in a salad bowl. Add olive oil and lemon juice and toss well. Season with salt and freshly ground black pepper, add grated lemon rind and toss again.

4. Just before serving, sprinkle with finely chopped chives, parsley and hard-boiled egg.

Italian Pepper Salad

900 g/2 lb large, firm peppers (green, red
   and yellow)
150 ml/$\frac{1}{4}$ pint olive oil
2 cloves garlic, finely chopped
lemon juice
salt and freshly ground black pepper

1. Place peppers under the grill as close to the heat as possible, turning them from time to time until the skin is charred on all sides. Then rub the charred skins off under running water. Remove stems and seeds.

2. Cut lengthwise into 2.5-cm/1-inch strips. Rinse well and drain.

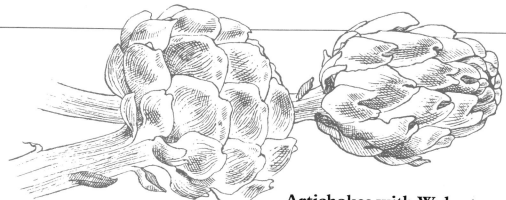

3. Place peppers in a salad bowl with olive oil and finely chopped garlic. Add lemon juice, salt and freshly ground black pepper, to taste. Chill for at least 1 hour before serving.

Mushroom and Bacon Hors-d'Oeuvre

450 g/1 lb button mushrooms
2 tablespoons lemon juice
225 g/8 oz green bacon, in 1 piece
2 tablespoons butter
2 tablespoons olive oil
½ Spanish onion, finely chopped
freshly ground black pepper
½ wine glass dry white wine
beurre manié (made by mashing 1
    tablespoon butter with 1 tablespoon flour
    to a smooth paste)
finely chopped parsley

1. Wash mushrooms, trim stalks and cut into quarters. Soak in a bowl of water with lemon juice until ready to use.

2. Dice green bacon.

3. Heat butter and olive oil in a large, thick-bottomed frying pan. Sauté finely chopped onion and diced green bacon in this until onion is transparent. Season to taste with freshly ground black pepper. Add quartered mushrooms and dry white wine and continue cooking over a low heat until mushrooms are tender but not soft. Stir in *beurre manié* and cook for a minute or two more, until sauce is thick. Serve, sprinkled with finely chopped parsley, in individual ramekins or little soufflé dishes.

Artichokes with Walnut Oil Dressing

4 artichokes
salt
juice of ½ lemon
freshly ground black pepper
finely chopped fresh herbs

WALNUT OIL DRESSING
150 ml/¼ pint double cream
salt and freshly ground black pepper
walnut oil
lemon juice

1. Remove the tough outer leaves of artichokes and trim tops of inner leaves. Trim the base and stem of each artichoke with a sharp knife. Cook until tender (30 to 40 minutes) in a large quantity of boiling salted water to which you have added the juice of ½ lemon. Artichokes are cooked when a leaf pulls out easily.

2. Turn artichokes upside down to drain.

3. Remove inner leaves of cooked artichokes, leaving a decorative outer ring of 2 or 3 leaves to form a cup around the heart of each artichoke. With the point of a spoon, remove choke from each artichoke. Season with salt and freshly ground black pepper and chill in the refrigerator.

4. To make Walnut Oil Dressing: whip double cream until stiff; flavour with salt, freshly ground black pepper and walnut oil and lemon juice, to taste.

5. Just before serving: pile artichoke hearts with whipped walnut cream filling and sprinkle with finely chopped herbs.

Choucroute Froide

1 Spanish onion, finely chopped
8 tablespoons olive oil
450 g/1 lb sauerkraut
300 ml/$\frac{1}{2}$ pint chicken stock
salt and coarsely ground black pepper
1 clove garlic, finely chopped
2 tablespoons wine vinegar
2 hard-boiled eggs, quartered
1 beetroot, cooked and sliced

1. Sauté finely chopped onion in 2 tablespoons olive oil until golden but not brown.

2. Place sauerkraut and onion in a heavy saucepan, and pour chicken stock over them. Simmer for 45 minutes.

3. Cool sauerkraut. Season to taste with salt and coarsely ground black pepper, and mix finely chopped garlic, remaining olive oil and the vinegar.

4. Serve garnished with quartered hard-boiled eggs and thin slices of cooked beetroot.

Cold Aubergine and Tomato Appetiser

4 aubergines
salt
6–8 ripe tomatoes
2 Spanish onions
freshly ground black pepper
olive oil

1. Peel aubergines and slice thinly. Sprinkle with salt and place slices under a weight for 30 minutes. Rinse thoroughly with cold water, drain and dry. Slice tomatoes and onions thinly. Keep separate.

2. Arrange a thin layer of onion slices in the bottom of a shallow baking dish, then a layer of aubergine slices, then one of tomato slices. Season with freshly ground black pepper. Repeat until all the vegetables are used up, ending with a layer of onion. Pour in olive oil until vegetables are barely covered. Bake in a very cool oven (120°C, 250°F, Gas Mark $\frac{1}{2}$) for about 3 hours, or until vegetables are cooked through. Chill and serve.

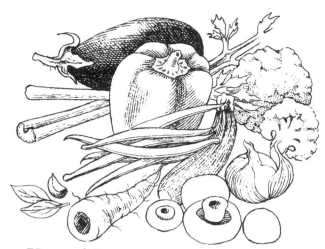

Vegetable Antipasto

Illustrated on page 280

2 courgettes
2 sticks celery
100 g/4 oz French beans
2 carrots
100 g/4 oz button mushrooms
6 small white onions
½ cauliflower
1 green pepper
1 red pepper
1 small aubergine
8 tablespoons olive oil
1 clove garlic, chopped
1–2 bay leaves
8 tablespoons tomato ketchup
4 tablespoons wine vinegar
2 tablespoons granulated sugar
2 level tablespoons prepared mustard
salt and freshly ground black pepper
lettuce leaves
finely chopped parsley

1. Cut the courgettes into 5-mm/¼-inch slices. Cut the celery into 2.5-cm/1-inch pieces. Slice the French beans into 2.5-cm/1-inch pieces. Scrape carrots and cut into 2.5-cm/1-inch pieces. Wipe the mushrooms with a damp towel and quarter. Cut the onions into quarters. Trim the cauliflower and break into small flowerets. Remove pith and seeds from the green and red peppers and cut into strips. Cut the unpeeled aubergine into small cubes.

2. Heat the olive oil in a large, heavy skillet. Add chopped garlic and sauté until golden. Remove garlic and discard. Add the bay leaves and all the vegetables and cook over medium heat until tender but still slightly crisp.

3. Stir in the tomato ketchup, wine vinegar, sugar, mustard and salt and freshly ground black pepper, to taste, and cook for another 5 minutes.

4. Cool and then chill in the refrigerator. Just before serving, correct seasoning with additional mustard, salt and freshly ground black pepper, if desired. The important thing to remember when preparing this dish is to observe the undercooking rule. All the vegetables should be *al dente*.

5. To serve: place vegetables on lettuce leaves and sprinkle with finely chopped parsley.

Devilled Carrot Appetiser

1 kg/2 lb small carrots
1 clove garlic, finely chopped
½ Spanish onion, finely chopped
6 tablespoons olive oil
6 tablespoons water
1 tablespoon wine vinegar
1 level tablespoon dry mustard
¼ level tablespoon powdered cumin
¼ level tablespoon paprika
¼ level tablespoon cayenne
salt and freshly ground black pepper
2 level tablespoons chopped parsley
lemon juice

1. Peel and slice carrots.

2. Sauté finely chopped garlic and onion in olive oil, stirring constantly, until vegetables are soft. Add sliced carrots and continue to cook, stirring for 2 minutes.

3. Add water, wine vinegar, spices, and salt and freshly ground black pepper, to taste, and simmer gently until carrots are tender.

4. Allow to cool. Sprinkle with finely chopped parsley and a little lemon juice just before serving.

24

Aubergine Omelette

1 medium-sized aubergine
salt
seasoned flour
olive oil
8–10 eggs
freshly ground black pepper
1 tablespoon water
2 level tablespoons butter

1. Wash aubergine, trim ends, and cut into 5-mm/ ¼-inch slices. Cut each slice into thin strips. Salt the strips and leave to sweat for 1 hour in a colander.

2. Rinse strips in cold water and squeeze them dry in a cloth. Toss aubergine strips in seasoned flour.

3. Heat 2 tablespoons olive oil in a frying pan and cook the strips until golden. Drain on absorbent paper. Keep warm.

4. Break eggs into a bowl and season to taste with salt and freshly ground black pepper.

5. Add water to eggs and beat with a fork or wire whisk just enough to mix yolks and whites.

6. Heat the omelette pan gradually on a medium heat until it is hot enough to make butter sizzle on contact.

7. Add 2 tablespoons olive oil and butter to heated pan and shake until butter is melted. When fat is sizzling, pour in the beaten eggs all at once. Quickly stir eggs for a second or two in the pan to assure even cooking just as you would for scrambled eggs. As omelette begins to set, add aubergine strips. Remove omelette from heat and, with one movement, slide the omelette towards the handle. When a third of the omelette has slid up the rounded edge of the pan, fold this quickly towards the centre with your palette knife. Raise the handle of the pan and slide opposite edge of omelette one-third up the side farthest away from the handle. Hold a heated serving dish under the pan, and, as the rim of the omelette touches the dish, raise the handle more

and more until the pan is turned upside down and your oval-shaped, lightly browned omelette rests on the dish. Pick up a small piece of butter on the point of a sharp knife and rub it over omelette. Serve immediately.

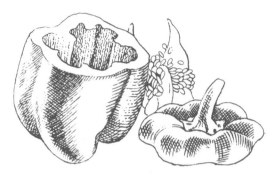

Italian Green Pepper Omelette

3 large green peppers
olive oil
salt and freshly ground black pepper
2 small cloves garlic, finely chopped
2 level tablespoons finely chopped parsley
8–10 eggs
1 tablespoon water
butter

1. Place green peppers in an ovenproof baking dish and bake them in a hot oven (230°C, 450°F, Gas Mark 8) for 20 to 30 minutes. Remove from oven and cover dish with a damp cloth for 10 minutes. Then, while peppers are still warm, remove skins carefully and cut peppers in halves. Scoop out seeds without damaging tender flesh of peppers. Cool and drain in a colander.

2. Cut peppers into strips and place in a shallow bowl. Add 3 tablespoons olive oil and season generously with salt and freshly ground black pepper. Sprinkle with finely chopped garlic and parsley and leave pepper strips to marinate in this mixture for at least 2 hours. Drain.

3. Break eggs into a bowl; season to taste with salt and freshly ground black pepper.

4. Prepare omelette as in Steps **5. 6.** and **7.** of Aubergine Omelette recipe (above), substituting green pepper strips for aubergine.

Russian Tomato Salad (see page 14)
Artichokes with Mustard Mayonnaise (see page 42)

Italian Antipasto Platter (see page 19)
Italian Vegetable Salad (see page 15)

Scrambled Eggs Provençale (see page 34)

Mushroom Salad with Chives (see page 16)

Red Pepper Omelette

4 tablespoons olive oil
½ Spanish onion, coarsely sliced
4 peppers (green, yellow and red), coarsely
  sliced
4 tomatoes, peeled and seeded
salt and freshly ground black pepper
8-10 eggs
2-4 level tablespoons freshly grated Gruyère
  cheese
2-4 level tablespoons freshly grated
  Parmesan cheese
2-4 level tablespoons butter

1. Heat olive oil in frying pan, add sliced onion and sauté, stirring from time to time, until onion is transparent. Add sliced and seeded peppers and cook over a low flame, stirring from time to time, until peppers are soft but not mushy.

2. Turn flame higher and stir in peeled and seeded tomatoes. Season generously with salt and freshly ground black pepper.

3. Break eggs into a bowl and beat with a whisk until foamy.

4. Pour eggs over vegetables, allow to set for a moment, then stir with a wooden spoon or spatula as you would for scrambled eggs. Sprinkle with finely grated cheese (Gruyère and Parmesan mixed) to bind mixture, and fold omelette into shape. Slide butter under omelette to add flavour, turn out on to a hot serving dish and serve immediately.

Hot Cauliflower Mousse

Illustrated on page 277

1 large cauliflower
salt
3 eggs
1 egg yolk
150 ml/¼ pint double cream
freshly ground black pepper
grated nutmeg
butter

GARNISH
**flowerets of cauliflower, poached
sprigs of fresh parsley or watercress
Hollandaise Sauce (see page 412)**

1. Clean cauliflower and cut into quarters. Cook in boiling salted water until just tender. Drain.

2. Preheat oven to moderate (180°C, 350°F, Gas Mark 4).

3. Put cooked cauliflower in the bowl of blender or food processor. Add eggs, egg yolk and cream. Season generously with salt, freshly ground black pepper and grated nutmeg. Put on lid of blender and blend until smooth.

4. Transfer mixture to a well-buttered soufflé dish with a band of aluminium foil tied around it, or a deep charlotte mould, and place in a roasting tin half full of boiling water on top of the cooker. Bring water to the boil again; then place the roasting tin in preheated oven and bake for 45 to 50 minutes, or until set.

5. Unmould mousse onto a heated serving dish. Garnish with sprigs of poached cauliflower and sprigs of parsley or watercress. Mask mousse with Hollandaise Sauce.

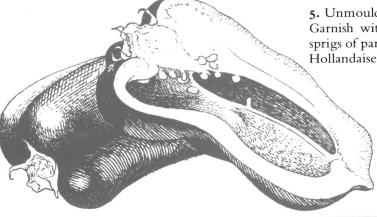

Egg Appetisers

How many of us today relegate the egg to the everyday breakfast basics of fried, boiled, poached or scrambled? Omelettes, soufflés and quiches use eggs to perfection to introduce a lunch or dinner menu (see Smoked Salmon Quiche, page 63). Ring the changes on the basic omelette by adding diced sautéed potatoes, courgettes or aubergines. Even scrambled eggs can make their mark as a first course of distinction. I remember a remarkable luncheon at the elegant Plaza Athenée in Paris which started off with a delicious version of scrambled eggs (3 eggs per person cooked in butter until soft and moist) mixed with diced truffles and asparagus, piled into a golden *croustade* of flaky pastry garnished with individual moulds of ham mousse and asparagus tips. Elegant and different, you'll agree. And yet, except for the diced truffles and the ham mousse, not too difficult or extravagant to make.

Taking a leaf from the Plaza Athenée's book, I have often served small hot pastry cases filled just before serving with scrambled eggs, lightly flavoured with a little grated Parmesan and tossed with diced ham and mushrooms, simmered in butter. Try this, too, with thin slivers of sliced smoked salmon or flaked smoked trout and sliced radishes.

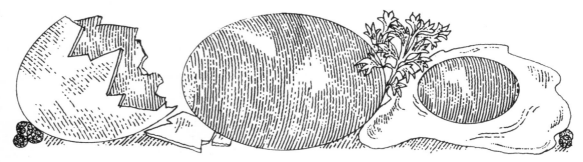

Oeufs moulés was a fashionable first course egg in nineteenth century France. Nothing more nor less than an egg baked in a *dariole* mould and then turned out before serving, these little egg turrets make a decorative first course today, especially if served with an appropriate sauce and placed in individual pastry cases, cooked artichoke hearts, mushroom caps or tomato cases.

Here again, the method is simplicity itself: butter individual *dariole* moulds generously. Break an egg into each mould; place moulds in a tin of hot water and cook in a moderate oven (180°C, 350°F, Gas Mark 4) for 15 minutes. The insides of the moulds can be sprinkled with finely chopped parsley, finely chopped chives blanched in boiling water, or finely chopped mushrooms simmered in butter.

To serve: turn out moulds into individual pastry cases and pour over any one of the three following sauces.

1. A purée of peeled, seeded and chopped tomatoes softened in butter with a hint of finely chopped shallot, thyme, salt and freshly ground black pepper.

2. A purée of poached artichoke hearts enriched with chicken *velouté* sauce and double cream.

3. A purée of poached asparagus tips enriched with chicken *velouté* and cream.

Or serve each **oeuf moulé** on a base of poached artichoke hearts, baked mushroom caps or tomato cases, and mask egg with a little well-flavoured Béchamel or Hollandaise sauce.

Stuffed Eggs with Green Mayonnaise

4-6 hard-boiled eggs
6 level tablespoons pounded buttered
    shrimps
6 level tablespoons mayonnaise (see page 417)
lemon juice
300-450 ml/½-¾ pint Green Mayonnaise (see
    Artichokes with Green Mayonnaise,
    page 19)
3 level tablespoons finely chopped fresh herbs

1. Shell hard-boiled eggs and cut them in half lengthwise. Remove yolks and mash them to a smooth thick paste with pounded buttered shrimps, mayonnaise and lemon juice, to taste.

2. Stuff each egg white with shrimp mixture, piling it up to re-form egg shape.

3. Arrange stuffed eggs on a bed of Green Mayonnaise in an *hors-d'oeuvre* dish. Sprinkle with finely chopped herbs.

Eggs in Aspic

Madeira Aspic (see Basic Meat Aspic,
    page 410)
8 fresh tarragon leaves
1 slice cooked ham, cut en julienne
4 poached eggs
2 level tablespoons each cooked peas, diced
    cooked turnip and diced cooked carrot
    (optional)

1. Coat the bottom of small individual moulds with Madeira Aspic; allow to set.

2. Pour boiling water over tarragon leaves; dry and arrange on aspic. Place 2 to 4 thin strips of ham across leaves, and dribble a little aspic over them to hold them in place.

3. Trim poached eggs with scissors and place in mould. Pour aspic over them to cover. Garnish, if desired, with cold cooked peas and diced cooked turnip and carrot. Cover with aspic. Chill. Unmould just before serving.

Oeufs en Cocotte

A popular first course today. Butter individual *cocottes* or soufflé dishes, break 1 or 2 eggs into each, flavour the eggs to taste with salt and freshly ground black pepper, cover each egg with a little hot cream, and bake in a preheated moderate oven (160°C to 180°C, 325°F to 350°F, Gas Mark 3 to 4) for 5 to 8 minutes, until the whites just begin to set and the yolks are still runny. The variations on this simple dish are infinite. I like the following:

1. Lightly sauté 4 to 6 tablespoons of diced chicken liver, Italian sausage or cooked ham in a little butter. Season generously with salt and freshly ground black pepper and divide among 4 to 6 individual ovenproof dishes or *cocottes*.

2. Sprinkle 1 or 2 eggs with a little finely grated cheese before adding 1 tablespoon double cream to each dish. Bake as above.

3. Spread a bed of creamed spinach in each ramekin or *cocotte*; add 1 or 2 eggs and 1 tablespoon double cream, to each dish. Bake as above and serve with a little tomato sauce.

Poached Eggs Hollandaise

1 recipe fingertip pastry (see Provençal
    Tomato and Onion Tart, page 66)
4 poached eggs
salt and freshly ground black pepper
butter
150 ml/¼ pint Hollandaise Sauce (see Fresh
    Asparagus Hollandaise, page 18)

1. Bake 4 individual pastry cases; remove from tins.

2. Place 1 poached egg in each case; season to taste with salt and freshly ground black pepper, and dot with butter. Warm through for a few minutes in a moderately hot oven (190°C, 375°F, Gas Mark 5).

3. Top each egg with 2 tablespoons Hollandaise Sauce and serve immediately.

32

Provençal Stuffed Eggs 'à la Tapénade'

8-10 black olives, stoned
4-5 anchovy fillets
4-5 level tablespoons tuna fish
1-2 level teaspoons Dijon mustard
2 tablespoons chopped capers
4-6 tablespoons olive oil
1 tablespoon cognac
freshly ground black pepper
4-6 hard-boiled eggs
finely chopped parsley
lettuce leaves
black olives for garnish

1. Pound stoned black olives, anchovy fillets and tuna fish in a mortar with mustard and capers. When the mixture has been blended to a smooth paste, put it through a fine sieve and whisk olive oil into it. Add cognac, and season to taste with freshly ground black pepper.

2. Cut hard-boiled eggs in half lengthwise and remove yolks. Blend yolks with *tapénade* mixture, adding a little more olive oil if necessary. Pipe egg hollows with mixture; sprinkle with finely chopped parsley and serve, garnished with lettuce leaves and black olives.

Note: The *tapénade* mixture keeps well in a covered jar and is excellent as a highly flavoured canapé spread.

Cold Oeufs Saumonées en Croûte

6 round rolls
butter
12 eggs
2 thin slices smoked salmon
6 level tablespoons double cream
salt and freshly ground black pepper
3 level tablespoons finely chopped parsley

1. Slice tops off rolls and pull out interiors of rolls with your fingers. Brush rolls inside and out with melted butter and bake in a moderate oven (180°C, 350°F, Gas Mark 4) until golden brown. Cool.

2. Mix eggs slightly until whites and yolks are well mixed, but do not beat them.

3. Cut thin slices of smoked salmon into thin strips and heat for a moment in 2 tablespoons butter.

4. Add eggs and cook, stirring constantly, over low heat. As eggs begin to set, add another 2 tablespoons butter and the cream. Season to taste with salt and freshly ground black pepper. Cool.

5. Stuff rolls with scrambled egg mixture and sprinkle with finely chopped parsley.

Oeufs Bénédictine

4 eggs
4 slices cooked ham
butter
4 slices white bread
150 ml/$\frac{1}{4}$ pint Hollandaise Sauce (see Fresh Asparagus Hollandaise, page 18)

1. Poach eggs and keep warm.

2. Cut 4 rounds of sliced ham just large enough to fit individual egg dishes. Warm in butter.

3. Toast bread and cut rounds of the same size. Butter toast rounds and place 1 in each heated egg dish.

4. Cover each round with warmed ham and top with a poached egg. Spoon over Hollandaise Sauce and serve immediately.

Surprise Eggs

4 eggs
8 level tablespoons grated Parmesan cheese
salt and white pepper
butter
4 level tablespoons double cream

1. Separate eggs. Beat the whites very stiff; add half the fully grated Parmesan and salt and white pepper, to taste. Mix well.

2. Butter individual ramekins or *cocottes*, and spoon an egg white into each. Use rather large dishes, as egg whites tend to rise like a soufflé. Make a depression with the back of your spoon for each egg yolk.

3. Place yolks in hollows (1 to each ramekin); cover each yolk with 1 tablespoon cream, and sprinkle with remaining grated cheese.

4. Bake in a hot oven (230°C, 450°F, Gas Mark 8) for 8 to 10 minutes.

Baked Eggs in Tomato Cups

4 large tomatoes
salt and freshly ground black pepper
4 eggs
butter

HOT CURRY SAUCE
2 level tablespoons butter
2 level tablespoons flour
150 ml/¼ pint milk
150 ml/¼ pint single cream
salt and white pepper
1 level teaspoon curry powder

1. Cut tops from tomatoes, remove pulp, and drain. Season insides of tomato cases with salt and a little freshly ground black pepper. Break an egg into each tomato case; dot with butter, and season with salt and freshly ground black pepper.

2. Bake in individual baking dishes in a moderately hot oven (190°C, 375°F, Gas Mark 5) until the eggs are firm. Serve topped with Hot Curry Sauce.

3. To make Hot Curry Sauce: melt butter in a thick-bottomed saucepan. Add flour and cook, stirring constantly, until well blended. Add milk and cream slowly, stirring constantly. Season to taste with salt, white pepper and curry powder. Cover and simmer gently for 8 minutes.

Scrambled Eggs

5 large eggs
salt and freshly ground black pepper
butter
6 level tablespoons double cream

1. Break eggs into a bowl and season to taste with salt and freshly ground black pepper. Mix eggs lightly with a fork, but do not beat them.

2. Heat 4 level tablespoons butter in the pan until it is sizzling but has not changed colour. Pour eggs into pan. Allow them to set slightly; then stir them constantly with a wooden spoon, running edge of spoon round the pan and drawing the eggs into the centre. Cook until creamy.

3. Then, with a wire whisk, whip double cream and a little diced butter into egg mixture until eggs are fluffy. Serve immediately on a hot plate.

Note: Good scrambled eggs need care and attention. Always heat the pan before adding butter. Use plenty of butter and make sure it is hot (but not coloured) before adding the eggs.

Scrambled Eggs with Cheese
Combine beaten eggs with grated Gruyère, Parmesan and double cream, to taste. Cook as in basic recipe above.

Scrambled Eggs with Buttered Shrimps
Warm shrimps through in their butter and fold into scrambled eggs cooked as in basic recipe.

Scrambled Eggs with Mushrooms
Sauté thinly sliced button mushrooms in butter until soft. Season generously with salt and freshly ground pepper, and fold into scrambled eggs when they are half cooked. Continue to cook as in basic recipe above. Garnish with sautéed mushroom caps.

Scrambled Eggs with Artichokes
Dice cooked artichoke hearts. Toss in butter, season generously with salt and freshly ground black pepper, and fold into scrambled eggs when they are half cooked. Continue to cook as in basic recipe. Garnish with finely chopped parsley.

34

Scrambled Eggs Provençale

Illustrated on page 28

8 anchovy fillets
4 slices white bread
butter
olive oil
8 eggs
salt and freshly ground black pepper
black olives
cayenne
2 tablespoons finely chopped parsley

1. Heat the oven.

2. Slice the anchovy fillets in half lengthwise.

3. Cut the bread into rounds about 7.5 cm/3 inches in diameter and sauté lightly in a little butter and olive oil until just golden. Place on a baking sheet and put into the oven to keep warm.

4. Break the eggs into a mixing bowl; add salt, freshly ground black pepper and cayenne to taste, and mix lightly. Scramble the eggs in butter and olive oil.

5. Spoon the scrambled eggs on to the fried toast rounds and garnish with a lattice-work of thin anchovy strips, halved black olives and finely chopped parsley.

Scrambled Egg Croustades

1 recipe shortcrust pastry (see page 420)
12 eggs
6 level tablespoons butter
100 g/4 oz cooked ham, diced
6 button mushrooms, quartered and
    sautéed in butter

1. Line individual *brioche* moulds thinly with pastry and bake until golden. Keep warm.

2. Scramble eggs (3 per person) in butter until creamy but still quite moist. Toss with diced cooked ham and sautéed mushrooms.

3. Fill pastry cases and serve immediately.

Variation: Bake twice as many pastry cases as you will need. Pile eggs, ham and mushrooms high in half of the cases and top with remaining cases, inverted to form pastry covers.

Baked Eggs and Bacon

8 eggs
4-6 tablespoons diced Cheddar cheese
4 rashers bacon, grilled and diced
salt and freshly ground black pepper
8 tablespoons double cream

1. Butter 4 individual *cocottes* or soufflé dishes; sprinkle a quarter of the diced cheese and diced grilled bacon over the bottom of each dish. Break 2 eggs into each dish.

2. Season to taste with salt and freshly ground black pepper, and top with 2 tablespoons double cream.

3. Bake in a moderate oven (180°C, 350°F, Gas Mark 4) for 15 minutes, or until egg whites are firm.

Deep-fried Eggs in Pastry

4-6 eggs
salt and freshly ground black pepper
puff pastry (see page 420)
2 egg yolks, well beaten
dried breadcrumbs
fat for deep-frying

1. Soft-boil eggs and place them in cold water. Shell eggs carefully, and sprinkle to taste with salt and freshly ground black pepper.

2. Roll out pastry very thinly and cut out oblong-shaped pieces large enough to enfold each egg. Wrap each egg in pastry, sealing the joins with a little beaten egg. Trim superfluous pastry edges with scissors, making sure it is not too thick in any one part.

3. **When ready to serve:** brush eggs with beaten egg yolks; toss them in fine breadcrumbs and fry them in hot fat until golden brown. Drain well and serve immediately.

Basic Omelette

5 large eggs
salt and freshly ground black pepper
1 tablespoon water
2 level tablespoons butter
4 level tablespoons whipped egg white
freshly grated Gruyère or Parmesan cheese

1. Break eggs into a bowl and season to taste with salt and freshly ground black pepper. Heat an omelette pan gradually on a medium heat until it is hot enough to make butter sizzle on contact. Add water to eggs and beat with a fork or wire whisk just enough to mix yolks and whites. Add butter to heated pan and shake until butter coats bottom of pan evenly. When butter is sizzling, pour in the beaten eggs all at once.

2. Quickly stir eggs for a second or two in the pan to assure even cooking just as you would for scrambled eggs. Then, if you want your omelette to be supremely light, stir in 2 tablespoons whipped egg white and a sprinkling of freshly grated Gruyère or Parmesan – not enough to give it a cheesy flavour, but just enough to intensify the eggy taste of your omelette.

3. And now is the time to start working: as eggs begin to set, lift edges with a fork or palette knife so that the liquid can run under. Repeat until liquid is all used up but the eggs are still moist and soft, keeping eggs from sticking by shaking pan during the above operation.

4. Remove eggs from heat and, with one movement, slide the omelette towards the handle. When a third of the omelette has slid up the rounded edge of the pan, fold this quickly towards the centre with your palette knife. Raise the handle of the pan and slide opposite edge of omelette one-third up the side farthest away from the handle. Hold a heated serving dish under the pan, and as the rim of the omelette touches the dish, raise the handle more and more, until the pan is turned upside down and your oval-shaped, lightly browned omelette rests on the dish.
French chefs usually 'finish' their omelettes by skimming the surface lightly with a knob of butter on the point of a knife. Serve immediately.

After one or two tries to achieve your cook's *tour de main*, you should be able to produce a delicious omelette every time, golden on the outside and as juicy as you could wish inside.

Anchovy Omelette

4-6 large eggs
1 tablespoon water
4-6 anchovy fillets, finely chopped
2 level tablespoons finely chopped parsley
1 tomato, peeled, seeded and chopped
olive oil
2 level tablespoons freshly grated Gruyère
  cheese
butter

1. Beat eggs with water until well mixed. Add chopped anchovy fillets, parsley and tomato.

2. Heat olive oil until sizzling in a preheated omelette pan. Remove pan from heat and pour in egg mixture. Return to heat and, shaking pan with one hand, stir egg mixture with fork in the other hand until eggs just begin to set. Sprinkle with freshly grated Gruyère and quickly stir eggs with a wide circular motion, shaking pan constantly to keep omelette from sticking.

3. When eggs are set but surface is still moist, roll omelette on to a hot plate by tilting pan, starting it away from edge at one side with a fork and letting it roll over itself. Pick up a small piece of butter on the point of a sharp knife and rub it over omelette. Serve immediately.

Omelette Provençale

2 tomatoes, peeled, seeded and finely
  chopped
1 clove garlic, finely chopped
1 small onion, finely chopped
8 sprigs fresh parsley, chopped
2 sprigs fresh tarragon, chopped
salt and freshly ground black pepper
2 tablespoons olive oil
4 eggs
2 level tablespoons butter

1. Combine finely chopped tomatoes, garlic onion, parsley and tarragon. Season with salt and freshly ground black pepper, and sauté in olive oil in a frying pan for about 10 minutes. Keep warm.

2. Beat eggs lightly, season with salt and pepper, and cook in butter as for Basic Omelette (see page 35). When eggs are still soft, spread vegetables in centre, fold omelette and serve at once on a heated dish.

Omelette Bénédictine

This is an excellent luncheon omelette if you have left-over *brandade de morue*.

4-6 large eggs
1 tablespoon water
butter or olive oil
6-8 level tablespoons Brandade de Morue
  (see page 94)

CREAM SAUCE
2 level tablespoons butter
2 level tablespoons flour
150 ml/¼ pint dry white wine
150 ml/¼ pint double cream
salt and freshly ground black pepper

1. Beat eggs with water until well mixed.

2. Heat butter or olive oil until sizzling in a preheated omelette pan. Remove pan from heat and pour in egg mixture. Return to heat and, shaking pan with one hand, stir egg mixture with fork in the other hand until eggs just begin to set.

3. When eggs are still soft, spread warmed *brandade de morue* over centre. Fold omelette; transfer to a heated dish, pour Cream Sauce over it and serve at once.

4. To make Cream Sauce: melt butter in the top of a double saucepan; stir in flour and cook, stirring constantly, until smooth. Add dry white wine and double cream, and stir until boiling. Reduce heat and cook, stirring from time to time, until smooth. Season to taste with salt and freshly ground black pepper.

Crêpes 'Alfredo' (see page 54)

French Onion Tart (see page 66); Spinach and Egg Tart (see page 67); Hot Mushroom Tart (see page 67);
Courgette and Bacon Tart (see page 64); Pizza Tart (see page 65)

Provençal Tomato and Onion Tart (see page 66)

Creamed Button Onion Tart (see page 63)

French Mushroom Tartlets (see page 64)

Cooked Appetisers from around the World

Asparagus Polonaise

1 kg/2 lb asparagus
pinch of sugar
salt and freshly ground black pepper
2 level tablespoons butter

POLONAISE SAUCE
100 g/4 oz butter
75 g/3 oz light breadcrumbs
2 hard-boiled eggs, finely chopped
2 level tablespoons finely chopped chives

1. Wash and trim asparagus. Lay it flat in a shallow saucepan and cook, covered, in a small amount of boiling water to which you have added sugar, salt, freshly ground black pepper and butter, until just tender – 10 to 15 minutes.

2. Drain asparagus and place on serving dish. Spoon Polonaise Sauce over it and serve immediately.

3. **To make Polonaise Sauce:** melt butter in a saucepan. Add breadcrumbs and sauté gently until light brown, then add finely chopped hard-boiled eggs and chives.

Italian Baked Asparagus

450 g/1 lb uncooked asparagus spears
4 level tablespoons butter
4 level tablespoons finely chopped onion
4 level tablespoons finely chopped celery
2 level tablespoons freshly grated Parmesan
  cheese
2 level tablespoons fresh breadcrumbs
4 canned Italian peeled tomatoes, diced
salt and freshly ground black pepper
pinch of oregano
pinch of thyme

1. Melt butter in the bottom of a rectangular baking dish. Line bottom with asparagus spears; sprinkle with finely chopped onion and celery, grated cheese and breadcrumbs and diced canned tomatoes, and season to taste with salt, pepper, oregano and thyme.

2. Cover and bake in a moderately hot oven (190°C, 375°F, Gas Mark 5) for about 45 minutes.

Délices au Gruyère

4 level tablespoons butter
flour
450 ml/¾ pint boiling milk
8 level tablespoons freshly grated Gruyère
  cheese
4 level tablespoons freshly grated Parmesan
  cheese
freshly grated nutmeg
2 egg yolks
salt and freshly ground black pepper
1 egg beaten with 2 tablespoons milk and
  1 tablespoon olive oil
fresh breadcrumbs
oil for frying

1. Melt butter in the top of a double saucepan. Stir in 4 level tablespoons flour and cook over water, stirring continuously with a wooden spoon, until smooth. Pour in boiling milk and mix with a whisk to make a thick sauce.

2. Simmer sauce for a few minutes longer. Add grated Gruyère and Parmesan and a little grated nutmeg, and continue cooking, stirring continuously, until cheese is completely blended.

3. Remove sauce from heat. Stir in egg yolks; season to taste with salt and freshly ground black pepper, and more nutmeg if desired. Continue to cook over water, stirring continuously, for 2 or 3 minutes, being careful not to let mixture boil. Spread in a rectangular baking tin and allow to cool. Cover with paper or foil and chill in refrigerator for 3 hours, or until needed.

4. Just before serving, cut into rectangles; flour lightly and dip in egg beaten with milk and olive oil. Drain, roll in fresh breadcrumbs and fry in hot oil until golden. Serve immediately.

42

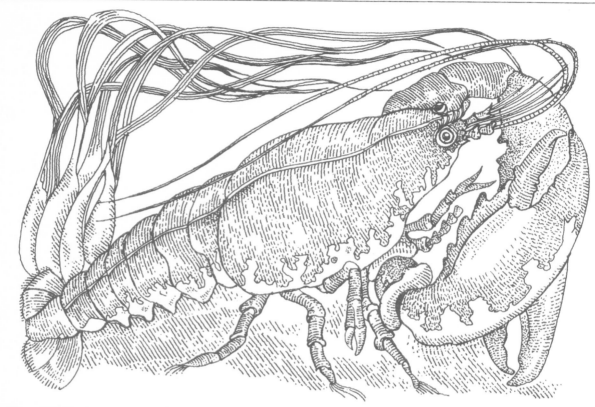

Bouillabaisse Salad 'Four Seasons'

2 lobsters (about 1 kg/2 lb each)
2 dozen mussels
16 prawns
450 g/1 lb crabmeat
75 g/3 oz chopped celery
1 lettuce
2 or 3 tomatoes, very thinly sliced
1 hard-boiled egg, finely chopped

DRESSING
250 ml/8 fl oz olive oil
175 ml/6 fl oz wine vinegar
4 tablespoons fish stock (reduced liquid in
   which shellfish were cooked, or canned
   clam juice)
½ Spanish onion, finely chopped
2 tablespoons dry white wine
1 tablespoon finely chopped chives
salt and freshly ground white pepper

1. All shellfish must be cooked and cooled before preparing salad.

2. In a shallow salad bowl, arrange celery, lobster and crabmeat in centre of bed of lettuce. Place mussels, prawns and sliced tomatoes alternately around edge of bowl.

3. To make the dressing: mix oil, vinegar, fish stock, onion, dry white wine and finely chopped chives. Season to taste with salt and freshly ground white pepper, and pour over salad.

4. Garnish with chopped egg and serve.

Artichokes with Mustard Mayonnaise
Illustrated on page 25

1. With a strong, sharp knife, slice all the leaves off level with the tips of the shortest ones. Strip away any tough outer leaves. Trim base and stem.

2. With a sharp-edged teaspoon, scoop and scrape out the fuzzy chokes, taking care not to leave a single fibre. Remember that these fibres are called 'chokes' for a very good reason.

3. While you are working on the artichoke, keep dipping it into a bowl of water heavily acidulated with lemon juice each time you cut open a fresh surface to prevent it turning brown. The artichoke contains peroxides and oxidising enzymes which cause it – and any steel utensil used with it – to discolour very quickly when exposed to the air. This is not dangerous, but it makes the artichoke look unattractive and spoils its flavour.

4. To a large pan of water add a handful of salt and some lemon juice (or a squeezed-out lemon half). Bring to the boil.

5. Immerse artichokes and simmer for 30 to 40 minutes, or until you can pull a leaf out easily.

6. Lift out artichokes and leave them to drain standing on their heads in a colander.

MUSTARD MAYONNAISE
2 egg yolks
1-2 level teaspoons Dijon mustard
salt and freshly ground black pepper
lemon juice
300 ml/½ pint olive oil

1. Have all ingredients at room temperature before you start. This is important: eggs straight from the refrigerator and cloudy olive oil are both liable to make a mayonnaise curdle.

2. Make sure that there are no gelatinous threads left on the egg yolks. Put yolks in a medium-sized bowl and set it in a pan or on a damp cloth on the table to hold it steady. Add mustard and a pinch each of salt and freshly ground black pepper, and work to a smooth paste with a spoon or a whisk.

3. Add a teaspoon of lemon juice and work until smooth again.

4. Pour olive oil into a measuring jug. With a teaspoon, start adding oil to egg yolk mixture a drop at a time, beating well between each addition.

5. Having incorporated about a quarter of the oil, step up the rate at which you add the remainder

of the oil, a teaspoon or two at a time, or a steady, fine trickle, beating strongly as you do so. If the mayonnaise becomes very thick before all the oil has been absorbed, thin it down again with more lemon juice or a few drops of cold water. Forcing olive oil into a very thick mayonnaise is another factor which may cause it to curdle. The finished mayonnaise should be thick and shiny, and drop from the spoon or whisk in heavy globs.

6. Correct seasoning, adding more salt, freshly ground black pepper or lemon juice if necessary.

7. If mayonnaise is not to be used immediately, beat in a tablespoon of boiling water to keep it from separating. Cover bowl tightly and leave at the bottom of the refrigerator until ready to use.

Carciofi alla Romana

6 small artichokes
lemon juice
3 level tablespoons finely chopped parsley
3 cloves garlic, mashed
3 level tablespoons finely chopped fresh mint
2-4 anchovy fillets, mashed
6 level tablespoons fresh breadcrumbs
salt and freshly ground black pepper
150 ml/¼ pint olive oil
300 ml/½ pint dry white wine

1. Trim rough outer leaves and stems of artichokes. Wash the artichokes in cold water. Open leaves by pressing artichokes against corner of kitchen table. Spread leaves, cut out 'chokes' (fuzzy centres) and discard them. Sprinkle with lemon juice to prevent exposed hearts turning black.

2. Mix parsley, garlic, mint, anchovies, breadcrumbs, and salt and freshly ground black pepper, to taste, with a little of the olive oil and wine. Stuff artichokes with this mixture and place them, heads down, in a shallow casserole just large enough to hold them. Pour over remaining oil and wine and cover with oiled paper. Bake in a moderately hot oven (190°C, 375°F, Gas Mark 5) for about 45 minutes, or until tender. Serve cold in their own juices as an *hors-d'oeuvre*, or hot as a vegetable, Roman style.

Herb-stuffed Mushrooms *Serves 4 to 6*
Mushrooms à la Grecque *Serves 4 to 6*
Spinach-stuffed Tomatoes *Serves 4*

44

Herb-stuffed Mushrooms

16–24 open mushrooms, according to size
4 shallots, finely chopped
1 clove garlic, finely chopped
225 g/8 oz sausagemeat
2 level tablespoons finely chopped chervil
  or parsley
2 level tablespoons finely chopped tarragon
¼ level teaspoon dried thyme
2 bay leaves, crumbled
salt and freshly ground black pepper
olive oil
dried breadcrumbs
2–4 level tablespoons finely chopped parsley

1. Wipe mushrooms clean with a damp cloth and trim stem ends. Remove stems carefully from caps and chop them finely. Mix thoroughly with shallots, garlic, sausagemeat and herbs, and season to taste with salt and freshly ground black pepper.

2. Sauté mixture in 2 tablespoons olive oil until golden.

3. Brush insides of mushroom caps with olive oil. Fill with sausage mixture and sprinkle lightly with breadcrumbs and finely chopped parsley.

4. Pour 6 tablespoons olive oil into an ovenproof *gratin* dish and heat through in the oven. Place stuffed mushroom caps in the hot oil and cook in a moderately hot oven (190°C, 375°F, Gas Mark 5) for 15 to 20 minutes.

Mushrooms à la Grecque

450 g/1 lb thickly sliced mushrooms
1 (142-g/5-oz) can tomato purée
2–3 tablespoons olive oil or butter
½ Spanish onion, finely chopped
½ clove garlic, finely chopped
salt and freshly ground black pepper

Serve hot as a vegetable, cold as an appetiser.

1. Combine 1 can tomato purée and 2 cans water in a saucepan with olive oil or butter, finely chopped onion and garlic, and salt and freshly

ground black pepper to taste. Mix well, cover pan and bring to the boil. Simmer gently over the lowest of heats, stirring from time to time, for about 30 minutes, adding a little more water if necessary.

2. Add sliced mushrooms to sauce and simmer for 10 minutes.

Spinach-stuffed Tomatoes

8 large tomatoes
16 level tablespoons hot cooked spinach
butter
salt and freshly ground black pepper
4 level tablespoons freshly grated Parmesan
  cheese

1. Slice tops off tomatoes; scoop out interiors carefully and discard.

2. Cook spinach, drain well and while hot rub twice through a fine sieve. Add butter, and season to taste with salt and freshly ground black pepper.

3. Fill tomatoes with the hot purée, sprinkle with freshly grated Parmesan and dot with butter. Arrange filled tomatoes in a buttered baking dish and bake in a moderate oven (180°C, 350°F, Gas Mark 4) for 5 minutes.

Moroccan Carrot Appetiser

1 kg/2 lb carrots, peeled and cut in quarters
   lengthwise
6 tablespoons water
6 tablespoons olive oil
2 cloves garlic
salt and freshly ground black pepper
1-2 tablespoons vinegar
$\frac{1}{4}$ level teaspoon cayenne
$\frac{1}{4}$ level teaspoon paprika
$\frac{1}{2}$ level teaspoon powdered cumin
1-2 tablespoons finely chopped parsley

1. Blanch peeled quartered carrots in water to cover until water boils. Drain.

2. Simmer carrots until tender in water and olive oil, with garlic, and salt and freshly ground black pepper, to taste.

3. Drain, add vinegar, and generous amounts of salt and freshly ground black pepper. Flavour to taste with cayenne, paprika and powdered cumin. Garnish with finely chopped parsley. Serve cold as an appetiser.

Tian à la Provençale

4 small aubergines
4 small courgettes
olive oil
2 green peppers
2 red peppers
2 yellow peppers
4 cloves garlic, finely chopped
4-6 level tablespoons finely chopped parsley
thyme and marjoram
8 tomatoes
·butter
4-6 level tablespoons fresh breadcrumbs

1. Cut aubergines and courgettes in thin strips, and sauté separately in olive oil.

2. Cut peppers (green, red and yellow) in rings, and sauté in olive oil. A few minutes before the end of cooking, sprinkle the aubergines and courgettes with half the finely chopped garlic and half the parsley, and add thyme and marjoram, to taste.

3. Cut tomatoes into thick rounds. Place them in a buttered *gratin* dish and cook *à la provençale* with remaining garlic and parsley, and the breadcrumbs.

4. Arrange cooked vegetables in a large ovenproof *gratin* dish, with the tomatoes in the centre, the aubergines on one side, and the courgettes on the other. Then place red, yellow and green pepper rings in a lattice over vegetables. Brown under the grill and serve immediately. Also good served cold.

Italian Pepper Appetiser

4-6 green and red peppers
6 tomatoes, peeled and diced
2 cloves garlic, finely chopped
1 (56-g/2-oz) can anchovy fillets, drained
   and finely chopped
4 tablespoons dried breadcrumbs
olive oil
salt and freshly ground black pepper
2 tablespoons butter

1. Cut peppers in half lengthwise and scoop out seeds and fibres.

2. Combine diced tomatoes, finely chopped garlic and anchovies, breadcrumbs and 4 to 6 tablespoons olive oil. Season with salt and freshly ground black pepper.

3. Stuff pepper halves with this mixture and arrange them in a well-oiled ovenproof baking dish. Dot with butter and bake in a moderate oven (180°C, 350°F, Gas Mark 4) for 45 to 50 minutes, until tender. Serve cold.

45

46

Grilled Peppers en Salade

4-6 green, red or yellow peppers
well-flavoured French Dressing (see Seafood
   Salad, page 16)
lettuce leaves
1 (56-g/2-oz) can anchovy fillets
finely chopped garlic
finely chopped parsley

1. Grill or roast peppers as close to the heat as possible, turning them until the skin is charred on all sides. Rub off skins under running cold water. Core, seed and slice peppers into thick strips and marinate in a well-flavoured French Dressing.

2. Serve as an appetiser salad on a bed of lettuce leaves with a lattice of anchovy fillets and a sprinkle of finely chopped garlic and parsley for garnish. Or serve in an *hors-d'oeuvre* dish with French Dressing only.

Note: Peppers prepared in this way will keep a long time under refrigeration if packed in oil in sterilised airtight jars.

Polynesian Pork Saté

1 kg/2 lb lean pork
6 Brazil nuts, grated
1 level tablespoon ground coriander seed
2 cloves garlic, finely chopped
1 level tablespoon salt
1 Spanish onion, grated
4 tablespoons lemon juice
1-2 level tablespoons brown sugar
4 tablespoons soy sauce
1 level teaspoon crushed black pepper (or
   freshly ground black pepper, to taste)
$\frac{1}{8}$ level teaspoon crushed hot red pepper

1. Cut pork into 2.5-cm/1-inch cubes. Combine remaining ingredients in a large mixing bowl. Add pork cubes and allow them to marinate in this mixture for at least 2 hours.

2. **When ready to serve:** thread pork on metal skewers and grill over charcoal or under a gas or electric grill until cooked through.

Javanese Steak Satés

675 g/1$\frac{1}{2}$ lb rump steak, 2.5 cm/1 inch thick
2 tablespoons soy sauce
6 tablespoons olive oil
2 tablespoons lemon juice
$\frac{1}{4}$ Spanish onion, finely chopped
1 clove garlic, finely chopped
1 level tablespoon powdered cumin
freshly ground black pepper

1. Cut steak into thin strips 7.5 cm/3 inches long, and marinate for at·least 4 hours in a mixture of soy sauce, olive oil, lemon juice, finely chopped onion and garlic, and powdered cumin.

2. Thread the beef on skewers and brush with marinade. Grill over charcoal or under a gas or electric grill until done, turning the skewers from time to time. Season to taste with freshly ground black pepper.

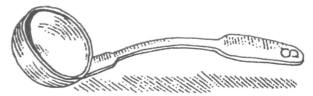

Pearl Buck's Sweet and Sour Spare Ribs

1.25 kg/2$\frac{1}{2}$ lb spare ribs of pork
450 ml/$\frac{3}{4}$ pint water
4 tablespoons soy sauce
salt
3 level tablespoons sugar or honey
3 tablespoons vinegar
1 level tablespoon cornflour
150 ml/$\frac{1}{4}$ pint water
2 tablespoons sake, or dry sherry and water
1 level teaspoon grated fresh ginger root

1. Cut ribs into separate pieces and cook in water with soy sauce and salt, to taste. Bring to the boil, turn down heat and allow to simmer for 1 hour.

2. Transfer to a frying pan, add remaining ingredients and fry until the gravy becomes translucent.

Marinated Smoked Salmon with Dill

225 g/8 oz sliced smoked salmon
1 level teaspoon whole black peppercorns
½ level teaspoon dill seed
1 bay leaf
300 ml/½ pint dry white wine
150 ml/¼ pint soured cream
2 level tablespoons prepared mustard
salt
lemon juice
1 tablespoon chopped chives
1 dill pickle, thinly sliced

1. Place salmon in a covered glass dish. Sprinkle with whole peppers and dill seed. Add bay leaf and cover with dry white wine. Place in refrigerator and allow salmon to marinate in this mixture overnight.

2. Just before serving, drain wine and spices from salmon. Place spices and half of the wine in a mixing bowl. Add soured cream and prepared mustard, and flavour to taste with salt and lemon juice.

3. Place salmon on a serving dish; cover with sauce and garnish with chopped chives and sliced pickle.

Soused Herrings

12 fresh herrings
1 Spanish onion, finely chopped
150 ml/¼ pint double cream
salt and freshly ground black pepper
2-3 level tablespoons pickling spice
dry cider or dry white wine
150 ml/¼ pint soured cream
½ cucumber, thinly sliced

1. Split herrings down the back; remove backbones carefully and stuff with their soft roes mixed with half the finely chopped onion, double cream, and salt and freshly ground black pepper, to taste.

2. Sprinkle half remaining chopped onion on the

bottom of a shallow ovenproof baking dish, season with 1 tablespoon pickling spice and arrange the fish on this bed, head to tail.

3. Cover with remaining spice and finely chopped onion. Pour in dry cider or dry white wine to cover and bake in a moderately hot oven (190°C, 375°F, Gas Mark 5), covered, until fish flakes easily with a fork. Cool, then remove fish. Strain cooking liquids and blend with soured cream. Season to taste with salt and freshly ground black pepper. Arrange fish on a serving dish; pour over cream sauce and garnish with thinly sliced cucumber.

George's Insalata 'La Morra'

225 g/8 oz raw potatoes
white wine vinegar
225 g/8 oz cooked breast of chicken
1 slice cooked ham, 5 mm/¼ inch thick
1 slice cooked tongue, 5 mm/¼ inch thick
50 g/2 oz Fontina, Caerphilly or Double
    Gloucester cheese
150 ml/¼ pint well-flavoured mayonnaise
    (see page 417)
6-8 level tablespoons whipped cream
salt and freshly ground black pepper
canned white truffles

1. Cut raw potatoes into matchsticks and boil them for 15 to 20 minutes in a mixture of water and white wine vinegar, three-fifths vinegar to two-fifths water. Drain and chill.

2. Cut chicken, ham, tongue and cheese into matchsticks. Combine with potatoes and dress with mayonnaise and whipped cream seasoned to taste with salt and freshly ground black pepper.

3. Just before serving, grate truffles over top of salad.

Note: Fontina cheese is firm, not crumbly, and slightly piquant without being strongly flavoured. Caerphilly or Double Gloucester are probably the nearest English equivalents.

47

48

Lentil Salad

225 g/8 oz lentils
1 Spanish onion, finely chopped
2 tablespoons olive oil
1 clove garlic
1 bay leaf
1 level teaspoon salt
1.4 litres/2½ pints water
4 tablespoons olive oil
2 tablespoons wine vinegar
salt and freshly ground black pepper
anchovy fillets
tomato wedges
black olives

DRESSING
½ Spanish onion, finely chopped
6 level tablespoons finely chopped parsley
1 level teaspoon prepared mustard
salt and freshly ground black pepper
olive oil
juice of ½ lemon

1. Soak lentils overnight in water to cover. Drain.

2. Sauté finely chopped onion in olive oil until transparent. Add garlic, bay leaf, salt and water, and simmer lentils in this stock for about 2 hours, or until tender. Drain and cool; then add olive oil and wine vinegar, and season to taste with salt and freshly ground black pepper.

3. **To make dressing:** combine finely chopped onion, parsley, mustard, salt and freshly ground black pepper in a bowl. Mix well and then pour in

Courgette Appetiser

4 level tablespoons finely chopped onion
4 level tablespoons finely chopped carrot
4 level tablespoons butter
150 ml/¼ pint dry white wine
150 ml/¼ pint water
2 garlic cloves, crushed
1 bouquet garni (2 sprigs parsley, 1 sprig thyme, 1 bay leaf)
12 courgettes, sliced and unpeeled

1. Combine finely chopped onion, carrot and butter in a saucepan with dry white wine and water. Add crushed garlic cloves and *bouquet garni*, and simmer for 15 minutes. Add sliced unpeeled courgettes, and simmer until tender.

2. Transfer courgettes to an earthenware dish. Pour *court-bouillon* over, chill and serve.

Aubergines au Gratin *Serves 4 to 6*
Potato Salad Niçoise *Serves 4 to 6*
Salade de Boeuf *Serves 4 to 6*

olive oil little by little, beating the mixture continuously, until sauce thickens. Flavour to taste with lemon juice.

4. Pour dressing over lentils and mix thoroughly. Garnish with anchovy fillets, tomato wedges and black olives.

Aubergines au Gratin

4 aubergines
salt
4 tablespoons olive oil
butter
1 Spanish onion, finely chopped
3 level tablespoons tomato purée
6 tomatoes, peeled, seeded and coarsely
  chopped
1–2 cloves garlic, finely chopped
3 level tablespoons finely chopped
  parsley
freshly ground black pepper
generous pinch each of allspice,
  cinnamon and sugar
dried breadcrumbs

1. Peel and dice aubergines, salt them liberally and leave to drain in a colander for 1 hour. Rinse off salt with cold water and shake diced aubergines dry in a cloth.

2. Combine olive oil and 2 tablespoons butter in a frying pan, and sauté aubergines until golden.

3. Remove from pan, and in the same oil fry onion until soft and just turning golden, adding more oil if necessary.

4. Add tomato purée, chopped tomatoes, and finely chopped garlic and parsley, and season to taste with salt, pepper, allspice, cinnamon and sugar. Simmer mixture, stirring occasionally, for 5 minutes.

5. Add diced aubergines to the mixture and pour into a buttered *gratin* dish (or individual soufflé dishes). Sprinkle with breadcrumbs, dot with butter and bake in a moderately hot oven (190°C, 375°F, Gas Mark 5) for 30 minutes.

This Turkish dish makes an excellent *hors-d'oeuvre*, served hot or cold.

Potato Salad Niçoise

1 kg/2 lb long thin salad potatoes
6–8 tablespoons olive oil
6–8 tablespoons dry white wine or beef
  consommé
2–3 tablespoons wine vinegar
6 level tablespoons finely chopped shallots
3 level tablespoons finely chopped parsley
salt and freshly ground black pepper
anchovy fillets
black olives
tomatoes

1. Boil long thin salad potatoes in their skins until cooked through. Peel and cut into thick slices. While still hot, pour over marinade of olive oil, dry white wine (or beef consommé) and wine vinegar. Add finely chopped shallots and parsley. Season to taste with salt and freshly ground black pepper.

2. Arrange anchovies in a latticework on top and place a black olive in the centre of each square. Garnish salad with a ring of tomato slices.

Salade de Boeuf

675 g/1½ lb boiled beef
6 gherkins, thinly sliced
6 level tablespoons finely chopped onion
6–8 tablespoons olive oil
2–3 tablespoons wine vinegar
salt and freshly ground black pepper
2 level tablespoons coarsely chopped
  gherkins
2 level tablespoons finely chopped parsley

Trim fat from beef and cut in small, thin slices. Mix with thinly sliced gherkins and finely chopped onion, and dress with olive oil, wine vinegar, and salt and freshly ground black pepper, to taste. Toss well and marinate in this mixture for at least 2 hours before serving. Garnish with chopped gherkins and parsley.

Hot and Cold Toasts and Canapés

50

Smoked Trout Canapés

4 smoked trout
double cream
olive oil
lemon juice
salt and freshly ground black pepper
sliced white bread
softened butter
finely chopped radishes
finely chopped parsley

1. Remove skin and bones from smoked trout and pound fillets to a paste in a mortar with 2 tablespoons each double cream and olive oil. Transfer mixture to an electric blender and add more cream and olive oil in equal quantities until mixture is of a spreadable consistency. Season to taste with lemon juice, salt and freshly ground black pepper. Chill.

2. Toast white bread and cut rounds of toast with a glass or biscuit cutter. Spread each round with softened butter and then cover generously with smoked trout mixture. Sprinkle with finely chopped radishes and parsley.

La Croûte Landaise

225 g/8 oz button mushrooms, sliced
6 level tablespoons butter
6 level tablespoons double cream
salt and freshly ground black pepper
4 fat slices brioche
4 thin rounds mousse de foie gras
1 egg yolk
150 ml/¼ pint Cream Sauce (see Omelette Bénédictine, page 36)
2 tablespoons freshly grated Parmesan cheese

1. Simmer sliced mushrooms in butter until soft. Purée them with cream; season to taste with salt and freshly ground black pepper.

2. Toast *brioche* slices. Spread each slice thickly with mushroom purée and place on a baking sheet. Top each 'toast' with a slice of *foie gras*. Add egg yolk to hot Cream Sauce and spoon over each 'toast'. Cover with freshly grated Parmesan and grill until golden.

Swiss Bacon and Mushroom Toasts *Serves 6*
L'Anchoïade-Hot Anchovy Canapés *Makes 8 to 12*
Brioches Farcies *Serves 4*

51

Swiss Bacon and Mushroom Toasts

12 thin slices white bread
225 g/8 oz Swiss cheese, grated
150 ml/¼ pint double cream
4 eggs
150 ml/¼ pint milk
8 level tablespoons butter

FILLING
12 rashers bacon
12–14 mushrooms, finely sliced
2 tablespoons butter
2 tablespoons lemon juice

1. To make filling for 6 sandwiches: fry bacon over moderate heat. Drain on kitchen paper. Sauté finely sliced mushrooms in butter and lemon juice. Use about 1 tablespoon mushrooms and 2 rashers trimmed bacon to fill each sandwich.

2. Trim crusts from bread. Mix Swiss cheese and cream and spread on all bread slices. Add a filling to half the bread slices; top with remaining slices, cheese side down. Beat eggs and milk with a fork. Dip sandwiches into egg mixture, coating both sides.

3. Heat butter until bubbling in a large frying pan; brown sandwiches on both sides over moderate heat. Serve with knife and fork or cut into bite-sized pieces.

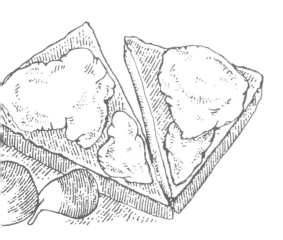

L'Anchoïade – Hot Anchovy Canapés

1 (56-g/2-oz) can anchovy fillets in oil
1 large clove garlic, crushed
1 tablespoon olive oil
2 level tablespoons softened butter
few drops lemon juice or cognac
freshly ground black pepper
4–6 thick slices white bread

1. Combine anchovy fillets, crushed garlic, olive oil and softened butter in a mortar, and pound to a smooth paste. Season to taste with a few drops of lemon juice or cognac and a little freshly ground black pepper.

2. Slice bread in half; toast on one side only and, while still hot, spread *anchoïade* paste on untoasted side, pressing paste well into bread. Toast in a hot oven for a few minutes just before serving.

Brioches Farcies

8 tiny brioches or 4 normal-sized ones
2 smoked sausages, finely chopped
50 g/2 oz ham, finely chopped
4 tablespoons milk
4 tablespoons cream
6–8 level tablespoons freshly grated Gruyère
   cheese
freshly ground black pepper
salt
1 tablespoon cognac

1. Cut caps off *brioches* and empty them. Pick apart interiors and combine with finely chopped meat of smoked sausages and ham. Add milk, cream and grated Gruyère and cook over a very low heat, stirring all the while, until you get a very thick paste. Add pepper, and a very little salt (sausages and ham are already rather salty). All this can be prepared in advance.

2. When ready to serve: reheat the mixture, stirring constantly. When it is very hot, remove from heat and stir in cognac; fill *brioches* with this mixture, replace caps and heat in the oven for a few minutes until warmed through.

52

Basic French Crêpes (for Savoury Fillings)

6 tablespoons plain flour
½ level teaspoon salt
2 eggs
450 ml/¾ pint milk
butter or oil
2 tablespoons cognac (optional)

1. Sift flour and salt into a mixing bowl. Beat eggs and add them to dry ingredients. Mix in the milk and 2 tablespoons melted butter or oil gradually to avoid lumps. Add cognac if desired. Strain batter through a fine sieve and let it stand for at least 2 hours before cooking. Batter should be as thin as cream. Add a little water if too thick.

2. For each *crêpe*, spoon about 2 tablespoons batter into buttered pan, swirling pan to allow to cover entire surface thinly. Brush a piece of butter around edge of hot pan with the point of a knife. Cook over a medium heat until just golden but not brown – about 1 minute each side. Repeat until all *crêpes* are cooked, stacking them on a plate as they are ready.

Italian Ham and Cheese Pancakes

½ recipe Basic French Crêpes (see above)
225 g/8 oz Mozzarella cheese
4 thin slices prosciutto (raw Parma ham)
butter
4 level tablespoons plain flour
300 ml/½ pint hot milk
salt
cayenne
½ level teaspoon ground nutmeg
300 ml/½ pint double cream
2 egg yolks, well beaten
150 ml/¼ pint well-flavoured Italian Tomato Sauce (see Polenta Pasticciata, page 71)

1. Make 8 to 12 *crêpes* before making ham and cheese filling.

2. Cut 8 to 12 thin slices Mozzarella cheese and put aside for later use. Dice the remaining cheese and the ham.

3. Melt 2 tablespoons butter in the top of a double saucepan. Stir in flour and cook over water, stirring constantly, until smooth. Add hot milk and continue to cook, stirring constantly, until thickened. Season to taste with salt, cayenne and nutmeg.

4. Combine cream and beaten egg yolks in a bowl. Pour in some of the hot sauce and whisk until smooth. Return cream and egg mixture to the saucepan, add diced cheese and ham, and cook over water until sauce is smooth, thick and golden. Do not let sauce boil after eggs are added or it will curdle. Let mixture cool.

5. Spread a thin coating of well-flavoured Italian Tomato Sauce over each pancake and then cover generously with cheese and ham filling. Roll pancakes and put them in a well-buttered rectangular baking dish. Chill until 1 hour before using.

6. When nearing time to serve, spoon a little Tomato Sauce over each pancake and top with a thin strip of Mozzarella cheese. Bake for 20 minutes in a moderate oven (180°C, 350°F, Gas Mark 4).

Italian Spinach Pancakes

½ recipe Basic French Crêpes (see above)
350 g/12 oz frozen spinach
butter
salt and freshly ground black pepper
225 g/8 oz Ricotta or cottage cheese
3 eggs, lightly beaten
freshly grated Parmesan cheese
150 ml/¼ pint double cream
freshly grated nutmeg
300 ml/½ pint well-flavoured Italian Tomato Sauce (see Polenta Pasticciata, page 71)

1. Make 8 to 12 *crêpes* before making the spinach and cheese filling.

2. Cook spinach with 2 tablespoons butter, and season to taste with salt and freshly ground black pepper. Drain thoroughly, and add Ricotta or cottage cheese, the beaten eggs, 25–50 g/1-2 oz grated Parmesan, cream and nutmeg, to taste.

3. Spread each pancake generously with spinach and cheese filling. Roll pancakes and put them in a well-buttered rectangular baking dish. Chill until 1 hour before using.

4. When nearing time to serve, brush each pancake with melted butter and sprinkle with freshly grated Parmesan. Bake for 20 minutes in a moderate oven (180°C, 350°F, Gas Mark 4). Serve with well-flavoured Italian Tomato Sauce.

Crêpes aux Fruits de Mer

½ recipe Basic French Crêpes (see page 52)
1–2 level tablespoons each freshly grated
    Gruyère and Parmesan cheese

SEAFOOD FILLING
3 level tablespoons finely chopped onion
3 level tablespoons finely chopped shallots
3 level tablespoons butter
3 level tablespoons finely chopped raw veal
    or cooked ham
3 level tablespoons plain flour
salt and freshly ground black pepper
¼ level teaspoon nutmeg and cayenne mixed
1 bay leaf, crumbled
3 level tablespoons chopped parsley
600 ml/1 pint warm milk
2 egg yolks, well beaten
4 level tablespoons double cream
2 tablespoons lemon juice
4–6 tablespoons dry white wine
3 level tablespoons freshly grated Parmesan
    cheese
450 g/1 lb diced freshly cooked lobster, crab
    or mussels, or a combination of the three

1. Make *crêpes* and cover them with waxed paper or foil to prevent them drying out.

2. To make seafood filling: sauté finely chopped onion and shallots in butter until transparent. Add finely chopped veal or ham and continue to cook, stirring constantly, for 2 to 3 minutes.

Sprinkle with flour and cook, stirring, for 2 minutes more. Season to taste with salt, freshly ground black pepper, nutmeg and cayenne pepper. Add crumbled bay leaf, chopped parsley and half the warm milk, and stir until well blended.

3. Transfer contents to the top of a double saucepan. Add remaining milk and cook over water for 1 hour, stirring from time to time. Strain into a bowl in which you have whisked egg yolks, double cream, lemon juice and white wine. Return to heat and cook until thickened. (Do not allow sauce to boil or eggs will curdle.) Stir in grated cheese and diced shellfish, and heat through.

4. To serve: top each *crêpe* with 2 tablespoons prepared filling, and roll loosely. Place in rows in a rectangular baking dish. Top with remaining sauce and 1 or 2 tablespoons each freshly grated Gruyère and Parmesan cheese. Place under a preheated grill and cook until golden brown.

Mushroom Fritters

100 g/4 oz plain flour
¼ level teaspoon salt
2 egg yolks
1 tablespoon melted butter
150 ml/¼ pint white wine, cider or ale
150 ml/¼ pint milk or water
2 egg whites, stiffly beaten
225 g/8 oz button mushrooms
juice of 1 lemon
salt and freshly ground black pepper
oil for frying

1. Sift flour and salt together, make a well in the centre, and into this pour the egg yolks and cool melted butter. Stir briskly, drawing the flour in by degrees and adding white wine, cider or ale, a little at a time. Let it stand for 1 hour.

2. When ready to cook, stir in milk or water and fold in the stiffly beaten egg whites.

3. Wash mushrooms and sprinkle with lemon juice and seasoning. Dip each mushroom in the batter and fry in hot oil until golden. Drain well and serve very hot.

54

Russian Blini

600 ml/1 pint milk
1 level tablespoon yeast
225 g/8 oz buckwheat flour (or half
  buckwheat and half plain flour)
½ level teaspoon salt
3 egg yolks
melted butter
1 level tablespoon sugar
3 egg whites, stiffly beaten
soured cream
caviar and lemon wedges (optional)

1. Heat half the milk until lukewarm and combine in a warm bowl with yeast. Sift flour together with salt, and add enough of this to the liquid to make a thick 'sponge'. Cover bowl. Stand in a warm place and let sponge rise for about 2½ hours.

2. Beat egg yolks and whisk into remaining milk. Add 2 tablespoons melted butter and the sugar, and add to raised sponge mixture with remaining sifted flour. Beat well and let stand, covered, for 30 minutes more.

3. When ready to serve, fold in stiffly beaten egg whites. Cook on a buttered griddle (I use an iron Swedish *plattar* pan with indentations. *Blini* should be about 7.5 cm/3 inches in diameter.

4. Serve *blini* hot with melted butter and soured cream, or for special occasions, with soured cream, caviar and lemon wedges.

Hard-boiled Egg Fritters

4 hard-boiled eggs
1 slice bacon, 5 mm/¼ inch thick
½ Spanish onion, finely chopped
4 level tablespoons butter
4 level tablespoons finely chopped parsley
450 ml/¾ pint cold well-flavoured Béchamel
  Sauce (see page 412)
salt and freshly ground black pepper
1 egg, beaten
dried breadcrumbs
oil or fat for frying
lemon wedges

1. Shell and chop eggs coarsely.

2. Chop bacon and sauté with finely chopped onion in butter until onion begins to colour.

3. Combine chopped eggs, bacon, onion and finely chopped parsley. Mix well and then stir into cold Béchamel Sauce. Season to taste with salt and freshly ground black pepper. Form mixture loosely into balls and chill.

4. When ready to cook, remove from refrigerator and re-form into more perfect shapes – patties, balls or cork shapes. Dip in beaten egg and then in breadcrumbs. Fry in hot oil until golden. Drain well and serve very hot with lemon wedges.

Crêpes 'Alfredo'
Illustrated on page 37

FILLING
1.75–2.25 kg/4–5 lb fresh spinach
butter
350 g/12 oz raw chicken (breast or legs)
2 small onions
½ clove garlic
150 ml/¼ pint double cream
salt and freshly ground black pepper

CRÊPE BATTER
125 g/4½ oz plain flour
300 ml/½ pint milk
3 eggs
2 level tablespoons melted butter

CHEESE SAUCE
100 g/4 oz butter
100 g/4 oz plain flour
1.15 litres/2 pints milk
350 g/12 oz Parmesan cheese, freshly grated
salt and freshly ground black pepper

1. Wash spinach well, removing any yellowed or damaged leaves. Drain and then remove stalks. Sauté spinach leaves in a pan with 4 level tablespoons butter, stirring constantly, until spinach 'melts'. Transfer to a large sieve and press out excess liquid.

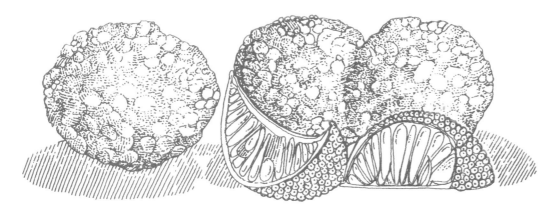

2. Remove skin from chicken, and cut meat into thin strips.

3. Chop onions and garlic finely and sauté in 2 level tablespoons butter over a low heat, stirring from time to time, until onions are transparent. Add chicken meat and continue to cook, stirring, until chicken is tender. Remove from heat.

4. Combine spinach and chicken and onion mixture and pass through the fine blade of a mincer. Add double cream and salt and freshly ground black pepper, to taste.

5. To make batter: combine flour, milk, eggs and melted butter in an electric blender and blend well. Pour batter into a bowl and leave to rest for at least 30 minutes before making crêpes.

6. To make savoury pancakes for Crêpes Alfredo: when ready to fry crêpes, cover an upturned soup plate with a folded cloth. Heat a small, heavy crêpe pan about 15 cm/6 inches in diameter. When it is very hot, rub entire surface very lightly with a wad of kitchen paper moistened with oil. Pour about 2 tablespoons batter into centre of hot pan, tilting it quickly so that it coats bottom of pan very thinly and evenly all over before it has had a chance to set. If you find you have used too much batter, pour excess back into the bowl once a thin layer has set on the bottom of the pan, and scrape away the 'trail' it leaves on the side of the pan. Then use a little less batter for the next crêpe. Cook steadily for 1

minute, drawing a spatula or the point of a knife round edges of crêpe to loosen it. As soon as small bubbles begin to form under the crêpe, flip it over and cook for 60 to 90 seconds longer. Slip out on the prepared plate and cover with the cloth. Continue in this manner until you have made 12 crêpes in all, with an extra one or two as a reserve, stacking them on top of each other under the cloth. Oil pan lightly between each crêpe.

7. To make sauce: melt butter in the top of a double saucepan. Stir in flour and cook over a low heat, stirring constantly until a pale *roux* is formed – about 2 minutes. Bring milk to the boil in a saucepan and add milk gradually to *roux*, stirring constantly so that no lumps form. Cook over lightly simmering water for 20 minutes. Then add freshly grated Parmesan, reserving 6 level tablespoons for later use. Season with salt and freshly ground black pepper to taste. Keep sauce warm.

8. To assemble crêpes: butter a large rectangular flameproof baking dish generously. Place 12 crêpes out on your working surface. Fill each crêpe generously with a few tablespoons of the spinach filling and roll up. Gently place crêpes side by side in the baking dish and put in a very cool to cool oven (120°C to 140°C, 250°F to 275°F, Gas Mark $\frac{1}{2}$ to 1).

9. Remove crêpes from oven; pour sauce over crêpes and sprinkle with remaining grated Parmesan. Place under grill for a few more minutes, or until sauce is bubbling. Serve immediately.

Soufflés

Easy Salmon Soufflé

4 tablespoons butter
3 tablespoons flour
300 ml/½ pint milk
8 tablespoons grated Parmesan cheese
1 (212-g/7½-oz) can salmon
little cream
salt
cayenne
4 egg yolks
5 egg whites

1. Melt butter in the top of a double saucepan. Add flour and stir until well blended. Add milk and continue cooking, stirring continuously, until the sauce has thickened. Stir in grated cheese and heat until cheese has melted into the mixture. Add canned salmon, pounded to a smooth paste with a little cream to make soufflé smooth. Heat through. Season generously with salt and cayenne.

2. Beat egg yolks in a bowl and pour hot salmon mixture over them, stirring until well blended.

3. Beat egg whites until stiff and gently fold them into mixture, a little at a time. Pour in a buttered and floured 20-cm/8-inch soufflé dish and set in a pan of hot water. Bake in a preheated moderate oven (180°C, 350°F, Gas Mark 4) for 25 to 30 minutes. Serve at once.

Mussel Soufflé

24 mussels
300 ml/½ pint dry white wine
3 level tablespoons finely chopped parsley
2 sprigs thyme
1 bay leaf
freshly ground black pepper
2 level tablespoons butter
2 level tablespoons flour
300 ml/½ pint hot milk
4 level tablespoons grated Parmesan cheese
salt
4 tablespoons mussel liquor
4 eggs

1. To prepare mussels: place mussels in a bowl and wash well under running water. Scrape each shell with a knife, removing all traces of mud, seaweed and barnacles. Discard any mussels with cracked, broken or opened shells: **they are dangerous**. Rinse again in running water and remove 'beards'.

2. To cook mussels: combine dry white wine, finely chopped parsley, thyme, bay leaf and freshly ground black pepper in a saucepan. Add mussels, cover saucepan and steam mussels, shaking the pan constantly until shells open.

3. Shell mussels, reserving liquor, and chop coarsely.

4. Melt butter in a saucepan, add flour and stir until smooth. Add hot milk and stir over low heat until thick. Remove from heat. Add grated Parmesan and season to taste with salt and freshly ground black pepper. Stir in chopped mussels and mussel liquor, and allow the mixture to cool slightly.

5. Separate eggs. Beat yolks lightly and stir into sauce. Beat whites until they are stiff but not dry, and fold into sauce. Pour into a 20-cm/8-inch soufflé dish around which you have tied greaseproof paper to make a high 'collar'.

6. Bake soufflé in a preheated moderate oven (180°C, 350°F, Gas Mark 4) for 45 minutes. Serve immediately.

Terrine d'Anguilles (see page 74)
Pâté aux Herbes (see page 79)

Fondant de Volaille 'Auberge du Père Bise'
(see page 77)

Arancini (see page 73)

Gnocchi alla Romana (see page 71)

Langouste Soufflé

2 live langoustes or lobsters (about 1 kg/2 lb
   each)
300 ml/½ pint Béchamel Sauce (see page 412)
fresh butter
paprika
salt and freshly ground black pepper
150 ml/¼ pint double cream
4 egg yolks
5 egg whites, stiffly beaten

1. Cook *langoustes* or lobsters in salted boiling
water for 25 minutes. Allow them to cool in their
own juices.

2. Cut shells in half and remove flesh. Pound
flesh in a mortar with 2 to 3 tablespoons each
thick Béchamel Sauce and butter. Season to taste
with paprika, salt and freshly ground black pepper.

3. Combine remaining Béchamel Sauce and
double cream in the top of a double saucepan. Add
pounded *langoustes* or lobsters and cook over
water, stirring constantly, until sauce is smooth
and thick.

4. Beat egg yolks in a bowl until well blended.
Stir in a little of the hot Béchamel Sauce and then
return egg mixture to remaining sauce. Cook over
water, stirring from time to time, until sauce is
thick. But do not allow sauce to boil, or it will
curdle. Remove from heat and beat until slightly
cooled. Then fold stiffly beaten egg whites into
the sauce; correct seasoning and fill empty
langouste shells with mixture.

5. Arrange buttered foil around shells to form a
'collar' so that mixture will not run over. Place
shells in a pan with a little hot water and cook in a
preheated moderate oven (180°C, 350°F, Gas
Mark 4) for about 20 minutes, or until soufflés are
puffed and golden.

Herring Soufflé

4 level tablespoons butter
2 level tablespoons flour
300 ml/½ pint milk
½ Spanish onion, finely chopped
2 level tablespoons finely chopped parsley
1 level tablespoon anchovy paste
salt
nutmeg
cayenne
175 g/6 oz cooked herring fillets, finely
   chopped
4 egg yolks, lightly beaten
5 egg whites

1. Melt 3 tablespoons butter in the top of a double
saucepan, add flour and stir until smooth. Add
milk and stir over low heat until thick. Remove
from heat.

2. Sauté finely chopped onion in remaining butter
until transparent. Combine with parsley and stir
into sauce. Add anchovy paste, and salt, nutmeg
and cayenne, to taste. Stir finely chopped cooked
herring fillets into soufflé mixture. Remove saucepan from heat and allow mixture to cool slightly.
Stir in lightly beaten egg yolks; blend well.

3. Beat whites until they are stiff but not dry, and
fold gently into sauce. Pour into a 20-cm/8-inch
soufflé dish around which you have tied greaseproof paper to make a high 'collar'. Bake soufflé
in a preheated moderate oven (180°C, 350°F, Gas
Mark 4) for 45 minutes. Serve immediately.

61

Quiche Lorraine

shortcrust pastry (see page 420)
4 eggs
150 ml/¼ pint double cream
150 ml/¼ pint milk
150 ml/¼ pint well-flavoured stock (chicken, beef or veal)
salt and freshly ground black pepper
freshly grated nutmeg
100 g/4 oz green bacon, or fat salt pork, cut in 1 piece
2 level tablespoons butter
100 g/4 oz Gruyère cheese, diced

1. Line pastry tin (or individual tins) with short-crust pastry. Prick bottom with a fork, brush with a little beaten egg and bake 'blind' for 15 minutes.

2. Whisk eggs in a bowl. Add cream, milk and stock and whisk until thick and lemon coloured. Flavour to taste with salt, freshly ground black pepper and freshly grated nutmeg.

3. Cut green bacon, or fat salt pork, into finger-shaped strips. Remove rind and blanch in boiling water for 3 minutes. Drain and sauté strips in butter until golden. Drain.

4. Arrange diced cheese and bacon or pork strips in bottom of pastry case. Pour over the cream and egg mixture and bake in a moderate oven (160°C, 325°F, Gas Mark 3) for 30 to 40 minutes, until the custard is set and golden brown. Serve hot.

Cassolette de Sole 'Mirabelle'

22 g/8 oz puff pastry (see page 420)
2 sole (450 g/1 lb each), filleted
2 shallots
butter
12 mussels
4 oysters, shelled
salt and freshly ground black pepper
1 glass dry white wine
300 ml/½ pint cream

1. Take 4 flan moulds 10 cm/4 inches across, roll the pastry out very thinly and line the moulds.

Bake 'blind' in a moderately hot oven (200°C, 400°F, Gas Mark 6) for 10 minutes, remove beans and return to a moderate oven (180°C, 350°F, Gas Mark 4) for 5 to 10 minutes.

2. Fold fillets over. Chop shallots finely, and put fish and shallots in a saucepan with a good-sized piece of butter, mussels, oysters, salt, freshly ground black pepper, wine and cream.

3. Allow to cook for 12 minutes, and then remove the fish and shellfish. Take the mussels out of their shells. Reduce the sauce until thick and add 2 tablespoons butter.

4. Warm the pastry cases in the oven for 2 minutes, fill with fish and shellfish, and pour the sauce over the top.

Artichoke Tarts Vinaigrette

4 cooked or canned artichoke hearts
4 hard-boiled eggs
1 thick slice cooked ham, diced
½ cucumber, peeled, seeded and diced
4 sticks celery, sliced
olive oil
wine vinegar
dry mustard
finely chopped garlic
salt and freshly ground black pepper
6 individual shortcrust pastry cases, baked 'blind' (see page 420)
finely chopped fresh herbs
mayonnaise (see page 417)

1. Dice artichoke hearts and hard-boiled eggs into large pieces and combine in a bowl with diced cooked ham, cucumber and celery.

2. Moisten liberally with a well-flavoured vinaigrette dressing made from 3 parts olive oil, 1 part wine vinegar, dry mustard, finely chopped garlic, salt and freshly ground black pepper, to taste.

3. When ready to serve: fill baked pastry cases with artichoke and egg. Sprinkle each tart with finely chopped fresh herbs and top with a dab of stiff mayonnaise.

Creamed Button Onion Tart

Illustrated on page 39

20-cm/8-inch shortcrust pastry case, baked 'blind' (see page 420)
melted butter (optional)

FILLING
675 g/2 lb tiny button onions
salt
300 ml/½ pint milk
1 bay leaf
3 black peppercorns
2 cloves
½ chicken stock cube
½ level teaspoon butter
½ level teaspoon flour
3 egg yolks
6 level tablespoons double cream
2 level teaspoons freshly grated Parmesan cheese
freshly ground black pepper
freshly grated nutmeg

1. To make filling: peel button onions. Put in a pan with cold salted water to cover. Bring to the boil over a moderate heat, boil for 2 minutes then drain thoroughly in a colander.

2. In another pan, combine milk with bay leaf, peppercorns, cloves and half a chicken stock cube. Bring to the boil, remove from heat and leave to infuse for 30 minutes, covered with a lid.

3. Add onions to infused milk and return to the heat. Bring to the boil again and poach gently for 5 to 7 minutes, until onions have softened but still hold their shape.

4. Place the prebaked tart case, still in its tin, on a baking sheet.

5. When onions are tender, remove them from the milk with a slotted spoon and arrange them side by side in the pastry case. Strain remaining milk through a fine sieve.

6. Melt butter in a heavy pan. Add flour and stir over a low heat for a minute or two until well blended to make a pale *roux*. Then gradually blend in strained milk, stirring constantly to make a smooth sauce, and simmer for a few minutes longer until thickened.

7. In a large bowl, beat egg yolks lightly with cream until well mixed. Gradually pour in a ladleful of hot sauce, beating all the while. Then pour all the sauce into the top of a double saucepan and stir over hot water until it thickens, taking great care not to let it come to the boil, or the egg yolks will curdle. Finally, stir in freshly grated Parmesan and season generously with salt, freshly ground black pepper and freshly grated nutmeg.

8. Spoon sauce over onions in tart case and bake in a moderate oven (180°C, 350°F, Gas Mark 4) for 30 minutes, or until filling has set and top is a rich golden colour. If tart has not browned by the time filling is firm, brush top lightly with melted butter and slip under a hot grill for a minute or two to colour it. Serve hot.

Smoked Salmon Quiche

4 eggs
150 ml/¼ pint double cream
150 ml/¼ pint milk
150 ml/¼ pint canned clam juice or well-flavoured fish stock
salt and freshly ground black pepper
grated nutmeg
8 individual shortcrust pastry cases (about 10 cm/4 inches in diameter)
thinly sliced smoked salmon
butter

1. Whisk eggs together with cream, milk and canned clam juice, or a well-flavoured fish stock. When well mixed, season to taste with salt, freshly ground black pepper and grated nutmeg.

2. Prick bottoms of pastry cases with a fork and bake 'blind' in a hot oven (230°C, 450°F, Gas Mark 8) for about 15 minutes, just long enough to set the crusts without browning them. Allow to cool.

3. Fill pastry cases with egg mixture. Cover with thin slices of smoked salmon and dot with butter. Bake in a moderate oven (160°C, 325°F, Gas Mark 3) for 30 to 40 minutes, and serve immediately.

64

Courgette and Bacon Tart

Illustrated on page 38

23- or 25-cm/9- or 10-inch shortcrust pastry case, baked 'blind' (see page 420)

FILLING
½ **Spanish onion**
2 tablespoons olive oil
100 g/4 oz green bacon, cut in 1 piece
4–6 small courgettes
salt and freshly ground black pepper
4 eggs
300 ml/½ pint cream
150 ml/¼ pint milk
freshly grated nutmeg
6 level tablespoons freshly grated Gruyère cheese

GARNISH
sprigs of fresh watercress (optional)

1. Chop onion finely and sauté in olive oil until soft, stirring constantly so that it does not take on colour. Remove onion from pan with a slotted spoon and reserve.

2. Cut green bacon into 5-mm/¼-inch slices and then cut each slice into 'fingers' about 5 mm/¼ inch thick. Sauté in oil until golden. Remove from pan with slotted spoon and reserve.

3. Wash courgettes and cut off tops and bottoms. Slice courgettes as thinly as you can and sauté slices in remaining fats until lightly coloured. Season to taste with salt and freshly ground black pepper. Remove from pan with slotted spoon and reserve.

4. Combine eggs, cream and milk in a mixing bowl and mix thoroughly. Season generously with salt, freshly ground black pepper and freshly grated nutmeg.

5. Sprinkle 2 level tablespoons grated Gruyère on the bottom of prepared pastry case. Combine sautéed onion, bacon and courgettes and spoon into pastry case. Sprinkle with 2 level tablespoons grated Gruyère and pour in egg and cream mixture.

6. Sprinkle with remaining Gruyère and bake in a moderate oven (160°C, 325°F, Gas Mark 3) for 30 to 40 minutes until the custard is set and is golden brown. Garnish if desired.

French Mushroom Tartlets

Illustrated on page 40

4–6 baked shortcrust pastry cases (see page 420)
450–675 g/1–1½ lb small button mushrooms
4 tablespoons butter
2 tablespoons olive oil
salt and freshly ground black pepper
pinch of cayenne
4–6 tablespoons Madeira
3 egg yolks
300 ml/½ pint double cream
finely chopped parsley

1. Wash or wipe the mushrooms and trim rough stem ends.

2. Sauté mushrooms in butter and olive oil for 3 minutes (the mushrooms should still be crisp). Season generously with salt and freshly ground black pepper, and a pinch of cayenne. Add Madeira and toss well. Remove pan from heat.

3. Whisk the egg yolks lightly and beat into the double cream. Cook the mixture in a double saucepan, stirring constantly, until mixture thickens. Be careful not to allow the cream to come to the boil, or the sauce will curdle. Add to the mushrooms in the pan and heat *gently*, stirring all the time.

4. To serve: place the baked pastry cases on a baking tray and fill each case with the mushroom and Madeira mixture. Spoon over any remaining Madeira sauce and place under the grill for a minute or two to heat through. Sprinkle with finely chopped parsley and serve immediately.

Prawn and Lobster Quiche

PASTRY
225 g/8 oz plain flour
1 level tablespoon icing sugar
generous pinch of salt
150 g/5 oz butter, diced and softened
1–2 tablespoons iced water

QUICHE FILLING
150 ml/¼ pint double cream
150 ml/¼ pint milk
150 ml/¼ pint canned clam juice
4 eggs
1 (198-g/7-oz) can lobster meat
100 g/4 oz prawns

1. To make pastry: sift flour, sugar and salt into a mixing bowl. Rub in softened butter a little bit at a time with the tips of the fingers until mixture resembles fine breadcrumbs. Do this very gently and lightly or mixture will become greasy and heavy. Add just enough iced water to make a good dough. Shape dough lightly into a flattened round, wrap in foil or polythene and put in refrigerator for at least 1 hour to ripen and become firm. If chilled dough is too firm for handling, leave at room temperature until it softens slightly. Then turn out on to a floured board and roll out in usual manner. Place in a 23-cm/9-inch pie tin and press out with fingertips. Prick with a fork, cover with a piece of foil and fill with dried beans. Bake 'blind' in a hot oven (230°C, 450°F, Gas Mark 8) for 15 minutes. Remove beans and foil. Allow pastry case to cool.

2. To make quiche filling and to serve: beat cream, milk, clam juice and eggs with a whisk. Place chunks of lobster and prawns on the baked pastry case. Pour the beaten egg mixture over the lobster and prawns. Bake in a moderate oven (160°C, 325°F, Gas Mark 3) for 30 to 40 minutes, until the custard is set and golden brown.

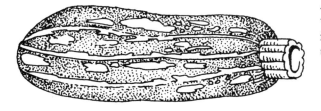

Pizza Tart

Illustrated on page 38

25-cm/10-inch shortcrust pastry case, baked 'blind' (see page 420)
1 egg yolk, lightly beaten

FILLING
6 large ripe tomatoes
olive oil
2 level tablespoons tomato purée
freshly ground black pepper
3 Spanish onions
2 level tablespoons butter
freshly chopped rosemary
2 level tablespoons Parmesan cheese
6–8 thin slices Mozzarella cheese
6–8 thin slices prosciutto
anchovy fillets and stoned black olives

1. Preheat oven to moderate (180°C, 350°F, Gas Mark 4).

2. To make filling: plunge tomatoes into boiling water for a minute to loosen skins; peel, seed and chop them. Heat 4 tablespoons olive oil in a deep frying pan; add tomatoes, tomato purée, and freshly ground black pepper, to taste. Simmer over a low heat until excess moisture is cooked away; mash occasionally with a wooden spoon to reduce tomatoes to a purée. Slice onions and simmer them separately in butter, together with a pinch of freshly chopped rosemary, until soft and golden, but do not let them brown.

3. Sprinkle bottom of pastry case with freshly grated Parmesan cheese. Add onions and cover with tomato purée. Arrange alternate slices of Mozzarella cheese and prosciutto around top of tart. Scatter anchovy fillets and black olives on cheese and ham. Brush olives and anchovies lightly with oil.

4. Bake tart for about 20 minutes. Serve hot, warm or cold as one large tart, cut in wedges, or in individual tart cases, as a first-rate appetiser or to hand around with drinks.

66

French Onion Tart

Illustrated on page 38

PÂTE BRISÉE PASTRY
225 g/8 oz plain flour
generous pinch of salt
1 level tablespoon icing sugar
150 g/5 oz butter, softened

ONION FILLING
2 Spanish onions
100 g/4 oz butter
2 level tablespoons flour
3 eggs
150 ml/¼ pint cream
150 ml/¼ pint milk
salt and freshly ground black pepper
freshly grated nutmeg

1. To make pâte brisée: sift flour, salt and sugar into a mixing bowl. Rub in the softened butter with the tips of the fingers until the mixture resembles fine breadcrumbs. Do this very gently and lightly or the mixture will become greasy and heavy. Roll into a ball and chill for 30 minutes or more.

2. To make onion filling: chop onions finely and sauté in butter until transparent. Cool. Add flour, eggs, cream and milk, and mix well. Season to taste with salt, freshly ground black pepper and freshly grated nutmeg.

3. Turn **pâte brisée** on to a floured board and knead or pat pastry lightly into a round. Place in a 25-cm/10-inch pie tin and press out with fingertips to line pie tin (no rolling is necessary). Flute edge of pastry and prick bottom with a fork to avoid air bubbles while cooking. Bake in a hot oven (230°C, 450°F, Gas Mark 8) for 10 minutes. Cool slightly.

4. Pour mixture into pastry case and cook in a moderate oven (160°C, 325°F, Gas Mark 3) for 30 to 40 minutes. Serve very hot.

5. If liked, garnish tart with bacon rolls stuffed with prunes.

Provençal Tomato and Onion Tart

Illustrated on page 39

4 tablespoons olive oil
6 large ripe tomatoes, peeled, seeded and chopped
4 level tablespoons tomato purée
1 clove garlic, finely chopped
freshly ground black pepper
3 Spanish onions, sliced
2 level tablespoons butter
freshly chopped rosemary
6-8 level tablespoons Parmesan cheese, freshly grated
salt
1 (56-g/2-oz) can anchovy fillets
black olives
olive oil

SAVOURY FINGERTIP PASTRY
225 g/8 oz plain flour
generous pinch of salt
1 level tablespoon icing sugar
150 g/5 oz butter, softened
1 egg yolk
4 tablespoons cold water
lightly beaten egg yolk to glaze

1. To make savoury fingertip pastry: sift flour, salt and sugar into a mixing bowl. Rub in the butter with the tips of the fingers until mixture resembles fine breadcrumbs. Do this very gently and lightly, or mixture will become greasy and heavy. Beat egg yolk and add cold water. Sprinkle over dough and work in lightly with your fingers. Shape moist dough lightly into a flattened round. Wrap in polythene and leave in refrigerator for at least 1 hour to ripen. If chilled dough is too firm for handling, allow to stand at room temperature until it softens slightly. Then turn it on to floured board and roll out as required.

2. Line a pie tin with pastry and flute the edge. Chill. Brush with a little lightly beaten egg yolk and bake in a hot oven (230°C, 450°F, Gas Mark 8) just long enough to set the crust without browning it. Allow to cool.

3. Heat olive oil in a pan; add chopped ripe tomatoes, peeled, seeded and chopped, tomato purée, finely chopped garlic and freshly ground black pepper, to taste. Cook over a low heat until excess moisture is cooked away, mashing occasionally with a wooden spoon to form a purée. Cool.

4. Simmer sliced onions in butter with a little freshly chopped rosemary until soft and golden, but not brown. Cool.

5. Combine tomato purée and onions and add 4–6 level tablespoons freshly grated Parmesan and salt and freshly ground black pepper, to taste.

6. Sprinkle bottom of pastry case with 2 level tablespoons freshly grated Parmesan; cover with tomato and onion mixture. Arrange anchovies in a lattice-work on top and place a black olive in the centre of each square. Brush olives and anchovies lightly with oil and bake in a moderate oven (180°C, 350°F, Gas Mark 4) for about 30 minutes.

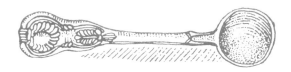

Spinach and Egg Tart
Illustrated on page 38

**23- or 25-cm/9- or 10-inch shortcrust pastry
 case, baked 'blind' (see page 420)**
350 g/12 oz frozen spinach, chopped
4 level tablespoons butter
salt and freshly ground black pepper
225 g/8 oz cottage cheese
3 eggs, lightly beaten
**25–50 g/1–2 oz Parmesan cheese, freshly
 grated**
8 level tablespoons double cream
freshly grated nutmeg
2 hard-boiled eggs, quartered

1. Sauté chopped spinach in butter for 5 minutes, stirring constantly. Season generously with salt

and freshly ground black pepper, to taste. Drain thoroughly and then add cottage cheese with beaten eggs, freshly grated Parmesan, double cream and grated nutmeg, to taste. Mix well.

2. Spread mixture in pastry case and bake the tart in a moderately hot oven (190°C, 375°F, Gas Mark 5) for 30 minutes or until crust is brown and the cheese custard mixture has set.

3. Garnish with quarters of hard-boiled eggs and serve immediately.

Hot Mushroom Tart
Illustrated on page 38

**20-cm/8-inch shortcrust pastry case, baked
 'blind' (see page 420)**
675 g/1½ lb mushrooms
1 Spanish onion
2 level tablespoons butter
2 tablespoons olive oil
1 level tablespoon flour
300 ml/½ pint single cream
2 eggs, beaten
2 tablespoons dry sherry
salt and freshly ground black pepper

1. Clean and quarter mushrooms; chop onion finely. Sauté mushrooms and onion in butter and olive oil until onion is transparent. Remove a quarter of mushrooms and reserve for garnish. Stir flour into remaining mixture and cook, stirring continuously, for 2 minutes.

2. Combine cream with beaten eggs, sherry and salt and freshly ground black pepper, to taste. Pour over mushroom and onion mixture and stir. Cool.

3. Pour mushroom mixture into prepared pastry case and bake in a moderately hot oven (190°C, 375°F, Gas Mark 5) until brown – about 30 minutes.

4. About 10 minutes before removing tart from oven, scatter reserved mushrooms on top of mushroom mixture. Brush with melted butter and return to oven.

Pasta

68

Spaghetti con Salsa Fredda

450 g/1 lb spaghetti
8 tomatoes, peeled, seeded and diced
2 cloves garlic, finely chopped
16 fresh basil leaves, chopped
4 level tablespoons chopped parsley
4–6 tablespoons warmed olive oil
salt and freshly ground black pepper
freshly grated Parmesan cheese

1. Cook spaghetti in boiling salted water until *al dente* – tender but still firm – about 12 to 15 minutes.

2. Mix together diced tomatoes, chopped garlic, basil and parsley. Moisten with olive oil; season generously with salt and freshly ground black pepper, and serve on drained hot spaghetti with freshly grated Parmesan.

Spaghetti con Pesto

450 g/1 lb spaghetti
salt
butter
freshly grated cheese (Romano or Parmesan)

PESTO SAUCE
2–3 cloves garlic, finely chopped
6–8 level tablespoons finely chopped fresh
  basil
6–8 level tablespoons finely chopped parsley
2–3 level tablespoons pine nuts
6–8 level tablespoons grated cheese
  (Romano or Parmesan)
olive oil
freshly ground black pepper

1. **To make Pesto Sauce:** pound finely chopped garlic, basil, parsley, pine nuts and grated cheese in a mortar until smooth. Gradually add olive oil and whisk until sauce is smooth and thick. Season to taste with freshly ground black pepper.

2. Cook spaghetti in rapidly boiling salted water until just tender – about 12 to 15 minutes. Drain and place on a hot serving dish. Spoon Pesto Sauce over and serve with a generous knob of butter and grated cheese.

Stuffed Cannelloni

450 g/1 lb flour
1 level teaspoon salt
3 eggs, well-beaten
4–5 tablespoons water
butter
freshly grated Parmesan cheese

FILLING
450 g/1 lb button mushrooms, chopped
225 g/8 oz cooked ham, chopped
1 Spanish onion, chopped
4 level tablespoons butter
2 tablespoons olive oil
4 level tablespoons freshly grated Parmesan
  cheese
4 level tablespoons double cream
salt and freshly ground black pepper
cinnamon

CHEESE SAUCE
2 tablespoons butter
2 tablespoons flour
600 ml/1 pint hot milk
4 tablespoons grated Parmesan cheese
salt and freshly ground black pepper

1. **To prepare cannelloni:** sift flour and salt into a large mixing bowl. Make a well in the centre and pour in beaten eggs. Add 2 tablespoons water, and mix flour and liquids together with your fingertips until the pasta dough is just soft enough to form into a ball, adding a tablespoon or two of water if the mixture seems too dry. Sprinkle a large pastry board with flour and knead the dough on this board with the flat of your hand until dough is smooth and elastic – about 15 minutes – sifting a little flour on your hand and the board from time to time. Divide dough into 4 equal parts and, using a rolling pin, roll out one piece at a time into paper-thin sheets. To do this, roll out in one direction, stretching the pasta dough as you go, and then roll out in the opposite direction. Sprinkle with flour, fold over and repeat. The dough should be just dry enough not to stick to the rolling pin. Repeat this process of rolling, stretching and folding the dough another 2 or 3 times. Repeat with other pieces of pasta dough. Allow to dry for 1 hour.

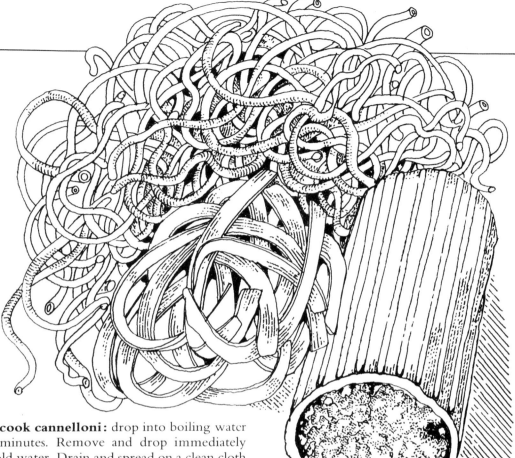

2. To cook cannelloni: drop into boiling water for 5 minutes. Remove and drop immediately into cold water. Drain and spread on a clean cloth to dry.

3. To make filling: sauté chopped mushrooms, ham and onion in butter and olive oil until vegetables are cooked through. Cool. Stir in freshly grated Parmesan, double cream and season to taste with salt, freshly ground black pepper and cinnamon.

4. To make Cheese Sauce: melt butter in the top of a double saucepan. Stir in flour to make a smooth *roux* then add hot milk gradually, stirring continuously. Season to taste with grated Parmesan, salt and freshly ground black pepper. Cook, stirring from time to time, until sauce is smooth and thick.

5. Place 2 tablespoons mushroom filling on each pasta square and roll pasta carefully around filling. Arrange filled cannelloni in a buttered shallow baking dish and cover with Cheese Sauce. Sprinkle generously with grated Parmesan and bake in a moderate oven (180°C, 350°F, Gas Mark 4) for about 30 minutes, or until golden brown.

Green Noodles alla Crema

3.5–4.5 litres/6–8 pints water
450 g/1 lb green noodles
salt
100 g/4 oz butter
100 g/4 oz Parmesan cheese, freshly grated
300 ml/½ pint double cream

1. Bring well-salted water to the boil in a large saucepan. Add green noodles and cook until *al dente* – tender but still firm – about 12 to 15 minutes.

2. While pasta is cooking, melt butter in a saucepan and stir in grated cheese and cream. Cook over a low heat, stirring constantly, until cheese melts and sauce is smooth.

3. Drain noodles and while still very hot, toss with the sauce. Serve noodles with additional grated Parmesan cheese.

70

Lasagne Verdi al Forno

450 g/1 lb green lasagne noodles
salt
butter
225 g/8 oz Mozzarella cheese, diced
50 g/2 oz Parmesan cheese, freshly grated
225 g/8 oz Ricotta cheese, crumbled

MEAT BALLS
450 g/1 lb lean beef, minced
4 eggs
½ loaf stale white bread
1 clove garlic, finely chopped
4 level tablespoons finely chopped parsley
salt and freshly ground black pepper

TOMATO SAUCE
1 Spanish onion, chopped
3 sticks celery, chopped
6 tablespoons olive oil
3 tablespoons tomato purée
1.5 kg/3 lb tomatoes, peeled, seeded and
   chopped
1 teaspoon sugar
2 cloves garlic, chopped
finely chopped parsley
salt and freshly ground black pepper
2 tablespoons butter

1. To make meat balls: combine beef and eggs
in a large bowl and mix well. Soak bread in water
until soft; squeeze dry and shred. Combine with
meat mixture, add garlic and parsley, and season
to taste with salt and freshly ground black pepper.
Form into marble-sized balls.

2. To make Tomato Sauce: sauté onion and
celery in oil in a large frying pan until soft.
Transfer to a larger pan and sauté meat balls in
remaining fat until golden. Add tomato purée to
remaining oil in pan and stir until smooth. Then
stir in chopped tomatoes and sugar and cook for 5
minutes, stirring constantly. Press mixture through
a fine sieve into a large saucepan. Add chopped
garlic and parsley, and simmer mixture for 1 hour.
Season with salt and freshly ground black pepper,
and add butter. Add meat balls and continue to
simmer 30 minutes longer, adding a little water
if sauce becomes too thick.

3. Cook the green lasagne, 6 to 8 at a time, in
boiling salted water until they are half done;
drain carefully. Line a well-buttered baking dish
with a layer of lasagne. Remove half the meat
balls from the Tomato Sauce with a perforated
spoon, and spoon over lasagne. Add a layer of
diced Mozzarella cheese, sprinkle generously with
grated Parmesan and crumbled Ricotta cheese,
and moisten with well-seasoned Tomato Sauce.
Repeat, using the same quantities, finishing with
Tomato Sauce. Dot with butter and bake in a
moderate oven (190°C, 375°F, Gas Mark 5) for
about 30 minutes.

Fettuccine alla Capricciosa

100 g/4 oz veal, finely chopped
100 g/4 oz butter
salt and freshly ground black pepper
150 ml/¼ pint red wine
300 ml/½ pint well-flavoured Italian Tomato
   Sauce (see Polenta Pasticciata, page 71)
225 g/8 oz peas
100 g/4 oz fresh or dried mushrooms, sliced
1-2 slices Parma ham, cut in thin strips
450 g/1 lb fettuccine (egg noodles)

1. Sauté finely chopped veal in half the butter until
golden. Add salt, freshly ground black pepper and
red wine, and simmer gently for 5 to 10 minutes.
Add Italian Tomato Sauce and continue cooking
over a low heat for 30 minutes.

2. Cook peas in boiling salted water until tender.
Drain and sauté with sliced mushrooms and ham in
remaining butter until mushrooms are cooked
through. Add to sauce.

3. Cook fettuccine in boiling salted water until
al dente – tender but still firm – about 12 to 15
minutes. Pour sauce over them and serve
immediately.

Polenta Pasticciata

450 g/1 lb yellow cornmeal
about 1.25 litres/2-2½ pints salted water
butter
8-10 tablespoons freshly grated Parmesan
    cheese
6-8 level tablespoons breadcrumbs
150 g/5 oz Mozzarella cheese, freshly grated

ITALIAN TOMATO SAUCE
2 Spanish onions, finely chopped
2 cloves garlic, finely chopped
4 tablespoons olive oil
6 level tablespoons Italian tomato purée
1 (793-g/1-lb 12-oz) can Italian peeled
    tomatoes
2 bay leaves
4 level tablespoons finely chopped parsley
¼ level teaspoon oregano
1 small strip lemon peel
6 tablespoons dry white wine
salt and freshly ground black pepper
1-2 tablespoons Worcestershire sauce

1. **To cook polenta:** bring water to the boil.
Pour the cornmeal in slowly, stirring constantly
with a wooden spoon. Continue cooking for 20
to 30 minutes, stirring frequently, until the polenta
is thick and soft and leaves the sides of the pan
easily. Add a little more water if necessary. Stir in
4 tablespoons butter and 6 to 8 tablespoons
freshly grated Parmesan.

2. Butter a shallow baking dish and sprinkle
generously with breadcrumbs and remaining
freshly grated Parmesan. Spread a quarter of the
polenta over it, cover with a quarter of the grated
Mozzarella, and dot with 1 tablespoon butter.
Repeat layers until all the ingredients are used up.

3. Bake in a moderately hot oven (190°C, 375°F,
Gas Mark 5) for 15 to 20 minutes, until well
browned. Serve with well-seasoned Tomato
Sauce.

4. **To make Italian Tomato Sauce:** sauté finely
chopped onions and garlic in olive oil in a large,
thick-bottomed frying pan until transparent and
soft but not coloured. Stir in tomato purée and

continue to cook for a minute or two, stirring
constantly. Pour in peeled tomatoes and add bay
leaves, parsley, oregano and lemon peel. Add dry
white wine, an equal quantity of water, and salt
and freshly ground black pepper, to taste. Simmer
gently, stirring from time to time, for 1 to 2 hours.
Just before serving, stir in Worcestershire sauce,
to taste.

Gnocchi alla Romana
Illustrated on page 60

225 g/8 oz Ricotta or cottage cheese
10-12 tablespoons butter
8 tablespoons freshly grated Parmesan
    cheese
3 egg yolks
4 tablespoons sifted flour
salt and freshly ground black pepper
freshly grated nutmeg

1. Sieve Ricotta or cottage cheese into a mixing
bowl.

2. Beat together 4 tablespoons each melted butter
and grated Parmesan, and 3 egg yolks, and stir
into cheese alternately with flour. Season to taste
with salt, and freshly ground black pepper and
nutmeg.

3. Spoon the mixture into a piping bag fitted with
a large plain nozzle. Hold piping bag over a
large saucepan full of boiling salted water and
force mixture through nozzle, cutting it in 2.5-
cm/1-inch pieces (gnocchi) with scissors. Cook
gnocchi for 6 or 7 minutes. Remove with a
perforated spoon and drain on a clean cloth.

4. When ready to serve, arrange gnocchi in overlapping rows in a well-buttered shallow casserole
or *gratin* dish. Pour 6 to 8 tablespoons melted
butter over them and sprinkle with remaining
Parmesan cheese. Bake in a moderate oven
(180°C, 350°F, Gas Mark 4) for 10 minutes, and
then brown under grill until golden.

Rice

Basic Italian Risotto *Serves 4 to 6*
Risotto con Funghi *Serves 4 to 6*
Saffron Rice with Avocado *Serves 4 to 6*

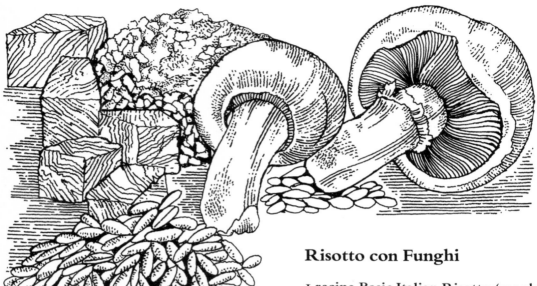

Risotto con Funghi

1 recipe Basic Italian Risotto (see above)
6-8 dried mushrooms
225 g/8 oz cooked ham, diced
6-8 level tablespoons freshly grated
   Parmesan cheese
butter

1. Soak dried mushrooms for several hours in hot water. Drain, cut into small pieces and combine with diced cooked ham.

2. Fold ham and mushroom mixture carefully into *risotto* cooked as in Basic Italian Risotto. Then stir in freshly grated Parmesan cheese.

3. Place rice in a well-buttered casserole. Cover and cook in a moderate oven (180°C, 350°F, Gas Mark 4) for about 20 minutes. Serve immediately.

Basic Italian Risotto

$\frac{1}{2}$ Spanish onion, finely chopped
4 tablespoons butter
350 g/12 oz rice
1-1.5 litres/1$\frac{1}{2}$-2 pints hot beef stock
$\frac{1}{2}$ level teaspoon powdered saffron
salt and freshly ground black pepper
freshly grated Parmesan cheese

1. Place chopped onion in a deep saucepan with butter. Cook slowly for 2 to 4 minutes, taking care that the onion does not become brown.

2. Add rice and cook over medium heat, stirring constantly with a wooden spoon. After a minute or so, stir in a cup of hot beef stock in which you have dissolved the powdered saffron.

3. Continue cooking, adding stock as needed and stirring from time to time, until rice is cooked – 15 to 18 minutes. Correct seasoning. By this time all the stock in the pan should have been absorbed by the rice, leaving rice tender but still moist. Serve immediately with extra butter and freshly grated Parmesan.

Saffron Rice with Avocado

$\frac{1}{2}$ teaspoon powdered saffron
6 tablespoons dry white wine
900 ml/1$\frac{1}{2}$ pints hot chicken stock
350 g/12 oz rice
salt and freshly ground black pepper
1 ripe avocado pear
juice of 1 lemon

1. Dissolve saffron in white wine. Add it to hot chicken stock and combine in a large saucepan with rice, salt and freshly ground black pepper, to taste.

2. Cover pan and simmer until all the liquid is absorbed and the rice is tender.

3. Cut avocado pear in half, lengthwise. Remove stone. Brush cut sides with lemon juice. Peel avocado with a sharp knife. Brush again with lemon juice to preserve colour. Dice avocado into a small bowl. Sprinkle with remaining lemon juice. Add salt and freshly ground black pepper, to taste. Toss well.

4. Transfer saffron rice to a heated bowl; garnish with diced avocado and serve immediately.

Chicken Liver Pilaff

butter
2 level tablespoons finely chopped onion
175 g/6 oz rice
600 ml/1 pint chicken stock
pinch of saffron
4 level tablespoons sultanas
salt and freshly ground black pepper
225 g/8 oz chicken livers
1 level tablespoon flour
300 ml/½ pint well-flavoured Brown Sauce
   (see page 411)
4 tablespoons Madeira wine

1. To prepare pilaff: melt 1 tablespoon butter in a thick-bottomed saucepan and simmer finely chopped onion for a minute or two. Add the rice and stir until rice is well coated with butter. Do not let it colour. Add the stock, saffron and sultanas, and season to taste with salt and freshly ground black pepper. Cover saucepan and simmer rice gently for 15 minutes, or until tender. Correct seasoning. Lightly stir in 1 tablespoon butter and press into well-buttered ring mould. Bake in a moderate oven (180°C, 350°F, Gas Mark 4) for 5 minutes.

2. To prepare chicken livers: cut green parts from livers. Wash livers carefully and pat dry in a clean cloth. Dice livers and toss them lightly in seasoned flour. Sauté in 2 tablespoons butter until

lightly browned. Pour in Brown Sauce and wine; season with salt and freshly ground black pepper. Simmer for a few more minutes, or until tender.

3. Turn rice ring out on a hot serving platter and fill with chicken livers.

Arancini
Illustrated on page 60

100 g/4 oz chicken livers, chopped
1 Spanish onion, finely chopped
1 clove garlic, finely chopped
4 tablespoons olive oil
salt and freshly ground black pepper
4-6 level tablespoons tomato purée
150 ml/¼ pint dry white wine
350 g/8 oz rice
butter
6-8 level tablespoons freshly grated
   Parmesan cheese
2 egg yolks, well beaten
2 eggs, well beaten
dried breadcrumbs
fat for deep-frying

1. Sauté chopped chicken livers, onion and garlic in olive oil until vegetables are transparent. Season to taste with salt and freshly ground black pepper. Add tomato purée diluted with dry white wine. Add enough water to make a creamy sauce, cover saucepan and simmer gently for 30 minutes.

2. Boil or steam rice in usual way until tender but not mushy. Drain well, butter lightly and season to taste with freshly grated Parmesan. Add well-beaten egg yolks and mix well.

3. Strain sauce from chicken livers into rice and mix well.

4. Form small balls the size of golf balls with seasoned rice mixture; then with your forefinger, dig a hole in the centre of each ball and put 1 teaspoon of liver mixture into each. Pinch shut and re-roll ball. Chill.

5. When ready to fry: dip *arancini* in beaten eggs and then in breadcrumbs, and fry until golden.

73

Terrines and Pâtés

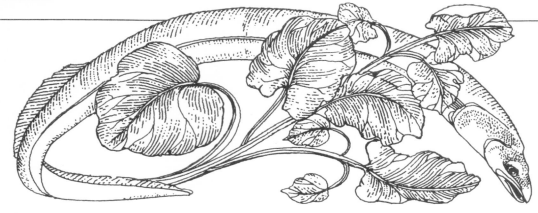

74

Terrine d'Anguilles
Illustrated on page 57

1 kg/2 lb fresh eel, skinned, boned and
   filleted
675 g/1½ lb whiting, skinned and filleted
450 g/1 lb sole, skinned and filleted
150 ml/¼ pint milk
salt and freshly ground black pepper
3 slices white bread
2 egg whites
750 ml/1¼ pints double cream
1 bunch watercress
parsley
dry white wine
butter

EEL JELLY
reserved eel bones
reserved eel stock
1 leaf gelatine
1 egg white
watercress or parsley stems

TO DECORATE
2 canned red pimientos
12 watercress leaves

CRÈME AU CRESSON
2 bunches watercress, with stems removed
salt
150 ml/¼ pint double cream
juice of 1 lemon or lime
freshly ground black pepper

1. Ask your fishmonger to kill and skin eel and
cut it into fillets. Ask him for the bones. (You'll
have to order your eel several days in advance.)

2. Cut eel fillets into even-sized pieces just long
enough to fit into a large oval deep pie dish.
Combine whiting, sole and the eel trimmings and
put through finest blade of your mincer twice.
Put mixture in a bowl and refrigerate for 1½ hours.

3. **To make panade:** bring milk to the boil in a
small saucepan. Season generously with salt and
freshly ground black pepper and remove from
heat. Trim crusts from three slices white bread
and shred into hot milk. Return pan to the heat
and bring to the boil again. Cool panade mixture.

4. **To make mousseline:** squeeze excess liquid
from panade mixture and beat into fish mousse.
Then beat in egg whites, one by one. When
mixture is smooth and thoroughly blended, place
bowl in a larger bowl containing ice, and gradually beat in double cream. Season to taste with
salt and freshly ground black pepper and refrigerate mousseline for 1½ hours to 'ripen' flavours.

5. **To test for flavour:** roll 2 tablespoons of the
mousseline mixture into a ball and place gently in
a saucepan with enough simmering water to just
cover it. Simmer it for a few minutes as you would
a *quenelle* until it is puffed and floats to the surface.
Cool and taste to see if you need to add a little
more seasoning.

6. **To prepare eel fillets:** remove stems from
bunch of watercress and the same amount of
parsley. Place stems and eel fillets in a flameproof
porcelainised shallow casserole or frying pan. Add
enough dry white wine to cover and bring gently
to the boil. Allow to gently bubble in the wine
for 2 minutes only. Remove pan from heat and
cool eel fillets in the stock.

7. To assemble terrine: generously butter a large deep oval pie dish or *terrine* (to hold 1 kg/2 lb *pâté*). Place a third of mousseline mixture in the bottom of the pie dish or *terrine*, gently spreading about 5 mm/¼ inch of the mixture around the sides of the dish. Chop parsley and watercress leaves and spread them on a large plate. Remove eel fillets from stock (reserving stock for later use) and roll fillets in the chopped herbs. Arrange half of the herbed eel fillets on the bed of mousseline mixture in the dish. Sprinkle with half of remaining chopped herbs, top with a third of the mousseline mixture and arrange remaining eel fillets on this bed. Sprinkle with remaining chopped herbs as above, and cover with remaining mousseline mixture.

8. Cover pie dish or *terrine* lightly with a double thickness of aluminium foil, then cover with a plate (or a folded wet tea towel). Place covered *terrine* in a roasting tin half filled with boiling water and cook for 1¾ hours in a cool oven (150°C, 300°F, Gas Mark 2).

9. Remove *terrine* from oven. Allow to cool and then place in the refrigerator for 24 hours.

10. To make eel jelly: place reserved eel bones in the stock and allow to bubble gently for 10 minutes only. Cool stock to lukewarm and add leaf gelatine to 'strengthen' jelly. Clarify the stock by boiling it for 3 minutes with the egg white and 4 to 6 stems of watercress or parsley. Strain through a fine muslin into a bowl and reserve for use.

11. To decorate terrine: cut 12 little diamonds from canned red pimiento. Blanch watercress leaves by placing them in cold water to cover and bring them to the boil. Drain. Remove *terrine* from the refrigerator. Spoon over enough clarified jelly (melt jelly by placing bowl in a pan of hot water) to just cover top of mousseline lightly. Allow to set, then decorate *terrine* with a ring of alternating pimiento 'diamonds' and watercress leaves. Gently spoon over enough of the jelly to keep leaves in place. **Note:** If any are displaced during this operation re-form pattern and allow to set, before brushing a final time with jelly. Return to refrigerator to set.

12. To make Crème au Cresson: place watercress leaves in blender with a generous pinch of salt. Blend at high speed for 1 second. Add double cream and blend for 1 second more. Then add lemon or lime juice, and salt and freshly ground black pepper, to taste. Blend for 1 second more. Serve in a sauceboat.

13. To serve terrine: cut in thin slices and serve cold with *Crème au Cresson*.

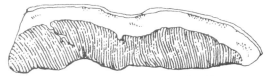

Terrine aux Foies de Volaille

225 g/8 oz lean pork
225 g/8 oz fat bacon
175 g/6 oz poultry livers
2 cloves garlic
4 small shallots
4 eggs, beaten
2 level tablespoons cornflour
3 tablespoons dry white wine
4 tablespoons Cointreau
salt and freshly ground black pepper
freshly grated nutmeg
1 sprig thyme
1 bay leaf
Madeira Aspic (see Basic Meat Aspic,
   page 410)

1. Put lean pork, fat bacon, poultry livers (chicken or duck, or a combination of the two) through the finest blade of your mincer, together with garlic and shallots. Combine mixture in a large bowl with beaten eggs, cornflour, dry white wine, Cointreau, and salt, freshly ground black pepper and grated nutmeg, to taste. Mix well.

2. Place a sprig of thyme, a bay leaf and the *pâté* mixture in an earthenware *terrine*. Cover the *terrine*, place in a pan of water and cook in a moderate oven (160°C to 180°C, 325°F to 350°F, Gas Mark 3 to 4) for about 1½ hours. At the end of the cooking, add Madeira Aspic.

The addition of Cointreau in this recipe removes any bitterness from the poultry livers.

Terrine of Pheasant

1 medium-sized pheasant
1 small onion, sliced
2 small carrots, sliced
2 sprigs parsley
1 bay leaf
salt
pinch of thyme
75 ml/3 fl oz Madeira
75 ml/3 fl oz cognac
225 g/8 oz fresh lean pork
450 g/1 lb fresh fat pork
1 egg, beaten
½ clove garlic, crushed
freshly ground black pepper
Madeira Aspic (see Basic Meat Aspic,
    page 410)

1. Split pheasant down the back. Open it out flat and cut the meat from each breast into strips. Place strips in a bowl with sliced onion, carrots, parsley, bay leaf, ½ teaspoon salt, a pinch of thyme, Madeira and cognac. Let meat marinate in this mixture for 2 hours, then drain. Strain marinade, reserving juices.

2. Cut remaining meat from the pheasant, and combine with lean pork and half the fat pork. Chop finely; add beaten egg, crushed garlic, ½ teaspoon salt, freshly ground black pepper, to taste, and the reserved marinade. Blend until very smooth.

3. Line a *terrine* or earthenware casserole with thin strips of remaining fat pork, thinly sliced. Spread a third of the meat mixture over the bottom, and arrange marinated strips on it. Add alternate layers of meat mixture and marinated strips. Then add alternate layers of meat mixture and breast mixture, finishing with the meat mixture.

4. Cover casserole. Place it in a pan of hot water and bake in a moderately hot oven (200°C, 400°F, Gas Mark 6) for about 1½ hours. Remove cover and place a weighted plate on the *terrine* to compress it gently as it cools.

5. When cold, unmould *terrine* and turn out on a

board. Scrape fat from surface. Wash and dry casserole, then return *terrine* to it, bottom side up. Pour Madeira Aspic around it, cooled but still liquid, and chill until set.

Pâté of Duck

1 tender duckling
450 g/1 lb veal
225 g/8 oz bacon, diced
4 level tablespoons savoury biscuit or
    cracker crumbs
salt and freshly ground black pepper
freshly grated nutmeg
1 egg, well beaten
1 glass dry sherry
100 g/4 oz thinly sliced bacon
1 onion, thinly sliced
1 lemon, thinly sliced
1 bay leaf
flour and water paste

1. Bone a tender duckling and cut the flesh into small pieces. Dice veal roughly, removing skin. Put veal, diced bacon and duck trimmings through the finest blade of your mincer twice to make a fine *farce*.

2. Add biscuit or cracker crumbs. Season to taste with salt, freshly ground black pepper and a little nutmeg, and moisten with well-beaten egg and sherry. Mix thoroughly.

3. Line a *terrine* with sliced bacon. Put in a layer of the *farce*, then some pieces of duck, more *farce*, and so on, until the dish is full. Cover with sliced bacon, and top with thin slices of onion and lemon, and a bay leaf. Put on the lid and seal the join with a paste made of flour and water. Bake in a moderate oven (180°C, 350°F, Gas Mark 4) for 1½ to 2 hours, until the pieces of duck feel quite tender when they are pierced with a skewer. (Remove pastry seal after 1½ hours to check on this.) Remove lid of *terrine* and place a weighted plate on the *pâté* to compress it gently as it cools. Chill in refrigerator for 2 to 3 days before serving.

Fondant de Volaille 'Auberge du Père Bise'

Illustrated on page 59

1 large capon (about 1.5 kg/3½ lb)
300 ml/½ pint dry sherry
2 tablespoons cognac
6-8 tablespoons Noilly
4 sprigs of thyme
1 bay leaf
4 sprigs of parsley
2 tablespoons port
4 shallots
2 carrots
½ Spanish onion
2 cloves garlic
6-8 peppercorns
225 g/8 oz pork fat
450 g/1 lb lean pork
2 level tablespoons coarse salt
freshly ground black pepper
225 g/8 oz foie gras
25 g/1 oz pistachio nuts
thin strips pork fat (about 450 g/1 lb)
diced foie gras (optional)
salted flour and water paste

1. Skin chicken and remove meat from bones, leaving breasts whole.

2. In a large porcelain bowl, combine sherry, cognac and Noilly with herbs, port, shallots, carrots and onions, all finely chopped, and garlic and peppercorns. Add chicken pieces and marinate in this mixture for at least 12 hours.

3. Dice pork fat and half the lean pork, and combine with coarse salt, and freshly ground black pepper, to taste. Refrigerate for 6 hours to prevent meat changing colour during cooking. Pass through the finest blade of your mincer.

4. Place chicken pieces in a roasting tin with remaining pork, diced, and roast in a hot oven (230°C, 450°F, Gas Mark 8) for 5 minutes, or until meat has coloured slightly. Strain marinade juices over meat and cook for 5 minutes more.

5. Remove chicken breasts and pass the remaining chicken pieces and pork juices through the finest blade of your mincer, blending in *foie gras* at the same time. Combine minced pork and pork fat with chicken mixture. Stir in pistachio nuts and remaining marinade juices, and place *pâté* mixture in refrigerator to 'relax' for 2 to 3 hours.

6. **When ready to cook:** line a large *terrine* or *pâté* mould with paper-thin strips of pork fat; fill a quarter full with *pâté* mixture; scatter diced *foie gras* over this for a really luxurious *terrine*, as served at Père Bise; cover with a layer of *pâté* mixture and place marinated chicken breasts on this. Repeat alternate layers of *pâté* mixture and diced *foie gras*, ending with *pâté* mixture. Top with thin strips of pork fat. Cover *terrine* and seal edges with a dough made of flour, water and salt, so that no moisture escapes. Place *terrine* in a pan of boiling water and bake in a moderate oven (160°C, 325°F, Gas Mark 3) for 1 hour. Keep *pâté* in refrigerator for 2 to 3 days before serving.

Home-made Pâté

225 g/8 oz cooked beef, lamb or veal
175 g/6 oz sausagemeat
2 slices white bread, trimmed
little milk
2 shallots, finely chopped
1 small onion, finely chopped
4 level tablespoons finely chopped parsley
2 egg yolks
salt and freshly ground black pepper
butter
gherkins or well-flavoured French Tomato
    Sauce (see page 416)

1. Put cooked beef, lamb or veal through a mincer with sausagemeat.

2. Soak bread in a little milk and squeeze almost dry. Add soaked bread to meat with finely chopped shallots, onion and parsley. Add egg yolks, and salt and freshly ground black pepper, to taste, and spoon mixture into a well-buttered *pâté* mould. Cook in a moderate oven (180°C, 350°F, Gas Mark 4) for 1 hour.

3. Serve cold with gherkins, or hot with well-flavoured French Tomato Sauce.

Terrine of Hare

675 g/1½ lb hare meat
butter
salt and freshly ground black pepper
pinch of nutmeg
2 level teaspoons finely chopped fresh thyme
   or 1 level teaspoon dried thyme
2 level tablespoons finely chopped parsley
150 ml/¼ pint dry white wine
2 tablespoons brandy
450 g/1 lb smoothly ground sausagemeat
slices of fat bacon
flour and water paste

1. Any remains of uncooked hare may be used to make a *terrine*. Remove all bones, trim the flesh and cut it in small pieces, and then weigh it.

2. Melt butter in a saucepan and sauté hare for a minute or two to stiffen outside; do not brown.

3. Place meat in a shallow bowl with salt, freshly ground black pepper and nutmeg, to taste, finely chopped thyme and parsley, and dry white wine and brandy. Marinate hare in this mixture for at least 2 hours.

4. The sausagemeat used should be very fine and smooth. If not sufficiently smooth when bought, put it through the mincer; pound it well and then sieve it.

5. Combine sausagemeat with the marinade liquids and the blood from the hare, if there is any, or the liver, pounded and sieved, to give the forcemeat the taste and darkish colour of the game. Mix well. Add marinated hare and mix again.

6. Line the bottom and sides of a *terrine* with thin slices of fat bacon, then put in the mixture, which should fill it, forming a mound on the top. Cover the top with more fat bacon and put on the lid. Seal round the join of lid and pot with a thick paste made of flour and water to keep in all the flavour of the meat while it is cooking. Make sure, however, that the little hole in the top of the lid is left open, or the *terrine* will burst in the cooking. If there is no hole in the lid, leave a small piece of the join unsealed.

7. **To cook terrine:** place it in a deepish pan with a little cold water round it and bring this to the boil over the heat. Then place it in the oven and cook until the meat is ready – 2 to 2½ hours. The water round the *terrine* should be kept boiling all the time; if it boils away, add more boiling water. Test the meat by running a needle in through the hole in the top, or if, on removing the cover, the fat on top looks quite clear and the meat moves about easily without adhering to the bottom and sides, it is sufficiently cooked. Remove cover and place a weighted plate on the *terrine* to compress it gently as it cools. Chill in the refrigerator for at least 3 days before serving to allow flavours to ripen.

To keep terrine: a *terrine* like this will keep for 2 to 3 months in the refrigerator if sealed with a layer of melted lard. Other kinds of game may be used instead of hare.

Chicken Liver Terrine

575 g/1¼ lb fresh chicken livers
6 tablespoons port
generous pinch of thyme
4 bay leaves
4 slices ham
350 g/12 oz sausagemeat
3 slices bread
little milk
150 ml/¼ pint dry white wine
½ clove garlic, finely chopped
freshly ground black pepper
thin rashers streaky bacon, or bacon and
   pork fat
melted lard

1. Place fresh chicken livers in a bowl, add port, a generous pinch of thyme, and 2 bay leaves, crumbled. Allow the livers to marinate in this mixture for at least 2 hours.

2. Put three-quarters of the chicken livers through a mincer with ham, sausagemeat, and bread which you have soaked in a little milk. Stir in dry white wine to make a rather wet mixture. Then add finely chopped garlic and freshly ground black pepper, to taste. Mix well.

3. Line a *pâté* mould with thin rashers of streaky bacon. For a more subtle flavour, ask your butcher to give you paper-thin strips of larding pork fat. Place the strips between 2 sheets of waxed paper, and pound them as thinly as possible. Then use thin strips of pork fat alternately with strips of streaky bacon to line your *pâté* mould.

4. Spread half of the liver and sausage mixture in the bottom of the mould. Add whole chicken livers, and cover with remaining liver and sausage mixture.

5. Top with thin strips of bacon and 2 bay leaves. Cover mould, place in a pan of boiling water and cook in a moderately hot oven (190°C, 375°F, Gas Mark 5) for $1\frac{1}{4}$ to $1\frac{1}{2}$ hours. Place a weight on *pâté* – all excess juices will pour over edges of mould – and allow to cool. When cold, coat with a little melted lard. Chill in refrigerator for 2 to 3 days before serving.

Pâté aux Herbes
Illustrated on page 57

450 g/1 lb pork
450 g/1 lb fresh or 100 g/4 oz frozen leaf
   spinach
salt
100 g/4 oz cooked ham
100 g/4 oz green bacon
100 g/4 oz cooked ox tongue
1 Spanish onion, finely chopped
2 cloves garlic, finely chopped
4 level tablespoons finely chopped basil
4 level tablespoons finely chopped parsley
4 level tablespoons finely chopped chervil
4 leaves rosemary, finely chopped
4 eggs, beaten
freshly ground black pepper
cayenne
freshly grated nutmeg
100 g/4 oz chicken livers
2 level tablespoons butter
150 ml/$\frac{1}{4}$ pint double cream
2 level tablespoons powdered gelatine
strips of pork fat
gherkins

1. Put pork through finest blade of mincer.

2. Cook spinach in boiling salted water for 5 minutes. Drain and press dry with hands to remove all water. Chop coarsely and put through mincer with pork again.

3. Dice ham, green bacon and ox tongue and combine with finely chopped onion, garlic and fresh herbs. (If you use dried herbs, use only half the quantity.) Stir in beaten eggs and add salt, freshly ground black pepper, cayenne and nutmeg to taste.

4. Chop chicken livers and sauté in 2 tablespoons butter until golden. Stir in cream and powdered gelatine which you have dissolved in a little water and mix well. Add to *pâté* mixture and mix well.

5. Line the bottom and sides of an ovenproof *terrine* with thin strips of pork fat. Press *pâté* mixture into *terrine*, cover with thin strips of pork fat and cook in a moderate oven (160°C, 325°F, Gas Mark 3) for 30 minutes. Lower heat to 150°C, 300°F, Gas Mark 2 and cook for another 30 to 40 minutes.

6. Remove from oven and cool. Serve cold, cut into slices, with gherkins.

Soups

Fresh Lettuce Soup I

2 lettuces
225 g/8 oz spinach leaves
6 spring onions
4 level tablespoons butter
1.15 litres/2 pints well-flavoured chicken
   stock
salt and freshly ground black pepper
1 egg yolk
4-6 level tablespoons double cream
fried croûtons of bread

1. Remove hard stalks and discoloured leaves
from lettuce and spinach. Wash the leaves well
and drain. Trim roots and most of the green from
onions. Slice vegetables thinly.

2. Melt butter in a saucepan and simmer sliced
vegetables gently for 15 minutes, stirring from
time to time. Add stock and bring to the boil.
Reduce heat, cover and simmer gently for 35
minutes. Correct seasoning.

3. Whisk egg yolk and cream in a soup tureen.
Add hot soup, stirring all the time. Serve with
croûtons.

Fresh Lettuce Soup II

2 lettuces
225 g/8 oz spinach leaves
3-4 spring onions
4 level tablespoons butter
600 ml/1 pint well-flavoured chicken stock
salt and freshly ground black pepper
300 ml/½ pint Béchamel Sauce (see page 412)
150 ml/¼ pint cream
4 level tablespoons finely chopped chervil
   or parsley
fried croûtons of bread

1. Remove hard stalks and discoloured leaves
from lettuce and spinach. Wash the leaves well
and drain. Trim roots and most of the green from
onions. Slice vegetables thinly.

2. Melt butter in a saucepan and simmer sliced
vegetables gently for 15 minutes, stirring from
time to time. Add stock and bring to the boil.
Reduce heat, cover and simmer gently for 35
minutes. Correct seasoning.

3. Add Béchamel Sauce and simmer for 10 minutes. Press through a fine sieve or blend in an
electric blender. Return purée to a clean saucepan.
Stir over a high heat until boiling. Add cream and
chervil or parsley, and serve with *croûtons.*

Chicken Soup with Matzoh Balls *Serves 4 to 6*
Chilled Spanish Soup *Serves 6 to 8*
Potage à la Bonne Femme *Serves 4 to 6*

Chicken Soup with Matzoh Balls

1.4 litres/2½ pints well-seasoned chicken stock

MATZOH BALLS
2 egg yolks
½ teaspoon salt
2 tablespoons melted chicken fat
4 level tablespoons finely chopped parsley
4 level tablespoons matzoh meal
2 egg whites, stiffly beaten

1. To make matzoh balls: beat egg yolks until light. Add salt and melted chicken fat, and beat again. Add finely chopped parsley and matzoh meal, and mix well. Then fold in beaten egg whites thoroughly. Chill dough for 15 minutes and form into very small balls.

2. Drop balls into boiling stock, cover and simmer for 20 minutes, or until tender.

Chilled Spanish Soup

Illustrated on page 85

2 slices white bread
8 large ripe tomatoes
1 cucumber
900 ml/1½ pints chicken broth, chilled
1 level teaspoon salt
freshly ground black pepper
2 tablespoons olive oil
2 tablespoons lemon juice
1-2 cloves garlic, finely chopped
4-6 level tablespoons finely chopped parsley
garlic croûtons
1 green pepper, seeded and chopped
4-6 spring onions, finely chopped
2 hard-boiled eggs, finely chopped

1. Trim crusts from bread and soak in cold water.

2. Peel, seed and chop tomatoes. Peel, seed and dice cucumber.

3. Combine chopped vegetables (saving half the tomatoes and a little cucumber for garnish) with soaked bread and well-flavoured chilled chicken broth. Season to taste with salt, freshly ground black pepper, olive oil, lemon juice and finely chopped garlic and parsley. Purée in an electric blender or pass through a fine sieve. Chill.

4. Serve with small accompanying bowls of garlic *croûtons*, finely chopped green pepper, spring onions, tomatoes, cucumber and hard-boiled eggs.

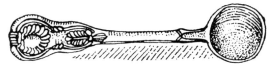

Potage à la Bonne Femme

4 level tablespoons butter
4-5 spring onions, thinly sliced
1 lettuce, shredded
½ cucumber, peeled, seeded and sliced into matchsticks
1 (227-g/8-oz) packet frozen peas
4-5 sprigs tarragon, chervil or sorrel, finely chopped
1.15 litres/2 pints chicken stock
2 egg yolks
150 ml/¼ pint cream
salt and freshly ground black pepper
fried bread croûtons

1. Melt butter in a saucepan. Add vegetables and herbs and simmer gently for about 5 minutes.

2. Bring chicken stock to the boil. Pour it over the vegetables and allow the soup to simmer gently for about 30 minutes, or until vegetables are quite tender.

3. Beat egg yolks and cream with a fork until well blended. Remove pan from the heat and strain egg and cream mixture into the soup, stirring constantly.

4. Return pan to heat and simmer, stirring constantly, until the yolks thicken, but do not let it come to the boil or your soup will curdle. Season to taste with salt and freshly ground black pepper. Serve with *croûtons*.

81

82

Hollandaise Soup

1 small turnip, diced
2 carrots, diced
½ cucumber, peeled, seeded and diced
1 (227-g/8-oz) packet frozen peas
2 level tablespoons butter
2 level tablespoons flour
1.15 litres/2 pints well-flavoured chicken
  stock
2 egg yolks
150 ml/¼ pint single cream
1 level tablespoon finely chopped parsley
  or tarragon
pinch of sugar
salt and freshly ground black pepper

1. Cook vegetables in separate saucepans of boiling salted water until just tender. Drain.

2. Melt the butter in a saucepan. Add the flour and cook, stirring with a wooden spoon, until smooth. Pour in the stock and simmer, stirring constantly, until soup is slightly thickened. Skim if necessary.

3. Remove saucepan from heat. Mix egg yolks and cream together and strain into soup, stirring constantly. Simmer gently over a low heat until the yolks thicken, but do not allow the soup to boil again or it will curdle.

4. Just before serving: add the chopped parsley or tarragon and a pinch of sugar, and season to taste with salt and freshly ground black pepper. Put the prepared vegetables into a hot soup tureen, pour the soup over them and serve immediately.

Crème Germiny

4 leaves sorrel
2 level tablespoons butter
600 ml/1 pint well-flavoured chicken
  consommé
8 egg yolks
4 level tablespoons double cream
salt and freshly ground black pepper

1. Wash and drain sorrel; shred finely. Simmer gently in butter until soft. Add chicken consommé and bring to the boil.

2. Combine egg yolks, double cream, and salt and freshly ground black pepper, to taste, in a large mixing bowl, and whisk with an egg beater until smooth. Pour hot consommé on to the egg mixture and mix well.

3. Pour mixture into a clean saucepan and simmer gently over a very low heat, stirring constantly, until smooth and thick. Do not let soup come to the boil or it will curdle.

Fresh Mushroom Soup

4 level tablespoons butter
3 level tablespoons flour
600 ml/1 pint chicken stock
300 ml/½ pint milk
225 g/8 oz mushrooms, washed and sieved
4 level tablespoons chopped parsley
juice of 1 lemon
150 ml/¼ pint double cream
salt and freshly ground black pepper

1. Melt butter in a saucepan. Add flour and cook gently for 3 to 4 minutes.

2. Add chicken stock; blend well and bring to the boil, stirring all the time. Add milk, sieved mushrooms, parsley and lemon juice, and cook for 5 minutes.

3. Stir in cream and season to taste with salt and freshly ground black pepper. Serve hot or cold.

Chilled Asparagus Soup

Illustrated on page 86

1 bunch fresh asparagus
¼ Spanish onion, finely chopped
4 tablespoons plus 450 ml/¾ pint chicken stock
4 level tablespoons butter
2 level tablespoons flour
salt and freshly ground black pepper
300 ml/½ pint double cream
2 level tablespoons finely chopped parsley
grated rind of ½ lemon

1. Cut the tips off asparagus and reserve for garnish. Break off tough white ends. Wash stalks and slice into 2.5-cm/1-inch segments.

2. Combine segments in a saucepan with finely chopped onion, 4 tablespoons chicken stock and butter, and simmer, covered, until tender.

3. Remove cooked asparagus segments. Stir in flour until well blended, add remaining chicken stock and cook, stirring continuously, until soup reaches boiling point. Season to taste with salt and freshly ground black pepper.

4. Return asparagus segments to thickened soup and purée in an electric blender or press through a fine sieve. Allow to cool, then chill.

5. Just before serving: add double cream and garnish with asparagus tips which you have cooked until tender and then chilled. Sprinkle with finely chopped parsley and grated lemon rind.

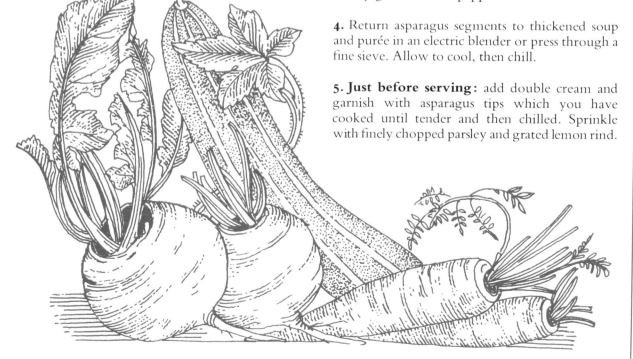

84

Spanish Summer Soup Salad

6 large ripe tomatoes
$\frac{1}{2}$ Spanish onion, thinly sliced
$\frac{1}{2}$ green pepper, seeded and thinly sliced
$\frac{1}{2}$ cucumber, peeled and thinly sliced
1 clove garlic, finely chopped
salt, Tabasco and freshly ground black
    pepper
6 tablespoons olive oil
3 tablespoons lemon juice
300–450 ml/$\frac{1}{2}$–$\frac{3}{4}$ pint chilled chicken
    consommé

GARNISH
2 tomatoes, peeled, seeded and diced
$\frac{1}{2}$ green pepper, seeded and diced
$\frac{1}{4}$ cucumber, peeled, seeded and diced
1 avocado pear, peeled, stoned, diced and
    brushed with lemon juice to preserve
    colour
garlic croûtons made from 4 slices white
    bread, diced and sautéed until crisp and
    golden in butter and olive oil
4 level tablespoons finely chopped chives
    or parsley

1. Seed tomatoes and dice coarsely. Combine in a salad bowl with thinly sliced Spanish onion, green pepper and cucumber. Season to taste with finely chopped garlic, salt, Tabasco and freshly ground black pepper, and marinate in olive oil and lemon juice in the refrigerator for at least 30 minutes.

2. Just before serving, add chilled chicken consommé.

3. Garnish with a sprinkling of diced tomato, green pepper, cucumber, avocado pear, garlic *croûtons*, and finely chopped chives or parsley.

Chilled Avocado Soup

1.75 litres/3 pints well-flavoured chicken
    stock
4 ripe avocado pears
lemon juice
salt and white pepper
6 drops Tabasco
150 ml/$\frac{1}{4}$ pint double cream

1. Chill stock thoroughly.

2. Peel and halve avocado pears and remove stones. Brush avocados generously on all sides with lemon juice as soon as you cut and peel them, to prevent discoloration.

3. Purée avocado halves with chilled stock until smooth, either in an electric blender, or by rubbing them together through a very fine sieve. Season to taste with salt and white pepper.

4. Add Tabasco and cream and blend thoroughly. Taste again for seasoning, adding a little more salt or Tabasco, if necessary, and lemon juice to taste.

Chilled Spanish Soup (see page 81)

Chilled Asparagus Soup (see page 83)
Maquereaux en Court-Bouillon (see page 95)

Brandade de Morue (Cream of Salt Cod) (see page 94)

Creamed Haddock (see page 97)

Watercress Vichyssoise *Serves 4 to 6*
Green Vegetable Soup with Cucumber *Serves 4 to 6*
Watercress and Mushroom Consommé *Serves 4 to 6*
Vegetable Consommé *Serves 4 to 6*

Watercress Vichyssoise

6 potatoes, peeled and sliced
3 large leeks, sliced
1½ bunches watercress
1 ham bone (optional)
1.75 litres/3 pints chicken stock (made with
 a stock cube)
salt and freshly ground black pepper
double cream, chilled
sprigs of watercress, to garnish

1. Cook sliced vegetables and watercress with ham bone in stock until done.

2. Blend in an electric blender, or purée through a fine sieve. Season with salt and freshly ground black pepper, and chill.

3. Just before serving, add chilled cream, to taste. Serve with sprigs of watercress.

Green Vegetable Soup with Cucumber

1 (113-g/4-oz) packet frozen peas
1 (227-g/8-oz) packet frozen leaf spinach
1.4 litres/2½ pints chicken consommé
8 level tablespoons butter
½ cucumber, peeled and seeded
2 egg yolks
150 ml/¼ pint double cream
salt and freshly ground black pepper
finely chopped parsley

1. Defrost peas and spinach leaves and simmer half of them in 4 tablespoons each chicken consommé and butter until cooked through. Drain and purée in an electric blender or push through a fine sieve.

2. Peel and seed cucumber and cut flesh into pea-sized dice. Combine diced cucumber with remaining peas and spinach leaves in remaining butter and cook gently until tender.

3. Beat egg yolks in a large bowl, stir in cream and puréed vegetables. Pour in remaining chicken consommé, whisking continuously, until well

mixed. Transfer to a clean saucepan and cook over a gentle heat, stirring, until green-tinted soup is smooth and thick. Do not let soup come to the boil, or it will curdle.

4. Just before serving, stir in cooked peas, spinach and diced cucumber. Season to taste with salt and freshly ground black pepper. Sprinkle with finely chopped parsley.

Watercress and Mushroom Consommé

1 bunch watercress
6-8 button mushrooms
900 ml-1.15 litres/1½-2 pints chicken stock
4-6 tablespoons port wine or Madeira
salt and freshly ground black pepper

1. Wash watercress and remove leaves from stems. Wash and trim mushrooms, slice thinly.

2. Bring chicken stock to the boil. Add watercress leaves and thinly sliced mushrooms and heat through. Add port or Madeira and salt and freshly ground black pepper, to taste. Serve immediately.

Vegetable Consommé

900 ml-1.15 litres/1½-2 pints beef consommé
4-6 sticks celery, thinly sliced
100 g/4 oz green beans, cut in 2.5-cm/1-inch
 segments
salt and freshly ground black pepper
2-4 level tablespoons chopped chives,
 or parsley

1. Bring beef consommé to the boil. Add thinly sliced celery and bean segments. Allow the soup to simmer gently for 20 minutes. Season with salt and freshly ground black pepper, to taste.

2. Add finely chopped fresh herbs and serve immediately.

89

90

Danish Cabbage Soup

1 cabbage (about 1 kg/2 lb)
1 Spanish onion
4 level tablespoons butter
1–2 level tablespoons brown sugar
900 ml/1½ pints beef stock
4–6 whole allspice
salt and freshly ground black pepper
1 (142-ml/5-fl oz) carton soured cream

1. Slice cabbage and onion thinly.

2. Melt butter in a saucepan, stir in brown sugar and simmer, stirring constantly, for 1 minute. Then add sliced vegetables and cook, stirring, until vegetables are lightly browned.

3. Add beef stock and allspice and salt and freshly ground black pepper, to taste. Simmer gently for 30 to 40 minutes, until cabbage is tender.

4. Stir in soured cream. Correct seasoning and serve immediately.

Carrot Vichyssoise 'Four Seasons'

5 potatoes, sliced
7 large carrots, sliced
2 large leeks, sliced
1 ham bone
1.4 litres/2½ pints chicken stock
1–2 level teaspoons sugar
1 level tablespoon salt
freshly ground black pepper
600 ml/1 pint double cream
raw carrot, cut in fine strips

1. Cook sliced vegetables and ham bone in stock until potatoes and carrots are tender.

2. Purée vegetables and stock in a blender, or push through a fine sieve.

3. Season to taste with sugar, salt and a pinch of freshly ground black pepper. Stir in cream, heat through – but do not allow to come to the boil.

4. Serve with a garnish of fine strips of raw carrot.

French Watercress Soup

4 level tablespoons butter
2 tablespoons olive oil
1 large onion, finely chopped
1 clove garlic, finely chopped
225 g/8 oz potatoes, peeled and thinly sliced
salt and freshly ground black pepper
1½ bunches watercress
300 ml/½ pint milk
300 ml/½ pint chicken stock
8–10 tablespoons single cream
2 egg yolks

1. Heat butter and olive oil until melted in a large, heavy saucepan. Sauté finely chopped onion and garlic over a moderate heat until transparent but not coloured.

2. Add sliced potatoes, sprinkle with salt and freshly ground black pepper and cover with 300 ml/½ pint water. Bring to the boil, reduce heat and simmer until potatoes are almost tender, 5 to 7 minutes.

3. Wash watercress carefully. Separate stems from leaves. Put about a quarter of the best leaves aside for garnish. Chop stalks coarsely and add them to the simmering pan, together with remaining leaves.

4. Stir in milk and chicken stock. Bring to the boil and simmer for 15 to 20 minutes, or until all the vegetables are very soft.

5. Rub soup through a fine wire sieve, or purée in an electric blender. Pour back into the rinsed-out saucepan, correct seasoning if necessary and reheat gently.

6. Blend cream with egg yolks. Pour into the heating soup and continue to cook, stirring constantly, until soup thickens slightly. Do not allow soup to boil once the egg yolks have been added, or they will scramble and ruin its appearance.

7. Shred reserved watercress leaves, sprinkle them over the soup and serve immediately.

Minestre Verde

Illustrated on page 280

225 g/8 oz dried haricot beans
4 rashers lean bacon
1 garlic clove
2.25 litres/2 quarts chicken stock
2 leeks
4-6 tomatoes
4 tablespoons olive oil
2 level tablespoons chopped herbs (parsley,
    basil, chives, oregano)
1 (100-g/4-oz) packet frozen peas
225 g/8 oz sliced green beans
1 potato, diced
salt and freshly ground black pepper
100-175 g/4-6 oz small elbow macaroni

GARNISH
2 level tablespoons finely chopped parsley
2 tablespoons olive oil
4-6 level tablespoons freshly grated
    Parmesan cheese

1. Place dried beans in a large saucepan, fill pan three-quarters full with cold water and bring to the boil. Remove pan from the heat and allow beans to stand in water for 1 hour.

2. Drain beans and put them in a large, clean saucepan with bacon and garlic and enough chicken stock (made with a cube) to cover. Simmer for $1\frac{1}{2}$ hours, adding more stock if necessary.

3. In the meantime, wash leeks carefully and chop. Peel and seed tomatoes and chop.

4. Sauté chopped leeks and tomatoes in olive oil until vegetables are soft. Add chopped herbs and cook for a few minutes more before adding peas, green beans and diced potato. Season with salt and freshly ground black pepper. Cook over a high heat for 10 minutes. Add reserved beans and their cooking liquid and elbow macaroni and cook until pasta is tender.

5. Stir in finely chopped parsley and olive oil. Sprinkle with grated Parmesan cheese.

Spanish Carrot Soup

675 g/$1\frac{1}{2}$ lb carrots
softened butter
6-8 tablespoons dry sherry
900 ml/$1\frac{1}{2}$ pints well-flavoured chicken stock
salt and freshly ground black pepper
2 egg yolks
300 ml/$\frac{1}{2}$ pint double cream

1. Peel carrots and cut into 1-cm/$\frac{1}{2}$-inch slices.

2. Heat 2 level tablespoons softened butter and cook carrots until golden, stirring frequently. Do not allow to scorch. Add 4 tablespoons dry sherry and 300 ml/$\frac{1}{2}$ pint chicken stock and bring to the boil. Reduce heat and simmer, covered, until the carrots are tender. Remove from the heat. Purée.

3. Return carrot purée to the heat, stir in 2 level tablespoons butter and remaining chicken stock, season with salt and freshly ground black pepper and simmer until heated through.

4. In another pan, melt 2 level tablespoons butter, beat in the egg yolks and double cream and add to the soup. Heat through, but do not allow soup to come to the boil. Just before serving, stir in 2 or more tablespoons dry sherry.

92

Prawn and Corn Chowder
Illustrated on page 280

1 (198-g/7-oz) can corn niblets
100 g/4 oz frozen Norwegian prawns
½ Spanish onion, finely chopped
2 level tablespoons butter
2.25 litres/4 pints chicken stock
freshly ground black pepper
1-2 tablespoons soy sauce
2 eggs, beaten
2-4 level tablespoons freshly chopped
   parsley

1. Drain corn niblets. Defrost prawns.

2. Sauté chopped onion in butter until soft; add chicken stock and corn niblets and simmer gently for 20 minutes. Then add prawns and continue to simmer for 10 more minutes.

3. Just before serving, add freshly ground black pepper and soy sauce to taste. Beat in eggs, sprinkle with chopped parsley and serve immediately.

Cream of Potato Soup

2 large Spanish onions
4 level tablespoons butter
6 medium potatoes
900 ml/1½ pints chicken stock
salt, freshly ground black pepper and nutmeg
300 ml/½ pint double cream
finely chopped chives

1. Peel onions and slice thinly. Sauté the onion rings gently in butter until soft. Do not allow to brown.

2. Peel and slice potatoes and add to onions with chicken stock, and salt, freshly ground black pepper and finely grated nutmeg, to taste, and simmer until vegetables are cooked.

3. Push the vegetables and stock through a wire sieve, or blend in an electric blender until smooth.

4. Just before serving, add cream and heat

through without boiling. Serve immediately sprinkled with chives.

Broccoli Cream Soup

2 (283-g/10-oz) packets frozen broccoli
1 stick celery, thinly sliced
1 small onion, thinly sliced
900 ml/1½ pints boiling chicken stock
generous pinch ground cloves
salt and freshly ground black pepper
about 300 ml/½ pint single cream

GARNISH
thin lemon slices
lightly salted whipped cream

1. Bring vegetables to boil in stock and simmer until tender.

2. Purée in electric blender or *mouli* or rub through fine sieve.

3. Add cloves, seasoning and thin with cream. Reheat, stirring, without boiling. Garnish with lemon slices topped with salted whipped cream.

Cream of Spinach Soup

1 kg/2 lb fresh spinach leaves
4 level tablespoons butter
salt and freshly ground black pepper
nutmeg
300 ml/½ pint double cream
600 ml/1 pint chicken stock (made with a
   cube)
finely chopped parsley
croûtons of fried diced bread

1. Wash the spinach leaves, changing water several times. Drain them thoroughly.

2. Put spinach in a thick-bottomed saucepan with butter, and cook gently, stirring continuously, until spinach is soft and tender.

3. Blend in an electric blender, or put through a

wire sieve. Season generously with salt, freshly ground black pepper and nutmeg.

4. Combine purée with cream and chicken stock, and heat through. Sprinkle with finely chopped parsley and fried diced bread. Serve immediately.

Cream of Onion Soup

6 Spanish onions
4 level tablespoons butter
sugar
600 ml/1 pint chicken stock (made with a
   cube)
300 ml/$\frac{1}{2}$ pint milk
2 tablespoons Cognac
$\frac{1}{2}$ level tablespoon Dijon mustard
300 ml/$\frac{1}{2}$ pint double cream
salt and freshly ground black pepper
nutmeg
croûtons made from 2 slices bread, diced
   and sautéed in butter until crisp and
   golden

1. Peel and slice onions thinly.

2. Heat butter in a large saucepan with a little sugar. Add the onion rings and cook them very, very gently over a low heat, stirring constantly with a wooden spoon, until the rings are just

beginning to turn colour. Add chicken stock and milk gradually, stirring constantly until the soup begins to boil. Then lower the heat, cover the pan, and simmer gently until onions are soft.

3. Blend to a smooth purée in an electric blender. Add cognac, mustard and double cream and season to taste with salt, freshly ground black pepper and nutmeg and heat through.

4. Pour soup into individual soup bowls. Sprinkle with *croûtons* and serve immediately.

93

Provençal Fish Salad

300 ml/½ pint well-flavoured mayonnaise
  (see page 417)
I clove garlic, finely chopped
1–2 anchovy fillets, finely chopped
2 level tablespoons finely chopped basil or
  tarragon
2 level tablespoons finely chopped parsley
1–2 level tablespoons finely chopped capers
lemon juice, to taste
675 g/1½ lb cold poached fish, diced
lettuce leaves
finely chopped parsley
black olives

1. Combine first 7 ingredients; toss diced cold poached fish lightly in sauce until well coated.

2. Arrange lettuce leaves around edges of a large shallow salad bowl; pile fish mixture into centre of bowl and garnish with finely chopped parsley and black olives.

Brandade de Morue (Cream of Salt Cod)

Illustrated on page 88

450 g/1 lb salt cod fillets (smoked haddock
  fillets make a delicious alternative)
1–2 cloves garlic, crushed
150 ml/¼ pint double cream
150 ml/¼ pint olive oil
1–2 boiled potatoes (optional)
juice and finely grated rind of ½ lemon
freshly ground black pepper
bread triangles fried in butter

1. Soak cod fillets overnight in a bowl under gently running water. Drain, put salt cod in a saucepan, cover with cold water and bring to the boil. Drain and return to pan. Cover with cold water and bring to the boil again. Turn off heat and allow to steep in hot water for 10 minutes. Strain cod, remove skin and bones, and flake fish with a fork.

2. Place cod fillets in electric blender with crushed garlic, 2 tablespoons cream and 4 tablespoons olive

oil, and blend (or work mixture to a smooth paste with a mortar and pestle), from time to time adding remainder of cream and olive oil alternately until they are completely absorbed and the *brandade* has the consistency of puréed potatoes. If mixture is too salty, add more potatoes, to taste.

3. Simmer mixture in a double saucepan or over water until heated through. Stir in lemon juice and grated peel, and season to taste with freshly ground black pepper.

Note: *Brandade de morue* may be served hot or cold. If hot, place in a mound on a warm serving dish and surround with bread triangles fried in butter.

Brandade de Saumon

675 g/1 lb fresh salmon
100 g/4 oz smoked salmon, chopped
I clove garlic, crushed
150 ml/¼ pint double cream
150 ml/¼ pint olive oil
lemon juice
Tabasco sauce
salt and freshly ground black pepper
bread triangles fried in olive oil or butter

1. Poach salmon until tender. Remove from water, drain and flake, removing bones and skin.

2. Place salmon flakes and chopped smoked salmon in electric blender with crushed garlic, 2 tablespoons cream and 4 tablespoons olive oil, and blend, adding remainder of cream and olive oil alternately from time to time, until the oil and cream are completely absorbed and the *brandade* is creamy smooth.

3. When ready to serve: simmer mixture in top of a double saucepan. Stir in lemon juice and Tabasco, to taste, and season generously with salt and freshly ground black pepper.

Note: *Brandade de saumon* may be served hot or cold. If hot, place in a mound on a warm serving dish and surround with bread triangles fried in olive oil or butter.

Maquereaux en Court-Bouillon

Illustrated on page 87

6 small mackerel
½ lemon, thinly sliced
4 carrots, scraped and diced
1 Spanish onion, diced
1 green pepper, seeded and diced
2 sprigs thyme
2 bay leaves
8 black peppercorns
4 cloves
600 ml/1 pint water
300-450 ml/½-¾ pint dry white wine
salt
2 tomatoes, peeled, seeded and diced

GARNISH
thin lemon wedges

1. Ask your fishmonger to clean mackerel and remove heads (to keep for the *court-bouillon*).

2. Make a *court-bouillon* with heads of fish, sliced lemon, carrots, diced onion and green pepper, thyme, bay leaves, peppercorns, cloves, water and dry white wine. Salt generously and cook for 30 minutes. Add diced tomatoes.

3. Place fish in a flat flameproof dish. Pour hot *court-bouillon* over them and cook fish in *court-bouillon* for about 15 minutes, or until they flake easily with a fork. Allow fish to cool in their liquor with aromatics.

4. Just before serving, garnish with thin lemon wedges.

Whitebait Fried in Lard

675 g/1½ lb whitebait
ice cubes and iced water
seasoned flour
lard for deep-frying
salt and freshly ground black pepper
lemon wedges

1. Put whitebait in a shallow bowl with ice cubes and a little iced water. Leave for 10 minutes.

2. Just before frying, spread fish on a clean tea towel to dry. Place on paper liberally dusted with well-seasoned flour and dredge with more flour. Place in a wire basket and shake off surplus flour. Then plunge the basket into very hot lard and fry quickly for 3 to 5 minutes, shaking basket continually to keep fish apart while cooking.

3. Lift basket from fat and shake it well before transferring fish to kitchen paper to drain. Place whitebait on a heated serving dish in a warm oven and repeat until all the whitebait are fried. Season with salt and freshly ground black pepper, and serve with lemon wedges.

New England Fish Balls

350 g/12 oz salt cod
2 level tablespoons grated onion
4 tablespoons milk or cream
freshly ground black pepper
350 g/12 oz cooked potatoes, mashed
2 eggs
flour
butter or olive oil
French Tomato Sauce (see page 416)

1. Soak cod overnight in a bowl under gently running water. Drain and place in a saucepan. Cover with cold water and bring slowly to the boil. Drain and return to saucepan. Cover with cold water and bring to the boil again. Remove from heat and allow to steep in hot water for 10 minutes. Drain and flake, removing skin and bones.

2. Combine grated onion, milk, (or cream), freshly ground black pepper, cod and mashed potatoes. Bind with raw egg. If mixture is too dry, add a little more milk.

3. Shape mixture into small balls, flour them and brown on both sides in a little hot butter or oil, or a combination of the two. Serve with Tomato Sauce.

Mousseline de Brochet Homardine

1 small lobster (about 350 g/12 oz)
olive oil
2 shallots, finely chopped
300 ml/½ pint dry white wine
150 ml/¼ pint Madeira
salt and freshly ground black pepper
2 level tablespoons flour
10 tablespoons butter
450 ml/¾ pint double cream
350 g/12 oz fresh pike (after skin and bones
   have been removed)
450 g/1 lb spinach
4 tablespoons chicken stock
4 large mushrooms
fresh breadcrumbs
crescents of flaky pastry (optional)

1. Cut lobster tail (shell and all) into slices; cut remaining body in half lengthwise and remove the coral. Carefully remove the intestinal tube. Sauté lobster pieces in olive oil over a high heat for 3 minutes. Add finely chopped shallots and moisten with dry white wine and Madeira. Season to taste with salt and freshly ground black pepper, and cook for 15 minutes. Remove lobster pieces from pan.

2. Add flour and 2 tablespoons butter to lobster coral. Mix well and add to pan juices, stirring until sauce is well blended. Pour sauce into the top of a double saucepan, add 150 ml/¼ pint double cream and allow to simmer over water until ready to serve.

3. To make mousseline: mince pike through the finest blade of your mincer. Place minced pike in a mortar, season to taste with salt and freshly ground black pepper, and pound it to a smooth paste, adding remaining double cream gradually to create a smooth, firm mousse. Oil 4 pieces of waxed paper. Divide pike mousse into 5 equal parts and put 1 portion of the mixture on each of 4 pieces of paper together with a *medaillon* of lobster tail (with shell removed). Fold each packet into a 'finger' 10 cm/4 inches long and 5 cm/2 inches thick. Poach them in simmering salted water for 15 minutes.

4. To make spinach mousses: wash spinach carefully, drain and cook with 4 tablespoons each butter and chicken stock. Drain until fairly dry. Put through the mincer with remaining pike *mousseline*. Season with salt and freshly ground black pepper, and mix well. Butter 4 individual aspic moulds and line with spinach mixture, placing remaining lobster meat, finely chopped, in the centre. Cover with the remaining spinach and poach in a *bain-marie* for 20 minutes.

5. To stuff mushroom caps: wash mushroom caps. Finely chop the stalks. Mix chopped stalks with 4 tablespoons softened butter, and stuff mushroom caps with this mixture. Sprinkle with freshly grated breadcrumbs and bake in a moderately hot oven (190°C, 375°F, Gas Mark 5) on a buttered baking sheet.

6. To serve: unfold the *mousselines* of pike. Arrange them in the centre of a long serving dish, mask with half the sauce (putting the rest in a sauceboat) and keep warm.

7. Remove lobster-filled spinach mousses carefully from the moulds and garnish the dish with them together with the mushroom caps. Add flaky pastry crescents if desired.

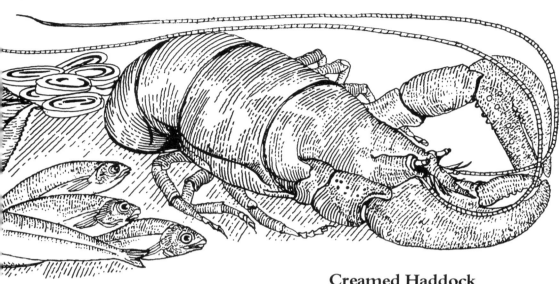

Sardines Farcies aux Épinards

1.5 kg/3 lb fresh spinach
olive oil
2 cloves garlic
1 Spanish onion, finely chopped
salt and freshly ground black pepper
18 fresh sardines (heads, tails and backbones
  removed)
fresh breadcrumbs

1. Wash spinach carefully and remove stems. Drain well and cook until limp. Place in a saucepan with 2 tablespoons olive oil, stirring constantly. Drain spinach and then chop finely with garlic.

2. Sauté finely chopped onion in 4 tablespoons olive oil until golden. Add finely chopped spinach and season to taste with salt and freshly ground black pepper. Mix well. Spread two-thirds of spinach mixture in the bottom of a *gratin* dish.

3. Place prepared sardines open side up on a clean tea towel. Place a tablespoon of reserved spinach mixture on each sardine half. Roll fish up tightly (starting at the head) and place them in rows on the bed of spinach. Sprinkle with breadcrumbs and then with olive oil, and bake in a moderate oven (190°C, 375°F, Gas Mark 5) for 20 minutes, or until done.

Creamed Haddock
Illustrated on page 88

1 kg/2 lb smoked haddock
milk
water
3 level tablespoons butter
3 level tablespoons flour
450 ml/¾ pint double cream
freshly ground black pepper
freshly grated nutmeg
100 g/4 oz small Norwegian prawns,
  defrosted
triangles of bread sautéed in butter

1. Cook haddock in equal quantities of milk and water until just tender. Allow to cool in stock. Drain, reserving stock, and remove bits of skin and bones from fish.

2. Melt butter in the top of a double saucepan. Stir in flour and cook over water for 3 minutes, stirring continuously until smooth. Add cream and stock the fish was cooked in, and continue to cook, stirring from time to time. Season to taste with freshly ground black pepper and a little grated nutmeg.

3. Fold prawns and haddock pieces (with skin and bones removed) into sauce and simmer gently until heated through. Serve in a shallow casserole, surrounded by triangles of bread sautéed in butter.

98

Anchovy Salad

225-350 g/8-12 oz salted anchovies
1 medium-sized onion, finely chopped
4 level tablespoons finely chopped parsley
4 thin slices lemon
4 tablespoons olive oil
4 tablespoons red wine
freshly ground black pepper

1. Wash anchovies in water until liquid is clear; dry them with a clean cloth and remove heads, tails and fins. Strip anchovy fillets from bones and place in a bowl. Add finely chopped onion, parsley and lemon slices.

2. Combine olive oil and red wine and pour over fillets. Season to taste with freshly ground black pepper and marinate anchovies for at least 2 hours before serving.

Filets de Sole au Vermouth

2 fillets of sole (about 675 g/1½ lb each)
melted butter
2 level tablespoons finely chopped onion
6 tablespoons dry vermouth
1 level tablespoon tomato purée
salt and freshly ground black pepper
150 ml/¼ pint double cream
1 truffle, or parsley, finely chopped
crescents of flaky pastry (see page 91)

1. Place fillets of sole in a well-buttered flameproof *gratin* dish. Scatter with finely chopped onion.

2. Blend vermouth, 6 tablespoons melted butter and tomato purée and pour over fish. Season to taste with salt and freshly ground black pepper. Cook over a high heat until fish flakes easily with a fork. Add double cream and simmer gently for a minute or two, shaking the pan continuously so that the sauce will thicken gradually.

3. **To serve:** place fish fillets on a heated serving dish. Pour over sauce, sprinkle with finely chopped truffle or parsley, and garnish with several crescents of flaky pastry. Serve immediately.

Rougets en Papillote 'Baumanière'

4 small rougets (red mullet),
  100-150 g/4-5 oz each
olive oil
salt and freshly ground black pepper
4 bay leaves
4 thin rashers bacon, grilled
fat or olive oil for deep-frying
4 slices lemon
4 anchovy fillets

SAUCE
4-5 egg whites
300 ml/½ pint double cream
4-5 anchovy fillets, mashed
salt and freshly ground black pepper
freshly grated nutmeg

1. *Rougets* are not gutted before cooking. Just sprinkle each fish with olive oil and season to taste with salt and freshly ground black pepper. Place 1 bay leaf on one side of fish and a thin rasher of grilled bacon on the other side.

2. Cut 4 pieces of greaseproof paper approximately 21 by 28 cm/8½ by 11 inches. Fold in half and cut in heart shapes. Open, brush with oil, and place prepared fish, bay leaf and bacon on one half. Fold paper shape over and seal edges well by crimping them together. Sauté *papillotes* in deep fat or olive oil for about 18 minutes.

3. Arrange *papillotes* on a serving dish. Open each one carefully and decorate *rougets* with lemon and anchovy. Serve with the following sauce.

4. **To make sauce:** beat egg whites until stiff and whip cream. Combine the two, add mashed anchovy fillets, and season to taste with salt, freshly ground black pepper and grated nutmeg. Cook over boiling water, skimming constantly, until heated through. Strain and serve hot.

Brochettes of Cod and Sole with Mustard Sauce *Serves 4*
Grilled Herrings
Bouillabaisse de Morue *Serves 6 to 8*

Brochettes of Cod and Sole with Mustard Sauce

2 thick cod steaks
2 small fillets of sole
salt
flour
oil for frying

MUSTARD SAUCE
2 level tablespoons butter
1 tablespoon olive oil
1 onion, coarsely chopped
1 bunch parsley stalks
salt and freshly ground black pepper
2 level tablespoons flour
300 ml/$\frac{1}{2}$ pint canned clam juice
150 ml/$\frac{1}{4}$ pint dry white wine
1–2 level tablespoons Dijon mustard

1. To make mustard sauce: heat butter and oil in a saucepan. Add chopped onion and parsley stalks, season to taste with salt and freshly ground black pepper, and sauté, stirring continuously, until onion is transparent. Sprinkle with flour and stir until well blended. Add clam juice and wine, and simmer gently for 20 minutes. Place mustard in the top of a double saucepan and strain stock over it, pressing onion and parsley stalks well against sieve with a wooden spoon. Mix well over water and continue to cook until sauce is thick and smooth.

2. When ready to serve: cut fish into 2.5-cm/1-inch squares and arrange them on small skewers. Salt and flour them, and deep-fry in very hot oil until golden. Serve *brochettes* immediately, accompanied by sauce.

Grilled Herrings

1. Clean and scale fresh herrings, taking care not to break the delicate skin underneath. Cut off heads. Wash and dry herrings carefully.

2. Make 2 shallow incisions on sides of each fish with a sharp knife.

3. Dip herrings in seasoned flour and then in melted butter. Sprinkle with lemon juice and grill on a well-oiled baking sheet for 5 to 8 minutes on each side, until they are cooked through. Serve immediately with lemon wedges or with Hollandaise Sauce (see Fresh Asparagus Hollandaise, page 18) or Mustard Hollandaise.

99

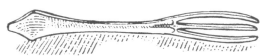

Bouillabaisse de Morue

675 g/1$\frac{1}{2}$ lb salt cod
2 Spanish onions, sliced
2 leeks (white parts only), sliced
4 tablespoons olive oil
4 tomatoes, peeled, seeded and diced
2 level tablespoons butter
1.15 litres/2 pints water
1 bouquet garni (2 sprigs thyme, 1 sprig fennel, 1 bay leaf)
1 strip orange peel
2 cloves garlic, crushed
$\frac{1}{4}$ level teaspoon powdered saffron
freshly ground black pepper
1 kg/2 lb potatoes, peeled and sliced
French bread
garlic
grated cheese
finely chopped parsley

1. Soak salt cod overnight. Drain and cut into large cubes.

2. Sauté sliced onions and leeks in olive oil until transparent. Simmer tomatoes in butter until smooth. Fill a large saucepan with water. Add vegetables with *bouquet garni*, orange peel, crushed garlic and saffron, and season to taste with freshly ground black pepper. Bring to the boil, add sliced potatoes, and when they are half cooked, add cubed salt cod. Lower heat and simmer *bouillabaisse* until cod is tender.

3. To serve: place slices of stale French bread rubbed with garlic and sprinkled with grated cheese in individual soup dishes. Pour over *bouillon*. Serve cod and potatoes on a separate serving dish, sprinkled with finely chopped parsley.

Steamed Salt Cod in the Italian Manner *Serves 4 to 6*
Poached Fillet of Sole with Grapes *Serves 4*
Baked Herrings

100

Steamed Salt Cod in the Italian Manner

1 kg/2 lb salt cod

SAUCE
**4 level tablespoons finely chopped Spanish
   onion
6 level tablespoons finely chopped parsley
2 cloves garlic, finely chopped
8 tablespoons olive oil
juice of ½ large lemon
pinch of monosodium glutamate
salt and freshly ground black pepper**

1. Soak cod overnight in a bowl under gently running water. Drain and put salt cod in a saucepan. Cover with cold water and bring to the boil. Drain and return to saucepan. Cover with cold water and bring to the boil again. Turn off heat and allow to steep in hot water for 10 minutes. Drain and remove skin and bones.

2. Combine first 5 sauce ingredients; add monosodium glutamate, and salt and freshly ground black pepper, to taste. Chill. When ready to serve, pour sauce over poached (or steamed) salt cod.

Poached Fillet of Sole with Grapes

**3 tablespoons softened butter
3 shallots or 1 small onion, finely chopped
8 fillets of sole
salt and freshly ground black pepper
150 ml/¼ pint dry white wine
150 ml/¼ pint fish stock (made with fish
   trimmings and ½ chicken stock cube)
150 ml/¼ pint thick Cream Sauce (see
   Omelette Bénédictine, page 36)
1 egg yolk
175 g/6 oz seedless white grapes
4-8 level tablespoons whipped cream**

1. Spread 2 tablespoons butter in a shallow pan and sprinkle with finely chopped shallots or onion. Season fillets of sole to taste with salt and freshly

ground black pepper. Roll them up, fasten with wooden cocktail sticks and arrange in the pan. Moisten with dry white wine and fish stock. Cover fish with a circle of buttered greaseproof paper cut the size of the pan, with a small hole in the middle. Bring to the boil, cover the pan and poach gently for 10 to 12 minutes. Remove wooden sticks from fillets and arrange fish on a heated dish.

2. Cook the fish liquor until it is reduced to about a quarter of the original quantity. Strain, add Cream Sauce mixed with egg yolk, and warm through until smooth. Do not allow to boil.

3. Simmer small seedless white grapes in a little water for a few minutes. Drain, simmer in 1 tablespoon butter and pour around fish.

4. Fold whipped cream into the sauce. Pour it over the fish and brown under a hot grill until golden.

Baked Herrings

1. Clean and scale fresh herrings, taking care not to break the delicate skin underneath. Cut off heads. Wash and dry herrings carefully.

2. Remove roes, detach skin and pound roes with an equal amount of softened butter. Force mixture through a fine sieve. Mix in 2 to 4 tablespoons fresh breadcrumbs, flavour with finely chopped parsley, and season to taste with salt and freshly ground black pepper.

3. Slit herrings down backbone with a sharp knife and remove backbone carefully, snipping both ends free with kitchen scissors.

4. Stuff herrings with roe mixture and place fish in a lightly-buttered shallow ovenproof dish. Sprinkle lightly with breadcrumbs, finely chopped parsley and melted butter.

5. Cover fish with buttered paper and bake in a moderately hot oven (200°C, 400°F, Gas Mark 6) for 15 to 20 minutes, until cooked through. Just before serving, brown under grill. Serve with lemon wedges.

Main Dishes

'In this competitive age,' wrote William Makepeace Thackeray in the last century, 'hospitality is being pressed into service and becoming an excuse for ostentation. Dinners are given mostly by way of revenge.'

The climax to this unhappy state of affairs was reached in America in the Gay Nineties, when a famous socialite decided to make her first big splash in Washington society. Abashed by rival political hostesses' habits of enfolding a costly jewelled or gold trinket in each guest's napkin, she decided that there was only one way to beat them at their own game. When her turn came to give a large dinner party, she wrapped a crisp new one hundred dollar bill in the napkin at each plate!

But the new trend in entertaining is away from big parties. The famous American publisher who had three guest lists for his equally famous parties – the 'A' list for Society; the 'B' list made up of actors, writers and other celebrities; and the 'C' list, a sort of catch-all for wits, favourite beauties and close friends – is a glamorous figure from a dead, dead past.

Small gatherings where everyone gets a chance to talk to everyone else are the new rule; intimate suppers for four, dinner parties for six to eight, country luncheons for eight to ten, buffet parties and after-theatre parties for eight to twenty. The result: a more friendly feeling, and conversation of a more thoughtful and informed calibre – except, of course, at the parties of the younger, cool set, where everyone sits on the floor and listens to records hour after hour, or at cocktail parties, where the talk is as impossible and improbable as it ever used to be. But one thing is true of today's parties: food is uppermost – everyone eats!

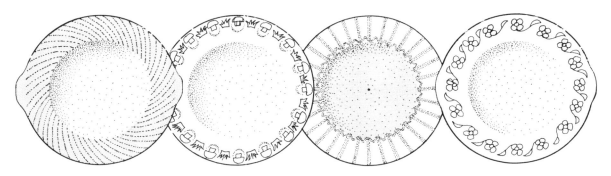

While some well-known hostesses explode like Roman candles with gimmicky party ideas to dazzle their guests, I much prefer the warm candlelight technique of the hostess who sees to every need but wastes no time on glittering pyrotechnics. Good seating, good food, good conversation: what more can anyone ask?

Well, I can tell you that asking your guests to 'come as you are' or 'as the person you hate' can backfire, and you may find that you are the one they hate most for such scandalous trickery. Entertaining, when properly done, needs no gimmicks. Try and mix people of all kinds and varieties at your parties – whether you are the guiding light behind a charity ball, tossing an after-theatre buffet at home, a highly perfected picnic in the country, or a dazzling dinner in town.

And give them something different. If you are entertaining visiting Americans, for instance, do not fall into the trap of giving them baked Virginia ham and candied sweet potatoes with marshmallows. Far better to lead them down the English byways of Star Gazey pie, Lancashire hotpot and old-fashioned treacle tart. The last thing in the world you want is to make visitors feel as though they were back at home. Far better that they should stagger about discussing the wonders of British cookery than merely observing that the English can turn out a damned fine hamburger!

To entertain with ease means planning as much do-it-ahead preparation as possible either in the morning or preferably the day before, so that you can then forget you are the host or hostess and just have fun.

Develop a repertoire of dishes that you do especially well and feel at ease in preparing. And then add a few new specialities to this list each year.

Do keep a record of the parties you give and the guests who attend each one. There is nothing worse for a guest than being served **paella** (no matter how delicious) every time he comes. In this way you can be sure you will not repeat your menus and serve the same people the same dishes each and every time.

If you are planning a new dish which sounds fabulous, try it out on the family or one or two close friends first. This gives you a chance to check on ingredients and on cooking times . . . and what is more important, allows you to add your own special touch to make the recipe more personally yours.

And remember, the true art of entertaining comes from knowing and being yourself. Do not struggle with a six-course dinner when informal casseroles are your *forte*. Being yourself means living by your own standards, not those of others. You can find fascinating ways, well within the scope of your own limitations, to entertain anyone, from a visiting diplomat to a visiting member of the family, without trying to do what is 'expected'.

A dinner party in Cannes, given one summer by the famous French *antiquaires* Grognot and Joinel in their luxury summer apartment overlooking the Old Port of Cannes, taught me what true simplicity can be. Four courses, if you count the gloriously simple green salad, made up this meal . . . and the only wine served with it was Sancerre, a *vin nouveau*, the perfect accompaniment. The first course was **rougets à la niçoise**, a dish of lightly grilled red mullet, followed by **poulet au blanc**, a tender chicken cooked in cream in the manner of Mère Blanc, well-known restaurant owner of Vonnas. A green salad with herbs and a **salade des fruits** completed this delicious meal. When one thinks of entertaining in terms as simple as these, it becomes more of a pleasure.

Entertaining in our day is so much easier than it was in Edwardian times. Of course, you may not have the scores of domestic servants that some families enjoyed in those days, but neither do you have twenty people sitting down for Sunday lunch, and your dinners do not have to go on for course after heavy course of complicated foods to keep up with the Joneses. Nor do you have to go twice a year to Baden-Baden to recover from these excesses. Today we have our electric equipment, the know-how of modern refrigeration, science and merchandising . . . and we have our four-course dinner with the continentally inspired casserole as star performer.

Although I entertain frequently, I like my parties to be simple and intimate, in keeping with the kind of life I live. Never any fussy cocktail bits with the drinks, but, for special occasions, bacon-wrapped prawns, prunes or chicken livers served hot, tiny *brioches* filled with *foie gras,* or iced celery stuffed with caviar and cream cheese – or no cocktail food at all but quantities of good food after: practically never more than four courses at any dinner party, but each course substantial and interesting in itself.

Two words of warning for the unwary: be realistic about your budget and stay within bounds. And stick to a dish you know you can do successfully with no last-minute grilling or warming up while your guests sit fidgeting at the table.

Fish

Marinated Cod Steaks

4 slices fresh cod, about 2.5 cm/1 inch thick
butter
onion
175-200 ml/6-7 fl oz canned clam juice or
   well-flavoured fish stock
salt and freshly ground black pepper
4 large potatoes, peeled

SAUCE
2 level tablespoons butter
2 level tablespoons flour
150 ml/$\frac{1}{4}$ pint canned clam juice, or well-
   flavoured fish stock
salt
cayenne
1 egg yolk
150 ml/$\frac{1}{4}$ pint double cream
juice of $\frac{1}{4}$ lemon

GARNISH
8 heart-shaped croûtons
4 rashers grilled bacon
2 level tablespoons finely chopped parsley

MARINADE 1
olive oil
dry white wine
finely chopped garlic
finely chopped parsley
1 bay leaf, crumbled
salt and freshly ground black pepper

MARINADE 2
1 onion, thinly sliced
$\frac{1}{2}$ lemon, thinly sliced
2-3 level tablespoons chopped parsley
1 bay leaf, crumbled
1 level teaspoon peppercorns
$\frac{1}{2}$ level teaspoon thyme
$\frac{1}{2}$ level teaspoon allspice
3 tablespoons vinegar
1 level tablespoon salt
300 ml/$\frac{1}{2}$ pint water

To make marinade 1: combine equal parts olive oil and dry white wine, flavoured with finely chopped garlic and parsley, crumbled bay leaf, salt and freshly ground black pepper, to taste.

To make marinade 2: combine sliced onion, sliced lemon, chopped parsley, crumbled bay leaf, peppercorns, thyme, allspice, vinegar, salt and water in a porcelain bowl.

1. Marinate cod slices for at least 4 hours in marinade 1 or 2.

2. Place marinated cod steaks in a well-buttered *gratin* dish with 1 tablespoon finely chopped onion and 2 to 4 tablespoons of the clam juice: place in double steamer, cover and steam until tender – 10 to 15 minutes. Or place in a saucepan on a bed of sliced onion with 125 ml/$\frac{1}{4}$ pint clam juice, or fish stock, and just enough water to cover fish. Season to taste with salt and freshly ground black pepper. Cover pan and bring to the boil, lower heat and simmer gently for 15 to 20 minutes, until fish flakes easily with a fork.

3. Scoop balls from potatoes with a potato scoop or melon baller. Boil them in salted water for 15 minutes. Drain and reserve.

4. **To make sauce:** heat butter in the top of a double saucepan, add flour and cook over water, stirring, until sauce is smooth and thick. Add canned clam juice and strained pan juices from fish. Season to taste with salt and cayenne, and simmer until smooth. Stir in egg yolk, cream and lemon juice, and simmer until thickened, being careful not to let sauce come to the boil. Strain through a fine sieve into a clean saucepan. Add potato balls to sauce and heat for 3 minutes, stirring from time to time.

5. **To serve:** place fish on a heated serving dish, garnish with *croûtons*, grilled bacon and finely chopped parsley, and serve accompanied by sauce.

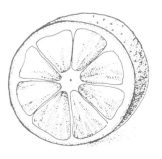

104

Marinated Salmon Steaks

4 fresh salmon steaks
50 g/2 oz butter
salt and freshly ground black pepper
paprika
2 level tablespoons dried breadcrumbs

MARINADE
1 Spanish onion, sliced
2 cloves garlic, finely chopped
2 sticks celery, sliced
2 bay leaves
4 tablespoons red wine vinegar
4 tablespoons olive oil
4 peppercorns

1. To make marinade: combine sliced onion, finely chopped garlic, sliced celery, bay leaves, red wine vinegar, olive oil and peppercorns in a large bowl.

2. Place salmon steaks in the marinade mixture and marinate for at least 2 hours.

3. Remove steaks from marinade, drain and place in a well-buttered ovenproof *gratin* dish. Brush with melted butter and sprinkle with salt, freshly ground black pepper and paprika. Sprinkle lightly with breadcrumbs, place under a preheated grill and grill for 5 minutes. Then bake in a moderate oven (160°C, 325°F, Gas Mark 3) for 5 to 10 minutes longer, until fish flakes easily with a fork.

Grilled Herrings with Mustard

4 fresh herrings
2-3 level tablespoons flour
salt and freshly ground black pepper
olive oil
French mustard
fresh breadcrumbs
4 tablespoons melted butter
boiled new potatoes

1. Clean and scale fresh herrings, taking care not to break the skin underneath. Cut off heads, wash and dry fish carefully.

2. Make 3 shallow incisions on sides of each fish with a sharp knife. Dip herrings in seasoned flour and brush them with olive oil. Grill on a well-oiled baking sheet for 3 to 4 minutes on each side.

3. Arrange herrings in a shallow ovenproof *gratin* dish and brush them liberally with French mustard. Sprinkle with fresh breadcrumbs and melted butter, and put in a very hot oven (240°C, 475°F, Gas Mark 9) for 5 minutes. Serve in the *gratin* dish with boiled new potatoes.

Grilled Sea Bass aux Herbes
Illustrated opposite

2 sea bass, cleaned
4 level tablespoons flour
olive oil
salt and freshly ground black pepper
2 sprigs each rosemary, fennel, parsley and thyme

1. Flour cleaned fish lightly and brush with olive oil. Season generously with salt and freshly ground black pepper.

2. Stuff cavities of fish with fresh herbs and grill for 3 to 5 minutes on each side, until fish flakes easily, basting fish with olive oil from time to time.

Grilled Sea Bass aux Herbes (see page 104)

Roast Leg of Pork Cooked Like Game (see page 152)

Spiedini di Vitello alla Romana (see page 138)

Roast Loin of Pork (see page 149)

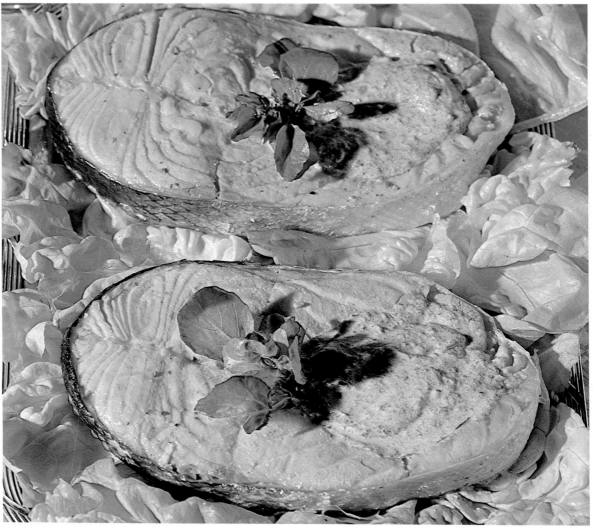

Cold Salmon with Watercress Mousseline (see page 111)

Fish Souvlakia (see page 109)

Oven Fried Plaice à la Niçoise

4-6 plaice, filleted
1 level tablespoon salt
300 ml/½ pint milk
100 g/4 oz dried breadcrumbs
4 level tablespoons finely chopped parsley
2 cloves garlic, finely chopped
freshly grated peel of ½ lemon
¼ level teaspoon dried thyme
4 tablespoons melted butter
paprika
lemon wedges

1. Add salt to the milk. Dip plaice fillets in the milk and then in the breadcrumbs, which you have mixed with finely chopped parsley, garlic, grated lemon peel and thyme.

2. Arrange the fish pieces in a well-buttered baking dish and pour the melted butter over them. Place the dish on the top shelf of a hot oven (230°C, 450°F, Gas Mark 8) for about 12 minutes. Sprinkle with paprika. Serve with lemon wedges.

Fish Souvlakia

Illustrated opposite

1 kg/2 lb fresh halibut, haddock or turbot
4 tomatoes, thinly sliced
2 onions, thinly sliced
Rice Pilaff (see below)

MARINADE SAUCE
6 tablespoons olive oil
6 tablespoons dry white wine
1-2 cloves garlic, finely chopped
½ onion, finely chopped
4 level tablespoons finely chopped parsley
1 level teaspoon oregano
salt and freshly ground black pepper

1. Combine Marinade Sauce ingredients in a mixing bowl. Cut fish into 3.5-cm/1½-inch squares and toss in marinade mixture to make sure each piece of fish is properly covered with marinade.

2. Place sliced tomatoes and onion on top of fish and cover bowl with a plate and refrigerate for at least 6 hours. Turn fish several times during marinating period.

3. When ready to cook, place fish on skewers alternating with tomato and onion slices. Dribble Marinade Sauce over fish and vegetables and cook over charcoal or under grill of your cooker until done. Turn skewers frequently, basting several times during cooking. Serve *souvlakia* with Rice Pilaff.

Rice Pilaff

350 g/12 oz long-grain rice
½ Spanish onion, finely chopped
butter
450 ml/¾ pint well-flavoured stock
thyme
salt and freshly ground black pepper

1. Wash rice; drain and dry with a cloth.

2. Sauté finely chopped onion in 4 tablespoons butter until a light golden colour. Add rice and continue to cook, stirring constantly, until it begins to take on colour.

3. Pour in hot stock, and season to taste with thyme, salt and freshly ground black pepper. Cover saucepan and place in a moderate oven (180°C, 350°F, Gas Mark 4) for 15 to 20 minutes, until the liquid has been absorbed and the rice is tender but not mushy. Serve with additional butter.

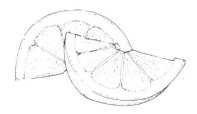

110

Baked Fresh Haddock

1 small fresh haddock (about 1.5 kg/3 lb)
¼ Spanish onion, finely chopped
8 button mushrooms, finely chopped
2–3 level tablespoons butter
2–3 level tablespoons finely chopped parsley
salt and freshly ground black pepper
150 ml/¼ pint double cream or dry white
    wine

1. Sauté finely chopped onion and mushrooms in butter until onion is transparent.

2. Have fish cleaned and scaled. Wipe it well with a damp cloth and place it in a well-buttered shallow baking dish in which you have sprinkled half the onion and mushroom mixture. Cover fish with remaining onions and mushrooms and season with finely chopped parsley, salt and freshly ground black pepper to taste. Pour over double cream or dry white wine. Bake in a moderately hot oven (190°C, 375°F, Gas Mark 5) until fish flakes easily with a fork. Serve immediately in the casserole.

Sautéed Salmon Steaks

4 fresh salmon steaks
2 tablespoons flour
4–6 level tablespoons butter
1 tablespoon olive oil
150 ml/¼ pint dry white wine
1 bay leaf
salt
white pepper
pinch of celery seed
2–4 level tablespoons finely chopped parsley

1. Choose centre cuts of salmon about 1.5 cm/¾ inch thick. Rub steaks well on both sides with flour.

2. Melt butter with olive oil in a heavy frying pan or French casserole, and when hot sauté steaks lightly. When steaks are light brown, add white wine and seasonings. Cover and simmer on top of stove until cooked, about 30 minutes, basting frequently. When salmon is cooked, sprinkle with finely chopped parsley and serve.

Salmon Brochettes

2-3 fresh salmon steaks (about 3.5 cm/1½
    inches thick)
6 tablespoons olive oil
2 tablespoons lemon juice
½ Spanish onion, finely chopped
4-6 level tablespoons finely chopped parsley
salt and freshly ground black pepper
4 small onions, sliced
4 tomatoes, sliced
16 small bay leaves
lemon juice

1. Cut fresh salmon steaks into bite-sized cubes
and marinate for at least 2 hours in olive oil, lemon
juice, finely chopped onion, parsley, salt and
freshly ground black pepper, to taste.

2. Place fish cubes on a skewer alternating with a
slice of onion, a slice of tomato and a bay leaf.
Grill over charcoal or under the grill, turning
frequently and basting from time to time with
marinade sauce.

3. To serve: remove cooked fish from skewer on
to serving plate and sprinkle with lemon juice.

Cold Salmon with Watercress Mousseline

Illustrated on page 108

4 fresh salmon steaks
600 ml/1 pint water
½ Spanish onion, sliced
1 stick celery, sliced
1 bay leaf
juice of 1 lemon
salt and freshly ground black pepper

WATERCRESS MOUSSELINE
2 bunches watercress
150 ml/¼ pint double cream
salt and freshly ground black pepper

1. Combine water, sliced onion, celery, bay leaf,
lemon juice, salt and freshly ground black pepper
to taste, in a wide saucepan. Bring to the boil, then
reduce heat and simmer gently for 15 minutes.

2. Add salmon steaks to the simmering liquid,
carefully placing them on the bottom of the
saucepan without letting them overlap. Cover pan
and simmer for 10 minutes, or until fish flakes
easily with a fork.

3. Chill the steaks in their own liquid and drain
just before serving. Serve with Watercress
Mousseline.

4. To make Watercress Mousseline: remove
leaves from watercress and place them in cold
water. Bring to the boil and then simmer for 10
minutes. Rinse well in cold water, drain and pass
through a fine sieve. Bring double cream to the
boil in a saucepan, add sieved watercress and
season to taste with salt and freshly ground black
pepper. Chill. Just before serving, whisk until
thick and smooth.

Sole en Papillote 'Festa del Mare' *Serves 4*
Baked English Trout with Bacon *Serves 4*
Stuffed Trout with White Wine *Serves 4 to 6*

112

Sole en Papillote 'Festa del Mare'

4 small sole, filleted
flour
salt and freshly ground black pepper
4 level tablespoons butter
2 tablespoons olive oil
4-6 button mushrooms, thinly sliced
4 tablespoons frozen prawns
4 tablespoons cockles
1 clove garlic, finely chopped
2 level tablespoons chopped parsley
150 ml/¼ pint dry white wine
150 ml/¼ pint double cream

1. Flour fillets and season to taste with salt and freshly ground black pepper. Sauté fillets gently on each side in butter and olive oil. Add sliced mushrooms, prawns, cockles, finely chopped garlic, parsley and dry white wine. Bring to the boil and reduce wine to half the original quantity. Add cream, lower heat and simmer gently for about 10 minutes, or until fish flakes with a fork.

2. To make papillotes: cut 4 pieces of paper (or foil) in pieces approximately 21 cm by 28 cm/8½ by 11 inches. Fold in half and cut into heart shapes. Open paper (or foil), brush with oil and place 4 fish fillets on each piece. Garnish with mushroom mixture and pour over sauce. Fold paper or foil shapes over and seal edges well by crimping them firmly together.

3. Place *papillotes* in an ovenproof dish, pour over a little olive oil and bake in a moderately hot oven (200°C, 400°F, Gas Mark 6) for 10 minutes. Arrange on a serving platter, slit edges of *papillotes*, roll back and serve immediately.

Baked English Trout with Bacon

4 fresh trout
8 rashers bacon, trimmed
salt and freshly ground black pepper
4 level tablespoons finely chopped parsley
4 tablespoons melted butter

1. Clean trout, split them open and remove backbones.

2. Cover the bottom of a flameproof *gratin* dish or shallow baking dish with bacon slices. Lay the split fish on the bacon cut sides down and sprinkle with salt, freshly ground black pepper and finely chopped parsley.

3. Dribble with melted butter and bake in a moderately hot oven (190°C, 375°F, Gas Mark 5) for 20 to 30 minutes, until fish flakes easily with a fork. Serve from baking dish.

Stuffed Trout with White Wine

4-6 fresh trout
225 g/8 oz cod or hake
4 large mushrooms, finely chopped
2 level tablespoons butter
2 tablespoons olive oil
1 egg white
salt and freshly ground black pepper
150-300 ml/¼-½ pint double cream
300 ml/½ pint fish stock or canned clam juice
300 ml/½ pint dry white wine
4 shallots, finely chopped

SAUCE
2 level tablespoons butter
2 level tablespoons flour
150 ml/¼ pint fish stock
300 ml/½ pint double cream
1 egg yolk
few drops of lemon juice
flour
butter

1. Slit trout carefully down the back, bone and empty them. Remove bones and skin from cod or hake.

2. Sauté finely chopped mushrooms in butter and olive oil.

3. Pound cod or hake to a smooth paste in a mortar, pass through a wire sieve and pound in mortar again with raw egg white. Season to taste with salt and freshly ground black pepper. Place mixture in a bowl over ice for 1 hour, gradually working in cream by mixing with a spatula from time to time. Add sautéed mushrooms to this mixture, and stuff fish.

4. Just before serving, poach stuffed trout in fish stock (or canned clam juice) and dry white wine with shallots, salt and freshly ground black pepper, to taste.

5. When trout are cooked, place on a heated serving dish and pour sauce over them.

6. To make sauce: reduce fish stock over a high heat to a quarter of the original quantity. Melt 1 level tablespoon butter in the top of a double saucepan, add flour and make a *roux*. Add fish stock and simmer until thickened. Stir in double cream and egg yolk. Whisk in a few drops of lemon juice and remaining butter. If sauce seems too thin, thicken with a *beurre manié*, made by mixing equal quantities of flour and butter to a smooth paste. Heat until sauce is smooth and thick, stirring constantly. Strain sauce over fish and serve immediately.

Turbot au Beurre Blanc

1 turbot (about 2.25 kg/5 lb), cleaned and prepared
well-flavoured Court-Bouillon (see page 411)

BEURRE BLANC
4 shallots, finely chopped
150 ml/¼ pint white wine vinegar
dry white wine
100-225 g/4-8 oz butter, diced
few drops of lemon juice
salt and freshly ground black pepper

1. Place a small whole turbot in a well-flavoured simmering *court-bouillon*. Bring gently to the boil, skim and lower heat until the liquid barely simmers. Poach for 25 to 35 minutes, until flesh flakes easily with a fork.

2. Remove fish from *court-bouillon*, drain and arrange on a hot serving dish. Serve immediately with *Beurre Blanc*.

3. To make Beurre Blanc: simmer chopped shallots in wine vinegar for 1 hour, adding a little dry white wine if it becomes too dry. Strain this reduced sauce into a small saucepan and whisk in diced butter over a high heat until sauce becomes thick and smooth. Do not let sauce separate, or all you will have is melted butter. Add a few drops of lemon juice and season to taste with salt and freshly ground black pepper.

Note: Few kitchens are equipped with a fish kettle or pan large enough to deal with a whole turbot, so ask your fishmonger to cut turbot into more manageable portions.

Turbot au Gratin

1 kg/2 lb poached turbot, flaked
225-350 g/8-12 oz well-flavoured Cream Sauce (see page 414)
butter
4-6 level tablespoons freshly grated Parmesan cheese

1. Bring well-flavoured Cream Sauce to the boil in the top of a double saucepan, add flaked turbot and heat through.

2. Pour turbot and sauce into a well-buttered, shallow flameproof dish. Sprinkle with grated cheese, dot with butter and glaze under a pre-heated grill until sauce is golden and bubbly. Serve immediately.

Beef

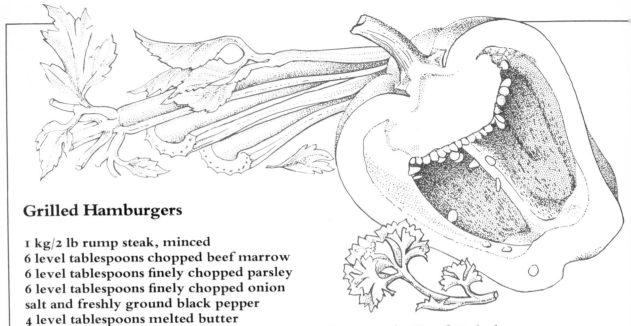

Grilled Hamburgers

1 kg/2 lb rump steak, minced
6 level tablespoons chopped beef marrow
6 level tablespoons finely chopped parsley
6 level tablespoons finely chopped onion
salt and freshly ground black pepper
4 level tablespoons melted butter

1. Combine minced beef, chopped beef marrow, parsley and onion; season to taste with salt and freshly ground black pepper.

2. Form mixture lightly into 4 large patties. Brush patties with melted butter and place under a grill for 4 to 5 minutes on each side.

Mixed Grill 'Skuets'

225 g/8 oz boned sirloin
225 g/8 oz boned shoulder of lamb
225 g/8 oz lamb's kidney
4 tablespoons olive oil
4 tablespoons lemon juice
1 large clove garlic, finely chopped
$\frac{1}{2}$ level teaspoon each dried thyme and sage
mushroom caps
small white onions, parboiled

1. Cut beef and lamb into 5-cm/2-inch cubes and cut kidney into thinner pieces.

2. Marinate meats in olive oil and lemon juice with finely chopped garlic and herbs for at least 1 hour.

3. Thread meats on skewers with mushroom caps and small parboiled onions. Grill, basting with the oil and lemon marinade, until cooked.

Burgundy Beef Kebabs

1.5 kg/3 lb steak
350 g/12 oz mushroom caps
2-3 green peppers, cut into 2.5-cm/1-inch
  squares

BURGUNDY MARINADE
150 ml/$\frac{1}{4}$ pint olive oil
6 tablespoons red Burgundy
2 tablespoons lemon juice
2 tablespoons soy sauce
1-2 cloves garlic, finely chopped
$\frac{1}{4}$ level teaspoon dry mustard
$\frac{1}{4}$ level teaspoon dried thyme
4 level tablespoons finely chopped celery
$\frac{1}{2}$ Spanish onion, coarsely chopped
salt and freshly ground black pepper

1. Cut meat into 2.5-cm/1-inch cubes.

2. Combine Burgundy Marinade ingredients in a large bowl. Add meat, stir well and refrigerate overnight. When ready to use, drain meat and reserve marinade.

3. When ready to grill: arrange beef cubes on long skewers, alternating with mushroom caps and green pepper squares. Grill over hot coals, turning meat and basting from time to time, until cooked as you like it.

California Beef Kebabs

1 kg/2 lb tender beef
4 tablespoons soy sauce
8 tablespoons olive oil
8 level tablespoons finely chopped onion
1-2 cloves garlic, crushed
freshly ground black pepper
$\frac{1}{4}$ level teaspoon powdered cumin
green and red pepper squares
button onions, parboiled
tomatoes, quartered

1. Cut beef into 2.5-cm/1-inch cubes and marinate in soy sauce, olive oil, chopped onion, garlic, freshly ground black pepper and powdered cumin for at least 2 hours.

2. When ready to cook, arrange beef on skewers alternating with squares of green and red peppers, small white onions and quartered tomatoes. Grill over hot coals, turning meat and basting from time to time, until cooked as you like it.

Pork and Beef Kebabs

450 g/1 lb pork, cut from leg
450 g/1 lb round beef steak
225 g/8 oz Spanish onions, finely chopped
salt and freshly ground black pepper
olive oil
4-6 tomatoes, halved
4-6 small onions, poached
2 baby marrows, sliced
4-6 mushroom caps

1. Have pork and beef cut into steaks about 2.5 cm/1 inch thick and cut steaks into 5-cm/2-inch squares. Combine meats and finely chopped Spanish onions in a bowl with salt, freshly ground black pepper and 6 to 8 tablespoons olive oil. Toss well, cover bowl and refrigerate overnight.

2. When ready to cook: remove meat from onion mixture (reserving onions for later use). Arrange pork and beef on 4 to 6 skewers alternating with tomato halves, poached onions, slices of baby marrow and a mushroom cap.

3. Brush meat and vegetables lightly with olive oil and cook over charcoal or under cooker grill until done, turning skewers frequently and basting several times during cooking. Roll skewers in reserved onion mixture and serve immediately.

Grilled Steak with Roquefort Butter

Illustrated on page 128

1 large rump steak (about 3 cm/1$\frac{1}{4}$ inches
   thick and weighing 675 g-1 kg/1$\frac{1}{2}$-2 lb)
freshly ground black pepper
butter
salt
25 g/2 oz Roquefort cheese
juice of $\frac{1}{2}$ lemon
4 level tablespoons finely chopped parsley,
   chervil or chives

1. Remove steak from refrigerator at least 30 minutes before cooking. Slit fat around side to prevent meat from curling during cooking.

2. Preheat grill for 15 to 20 minutes.

3. Sprinkle both sides of steak with freshly ground black pepper and spread with 2 to 4 level tablespoons softened butter.

4. Rub hot grill with a piece of suet, place steak on grid and grill for 4 minutes on each side for a rare steak, 5 minutes on each side for medium, and for 6 to 8 minutes if you prefer steak to be well-done. Sprinkle with salt, to taste.

5. Cream Roquefort cheese and 50 g/2 oz butter with lemon juice and finely chopped parsley, chervil or chives. Season with salt and freshly ground black pepper, to taste.

6. Transfer steak to a heated serving platter and top with Roquefort butter.

116

Japanese Teriyaki 'Pan American'

675 g/1½ lb rump steak
2–4 tablespoons soy sauce
4 tablespoons sake or medium sherry
   diluted with water
4 tablespoons chicken stock
honey
freshly ground black pepper

1. Cut steak into 2.5-cm/1-inch cubes and marinate for at least 30 minutes in a mixture of soy sauce, *sake* (or medium sherry diluted with a little water), chicken stock and flavour to taste with honey.

2. Thread the beef on skewers and brush with marinade. Grill over charcoal or under the grill until meat is cooked to your liking, turning the skewers from time to time. Season with freshly ground black pepper, to taste.

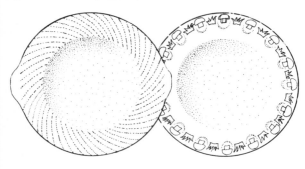

Grilled Steak 'Fines Herbes'

1 large rump steak (about 3 cm/1¼ inches
   thick and weighing 675 g–1 kg/1½–2 lb)
freshly ground black pepper
butter
salt
2 level tablespoons chopped chives
2 level tablespoons chopped parsley
¼ lemon
thin slices of beef marrow

1. Remove steak from refrigerator at least 30 minutes before cooking. Slit fat in several places around side to prevent meat from curling during cooking.

2. Preheat grill for 15 to 20 minutes.

3. Sprinkle both sides of steak with freshly ground black pepper and spread with 2 to 4 level tablespoons softened butter.

4. Rub hot grill with a piece of suet, place steak on grid and grill for 4 minutes on each side for a rare steak, 5 minutes on each side for medium, and for 6 to 8 minutes if you prefer steak to be well-done. Sprinkle with salt, to taste.

5. Make a sauce of 6 level tablespoons butter combined with chopped chives, parsley and pan juices. Season with lemon juice, salt and freshly ground black pepper, to taste.

6. Transfer steak to a heated serving platter and pour sauce over it. Top with slices of beef marrow poached for 4 minutes in salted water.

Beefsteak with Oyster Sauce

1 large thick rump steak (about 3 cm/1¼
   inches thick and weighing 675 g–1 kg/
   1½–2 lb)
freshly ground black pepper
softened butter

OYSTER SAUCE
12 oysters
2 level tablespoons butter
1–2 tablespoons lemon juice
salt
cayenne
2 egg yolks
6 level tablespoons double cream
Worcestershire sauce

1. Remove steak from refrigerator at least 30 minutes before cooking. Slit fat in several places around sides to prevent meat from curling during cooking.

2. Preheat grill for 15 minutes.

3. Sprinkle both sides of steak with freshly ground black pepper and spread with softened butter. Grill on each side for 4 minutes for a rare steak, 5 minutes for medium, and for 6 to 8 minutes to be well-done. In the meantime, make the sauce.

4. To make Oyster Sauce: remove oysters from shells, saving the liquor. Combine oysters and liquor in a saucepan with butter, lemon juice, salt and cayenne to taste. Simmer gently for 2 to 3 minutes until the oysters begin to curl up. Remove pan from heat and stir in egg yolks beaten with cream. Add a little Worcestershire sauce, to taste, and heat through, but do not allow to come to a boil again or sauce will curdle. Keep sauce warm over hot water.

5. To serve: place steak on hot serving dish and surround with Oyster Sauce.

Steak Poele 'Paul Chêne'

4 thick steaks
salt and freshly ground black pepper
4 level tablespoons butter
2 tablespoons hot beef stock
juice of $\frac{1}{2}$ lemon
2 level tablespoons finely chopped parsley
2 level tablespoons finely chopped chervil or chives

1. Season steaks generously with salt and freshly ground black pepper, and sauté on both sides in butter until cooked as you like them.

2. Place steaks on a heated dish. Add hot stock and lemon juice to pan juices and pour over the meat. Sprinkle with finely chopped herbs and serve immediately.

Pepper Steak

4 thick fillet steaks
salt
2 level tablespoons crushed peppercorns
4 level tablespoons butter
2 tablespoons olive oil
dash of cognac
8 tablespoons well-flavoured veal stock
4 level tablespoons double cream

1. Flatten steaks and season to taste with salt. Press crushed peppercorns well into each side of meat. Sauté steaks on each side in 2 tablespoons

butter and 1 tablespoon olive oil until tender. Remove and keep warm.

2. Add a dash of cognac to the pan, pour in veal stock and cook over a high heat, stirring occasionally, until stock is reduced to half of the original quantity. Add remaining butter and shake pan vigorously until butter is amalgamated into sauce. Add cream and continue to shake pan until sauce is rich and smooth.

3. Pour sauce over steaks and serve immediately.

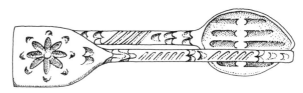

Entrecôtes Bercy

2 sirloin steaks (about 450 g/1 lb each)
sprigs of fresh watercress

BERCY SAUCE
100g/4 oz beef marrow, diced
4 shallots, finely chopped
300 ml/$\frac{1}{2}$ pint dry white wine
225 g/8 oz softened butter, diced
4 level tablespoons finely chopped parsley
2 tablespoons lemon juice
salt and freshly ground black pepper

1. To make Bercy Sauce: poach diced beef marrow in boiling water, drain and cool. Simmer finely chopped shallots in white wine until the liquid is reduced to a third of the original quantity. Remove from heat and whisk until slightly cooled, then with pan over hot but not boiling water, gradually whisk in diced softened butter stirring continuously until sauce is thickened. Stir in diced beef marrow, finely chopped parsley, lemon juice, and season to taste with salt and freshly ground black pepper.

2. Grill steaks for 2 to 3 minutes on each side for rare, 4 minutes for medium and 5 to 6 minutes for well-done. Place on a heated serving dish and garnish with sprigs of fresh watercress. Serve immediately with Bercy Sauce.

118

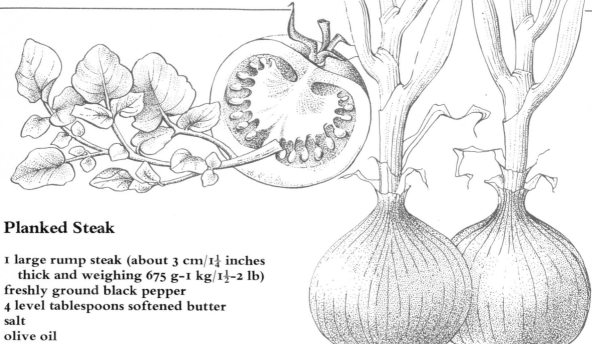

Planked Steak

1 large rump steak (about 3 cm/1¼ inches
    thick and weighing 675 g-1 kg/1½-2 lb)
freshly ground black pepper
4 level tablespoons softened butter
salt
olive oil
Glazed Onions (see below)
Grilled Tomatoes (see below)
buttered peas
Pommes de Terre Duchesse (see page 119)
sprigs of watercress

1. Remove steak from refrigerator at least 30 minutes before cooking. Slit fat in several places around side to prevent meat from curling during cooking.

2. Preheat grill for 15 to 20 minutes.

3. Sprinkle both sides of steak with freshly ground black pepper and spread with softened butter.

4. Rub hot grill with a piece of suet and place steak on grid. Grill on each side for 4 minutes for a rare steak, 5 minutes for medium, and for 6 to 8 minutes to be well-done. Sprinkle with salt, to taste.

5. Place steak on a plank or wooden platter that has been oiled thoroughly with olive oil and heated in the oven. Arrange Glazed Onions, Grilled Tomatoes and buttered peas around steak, and garnish with a ring of Pommes de Terre Duchesse. Brown under grill and garnish with fresh watercress.

Glazed Onions

12 small onions
salt
1 tablespoon butter
1 tablespoon granulated sugar

1. Cook small white onions in boiling salted water until they are tender and drain well.

2. Melt butter in a saucepan, add sugar and stir until well blended. Add onions and cook slowly until they are glazed. Keep warm.

Grilled Tomatoes

6 large ripe tomatoes
butter
salt and freshly ground black pepper
dried oregano
1-2 tablespoons breadcrumbs
1 teaspoon finely chopped chives or onion
1-2 tablespoons freshly grated Parmesan
    cheese

1. Cut tomatoes in half.

2. Place tomato halves in a buttered baking dish. Season to taste with salt, freshly ground black pepper and dried oregano. Sprinkle with breadcrumbs, finely chopped chives or onion, and freshly grated Parmesan. Dot tomatoes with butter and grill them 7.5 cm/3 inches from the heat until tender.

Pommes de Terre Duchesse

1 kg/2 lb potatoes
salt
2–4 level tablespoons butter
2 eggs
2 egg yolks
freshly ground black pepper
freshly grated nutmeg

1. Peel potatoes and slice them thickly. Cover and cook them in simmering salted water until soft but not mushy. Drain well and return potatoes to pan and remove all moisture by shaking pan over heat until they are dry.

2. Rub potatoes through a fine sieve and add butter, beating with a wooden spoon until mixture is very smooth.

3. Combine eggs and egg yolks, and gradually beat into potato mixture. Season to taste with salt, freshly ground black pepper and freshly grated nutmeg. Beat until mixture is very fluffy.

Tournedos en Croûte

4 tournedos
4 level tablespoons butter
2 tablespoons olive oil
4 mushrooms finely chopped
100 g/4 oz pâté de foie gras, crumbled
salt and freshly ground black pepper
2–4 tablespoons dry sherry or Madeira
Flaky Pastry (see page 421)
1 egg, separated

1. Sauté *tournedos* in 2 level tablespoons butter and olive oil for about 3 minutes on each side. Remove from pan and allow to cool.

2. Sauté mushrooms in the remaining butter until golden. Add crumbled *pâté de foie gras* and sauté the mixture until lightly browned. Season to taste with salt and freshly ground black pepper, and enough sherry or Madeira to bind the mixture. Spread the top of each *tournedos* thinly with this mixture and allow to cool.

3. Cut 4 rounds of flaky pastry 2.5 cm/1 inch larger in diameter than the meat, and the same number about 3.5 cm/1½ inches larger in diameter.

4. Lay *tournedos* on the smaller rounds and cover them with the larger ones. Brush pastry edges with lightly beaten egg white and press together firmly. Decorate pastry tops with cut out leaves, etc. and paint with lightly beaten egg yolk.

5. Bake in a moderately hot oven (200°C, 400°F, Gas Mark 6) for 15 to 20 minutes, or until the pastry is golden.

Note: For a more inexpensive version of this dish, substitute the *foie gras* with ½ Spanish onion and 2 thin slices of cooked ham, both finely chopped and sautéed in butter until golden.

Tournedos 'En Boite'

4 thickly cut tournedos
4 level tablespoons butter
6 finely chopped shallots
French mustard
Worcestershire sauce
pinch of rosemary
salt and freshly ground black pepper
4 tablespoons cognac

1. Place well-trimmed *tournedos* in 4 individual flameproof casseroles with butter and finely chopped shallots, flavoured to taste with French mustard and Worcestershire sauce.

2. Cover and cook for about 5 minutes then drain fat, turn *tournedos* over and add a pinch each of rosemary, salt and freshly ground black pepper to each casserole. Pour cognac over meat, cover and continue cooking for a few minutes longer. Serve in casseroles.

Steak in Beer *Serves 4*
Texas Beef with Oysters *Serves 4 to 6*
Mr Pickwick's Boiled Dinner *Serves 8 to 10*

120

Steak in Beer

1 thick rump steak (1 kg/2 lb)
4 tablespoons olive oil
1 clove garlic, finely chopped
salt and freshly ground black pepper
450 g/1 lb button mushrooms, sliced
4–6 level tablespoons butter
juice of $\frac{1}{4}$ lemon
2 level tablespoons flour
300 ml/$\frac{1}{2}$ pint beer
1–2 teaspoons soy sauce

1. Brush steak with olive oil, sprinkle with $\frac{1}{2}$ clove finely chopped garlic and season to taste with salt and freshly ground black pepper. Allow steak to absorb these flavours for at least 1 hour. Grill until medium rare.

2. A few minutes before the steak is done, sauté sliced mushrooms in butter and lemon juice until tender. Add flour and stir until well blended then pour in beer. Bring the mixture to the boil. Add soy sauce and remaining finely chopped garlic and season to taste with freshly ground black pepper.

3. Place steak on a heated serving dish and pour bubbling mushroom and beer sauce over meat. Serve immediately.

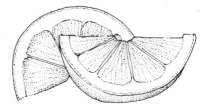

Texas Beef with Oysters

Illustrated on page 125

1.5 kg/3 lb sirloin joint
4 tablespoons softened butter
freshly ground black pepper
salt
1 dozen fresh oysters, drained
2 tablespoons finely chopped parsley
lemon wedges

1. Rub joint with softened butter and freshly ground black pepper, to taste. Roast in a hot oven (220°C, 425°F, Gas Mark 7) for 15 minutes. Reduce the heat to moderately hot (190°C, 375°F, Gas Mark 5) and continue to roast for 1 hour.

2. Remove joint from the oven. Season to taste with salt, and place the drained fresh oysters over the meat. Cook for a further 5 to 10 minutes, or until the oysters plump up and begin to crinkle at the edges. Sprinkle with finely chopped parsley, and serve with lemon wedges.

Mr Pickwick's Boiled Dinner

1.75 kg/4 lb shoulder of beef
450 g/1 lb salt pork
2 bay leaves
6 peppercorns
1 boiling chicken, drawn
1 loin of pork
8 large carrots, scraped
8 medium onions, peeled
8 large potatoes, peeled
8 small turnips, peeled and quartered

HORSERADISH CHANTILLY
whipped cream
salt
freshly grated horseradish

1. Ask your butcher to bone and tie beef. Place in a large stockpot or heavy-bottomed saucepan with just enough cold water to cover and bring to the boil. Skim and reduce heat to a simmer. Add salt pork, bay leaves and peppercorns, cover and simmer over the lowest of heats for 3 to 4 hours, skimming from time to time, until meat is tender. Add chicken and fresh pork after first hour.

2. Cool slightly and skim off any excess fat. Add carrots, onions, potatoes and turnips and cook for 20 to 30 minutes, until vegetables are tender.

3. Serve the beef, pork, salt pork and chicken on a platter garnished with vegetables. Accompany with Horseradish Chantilly.

4. To make Horseradish Chantilly: stir salt into whipped cream and add freshly grated horseradish to taste.

Rare Fillet Stroganoff 'Four Seasons' *Serves 4 to 6*
Barbecued Beef in Foil *Serves 4*
Beef and Pork Loaf *Serves 8*

121

Rare Fillet Stroganoff 'Four Seasons'

Illustrated on page 128

8-12 slices fillet of beef
4 tablespoons melted butter
paprika
rich beef stock or jus de viande
1-2 tablespoons brandy
1 tablespoon dry sherry
125 ml/¼ pint soured cream
lemon juice
salt and freshly ground black pepper

1. Sauté beef in melted butter for a minute or two on each side. Sprinkle with paprika, add rich beef stock or *jus de viande*. Cover and simmer gently until meat is done to your liking.

2. Remove meat and keep warm. Add brandy and sherry to juices and reduce sauce to the desired consistency. Add soured cream, being careful not to bring sauce to the boil after soured cream is added. Sprinkle lemon juice to taste into sauce, add salt and freshly ground black pepper if necessary.

Barbecued Beef in Foil

1 kg/2 lb round of beef
olive oil
4 medium-sized onions, quartered
4 medium-sized carrots

TOMATO BARBECUE SAUCE
½ small onion
1 clove garlic
1 sprig parsley
150 ml/¼ pint tomato ketchup
2 tablespoons wine vinegar
2 tablespoons olive oil
1 teaspoon Worcestershire sauce
freshly ground black pepper

1. To make Tomato Barbecue Sauce: finely chop onion, garlic and parsley and put in a large screw-top jar with all the other ingredients. Cover and shake vigorously until all ingredients are well blended. Allow to stand for 24 hours before using.

2. Brush round of beef on both sides with oil and grill until well browned on both sides.

3. Place it on a double sheet of foil large enough to fold over roast. Add quartered onions and carrots, and coat with Tomato Barbecue Sauce. Fold foil over roast and cook for 45 to 60 minutes, until meat is tender.

Beef and Pork Loaf

1 kg/2 lb each lean beef and pork
1 Spanish onion, quartered
100 g/4 oz fresh breadcrumbs
milk
1 (227-g/8-oz) can Italian tomatoes
3 eggs, well beaten
2 bay leaves, crumbled
salt and freshly ground black pepper
thyme
6-8 tablespoons heated stock
French Tomato Sauce (see page 416)

1. Put beef, pork and quartered onion through mincer twice and mix well with fresh breadcrumbs which you have moistened with a little milk. Then add canned tomatoes, well-beaten eggs, crumbled bay leaves, salt, freshly ground black pepper and thyme, to taste. Mix well.

2. Put mixture in a well-greased baking dish, or pat into a loaf shape on a greased baking sheet or oiled board. Bake in a moderate oven (160°C, 325°F, Gas Mark 3) for at least 1 hour, basting occasionally with a little hot stock. Serve with French Tomato Sauce.

122

Mrs Beeton's Cottage Pie

1 kg/2 lb minced raw beef
1½ Spanish onions, chopped
butter
6 medium-sized carrots, minced
2 level tablespoons tomato purée
2-4 level tablespoons finely chopped herbs
  (parsley, thyme, bay leaf, chervil, or
  sage, etc.)
beef stock
salt and freshly ground black pepper
450 g/1 lb potatoes, cooked

1. Sauté chopped onions in butter until transparent then add minced beef and sauté stirring continuously, until brown.

2. Stir in minced carrot, tomato purée and finely chopped herbs. Add sufficient beef stock to cover and season to taste with salt and freshly ground black pepper. Simmer for 30 to 40 minutes, until meat is tender. Place meat mixture in a well-buttered deep oval pie dish.

3. Mash cooked potatoes and season to taste with clarified butter, salt and freshly ground black pepper. Pile mixture on meat and brown in a moderately hot oven (200°C, 400°F, Gas Mark 6) for 8 to 10 minutes, until golden.

Fresh or Salt Brisket with Horseradish Sauce

1.5-1.75 kg/3-4 lb fresh or salt beef brisket
2 Spanish onions, each stuck with a clove
4 large carrots
2 bay leaves
salt and freshly ground black pepper

HORSERADISH SAUCE
2 level tablespoons butter
2 level tablespoons flour
300 ml/½ pint hot milk
150 ml/¼ pint reduced stock from brisket
4-6 level tablespoons grated horseradish
1 tablespoon lemon juice
salt and freshly ground black pepper

1. Place meat in a casserole with onions, carrots and bay leaves, and cover with water. Season with salt (no salt if salt beef is used) and freshly ground black pepper and bring gently to the boil. Skim; lower heat and simmer very gently for 3 to 4 hours, until meat is tender. Cool in stock.

2. Slice meat thinly and reheat in stock just before serving. Serve with Horseradish Sauce.

3. To make Horseradish Sauce: melt butter in the top of a double saucepan, add flour and cook for 1 minute, stirring constantly, until smooth. Add hot milk and reduced stock from brisket (reduce 300 ml/½ pint stock to half of its original quantity) stirring continuously until mixture comes to the boil. Drain horseradish, add it to sauce with lemon juice, and season to taste with salt and freshly ground black pepper.

Old English Beefsteak and Kidney Pie *Serves 4 to 6*
Steamed Beef – Chinese Style *Serves 2 to 4*
Island Paper-wrapped Beef *Serves 2 to 3*

123

Old English Beefsteak and Kidney Pie

Illustrated on page 128

1 kg/2 lb thick beefsteak, cut into 3.5-cm/
   1½-inch cubes
350 g/12 oz calf's kidney
4 level tablespoons plain flour
1 level tablespoon salt
¾ level teaspoon freshly ground black
   pepper
6 level tablespoons butter or suet
1 Spanish onion, finely chopped
300 ml/½ pint rich beef stock
1 bay leaf
1 level tablespoon chopped parsley
¼ level teaspoon each powdered cloves and
   marjoram
Flaky Pastry (see page 421)

1. Clean kidney, split in half, remove fat and large tubes, and soak in salted water for 1 hour. Dry kidney and cut into 5-mm/¼-inch slices.

2. Mix flour, salt and ½ level teaspoon freshly ground black pepper, and roll beef and kidneys in this mixture.

3. Melt butter or suet in a thick-bottomed casserole and sauté finely chopped onion until golden. Add the beef and kidneys, and brown them thoroughly, stirring almost constantly. Moisten with beef stock and add remaining freshly ground black pepper, bay leaf, chopped parsley, powdered cloves and marjoram. Mix well, cover casserole and simmer over a low flame for 1 to 1¼ hours, until meat is tender. If liquid is too thin, thicken with a little flour mixed to a paste with water.

4. Butter a deep baking dish, place a pie funnel in centre of dish, add meats and liquid and allow to cool.

5. In the meantime, make flaky pastry and place over meat, moistening and pinching edges to dish. Make vents in the pastry to allow steam to escape and bake in a hot oven (230°C, 450°F, Gas Mark 8) for 10 minutes. Lower heat to moderately hot (190°C, 375°F, Gas Mark 5) and continue baking for 15 minutes, or until pastry crust is golden.

Steamed Beef – Chinese Style

450 g/1 lb beefsteak
1 teaspoon cornflour
salt and freshly ground black pepper
2 teaspoons soy sauce
1 tablespoon oil
2 tablespoons sherry
1 teaspoon wine vinegar
2 spring onions

1. Slice beefsteak across the grain into thin strips and place in a bowl.

2. Blend cornflour, salt, freshly ground black pepper, soy sauce, oil, sherry and vinegar, and pour over beef. Chop the onions very finely and sprinkle over top. Cover tightly and let stand for at least 1 hour.

3. When ready to cook: place bowl of beef on a stand over a saucepan of boiling water. Cover saucepan and steam until beef is tender. Serve immediately.

Island Paper-wrapped Beef

350 g/12 oz tender beefsteak
3 tablespoons sake or dry sherry
3 tablespoons soy sauce
1 level tablespoon cornflour
1 Spanish onion, finely chopped
oiled paper
peanut oil for frying

1. Slice beef thinly across the grain and marinate in *sake* (or dry sherry), soy sauce, cornflour and finely chopped onion for 10 to 15 minutes, stirring from time to time.

2. Divide the beef into equal portions on 10-cm/4-inch squares of oiled paper (18 to 20 squares) and fold securely into little packets.

3. Deep-fry the packages in hot oil for 2 minutes and serve hot, just as they are in their little paper jackets.
Serves 4 to 5 as an appetiser, if one or two other dishes are served.

Chinese Steak with Green Peppers *Serves 2 to 4*
Roast Prime Ribs of Beef *Serves 8 to 10*
Roast Beef 'Redbridge' *Serves 4*

124

Chinese Steak with Green Peppers

450 g/1 lb rump steak
4 tablespoons corn or peanut oil
1 small clove garlic
¼ Spanish onion, diced
1 green pepper, diced
salt and freshly ground black pepper
¼ teaspoon ginger
1 level tablespoon cornflour
150 ml/¼ pint well-flavoured stock
1-2 teaspoons soy sauce

1. Cut steak diagonally across the grain into thin slices, then cut into strips about 5 cm/2 inches long.

2. Heat oil in frying pan over medium heat. Place garlic clove in hot oil and remove after 3 minutes. Add meat to oil and stir-fry over medium heat until meat starts to brown. Mix in onion, green pepper, salt, freshly ground black pepper and ginger, and cook over medium heat, stirring constantly until tender – about 3 minutes.

3. Blend cornflour with stock and soy sauce. Stir mixture into frying pan, bring to the boil and cook, stirring constantly, until liquid is thickened. Serve over rice.

Roast Prime Ribs of Beef

Illustrated on page 126

1 rib roast of beef (2.25-3.5 kg/5-8 lb)
2 cloves garlic, cut in slivers
2 bay leaves, crumbled
4-6 level tablespoons butter or fat
freshly ground black pepper
1 flattened piece of beef suet, to cover roast
4-6 tablespoons red wine or water
salt

1. Make 8 incisions in rib roast near the bone with the point of a sharp knife. Insert a sliver of garlic and a segment of bay leaf into each incision.

2. Spread beef with butter or fat and sprinkle with freshly ground black pepper. Tie a flattened layer of beef suet over the top and allow meat to absorb flavours for 2 hours before roasting.

3. Preheat oven to hot (220°C, 425°F, Gas Mark 8).

4. When ready to roast, place the meat on a rack over a roasting tin, resting meat on the bone ends, and roast for 15 minutes, then reduce oven to moderate (160°C, 325°F, Gas Mark 3). Add warmed red wine or water to pan and continue to roast, basting frequently, allowing 15 to 18 minutes per half kilo/per lb if you like your beef rare, 20 to 25 minutes per half kilo/per lb for medium, and 28 to 32 minutes per half kilo/per lb if you prefer it well-done.

5. When meat is cooked to your liking, season to taste with salt and additional pepper, remove to a warm serving platter and let it stand for 15 to 20 minutes at the edge of the open oven before carving. During this time the beef sets, the cooking subsides and the roast is ready for carving.

6. In the meantime, spoon off the excess fat in the roasting tin and using the pink juices that pour from the roast as it sets, stir all the crusty bits into it to make a clear sauce. Bring to the boil, reduce heat and simmer for 1 or 2 minutes. Strain and serve in a sauceboat with roast.

Roast Beef 'Redbridge'

4 thick slices rare roast beef
2 level tablespoons butter
1 tablespoon olive oil
meat juices left over from roast, skimmed of fat
1-2 level tablespoons Dijon mustard
4-6 tablespoons red wine
freshly ground black pepper
finely chopped chives

1. Melt butter and oil in a large frying pan and sauté beef slices until warmed through.

2. In the meantime, whisk meat juices with mustard until well blended. Pour over meat and allow to sizzle for a moment, then pour in red wine and turn up heat to reduce sauce. Season to taste with a little freshly ground black pepper and finely chopped chives.

Texas Beef with Oysters (see page 120)

Roast Prime Ribs of Beef (see page 124)

Rare Fillet Stroganoff 'Four Seasons' (see page 121)

Grilled Steak with Roquefort Butter (see page 115)

Old English Beefsteak and Kidney Pie (see page 123)

Roast Fillet of Beef

1 fillet of beef (1.75-2.75 kg/4-6 lb), stripped
   of fat
olive oil or melted butter
freshly ground black pepper
salt
mushrooms, sautéed in butter
baked potatoes

Fillet of beef, the most tender of all beef cuts,
cooks in a short time. At its best when served
crusty brown outside and pink to rare inside, it
should be roasted in a hot oven.

1. **To roast fillet:** place fillet on rack in a shallow
roasting tin, tucking narrow end of fillet under to
make the roast evenly thick. Brush generously
with olive oil or melted butter and season with
freshly ground black pepper. Roast in a hot oven
(230°C, 450°F, Gas Mark 8) for 45 to 60 minutes,
until beef is cooked to your liking.

2. Slice in 2.5-cm/1-inch slices, season with salt,
and serve with sautéed mushrooms and baked
potatoes.

Braised Beef in Pastry

1 boned loin of beef (about 1.5 kg/3 lb)
100 g/4 oz butter
2 tablespoons olive oil
100 g/4 oz unsmoked bacon, diced
300 ml/½ pint dry white wine
300 ml/½ pint well-flavoured beef stock
1 beef bone, sawn in pieces
1 calf's foot, split
salt and freshly ground black pepper
1 Spanish onion, finely chopped
450 g/1 lb button mushrooms, finely
   chopped
300 ml/½ pint well-flavoured Béchamel
   Sauce (see page 412)
Puff Pastry (see page 420)
1 egg, beaten

1. Melt half the butter in a thick-bottomed ovenproof casserole. Add olive oil and diced bacon, and
sauté meat in this amalgamation of fats until well
browned on all sides. Add dry white wine, stock,
beef bone, calf's foot and barely enough hot water
to cover the meat. Season to taste with salt and
freshly ground black pepper. Cover casserole and
simmer gently for 3½ to 4 hours.

2. Remove the meat from the liquid, raise heat and
boil the stock with bones and calf's foot until the
sauce is reduced to a third of the original quantity.

3. Sauté finely chopped onion and mushrooms in
remaining butter until onion is transparent. Add
vegetable mixture to well-flavoured Béchamel
Sauce and allow to cool.

4. Cut beef into slices and spread each slice thickly
with Béchamel Sauce. Re-form the spread slices
into a roast, slip a metal skewer as a marker between each slice. Divide the pastry in half, roll out
each piece thinly and place roast on one half of
pastry. Cover with remaining pastry, allowing
handles of skewers to pierce through pastry, and
seal edges well with beaten egg. Decorate with
pastry leaves. Bake in a moderately hot oven
(200°C, 400°F, Gas Mark 6) for about 40 minutes,
or until pastry is cooked through and golden
brown.

5. Strain sauce and serve with roast.

6. **To carve roast:** remove metal skewer
markers from roast one by one, and slice pastry
through where skewer was. In this way each piece
of pre-sliced meat will have its own pastry case.

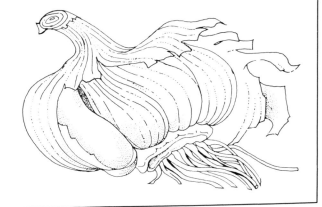

Lamb

Brochettes de Mouton *Serves 4*
Lamb Steaks with Béarnaise Sauce *Serves 6*
Herb-breaded Lamb Cutlets *Serves 4 to 6*
Lamb Chops en Croûte 'Rainbow Room' *Serves 8*

130

Brochettes de Mouton

1 kg/2 lb tender lamb
300 ml/½ pint olive oil
6 tablespoons lemon juice
1-2 level tablespoons honey
1 clove garlic, crushed
2 bay leaves, crushed
salt and freshly ground black pepper
green and red pepper squares
button onions, parboiled
tomatoes, quartered

1. Cut lamb into 2.5-cm/1-inch cubes.

2. Combine olive oil with lemon juice, honey, crushed garlic and bay leaves. Season to taste with salt and freshly ground black pepper, and marinate lamb in this mixture for 2 to 4 hours.

3. Thread cubes of meat on skewers alternately with squares of green and red peppers, button onions and quartered tomatoes, and grill for 15 to 20 minutes, brushing frequently with the marinade.

Lamb Steaks with Béarnaise Sauce

3 tender lamb steaks, cut from leg of
    baby lamb
salt and freshly ground black pepper
3-6 level tablespoons butter or lard
watercress
Béarnaise Sauce (see page 414)

1. Ask your butcher to cut 3 tender lamb steaks about 2.5 cm/1 inch thick from the large end of a leg of lamb. Bone the remainder and cut into 2.5-cm/1-inch cubes, and use for a curried lamb dish with rice.

2. Flatten lamb steaks with a cleaver and season with salt and freshly ground black pepper.

3. Melt butter or lard in a thick-bottomed frying pan. Place lamb steaks in pan and sauté in the hot fat for 6 minutes per side. Transfer to a heated serving dish and garnish with sprigs of fresh watercress. Serve immediately with Béarnaise Sauce.

Herb-breaded Lamb Cutlets

4-6 lamb cutlets or chops
100-175 g/4-6 oz dried breadcrumbs
2 level tablespoons finely chopped parsley
¼ level teaspoon dried thyme
¼ level teaspoon dried marjoram
grated rind of ½ lemon
salt and freshly ground black pepper
2 eggs, well beaten
4 tablespoons olive oil

1. Combine breadcrumbs, finely chopped parsley, dried thyme, marjoram and freshly grated lemon rind. Mix well.

2. Season lamb cutlets generously with salt and freshly ground black pepper. Dip in well-beaten egg and then coat with breadcrumb mixture.

3. Heat olive oil in a frying pan and sauté lamb cutlets over a low heat until they are well browned on both sides.

Lamb Chops en Croûte 'Rainbow Room'

8 lamb chops, 3.5 cm/1½ inches thick
salt and freshly ground black pepper
olive oil
275 g/10 oz Puff Pastry (see page 420)
1 egg, beaten

DUXELLES
2 level tablespoons finely chopped shallots,
    or onion
4 level tablespoons butter
1 tablespoon olive oil
275 g/10 oz mushrooms, finely chopped
2 tablespoons Demi-glace or Brown Sauce
    (see page 411)
2 tablespoons finely chopped parsley
breadcrumbs, optional

1. Trim all fat from lamb chops and season with salt and freshly ground black pepper. Brown on both sides in a hot pan with a little olive oil. Chops should remain very rare on the inside. Cool.

2. To make duxelles: sauté chopped shallots, or onion, in butter and oil until transparent. Add chopped mushrooms (stalks and peels will do) and stir over a medium heat until moisture has evaporated. Add Demi-glace or Brown Sauce and finely chopped parsley. Let simmer for 5 minutes. Breadcrumbs may be added to achieve desired consistency.

3. Roll out puff pastry into 8 circles big enough to encase chops. Spread *duxelles* of mushrooms on top of chops. Place 1 chop on each circle of pastry and wrap around, leaving bone out. Moisten join with water and seal securely. Brush with beaten egg and bake in a moderately hot oven (200°C, 400°F, Gas Mark 6) for 15 minutes.

Grilled Lamb Cutlets 'Reforme'

8 small lamb cutlets
freshly ground black pepper
softened butter
salt

SAUCE
1-2 tablespoons vinegar
2 level tablespoons sugar
25 g/1 oz crushed peppercorns
1 onion, finely chopped
300 ml/½ pint well-flavoured Brown Sauce
    (see page 411)
100 g/4 oz tongue, cut en julienne
1 small beetroot, cut en julienne
white of 1 hard-boiled egg, cut en julienne
2 gherkins, cut en julienne

1. Remove lamb cutlets from refrigerator at least 30 minutes before cooking and trim fat.

2. Preheat grill.

3. Sprinkle both sides of cutlets with freshly ground black pepper, and spread with softened butter. Grill over charcoal or under grill until cooked. Sprinkle with salt and serve immediately

4. To make sauce: place vinegar, sugar, crushed peppercorns and finely chopped onion in a saucepan, and reduce over a high heat until onion is soft and highly flavoured. Add Brown Sauce and simmer for a few minutes. Strain and add slivers of tongue, beetroot, white of hard-boiled egg and gherkins.

Grilled Lamb Chops

Illustrated on page 148

8-10 tenderloin lamb chops
suet
lemon juice
rosemary or oregano
salt and freshly ground black pepper

1. Ask your butcher to trim a loin of baby lamb into 8 or 10 chops.

2. Preheat grill for 15 to 20 minutes. Rub grid with a piece of suet.

3. Place chops on grid, sprinkle with lemon juice and season to taste with rosemary or oregano, salt and freshly ground black pepper. Grill for 3 to 5 minutes on each side. Serve immediately.

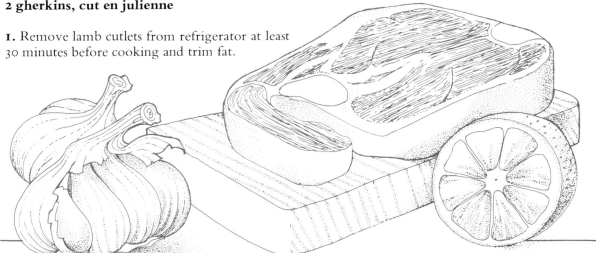

Carré d'Agneau Persillé *Serves 4 to 6*
Lamb and Bacon Kebabs *Serves 6*
Leg of Lamb in Pastry 'L'Oustau de la Baumanière' *Serves*

Carré d'Agneau Persillé

Illustrated on page 145

2 loins of baby lamb
softened butter
salt and freshly ground black pepper
100 g/4 oz fresh breadcrumbs
4 tablespoons finely chopped parsley
½ level teaspoon dried thyme
½ level teaspoon dried marjoram
grated rind of ½ lemon
grilled whole tomatoes
watercress

1. Spread loins of lamb with softened butter and season generously with salt and freshly ground black pepper. Place in a roasting tin and roast in a moderately hot oven (200°C, 400°F, Gas Mark 6) for 15 minutes. Remove from oven and cool.

2. Make a paste of breadcrumbs, chopped parsley, thyme, marjoram, lemon rind and softened butter, and coat sides of lamb thickly with this mixture.

3. Twenty minutes before serving, return loins of lamb to a moderately hot oven and roast for 20 minutes.

4. Serve garnished with grilled whole tomatoes and watercress.

Lamb and Bacon Kebabs

Illustrated on page 148

675 g–1 kg/1½–2 lb boneless leg of lamb
4 tablespoons clear honey
2 tablespoons olive oil
2 tablespoons lemon juice
4 cloves garlic, crushed
2 tablespoons soy sauce
16 button onions, peeled
about 450 g/1 lb streaky bacon
2 large green peppers
8 black olives, stoned
2 large tomatoes, quartered

1. Cut lamb into 2.5-cm/1-inch cubes, discarding fat and gristle. You should have about 40 cubes. Put them in a bowl.

2. Combine next 5 ingredients with 300 ml/½ pint hot (not boiling) water. Pour over lamb and marinate for at least 1 hour.

3. Blanch button onions for 1 minute; drain well.

4. Stretch each bacon rasher out thinly with the back of a knife, and cut into pieces long enough to wrap around lamb cubes.

5. Halve, seed and core peppers. Cut each half into 3 strips and each strip in half (24 pieces).

6. Remove lamb from marinade and wrap each cube in a strip of bacon.

7. Assemble eight 25-cm/10-inch skewers as follows: 1 piece of pepper, 1 cube of lamb, 1 button onion, lamb, pepper, lamb, onion, lamb, pepper, lamb, black olive.

8. Barbecue skewers over hot coals, or under grill, turning occasionally and brushing with marinade. They will take 15 to 20 minutes.

9. Two or three minutes before the end of cooking time, spear a piece of tomato on to each skewer.

Leg of Lamb in Pastry 'L'Oustau de la Baumanière'

1 small leg of lamb, or piece of leg near bone (1.5 kg/3 lb)
2 lamb's kidneys, diced
butter
65 g/2½ oz mushrooms, sliced
1–2 truffles, diced (optional)
thyme and rosemary
salt and freshly ground black pepper
1–2 tablespoons Armagnac or good brandy
Flaky Pastry (see page 421)
1 egg yolk, slightly beaten

1. Ask your butcher to bone lamb, leaving shank end bone intact, so that you can stuff lamb. **Note:** if young lamb is not available, ask butcher to cut off 1-kg/3-lb piece near shank end, reserving top end of leg for lamb steaks or to cut into cubes for brochettes. Ask him to leave shank and bone intact.

2. Sauté kidneys in 2 tablespoons butter in a thick-bottomed frying pan for 1 minute. Add sliced mushrooms and diced truffles, and season to taste with thyme, rosemary, salt and freshly ground black pepper. Simmer, stirring constantly, for 1 or 2 minutes more. Sprinkle with Armagnac, or a good brandy.

3. Stuff leg of lamb with this mixture, reshape and stitch or tie opening with heavy thread. Sprinkle lamb with salt and freshly ground black pepper, and roast in a moderately hot oven (190°C, 375°F, Gas Mark 5) for 25 to 35 minutes, until half cooked.

4. Cool, rub with 2 tablespoons softened butter and wrap in thinly rolled Flaky Pastry. Brush with cold water and bake in a hot oven (230°C, 450°F, Gas Mark 8) for 20 minutes more. Brush with slightly beaten egg yolk and continue baking until the crust is browned and pastry is cooked.

Breaded Lamb Fingers Saint Germain

1–1.25 kg/2–2½ lb breast of lamb
1 Spanish onion, quartered
4 large carrots, quartered
450 ml/¾ pint well-flavoured veal or chicken stock
salt and freshly ground black pepper
flour
2 eggs, well beaten
breadcrumbs
4–6 tablespoons clarified butter
purée of green peas
Béarnaise Sauce (see page 414)

1. Poach lamb with Spanish onion and carrots in well-flavoured veal or chicken stock until tender, 1½ to 2 hours.

2. Carefully pull out the bones and place the meat on a flat dish, top with another dish and weight it lightly.

3. When cold, cut meat into thin strips about 3.5 cm/1½ inches wide. Trim strips neatly, season to taste with salt and freshly ground black pepper.

Roll strips in flour, dip in beaten egg and then roll in breadcrumbs.

4. Heat clarified butter in a thick-bottomed frying pan and sauté strips until golden brown. Arrange strips in a ring round a purée of green peas. Serve with Béarnaise Sauce.

Crown Roast of Lamb
Illustrated on page 146

1 crown roast of lamb, 16-rib (made from rib sections of two loins of lamb)
2 cloves garlic, slivered
1–2 level teaspoons rosemary
juice of 1 lemon
salt and freshly ground black pepper
softened butter
paper frills, or button mushroom caps simmered in butter
creamed button onions or buttered peas, or glazed button onions and mushrooms
finely chopped mint

1. Cut small slits in the lamb and insert slivers of garlic. Rub meat with rosemary and lemon juice, and sprinkle generously with salt and freshly ground black pepper. Brush with softened butter.

2. Cover tips of the crown's bones with foil to prevent them from burning as the roast cooks. Place the meat on a rack in an open roasting tin.

3. Cook crown of lamb in a cool oven (150°C, 300°F, Gas Mark 2) for about 2 to 2½ hours – it should be rare when served. Remove foil and replace with paper frills or mushroom caps simmered in butter. Fill the centre of the crown with creamed button onions or buttered peas, or a combination of glazed button onions and mushrooms; sprinkle with finely chopped mint and serve immediately.

133

Bourbon Barbecued Lamb *Serves 6*
Selle d'Agneau au Romarin *Serves 4 to 6*
Rack of Lamb with Harem Pilaff 'Rainbow Room'
Serves 4 to 6

134

Bourbon Barbecued Lamb

I small leg of lamb, boned but not tied

MARINADE
150 ml/¼ pint bourbon whisky
150 ml/¼ pint olive oil
2 cloves garlic, finely chopped
2 bay leaves, crumbled
¼ level teaspoon each dried thyme,
   tarragon and rosemary
salt and freshly ground black pepper

I. Marinate lamb for 12 hours in marinade ingredients, turning meat several times during this period.

2. When ready to grill, build charcoal fire and burn until flames have subsided and coals are covered with ash. Drain lamb, reserving marinade. Place it on grill about 18 cm/7 inches from coals, and barbecue for 45 to 50 minutes, turning meat and brushing it with marinade every 10 minutes.

3. To serve: slice in thin strips and serve with rice.

Selle d'Agneau au Romarin

I saddle of lamb (1.5–1.75 kg/3½–4 lb, when
   trimmed)
salt and freshly ground black pepper
12 sprigs fresh rosemary
olive oil or melted butter

SAUCE
4 sprigs fresh rosemary
150 ml/¼ pint water
150 ml/¼ pint well-flavoured gravy
225 g/8 oz softened butter, diced
2 tablespoons cognac
salt and freshly ground black pepper

I. Preheat oven to very hot (240°C, 475°F, Gas Mark 9).

2. Season saddle of lamb with salt and freshly ground black pepper. Tie 12 sprigs of fresh rosemary to it and sprinkle lightly with olive oil or melted butter.

3. Roast lamb in preheated very hot oven for 15 minutes; reduce heat to moderately hot (200°C, 400°F, Gas Mark 6) and cook for 16 to 20 minutes per half kilo/per lb for pink; 20 to 25 minutes per half kilo/per lb for well-done. Serve with sauce.

4. To make sauce: place rosemary and water in a saucepan and bring to the boil. Reduce water to about 4 tablespoons over a high heat. Heat gravy in the top of a double saucepan, add 2 tablespoons reduced rosemary water to this and then, over hot but not boiling water, beat in diced softened butter until sauce is thick and smooth. Add cognac and salt and freshly ground black pepper to taste.

Rack of Lamb with Harem Pilaff 'Rainbow Room'

2 racks of baby lamb, trimmed
salt and freshly ground black pepper
I level tablespoon English mustard
3 tablespoons dry white wine
8 level tablespoons fresh breadcrumbs
4 level tablespoons finely chopped parsley
I level tablespoon finely chopped garlic

HAREM PILAFF
4 level tablespoons finely chopped onion
100 g/4 oz fresh butter
225 g/8 oz rice
4 tablespoons white wine
900 ml/1½ pints beef stock
salt
100 g/4 oz button mushrooms, sliced
100 g/4 oz avocado pear, diced
½ level tablespoon finely chopped garlic
100 g/4 oz tomatoes, peeled, seeded and diced
¼ level teaspoon oregano
salt and freshly ground black pepper
75 g/3 oz raw chicken livers, diced

I. Season trimmed racks of lamb generously with salt and freshly ground black pepper and roast in a moderately hot oven (200°C, 400°F, Gas Mark 6) for 20 minutes.

2. Form a paste with English mustard and dry white wine. Brush racks of lamb with paste, then pat on mixture of breadcrumbs and finely chopped parsley and garlic. Return meat to oven and roast for 8 to 10 minutes. Serve with Harem Pilaff.

3. To make Harem Pilaff: sauté finely chopped onion in half the butter for 1 minute. Add rice and stir for another minute. Pour white wine and beef stock over rice and season with salt. Bring to the boil, cover casserole and let simmer for 18 minutes. Stir once only with a fork. In the meantime, sauté mushrooms in 2 tablespoons butter for 3 minutes then add diced avocado and finely chopped garlic. Sauté for 1 minute, add diced tomatoes and oregano, and season to taste with salt and freshly ground black pepper. Let simmer for 5 minutes. In another pan, sauté chicken livers in remaining butter and add to the finished rice, stirring with a fork.

4. Form rice into a ring, and fill centre with avocado and mushroom mixture.

Roast Leg of Lamb with Rosemary

1 leg of lamb (2.25-2.75 kg/5-6 lb)
2 fat cloves garlic, slivered
1-2 level teaspoons dried rosemary
juice of 1 lemon
6 level tablespoons softened butter
salt and freshly ground black pepper
freshly grated nutmeg

1. Preheat oven to moderately hot (190°C, 375°F, Gas Mark 5).

2. Cut small slits in the lamb and insert slivers of garlic.

3. Combine rosemary with lemon juice, softened butter, salt, freshly ground black pepper and freshly grated nutmeg, to taste. Spread leg of lamb with this mixture and place on a rack in an open roasting tin. Place meat in oven.

4. Reduce oven heat to cool (150°C, 300°F, Gas Mark 2) and roast meat, uncovered, for 20 to 25 minutes per half kilo/per lb.

5. Transfer lamb to a heated serving dish and allow to stand for 20 minutes before carving.

Trader Vic's Indonesian Lamb Roast

1 best end of lamb (about 8 ribs)

JAVANESE SATÉ SAUCE
1 large Spanish onion, finely chopped
½ level tablespoon salt
½ level tablespoon garlic salt
pinch of monosodium glutamate
1 level tablespoon Trader Vic's Saté Spice
(or ½ level tablespoon curry powder and
¼ level teaspoon each powdered turmeric,
coriander and chilli powder)
juice of 1 lemon
1-3 level tablespoons honey
freshly ground black pepper

1. Cut best end of lamb into 4 portions. Trim all the fat to the rib bones. Wrap the bone ends with foil to prevent burning.

2. To make sauce: combine all ingredients in a large porcelain bowl.

3. Marinate lamb in Javanese Saté Sauce for at least 12 hours.

4. When ready to serve: barbecue lamb in a moderately hot oven (190°C, 375°F, Gas Mark 5) for 18 to 20 minutes, or until tender. Remove foil and serve.

Kidney

Lamb's Kidneys en Brochette

8-12 lamb's kidneys
4-6 tablespoons melted butter
salt and freshly ground black pepper
fresh breadcrumbs
garlic butter
4 rashers grilled bacon
sprigs of watercress
boiled new potatoes

1. Split kidneys in half from rounded edge and remove thin outer skin. Open them out and run skewer through them to keep them open.

2. Brush with melted butter, season with salt and freshly ground black pepper, and sprinkle generously with breadcrumbs. Place under a grill and cook for 10 to 15 minutes, until cooked.

3. Just before serving: place a knob of garlic butter on each kidney half. Garnish with grilled bacon and watercress. Serve with boiled new potatoes.

Lamb's Kidneys with Port Wine

8-12 lamb's kidneys
butter
$\frac{1}{2}$ Spanish onion, finely chopped
4 level tablespoons finely chopped parsley
salt and freshly ground black pepper
4-6 button mushrooms, thinly sliced
1 level teaspoon flour
4-6 tablespoons port
4 croûtons fried in butter, or cooked rice

1. Clean kidneys of fibres and fat and slice thinly.

2. Melt 4 level tablespoons butter in a frying pan and add finely chopped onion and parsley. Sauté, stirring constantly, for a few minutes. Season to taste with salt and freshly ground black pepper.

3. Add kidneys and sliced mushrooms and continue to cook, stirring continuously, until tender.

4. Make a *beurre manié* by mashing flour to a smooth paste with 2 level teaspoons butter. Stir *beurre manié* into kidneys, stir in port, and cook, stirring constantly, until well blended. Serve with *croûtons* fried in butter, or cooked rice.

Rognons au Porto 'La Paillote'

4 calf's kidneys
butter
½ Spanish onion, finely chopped
2-4 tablespoons parsley, finely chopped
salt and freshly ground black pepper
4-6 button mushrooms, thinly sliced
1-2 level teaspoons flour
2-4 tablespoons port
baked pastry case or cooked rice

Steps 1 to 3, as for Lamb's Kidneys with Port Wine.

4. Make a *beurre manié* by mashing flour to a smooth paste with 2 level teaspoons butter. Stir *beurre manié* into kidneys, stir in port and cook, stirring constantly, until well blended. Serve in a baked pastry case or ring of cooked rice.

Rognons Flambés

8-12 lamb's kidneys
6 level tablespoons butter
4 level tablespoons finely chopped onion
1 level tablespoon Dijon mustard
salt and freshly ground black pepper
6 tablespoons port
cognac
4 level tablespoons finely chopped parsley
juice of ½ lemon
boiled new potatoes

1. Remove thin outer skins from kidneys.

2. Sauté quickly in half the butter with finely chopped onion until kidneys stiffen and begin to brown. Dice kidneys (the interiors will still be raw). Melt remaining butter in a thick-bottomed frying pan and add diced kidneys, onion, Dijon mustard, salt and freshly ground black pepper. Stir over a high heat for a minute or two then add port. Reduce heat and allow to simmer, stirring continuously, until kidneys are tender.

3. Sprinkle kidneys with cognac and ignite, allow the flames to die down, stirring continuously. Do not allow sauce to boil at any time during its preparation, or kidneys will be tough.

4. Just before serving, sprinkle with finely chopped parsley and lemon juice. Serve with boiled new potatoes.

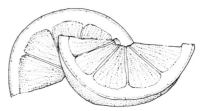

Rognons Sautés au Vin Rouge

8-12 lamb's kidneys
100 g/4 oz mushrooms, sliced
4 level tablespoons butter
1 Spanish onion, finely chopped
150 ml/¼ pint red wine
4 level tablespoons Demi-glace or Brown Sauce (see page 411)
2-4 level tablespoons finely chopped parsley

1. Sauté sliced mushrooms in butter until golden, remove and keep warm.

2. Sauté chopped onion in pan until transparent, add kidneys, cut in small pieces, and simmer lightly for a minute or two. Pour red wine over meat and cook, stirring until sauce bubbles.

3. Reduce heat, stir in Demi-glace or Brown Sauce, and allow to simmer for a minute, until reduced to half the original quantity.

4. Stir in cooked mushrooms, sprinkle with parsley and serve.

137

138

Spiedini di Vitello alla Romana
Illustrated on page 107

4 thin veal escalopes
4 slices prosciutto (Parma ham)
4 slices Parmesan or Gruyère cheese
salt and freshly ground black pepper
unsliced bread
butter
olive oil
dry vermouth or dry white wine
shredded lettuce

1. Place each piece of veal between 2 sheets of waxed paper and flatten them with a wooden mallet, or with the flat side of a cleaver.

2. Place a thin slice of *prosciutto* (Parma ham) and a thin slice of Parmesan or Gruyère cheese on each escalope. Season to taste with salt and freshly ground black pepper, and roll up.

3. Cut 6 cubes of bread from a whole loaf approximately to the size of the meat rolls. Trim crusts.

4. Spear a piece of bread on a metal skewer; add a veal roll, then a piece of bread, then another veal roll, and finally a piece of bread.

5. When ready to serve, sauté the skewered *spiedini* in butter with just a little olive oil for about 10 minutes. When the meat begins to take on a little colour, add a little dry vermouth or white wine to the pan and allow to sizzle for a few minutes. Serve on a bed of shredded lettuce or Saffron Rice.

Saffron Rice

1 level tablespoon butter
1 Spanish onion
225 g/8 oz rice
150 ml/¼ pint chicken stock, strained
salt and freshly ground black pepper
freshly grated nutmeg
generous pinch saffron

1. Melt butter in a saucepan; add finely chopped onion and stir over the heat until transparent.

2. Stir in rice. Add strained chicken stock and salt, freshly ground black pepper, a little freshly grated nutmeg and saffron, to taste, and simmer gently, covered, for about 25 minutes, or until rice is tender but not mushy.

Medaillons de Veau 'Orloff'

6 slices fillet of veal (about 100 g/4 oz each)
salt and freshly ground black pepper
flour
butter
6 shallots
8 tablespoons dry white wine
8 tablespoons port
8 tablespoons stock

1. Season fillets with salt and freshly ground black pepper and dust them lightly with flour. Sear on both sides in a shallow pan containing 4 tablespoons melted butter. Lower the heat and cook slowly for 10 to 12 minutes. Remove from pan and keep hot.

2. Chop the shallots and soften them in the pan juices, add the white wine and port. Reduce by half over a high heat and add the stock.

3. When hot but not boiling, remove from the heat and stir in 2 to 4 tablespoons butter in small pieces. Pour sauce over the steaks. Serve immediately.

Côtes de Veau Grandmère 'Petite Auberge' *Serves 4*
Sweetbreads à la Royale *Serves 4*
Costolette di Vitello alla Valdostana *Serves 6*

Côtes de Veau Grandmère 'Petite Auberge'

4 thick veal chops
salt and freshly ground black pepper
2 level tablespoons butter
2 tablespoons olive oil
16 button onions
100 g/4 oz bacon, diced
8 button mushrooms, cut in quarters
4 tablespoons well-flavoured beef stock or
    glace de viande
2-4 level tablespoons finely chopped parsley

1. Season veal chops to taste with salt and freshly ground black pepper, and sauté in butter and olive oil until golden on both sides. Cover pan and simmer chops gently for about 10 minutes.

2. Place button onions and diced bacon in cold water and bring to the boil. Drain, and add to chops with quartered mushrooms. Simmer gently, uncovered, for about 5 minutes. Add well-flavoured beef stock or *glace de viande*. Sprinkle with finely chopped parsley and serve immediately.

Sweetbreads à la Royale

2 pairs sweetbreads
salt
juice of $\frac{1}{2}$ lemon
1 Spanish onion, coarsely chopped
2 carrots, coarsely chopped
butter
2 level tablespoons flour
freshly ground black pepper
4 tablespoons cognac
8 tablespoons dry white wine
150 ml/¼ pint well-flavoured chicken stock
2 tablespoons double cream
8 tablespoons port
4 mushroom caps, sautéed in butter

1. Soak sweetbreads in cold water for 1 hour, changing water when it becomes tinged with pink. Blanch them for 15 minutes in simmering salted water to which you have added lemon juice. Drain and cool, then trim and cut into slices 5 cm/2 inches thick.

2. Sauté chopped onion and carrots in a little butter until golden. Remove and keep warm.

3. Flour sweetbreads lightly, add to pan with a little more butter and sauté until golden. Spoon vegetables over sweetbreads, season to taste with salt and freshly ground black pepper. Cover with buttered paper and place in a moderately hot oven (190°C, 375°F, Gas Mark 5) for 10 minutes. Remove paper, flame with heated cognac and remove sweetbreads to a heated serving dish. Keep warm.

4. Add dry white wine to the pan and cook over a high heat, stirring continuously and scraping all crusty bits from sides of pan, until sauce is reduced to half the original quantity. Add chicken stock and simmer gently for 5 minutes, strain then add cream and port. Correct seasoning and pour sauce over sweetbreads. Top with sautéed mushroom caps.

Costolette di Vitello alla Valdostana

6 large veal cutlets
175 g/6 oz Fontina cheese, thinly sliced
canned white truffles, thinly sliced
salt and freshly ground black pepper
flour
2 eggs, beaten
breadcrumbs
butter
1 tablespoon olive oil
boiled rice
freshly grated Parmesan cheese

1. Slice the cutlets with a sharp knife to make a pocket with both parts still attached to the bone. Stuff this pocket with thin slices of Fontina cheese and white truffle. Season to taste with salt and freshly ground black pepper. Press the pocket shut, beating the edges to seal them properly.

2. Flour the cutlets, roll them in beaten egg and then in breadcrumbs. Sauté cutlets gently in 3 tablespoons butter and 1 tablespoon olive oil until they are a rich golden brown. Serve with boiled rice dressed with butter and freshly grated Parmesan.

Veal Parmesan 'Four Seasons' *Serves 8*
Veal Medaillons with Pommes de Terre Macaire
Serves 4 to 6
Veal Chops aux Fines Herbes *Serves 4 to 6*

140

Veal Parmesan 'Four Seasons'

16 thin escalopes of veal
flour
3 eggs, well beaten
100 g/4 oz fresh breadcrumbs
225 g/8 oz freshly grated Parmesan cheese
grated rind of 5 lemons
olive oil or butter

1. Dip thin slices of veal in flour, then in beaten egg, and finally in a mixture of breadcrumbs, Parmesan and lemon rind.

2. Sauté veal slices on both sides in oil or butter until golden brown. Serve immediately.

Veal Medaillons with Pommes de Terre Macaire

4-6 veal chops
salt and freshly ground black pepper
flour
4 level tablespoons butter
1 tablespoon olive oil
4-6 tablespoons port
stock (see method)
4 level tablespoons sultanas

POMMES DE TERRE MACAIRE
1 kg/2 lb medium-sized potatoes
175 g/6 oz softened butter
salt and freshly ground black pepper

1. **To make Pommes de Terre Macaire:** bake potatoes in a moderately hot oven (200°C, 400°F, Gas Mark 6) for 40 to 50 minutes. Cut them in half and scoop out the pulp. Using a fork, mash this pulp up with the softened butter. Season generously with salt and freshly ground black pepper. Spread mixture in well-buttered individual patty tins just the size of the *medaillons* (see below). Return to the oven and bake for 25 to 30 minutes to form well-browned potato cakes.

Note: potato cakes can be kept warm in a low oven while you prepare *medaillons*.

2. Trim bones from veal chops to make veal rounds. Season veal rounds with salt and freshly ground black pepper, dust with flour and sauté in butter and olive oil until tender.

3. Remove veal and keep warm, pour off excess butter and add port and a little well-flavoured stock (made with veal bones, 1 bay leaf, ½ chicken stock cube and a little water), stirring in all the crusty bits from the sides of the pan.

4. **To serve:** unmould potato cakes on to a heated serving dish, top with veal *medaillons* and mask with port sauce in which you have heated some sultanas, previously soaked overnight in a little port. Serve immediately.

Veal Chops aux Fines Herbes

4-6 veal chops
salt and freshly ground black pepper
butter
2 tablespoons olive oil
6 tablespoons dry white wine
2 level tablespoons finely chopped shallots,
  or onion
150 ml/¼ pint well-flavoured veal or chicken
  stock
1 level tablespoon flour
2 level tablespoons mixed fines herbes
  (parsley, chervil and tarragon), finely
  chopped

1. Season veal chops generously with salt and freshly ground black pepper. Sauté gently on both sides in 2 tablespoons each butter and olive oil until almost tender.

2. Add dry white wine and finely chopped shallots or onion, and continue cooking until done. Transfer to a heated serving dish and keep warm.

3. Reduce dry white wine and pan juices over a high heat to half of the original quantity. Heat the well-flavoured stock, thicken with a *beurre marie* made by mashing together 1 tablespoon each butter and flour and add to the pan juices. Stir in finely chopped *fines herbes* and pour over chops. Serve immediately.

Italian Veal Cutlets au Gratin

8 thin escalopes of veal
150 ml/¼ pint double cream
4 level tablespoons freshly grated Parmesan
   cheese
100 g/4 oz Mozzarella cheese, diced
100 g/4 oz cooked ham, diced
2 eggs
salt and freshly ground black pepper
2 level tablespoons butter
2 tablespoons oil

1. Combine cream, grated Parmesan and diced Mozzarella cheese and ham in the top of a double saucepan. Cook over hot water, stirring constantly until cheese melts.

2. Beat eggs in a bowl, then whisk in hot cheese mixture and season to taste with salt and freshly ground black pepper.

3. Melt butter and oil in a thick-bottomed frying pan and brown veal escalopes on both sides. Season with salt and freshly ground black pepper. Place 2 escalopes in each of 4 individual *gratin* dishes and spoon cheese mixture over them. Grill until sauce is well browned and bubbling.

Noix de Veau Farcie

1 noix de veau (a piece of topside of leg or
   rump), trimmed of fat, boned and rolled
   into a compact shape 10–14 cm/4–5½
   inches in diameter, about 1.5 kg/3 lb
salt and freshly ground black pepper
crushed rosemary
softened butter
8 button mushroom caps, sliced
450 ml/¾ pint Sauce Suprême (see page 413)
4–6 level tablespoons freshly grated
   Parmesan cheese
4 thin slices pâté de foie gras, diced
thin slices of white truffle
melted butter

1. Season veal with salt, freshly ground black pepper and crushed rosemary. Spread meat with softened butter and roast in a moderately hot

oven (190°C, 375°F, Gas Mark 5) for about 18 to 20 minutes per half kilo/per lb, basting frequently. Add a little hot water if fat tends to scorch.

2. Cut a thin slice off the top of the meat and then carefully cut out the interior with a sharp knife (as you would for a *brioche farcie* or a *vol-au-vent*), leaving a thin shell of meat.

3. Slice veal taken from *noix* into thin strips or scallops, and sauté for a few minutes in butter with sliced mushrooms. Add 300 ml/½ pint Sauce Suprême flavoured with freshly grated Parmesan, and fold in diced *pâté de foie gras* and sliced truffle.

4. Fill the meat shell with this mixture, replace the cover and brush with melted butter. Return to the oven for several minutes to glaze. Serve immediately with remaining Sauce Suprême.

Roast Loin of Veal

1 loin of veal (1.5 kg/3 lb when boned,
   rolled and tied)
salt and freshly ground black pepper
4 level tablespoons softened butter
crushed rosemary
crumbled bay leaves
150 ml/¼ pint dry white wine
1 level tablespoon tomato purée

1. Ask your butcher to bone, trim and tie a loin of veal. Season loin of veal to taste with salt and freshly ground black pepper. Spread with softened butter and sprinkle with crushed rosemary and crumbled bay leaves. Roast the meat in a moderate oven (160°C, 325°F, Gas Mark 3) for about 30 minutes per half kilo/per lb, or until juices run clear, basting frequently. The meat should be moist but not pink. Add a little hot water if fat tends to scorch during cooking.

2. Remove veal from oven and skim excess fat from juices left in roasting tin. Add dry white wine and tomato purée to pan juices and cook on top of the cooker, scraping bottom and sides of tin with a wooden spoon to dislodge any crusty morsels stuck there. Allow to simmer for 2 to 3 minutes. Correct seasoning, strain and serve with the roast.

Danish Meat Balls (Frikadeller) *Serves 4 to 6*
Italian Roast Leg of Veal *Serves 6 to 8*
Roast Loin of Veal with Breadcrumbs *Serves 6*

142

Danish Meat Balls (Frikadeller)

350 g/12 oz finely ground veal
225 g/8 oz finely ground pork
100 g/4 oz flour
450 ml/¾ pint milk
1 egg, beaten
salt and freshly ground black pepper
½ level teaspoon ground cloves
1 medium-sized onion, finely chopped and
    sautéed in butter
butter and oil for frying

1. Combine finely ground meats and flour, mixing well. Add milk little by little, stirring well to make a smooth paste. Stir in egg and season to taste with salt, freshly ground black pepper, ground cloves, and finely chopped onion which you have sautéed in butter until transparent.

2. Form mixture into small balls about 2.5 cm/1 inch in diameter and fry *frikadeller* evenly on all sides in butter and oil until cooked through.

Italian Roast Leg of Veal

1 leg of veal (2–2.75 kg/4½–6 lb), boned and
    tied
salt and freshly ground black pepper
dried thyme
225 g/8 oz unsmoked bacon, thinly sliced
2 cloves garlic
4 carrots, thinly sliced
1 Spanish onion, thinly sliced
2 bay leaves
100 g/4 oz butter
300 ml/½ pint dry white wine
2–3 level tablespoons tomato purée
beurre manié (see method)

1. Lard the veal with fat and tie it securely into a neat roast.

2. Two hours before cooking veal, remove it from refrigerator. Rub meat with salt, freshly ground black pepper and dried thyme, and allow meat to absorb flavour for a minimum of 2 hours.

3. When ready to cook veal, cover meat with thin bacon slices and put it in a roasting tin. Surround veal with garlic cloves, sliced carrots, onion and bay leaves. Melt the butter, combine with wine and tomato purée and pour over meat. Roast in a moderate oven (160°C, 325°F, Gas Mark 3) for 20 minutes per half kilo/per lb or until veal is well-done but juicy, basting frequently.

3. Skim fat from surface of pan juices and thicken gravy slightly with a *beurre manié*, made by mashing together 1 tablespoon each butter and flour.

Roast Loin of Veal with Breadcrumbs

1 loin of veal (1.5 kg/3 lb when boned,
    rolled and tied)
6 rashers unsmoked bacon
4 level tablespoons softened butter
1 Spanish onion, finely chopped
2 carrots, finely chopped
2 sticks celery, finely chopped
salt and freshly ground black pepper
450 ml/¾ pint well-flavoured stock
1 egg, well beaten
6–8 level tablespoons breadcrumbs
2–4 level tablespoons freshly grated
    Parmesan cheese

1. Line roasting tin with rashers of bacon and place rolled veal on the bacon. Spread meat with softened butter and surround it with chopped onion, carrots and celery. Season meat generously with salt and freshly ground black pepper, and roast in a hot oven (230°C, 450°F, Gas Mark 8) until well browned on all sides.

2. Add stock, reduce oven heat to cool (150°C, 300°F, Gas Mark 2) and continue roasting the meat for 1½ to 2 hours, until it is cooked, basting frequently.

3. Remove strings from roast, and brush top and sides with egg. Sprinkle with breadcrumbs and Parmesan and return to the oven for 15 minutes, or until crumbs are golden.

4. Reduce pan juices over high heat, strain and serve with roast.

Liver

Swiss Liver Brochettes

4-6 thin slices fresh calf's liver
16 sage leaves
6 level tablespoons butter
2 tablespoons olive oil
½ Spanish onion, finely chopped
4-6 potatoes
salt and freshly ground black pepper

1. Cut thin slices of liver into 20 even-sized rectangles. Place each rectangle alternately with sage leaf on metal skewers, allowing 5 liver pieces to each skewer. Heat a little butter and olive oil in a thick-bottomed frying pan, and sauté finely chopped onion until transparent. Add liver *brochettes* and sauté, covered, until brown and tender.

2. Peel potatoes and grate coarsely.

3. Heat remaining butter and oil in frying pan. (I like to use an oval pan for this recipe as the *brochettes* look so attractive on an oval potato cake.) Add potatoes and season generously with salt and freshly ground black pepper. Simmer gently, covered, shaking pan from time to time to prevent sticking, until potato cake is crisp and brown on the bottom. Invert potato cake on to a plate and then slide cake into frying pan to brown other side.

4. To serve: arrange the *brochettes* on the potato cake.

Le Foie Chaud Pommes

675 g/1½ lb fresh calf's liver, sliced
1 kg/2 lb tart eating apples, cored, peeled
  and quartered
1 glass white Alsatian wine
100 g/4 oz dried currants, soaked in wine
¼ teaspoon cinnamon
salt and freshly ground black pepper
pinch of ground cloves
pinch of powdered thyme
1 level tablespoon flour
4 level tablespoons butter
finely chopped parsley

1. Simmer peeled and quartered apples in white

Alsatian wine until tender. Add the currants, which you have soaked in wine, and the cinnamon and keep warm.

2. Season sliced liver with salt, freshly ground black pepper, ground cloves and powdered thyme. Sprinkle with flour, and brown in butter for 3 minutes.

3. Arrange the *compote* of warm apples on a heated serving dish, place sautéed liver slices on top and garnish with finely chopped parsley.

Calf's Liver with Avocado 'Four Seasons'

12 thin slices calf's liver
2-3 avocado pears
juice of three lemons
flour
salt and freshly ground black pepper
225 g/8 oz butter
8 tablespoons beef or veal stock
½ level teaspoon thyme

1. Peel avocados, remove stones and cut thinly into 12 slices. Brush each slice with a little lemon juice to preserve colour.

2. Slice calf's liver thinly.

3. Dip sliced avocado and calf's liver in flour well seasoned with salt and freshly ground black pepper. Sauté very quickly in a little butter. Arrange on platter.

4. Brown remaining butter in saucepan, add remaining lemon juice, beef or veal stock and thyme. Pour over liver.

Pork and Ham

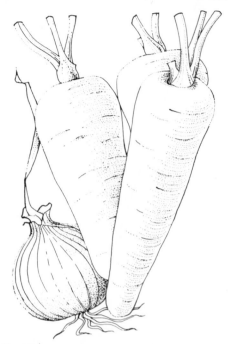

Pork Chops in Red Wine

4-6 good-sized pork chops
salt and freshly ground black pepper
flour
2 level tablespoons butter
2 tablespoons olive oil
4 level tablespoons finely chopped shallots,
      or onion
150 ml/¼ pint red wine
2-4 level tablespoons finely chopped parsley

1. Trim excess fat from pork chops and season them generously with salt and freshly ground black pepper. Dust with flour and sauté gently in butter and olive oil until brown on both sides.

2. Transfer the pork chops to a heated serving dish, pouring off excess fat from pan. Add finely chopped shallots, or onion, and red wine to the pan and cook slowly, stirring in all the crusty bits from sides and bottom of the pan. Skim fat and cook sauce until reduced to half of the original quantity.

3. Correct seasoning and pour over chops. Sprinkle with finely chopped parsley and serve immediately.

Pork Chops 'Avesnoise'

4 thick pork chops, cut from the loin
2 tablespoons olive oil
2 level tablespoons butter
salt and freshly ground black pepper
100 g/4 oz Gruyère cheese, freshly grated
1-2 level teaspoons Dijon mustard
double cream

1. Trim excess fat from 4 good-sized pork chops and sauté them gently with a little oil and butter in a thick-bottomed frying pan. Season to taste with salt and freshly ground black pepper.

2. When cooked, remove from pan and allow to cool. Make a *pommade* of finely grated Gruyère (about 6 tablespoons) mixed with mustard and just enough double cream to make a smooth mixture of spreading consistency. Place chops on a grill pan and spread generously with cheese *pommade*. Glaze quickly under the grill until cheese mixture is bubbling and golden. Serve immediately.

Indonesian Skewered Pork

1.5-kg/3 lb loin of pork, boned but not tied
salt and freshly ground black pepper
2 level teaspoons coriander
2 level teaspoons cumin seed
1 Spanish onion, finely chopped
2 level teaspoons brown sugar
4 tablespoons soy sauce
4 tablespoons lemon juice
¼ level teaspoon powdered ginger

1. Cut pork into 2.5-cm/1-inch cubes and combine in a porcelain bowl with remaining ingredients. Mix well and allow pork cubes to marinate in this mixture for at least 4 hours, turning from time to time so that it becomes impregnated with all the flavours.

2. When ready to grill: drain and reserve marinade. Arrange 4 to 6 cubes of meat on each skewer, brush with marinade and grill for 5 minutes. Turn pork and baste with marinade every 5 minutes until pork is done – 20 to 25 minutes in all.

Carré d'Agneau Persillé (see page 132)

Crown Roast of Lamb (see page 133)

Lamb and Bacon Kebabs (see page 132)

Grilled Lamb Chops (see page 131)

Roast Loin of Pork Normande

1 loin of pork (7-8 cutlets)
salt and freshly ground black pepper
dried thyme
freshly grated nutmeg
4-6 tablespoons apple cider
4-6 level tablespoons apple jelly
flour and butter
watercress
**4 eating apples, cored and thinly sliced,
    sautéed in 4 level tablespoons butter**

1. Rub pork with salt, freshly ground black pepper, thyme, and a sprinkling of nutmeg. Arrange meat fat side up and brown in a hot oven (230°C, 450°F, Gas Mark 8) for 10 minutes. Reduce heat to moderate (180°C, 350°F, Gas Mark 4) and continue to roast until meat is cooked, basting with blended cider and jelly for the first $1\frac{1}{2}$ hours of cooking time.

2. Remove excess fat from the pan, adding a little water or cider if fat starts to scorch. Make gravy by thickening pan drippings with a little flour kneaded with an equal amount of butter. Serve with watercress and thinly sliced sautéed apples.

Roast Loin of Pork

Illustrated on page 107

1 loin of pork (7-8 cutlets)
1-2 cloves garlic, cut in slivers
2-3 bay leaves, crumbled
6 level tablespoons softened butter
crumbled thyme and rosemary
Dijon mustard
salt and freshly ground black pepper
flour
butter
watercress
puréed potatoes

1. Ask your butcher to remove rind from pork without removing fat.

2. Make incisions the length of the loin, near the bone, with a sharp knife. Insert a sliver of garlic and a segment of bay leaf into each incision.

3. Mix softened butter, crumbled thyme, rosemary and mustard, to taste, into a smooth paste, and rub well into pork several hours before roasting. Season to taste with salt and freshly ground black pepper, and let stand at room temperature to absorb flavours.

4. Arrange the meat fat side up and brown in a hot oven (230°C, 450°F, Gas Mark 8) for 15 minutes. Reduce the oven heat to moderate (180°C, 350°F, Gas Mark 4) and continue to roast until the meat is cooked.

5. Remove excess fat from the pan and thicken pan drippings with a little flour kneaded with an equal amount of butter. Garnish with sprigs of watercress, and serve with puréed potatoes.

Chinese Fried Pork Pellets

450 g/1 lb pork fillet
$\frac{1}{2}$ teaspoon salt
pinch of monosodium glutamate
1-2 tablespoons sake or dry sherry
corn or peanut oil for frying

BATTER
1 egg white
6 level tablespoons cornflour
3 tablespoons soy sauce
2 tablespoons sake
2 teaspoons ginger syrup

1. Cut pork into bite-sized pieces, place in a bowl and season with salt, monosodium glutamate and *sake* or dry sherry.

2. To make batter: beat egg white in a bowl until stiff, add cornflour mixed with soy sauce, *sake* and ginger juice, and mix well to make batter.

3. Heat oil for deep-frying to 180°C/350°F.

4. Coat pork well with batter and fry until crisp and golden.

Serves 4, if served with two or more other Chinese dishes. Double quantities if served alone as a main course.

Chinese Pork with Watercress *Serves 2 to 3*
Filet de Porc en Croûte *Serves 4*
Roast Loin of Pork Boulangère (High Heat Method)
Serves 4

150

Chinese Pork with Watercress

4 bunches watercress
I level teaspoon salt
juice of ½ lemon
4 tablespoons corn oil
I small clove garlic, finely chopped
450 g/I lb fillet of pork, thinly sliced
2-3 tablespoons soy sauce
I tablespoon sake or dry sherry

I. Trim watercress stems and wash well, picking out any yellowed or damaged leaves. Drain. Soak for 30 minutes in cold water to which you have added salt and lemon juice. Drain, rinse in clean water and dry.

2. When ready to serve: heat oil in frying pan, add garlic and thin pork slices, and brown the meat quickly on all sides. Add the soy sauce, *sake* or dry sherry, and watercress, and cook, stirring constantly, until the juices begin to boil. Cover pan and cook for 2 minutes longer. Serve immediately.
Serves 4 to 6, if served with two or more other Chinese dishes.

Filet de Porc en Croûte

I fillet of pork (about 400-450 g/14-16 oz)
salt and freshly ground black pepper
Puff Pastry (see page 420)
50 g/2 oz Parma ham, sliced very thinly
beaten egg

DUXELLES
450 g/I lb button mushrooms, finely
  chopped
I Spanish onion, finely chopped
4 level tablespoons butter
salt and freshly ground black pepper
powdered thyme
2-3 level tablespoons freshly chopped
  parsley
4-6 level tablespoons fresh breadcrumbs
2 eggs, well beaten

I. Season fillet lightly with salt and freshly ground black pepper, and seal it quickly on all sides. Cool.

2. To make duxelles: sauté finely chopped mushrooms and onion in butter, season to taste with salt, freshly ground black pepper and powdered thyme. Add freshly chopped parsley and fresh breadcrumbs. Stir in beaten eggs, mix well and heat through. Turn out into a small pan and set aside to cool.

Note: This filling should be prepared in advance.

3. Roll out puff pastry about 3 mm/⅛ inch thick, in a shape 5 cm/2 inches longer than the fillet and about 25 cm/10 inches wide. Place fillet in centre of pastry, spread evenly with the *duxelles* and top with thin slices of ham. Fold one side of pastry over the pork, spread a little beaten egg over the upper surface and then fold over the second side of the pastry, overlapping the first. Roll pastry ends out flat, spread with beaten egg on the upper side and fold the ends over the roll. Place pastry-wrapped fillet in a baking tin with the folded ends down. Brush the surface with beaten egg and decorate with lattice strips of leaves cut from pastry scraps. Brush pastry again with beaten egg and prick lightly with a fork. Bake in a moderately hot oven (200°C, 400°F, Gas Mark 6) for about 40 minutes.

Roast Loin of Pork Boulangère
(High Heat Method)

I loin of pork (7-8 cutlets)
salt and freshly ground black pepper
butter
2 level tablespoons flour
6-8 large potatoes
I Spanish onion, finely chopped
2-4 level tablespoons finely chopped parsley
hot light stock or water

I. Season pork generously with salt and freshly ground black pepper and place it on the rack of a roasting tin. Roast in a hot oven (220°C, 425°F, Gas Mark 7) for I hour, or until pork is half cooked, basting from time to time.

2. Remove pork and roasting rack from tin and skim off excess fat. Thicken pan gravy with a *beurre manié* of 2 level tablespoons each butter and flour mashed together to a smooth paste. Pour into a small saucepan and reserve.

3. Peel and slice potatoes thinly, and place them in roasting tin with finely chopped onion, parsley, salt and freshly ground black pepper, to taste. Spread potatoes with 4 tablespoons softened butter, and place pork roast on top, adding just enough hot stock (or water) to cover the potatoes. Bring the liquid to the boil, return roasting tin to a moderately hot oven (200°C, 400°F, Gas Mark 6) and cook for 1 to 1½ hours longer, until meat is done. The liquid should almost have completely cooked away, and the potatoes nicely browned on top.

4. Reheat pan gravy and serve with roast potatoes.

Barbecued Loin of Pork

1 loin of pork
¼ level teaspoon dry mustard
¼ level teaspoon ground coriander
¼ level teaspoon ground cloves
2 cloves garlic, finely chopped
¼ level teaspoon freshly ground black pepper
4 tablespoons olive oil
4 tablespoons soy sauce
4 tablespoons vinegar
6 tablespoons water
2 level tablespoons sugar
1 small fresh pineapple

GARNISH
diced fresh pineapple
sliced cucumber
watercress and parsley sprigs

1. Ask your butcher to cut backbone from ribs.

2. Mix mustard, coriander, cloves, garlic, freshly ground black pepper, olive oil, soy sauce, vinegar, water and sugar together in a saucepan. Bring to the boil, lower the heat and simmer for 30 minutes.

3. Peel pineapple, reserving flesh for garnish. Place loin in a roasting tin, brush with marinade and cover with pineapple skin. Roast meat in a moderate oven (180°C, 350°F, Gas Mark 4) for about 2 hours, or until cooked, basting frequently with hot barbecue sauce.

4. Garnish with diced fresh pineapple, sliced cucumber, watercress and parsley sprigs.

Roast Leg of Pork Cooked Like Game
Jambon à la Crème du Relais Fleuri *Serves 4*
Ham Steaks 'Forum of the Twelve Caesars' *Serves 6*

152

Roast Leg of Pork Cooked Like Game

Illustrated on page 106

1 leg of pork
olive oil
2 Spanish onions, thinly sliced
4 cloves garlic, thinly sliced
1 bottle red Burgundy
peel of 1 orange
300 ml/½ pint chicken stock

AROMATIC SPICE MIXTURE
1 level teaspoon salt
½ level teaspoon powdered nutmeg
¼ level teaspoon powdered cloves
2 bay leaves, crumbled
½ level teaspoon thyme
12 peppercorns, crushed

1. Ask your butcher to trim a leg of fresh pork to the shape of a ham, and to score the fat.

2. Rub the pork with olive oil and then with aromatic spice mixture. Place pork on a serving dish large enough to hold it, and keep in refrigerator for 24 hours to allow flavours to permeate meat.

3. Remove pork from refrigerator; place it in a large deep container with sliced onions and garlic, red wine, 150 ml/¼ pint olive oil, orange peel and chicken stock. Marinate pork in this mixture for 3 to 4 days, turning the meat in the marinade twice each day.

4. Preheat oven to moderate (160°C, 325°F, Gas Mark 3). When ready to cook roast, remove pork from marinade (reserve marinade for later use) and pat meat dry with absorbent paper. Sprinkle with olive oil and place meat on rack in roasting tin. Roast for 25 minutes per half kilo/per lb, or until the meat is cooked through.

5. To make sauce: cook reserved marinade juices over a high heat until reduced by half; strain into a bowl and serve with meat.

6. Transfer meat to a heated platter and keep warm. Strain pan juices into sauce.

Jambon à la Crème du Relais Fleuri

4 thick slices cooked ham
2 level tablespoons butter
2 level tablespoons flour
150 ml/¼ pint port
150 ml/¼ pint chicken stock
freshly ground black pepper
1 egg yolk
150 ml/¼ pint thick cream
salt
2 level tablespoons finely chopped parsley

1. To prepare cream sauce: make a *roux blond* with butter and flour. Add port, chicken stock and freshly ground black pepper, to taste. Simmer until sauce is reduced and is rich and thick. Remove from heat and cool. When sauce is barely warm, combine egg yolk and cream and whisk into sauce. Correct seasoning, adding salt and more pepper, if necessary.

2. Warm ham in a cool oven (150°C, 300°F, Gas Mark 2) for 15 to 20 minutes.

3. When ready to serve: heat sauce, but do not allow to come to the boil, as it will curdle.

4. To serve: arrange ham slices on a warm serving dish and pour sauce over them. Sprinkle with chopped parsley and serve immediately.

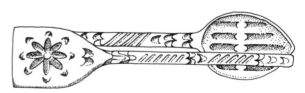

Ham Steaks 'Forum of the Twelve Caesars'

4-6 thick slices ham (about 225 g/8 oz each)
450 g/1 lb Italian spiced mustard fruit (frutta di Cremona)
300 ml/½ pint clear honey, heated
12 walnuts

1. Grill ham steaks on one side for about 3 minutes. Turn and grill other side for 1½ minutes.

Ham Steaks Stuffed with Sweet Potatoes *Serves 4*
Sausages and Mash *Serves 3 to 4*
Boiled Salt Pork *Serves 4*

153

2. Arrange segments of mustard fruit on top of steaks and place under grill for 1 to 2 minutes more. Remove from grill, place steaks on a heated serving dish and pour heated honey over them. Garnish each steak with 2 or 3 walnuts. Serve immediately.

Ham Steaks Stuffed with Sweet Potatoes

4 thick slices ham (about 225 g/8 oz each)
1 (425-g/15-oz) can sweet potatoes
4 tablespoons melted butter
grated rind of ½ lemon
grated rind of ½ orange
¼ level teaspoon powdered cinnamon
2-4 tablespoons bourbon or rum
salt and freshly ground black pepper
2-4 level tablespoons brown sugar

1. Mash sweet potatoes with melted butter and flavour with grated lemon and orange rind, cinnamon, bourbon or rum, salt and freshly ground black pepper, to taste.

2. Spread the stuffing thickly on 2 ham steaks and top with remaining steaks. Sprinkle the steaks with a little brown sugar and season with freshly ground black pepper. Wrap loosely in foil and bake in a moderate oven (160°C, 325°F, Gas Mark 3) for 1 hour.

Sausages and Mash

450 g/1 lb pork sausages
2-4 level tablespoons lard
butter
salt and freshly ground black pepper
¼ level teaspoon powdered thyme
¼ level teaspoon powdered sage
2 egg yolks
milk or single cream
675 g/1½ lb potatoes, cooked and mashed
beaten egg (optional)
2-4 tablespoons breadcrumbs

1. Blanch sausages by putting them in a saucepan with cold water and bringing them quickly to

the boil. Drain, remove their skins and cut each one into 3 pieces. Sauté pieces in lard for a minute or two to brown them.

2. Place sausages in a buttered pie dish or oven-proof baking dish and sprinkle them with salt, freshly ground black pepper, powdered thyme and powdered sage.

3. Combine yolks with 4 tablespoons milk or cream, and beat into potato mixture. Season to taste with salt and freshly ground black pepper.

4. Spread potato mixture over sausages. Brush with milk or beaten egg, sprinkle with breadcrumbs and bake in a moderately hot oven (190°C, 375°F, Gas Mark 5) for 20 to 30 minutes, until potatoes are golden brown.

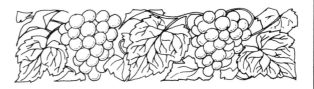

Boiled Salt Pork

1.25 kg-1.5 kg/2½-3 lb pickled or salted pork
2 Spanish onions
6 carrots
12 parsnips or 6 turnips

1. Choose a nice piece of pickled pork or salted pork. Wash it, cover with cold water and soak for 24 hours, changing water several times.

2. When ready to cook, place meat in a saucepan with enough warm water to cover it. Bring slowly to the boil, skim well and then simmer gently until tender, allowing 25 minutes per half kilo/per lb and 25 minutes over.

3. After skimming, add onions, carrots, and parsnips or young turnips.

4. When ready to serve: place the meat on a hot serving dish, strain some of the liquid around it and garnish with vegetables. Use remaining liquid to make pear or lentil soup.

154

Basic Boiled Chicken

1 boiling chicken, cleaned and trussed
½ lemon
butter
salted water or stock
1 Spanish onion stuck with cloves
2 carrots
2 sticks celery
1 bay leaf
300 ml/½ pint English Parsley Sauce (see
  page 414) or Chicken Velouté Sauce (see
  page 410) or Celery Sauce (see page 413)
bacon rolls or quartered hard-boiled eggs

1. Rub cleaned and trussed boiling chicken with
the cut side of the lemon half and wrap it in a
piece of well-buttered waxed paper to keep it a
good colour.

2. Put the chicken in boiling salted water, or
better yet, a little light stock, with 1 Spanish onion
stuck with cloves, carrots, celery and bay leaf.
Bring to the boil and allow it to simmer slowly
until tender from 2 to 3 hours, depending on age
and size of chicken. Unless cooked slowly, the
flesh will become hard and tasteless.

3. When chicken is tender, remove from stock to a
hot dish. Remove paper and string from chicken,
and mask it with English Parsley, Chicken
Velouté or Celery Sauce. Garnish with little rolls
of bacon or quartered hard-boiled eggs.

Basic Steamed Chicken

1 roasting chicken
½ lemon
salt and freshly ground black pepper
4 tablespoons melted butter
4 tablespoons chicken stock
2 tablespoons finely chopped onion
English Parsley Sauce (see page 414) or
  Velouté Sauce (see page 410) or Celery
  Sauce (see page 413)

1. Rub cleaned and trussed chicken with cut side of
½ lemon and sprinkle with salt and freshly ground
black pepper, to taste. Place it in a *gratin* dish just

large enough to hold it and add butter, chicken
stock and finely chopped onion. Place *gratin* dish
in a large double steamer over 7.5 cm/3 inches of
rapidly boiling water. Cover tightly and steam
for 1 to 2 hours, depending on size of chicken.
Serve with Parsley, Velouté or Celery Sauce.

Chicken Baked in Salt

Illustrated on page 167

1 tender roasting chicken (about 1.5 kg/3 lb
  when dressed)
1.75 kg/4 lb coarse sea salt
softened butter or olive oil
salt and freshly ground black pepper

STUFFING
chicken liver
100 g/4 oz bacon
100 g/4 oz fresh pork
2 cloves garlic, finely chopped
100 g/4 oz dried breadcrumbs
milk or stock, to moisten
4 level tablespoons finely chopped parsley
½ level teaspoon dried tarragon
generous pinch of mixed spice
salt and freshly ground black pepper
butter
2 eggs

1. To make stuffing: put chicken liver, bacon,
fresh pork and garlic through the finest blade of
your mincer. Moisten breadcrumbs with a little
milk or stock; combine with minced meats and
add finely chopped parsley, dried herbs and mixed
spice. Mix well, adding more milk or stock if
necessary to make a fairly loose mixture. Season
generously with salt and freshly ground black
pepper and simmer in a little butter until mixture
is partially cooked. Remove from pan and beat
in 2 eggs.

2. To stuff chicken: loosen the skin at the neck
end of a cleaned and trussed roasting chicken as
much as possible from the breast. Insert stuffing
over the flesh of the breast and fill the loose skin of
the neck with as much as it will hold. Fold the skin
over and fasten with 1 or 2 stitches. Stuff the body
cavity as well.

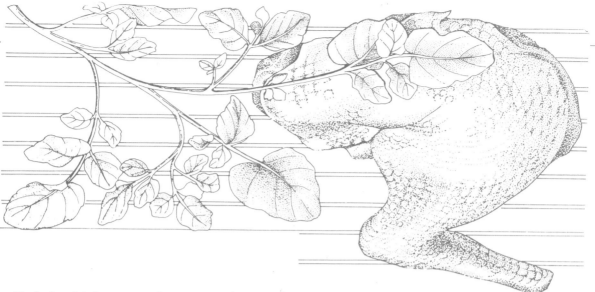

3. To bake chicken: spread coarse sea salt 2.5 cm/ 1 inch thick on the bottom of casserole. Rub chicken lightly with a little softened butter or olive oil and season generously with salt and freshly ground black pepper. Wrap chicken lightly in greaseproof paper and place on bed of sea salt. Pour sea salt around chicken to the top of casserole, mounding salt up to completely cover bird. Place cover on casserole and place in a moderately hot oven (200°C, 400°F, Gas Mark 6) for $1\frac{1}{2}$ hours.

4. To serve: remove casserole cover, break salt crust and remove excess salt from casserole. Lift out chicken, remove greaseproof paper from bird and place chicken on a heated serving platter.

Lemon Grilled Chicken

3 young frying chickens, quartered
salt and freshly ground black pepper

LEMON BARBECUE SAUCE
150 ml/$\frac{1}{4}$ pint olive oil
8 tablespoons lemon juice
4 level tablespoons finely chopped onion
1-2 level teaspoons dried tarragon
1-2 level teaspoons finely chopped parsley
salt and freshly ground black pepper
Tabasco sauce

1. Sprinkle chicken with salt and freshly ground black pepper, and marinate in Lemon Barbecue Sauce for at least 4 hours.

2. When ready to grill, drain chicken pieces and brush with reserved marinade juices. Grill slowly until tender – 45 minutes – turning chicken pieces and basting from time to time.

Grilled Spring Chicken

2 tender poussins (young chickens)
salt and freshly ground black pepper
paprika
lemon juice
melted butter
4 level tablespoons browned breadcrumbs
sprigs of watercress
lemon wedges

Only very young and tender chickens can be cooked in this way.

1. Split cleaned chickens open through the back, flatten and trim birds, cutting off feet and wing-tips. Wipe with a damp cloth, and season generously with salt, freshly ground black pepper, paprika and a little lemon juice. Skewer birds open, brush both sides with melted butter and sprinkle with fine browned breadcrumbs.

2. Grill over charcoal or under grill for 25 to 30 minutes, turning the birds occasionally and basting frequently with melted butter.

3. Serve very hot, garnished with watercress and lemon wedges.

156

Roast Chicken with Stuffing

1 roasting chicken, cleaned and trussed
stuffing (see choice of stuffings below)
2 rashers fat bacon
butter
sifted flour
watercress
lemon juice
salt
300 ml/$\frac{1}{2}$ pint chicken stock
freshly ground black pepper
300 ml/$\frac{1}{2}$ pint English Bread Sauce (see
   page 410)

1. Loosen the skin at the neck end of a cleaned and trussed roasting chicken as much as possible from the breast. Insert stuffing over the flesh of the breast and fill the loose skin of the neck with as much as it will hold. Fold the skin over and fasten with 1 or 2 stitches. Stuff body cavity as well.

2. Tie 1 or 2 rashers of fat bacon over the breast, making 1 or 2 slits in the bacon to prevent it from curling. Cover the bird with waxed paper and roast in a moderate oven (160°C, 325°F, Gas Mark 3), basting frequently with butter for 1 to $1\frac{1}{2}$ hours, depending on size and age of the bird. Test it by feeling the flesh of the leg; if it gives way to pressure it is ready.

3. A few minutes before the end of cooking time, remove the paper and bacon and sprinkle the breast lightly with sifted flour. Baste well, and brown quickly.

4. When ready to serve: put bird on a hot serving dish, remove the trussing string, and garnish with watercress seasoned with lemon juice and salt, to taste.

5. Pour off the fat from the roasting tin in which bird was roasted, add chicken stock and stir over a high heat until boiling, scraping in any brown bits from sides of pan. Season to taste with salt and freshly ground black pepper, and serve in a sauceboat.

6. Serve with English Bread Sauce.

Stuffing I: French

liver and heart of bird, finely chopped
1 Spanish onion, finely chopped
2 tablespoons olive oil
2 level tablespoons butter
3 slices white bread, diced
3 level tablespoons finely chopped parsley
salt and freshly ground black pepper
pinch of cayenne
1 egg, beaten
4 tablespoons dry white wine

1. Sauté finely chopped liver, heart and onion in olive oil and butter until golden.

2. Add diced bread and finely chopped parsley and cook for a few minutes, stirring continuously.

3. Season with salt and freshly ground black pepper and cayenne. Transfer mixture to a mixing bowl and allow to cool. Just before stuffing bird, stir in beaten egg and dry white wine.

Stuffing II: Moroccan

$\frac{1}{2}$ onion, finely chopped
$\frac{1}{4}$ clove garlic, finely chopped
2 level tablespoons butter
2 level tablespoons olive oil
65 g/$2\frac{1}{2}$ oz fresh breadcrumbs
2 level tablespoons finely chopped parsley
4 level tablespoons slivered toasted almonds
4 level tablespoons seedless raisins, soaked
   in hot water
salt and freshly ground black pepper
$\frac{1}{4}$ level teaspoon cumin seed
$\frac{1}{4}$ level teaspoon ground ginger
$\frac{1}{4}$ level teaspoon ground cinnamon
$\frac{1}{4}$ level teaspoon cayenne
1 egg, beaten
4 tablespoons chicken stock

1. Sauté finely chopped onion and garlic in butter and olive oil until the vegetables are soft.

2. Add the breadcrumbs and finely chopped parsley and continue to cook, stirring continuously over a low heat, for a few more minutes.

3. Transfer mixture to a mixing bowl and stir in slivered toasted almonds and soaked raisins.

4. Season with salt and freshly ground black pepper, cumin seed, ground ginger, cinnamon and cayenne. Add beaten egg and chicken stock and mix well.

Poulet Sauté 'Quaglino's'

1 tender chicken (1.25-1.5 kg/2½-3 lb)
salt and freshly ground black pepper
4 level tablespoons butter
1 bouquet garni (2 parsley roots, 1 sprig thyme, 1 bay leaf)
2 level tablespoons finely chopped onion
1 small clove garlic
1 glass dry white wine
450 g/1 lb ripe red tomatoes, peeled, seeded and chopped
4 button mushrooms, simmered in butter and lemon juice

1. Cut chicken into serving pieces, reserving backbone. Season well with salt and freshly ground black pepper, and put chicken pieces flesh side down in a sauté pan or thick-bottomed frying pan just large enough to hold them comfortably. Sauté chicken pieces in butter until they are browned on all sides – about 10 minutes.

2. Add backbone and *bouquet garni*, cover pan and simmer gently for 20 minutes. Remove wings and breasts after 15 minutes. They are the most delicate, and cook most quickly. Keep warm.

3. Remove remaining pieces and sauté finely chopped onion in pan juices until transparent. Add garlic and dry white wine, and continue cooking until wine is reduced to half of the original quantity.

4. Add tomatoes and simmer for 5 minutes more.

5. Return sautéed chicken to the pan, cover and

allow to simmer gently over the lowest of heats for 5 minutes. Do not allow liquid to boil or your chicken will be tough.

6. Garnish with button mushrooms which you have simmered in butter and lemon juice. Serve immediately.

Chicken Stuffed with Grapes
Illustrated on page 166

1 roasting chicken (1.75-2.25 kg/4-5 lb)
butter
salt
freshly ground black pepper
dry white wine

STUFFING
1 Spanish onion, finely chopped
4 cloves garlic, finely chopped
butter
4 slices dry bread, crumbled
100-175 g/4-6 oz white seedless grapes
6 tablespoons melted butter
2 level tablespoons finely chopped parsley
¼ level teaspoon dried sage
salt and freshly ground black pepper

1. To make stuffing: sauté onion and garlic in a little butter and combine with crumbled bread, grapes, melted butter, finely chopped parsley and sage. Season to taste with salt and freshly ground black pepper.

2. Rub chicken on the inside with salt and stuff with the grape stuffing.

3. Skewer the opening. Truss the chicken and rub it with butter, salt and freshly ground black pepper. Roast the bird in a moderate oven (160°C, 325°F, Gas Mark 3) for 1½ to 2 hours, until cooked, basting from time to time with a little dry white wine.

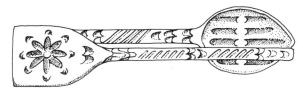

157

158

Chicken Sauté Alexandra

1 tender chicken (1.25–1.5 kg/2½–3 lb)
salt and freshly ground black pepper
4 level tablespoons butter
1 bouquet garni (2 parsley roots, 1 sprig
    thyme, 1 bay leaf)
150 ml/¼ pint chicken stock
150 ml/¼ pint Chicken Velouté Sauce (see
    page 410)
4 level tablespoons cooked puréed onions
4 level tablespoons double cream

1. Cut chicken into serving pieces, reserving back-bone. Season well with salt and freshly ground black pepper, and put chicken pieces, flesh side down, in a sauté pan or thick-bottomed frying pan just large enough to hold them comfortably. Add 2 tablespoons butter and sauté chicken pieces until they are browned on all sides – about 10 minutes.

2. Add backbone and *bouquet garni*, cover pan and simmer gently for 20 minutes. Remove wings and breasts after 15 minutes. They are the most deli-cate, and cook most quickly. Keep warm.

3. Remove remaining pieces of chicken, add chicken stock to pan juices and reduce to half of the original quantity.

4. Stir in Chicken Velouté Sauce to which you have added cooked puréed onions, double cream and remaining 2 tablespoons butter. Strain the sauce over chicken pieces and heat through.

Poulet Sauté à la Crème

1 tender chicken (1.25–1.5 kg/2½–3 lb)
salt and freshly ground black pepper
4 level tablespoons butter
1 bouquet garni (2 parsley roots, 1 sprig
    thyme, 1 bay leaf)
300 ml/½ pint double cream

1. Cut chicken into serving pieces, reserving backbone. Season well with salt and freshly ground black pepper, and put chicken pieces, flesh side down, in a sauté pan or thick-bottomed frying pan just large enough to hold them com-fortably. Add 2 tablespoons butter and sauté chicken pieces until they are browned on all sides – about 10 minutes.

2. Add backbone and *bouquet garni*, cover pan and simmer gently for 20 minutes. Remove wings and breasts after 15 minutes. They are the most deli-cate, and cook most quickly. Keep warm.

3. Remove remaining pieces, add cream to pan juices and reduce to half of the original quantity. Stir in remaining 2 tablespoons butter and strain.

4. Add chicken pieces to strained sauce, heat through and serve.

Poulet à la Marengo

1 tender chicken
salt and freshly ground black pepper
2 level tablespoons butter
2 tablespoons olive oil
2 shallots, finely chopped
1 level tablespoon flour
1 glass dry sherry
4 level tablespoons tomato purée
1 bouquet garni (4 sprigs parsley, 1 stick
   celery, 1 bay leaf)
12 button mushrooms, sliced
well-flavoured chicken stock
lemon juice
cayenne
croûtons of fried bread or crescents of
   flaky pastry

1. Cut chicken into serving pieces, removing as much of the skin as possible. Season pieces with salt and freshly ground black pepper, and sauté in butter and olive oil until golden.

2. Sprinkle with finely chopped shallots and flour, and continue to cook, shaking pan, until shallots are transparent. Then add dry sherry, tomato purée, *bouquet garni*, sliced mushrooms and enough well-flavoured stock to cover. Cover and simmer gently in a moderate oven (160°C, 325°F, Gas Mark 3) until chicken is tender.

3. To serve: arrange chicken pieces on a heated serving dish. Skim fat from sauce, add lemon juice and cayenne to taste, and strain sauce over chicken pieces. Garnish with sliced mushrooms and *croûtons* or pastry crescents, and serve immediately.

Poulet Sauté à l'Estragon

159

1 plump chicken
4 tablespoons olive oil
6 level tablespoons finely chopped shallots
1 wine glass very dry white wine
100 ml/4 fl oz water
salt and freshly ground black pepper
450 g/1 lb potatoes, peeled and diced
8 level tablespoons butter
finely chopped fresh tarragon
finely chopped parsley

1. Clean a fine fat chicken and cut it in serving pieces (drumsticks, thighs, wings, and the carcass, cut into 4 or 6 pieces).

2. Sauté chicken pieces in olive oil in a heavy-bottomed ovenproof casserole or iron *cocotte*, turning pieces often until they are evenly golden on all sides.

3. Drain off surplus oil, add finely chopped shallots and stir well, cooking for another minute or two, until shallots are transparent. Add dry white wine and water (the water is to remove the acidity of the wine), and season to taste with salt and freshly ground black pepper. Cover and cook for about 20 minutes, by which time the sauce should be reduced to half of the original quantity. If not, reduce it over a high heat.

4. In the meantime, sauté diced potatoes in 4 tablespoons butter in a frying pan until they are golden.

5. Place chicken pieces on a warm serving dish, add diced cooked potatoes and keep warm.

6. Add finely chopped tarragon and remaining butter to sauce in the casserole. Stir well, taste and correct seasoning. Pour sauce over the diced potatoes and the chicken pieces. Sprinkle with finely chopped parsley.

7. When you serve this dish, mix a little sauce into the potatoes so that they will be well moistened by it. Your sauce should not be too liquid, and there should only be about 2 tablespoons per person.

160

Chicken with Dumplings

1 large boiling chicken (1.75-2.25 kg/4-5 lb)
1.15 litres/2 pints water
salt
4 carrots
1 Spanish onion stuck with 1 clove
2 sticks celery

SAUCE
3 level tablespoons butter
3 level tablespoons flour
300 ml/½ pint milk

DUMPLINGS
225 g/8 oz self-raising flour, sifted
½ level teaspoon salt
8 level tablespoons melted chicken fat,
   or butter
4 level tablespoons finely chopped parsley
about 150 ml/¼ pint milk

1. To cook chicken: bring water to the boil in a large saucepan. Cut chicken into serving pieces and add to the boiling water with salt and vegetables. Bring to the boil again. Skim, reduce heat and simmer chicken very gently for 3 hours, or until tender. Remove chicken and vegetables from stock. Skim fat from stock, reserving 8 level tablespoons for dumplings. **Note:** if there is not enough chicken fat, make up the amount with melted butter. Strain stock and reserve.

2. To make sauce: melt butter in a small saucepan. Stir in flour until smooth, add milk and cook, stirring constantly until sauce is smooth. Measure 1¼ pints of the chicken stock into a large casserole. Bring to the boil and add cream sauce to stock, stirring constantly. Bring to the boil again and simmer for 5 minutes. Add chicken pieces to sauce.

3. To make dumplings: sift self-raising flour and salt into a mixing bowl. Stir in 8 tablespoons melted chicken fat or butter, and the finely chopped parsley with a fork. Add milk a little at a time, stirring with a fork, or your fingers, until mixture is just dampened. Drop a tablespoonful at a time on to chicken pieces in gently bubbling sauce. Cover and cook for 20 to 25 minutes, until dumplings are cooked through.

Chicken Fricassée

1 tender chicken
juice of 1 lemon
salt
chicken stock
salt and freshly ground black pepper
1 bouquet garni
dry white wine
8 small white onions
2-4 level tablespoons finely chopped parsley
croûtons of bread fried in butter

SAUCE
3 level tablespoons butter
3 level tablespoons flour
8 button mushrooms, sliced
2 egg yolks
double cream (optional)

1. To whiten chicken: clean and wash chicken, cut into serving pieces and put in a saucepan with half the lemon juice and enough cold salted water to cover. Bring to the boil, remove from heat and drain. Plunge into cold water for 5 minutes. Drain.

2. Place chicken in a saucepan with sufficient chicken stock to cover. Add salt, freshly ground black pepper, *bouquet garni*, dry white wine and onions. Bring to the boil, skim and reduce heat; simmer gently until chicken is tender. Remove chicken pieces and onions to a clean casserole and keep warm. Strain and reserve stock for sauce.

3. To make sauce: melt butter in the top of a double saucepan, add flour and stir until smooth. Pour in strained chicken stock and stir over water until boiling. Add sliced mushrooms and simmer gently for 15 minutes. Combine yolks with remaining lemon juice and a little double cream if desired, and stir in a little of the hot sauce. Pour egg and lemon mixture into double saucepan and stir until thick and smooth. Do not allow to boil or sauce will curdle.

4. To serve: place hot cooked chicken pieces and onions in a heated serving bowl. Pour sauce over them and garnish with finely chopped parsley and *croûtons* of fried bread. Serve immediately.

Chicken Breasts with Foie Gras

breasts of 2 young chickens
4 level tablespoons butter
2 tablespoons olive oil
4 level tablespoons foie gras
450 ml/¾ pint double cream
salt and freshly ground black pepper

1. Separate each half chicken breast into 2 *suprêmes* and sauté them gently in butter and olive oil, covered, until tender but not brown.

2. In the meantime, mix *foie gras* with 4 tablespoons double cream until smooth. Season generously with salt and freshly ground black pepper. Reserve.

3. To finish dish: remove chicken pieces from pan when cooked through. Keep warm. Add remaining cream to pan and bring to the boil. Blend *foie gras* mixture into the sauce and cook, stirring continuously, until smooth. Correct seasoning, pour sauce over chicken pieces and serve immediately.

Twice-Fried Chicken

1 tender chicken (about 1.5 kg/3½ lb)
4 tablespoons soy sauce
8 tablespoons sake or dry sherry diluted
    with a little water
1 level teaspoon sugar
1 level teaspoon fresh root ginger, finely
    chopped
fat or oil for frying
cornflour, sifted

1. Bone chicken and cut the meat into 2.5-cm/ 1-inch pieces.

2. Combine soy sauce, *sake* (or dry sherry diluted with a little water), sugar and ginger. Marinate chicken pieces in this mixture for at least 2 hours. Drain the chicken thoroughly, reserving marinade juices.

3. Dry the chicken pieces and fry in deep fat until golden. Remove from fat and drain.

4. Add chicken to marinade juices, stirring well so that all pieces are coated by marinade. Allow to stand in marinade for at least 15 minutes. Drain the chicken pieces.

5. Dust lightly with sifted cornflour and fry again in deep fat until crisp and golden brown.

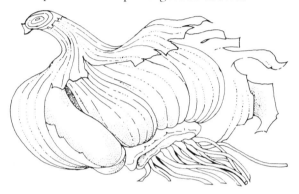

Fried Chicken Strips

450 g/1 lb raw chicken breast
1 egg, beaten
2 tablespoons finely chopped onion
1 clove garlic, finely chopped
2 level tablespoons cornflour
1 tablespoon soy sauce
1 tablespoon sake
2 level teaspoons sugar
salt
fat for deep-frying
finely chopped parsley

1. Remove skin from chicken breast and slice across grain into strips, 5 mm/1¼ inches wide.

2. Place chicken strips in a bowl; add beaten egg, and finely chopped onion and garlic. Sprinkle with cornflour, soy sauce, *sake*, sugar, and salt, to taste. Mix well. Marinate chicken strips in this mixture for 10 to 15 minutes.

3. Fry strips, one at a time, in deep hot fat until golden. Drain.

4. Just before serving, fry again. Garnish with finely chopped parsley and serve immediately.
Serves 4 in a Chinese meal or 2 as a main course on its own.

162

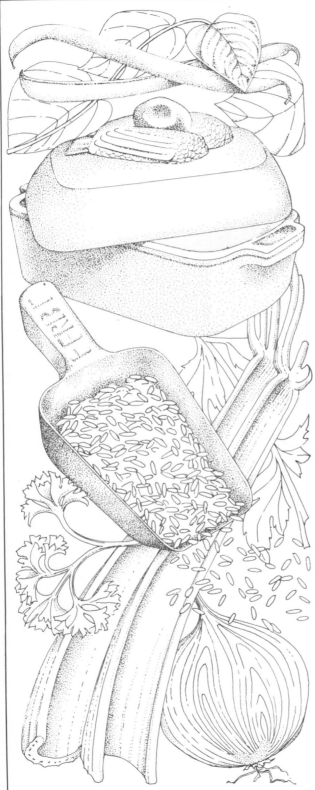

Boiled Chicken with Rice

Illustrated on page 165

1 fat chicken
1 Spanish onion, stuck with 2 cloves
2 large carrots
1 bouquet garni (celery leaves, 2 sprigs
    parsley, 2 sprigs thyme)
2 sticks celery
1 glass dry white wine
1.15 litres/2 pints white stock (chicken or
    veal, or both)
salt and black peppercorns

RICE
1 tablespoon butter
1 Spanish onion, finely chopped
225 g/8 oz rice
300 ml/$\frac{1}{2}$ pint strained chicken stock
600 ml/1 pint hot water
salt and freshly ground black pepper

CREAM SAUCE
2 tablespoons flour
2 tablespoons butter
150 ml/$\frac{1}{4}$ pint strained chicken stock
450 ml/$\frac{3}{4}$ pint double cream
salt and freshly ground black pepper
freshly grated nutmeg

GARNISH
cooked carrots
cooked green beans

1. Clean, singe and truss chicken; place in a casserole with an onion stuck with cloves. Add carrots, *bouquet garni* and celery, and moisten with dry white wine and a good white stock. Season to taste with salt and a few peppercorns and simmer gently for about 1$\frac{1}{2}$ hours, or until tender.

2. Remove chicken and keep warm. Strain chicken stock, and use for cooking rice and for cream sauce.

3. To prepare rice: Melt butter in a saucepan, add finely chopped onion and stir for a minute over heat until transparent. Stir in rice. Add 300 ml/$\frac{1}{2}$ pint strained chicken stock and hot water; season to taste with salt and black pepper. Simmer very gently, covered, for about 25 minutes, or until tender but not mushy.

4. To make cream sauce: Make a white *roux* with flour and butter; add 150 ml/¼ pint chicken stock and double cream, and bring slowly to the boil, stirring constantly. Simmer, stirring from time to time, until sauce is thick and smooth. Remove from heat. Season to taste with salt, black pepper and nutmeg.

5. To serve: Place boiled chicken in the centre of a large heated serving platter. Surround with colourful clusters of cooked whole carrots, green beans and rice. Pour a little cream sauce over chicken and serve the rest separately.

Spanish Fried Chicken

4 chicken breasts
2 leeks (white parts only), finely chopped
4 sprigs parsley
1 bay leaf
150 ml/¼ pint dry white wine
150 ml/¼ pint chicken stock
salt and freshly ground black pepper
300 ml/½ pint Béchamel Sauce (see page 412)
flour
2 eggs, well beaten
fine breadcrumbs
oil for frying

SPINACH PURÉE
1 kg/2 lb spinach
4 tablespoons butter
4 tablespoons chicken stock
freshly ground black pepper
Béchamel Sauce (see page 412)
2 egg yolks, well beaten
salt

1. Place chicken breasts in a well-buttered shallow *gratin* dish with finely chopped leeks, parsley, bay leaf, equal parts dry white wine and chicken stock, salt and freshly ground black pepper, to taste. Cover with a piece of well-buttered foil and poach in a moderately hot oven (200°C, 400°F, Gas Mark 6) until tender. Allow chicken to cool in dish in which it was cooked, then drain.

2. Coat each breast with well-flavoured Béchamel Sauce and allow to cool on a wire rack until sauce is firm.

3. Dip each breast in flour, then in beaten egg, and then toss in fine breadcrumbs, pressing breadcrumbs well against chicken breast with a spatula.

4. To make spinach purée: wash spinach several times in cold water. Combine in a large saucepan with butter, chicken stock, and freshly ground black pepper, to taste. Cook over a high heat, stirring constantly, until spinach is tender – about 5 minutes. Drain and squeeze dry, chop and then purée in electric blender. Combine spinach with a little Béchamel Sauce and beaten egg yolks. Correct seasoning and reheat in the top of a double saucepan until ready to use.

5. Just before serving, fry chicken breasts in deep hot oil until golden. Serve on bed of puréed spinach.

Japanese Chicken

1 tender chicken (about 1.5 kg/3½ lb)
2-4 tablespoons soy sauce
4-6 tablespoons sake or dry sherry diluted with a little water
1 level tablespoon brown sugar
15 g/½ oz root ginger, finely chopped
2 shallots, finely chopped
4 slices lemon, coarsely chopped
1 clove garlic, coarsely chopped
cornflour
4 tablespoons peanut or olive oil

1. Combine soy sauce, *sake* (or sherry and water), sugar, chopped root ginger, shallots, lemon and garlic.

2. Cut chicken into serving pieces and dust with a little cornflour. Marinate in mixture for at least 4 hours, turning chicken in juices from time to time.

3. Place chicken in a shallow baking dish and sprinkle with peanut or olive oil. Bake in a moderate oven (160°C, 325°F, Gas Mark 3) for 1 to 1½ hours, basting from time to time.

164

Turkey with Orange Sauce

1 medium-sized turkey (about 4.5 kg/10 lb)
1 orange
1 Spanish onion
2 tablespoons olive oil
salt and freshly ground black pepper
$\frac{1}{4}$ level teaspoon dried rosemary
$\frac{1}{4}$ level teaspoon dried oregano
100 g/4 oz butter, melted
4–6 rashers unsmoked bacon
150 ml/$\frac{1}{4}$ pint dry white wine
juice of 2 oranges
1 clove garlic, finely chopped
1 chicken stock cube

ORANGE SAUCE
turkey giblets
1 Spanish onion, coarsely chopped
1 bay leaf
4 sprigs celery leaves
4 sprigs parsley
salt and freshly ground black pepper
150 ml/$\frac{1}{4}$ pint dry white wine
2 tablespoons butter
2 tablespoons flour
stock from giblets
pan juices

1. Dice unpeeled orange; peel and dice onion. Toss in a mixing bowl with olive oil, salt, freshly ground black pepper, rosemary and oregano.

2. Stuff bird loosely with this mixture. Brush bird with a little melted butter and season generously with salt and freshly ground black pepper. Place in a roasting tin, breast side up. Cover breast with bacon slices and roast bird in a moderate oven (160°C, 325°F, Gas Mark 3) for 30 minutes. Baste turkey with basting sauce made of remaining melted butter, dry white wine and orange juice, seasoned with finely chopped garlic, chicken stock cube, salt and freshly ground black pepper, to taste. Cover loosely with foil and continue to cook for 3 to 4 hours, basting frequently, until turkey is tender. Remove and discard orange and onion stuffing before serving.

3. To make Orange Sauce: wash giblets, and combine neck, heart and gizzard in a saucepan with coarsely chopped onion, bay leaf, celery leaves, parsley, salt and freshly ground black pepper, dry white wine and enough water to cover. Bring to the boil, skim, lower heat and simmer for 1$\frac{1}{2}$ hours, adding more water from time to time. Add liver and continue cooking for 30 minutes more. Remove heart, gizzard and liver, and chop pieces coarsely. Melt butter in the top of a double saucepan. Add flour and stir until smooth. Add strained stock from giblets and pan juices (with fat removed), and cook over water, stirring constantly, until sauce is smooth and thick. Add chopped giblets and heat through; correct seasoning and serve with turkey.

Devilled Duck, Chicken or Turkey

6 portions cold roast duck, chicken or turkey
100 g/4 oz softened butter
1 level tablespoon Dijon mustard
1 level teaspoon English mustard
2 level tablespoons chutney
1 level teaspoon curry powder
1–2 tablespoons lemon juice
salt
cayenne

1. Score poultry with a sharp knife.

2. Combine butter, mustards, chutney, curry powder and lemon juice in a mortar, and pound to a smooth paste. Season to taste with salt and cayenne.

3. Spread mixture on cold duck, chicken or turkey, and grill until sizzling hot.

Boiled Chicken with Rice (see page 162)

Chicken Stuffed with Grapes (see page 157)
Chicken Baked in Salt (see page 154)

Roast Game Birds

Roast Duckling Farci à la Grecque

1 Aylesbury duckling (about 2.25 kg/5 lb)
175 g/6 oz bourgoùrie (Greek ground wheat)
well-flavoured chicken stock
1 Spanish onion, unpeeled
duck's liver, heart and gizzard
butter
4 level tablespoons finely chopped shallots
   or onion
2 level tablespoons dried currants
4-6 level tablespoons blanched almonds,
   chopped
grated rind of 1 orange
sage
salt and freshly ground black pepper
flour
dry white wine
orange juice

1. Simmer *bourgourie* in chicken stock with 1 unpeeled Spanish onion until tender, then drain. Remove onion, peel and chop finely.

2. Chop liver, heart and gizzard, and sauté in butter with finely chopped shallots. Soak currants in a little hot water until soft. Drain.

3. Combine *bourgourie*, chopped onion, giblets, currants and chopped almonds in a bowl, and mix well. Add grated orange rind and rubbed sage, salt and freshly ground black pepper, to taste. Then add 4 tablespoons melted butter and mix well.

4. Stuff cleaned and trussed duck with this mixture and sew up the opening.

5. Place duck, breast side up on a rack in a roasting tin. Cover breast of the bird with buttered foil and roast in a moderate oven (180°C, 350°F, Gas Mark 4) for 1½ to 1¾ hours. Baste frequently with butter or dripping. Remove foil 20 minutes before removing duck from the oven. Dredge breast with flour and leave in oven until well browned. Transfer to a hot serving dish, remove trussing threads and strings. Skim fat from pan juices in roasting tin, stir in a little dry white wine and orange juice. Bring to the boil on top of the cooker, stirring in all crusty bits from sides and bottom of pan.

Reduce heat and simmer for 2 to 3 minutes. Strain into sauceboat and serve with duck.

Caneton de Colette

1 plump duck (about 2.25 kg/5 lb)
1-2 duck livers
butter
salt and freshly ground black pepper
allspice
½ glass cognac
½ glass port
stock (optional)

1. Clean, singe and truss a plump duck. Remove wishbone to help carving, and roast duck in a moderately hot oven (200°C, 400°F, Gas Mark 6) for 25 minutes, or until flesh is pink when cut.

2. Sauté duck livers in butter for a minute or two until they stiffen but are not cooked through. Add pan juices from duck, then mash livers with a fork and season generously with salt, freshly ground black pepper and allspice. Pour warmed cognac and port over sauce, ignite and reduce over a high heat to three-quarters of the original quantity.

3. Remove drumsticks and wings from duck, and sauté in butter until cooked through.

4. Remove breast of duck, cut into long fine strips and sauté in butter. Arrange in centre of heated serving dish.

5. Cut carcass in half and press in a duck press to obtain as much blood and juices as possible (or cut duck carcass into 4 to 6 pieces and press each piece with pincers to obtain juices). Mix these juices with mashed livers, adding a little stock if necessary, and heat through until bubbling.

6. Arrange drumsticks and wings on serving dish. Correct seasoning of sauce and strain through a fine sieve over strips of meat and drumsticks.

170

Duck en Gelée

1 tender duckling
6 level tablespoons butter
2 tablespoons olive oil
8 tablespoons dry white wine
600 ml/1 pint well-flavoured chicken stock
1 calf's foot, split in two
salt and freshly ground black pepper
1 bouquet garni (2 sprigs parsley, 2 sprigs
**   thyme, 1 stick celery, 2 bay leaves)**
12 cubes fat bacon
12 young turnips
12 button mushrooms
12 button onions
100 g/4 oz lean beef, minced
whites and shells of 2 eggs
2 level tablespoons gelatine
green salad

1. Clean duckling, cut into serving pieces. Sauté in 4 level tablespoons butter and 2 tablespoons olive oil in a flameproof casserole until golden on all sides. Moisten with dry white wine and bring to the boil. Add chicken stock, calf's foot, salt, freshly ground black pepper and a *bouquet garni*. Reduce heat and simmer gently for 30 minutes, skimming from time to time.

2. Sauté bacon cubes in remaining butter until golden. Remove, and sauté turnips in resulting fat until golden.

3. Combine sautéed bacon and turnips with button mushrooms and onions, and add to duckling. Cover and simmer for about 1½ hours, or until duckling is tender and vegetables are cooked through, basting duckling from time to time.

4. Remove duckling to an oval *terrine* just large enough to hold it, and surround with bacon cubes, turnips, mushrooms and onions.

5. To clarify stock: strain stock into a clean saucepan; add minced beef and the whites and shells of 2 eggs and bring gradually to the boil over a low heat, stirring frequently. Stop stirring when thick pad of foam forms on top of liquid. Simmer for 30 minutes. Whilst hot, strain stock through a sieve lined with a wet flannel cloth.

6. Soften gelatine in a little cold water and stir into the hot stock. Pour over duckling, covering it. **Note:** if there is not enough liquid to cover duckling completely, add equal quantities chicken stock and dry white wine. Allow to set for 12 hours before unmoulding. Serve with a green salad.

Roast Stuffed Goose

1 fat goose (3.5-4.5 kg/8-10 lb)
melted butter
salt and freshly ground black pepper
4-6 tablespoons Calvados or cognac
dried breadcrumbs

STUFFING
1 Spanish onion, finely chopped
4 level tablespoons butter
2 tablespoons olive oil
225 g/8 oz sausagemeat
4 level tablespoons finely chopped parsley
2 eggs, well beaten
juice of ½ lemon
crushed dried thyme and sage
salt and freshly ground black pepper
50-75 g/2-3 oz dried breadcrumbs

Note: If goose is frozen, leave in the original wrappings and thaw for 48 hours in the refrigerator. Remove wrapping and drain liquids from cavity of goose.

Or, remove wrappings from frozen goose and thaw overnight in a container of water. Drain.

Then chop off tips of wings. Cut all excess fat from cavity and reserve for frying potatoes or some other use. Remove giblets and save for goose stock or sauce.

The gizzard, heart and liver are also good braised with goose fat and finely chopped onion and sliced thinly to be served with salad greens (young lettuce and spinach leaves, *mache* and curly endive) as an appetiser salad.

1. To make stuffing: sauté finely chopped onion in butter and olive oil until transparent. Add

Roast Goose with Sage and Onion Stuffing

1 fat goose (3.5-4.5 kg/8-10 lb)
apple sauce

STUFFING
225 g/8 oz butter
450 g/1 lb Spanish onions, chopped
175 g/6 oz celery, chopped
1 small loaf, freshly grated
2 eggs, well beaten
1 large cooking apple, peeled, cored and
  diced
1 level tablespoon powdered sage
salt
freshly ground black pepper

sausagemeat and sauté with onion until golden. Combine onion and sausage mixture in a bowl with finely chopped parsley. Stir in eggs, lemon juice, thyme, sage, salt and freshly ground black pepper, to taste. Add breadcrumbs and mix well.

2. Stuff and tie goose, brush lightly with melted butter and season generously with salt and freshly ground black pepper. Roast in a moderately hot oven (200°C, 400°F, Gas Mark 6) for 15 minutes. Reduce heat to moderate (150°C, 300°F, Gas Mark 2) and continue roasting until goose is tender – about 25 minutes per half kilo/per lb.

3. Skim off fat several times during cooking and baste goose with pan juices. The reserved fat will keep indefinitely in a cool place.

4. If you cover goose with foil, remove foil at least 45 minutes before end of cooking time. Flame goose with heated Calvados or cognac 15 minutes before the end of cooking time, then sprinkle lightly with dried breadcrumbs. Raise oven heat to hot (230°C, 450°F, Gas Mark 8) and cook for 15 minutes.

See Note for Roast Stuffed Goose.

1. To make stuffing: melt butter, and sauté onions and celery until golden. Combine with breadcrumbs, beaten eggs, diced apple, sage, salt and freshly ground black pepper, to taste.

2. Lightly stuff the goose. Truss and place on a rack in a shallow roasting tin. Roast in a cool oven (150°C, 300°F, Gas Mark 2) for about 25 minutes per half kilo/per lb. Prick the skin occasionally to let the fat run out. Skim fat from roasting tin from time to time. Serve goose with apple sauce.

Game

172

Grilled Quail

8 quail
salt and freshly ground black pepper
melted butter
8 croûtons fried bread
watercress
English Bread Sauce (see page 410)

1. Split quail through the backbone and lay them flat without separating the halves.

2. Wipe them carefully and season generously with salt and freshly ground black pepper. Brush with butter and grill for 5 to 6 minutes on one side. Turn birds; brush with butter and grill for 5 to 6 minutes on the other side, until tender.

3. When quail are ready to be served, place each bird on a *croûton* of bread fried in butter until golden; garnish with sprigs of watercress. Serve English Bread Sauce separately.

Cailles en Caisses

4–8 quail, according to size
1 (60-g/2⅜-oz) can mousse de foie gras
truffles
2 level tablespoons butter
1 tablespoon olive oil
2 small carrots, diced
1 medium-sized onion, diced
salt and freshly ground black pepper
well-flavoured stock (optional)
Brown Chaudfroid Sauce (see page 411)
chopped Aspic Jelly (see page 410)

1. Bone quail and stuff them with *mousse de foie gras*, putting a truffle or part of a truffle in the centre of each. Sew them up, making them as neat a shape as possible.

2. Braise birds in butter and olive oil with diced carrots and onion for 15 to 20 minutes or poach them in a little well-flavoured stock with diced carrot and onion until tender. Season with salt and freshly ground black pepper. Remove pan from heat and cool. Remove trussing threads and coat each quail with Brown Chaudfroid Sauce.

3. When set, place each bird in an individual shallow ramekin or soufflé dish just large enough to hold it. Garnish with chopped aspic jelly.

Roast Guinea Fowl

2 guinea fowl
½ Spanish onion, halved
½ lemon, halved
6 juniper berries, crushed
½ level teaspoon dried thyme
salt and freshly ground black pepper
melted butter
watercress

1. Divide the onion, lemon, juniper berries and thyme between the two birds and use to stuff the cavity in each.

2. Skewer openings and truss birds. Season with salt and freshly ground black pepper, and roast in a moderate oven (160°C, 325°F, Gas Mark 3) for 50 to 60 minutes, until tender, basting birds with melted butter every 10 minutes. Serve garnished with sprigs of watercress.

Herbed Guinea Fowl

2 guinea fowl
2 cloves garlic, finely chopped
½ level teaspoon dried thyme
6 level tablespoons softened butter
grated peel of ¼ lemon
lemon juice
salt and freshly ground black pepper

1. Cut guinea fowl into quarters.

2. Pound garlic, thyme, butter and lemon peel to a smooth paste with lemon juice, salt and freshly ground black pepper, to taste.

3. Rub birds with this mixture and place in a well-buttered *gratin* dish. Cook in a moderately hot oven (190°C, 375°F, Gas Mark 5) for 40 to 50 minutes, until tender.

4. Cool; wrap loosely in foil until ready to use.

Roast Grouse with Juniper Berries

4 young grouse (225-450 g/½-1 lb each)
4 level tablespoons softened butter
8-12 juniper berries, crushed
juice of 1 lemon
salt and freshly ground black pepper
8 thin rashers bacon
4 croûtons big enough to serve as base for grouse
clarified butter
1 tablespoon olive oil
1-2 tablespoons cognac
watercress
redcurrant jelly

1. Combine softened butter, crushed juniper berries and lemon juice in a mixing bowl; add salt and a generous amount of freshly ground black pepper, to taste.

2. Rub birds inside and out with this mixture. Tie 2 thin rashers of fat bacon over the breast of each bird and roast in a hot oven (220°C, 425°F, Gas Mark 7) for 20 to 25 minutes.

3. When birds are half cooked, remove livers and mash them slightly. Place in roasting tin to cook with grouse until birds are tender. Skim fat from tin.

4. Just before serving, fry *croûtons* in a little clarified butter and olive oil until golden. Spread with mashed livers and crusty bits from roasting tin which you have seasoned to taste with cognac, salt and freshly ground black pepper, to taste.

5. To serve: remove bacon and string, place each bird on a garnished *croûton* and arrange on a heated serving dish. Serve with watercress and redcurrant jelly.

Spatchcocked Grouse

4 young grouse (225-450 g/½-1 lb each)
salt and freshly ground black pepper
2 level tablespoons finely chopped parsley
2 level tablespoons finely chopped shallots (optional)
melted butter
dried thyme or crushed juniper berries
Maître d'Hôtel Butter (see below)
game potato chips or grilled mushrooms

Only very young and tender birds can be prepared in this way.

1. Split them through the back without separating the halves, wipe the pieces carefully with a damp cloth and skewer them open. Season generously with salt, freshly ground black pepper and finely chopped parsley and shallots (optional). Brush birds with melted butter and season with a little dried thyme or crushed juniper berries.

2. Grease grid and make it very hot. Place birds on it and grill them over a high heat, turning them occasionally and brushing them with more butter when necessary. Cooking time will depend very much on the size and thickness of the grouse.

3. When cooked to your liking (grouse should never be overcooked), place the birds on a very hot dish with a pat of Maître d'Hôtel Butter on the top of each one. Garnish with game potato chips or grilled mushrooms.

Maître d'Hôtel Butter

100 g/4 oz butter
1 tablespoon finely chopped parsley
1 tablespoon lemon juice
salt and freshly ground black pepper

Cream butter with finely chopped parsley and lemon juice. Season to taste with salt and freshly ground black pepper. Chill.

174

Game Pie

2 partridges or pheasants
350 g/12 oz veal cutlets
225 g/8 oz cooked ham
6 tablespoons cognac
6 tablespoons red wine
2 level tablespoons finely chopped parsley
4 level tablespoons finely chopped onion
salt and freshly ground black pepper
butter
3 tablespoons olive oil
100 g/4 oz button mushrooms, quartered
$\frac{1}{4}$ level teaspoon dried thyme
1 bay leaf
300 ml/$\frac{1}{2}$ pint well-flavoured game stock
Puff Pastry (see page 420)
1 egg yolk

1. Cut partridges (or pheasants) into serving pieces, removing bones where possible.

2. Cut veal and ham into 1-cm/$\frac{1}{2}$-inch strips.

3. Marinate meats in cognac and red wine for at least 4 hours, with finely chopped parsley, onion, salt and freshly ground black pepper, to taste.

4. Preheat oven to hot (230°C, 450°F, Gas Mark 8).

5. Line a deep pie dish with strips of ham and veal. Sauté partridge or pheasant pieces in 3 tablespoons each butter and olive oil until golden, then place them on this bed. Top with quartered mushrooms, and season generously with salt, freshly ground black pepper, dried thyme and a bay leaf. Pour over marinade juices and game stock, and dot with 2 tablespoons diced butter.

6. Cover pie dish with a double thickness of aluminium foil; place in preheated oven and cook for 20 minutes. Reduce heat to moderate (180°C, 350°F, Gas Mark 4) and continue to cook for 45 minutes, or until meats are tender. Remove from oven and cool.

7. Line the rims of the pie dish with strips of puff pastry, and then cover pie with remaining pastry. Make a hole in the centre and decorate with pastry leaves. Brush with egg yolk and cook in a hot oven (230°C, 450°F, Gas Mark 8) for 10 minutes, or until pastry begins to brown, then reduce heat to moderate (180°C, 350°F, Gas Mark 4) and continue cooking for 20 to 30 minutes, until the pastry is brown and crisp.

Roast Wild Duck

2 wild ducks
salt and freshly ground black pepper
dried thyme
2 oranges
2 tart apples
2 Spanish onions
8 rashers bacon
300 ml/$\frac{1}{2}$ pint port

GARNISH
orange slices
watercress

SAUCE
2 level tablespoons flour
juice of 1 orange
juice of 1 lemon
port
salt and freshly ground black pepper

1. Clean, pluck and singe wild ducks. Rub cavities with salt, freshly ground black pepper and dried thyme.

2. Chop unpeeled oranges, apples and onions coarsely, and stuff ducks loosely with this flavouring mixture, keeping any remaining mixture for placing around ducks in roasting tins. Place ducks, breast sides up, on rack in roasting tins, cover the breasts with bacon and pour port into the tins.

3. Roast ducks in a hot oven (230°C, 450°F, Gas Mark 8) for 20 minutes, basting several times with port.

4. Remove bacon, baste well with pan juices and continue roasting for 10 to 15 more minutes until ducks are tender but rare. Crisp skins under grill, then transfer ducks to a heated serving dish and keep warm.

5. To make sauce: skim most of fat from pan juices, and stir in flour which you have dissolved in orange and lemon juice. Stir over a high heat, incorporating all crusty bits, until sauce thickens. Then add port, salt and freshly ground black pepper, to taste.

6. To serve: garnish ducks with orange slices and fresh watercress. Serve.

Roast Pheasant

2 tender pheasants (about 1.25 kg/2½ lb each)
salt and freshly ground black pepper
2 slices fat salt pork or fat bacon
chicken stock
red wine
watercress
English Bread Sauce (see page 410) or
  browned breadcrumbs

STUFFING
1 cooking apple
4 tablespoons softened butter
juice of ½ lemon
4 tablespoons finely chopped onion
2 tablespoons olive oil
salt and freshly ground black pepper

GRAVY
150 ml/¼ pint chicken stock
2 tablespoons redcurrant jelly
2 tablespoons fresh breadcrumbs

1. To make stuffing: grate apple coarsely and combine with softened butter, lemon juice and finely chopped onion which you have softened in olive oil. Season generously with salt and freshly ground black pepper.

2. Stuff birds with this mixture. Season with salt and freshly ground black pepper. Tie a thin slice of fat salt pork or bacon over the breasts and roast in a moderate oven (180°C, 350°F, Gas Mark 4) for about 1 hour, or until tender, basting from time to time with chicken stock and red wine.

3. To make gravy: skim fat from pan juices and combine 150 ml/¼ pint of the pan juices

(made up, if necessary with water and red wine), with stock, redcurrant jelly and breadcrumbs. Simmer gently, stirring, until thickened.

4. To serve: remove bacon and strings and transfer birds to a heated serving dish. Garnish with watercress and serve with gravy and English Bread Sauce or browned breadcrumbs.

Pheasant Mousse

175 g/6 oz pheasant breast, cooked
50 g/2 oz ham
150 ml/¼ pint extra thick White Sauce (see
  page 413)
2 eggs
4 level tablespoons softened butter
1–2 tablespoons dry sherry
salt and freshly ground black pepper
pinch of nutmeg
grated lemon rind
150 ml/¼ pint double cream, stiffly whipped
clarified butter
a few cooked green peas, or finely chopped
  parsley and truffles
French Tomato Sauce (see page 416)

1. Mince pheasant with ham, and pound until smooth in a mortar with Extra-thick White Sauce, 2 eggs and softened butter.

2. Rub mixture through a fine sieve into a bowl. Add sherry, salt, freshly ground black pepper, nutmeg and grated lemon rind. Mix well, then fold in stiffly whipped cream.

3. Grease a plain mould with clarified butter and decorate with cooked green peas, or finely chopped parsley and truffles cut in fancy shapes. Pour in the pheasant mixture and cover with greased greaseproof paper. Place mould in a pan two-thirds full of boiling water and cook in a moderate oven (180°C, 350°F, Gas Mark 4) until mousse is firm to the touch.

4. Allow mousse to stand for a few minutes after removing it from the oven. Turn out carefully on to a serving dish and pour French Tomato Sauce around it.

Grilled Venison Steaks

4 venison steaks
salt and freshly ground black pepper
2 bay leaves, crumbled
4 tablespoons olive oil
2 tablespoons lemon juice
6 level tablespoons softened butter
red or blackcurrant jelly

1. Choose the steaks from the leg if possible, cut from 1.5-2.5 cm/¾-1 inch in thickness. Trim them neatly and season with salt, freshly ground black pepper and crumbled bay leaves. Marinate them in olive oil and lemon juice for 2 hours.

2. Drain and grill as you would beef, turning them often and allowing rather longer than for a beef steak. Venison must be served immediately, or it will become tough.

3. To serve: transfer steaks on to a heated serving dish and garnish with softened butter to which you have added red or blackcurrant jelly, to taste.

Marinated Venison Steaks

4 thick steaks of venison, cut from the loin
salt and freshly ground black pepper
½ Spanish onion, sliced
2 carrots, sliced
4 sprigs parsley
2 bay leaves
thyme and rosemary
150 ml/¼ pint dry white wine
8 tablespoons olive oil
2 tablespoons butter

SAUCE
2 tablespoons butter
2 shallots, finely chopped
1 tablespoon flour
6 tablespoons marinade juices, strained
200 ml/7 fl oz soured cream
lemon juice
freshly ground black pepper

1. Season venison steaks generously with salt and freshly ground black pepper, and combine in a bowl with sliced onion and carrots, parsley, bay leaves, thyme and rosemary. Moisten with dry white wine and 6 tablespoons olive oil. Place bowl in the refrigerator and marinate steaks for 24 to 48 hours, turning them occasionally.

2. To cook steaks: remove venison from marinade, reserving marinade juices for further use, and pat dry. Heat 2 tablespoons each olive oil and butter in a large thick-bottomed frying pan, and sauté venison over a high heat for about 3 minutes on each side. Remove and keep warm.

3. To make sauce: drain excess fat from frying pan, add 2 tablespoons butter and sauté finely chopped shallots until soft. Sprinkle with flour and cook, stirring, until the *roux* is lightly browned. Add 6 tablespoons strained marinade juices, the soured cream, lemon juice and freshly ground black pepper, to taste.

4. Serve steaks on a heated serving dish with sauce.

Woodcock au Fumet

2 woodcock
2 rashers bacon
salt and freshly ground black pepper
olive oil
2 shallots, finely chopped, or ¼ Spanish onion, finely chopped
300 ml/½ pint champagne
300 ml/½ pint port
2 level tablespoons tomato purée
2 slices white bread
butter
4 level tablespoons sieved pâté de foie gras
2 tablespoons cognac

1. Hang woodcock for 4 to 6 days.

2. Clean and draw birds, reserving the livers. Truss legs close to the body and tie a rasher of bacon around each bird. Season generously with salt and freshly ground black pepper, and roast in a hot oven (220°C, 425°F, Gas Mark 7) for 10 to 15 minutes. Cut threads and discard bacon. Cut 2 *suprêmes* (breast and wings) and legs from birds, and reserve.

176

3. Chop carcasses finely and put them in a sauce-pan with a little olive oil and finely chopped shallots, or onion. Simmer until shallots are soft. Add champagne, port and tomato purée, and continue cooking for a few minutes.

4. Chop the raw livers and add them, together with the juices in the roasting tin in which the birds were cooked, to the chopped carcasses; simmer sauce for 30 minutes.

5. Cut bread slices in half, trim crusts and sauté slices in butter until golden. Spread with sieved *foie gras*. Place them on a heated serving dish.

6. Warm woodcock *suprêmes* and legs through in a little butter, sprinkle with cognac and flame.

7. To serve: arrange woodcock pieces on *canapés* and rub sauce over birds through a fine sieve. Serve immediately.

Partridge en Salade

2 partridges
150 ml/¼ pint olive oil
4 level tablespoons finely chopped shallots
  or onion
wine vinegar
4 level tablespoons finely chopped chervil or
  parsley
salt and freshly ground black pepper
dry mustard
2 apples, peeled and diced
2 sticks celery, sliced

1. Roast partridges in a moderately hot oven (200°C, 400°F, Gas Mark 6) for 18 to 20 minutes. Cut into serving pieces. Slice breasts.

2. Combine partridge pieces in a bowl with olive oil and finely chopped shallots, or onion. Marinate in this mixture for at least 12 hours, turning pieces from time to time.

3. When ready to serve, remove partridges from marinade and arrange them in a serving bowl. Make a well-flavoured *vinaigrette* with the oil in the dish by adding wine vinegar, finely chopped

chervil or parsley, salt, freshly ground black pepper and dry mustard, to taste. Pour *vinaigrette* mixture over partridges and add diced apples and celery. Toss and serve.

177

Lièvre à la Broche 'Paul Bocuse'

1 young hare (about 2 kg/4½ lb)
salt and freshly ground black pepper
powdered thyme and rosemary
Dijon mustard
olive oil
Rice Pilaff (see page 109)

SAUCE
2 shallots, finely chopped
pan juices
2 tablespoons wine vinegar
450 ml/¾ pint soured cream
2 juniper berries, crushed

1. Do not marinate hare. Rub it with a damp cloth and put it on a spit. Season the hare inside and out with salt, freshly ground black pepper, powdered thyme and rosemary, to taste, then coat it generously with Dijon mustard. Sprinkle with a little olive oil and roast it on the spit for 35 to 40 minutes, or until the hare is tender but the flesh is still rose-coloured. Make sure there is a pan under the hare to catch the juices as it cooks.

2. To make sauce: simmer finely chopped shallots in pan juices until soft. Add wine vinegar and scrape all the crusty bits from the sides of the pan. Then add soured cream and crushed juniper berries, and reduce the sauce to one-third of the original quantity. Strain.

3. Serve the hare with sauce and a Rice Pilaff.

Casseroles

French cooks are famous for their superb casseroles of meat, fish and poultry, enhanced with the subtle flavour of aromatic herbs and simmered gently in a sauce made rich with good stock, cream or wine. It is perhaps just this use of herbs and wines, and the words so often called on to describe these dishes – rich, unctuous, exotic, sophisticated – that have made the less adventurous cook too intimidated to attempt them.

For the uninitiated to whom cooking with wine may seem as extravagant as it is difficult, the well-known author and gourmet, Paul Gallico, set down this golden rule to dispel once and for all any misunderstanding: 'The only difference between cooking with wine and not cooking with wine is that you pour some wine in.'

My first contact with French food and wine was as dramatic and complete as any I have had since. It was in the winter of 1944, in the little river town of Duclair, just a few miles from Rouen. The dimly lit windows of a riverside inn beckoned the four travel-stained soldiers of the U.S. Army standing on the *quai*. We were young – not one of us over twenty-one – weary of the training, travel and camp life that were to prepare us for the push ahead, and hungry for food other than our army rations, for faces other than our camp companions, and for that something else which we all felt was waiting for us somewhere in this war-spoiled terrain of Northern France – the spirit of France itself.

This was to be our first meal in France, not perhaps as it should have been, but as the fortunes of war and of the pot would permit. The innkeeper, surprised to find soldiers asking for anything other than beer or Calvados, claimed at first that he had nothing to serve us. Then, taking pity on our youth and the fact that we had journeyed thousands of miles for this encounter, he disappeared for a moment or two into the cellars, to return with a slim white earthenware terrine and two dust-covered bottles – all that he could find to offer us – the *pâté* made for himself and his wife, and the wine hidden from the Germans behind bricked-over alcoves in the cellar.

The *pâté* was a home-made terrine of duck, its top covered with the rich golden-white fat of its own body, which had simmered slowly in the oven with a little wine to cover; the fillets of its breast and liver marbled the rich red-stained meat as we cut into it. Crusty bread and glasses of cellar-cooled claret completed this unforgettable meal, the perfect introduction to the pleasures of French food and wines, for *pâté de canard*, as made in Duclair, is one of the most famous dishes of Normandy, and Chantemerle, the wine he found for us that night, one of the noblest wines of all France.

Good food and wine have been the symbols of French living since they emerged together from the monasteries at the end of the Dark Ages. And they have been linked inextricably ever since.

Guardians of the pleasures of the tables as much as of the learning of the past, the monks kept the secrets of the gourmets safe for a thousand years after the Roman Empire collapsed. The kings of those days were merely chiefs; the barons taken up with wars. Not for them the finer points of the table.

But the traditions of good living persisted behind monastery walls. The strictest orders, though fasting themselves, provided hospitality for the great on pilgrimages or on their way to the wars, and for merchants traversing the ancient trade routes of Europe from the South to the Hanseatic Ports.

In their guests' refectories a more sophisticated cuisine persisted, and wine played its part in full. For as the great Cistercian and Benedictine monastries cleared the wooded lands presented to them over the centuries, they planted them with vines. Some of the most famous vineyards in Burgundy – Clos Vougeot, for instance, belonged to the Abbey of Citeaux – were tended by monks forbidden by their order to drink the wines they produced. But they were not forbidden to sell them, and strategic gifts of their finest vintages to popes and kings often led to miraculous advancements for the clergy.

Equal miracles can be produced today by the marriage of the right wine with the right food. For the balance is important. In the districts where wine is grown and where cooking reaches its peak, a rustic cuisine accompanies the coarser wines; subtle cooking, the light wines; and rich full fare, the full-bodied vintages.

During the past few years there has been a revolution at our tables: the British are becoming a nation of wine drinkers. Not just for special occasions and holidays, but for everyday living. It is no longer the hallmark of the connoisseur to have a bottle of wine on the table. And the British housewife is catching up with her French counterpart, who has known this little kitchen secret all along: to make an everyday dish an event, just add a little wine.

The bouquet and flavour of a good table wine will vastly improve the quality of your cooking. Learn to cook with the same quality wines that you like to drink. There is no such thing as a good cooking wine; any wine that is fit to cook with is fit to drink. And a note to teetotallers . . . the cooking evaporates the alcohol in the wine and only the wonderful flavour remains.

Use wine to tenderise as well as flavour the type of dish that has made France famous – superb slow-cooking casseroles of meat, poultry and game, seized in a little butter or olive oil, enhanced with the flavour of aromatic herbs, and then simmered gently for hours in a sauce enriched with good stock and fine wine.

Let wine add flavour to soups, sauces, stews and salads. Lace a thick soup with dry sherry or Madeira; add a little dry white wine to a salad dressing for fish or potatoes; combine white wine with powdered saffron and a well-flavoured French dressing for a Spanish-style salad of fish and shellfish cooked in a *court-bouillon* of white wine and water, spiked with vinegar and flavoured with onion, carrots, lemon peel and bay leaf.

Louis Outhier, handsome young chef-proprietor of the Oasis restaurant in La Napoule, just along the coast from Cannes, who trained with the famous Fernand Point at Vienne, uses wine to advantage in his sauces. He is one of the best chefs along the Coast, and the hard-to-find Oasis – it is in a back street just off the coastal road – is one of the most rewarding stop-offs for discerning visitors. There you can enjoy the specialities of the chef – **loup de mer en croûte**, a freshly caught sea bass half cooked in a white wine *court-bouillon*, placed on a large board, its form, fins, tail, eyes and scales remodelled in *brioche* pastry, and baked until golden in the oven. This masterpiece is served at the table, letting out all its aroma as it is cut before your eyes. Louis Outhier's **lobster belle aurore** is lobster poached in a white wine *court-bouillon* flavoured with onion, carrot, tomato and cognac. The lobster is split, the meat removed from the shell, sliced and combined with the *court-bouillon*, reduced to a thick sauce and blended with equal parts of fresh cream and sauce Hollandaise. The whole is returned to the half-shell, sprinkled with freshly grated Parmesan and browned quickly under the grill.

Sauces with a red wine base can add distinctive savour to delicious hurry-up dishes too; try **ouefs en meurette,** poached eggs served on *croûtons* of fried bread and covered with a red wine sauce, or roast beef *à la bordelaise*, thin slices of rare roast beef simmered in butter and then bathed in a red wine sauce. Beefsteak *à la bordelaise* – rare beefsteak served with a red wine sauce – is a wonderful variation on the grilled meat theme. Even hamburgers and meat loaf are greatly improved by the addition of this simple sauce.

Seafood

Cod Steaks Baked with Saffron *Serves 4*
Smoked Haddock Casserole *Serves 4 to 6*
Baked Plaice with Mushrooms *Serves 4*

180

Cod Steaks Baked with Saffron

1 Spanish onion, finely chopped
4 level tablespoons butter
4 level tablespoons fresh breadcrumbs
salt and freshly ground black pepper
2 tablespoons olive oil
4 medium-sized cod steaks
150 ml/¼ pint chicken stock
¼–½ level teaspoon saffron
150 ml/¼ pint dry white wine
juice of ½ lemon
2 level tablespoons finely chopped parsley

1. Sauté finely chopped onion in butter until onion is soft. Add breadcrumbs and cook for 5 minutes more. Season with salt and freshly ground black pepper. Remove onion and breadcrumb mixture with a slotted spoon and reserve.

2. Add olive oil to casserole; place cod steaks in casserole, season with salt and freshly ground black pepper and sauté for 3 minutes on each side. Spoon onion and breadcrumb mixture around steaks.

3. Heat chicken stock with saffron and pour over cod steaks. Pour over dry white wine, cover casserole, and cook in a moderate oven (180°C, 350°F, Gas Mark 4) for 20 minutes. Remove cover from casserole and continue to cook for 5 or 10 minutes longer. Just before serving, sprinkle cod steaks with lemon juice and finely chopped parsley.

Smoked Haddock Casserole

1 kg/2 lb smoked haddock
water and milk, to cover
butter
3 level tablespoons flour
450 ml/¾ pint cream
¼–½ level teaspoon turmeric
freshly ground black pepper
freshly grated nutmeg
2 level tablespoons finely chopped parsley
triangles of bread

1. Soak haddock in cold water for 2 hours. Drain

haddock, put it in a saucepan and cover with equal amounts of water and milk. Bring to a fast boil. Remove from heat and allow to stand for 15 minutes. Drain haddock, reserving stock.

2. Melt 3 level tablespoons butter in the top of a double saucepan. Stir in flour and cook over water for 3 minutes, stirring continuously, until smooth. Add cream and enough turmeric (dissolved in a little hot water) to give a rich golden colour to the sauce. Continue to cook, stirring from time to time.

3. Boil 300 ml/½ pint haddock stock to reduce it to half its original quantity and add enough of this highly-flavoured stock to give savour to your sauce. Season to taste with freshly ground black pepper and a little grated nutmeg.

4. Remove skin and bones from haddock and break into large pieces. Arrange pieces in a shallow flameproof casserole, pour over sauce and simmer very gently until ready to serve.

5. Sprinkle with finely chopped parsley and serve in the casserole surrounded by triangles of bread which you have sautéed in butter.

Baked Plaice with Mushrooms

300 ml/½ pint milk
salt
8-12 fresh fillets of plaice
dried breadcrumbs
butter
dried tarragon
freshly ground black pepper
225 g/8 oz button mushrooms, thinly sliced
4 level tablespoons finely chopped shallots
4 tablespoons melted butter
juice of ½ lemon

1. Flavour milk with salt. Dip plaice fillets in the milk and then in the breadcrumbs. Set aside.

2. Butter an ovenproof shallow casserole. Lay prepared fillets in it and season with dried tarragon, salt and freshly ground black pepper, to taste.

3. Sauté thinly sliced mushrooms and finely chopped shallots in 4 tablespoons butter until vegetables begin to turn colour; scatter over fish. Dribble the melted butter and lemon juice over them and bake in a hot oven (220°C, 425°F, Gas Mark 7) until fish flakes easily with a fork.

Curried Plaice with Rice

**8-12 fillets of plaice
butter
1 Spanish onion, finely chopped
1½ level tablespoons curry powder
salt and freshly ground black pepper
juice of ½ lemon
300 ml/½ pint well-flavoured Béchamel
   Sauce (see page 412)
300 ml/½ pint dry white wine, reduced over
   a high heat to ⅓ the original quantity
boiled rice to serve**

1. Slice each fillet into 3 pieces.

2. Melt 2 tablespoons butter in a shallow flame-proof casserole; add finely chopped onion and sauté until transparent. Stir in 1 level tablespoon curry powder, and season to taste with salt and freshly ground black pepper.

3. Spread onion mixture over the bottom of casserole and arrange fish pieces on top. Dot with butter, cover casserole and cook for 10 minutes over a medium heat. Remove cover, sprinkle with remaining curry powder and lemon juice.

4. Flavour Béchamel Sauce with reduced white wine and pour over fish to cover it. Cover casserole and simmer over a low heat for 15 minutes. Serve with boiled rice.

182

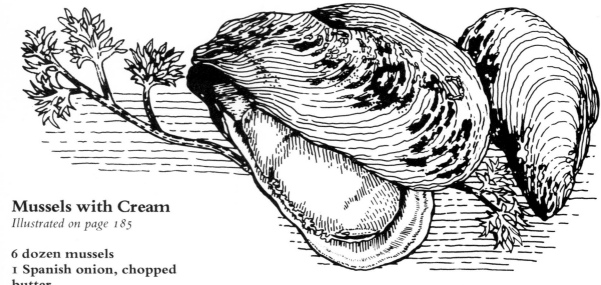

Mussels with Cream
Illustrated on page 185

6 dozen mussels
1 Spanish onion, chopped
butter
300 ml/½ pint dry white wine
2-3 sprigs parsley
1 sprig thyme
1 bay leaf
freshly ground black pepper
1 level tablespoon flour
6 level tablespoons double cream
2 level tablespoons chopped parsley

1. Scrape, beard and wash mussels thoroughly.

2. Sauté chopped onion in 2 level tablespoons butter in a large casserole until transparent but not coloured.

3. Add wine, parsley, thyme and bay leaf, and freshly ground black pepper, to taste, and simmer gently for 10 minutes. Add mussels to this mixture. Cover casserole and steam, shaking constantly, until mussel shells open.

4. Pour off cooking liquid into a small saucepan and reduce over a high heat to half the original quantity. Thicken sauce by adding a *beurre manié*, made by creaming together 2 tablespoons butter and 1 tablespoon flour. Cook over high heat, stirring constantly, until sauce is smooth. Add double cream, correct seasoning and pour sauce over mussels. Sprinkle with a little finely chopped parsley. Bring to the boil, remove from heat and serve immediately.

Sole au Chablis 'Hôtel de la Côte d'Or'

2 sole (about 450 g/1 lb each)
bones, head and trimmings from fish
150 ml/¼ pint water
salt and freshly ground black pepper
1 bouquet garni (1 bay leaf, 1 sprig thyme,
    4 sprigs parsley)
butter
2 shallots or small white onions, finely
    chopped
150 ml/¼ pint dry white Chablis

1. Ask your fishmonger to fillet the sole and give you the bones, head and trimmings to make a fish *fumet*. Simmer bones and trimmings for 15 minutes in water flavoured to taste with salt, freshly ground black pepper and a *bouquet garni*. Strain and reserve liquid.

2. Place fillets of sole in a well-buttered ovenproof *gratin* dish or shallow casserole. Sprinkle with finely chopped shallots (or onions) and add Chablis (or other dry white Burgundy), fish *fumet* and salt to taste. Cover with buttered paper and bake in a moderately hot oven (190°C, 375°F, Gas Mark 5) for about 15 minutes.

3. Arrange poached fillets on a heated serving dish; put fish liquor into a small saucepan and reduce over a high heat to half the original quantity. Whisk in 2 to 4 tablespoons butter, correct seasoning and strain sauce over sole. Serve immediately.

Turbot Baked in Cream

4 thick slices turbot
butter
salt and freshly ground black pepper
600 ml/1 pint double cream
lemon juice
Dijon mustard
Worcestershire sauce

1. Place turbot slices in a well-buttered ovenproof baking dish or shallow casserole, and season generously with salt and freshly ground black pepper.

2. Season cream to taste with lemon juice, Dijon mustard and Worcestershire sauce. Pour over fish and cover with buttered paper or a piece of foil. Place baking dish in a tin of boiling water in a moderately hot oven (190°C, 375°F, Gas Mark 5) for 15 to 20 minutes, until fish flakes easily with a fork.

3. To serve: transfer turbot to a heated serving dish, correct seasoning of sauce and strain over fish. Serve immediately.

Baked Fish with Mustard Sauce

1 white fish (1.5 kg/3 lb)
300 ml/½ pint dry white wine
150 ml/¼ pint water
2 tablespoons olive oil
4 level tablespoons finely chopped parsley
6 level tablespoons finely chopped shallots
2-3 level teaspoons dry mustard
salt and freshly ground black pepper

1. Clean and score fish and place in a baking dish.

2. Combine dry white wine, water, olive oil, finely chopped parsley and shallots with dry mustard that has been mixed with a little hot water.

Season to taste with salt and freshly ground black pepper, and pour liquid over fish.

3. Bake in a moderate oven (180°C, 350°F, Gas Mark 4) for 30 to 40 minutes, until the fish flakes easily at the touch of a fork, basting it every 10 minutes. Remove the fish to a heated serving platter, pour the basting sauce over the fish and serve.

Italian Fish Casserole

750 ml/1¼ pints well-flavoured chicken stock
225 g/8 oz long-grained rice
300 ml/½ pint well-flavoured Italian Tomato Sauce (see page 415)
675 g/1½ lb assorted fish, cut into pieces
butter
4 level tablespoons finely chopped parsley
salt and freshly ground black pepper
2 level tablespoons freshly grated Parmesan cheese
green salad to serve

1. Bring chicken stock to the boil, add rice and simmer until cooked through.

2. Prepare well-flavoured Tomato Sauce.

3. Remove any bones from the fish, add fish pieces to sauce and simmer until fish flakes easily with a fork.

4. Butter a shallow ovenproof *gratin* dish. Fill with rice mixed with finely chopped parsley. Season to taste with salt and freshly ground black pepper, and dot with knobs of butter. Arrange pieces of cooked fish on bed of rice, mask with sauce, sprinkle with grated cheese and put in a moderately hot oven (190°C, 375°F, Gas Mark 5) for 10 minutes. Serve with a green salad.

184

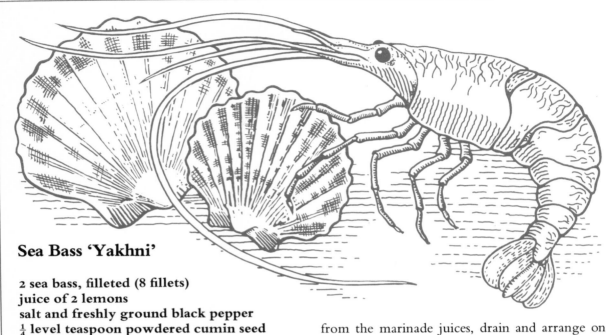

Sea Bass 'Yakhni'

2 sea bass, filleted (8 fillets)
juice of 2 lemons
salt and freshly ground black pepper
¼ level teaspoon powdered cumin seed
Pilaff rice (see recipe below)

YAKHNI SAUCE
4 tablespoons olive oil
1 large Spanish onion, finely chopped
2 bay leaves
4-6 tablespoons finely chopped parsley
4 tablespoons finely chopped celery leaves
2 cloves garlic, finely chopped
450 g/1 lb tomatoes, peeled, seeded and
    finely chopped
1 tablespoon tomato purée

1. Combine lemon juice, salt, freshly ground black pepper and powdered cumin in a bowl, and marinate fish fillets in the mixture for at least 1 hour, turning fillets occasionally.

2. To make Yakhni Sauce: heat oil in a shallow pan and sauté onion until transparent. Add bay leaves and finely chopped parsley, celery leaves and garlic, and simmer until vegetables begin to take on colour. Add tomatoes and tomato purée and simmer for 30 minutes longer, stirring from time to time.

3. To cook fish: 30 minutes before serving, spread half of the Yakhni Sauce over the bottom of a large ovenproof dish. Remove the fish fillets

from the marinade juices, drain and arrange on the sauce. Pour over remaining sauce, cover with a piece of oiled paper and bake in a moderately hot oven (190°C, 375°F, Gas Mark 5) for 30 minutes, or until fish flakes with a fork. Serve hot with pilaff rice.

Pilaff Rice

350 g/12 oz long-grain rice
½ Spanish onion, finely chopped
butter
450 ml/¾ pint well-flavoured stock
thyme
salt and freshly ground black pepper

1. Wash rice; drain and dry with a cloth.

2. Sauté finely chopped onion in 4 tablespoons butter until a light golden colour. Add rice and continue to cook, stirring constantly, until it begins to take on colour.

3. Pour in hot stock, and season to taste with thyme, salt and freshly ground black pepper. Cover pan and place in a moderate oven (180°C, 350°F, Gas Mark 4) for 15 to 20 minutes, until the liquid has been absorbed and the rice is tender but not mushy. Serve with additional butter.

Mussels with Cream (see page 182)

Dried Vegetable Harvest

Mexican Beans (see page 232)

Boston Baked Beans (see page 231)

Aubergine and Minced Lamb Casserole (see page 228)

Pot-au-feu de Poissons

4 sticks celery, cut into 5-cm/2-inch
  segments
4 carrots, cut into 5-cm/2-inch segments
4 leeks, cut into 5-cm/2-inch segments
butter
salt and freshly ground black pepper
600 ml/1 pint chicken stock
bones and trimmings from fish
575 g/1½ lb turbot fillets
575 g/1½ lb sole fillets
4-6 scallops
100 g/4 oz tiny Norwegian prawns
2 level tablespoons flour
300 ml/½ pint double cream
2 level tablespoons finely chopped parsley
2 level tablespoons finely chopped chives

1. Cut celery, carrot and leek segments into thin
'matchstick' strips. Sauté vegetables in 2 level
tablespoons butter in a shallow flameproof casserole for a few minutes, season with salt and
freshly ground black pepper. Add half the chicken
stock and simmer until vegetables are just tender.
Remove vegetables from casserole with a slotted
spoon. Keep warm.

2. Add remaining chicken stock to casserole with
bones and trimmings from fish, season well with
salt and freshly ground black pepper and bring to
the boil. Skim, remove fish bones and trimmings
and poach turbot fillets in stock until fish flakes
with a fork. Remove and keep warm.

3. Add sole fillets to the casserole and poach for
several minutes until fish flakes with a fork.
Remove and keep warm.

4. Add scallops and prawns to the casserole and
poach for several minutes until scallops are cooked.
Remove scallops and prawns and keep warm.

5. Reduce cooking liquids over a high heat to one-
third of the original quantity.

6. In the meantime, melt 2 level tablespoons
butter in the top of a double saucepan over direct
heat. Add flour and cook, stirring constantly until
the *roux* is well blended. Then stir in reduced

fish stock and double cream and cook over simmering water, stirring from time to time, until
sauce is smooth and thick. Correct seasoning.

7. **To assemble Pot-au-feu:** divide the hot
seafood between 4 to 6 shallow bowls, arrange
poached vegetables decoratively among the serv-
ings, and top seafood and vegetables with the
sauce. Sprinkle each bowl with a little finely
chopped parsley and chives.

Brodet – a Red Fish Stew

2 Spanish onions, thinly sliced
6 tablespoons olive oil
3 level tablespoons tomato purée
hot water
1.25 kg/2½ lb assorted fish, cut into pieces
300 ml/½ pint red wine
salt and freshly ground black pepper
100 g/4 oz cooked prawns
2 level tablespoons butter
4 level tablespoons finely chopped parsley
2 cloves garlic, finely chopped
grated rind of ½ lemon

1. Sauté sliced onions in olive oil in a large flameproof casserole until onions are soft and transparent. Stir in tomato purée diluted in 4 tablespoons
hot water. Add fish pieces and continue to cook,
shaking casserole from time to time to keep fish
from sticking to bottom of casserole.

2. Add red wine to casserole and enough hot
water to just cover fish. Season generously with
salt and freshly ground black pepper and continue
to cook gently, shaking pan from time to time,
until fish flakes easily with a fork.

3. Sauté prawns in butter, finely chopped parsley
and garlic, and grated lemon rind. Sprinkle over
fish and serve immediately.

190

Mexican Fish Bake

1 kg/2 lb fish (cod, halibut, etc.)
butter
2 Spanish onions, sliced
6-8 tomatoes, thickly sliced
salt
paprika and cayenne
2 canned pimientos, cut in thin strips
300 ml/½ pint dry white wine
6-8 tablespoons olive oil

1. Clean fish and cut into pieces. Butter an oven-proof casserole generously and arrange fish, sliced onions and tomatoes in casserole in alternating layers – seasoning each layer with salt, paprika and cayenne, to taste.

2. Garnish the top layer with thin strips of pimiento and pour over wine and olive oil.

3. Bake fish and vegetables in a moderate oven (160°C, 325°F, Gas Mark 3) for 30 to 40 minutes, until fish flakes easily with a fork.

Egyptian Fish Taguen for One

2 tablespoons olive oil
1 small onion, finely chopped
1 small clove garlic, finely chopped
100 g/4 oz short-grain rice
1 fillet of sea bass, turbot or halibut,
    weighing about 175 g/6 oz
salt and freshly ground black pepper
300 ml/½ pint well-flavoured fish stock
1-2 Italian canned tomatoes, chopped
lemon slices

1. Heat the oil and add the onion and garlic. When the vegetables start to take on colour, add the rice and cook until it turns golden brown.

2. Place half the rice in a small earthenware casserole and top with fish. Season to taste with salt and freshly ground black pepper. Add remainder of rice and pour over all the fish stock and chopped tomato. Cook, covered, in a moderately hot oven (200°C, 400°F, Gas Mark 6) for 45 minutes to 1 hour. Serve garnished with lemon slices.

Prawn and Scallop Casserole

6 scallops
½ chicken stock cube
1 tablespoon lemon juice
350 g/12 oz prawns in their shells
dry white wine (optional)

SAUCE
butter
3 tablespoons flour
600 ml/1 pint hot milk
1 clove garlic, finely chopped
¼ level teaspoon dry mustard
1 level tablespoon tomato purée
freshly grated Gruyère cheese
salt and freshly ground black pepper
225 g/8 oz button mushrooms, quartered
2 level tablespoons finely chopped parsley

1. To make sauce: melt 3 tablespoons butter in the top of a double saucepan, stir in flour and cook over water, stirring constantly, until smooth. Add hot milk, stirring constantly, until well blended. Lower heat and simmer for 20 minutes. Then add finely chopped garlic, dry mustard, tomato purée, coarsely grated Gruyère and salt and freshly ground black pepper, to taste. Continue cooking, stirring constantly, until cheese melts.

2. Poach scallops for 10 minutes in just enough water to cover them to which you have added ½ chicken stock cube, lemon juice and salt and freshly ground black pepper, to taste. Drain, reserving liquid.

3. Poach prawns in their shells in remaining stock from scallops, adding more water (or water and dry white wine), to just cover prawns. Drain, reserving liquid.

4. To assemble casserole: peel prawns, slice scallops thinly and add prawns and sliced scallops to sauce. Sauté button mushrooms in 2 level tablespoons butter in a flameproof casserole. Strain 150 ml/¼ pint of liquid left from cooking shellfish into casserole and continue to simmer for 1 minute. Pour in prawns and scallops in sauce. Taste, correct seasoning and heat through. Garnish, just before serving, with chopped parsley.

Beef

Estouffade de Boeuf

1 large piece bacon rind, or fresh pork fat
1.5 kg/3½ lb lean beef
4 cloves garlic, cut into slivers
salt and freshly ground black pepper
1 bouquet garni (1 stick celery, 2 sprigs
  parsley, 2 sprigs thyme)
1 bay leaf
1 strip orange peel
225 g/8 oz green bacon, in 1 piece, diced
2 Spanish onions, halved
4 cloves
4 carrots, sliced lengthwise
8 shallots
4 tablespoons cognac
150 ml/¼ pint rich beef stock
good red wine

1. Lay a good-sized strip of bacon rind or fresh pork fat in the bottom of an ovenproof casserole. Stud meat with garlic slivers and rub with salt and freshly ground black pepper. Place on protective 'bed' of bacon rind and surround with *bouquet garni*, bay leaf, orange peel, diced green bacon, halved onions stuck with cloves, sliced carrots and shallots. Moisten with cognac and rich beef stock and add red wine until meat is practically covered.

2. Cover the casserole and cook in a moderately hot oven (190°C, 375°F, Gas Mark 5) for 1 hour. Reduce oven temperature to very cool (120°C, 250°F, Gas Mark ½) and cook until tender. Skim fat from sauce and remove *bouquet garni* before serving.

Pampas Beef with Olives

1.75 kg/4 lb lean beef
flour
5 tablespoons butter
4 tablespoons olive oil
salt and freshly ground black pepper
225 g/8 oz bacon, diced
2 cloves garlic
2 carrots, sliced
450 g/1 lb button onions
2 level tablespoons chopped parsley
2 bay leaves
2 sprigs thyme
1 small piece orange peel
1 bottle good red wine
12 ripe olives, stoned
12 mushrooms, sliced

1. Cut beef into large cubes, roll them in flour, and brown on all sides in 4 tablespoons butter and olive oil. Transfer to a casserole, and season to taste with salt and freshly ground black pepper.

2. Sauté diced bacon, garlic, carrots and onions in remaining fat until bacon is crisp and vegetables are golden. Transfer to casserole with meat. Add parsley, bay leaves, thyme and orange peel, and gradually moisten with 1 bottle of good red wine. Cook in a cool oven (150°C, 300°F, Gas Mark 2) for 1½ to 2 hours until meat is almost done.

3. Correct seasoning. Stir in, little by little, a *beurre manié* made with 1 level tablespoon flour blended to a paste with the same amount of butter. Add stoned ripe olives and sliced mushrooms, cover and allow to simmer in a cool oven or on the charcoal grill until mushrooms are cooked and meat is tender.

192

Boeuf en Daube

1.5 kg/3 lb lean top rump of beef
3 cloves garlic
100 g/4 oz fat salt pork
3 tablespoons olive oil
4 shallots, finely chopped
4 tomatoes, peeled, seeded and coarsely
 chopped
2 cloves garlic, finely chopped
12 button onions
100 g/4 oz button mushrooms, quartered
4 sprigs parsley
300 ml/½ pint rich beef stock
flour and water

MARINADE
3 slices lemon
1 bay leaf
pinch of thyme
1 level teaspoon finely chopped herbs
 (chives, tarragon, parsley)
150 ml/¼ pint dry white wine
1 tablespoon olive oil
salt and freshly ground black pepper

1. Make 6 small incisions in beef with a sharp
knife and bury half a clove of garlic in each.

2. Combine ingredients of marinade mixture in a
mixing bowl, and marinate meat in this mixture,
turning occasionally, for 12 hours.

3. Remove rind from piece of fat salt pork. Dice
pork and sauté in olive oil until golden. Remove
pork bits, and brown beef well on all sides in the
resulting amalgamation of fats.

4. Place pork rind in the bottom of an ovenproof
casserole. Place beef on it and surround with
sautéed pork bits, finely chopped shallots, peeled,
seeded and coarsely chopped tomatoes, garlic,
button onions, quartered button mushrooms and
parsley. Strain the marinade juices over the meat
and add beef stock.

5. Seal the casserole hermetically (make a thick
paste of flour and water, shape it into a long,
narrow roll and fit it round the edge of the
casserole; press lid of casserole firmly into this

pastry band and seal). Cook in a very cool oven
(120°C, 250°F, Gas Mark ½) for 4 to 5 hours.
Serve from the casserole.

Beef Stew with Parsley Dumplings

1.5 kg/3½ lb stewing beef
flour
salt and freshly ground black pepper
2 level tablespoons butter or lard
2 tablespoons olive oil
hot water or beef stock (made with a stock
 cube)
12 button onions
12 small carrots
1 level tablespoon cornflour, dissolved in a
 little stock

PARSLEY DUMPLINGS
100 g/4 oz flour, sifted
2 level teaspoons baking powder
½ level teaspoon salt
2 level tablespoons butter
1 egg, beaten
2 level tablespoons finely chopped parsley
150 ml/¼ pint milk

1. Cut meat into 5-cm/2-inch cubes. Dredge in
flour seasoned to taste with salt and freshly ground
black pepper.

2. Heat fat and oil in a thick-bottomed flameproof
casserole, and sauté meat until well browned on
all sides. Add 600 ml/1 pint hot water or stock,
cover casserole tightly and simmer gently for 1½
to 2 hours, until beef is tender. About 30 minutes
before the end of cooking time, add onions and
carrots, and more liquid if necessary.

3. Cover and continue to cook for 15 minutes.
Drop parsley dumplings gently on top of stew,
cover casserole and finish cooking.

4. **To make parsley dumplings:** combine sifted
flour, baking powder and salt in a mixing bowl.
Cut in butter with a pastry blender or with 2
knives. Combine beaten egg, parsley and milk,
and stir into flour to make a soft dough. Scoop
out dumpling mixture with a wet serving spoon,

and drop quickly by the spoonful on to meat and vegetables in casserole, leaving a little space at sides for steam to circulate. Cover casserole and steam gently for 15 minutes.

5. To serve: arrange meat, vegetables and dumplings on a heated serving dish and keep warm. Thicken gravy with cornflour which you have dissolved in a little stock.

Boeuf Sauté à la Bourguignonne 'Alexandre Dumaine'

1.25 kg/2½ lb beef
½ bottle red wine
225 g/8 oz carrots, sliced
25 g/1 oz shallots, finely chopped
50 g/2 oz onion, finely chopped
1-2 sprigs thyme
1-2 bay leaves
225 g/8 oz unsmoked bacon
12 button onions
12 baby carrots
1 level tablespoon flour
1 glass water
2-4 cloves garlic
1 bouquet garni (1 stick celery, 2 sprigs thyme, 1 bay leaf, 2 sprigs parsley)
salt and freshly ground black pepper
12 button mushrooms
butter

1. Cut beef into bite-sized pieces and marinate overnight in red wine with carrots, shallots, onion, thyme and bay leaves. Drain well.

2. Dice bacon and brown in a *cocotte* with small onions and carrots. When these are lightly coloured, remove them together with the bacon, and sauté drained beef in remaining fat until brown. Sprinkle with flour, and add red wine from marinade and a glass of water.

3. Return diced bacon, onions and carrots to the pan, and add garlic and a *bouquet garni*. Season to taste with salt and freshly ground black pepper. Simmer gently until meat is tender and the sauce reduced to half the original quantity – about 2¾ to 3 hours.

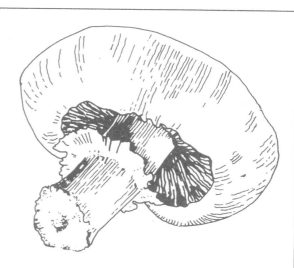

193

4. Brown mushrooms in butter and add to meat about 10 minutes before end of cooking.

Potted Tournedos

2 level tablespoons butter
4 thickly cut tournedos
6 shallots, finely chopped
French mustard
Worcestershire sauce
dried rosemary
salt and freshly ground black pepper
4 tablespoons cognac

1. Melt 1 level tablespoon butter in a frying pan and sauté tournedos (thick slices of fillet of beef, trimmed and tied with a thin strip of fat) for ½ to 1 minute on each side. Remove string and place in 4 individual ovenproof casseroles; keep warm.

2. Add remaining butter to pan and sauté finely chopped shallots until transparent. Add mustard and Worcestershire sauce, to taste, to the shallots; mix well and pour over tournedos.

3. Cover casseroles and cook for about 10 minutes in a hot oven (230°C, 450°F, Gas Mark 8). Drain off fat, turn tournedos over and add a pinch of rosemary, salt and freshly ground black pepper, to taste, to each casserole. Pour 1 tablespoon cognac over each tournedos and continue cooking for a few minutes longer. Serve in the casseroles.

Boeuf à l'Ail *Serves 6*
Flanders Carbonnade of Beef *Serves 4 to 6*
Stufatino di Manzo *Serves 4*

194

Boeuf à l'Ail

1.75 kg/4 lb beef (rump or top round)
4 level tablespoons butter
2 tablespoons olive oil
450 g/1 lb tomatoes, peeled, seeded and
   chopped
2–3 level tablespoons tomato purée
2 sprigs thyme
2 bay leaves
salt and freshly ground black pepper
4 cloves garlic
water, stock or dry white wine
noodles or boiled new potatoes to serve

1. Cut beef into cubes about 5 cm/2 inches square. Sauté cubes in butter and olive oil until well browned. Add tomatoes, tomato purée, thyme and bay leaves, and season to taste with salt and freshly ground black pepper.

2. Do not peel garlic; just smash cloves with the heel of your hand and add them to the casserole.

3. Simmer beef gently for about 3 hours, adding a little hot water, stock or white wine if meat becomes dry. Serve with noodles or new potatoes.

Flanders Carbonnade of Beef

1.25 kg/2½ lb beef (rump or round)
flour
225 g/8 oz green bacon
butter
olive oil
3 Spanish onions, sliced
150 ml/¼ pint boiling water
450 ml/¾ pint beer
2 level tablespoons finely chopped parsley
1 level teaspoon thyme
2 tablespoons wine vinegar
boiled potatoes to serve

1. Cut beef into 3.5-cm/1½-inch squares and flour lightly.

2. Dice green bacon and sauté gently in butter and olive oil in a large thick-bottomed frying pan. Transfer bacon to a large ovenproof casserole.

3. Sauté sliced onions in remaining fat until transparent and add to meats in casserole. Drain off fat, pour boiling water into frying pan and bring to the boil again, stirring in all the crusty bits from the sides of the pan. Pour over meat and vegetables.

4. Add beer, finely chopped parsley and thyme to casserole. Cover and cook in a cool oven (150°C, 300°F, Gas Mark 2) for about 2 hours. Just before serving, stir in wine vinegar. Serve with boiled potatoes.

Stufatino di Manzo

Illustrated on page 200

2 level tablespoons lard
2 level tablespoons olive oil
350 g/12 oz fat salt pork, cut into fingers
8 button mushrooms
8 button onions, poached until just tender
2 large Spanish onions, chopped
2 cloves garlic, chopped
4 level tablespoons flour
½ level teaspoon dried marjoram
salt and freshly ground black pepper
1.25 kg/2½ lb lean beef, cut into 3.5-cm/
   1½-inch cubes
150 ml/¼ pint red wine
4 level tablespoons tomato purée, diluted in
   water
1 strip orange peel

1. Melt lard and olive oil in a large, thick-bottomed pan or flameproof casserole. Add fingers of salt pork, button mushrooms and poached button onions, chopped onion and garlic, and sauté, stirring constantly, until golden. Remove salt pork and vegetables with a perforated spoon and reserve.

2. Combine flour and marjoram and salt and freshly ground black pepper, to taste, in a large bowl. Add meat and toss until cubes are coated with seasoned flour.

3. Add floured meat to casserole and cook, stirring frequently, until meat is well browned on all sides.

4. Now add red wine (one of the rougher Italian ones) and continue cooking until the wine is reduced to half the original quantity.

5. Add diluted tomato purée and strip orange peel. Cover casserole and simmer very gently for about 2 hours, or until the meat is tender and the sauce thick and richly coloured. Thirty minutes before serving add reserved bacon, aromatics and mushrooms and onions.

Note: A tablespoon or two of red wine just before serving will add extra *bouquet* to this dish.

Beef Marinated in Beer

1.75 kg/4 lb beef (rump or round)
4 tablespoons olive oil
2 level tablespoons brown sugar
2 level tablespoons flour
4 tablespoons red wine
4 level tablespoons double cream

BEER MARINADE
1 bottle beer (pale or brown ale)
600 ml/1 pint water
4 tablespoons olive oil
1 Spanish onion, sliced
6 carrots, sliced
2 bay leaves
6 peppercorns
2 cloves
1 level teaspoon allspice
salt

1. To make beer marinade: combine beer, water, olive oil, sliced onion and carrots, bay leaves and seasonings in a large mixing bowl.

2. Place beef in this marinade and marinate in the refrigerator for 2 or 3 days, turning meat once or twice each day.

3. When ready to cook: remove meat from marinade and drain, reserving marinade. Heat olive oil in a flameproof casserole just large enough to hold beef. Add meat, and brown on all sides. Pour 300 ml/½ pint marinade juices with vegetables and seasonings over meat. Cover cas-

serole and cook for 1¾ hours in a cool oven (150°C, 300°F, Gas Mark 2), adding more marinade juices during cooking if necessary.

4. Remove casserole from oven. Sprinkle meat with brown sugar and simmer on top of the cooker, uncovered, for 15 minutes longer, turning meat until sugar has melted and browned.

5. Stir flour into remaining marinade juices. Add red wine and pour over meat. Return casserole to oven, uncovered, for 30 minutes, or until sauce has thickened. Remove meat to a serving dish. Strain sauce and skim off any fat. Stir in double cream and pour over meat. Serve immediately.

Magyar Slow-cooked Beef Casserole

225 g/8 oz dried red beans
100 g/4 oz rice
1.25 kg/2½ lb beef, cut into 3.5-cm/1½-inch cubes
lard
salt and freshly ground black pepper
2 bay leaves
3 large tomatoes, cut in quarters
3 Spanish onions, thinly sliced
3 large carrots, thinly sliced
2 cloves garlic, chopped

1. Soak dried red beans overnight in cold water. Drain. Cook rice and beans in boiling salted water for 8 minutes. Drain.

2. Sauté beef in 4 level tablespoons lard until golden on all sides. Season generously with salt and freshly ground black pepper.

3. Place beef in a large flameproof casserole with partially cooked beans, bay leaves, quartered tomatoes, thinly sliced onions and carrots, chopped garlic and partially cooked rice. Add enough water to cover generously and bring liquid gently to the boil on top of the cooker. Skim.

4. Cover casserole and cook in a cool oven (150°C, 300°F, Gas Mark 2) for at least 3 hours, or until meat and vegetables are meltingly tender.

196

Yankee Pot Roast

1.75-2.75 kg/4-6 lb lean brisket of beef,
   in 1 piece
2 level tablespoons lard
2 tablespoons olive oil
600 ml/1 pint well-flavoured beef stock
4 large or 8 small carrots, quartered
2 Spanish onions, quartered
1 large or 2 small turnips, quartered
4 whole cloves
2 whole allspice
2 bay leaves
salt and freshly ground black pepper
freshly grated nutmeg

GARNISH
12 small carrots
12 small onions
3 large or 6 small turnips, quartered
stock or stock and water
6 potatoes

1. Brown beef well on all sides in lard and olive oil in a thick-bottomed flameproof casserole. Pour beef stock into the casserole and bring to the boil. Skim, then reduce heat. Add carrots, onions, turnip, cloves, allspice, bay leaves and salt, freshly ground black pepper and freshly grated nutmeg, to taste. Cook very gently for 2½ to 3 hours, until the meat is tender, making sure that the liquid barely simmers (to avoid the meat becoming tough) and only turning roast once during the cooking time.

2. Transfer meat to a heated serving dish and keep warm.

3. Thirty minutes before serving time, prepare the garnish. Poach prepared small carrots and onions and quartered turnips in a little stock, or stock and water, until just tender. Boil potatoes.

4. Garnish meat with freshly boiled vegetables.

5. Skim fat from sauce in casserole. Strain sauce into a small saucepan, thicken if desired and season with salt and freshly ground black pepper and nutmeg, to taste. Reheat and serve with meat and vegetables.

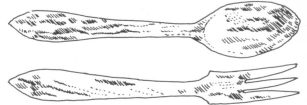

Carne Assada (Portuguese Pot Roast)

Illustrated on page 198

1.75 kg/4 lb rolled beef (round or rump), in
   1 piece
450 ml/¾ pint red wine
juice of ½ lemon
6 tablespoons olive oil
2 cloves garlic, finely chopped
1 level teaspoon salt
1 level teaspoon paprika
½ level teaspoon freshly ground black
   pepper
2 bay leaves
2 cloves
1 level tablespoon flour

GARNISH
fried potatoes
asparagus tips
halved hard-boiled eggs

1. Marinate beef overnight in red wine, lemon juice and 2 tablespoons olive oil, flavoured with garlic, salt, paprika, freshly ground black pepper, bay leaves and cloves.

2. Drain, reserving the juices. Brown meat in a flameproof casserole in the remaining olive oil. Add marinade juices. Cover casserole and cook in a moderate oven (160°C, 325°F, Gas Mark 3) for 2½ hours. Uncover casserole, baste meat with pan juices and continue to cook until meat is tender – about 30 minutes.

3. **To serve:** remove beef to a heated serving dish and keep warm. Thicken pan juices with flour, correct seasoning and strain. Arrange fried potatoes, cooked asparagus tips and halved hard-boiled eggs around carved meat. Pour a little sauce over meat and asparagus tips and serve remaining sauce separately.

Choucroute Garnie au Champagne (see page 222)

Carne Assada (Portuguese Pot Roast) (see page 196)

Veal Birds (see page 210)

Stufatino di Manzo (see page 194)

Lamb Blanquette with Ham (see page 205)

Beef Vindaloo

2 Spanish onions, finely chopped
2 cloves garlic, finely chopped
olive oil
1 level tablespoon ground coriander seed
1 level teaspoon ground turmeric
1 level teaspoon freshly ground black
  pepper
$\frac{1}{2}$ level teaspoon powdered mustard
$\frac{1}{2}$ level teaspoon ground cumin seed
$\frac{1}{4}$ level teaspoon ground red pepper
$\frac{1}{4}$ level teaspoon ground ginger
grated peel and juice of $\frac{1}{2}$ lemon
1.25 kg/$2\frac{1}{2}$ lb shin of beef
flour
600 ml/1 pint light beef stock (made with a
  stock cube)
salt
rice to serve

1. Sauté finely chopped onions and garlic in 4
tablespoons olive oil in a flameproof casserole
until onion is transparent. Add spices and lemon
peel and juice and simmer, stirring constantly, for
2 to 3 minutes.

2. Cut beef into 2.5-cm/1-inch cubes, dust lightly
with flour and add to lemon spice mixture. Stir
well and cook for 10 minutes, adding a little more
olive oil if necessary. Then add beef stock and
salt to taste, cover casserole and simmer gently
until beef is tender. Serve with rice.

Boeuf à la Corse 'Chez Victor, aux Deux Marches'

201

1.25 kg/$2\frac{1}{2}$ lb lean beef
$\frac{1}{2}$ calf's foot
225 g/8 oz unsmoked bacon, in 1 piece
2 tablespoons olive oil
2 level tablespoons butter
2 tablespoons cognac
2–3 level tablespoons tomato purée
1 Spanish onion, quartered
2 cloves garlic
1 bouquet garni (2 sprigs parsley, 2 sprigs
  thyme, 1 bay leaf, 1 stick celery)
salt and freshly ground black pepper
1 bottle red wine
125 g/$4\frac{1}{2}$ oz dried mushrooms
75-100 g/3-4 oz green olives, stoned
2-3 level tablespoons finely chopped parsley

1. Cut beef into cubes about 5 cm/2 inches square.

2. Put calf's foot and bacon in a pan of cold water
and bring to the boil. Drain and dry well.

3. Heat olive oil and butter in a large thick-
bottomed flameproof casserole. Add beef, calf's
foot and bacon, and sauté until meats are golden
brown. Add cognac, and flame. Then add tomato
purée, onion, garlic and *bouquet garni*, and season
to taste with salt and freshly ground black pepper.
Add just enough red wine to cover the meat.
Cover casserole and simmer gently for $1\frac{1}{2}$ hours,
adding hot water occasionally if necessary.

4. Then add dried mushrooms, which have been
soaked for 30 minutes in warm water, and stoned
olives. Continue to cook for 15 minutes.

5. Remove *bouquet garni*, sprinkle with finely
chopped parsley and serve in the casserole.

202

Hochepot de Queue de Boeuf

1 large oxtail
225 g/8 oz butter
4 medium-sized onions, sliced
3 large carrots, sliced
3 cloves garlic, crushed
1 glass good brandy
1 bottle Chablis
600 ml/1 pint rich beef stock
salt and freshly ground black pepper
1 bouquet garni (2 sprigs parsley, 2 sprigs
    thyme, 2 bay leaves, 1 stick celery)
24 button mushrooms
100 g/4 oz fat salt pork, diced
24 tiny onions
sugar
finely chopped parsley
purée of peas or chestnuts

1. Cut large oxtail into 10-cm/4-inch segments and blanch in cold water for at least 6 hours. Drain well and dry lightly with a clean towel.

2. Melt 4 tablespoons butter in a large thick-bottomed saucepan or flameproof casserole, and sauté the pieces of oxtail with sliced onions and carrots until golden. Then add crushed garlic. Cover casserole for 2 minutes, pour in brandy, and flame. Put out the flames with a bottle of dry Chablis. Add just enough rich beef stock to cover the pieces of oxtail. Add salt, freshly ground black pepper, and a *bouquet garni*, and simmer for 3 hours.

3. Strain sauce into a bowl through a fine sieve.

4. Place pieces of oxtail in a clean casserole and garnish with mushrooms which you have sautéed lightly in 2 tablespoons butter, diced fat salt pork which you have sautéed in 2 tablespoons butter, and onions which you have simmered until tender in a little water with the remaining butter and a little sugar.

5. Skim fat from surface of sauce, then pour sauce over the meat and vegetables. Bring slowly to the boil, cover the casserole and cook in a moderate oven (160°C, 325°F, Gas Mark 3) for 1 hour. When the *hochepot* is done, the meat should be meltingly tender and the sauce rich and smooth, and slightly thick without the aid of flour or a *beurre manié*.

6. Sprinkle with chopped parsley and serve from the casserole with a purée of peas or chestnuts.

Chili con Carne with Red Wine

1 kg/2 lb minced lean beef
1 Spanish onion, finely chopped
2 cloves garlic, chopped
2-3 level tablespoons bacon fat
1 (425-g/15-oz) can Italian peeled tomatoes
300 ml/$\frac{1}{2}$ pint red wine
3 level tablespoons Mexican chili powder*
1 level tablespoon flour
2 bay leaves, crumbled
$\frac{1}{4}$ level teaspoon powdered cumin
$\frac{1}{2}$ level teaspoon oregano
salt and freshly ground black pepper
2 (432-g/15$\frac{1}{4}$-oz) cans red kidney beans,
    drained
boiled rice to serve

*Note: Spice Islands brand or Twin Trees or McCormicks – not powdered chillies.

1. Sauté minced meat, chopped onion and chopped garlic in bacon fat until brown in a thick-bottomed flameproof casserole.

2. Add Italian canned tomatoes (with their juice) and red wine; bring again to the boil. Skim, cover casserole and simmer very gently for about 1 hour.

3. Blend chili powder with flour in a little of the hot pan juices and add to the casserole at the same time as crumbled bay leaves, cumin, oregano and salt and freshly ground black pepper, to taste.

4. Simmer over a low heat until meat is tender. Check seasoning; add canned red kidney beans and heat through. Serve with boiled rice.

Lamb

Daube de Mouton

1 leg of lamb
225 g/8 oz bacon, thinly sliced, and
225 g/8 oz bacon, in 1 piece
olive oil
salt and freshly ground black pepper
dried thyme
marjoram
crumbled bay leaves
4-6 level tablespoons finely chopped onion
1 bouquet garni (2 sprigs parsley, 2 sprigs thyme, 1 stick celery, 1 bay leaf)
1 strip dried orange peel
well-flavoured stock
flour and water paste

MARINADE
red wine
4 tablespoons olive oil
2 carrots, finely chopped
1 Spanish onion, finely chopped
4 cloves garlic, smashed
1 bay leaf
2 sprigs thyme
1 sprig rosemary
4 sprigs parsley
salt and freshly ground black pepper

1. Bone leg of lamb and cut it into large pieces weighing about 75 g/3 oz each.

2. Cut half the bacon slices into 5-mm/¼-inch strips. Lard each of the lamb pieces with 2 strips of bacon which you have rubbed with a little olive oil, salt, freshly ground black pepper, dried thyme, marjoram and crumbled bay leaf.

Note: If you do not have a larding needle, cut 2 holes in meat cubes with a thin-bladed knife and insert strips of well-seasoned bacon into holes with the point of a skewer.

3. To marinate meat: place prepared lamb cubes in a large earthenware bowl and add just enough red wine to cover meat. Add 4 tablespoons olive oil, finely chopped carrots and Spanish onion, garlic, bay leaf, thyme, rosemary and parsley, and salt and freshly ground black pepper, to taste. Marinate for at least 4 hours.

4. To cook daube: dice uncut bacon and blanch it with remaining bacon slices. Cover the bottom of a large earthenware ovenproof casserole with a layer of lamb cubes. Sprinkle with 4 tablespoons finely chopped onion and half the diced blanched bacon, and season with a pinch of dried thyme and crumbled bay leaf. Cover with a layer of lamb and sprinkle with onions, bacon and dried herbs as above. Drop in a *bouquet garni* and a strip of dried orange peel. Then cover with a final layer of lamb cubes right to the very top of the casserole. Pour in strained marinade juices and a little stock. Top with remaining thin bacon slices, cover casserole and wrap a band of paste (made with flour and water) around join to seal it completely. Cook for 2½ to 3 hours in a cool oven (150°C, 300°F, Gas Mark 2).

5. To serve: remove pastry seal and the cover then remove bacon strips and *bouquet garni*. Skim and serve *daube* from casserole.

Lamb en Cocotte

1 loin of lamb, boned and rolled
thin strips of bacon
2 level tablespoons butter
2 tablespoons olive oil
2 large carrots, sliced
2 Spanish onions, sliced
salt and freshly ground black pepper
1 glass dry white wine or water
2-4 tomatoes, quartered

1. Lard rolled loin of lamb with thin strips of bacon.

2. Melt butter and olive oil in a thick-bottomed *cocotte* or casserole just large enough to hold lamb and add sliced carrots and onions. Simmer, stirring, until onion is transparent. Add meat and season to taste with salt and freshly ground black pepper. Sauté lamb until golden on all sides.

3. Transfer casserole to a moderate oven (160°C, 325°F, Gas Mark 3) and cook, uncovered, for 1½ to 2 hours, until lamb is tender, adding a little dry white wine or hot water if necessary to prevent *cocotte* from scorching. When meat is half cooked, add quartered tomatoes.

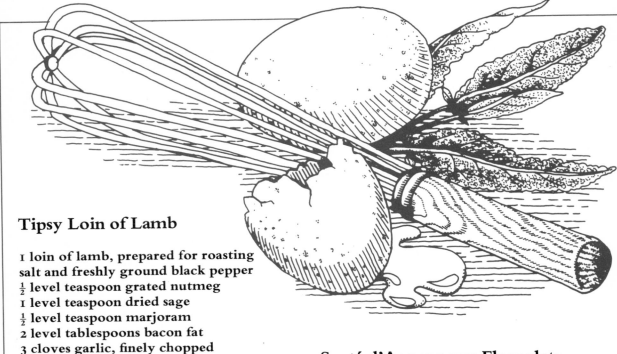

Tipsy Loin of Lamb

1 loin of lamb, prepared for roasting
salt and freshly ground black pepper
$\frac{1}{2}$ level teaspoon grated nutmeg
1 level teaspoon dried sage
$\frac{1}{2}$ level teaspoon marjoram
2 level tablespoons bacon fat
3 cloves garlic, finely chopped
4 level tablespoons finely chopped parsley
bouquet garni (1 bay leaf, 1 sprig thyme, 2
  sprigs green celery leaves)
claret
450 ml/$\frac{3}{4}$ pint beef stock
1 level tablespoon flour
1 level tablespoon butter

1. Rub lamb well on all sides with salt and freshly ground black pepper, nutmeg, sage and marjoram.

2. Sear meat in hot bacon fat with finely chopped garlic and parsley. Place roast in a flameproof oval casserole. Add *bouquet garni*, tied with heavy white thread. Cover meat with claret and cook uncovered in a moderately hot oven (190°C, 375°F, Gas Mark 5), allowing 30 to 35 minutes per half kilo/per lb. Turn meat occasionally. When meat is done, the wine will have evaporated.

3. Remove meat and keep warm. Pour beef stock into casserole with pan juices, and reduce over a high heat to half the original quantity.

4. Brown flour in butter and mix with a little stock until smooth. Stir this *roux* into remaining stock and cook, stirring constantly, until sauce is thick and smooth. Correct seasoning and serve with meat.

Sauté d'Agneau aux Flageolets 'Nouvelle Cuisine'

1 rack of lamb, trimmed
salt and freshly ground black pepper
1 bay leaf
olive oil
1 (340-g/12-oz) can flageolets
butter
2 level tablespoons finely chopped parsley or
  chives

SAUCE
bones and trimmings from rack of lamb
$\frac{1}{2}$ chicken stock cube
2 level tablespoons tomato purée
$\frac{1}{2}$ Spanish onion, finely chopped
1 bay leaf
4 tablespoons dry white wine
1 level teaspoon flour
1 level teaspoon butter
freshly ground black pepper
salt

1. Cut meat from bones of lamb, making a 'fillet' of lamb. Cut the 'fillet' into 2.5-cm/1-inch thick slices. Trim each slice into three or four even-sized cubes, according to size of lamb. Reserve bones and meat trimmings and scraps for sauce.

2. Season lamb cubes generously with salt and freshly ground black pepper, add bay leaf and 4 level tablespoons olive oil. Toss well and leave lamb to marinate for at least 2 hours.

3. **To make sauce:** chop lamb bones coarsely and place in a thick-bottomed saucepan, or small flameproof casserole, with the lamb trimmings, $\frac{1}{2}$ chicken stock cube, tomato purée, finely chopped onion, bay leaf and wine. Add water to just cover and simmer gently until meat on bones is cooked through. Strain stock into clean saucepan and cook over a high heat until it is reduced to half its original quantity. Whisk in *beurre manié*, made by mashing 1 level teaspoon each flour and butter to a smooth paste. Season with freshly ground black pepper, and salt. Keep warm.

4. **When ready to cook lamb:** drain canned *flageolets*, season with salt and freshly ground black pepper and sauté for a few minutes in butter. Sear lamb in oil on all sides until golden brown but still quite rare. Pour off excess fats, add sauce and then add *flageolets* and bring to the bubble. Sprinkle with finely chopped parsley or chives and serve immediately.

Lamb Blanquette with Ham

Illustrated on page 200

1 kg/2 lb boned shoulder or leg of lamb
225 g/8 oz cooked ham, in 1 piece
2 tablespoons olive oil
12 button onions
1 bouquet garni (2 sprigs parsley, 1 stick
   celery, 2 bay leaves, 2 sprigs thyme)
600 ml/1 pint boiling water or light stock
salt and freshly ground black pepper
4 level tablespoons butter
12 button mushrooms
2 level tablespoons flour
2 egg yolks
150 ml/$\frac{1}{4}$ pint cream
juice of $\frac{1}{2}$ lemon

1. Cut lamb and ham into cubes and place in a flameproof casserole. Sauté in olive oil until golden. Add onions and stir for 2 minutes. Then add the *bouquet garni*. Add boiling water or light stock, season generously and reduce heat until liquid barely simmers. Cover casserole and simmer for 1 to 1$\frac{1}{2}$ hours until meat is tender.

2. Drain cooking stock into a bowl; discard *bouquet garni* and place meat in a clean casserole to keep warm.

3. Melt 2 level tablespoons butter in a small pan and sauté mushrooms for 5 minutes, stirring occasionally. Add to the meat.

4. Make a *roux* with 2 level tablespoons butter and 2 level tablespoons flour in the top of a double saucepan. Add strained stock and stir over water until sauce is smooth and thick. Remove from heat.

5. Blend egg yolks, cream and lemon juice and 'finish' sauce by adding a quarter of the hot stock to egg and cream mixture. Pour this mixture into remaining stock and heat through until thick. Add salt and freshly ground black pepper if desired. Strain sauce through a fine sieve over the meat, heat through and serve immediately.

Irish Stew

1.5 kg/3 lb shoulder of mutton
450 g/1 lb onions
1 kg/2 lb potatoes
salt and freshly ground black pepper
light stock
3 level tablespoons chopped parsley

1. Cut mutton in 6-cm/2$\frac{1}{2}$-inch cubes; peel and slice onions thinly. Peel and slice potatoes thickly.

2. Place a layer of sliced onions on the bottom of a flameproof casserole. Cover with a layer of meat, then a layer of potatoes, and continue filling casserole in alternate layers, finishing with potatoes. Season each layer with salt and freshly ground black pepper. Add light stock, to cover. Bring to the boil, skim and lower heat. Simmer very gently, covered, until tender – almost 3 hours.

3. Just before serving, sprinkle with chopped parsley.

206

Shoulder of Lamb Camarguaise

1 shoulder of lamb
salt and freshly ground black pepper
butter
olive oil
well-flavoured stock
2–3 level tablespoons tomato purée
mushroom stalks
bouquet garni (2 sprigs parsley, 2 sprigs
    thyme, 1 bay leaf)

MARINADE
3 tablespoons olive oil
450 ml/¾ pint dry white wine
2 Spanish onions, chopped
4 large carrots, chopped
2 cloves garlic, smashed

RISOTTO STUFFING
225 g/8 oz short-grain rice
salt
1 canned pimiento, cut in thin strips
6 black olives, stoned and cut in strips
6 button mushroom caps, thinly sliced
3 level tablespoons butter
freshly grated Gruyère cheese
freshly ground black pepper

1. Ask your butcher to bone lamb; do not let him tie it. Ask for bones. Season boned shoulder of lamb generously with salt and freshly ground black pepper. Place lamb in a porcelain or earthenware casserole with marinade ingredients. Marinate lamb in this mixture for at least 8 hours, turning meat from time to time.

2. **To make risotto stuffing:** cook short-grain rice in boiling salted water until it is tender but not mushy. Drain well. Simmer strips of pimiento, olives and mushrooms in butter until soft. Combine with rice and season to taste with freshly grated Gruyère, salt and freshly ground black pepper.

3. **To stuff lamb:** drain lamb, reserving vegetables and juices of marinade. Wipe lamb dry and lay out on a table. Season with salt and freshly ground black pepper, and lay risotto stuffing down centre of meat. Tie up meat.

4. Brown lamb well on all sides in butter and olive oil. Place it in a flameproof casserole with bones and the vegetables of the marinade. Add marinade juices and well-flavoured stock to cover lamb. Stir in tomato purée, mushroom stalks and *bouquet garni*. Bring to the boil, lower heat and cover casserole. Simmer lamb gently for 2 hours.

5. Remove lamb from casserole and keep warm. Bring stock to the boil and cook until reduced to half the original quantity. Strain through a fine sieve. Thicken if necessary with a little *beurre manié*, made by mashing together equal quantities of flour and butter, and keep warm.

6. **To serve:** remove strings from lamb and place it on a heated serving dish. Pour a little sauce over lamb and serve immediately with the remaining sauce in a sauceboat.

Turkish Lamb Casserole with Green Beans

1 Spanish onion, finely chopped
2 level tablespoons butter
4 tablespoons olive oil
1.25 kg/2½ lb lamb, cut from leg
flour
salt and freshly ground black pepper
6 tomatoes, peeled, seeded and coarsely
    chopped
600 ml/1 pint chicken stock (made with a
    stock cube)
450 g/1 lb green beans
juice of ½ lemon (optional)

1. Sauté finely chopped onion in butter and olive oil in a flameproof casserole until onion is transparent.

2. Cut meat into even-sized cubes; roll in seasoned flour and add to onion. Simmer gently, stirring from time to time, until meat absorbs onion juices.

3. Add chopped tomatoes and chicken stock. Cover casserole and simmer gently over a low heat for 30 minutes.

4. Slice green beans into 2.5-cm/1-inch segments and add to casserole. Cover casserole again and continue to cook, over a moderate flame, until beans are tender. Correct seasoning, adding lemon juice, and salt and freshly ground black pepper, if desired.

Braised Stuffed Shoulder of Lamb

1 shoulder of lamb
olive oil
salt and freshly ground black pepper
lemon juice
flour
butter
beef, veal or chicken stock, or dry white
  wine
½ calf's foot (optional)

STUFFING
225 g/8 oz sausagemeat
½ Spanish onion, finely chopped and sautéed
  in butter
2 level tablespoons butter
2 level tablespoons finely chopped parsley
1 egg, beaten
225 g/8 oz spinach, chopped and sautéed in
  butter
salt and freshly ground black pepper
cumin or coriander

1. Ask your butcher to bone and trim a shoulder of lamb ready for rolling. Do not let him roll this.

2. Brush lamb with olive oil, and season to taste with salt and freshly ground black pepper. Sprinkle with lemon juice.

3. To make stuffing: in a large mixing bowl combine sausagemeat, finely chopped onion

which you have sautéed in butter until transparent, finely chopped parsley, beaten egg, sautéed spinach, and salt, freshly ground black pepper and spices to taste. Mix well.

4. Lay this stuffing on meat; roll up and sew up with fine string. Dust the lamb with flour and brown meat slowly on all sides in equal quantities of olive oil and butter in an oval *cocotte* or flameproof casserole just large enough to hold it.

5. Moisten the lamb with a little hot stock (beef, veal or chicken), dry white wine, or even hot water. Cover casserole, lower heat and cook for 1½ to 2 hours, adding a little more liquid from time to time if necessary.

Note: If thicker sauce is desired, add half a calf's foot after meat is browned.

Lamb Stew with Courgettes

1.25 kg/2½ lb boned shoulder of lamb
4 tablespoons olive oil
1 Spanish onion, finely chopped
1 (793-g/1 lb 12-oz) can Italian peeled
  tomatoes
2-4 level tablespoons tomato purée, diluted
  in water
2-4 level tablespoons finely chopped parsley
oregano
salt and freshly ground black pepper
1 kg/2 lb courgettes
4 level tablespoons butter

1. Cut lamb into 5-cm/2-inch cubes. Heat oil in a thick-bottomed flameproof casserole and brown lamb on all sides. Add chopped onion and cook until lightly browned.

2. Add tomatoes and diluted tomato purée and season to taste with chopped parsley, oregano, salt and freshly ground black pepper. Bring to the boil, reduce heat and cover casserole. Simmer gently for 1 hour.

3. Brown courgettes in butter, add them to the casserole and continue cooking for 30 minutes longer, or until meat and vegetables are cooked.

208

Old Fashioned Mutton Stew

This mutton stew is prepared in a special way. The boned neck of mutton is particularly suitable for stews because it is juicy and gelatinous.

1 kg/2 lb boned shoulder of mutton
1 kg/2 lb boned breast or neck of mutton
3 Spanish onions, thinly sliced
6 large baking potatoes, peeled and sliced
1 bouquet garni (2 sprigs parsley, 2 sprigs thyme, 1 stick celery, 1 bay leaf)
salt and freshly ground black pepper
4 leeks, thinly sliced
16 small potatoes, pared into regular oval shapes
16 small white onions, blanched
butter
4 level tablespoons freshly chopped parsley
Worcestershire sauce to serve

1. Cut meat into squares 100–150 g/4–5 oz each. In order to keep mutton white, soak in cold water for a few hours or blanch just before making stew.

To blanch mutton: put meat in a large pan and add water to cover. Bring to the boil, drain immediately, refresh with cold water and drain again.

2. Arrange alternate layers of meat, sliced onions and sliced potatoes in a large flameproof casserole. Add *bouquet garni* and season to taste with salt and freshly ground black pepper. Top with thinly sliced leeks.

3. Add just enough water to cover. Cover casserole and simmer for about 1½ hours or until meat is tender. Then remove meat from casserole and add small potatoes and small onions. Add more water, if necessary, and correct seasoning. Cover casserole with a piece of buttered paper and then cover with lid. Simmer for 20 to 30 minutes, until vegetables are cooked. Return meat to casserole and heat through. Sprinkle with chopped parsley just before serving. Serve in the casserole, accompanied with Worcestershire sauce.

Note: The starchy baking potatoes, onions and leeks should disintegrate to a flavoursome sauce.

Navarin de Mouton aux Aromates

1.5 kg/3 lb boned shoulder or breast of lamb, or a combination of the two
2 level tablespoons butter
2 tablespoons olive oil
2 Spanish onions, quartered
2 level tablespoons flour
granulated sugar
salt and freshly ground black pepper
4 small turnips, quartered
1 bouquet garni (2 sprigs parsley, 2 sprigs thyme, 1 bay leaf)
300 ml/½ pint light stock
4 level tablespoons tomato purée, diluted in water
12 small white onions
100 g/4 oz unsmoked bacon, diced
12 small potatoes, peeled
100 g/4 oz fresh peas
4 anchovy fillets, finely chopped
4 tablespoons finely chopped parsley
2 large cloves garlic, finely chopped
grated rind of 1 lemon

1. Cut lamb into cubes and brown in butter and olive oil with quartered onions.

2. Remove some of the fat; blend in flour, stirring over low heat until slightly thickened. Sprinkle with a generous pinch or two of granulated sugar to give a deeper colour to the sauce, and season to taste with salt and freshly ground black pepper.

3. Add quartered turnips and *bouquet garni*. Stir in stock and diluted tomato purée. Simmer, covered, in a moderate oven (180°C, 350°F, Gas Mark 4) for 1 hour.

4. Drain the pieces of lamb in a sieve, reserving sauce, and remove bits of skin and bones which have separated from meat during cooking.

5. Allow sauce to cool; skim off fat, and strain the sauce into a clean casserole. Add pieces of lamb. Then glaze button onions, blanch and sauté diced unsmoked bacon, peel potatoes, shell peas, and add all these to the stew. Bring to the boil and cook, covered, in a moderate oven for 30 to 40 minutes, until vegetables are cooked and lamb is tender. Correct seasoning and sprinkle with finely chopped anchovies, parsley, garlic and grated lemon rind. Serve from casserole.

Lamb Curry with Yogurt

1.25 kg/2½ lb boned shoulder of lamb, cut
    into 6-cm/2½-inch cubes
2 level tablespoons butter
2 tablespoons olive oil
2 Spanish onions, chopped
2 cloves garlic, finely chopped
300 ml/½ pint yogurt
1 level tablespoon curry powder
¼ level teaspoon each ginger and turmeric
⅛ level teaspoon each paprika and cayenne
1 level tablespoon flour
sea salt and freshly ground black pepper
light stock (optional)

1. Heat butter and olive oil in a thick-bottomed flameproof casserole. Add chopped onions and garlic, and sauté until vegetables are transparent. Remove vegetables and reserve.

2. Add the meat to the casserole and brown on all sides. Return the onion and garlic, stir in yogurt, spices and flour, and season to taste with salt and freshly ground black pepper. Simmer until tender – about 40 minutes. If desired, thin the sauce with a little light stock before serving.

Veal

210

Veal Chops en Casserole

4-6 thick veal chops
salt and freshly ground black pepper
2 level tablespoons butter
2 tablespoons olive oil

VELOUTÉ SAUCE
2 level tablespoons butter
2 level tablespoons flour
300 ml/½ pint well-flavoured stock

1. Season veal chops generously with salt and freshly ground black pepper.

2. Heat butter and olive oil in a shallow flame-proof earthenware casserole, and simmer veal chops gently on both sides in a moderate oven (160°C, 325°F, Gas Mark 3) until chops are tender.

3. To make Velouté Sauce: melt butter in the top of a double saucepan; stir in flour and cook over water, stirring constantly until smooth. Stir in hot stock and cook, stirring from time to time, until sauce is smooth and thickened.

4. Five minutes before serving, pour sauce over chops. Correct seasoning and serve in the casserole.

Veal with Rosemary

1 rump roast of veal, boned, rolled and tied
salt and freshly ground black pepper
dried thyme
flour
2 level tablespoons butter
2 level tablespoons olive oil
150 ml/¼ pint dry white wine
150 ml/¼ pint water
2 cloves garlic, finely chopped
3 sprigs fresh rosemary
2 Spanish onions, quartered
6 carrots, quartered

1. Season roast generously with salt, freshly ground black pepper and thyme. Dredge with flour. Heat butter and olive oil in a thick-bottomed flameproof casserole, and brown meat on all sides.

2. Add dry white wine, water, finely chopped garlic and rosemary. Cover casserole and cook in a moderate oven (160°C, 325°F, Gas Mark 3) for 1½ hours.

3. Add quartered onions and carrots, and continue to cook until meat and vegetables are tender – 30 to 40 minutes more.

4. Remove roast and vegetables to a heated serving dish. Slice meat and serve with pan juices.

Veal Birds
Illustrated on page 200

12 thin slices veal cutlet
5 level tablespoons butter
1 Spanish onion, finely chopped
100 g/4 oz mushrooms, finely chopped
450 ml/¾ pint well-flavoured stock
1 bay leaf
3-4 celery tops
3-4 sprigs parsley
1 level tablespoon flour
salt and freshly ground black pepper

FORCEMEAT STUFFING
100 g/4 oz fresh breadcrumbs
50 g/2 oz suet, freshly grated
4 level tablespoons finely chopped fresh parsley
½ level teaspoon each dried thyme, marjoram and basil
½ level teaspoon grated lemon rind
2 eggs
salt and freshly ground black pepper
water or dry white wine (optional)

1. To make forcemeat stuffing: mix together breadcrumbs, freshly grated suet, finely chopped fresh parsley, dried herbs, lemon rind and eggs. Season generously with salt and freshly ground black pepper. If mixture seems too dry, add a little water or dry white wine.

2. Beat thin slices of veal with a rolling pin to flatten and tenderise them. Spread forcemeat mixture on each piece of meat, roll up and secure with very fine string.

3. Heat 2 tablespoons butter in a thick-bottomed saucepan and sauté finely chopped onion and mushrooms until onion is transparent.

4. Remove vegetables, add 2 tablespoons butter to pan and cook veal 'birds' over a moderate heat until well browned. Pour in stock and add sautéed mushrooms and onions, bay leaf, celery tops and parsley. Cover pan and simmer gently for 30 to 40 minutes, or until meat is tender.

5. Just before serving, remove strings from veal birds and thicken gravy with a *beurre manié*, made by mashing together 1 tablespoon butter and 1 tablespoon flour. Correct seasoning and serve immediately.

Braised Shoulder of Veal

1 shoulder of veal (about 1.25 kg/2½ lb)
salt and freshly ground black pepper
2-3 level tablespoons butter
2-3 tablespoons olive oil
100 g/4 oz onions
4 carrots
2 sticks celery
3 cloves garlic
2-3 level tablespoons flour
2 bay leaves
450 ml/¾ pint water
450 ml/¾ pint dry white wine
watercress

1. Season veal generously with salt and freshly ground black pepper. Heat butter and olive oil in a large flameproof casserole and brown veal on all sides in fat. Remove veal.

2. Chop onions, carrots, celery and garlic, and brown them in the pan, stirring constantly.

Sprinkle with flour and stir until flour is absorbed by the *mirepoix* of vegetables.

3. Return veal to the pan and add bay leaves, water and dry white wine. Cover the casserole and cook in a moderate oven (160°C, 325°F, Gas Mark 3) for 1½ hours. Turn the meat at least once during cooking time.

4. When veal is tender, strain pan juices into a clean saucepan and reduce the sauce over high heat to half the original quantity. Season the sauce to taste, adding a little more white wine (or cognac) if desired. The flavour of the sauce should be quite pronounced to enhance the rather mild taste of the veal.

5. Carve half the braised veal into rather thick slices. Arrange slices on a heated serving platter with remaining unsliced veal. Spoon some of the sauce over the meat and garnish dish with sprigs of fresh watercress. Serve remaining sauce separately.

Veau à la Ménagère

1.25 kg/2½ lb veal, in 1 piece
4 level tablespoons butter
2 level tablespoons flour
hot water or light stock
1 bay leaf
thyme
salt and freshly ground black pepper
12 mushroom caps
1 (227-g/8-oz) packet frozen peas
12 button onions, blanched
12 small carrots, blanched

1. Melt butter in the bottom of a flameproof casserole. Stir in flour and allow to colour, stirring continuously. Brown veal in this on all sides.

2. Add hot water or light stock and stir constantly until liquid comes to the boil. Add bay leaf, thyme and salt and freshly ground black pepper, to taste. Simmer gently, covered, for 1 hour.

3. Add mushroom caps, peas, and blanched button onions and small carrots. Continue to cook until meat and vegetables are tender.

Veal in Soured Cream

**1.5 kg/3 lb lean veal, cut from shoulder or
   leg
salt and freshly ground black pepper
4 level tablespoons butter
2 tablespoons olive oil
1 level tablespoon flour
300 ml/½ pint soured cream
¼ level teaspoon paprika
2–4 level tablespoons finely chopped onion
225 g/8 oz button mushrooms, quartered
boiled rice to serve**

1. Cut veal into 3.5-cm/1½-inch cubes. Season generously with salt and freshly ground black pepper, rubbing seasoning well into meat.

2. Heat 2 tablespoons each butter and oil in a thick-bottomed frying pan, and sauté meat, 4 to 6 pieces at a time, until lightly browned on all sides.

3. Place meat in a flameproof casserole; add flour to fat remaining in pan and cook, stirring constantly, until smooth. Then add soured cream and cook, stirring, until well blended. Season to taste with salt, freshly ground black pepper and paprika.

4. Melt remaining butter in a separate saucepan and simmer chopped onion until golden. Add quartered mushrooms and simmer over a low heat for 5 minutes.

5. Combine mushroom-onion mixture with soured cream sauce; add a little hot water if necessary, and pour over veal. Cover casserole and bake in a moderate oven (160°C, 325°F, Gas Mark 3) for 1 hour, or until meat is tender. Serve with boiled rice.

Veal Fricassée

1.5 kg/3 lb rump or shoulder of veal
lemon juice
butter
2 Spanish onions, chopped
4 large carrots, sliced
2 level tablespoons flour
450 ml/$\frac{3}{4}$ pint dry white wine
well-flavoured veal or chicken stock
salt and freshly ground black pepper
1 bouquet garni (2 sprigs parsley, 2 sprigs
    thyme, 1 bay leaf)
4 leeks, cut in thin strips
12 button mushroom caps
4 egg yolks
400 ml/14 fl oz double cream
1 level tablespoon each finely chopped
    tarragon, chervil and parsley
freshly grated nutmeg

1. Cut veal into 3.5-cm/$1\frac{1}{2}$-inch cubes and soak for 12 hours in cold water with a little lemon juice. Change water 2 or 3 times.

2. Sauté blanched veal pieces in butter in a deep flameproof casserole until golden. Add onion and carrots and continue to simmer, stirring from time to time, until onion is transparent. Sprinkle with flour and sauté a few minutes more. Add dry white wine and just enough well-flavoured stock to cover meat. Season with salt and freshly ground black pepper, and bring to the boil. Remove any scum that forms on the surface with a perforated spoon as you would for a *pot-au-feu*. Add *bouquet garni*. Reduce heat, cover casserole and simmer gently over a very low heat or in a cool oven (150°C, 300°F, Gas Mark 2) for $1\frac{1}{2}$ hours, or until tender.

3. Wash leeks thoroughly and cook in a little salted water until tender. Drain and keep warm in a little butter.

4. Simmer mushroom caps in a little butter and lemon juice, and keep warm.

5. Whisk egg yolks with double cream. Pour a little of the hot stock into the cream and egg mixture, whisking to prevent eggs from curdling.

Then add mixture to hot stock in casserole and heat through, being careful not to let mixture come to the boil.

6. Stir mushroom caps, leeks and finely chopped herbs carefully into the fricassée. Season with a little grated nutmeg and keep warm in the oven until ready to serve.

Pot-roasted Veal with Anchovies

1 leg of veal (about 2.75 kg/6 lb)
1 (56-g/2-oz) can anchovy fillets, cut in thin
    strips
2 cloves garlic, cut in thin strips
butter
salt and freshly ground black pepper
4-6 cloves
2 Spanish onions, sliced
2 bay leaves
150 ml/$\frac{1}{4}$ pint dry white wine
150 ml/$\frac{1}{4}$ pint water
4 level tablespoons fine breadcrumbs
1 level tablespoon flour

1. Trim and wipe leg of veal. Make small incisions all over the surface with tip of a sharp knife; stuff incisions with thin anchovy and garlic strips. Rub with 2 tablespoons softened butter, sprinkle with salt and freshly ground black pepper, and insert cloves.

2. Place roast in an ovenproof casserole and surround with sliced onions, bay leaves, dry white wine, water and 2 tablespoons butter. Cover casserole and roast in a moderate oven (160°C, 325°F, Gas Mark 3) for about $3\frac{1}{2}$ hours, basting with pan juices from time to time.

3. Turn roast over, dust with breadcrumbs, dot with 2 tablespoons butter and roast 15 minutes longer, or until crumbs are browned.

4. Transfer veal to a heated serving dish and keep warm. Stir *beurre manié* – made by mashing together 1 tablespoon each flour and butter – into pan juices, and cook, stirring constantly, until sauce is thick. Strain gravy around roast and serve immediately.

Osso Buco à l'Orange

4-6 thick slices shin of veal
flour
salt and freshly ground black pepper
4-6 tablespoons olive oil
4 cloves garlic, finely chopped
1 Spanish onion, finely chopped
150 ml/¼ pint boiling chicken or veal stock
150 ml/¼ pint dry white wine
6 level tablespoons tomato purée
6 anchovy fillets, finely chopped
6 level tablespoons finely chopped parsley
grated rind of 1 orange
grated rind of ½ lemon

RISOTTO ALLA MILANESE
½ Spanish onion, finely chopped
4 tablespoons butter
350 g/12 oz rice
hot chicken or veal stock
½ teaspoon powdered saffron
salt and freshly ground black pepper

1. Choose shin of veal with plenty of meat and ask for it to be sawn into pieces 5 cm/2 inches thick. Dredge pieces with flour, season generously with salt and freshly ground black pepper, and simmer in olive oil until lightly browned on all sides.

2. Add 1 clove garlic and 1 Spanish onion, finely chopped. Pour boiling stock, white wine and tomato purée over meat, cover pan and simmer gently for 1½ hours.

3. Add anchovy fillets and the remaining garlic cloves, both finely chopped. Blend thoroughly, heat through and serve sprinkled with finely chopped parsley and grated orange and lemon rind. Serve with *Risotto alla Milanese*.

4. To cook Risotto alla Milanese: place finely chopped Spanish onion in a deep saucepan with butter. Cook slowly for 2 to 4 minutes, taking care that the onion does not become brown. Add rice and cook over medium heat, stirring constantly with a wooden spoon. After a minute or so, stir in 250 ml/8 fl oz hot chicken or veal stock in which you have dissolved ½ teaspoon powdered

saffron. Continue cooking, adding stock as needed and stirring from time to time, until rice is cooked – 15 to 18 minutes. Correct seasoning. By this time all the stock in the pan should have been absorbed, leaving rice tender but still moist.

Noix de Veau à la Bourgeoise

bacon, cut in thin strips
2 tablespoons cognac
2 level tablespoons finely chopped parsley
dried thyme
salt and freshly ground black pepper
1.25-1.5 kg/2½-3 lb noix de veau (topside of leg), trimmed of fat and tied
pork fat
3-4 onions
3-4 large carrots
6-8 sprigs parsley
1 bouquet chives
300 ml/½ pint beef, veal or chicken stock

SAUCE
2 level tablespoons butter
1 level tablespoon flour
4-6 tablespoons dry white wine
300 ml/½ pint stock
4 tablespoons butter, diced

1. Marinate thin strips of bacon in cognac with finely chopped parsley, and dried thyme, salt and freshly ground black pepper, to taste, for at least 2 hours.

2. Lard the veal with these pieces.

3. Place several thin pieces of pork fat in a casserole (I use an oval Le Creuset casserole for this) and place veal on top. Surround with onions, carrots, parsley and chives, and moisten with well-flavoured stock. Cook over a medium heat until liquid begins to boil. Reduce heat, cover casserole and simmer for 1½ to 2 hours, until veal is tender. Remove veal to a heated serving dish and keep warm.

4. Reduce pan juices over high heat to a quarter of original quantity and glaze veal with several tablespoons of this sauce. Keep warm.

5. To make sauce: melt butter in the top of a double saucepan, add flour and stir until smooth. Add dry white wine, the remaining pan juices and stock, and cook over water, stirring constantly, until smooth. Reduce sauce over a high heat, stirring from time to time. Whisk in diced butter. Serve with the roast.

Tendrons de Veau en Terrine

1.25 kg/2½ lb breast of veal, cut into cutlets
lemon juice
4 level tablespoons butter
2 level tablespoons flour
450 ml/¾ pint well-flavoured Velouté Sauce
  (see page 410)
1 bouquet garni (2 sprigs parsley, 2 sprigs
  thyme, 1 bay leaf)
4-6 peppercorns
8 button onions, blanched
4 sweetbreads, blanched and sliced
8 button mushroom caps
2 egg yolks
2 level tablespoons finely chopped parsley

1. Soak veal 'cutlets' overnight in water and the juice of 1 lemon.

2. Drain and sauté in butter until they begin to stiffen. Sprinkle with flour and continue to cook, stirring constantly, until veal begins to take on a little colour. Moisten with Velouté Sauce, add *bouquet garni*, peppercorns and blanched button onions, and simmer, covered, for 1 hour.

3. Then add sliced blanched sweetbreads and button mushroom caps, and continue to cook for 45 to 60 minutes longer.

4. Strain, reserving sauce, and place veal, sweetbreads and vegetables in a clean *terrine*.

5. Mix egg yolks with juice of ½ lemon and add a little of the hot sauce to this mixture. Pour egg mixture into rest of hot sauce and cook, stirring constantly, until thick and smooth. Do not allow the sauce to boil, or the yolks will curdle. Pour sauce over veal and sweetbreads, sprinkle with finely chopped parsley and serve.

Fillet of Pork with Turnips
Smothered Pork Chops *Serves 4 to 6*
Pork Chops in Cider *Serves 4 to 6*

Pork and Ham

216

Fillet of Pork with Turnips

1 fillet of pork
6 tablespoons water
salt and freshly ground black pepper
18-24 baby turnips
4 level tablespoons butter
fat from pork
2 level tablespoons sugar
150 ml/¼ pint beef stock flavoured with 1-2
   tablespoons tomato purée

1. Ask your butcher to trim and tie a fillet of pork. Put it in a casserole with water, and season to taste with salt and freshly ground black pepper. Cook uncovered in a moderately hot oven (200°C, 400°F, Gas Mark 6) for 20 minutes, or until meat is nicely browned.

2. Blanch turnips in boiling water for 10 minutes, then drain. Sauté turnips in a large thick-bottomed casserole with butter and a little fat from the roast. Sprinkle with sugar and season to taste with salt and freshly ground black pepper. Simmer, shaking pan from time to time, until turnips are glazed.

3. **When pork is three-quarters cooked:** skim off excess fat, surround with glazed turnips and moisten with tomato-flavoured stock. Cover pan and simmer in a moderate oven (160°C, 325°F, Gas Mark 3) for 20 to 30 minutes or until pork is tender, turning meat from time to time.

Smothered Pork Chops

4-6 loin pork chops
butter
2 level tablespoons olive oil
salt and freshly ground black pepper
dried thyme
4 large potatoes, peeled and thinly sliced
2 large Spanish onions, thinly sliced
450 ml/¾ pint well-flavoured beef stock
4 level tablespoons finely chopped parsley
6 level tablespoons fresh breadcrumbs

1. Sauté pork chops in 2 level tablespoons softened butter and olive oil in a large flameproof casserole for 5 minutes on one side. Season generously with salt, freshly ground black pepper and dried thyme, and sauté gently for 5 minutes on other side.

2. Spread thinly sliced potatoes over chops. Season with salt and freshly ground black pepper and dried thyme. Spread thinly sliced onions over potatoes and pour over well-flavoured beef stock. Cover casserole and cook in a moderately hot oven (190°C, 375°F, Gas Mark 5) for 35 minutes, or until vegetables and meat are well cooked. Add a little more beef stock or water, during cooking time, if necessary.

3. Remove cover and sprinkle with finely chopped parsley and breadcrumbs. Dribble with melted butter and continue to bake for 10 minutes, or until crumbs are lightly browned.

Pork Chops in Cider

4-6 pork chops
salt and freshly ground black pepper
2 level tablespoons butter
2 tablespoons olive oil
¼ level teaspoon powdered basil
¼ level teaspoon powdered marjoram
¼ level teaspoon powdered thyme
2 Spanish onions, finely chopped
150 ml/¼ pint cider
150 ml/¼ pint water

1. Trim excess fat from pork chops, season generously with salt and freshly ground black pepper, and sauté in butter and olive oil until brown on both sides.

2. Transfer chops to an ovenproof baking dish and sprinkle with basil, marjoram and thyme.

3. Simmer finely chopped onions in remaining fat until transparent. Add to pork chops and moisten with cider and water. Cover the casserole and bake in a moderate oven (180°C, 350°F, Gas Mark 4) for 45 to 60 minutes, until tender. Serve from the casserole.

Duck en Daube (see page 242)

Chicken en Cocotte (see page 233)

Pineapple Duck (see page 243)   Arroz con Pollo (see page 241)

Moroccan Chicken (see page 239)

Pork à la Berrichonne
Flemish Pork Casserole *Serves 4*
Ham and Lentil Casserole *Serves 4 to 6*

Pork à la Berrichonne

½ leg of pork, boned and rolled (about
  1.75–2.25 kg/4–5 lb)
600 ml/1 pint dry white wine
salt and freshly ground black pepper
4 carrots, sliced
1 Spanish onion, finely chopped
2 cloves garlic, finely chopped
4 sprigs thyme
6 sage leaves
1 bay leaf
2 level tablespoons butter
300 ml/½ pint stock

1. Marinate pork overnight in a porcelain or glass bowl in dry white wine with salt, freshly ground black pepper, sliced carrots, finely chopped onion and garlic, and herbs.

2. The next day, remove pork from marinade, wipe dry and sauté in butter in a thick-bottomed flameproof casserole until golden on all sides. Pour off butter and moisten with marinade juices. Simmer uncovered in a moderate oven (160°C, 325°F, Gas Mark 3) for 2 hours until the liquid is reduced. Lower the oven heat to cool (140°C, 275°F, Gas Mark 1). Add the stock, cover and simmer for 45 to 60 minutes, until pork is tender.

3. Remove roast and keep warm. Strain juices through a fine sieve, reheat the sauce and serve with the roast.

Flemish Pork Casserole

4 thick pork chops
4 tablespoons butter
4 tart eating apples
6 sprigs rosemary, chopped
salt and freshly ground black pepper
watercress

1. Trim excess fat from chops, season and brown slowly on both sides in 2 tablespoons butter.

2. Peel apples and cut into eighths.

3. Put the half-cooked chops in a shallow oven-proof casserole, sprinkle with rosemary, salt and freshly ground black pepper, and arrange mounds of apples around them. Sprinkle over remaining butter, melted, and bake in a moderately hot oven (190°C, 375°F, Gas Mark 5) for about 30 minutes, or until pork is thoroughly cooked.

4. Decorate the chops with paper ruffs, garnish with watercress and serve from the casserole.

Ham and Lentil Casserole

225 g/8 oz dried lentils
cooked ham bone (or 225 g/8 oz bacon, in
  1 piece)
2 Spanish onions, quartered
2 bay leaves
2 cloves garlic
4 sticks celery, thickly sliced
4 carrots, thickly sliced
salt and freshly ground black pepper
900 ml/1½ pints chicken stock (made with
  a stock cube)
6 frankfurters
4 level tablespoons finely chopped spring
  onion tops
4 level tablespoons finely chopped parsley
soured cream to serve

1. Put lentils in a large bowl, cover with cold water, and soak for several hours, or overnight.

2. Drain lentils and put them in a large ovenproof casserole. Add ham shank or bacon piece, quartered onions, bay leaves, garlic and thickly sliced celery and carrots. Season with salt and freshly ground black pepper, to taste. Add chicken stock, cover casserole and cook in a moderate oven (180°C, 350°F, Gas Mark 4) for 1 hour, adding a little more stock if necessary.

3. Add frankfurters, cover casserole and continue to cook for 30 to 45 minutes, until lentils are meltingly tender.

4. To serve: remove ham bone and cut off meat (or remove bacon piece and cut it into slices). Return meat to casserole and correct seasoning. Sprinkle with chopped spring onion tops and parsley and serve immediately with soured cream.

Cassoulet

675 g/1½ lb dried white haricot beans
450 g/1 lb green bacon, in 1 piece
2 Spanish onions
1 sprig thyme
1 bay leaf
6 cloves garlic
2 tablespoons lard
salt and freshly ground black pepper
675 g/1½ lb boned loin or shoulder of lamb
2 level tablespoons butter
2 tablespoons olive oil
8 saucisses de Toulouse or pork sausages
1 loin of pork (8 thin chops)
8 pieces preserved goose or duck (optional)
8 tomatoes, peeled and seeded
300 ml/½ pint well-flavoured Tomato
   Sauce (see page 415)
2 level tablespoons pork or goose fat
fresh breadcrumbs

1. To half-cook beans: soak haricot beans overnight. Drain and cook them for 30 minutes in water with bacon, onions, thyme, bay leaf, 3 cloves garlic, lard, and salt and freshly ground black pepper, to taste. Drain, reserving bean stock.

2. To prepare meats: cut lamb into serving pieces and sauté in butter and olive oil in a large flameproof casserole until golden. Remove lamb pieces with a slotted spoon and reserve. Prick the sausages and sauté in fats until golden. Remove and reserve. Then place pork loin in the casserole and sauté over a high heat until golden on all sides. Place casserole in a moderate oven (180°C, 350°F, Gas Mark 4) and roast until well cooked.

3. To assemble dish: place lamb pieces in bottom of a large earthenware casserole and put loin of pork in centre. Add half-cooked beans. Add preserved goose or duck, if desired, and bacon (cut into slices), remaining garlic and tomatoes. Top with more beans, then add sausages and a thin layer of beans (the sausages should not be entirely covered). Pour over the tomato sauce, add 300–600 ml/½–1 pint bean stock and 2 tablespoons pork or goose fat. Sprinkle generously with breadcrumbs and cook in a cool oven (150°C, 300°F, Gas Mark 2) for 2½ hours. Cover dish with aluminium foil after the first hour of cooking so that it does not form too thick a crust.

Choucroute Garnie au Champagne
Illustrated on page 197

fat salt pork, thinly sliced
2 Spanish onions, sliced
4 cloves garlic, coarsely chopped
1.75 kg/4 lb sauerkraut, well washed
450 g/1 lb salt pork, in 1 piece
freshly ground black pepper
4-6 juniper berries
champagne or white wine
1 boned loin of pork
1 large Lorraine sausage, or 1 Cotechino
   sausage and 4-8 other sausages (Bratwurst,
   Knockwurst, frankfurters, saucisses de
   Toulouse)
boiled potatoes to serve

1. Line a deep earthenware casserole or stockpot with thinly sliced fat salt pork. Add half the sliced onions and chopped garlic. Place a thick layer of well-washed and drained sauerkraut on top with a large piece of salt pork. Grind plenty of black pepper over it, sprinkle with juniper berries, and add remaining onions and garlic. Cover with remaining sauerkraut and add just enough champagne (or white wine) to cover the sauerkraut. Cover and cook in a cool oven (150°C, 300°F, Gas Mark 2) for 4 to 6 hours.

2. A loin of pork, fresh or smoked, is excellent with *choucroute*. Add it to the *choucroute* about 2½ hours before serving.

3. Half an hour later add a large Lorraine sausage (or a Cotechino sausage, and a selection of small sausages as available).

4. To serve: heap the *choucroute* in the middle of a platter and arrange slices of meat and sausages around it. For those with a taste for the spectacular – place an unopened half-bottle of champagne, with only the wires removed, in the centre of the hot sauerkraut just before bringing it to the table. Then watch the warmed champagne gush out over the sauerkraut. Serve with boiled potatoes.

Petit Salé aux Choux *Serves 4 to 6*
Potée Bourguignonne *Serves 6*
Ham and Egg Luncheon Casserole *Serves 4 to 6*

Petit Salé aux Choux

675 g/1½ lb pickled or salted pork
1 bouquet garni (2 sprigs parsley, 2 sprigs
    thyme, 2 bay leaves)
1 Spanish onion, stuck with 2 cloves
peppercorns
1 medium-sized cabbage
boiled potatoes (optional)

1. Wash pickled or salted pork and soak, covered, for 24 hours in cold water, changing water several times.

2. Put fresh water in a large flameproof casserole, add meat and bring gently to the boil. Skim well and add *bouquet garni*, onion stuck with cloves, and peppercorns.

3. Clean cabbage and cut into wedges, and add it to the boiling liquid. Reduce heat and simmer meat and vegetables for about 2 hours.

4. Remove cabbage and drain well. Place it in a shallow serving bowl, place meat on top and surround, if desired, with boiled potatoes. The pot liquor will serve to make lentil or pea soup.

Potée Bourguignonne

675 g/1½ lb pickled or salted pork
6 sausages
100 g/4 oz bacon, in 1 piece
225 g/8 oz turnips
225 g/8 oz carrots
1 Spanish onion
1 bouquet garni (2 sprigs parsley, 2 sprigs
    thyme, 1 bay leaf, 1 stick celery)
peppercorns
1 small cabbage
450 g/1 lb small potatoes, peeled

1. Soak meat, covered, in cold water for 24 hours, changing water several times.

2. Put the salt pork, sausages and bacon in a flame-proof casserole with cold water. Bring gently to the boil. Skim and simmer gently for 30 minutes, skimming from time to time.

3. Peel turnips, carrots and Spanish onion. Add vegetables to *pot-au-feu* with *bouquet garni* and peppercorns. Skim. Reduce heat and simmer for 1 hour.

4. Cut cabbage into 6 wedges. Cook in gently simmering salted water until just tender. Drain. Add peeled potatoes to casserole and continue to cook for 40 minutes longer. Just before serving, put cabbage wedges in casserole and heat through.

5. To serve potée: remove vegetables from *bouillon* with a slotted spoon. Place cabbage in a shallow serving bowl, place the salt pork on it and surround with sausages, bacon cut into thin slices, and vegetables. Moisten with a little *bouillon*. The remaining *bouillon* will serve as the base for an excellent soup.

Ham and Egg Luncheon Casserole

6 eggs
2–3 Spanish onions
2 level tablespoons butter
2 tablespoons olive oil
225 g/8 oz ham, in 1 piece, cut into dice
450 ml/¾ pint light Béchamel Sauce (see
    page 412)
salt and freshly ground black pepper
2 level tablespoons finely chopped parsley

1. Hard-boil the eggs for 15 minutes in boiling water. Remove shells and slice.

2. Slice onions and sauté in butter and olive oil in a shallow flameproof casserole until they are soft and golden; do not let them brown.

3. Add diced ham and continue to cook, stirring, until onions just start to turn colour. Add hot Béchamel Sauce to onion and ham mixture and stir well. Fold in the egg slices and add salt and freshly ground black pepper, to taste. Heat through, sprinkle with finely chopped parsley and serve immediately.

223

Vegetable

Braised Celery

2 heads celery
½ Spanish onion, thinly sliced
2 small carrots, thinly sliced
butter
150 ml/¼ pint chicken stock
salt and freshly ground black pepper
1 level tablespoon flour
finely chopped parsley

1. Clean celery, cut each head in half lengthwise and trim off tops. Blanch celery in boiling water for 10 minutes.

2. Drain carefully and put in a flameproof casserole with thinly sliced onion, carrots, 2 level tablespoons butter and chicken stock. Season to taste with salt and freshly ground black pepper. Cover casserole and cook gently until tender (30 to 40 minutes), adding a little more stock, if necessary.

3. Five minutes before you remove vegetables from heat, mix 1 tablespoon each butter and flour to a smooth paste and stir into pan juices to thicken sauce. Just before serving sprinkle with finely chopped parsley.

French Potato and Cheese Casserole

675 g-1 kg/1½-2 lb new potatoes
butter
150 ml/¼ pint well-flavoured beef stock
6 level tablespoons freshly grated Gruyère cheese
2 level tablespoons freshly grated Parmesan cheese
salt and freshly ground black pepper

1. Butter an ovenproof shallow casserole.

2. Peel and slice potatoes thinly and soak in cold water for a few minutes. Drain and dry thoroughly with a clean tea towel. Place a layer of sliced potatoes on bottom of casserole in overlapping rows. Pour over a quarter of the stock, sprinkle with 2 tablespoons grated cheese (mixed Gruyère and Parmesan), dot with butter and season to taste with salt and freshly ground black pepper (not too much salt). Continue this process until casserole is full, finishing with a layer of grated cheese. Dot with butter and cook in a moderate oven (180°C, 350°F, Gas Mark 4) for about 1 hour, or until potatoes are cooked through. If top becomes too brown, cover with aluminium foil. Serve very hot.

Braised Chicory

8 heads chicory
butter
½ Spanish onion, thinly sliced
2 small carrots, thinly sliced
150 ml/¼ pint chicken stock
salt and freshly ground black pepper
juice of ½ lemon or orange
1 level tablespoon butter
½ level tablespoon flour

1. Trim root ends of chicory and wash well in cold water. Drain.

2. Heat 4 tablespoons butter in a shallow flameproof casserole. Add raw chicory, thinly sliced onion, carrots and chicken stock. Season to taste with salt and freshly ground black pepper. Cover vegetables with buttered paper. Cover casserole and simmer over a very low heat or in a moderate oven (180°C, 350°F, Gas Mark 4) for 40 minutes, or until tender, adding a little more stock, if necessary.

3. Turn vegetables from time to time and, 20 minutes after putting casserole in the oven, sprinkle vegetables with the juice of ½ lemon or orange.

4. Five minutes before you remove vegetables from heat, mix 1 tablespoon each butter and flour to a smooth paste and stir into pan juices to thicken sauce.

Saffron Cabbage and Ham Casserole

1 small white cabbage
1 small green cabbage
600 ml/1 pint brown stock
225 g/8 oz cooked ham, cut into slivers
1 Spanish onion, thinly sliced
butter
½ level teaspoon saffron
salt and freshly ground black pepper
¼ level teaspoon cayenne

1. Cut cabbages into eighths and soak in salted water for 30 minutes.

2. Drain well and then arrange in a large flameproof casserole. Pour over stock, cover casserole and simmer in stock for 10 to 15 minutes, until cabbage is just about half done.

3. Sauté ham slivers and thinly sliced onion in a little butter for a few minutes, until onion is soft.

4. Mix saffron with a little hot water and add it to the cabbage together with sautéed ham and onion. Season with salt, freshly ground black pepper and cayenne. Mix thoroughly and simmer until cabbage is tender and not mushy. If it gets too dry while cooking, add a little more stock.

Scalloped Cabbage Casserole

1 cabbage
salt
4 level tablespoons butter
300 ml/½ pint Béchamel Sauce (see page 412)
freshly ground black pepper
4-6 level tablespoons freshly grated
**   Parmesan cheese**
150 ml/¼ pint double cream
¼ chicken stock cube
freshly grated nutmeg

1. Shred cabbage and soak in salted cold water for 30 minutes. Drain well. Melt butter in a flameproof casserole, add shredded cabbage and simmer, covered, until cabbage is just tender but not browned.

2. Remove half the simmered cabbage. Pour over cabbage remaining in the casserole half the quantity of Béchamel Sauce. Sprinkle with freshly ground black pepper and half the grated Parmesan.

3. Add remaining cabbage, pour remaining sauce over the top and add more freshly ground black pepper and remainder of Parmesan.

4. Simmer double cream with ¼ chicken stock cube and then pour over cabbage. Sprinkle with a little freshly grated nutmeg. Place casserole in a moderate oven (180°C, 350°F, Gas Mark 4) and cook until the casserole bubbles and the top is golden brown – about 30 minutes.

226

Cabbage Casserole

1 green cabbage (about 1 kg/2 lb)
salt
1 level tablespoon cornflour
450 ml/¾ pint milk
coarsely grated Gruyère cheese
butter
freshly ground black pepper
freshly grated nutmeg

1. Remove and discard discoloured outer leaves from green cabbage. Wash, core and shred cabbage, and soak in cold salted water for 30 minutes. Drain and cook, covered, in a small amount of boiling salted water until just tender. Drain.

2. Mix cornflour with a little hot milk. Bring remaining milk to the boil in the top of a double saucepan, stir in cornflour mixture and cook over boiling water until mixture thickens. Add 6 level tablespoons grated Gruyère, 4 level tablespoons butter, and salt, freshly ground black pepper and nutmeg, to taste. Stir into cabbage and mix well.

3. Turn the mixture into a well-buttered shallow casserole; sprinkle with 2 level tablespoons grated Gruyère, dot with butter and brown lightly in the oven.

Steamed Stuffed Cabbage

1 Savoy cabbage
butter
Italian Tomato Sauce (see page 415)

STUFFING
1 Spanish onion, chopped
butter
225 g/8 oz button mushrooms, chopped
450 g/1 lb cooked ham, pork or veal,
  'finely chopped
8 level tablespoons cooked rice
salt and freshly ground black pepper
freshly grated nutmeg
little chicken stock

1. To make stuffing: sauté chopped onion in 4 tablespoons butter until transparent. Add mush-

rooms and simmer, stirring constantly, until soft. In another pan, sauté ham in 2 tablespoons butter until golden. Combine ham with vegetables and rice, and season generously with salt, freshly ground black pepper and nutmeg. Moisten with chicken stock.

2. Wash, trim and core cabbage. Place it in a large saucepan, cover with water and bring to the boil. Drain well.

3. Cut out centre of cabbage in a circle with a diameter of about 6 cm/2½ inches, and scoop out to form a cup. Beginning with the outer leaves, separate leaves one by one and fill each leaf with 1 to 2 tablespoons stuffing. Spoon remaining stuffing into cavity.

4. Place cabbage in a well-buttered ovenproof dish, cover loosely with foil and steam over boiling water in a covered pan until tender. Serve with Italian Tomato Sauce.

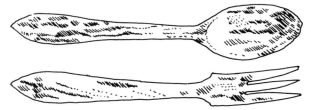

Braised Stuffed Lettuce Leaves

2 lettuces
2 level tablespoons butter
100 g/4 oz raw rice
600 ml/1 pint hot beef stock
1 Spanish onion, finely chopped
6-8 button mushrooms, finely chopped
2 tablespoons olive oil
100 g/4 oz ham, finely chopped
salt and freshly ground black pepper
2 level tablespoons tomato purée
2 level tablespoons finely chopped parsley

1. Separate lettuce leaves and wash well. Drain. Pour over boiling water to soften leaves. Drain.

2. Melt butter in a thick-bottomed frying pan. Add the rice and sauté until golden. Add half the hot beef stock to cover rice (adding a little water, if necessary), and cook, stirring constantly, until mixture comes to the boil. Reduce heat, cover the pan and cook slowly for about 15 minutes, adding a little more beef stock if necessary.

3. Sauté the chopped onion and mushrooms in oil in another frying pan and add to rice mixture. Mix in the finely chopped ham. Season generously with salt and freshly ground black pepper.

4. Place equal quantities of the rice and ham mixture on each lettuce leaf and roll them up, tucking ends in to form a neat 'package'. Arrange lettuce packets in a shallow ovenproof casserole.

5. Blend tomato purée with remaining hot beef stock. Pour over the lettuce packages, cover casserole and cook in a moderately hot oven (190°C, 375°F, Gas Mark 5) for 30 minutes, or until done, basting frequently. Sprinkle with finely chopped parsley and serve from the casserole.

Courgette Casserole

1 kg/2 lb courgettes, sliced
salt
1 Spanish onion, finely chopped
butter
2 eggs
8 level tablespoons soured cream
8 level tablespoons freshly grated Gruyère
  cheese
freshly ground black pepper
2 level tablespoons dried breadcrumbs

1. Simmer courgettes in a little salted water in a covered saucepan until tender but still crisp – about 5 minutes. Drain and whisk in an electric blender.

2. Sauté onion in butter until transparent. Add to courgette mixture with eggs, soured cream and 3 tablespoons grated cheese, and blend again. Season generously with salt and freshly ground black pepper.

3. Butter a shallow ovenproof casserole, line it with 3 tablespoons grated cheese and pour in the courgette mixture.

4. Mix breadcrumbs with remaining cheese and sprinkle over the top. Bake in a moderate oven (160°C, 325°F, Gas Mark 3) for 30 to 40 minutes, until set.

227

Tunisian Pepper and Tomato Casserole

2 Spanish onions
olive oil
6 ripe tomatoes, sliced
3 red or green peppers, diced
1 (100-g/3¼-oz) can tomato purée
1–2 cloves garlic
salt and freshly ground black pepper
⅛–¼ level teaspoon each cayenne and paprika
4 eggs
powdered cumin

1. Slice onions thickly and sauté in 6 tablespoons olive oil until golden. Add sliced tomatoes, diced peppers, tomato purée and garlic, and simmer vegetables until soft and cooked through.

2. Add 4 tablespoons olive oil, season to taste with salt, freshly ground black pepper, cayenne and paprika, and simmer for 5 minutes more.

3. To serve: spoon softened vegetables into individual casseroles or ovenproof serving dishes. Break 1 egg into each dish and bake in a moderately hot oven (200°C, 400°F, Gas Mark 6) until eggs are just set – about 10 minutes. Sprinkle with a little powdered cumin.

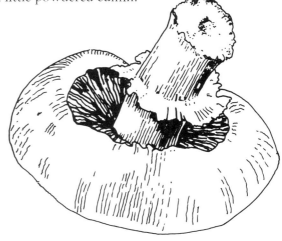

228

French Aubergine Casserole

1 kg/2 lb aubergines
2 Spanish onions, finely chopped
4 cloves garlic, finely chopped
600–900 ml/1–1½ pints chicken stock
salt and freshly ground black pepper
1 bay leaf
100 g/4 oz finely grated Gruyère cheese
4–6 eggs (1 per person)
garlic croûtons

1. Cut the aubergines (unpeeled) into small cubes. Combine with finely chopped onions and garlic in an ovenproof casserole. Add chicken stock, to cover. Season with salt and freshly ground black pepper, to taste, and add bay leaf. Cook in a moderately hot oven (190°C, 375°F, Gas Mark 5) for 20 minutes, stirring once during cooking time. When vegetables are tender, sprinkle with grated Gruyère and cook for 5 minutes more.

2. Just before serving, break 1 egg per person into a small saucer, slide gently into the casserole and continue to cook until egg whites are firm, about 5 minutes.

3. Serve hot with lightly flavoured garlic *croûtons*.

Aubergine and Minced Beef Casserole

1 large onion, coarsely chopped
butter
675 g/1½ lb minced lean beef
150 ml/¼ pint tomato purée
450 ml/¾ pint water
1 level teaspoon salt
¼ level teaspoon freshly ground black pepper
4 medium-sized aubergines, sliced

1. Sauté chopped onion in 4 tablespoons butter until golden. Add the meat and cook, stirring continuously, until it is browned.

2. Combine the tomato purée with the water, add salt and freshly ground black pepper, and pour sauce over meat. Bring to the boil and simmer for 5 minutes. Remove mixture.

3. Sauté aubergine slices in 8 tablespoons butter and place a layer of aubergine in the bottom of a well-buttered casserole.

4. Using a slotted spoon, add a layer of drained beef, another layer of aubergine, then beef, and so on, until all the beef and aubergines have been used up. Pour over the remaining sauce and bake, uncovered, in a moderate oven (180°C, 350°F, Gas Mark 4) until aubergines are tender. Serve hot.

Aubergine and Minced Lamb Casserole

Illustrated on page 188

1 Spanish onion, finely chopped
2 cloves garlic, finely chopped
olive oil
675 g/1½ lb cooked lamb, minced
225 g/8 oz mushrooms, chopped
6 tomatoes, peeled, seeded and chopped
4 level tablespoons finely chopped parsley
salt and freshly ground black pepper
1–2 level tablespoons tomato purée
6 tablespoons rich beef or veal stock
4–6 aubergines, unpeeled
flour
4–6 tablespoons grated Parmesan cheese
2 eggs
1 (142-ml/5-fl oz) carton yogurt

1. Sauté onion and garlic in 4 tablespoons olive oil until transparent. Add lamb and continue cooking, stirring from time to time, until brown. Add chopped mushrooms, tomatoes, parsley, and salt and freshly ground black pepper, to taste, and cook until onion is tender.

2. Dilute tomato purée in stock. Add to meat and vegetable mixture and simmer for 10 minutes.

3. Slice aubergines, unpeeled, in thin slices. Dust with flour and fry on both sides in hot olive oil; drain on absorbent paper. Line a baking dish with slices of aubergine. Spread a layer of stuffing mixture on them, sprinkle lightly with grated Parmesan cheese and cover with a layer of aubergines. Continue this process until baking dish is full, ending with a layer of aubergines.

4. Beat eggs and blend in 2 level tablespoons flour. Add yogurt and whisk to a creamy sauce. Pour this sauce over meat and vegetable mixture. Sprinkle with grated Parmesan cheese and bake in a moderately hot oven (190°C, 375°F, Gas Mark 5) until the top has browned nicely. Serve hot. It is also very good cold and can be reheated successfully.

Ratatouille

8 tablespoons olive oil
2 Spanish onions, sliced
2 cloves garlic, finely chopped
2 green peppers, sliced
2 small aubergines, sliced
4 courgettes, sliced
8 ripe tomatoes, peeled, seeded and chopped
salt and freshly ground black pepper
4 level tablespoons chopped parsley
$\frac{1}{4}$ level teaspoon dried marjoram
$\frac{1}{4}$ level teaspoon dried basil

1. Heat olive oil in a large thick–bottomed flame-proof casserole. Add sliced onions and garlic and sauté until vegetables soften.

2. Add sliced green peppers and aubergines and continue to cook, stirring from time to time. Ten minutes later, stir in sliced courgettes and peeled, seeded and chopped tomatoes. Reduce heat, cover casserole and simmer vegetables gently for 30 minutes.

3. Season to taste with salt and freshly ground black pepper, add chopped parsley, marjoram and basil and cook, uncovered, for about 10 to 15 minutes more. Serve hot from the casserole.

230

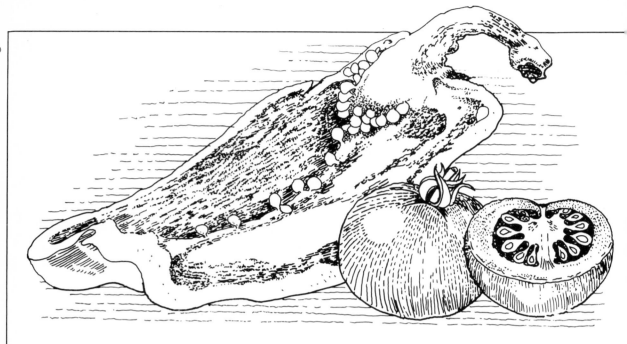

Baked Corn and Courgette Casserole

1 Spanish onion, finely chopped
1 clove garlic, finely chopped
4 level tablespoons butter, melted
1 green pepper, diced
450 g/1 lb courgettes, thinly sliced
2 (312-g/11-oz) cans sweet corn niblets
dried oregano and marjoram
salt and freshly ground black pepper
300 ml/½ pint Italian Tomato Sauce (see
    page 415)

1. Sauté finely chopped onion and garlic in butter in a flameproof casserole until vegetables are transparent. Add diced green pepper and continue to sauté, stirring constantly, until vegetables just begin to change colour. Then add finely sliced courgettes and continue to sauté, stirring continuously, until courgettes begin to soften.

2. Drain corn niblets and add to casserole with dried oregano, or marjoram, and salt and freshly ground black pepper, to taste.

3. Pour over Italian Tomato Sauce and cook, uncovered, in a moderate oven (180°C, 350°F, Gas Mark 4) for about 45 minutes.

Peas and Pasta Luncheon Casserole

2 (227-g/8-oz) packets frozen peas
225 g/8 oz small shell pasta
salt
4 level tablespoons butter
½ Spanish onion, finely chopped
1 clove garlic, finely chopped
100 g/4 oz cooked ham, cut into pea-sized
    dice
2 level tablespoons finely chopped parsley
1 chicken stock cube
freshly ground black pepper
freshly grated Gruyère cheese

1. Defrost peas.

2. Cook pasta shells in salted boiling water until just tender. Drain.

3. Melt butter in a large shallow flameproof casserole. Add finely chopped onion and garlic and simmer gently until vegetables are soft. Add diced cooked ham, pasta shells and finely chopped parsley and cook over a low heat, stirring, for several minutes.

4. In the meantime dissolve chicken stock cube in 150 ml/¼ pint hot water and add to casserole with defrosted peas. Season with salt and freshly ground black pepper. Cover casserole and continue to cook for 10 to 15 minutes, until peas are tender.

5. Serve from casserole, with freshly grated Gruyère cheese.

Creole Rice Casserole

225 g/8 oz rice
butter
olive oil
600 ml/1 pint chicken stock
salt and freshly ground black pepper
1 green pepper, diced
1 Spanish onion, chopped
1 (793-g/1 lb 12-oz) can Italian peeled
    tomatoes
4 level tablespoons finely chopped parsley
2 bay leaves, crumbled
4–6 tomatoes, sliced
½ level teaspoon dried oregano
6 level tablespoons freshly grated Gruyère
    cheese
4 level tablespoons freshly grated Parmesan
    cheese

1. Sauté rice in 2 tablespoons each butter and olive oil until rice becomes translucent. Add chicken stock and simmer until rice is just tender. Add more butter, and salt and freshly ground black pepper, to taste.

2. Sauté diced green pepper and chopped onion in 2 tablespoons each butter and olive oil in a large shallow flameproof casserole until vegetables are soft.

3. Chop canned tomatoes coarsely and add, with juices, to casserole. Then stir in chopped parsley, bay leaves and salt and freshly ground black pepper, to taste. Simmer for 3 minutes.

4. Add hot butter-cooked rice to casserole, mix well and top with a layer of overlapping tomato slices. Sprinkle with oregano and freshly grated Gruyère and Parmesan cheese and cook in a moderate oven (180°C, 350°F, Gas Mark 4) for 25 to 30 minutes until cheese has melted and is bubbling brown.

Boston Baked Beans

Illustrated on page 187

675 g/1½ lb haricot beans
450 g/1 lb salt pork or fat bacon
2 onions, finely chopped
2 level teaspoons dry mustard
salt and freshly ground black pepper
4 level tablespoons dark treacle
4 tablespoons Demerara sugar
600 ml/1 pint boiling water from beans
4 level tablespoons tomato ketchup
2 level tablespoons bacon fat
sautéed onion rings, cooked sausages and
    frankfurters (optional)

1. Soak the beans overnight in cold water.

2. Drain, cover again with fresh water, and allow to simmer on a low heat for about 1 hour, or until the skins of the beans burst when blown upon. Drain again, saving about 600 ml/1 pint of the liquid.

3. Scald the salt pork quickly; drain pork and cut slashes in the rind with a sharp knife.

4. Cut pork in 2 pieces; place 1 piece in bottom of a large casserole, add beans and bury remainder of pork in the beans so that the rind just shows.

5. Mix finely chopped onions, mustard, salt, freshly ground black pepper, treacle and sugar with reserved bean water, and bring to the boil. Pour this mixture over the beans, to cover. If necessary, add more boiling water. Place lid on casserole and bake in a cool to moderate oven (150–160°C, 300–325°F, Gas Mark 2–3) for 6 hours. From time to time add more boiling water, so that beans are kept covered and moist.

6. **One hour before serving:** stir 2 to 4 tablespoons tomato ketchup into the beans, drip the hot melted bacon fat over them and cook for 1 hour in a moderate oven, uncovered, to colour beans and brown pork. If desired, add sautéed onion rings, cooked sausages and frankfurters just before serving.

232

Mexican Beans

Illustrated on page 187

450 g/1 lb red kidney beans
1 Spanish onion, finely chopped
2 cloves garlic, finely chopped
salt
2 level tablespoons butter
1 level tablespoon flour
½ level teaspoon cumin powder
2 level tablespoons Mexican chili powder*
1 bouquet garni (2 sprigs parsley, 2 sprigs thyme, 1 stick celery, 1 bay leaf)
300 ml/½ pint beef stock
freshly ground black pepper

* Spice Islands brand or Twin Trees or McCormicks – not powdered chillies.

1. Place kidney beans in a large saucepan. Fill pan with water and bring gently to the boil. Remove saucepan from heat and let beans soak in hot water for 1 hour.

2. Drain, and simmer with finely chopped onion and garlic in salted water in a large casserole. After about 1 hour of cooking, taste them. If they are cooked, drain; if not, continue to simmer until they are tender, but do not let them burst. Drain.

3. Mix butter, flour, cumin powder and Mexican chili powder (a combination of powdered chillies, cumin, salt, flour and garlic) to a smooth paste.

4. Combine cooked beans and chili paste in a saucepan and add *bouquet garni*, beef stock, and salt and freshly ground black pepper, to taste. Simmer, stirring gently from time to time, for about 45 minutes, until sauce is smooth and rich.

5. Remove *bouquet garni*. Serve immediately.

Red Beans and Bacon

450 g/1 lb red kidney beans
2 Spanish onions, chopped
1 bouquet garni (2 sprigs parsley, 2 sprigs thyme, 1 stick celery, 1 bay leaf)
1 strip orange peel
450 g/1 lb bacon, in 1 piece
150–300 ml/¼–½ pint red wine
4-6 tablespoons olive oil
salt and freshly ground black pepper

1. Place kidney beans in a large saucepan. Fill pan with water and bring gently to the boil. Remove pan from heat and let beans soak for 1 hour.

2. Drain; simmer beans with chopped onions, *bouquet garni*, orange peel and bacon in water to cover in a large casserole until beans are almost cooked through – 45 to 60 minutes. Beans should remain fairly firm, otherwise they will break in subsequent cooking. Add a little more water from time to time, if necessary. Remove bacon and keep warm. Drain beans, reserving liquid.

3. Combine drained beans with about 150 ml/¼ pint of the reserved bean liquor in a clean casserole. Add red wine, olive oil and salt and freshly ground black pepper, to taste, and simmer gently, stirring beans from time to time, for about 10 minutes, or until beans have absorbed flavour. Remove *bouquet garni*.

4. Slice bacon; add to the casserole and serve immediately.

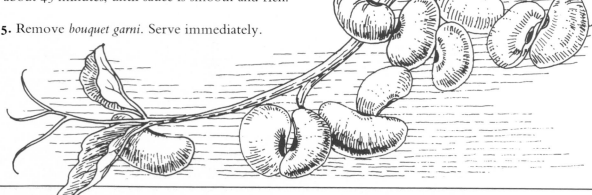

Poultry

Chicken en Cocotte

Illustrated on page 218

1 tender chicken (about 1.5 kg/3½ lb)
salt and freshly ground black pepper
225 g/8 oz fat bacon, in 1 piece
2 level tablespoons butter
2 tablespoons olive oil
1 Spanish onion, finely chopped
1 clove garlic, finely chopped
1 bouquet garni (2 sprigs parsley, 2 sprigs thyme, 1 bay leaf)
300 ml/½ pint dry white wine

1. Cut chicken into serving pieces and season to taste with salt and freshly ground black pepper.

2. Cut bacon into 'fingers', about 5 mm/¼ inch thick.

3. Heat butter and oil in an iron *cocotte* or a heavy casserole and sauté bacon 'fingers' until golden.

4. Remove bacon and reserve. Add finely chopped onion and garlic and cook over a medium heat, stirring constantly, until soft. Remove with a slotted spoon. Add chicken pieces to casserole and brown them on all sides.

5. Return bacon, onion and garlic to the pan, then add *bouquet garni* and dry white wine. Cover the casserole and let the chicken simmer over a very low heat until it is tender. Add a little chicken stock (made with a cube), during the cooking, if the sauce reduces too quickly.

Braised Chicken with Tomatoes

1 tender chicken (about 1.5 kg/3½ lb)
2 tablespoons olive oil
4 level tablespoons butter
450 g/1 lb tomatoes, peeled, seeded and coarsely chopped
1 clove garlic, finely chopped
6 level tablespoons finely chopped onion
salt and freshly ground black pepper
300 ml/½ pint well-flavoured chicken stock
4-6 tablespoons dry sherry
2 level tablespoons finely chopped parsley

1. Prepare and truss chicken.

2. Melt olive oil and 2 level tablespoons butter in a thick-bottomed flameproof casserole, and brown chicken in it on all sides.

3. Melt remaining butter in a frying pan, and sauté tomatoes, garlic and onion until onion is soft.

4. Add vegetables to the browned chicken, season with salt and freshly ground black pepper, and pour in the stock. Cover casserole, place in a moderate oven (160°C, 325°F, Gas Mark 3) for 1½ to 2 hours until chicken is tender. If necessary, a little more stock may be added during the cooking.

5. To serve: place chicken on a hot serving dish and remove trussing thread or string. Skim fat from tomatoes, add dry sherry and correct seasoning. Sprinkle with finely chopped parsley and pour sauce around the chicken.

234

Chicken en Casserole

1 chicken (about 1.5 kg/3½ lb)
6 small white onions
4 carrots, diced
2 turnips, diced
2 sticks celery, sliced
2 bay leaves
300 ml/½ pint well-flavoured chicken stock
salt and freshly ground black pepper

1. Prepare and truss chicken. Put it in an oven-proof casserole with peeled white onions, diced carrot and turnip, sliced celery and bay leaves.

2. Heat chicken stock and add to casserole. Cover and cook in a moderate oven (160°C, 325°F, Gas 1½ to 2 hours, until the chicken is quite tender, basting occasionally with the stock. Season with salt and freshly ground black pepper.

3. Cut chicken into serving pieces. Serve in casserole.

Saffron Chicken Casserole

1 chicken (about 1.5 kg/3½ lb)
100 g/4 oz butter
1 Spanish onion, finely chopped
1 chicken stock cube
¼-½ level teaspoon saffron
salt and freshly ground black pepper
hot water
300 ml/½ pint cream
4 egg yolks

1. Cut chicken into 8 serving pieces. Melt butter in a large flameproof casserole, and sauté chicken pieces gently on all sides without letting them colour.

2. Add finely chopped onion, crumbled chicken stock cube, saffron, and salt and freshly ground black pepper, to taste. Cover with hot water and simmer gently for 50 to 60 minutes, until tender.

3. Just before serving, whisk cream and egg yolks together in a large bowl. Remove chicken pieces with a slotted spoon. Strain a little hot chicken stock into cream and egg mixture and whisk. Strain remainder of stock into bowl, pressing all juices through sieve.

4. Clean casserole, return chicken pieces to it and pour creamy mixture over chicken. Heat through for 5 minutes, stirring continuously, being careful that sauce never comes to the boil or the sauce will curdle. Correct seasoning and serve immediately.

Summer Saffron Chicken

1 tender chicken (about 1.5 kg/3½ lb)
butter
12 small onions
1 level tablespoon flour
½ level teaspoon saffron
salt and freshly ground black pepper
1 bouquet garni (2 sprigs parsley, 2 sprigs thyme, 1 bay leaf)
24 button mushrooms
juice of 2 lemons
2 egg yolks
300 ml/½ pint double cream

1. Cut chicken into 8 serving pieces and sauté in 4 to 6 tablespoons butter with onions in a large flameproof casserole until chicken pieces just begin to turn colour. Sprinkle chicken pieces and onions with flour and add just enough water to cover chicken. Season with saffron, and salt and freshly ground black pepper, to taste. Add *bouquet garni,* cover casserole and cook for about 1½ hours, or until chicken is tender.

2. Remove chicken and onions to a deep serving dish or clean casserole. Strain stock into a clean saucepan and reserve.

3. Sauté button mushrooms in 2 tablespoons butter and juice of 1 lemon until tender and add to chicken and onions. Chill.

4. Whisk egg yolks, juice of 1 lemon and 150 ml/¼ pint double cream in a bowl. Bring stock to the boil, and add, whisking vigorously, a ladle of boiling stock to the cream and egg mixture. Pour mixture into the hot stock, bring gently to the boil, whisking well, until sauce is thick and creamy. Strain sauce through a fine sieve into a clean bowl and allow to cool. Chill.

5. When ready to serve, whisk remaining cream into cold saffron sauce, correct seasoning and spoon over chicken and vegetables. Toss well.

Poulet aux Concombres

4 medium-sized carrots
1 Spanish onion
1 tender chicken (about 1.5 kg/3½ lb),
   with giblets
melted butter
¼ level teaspoon powdered thyme
1 bay leaf, crumbled
salt
2 large firm tomatoes, peeled, seeded and
   coarsely chopped
1 cucumber
freshly ground black pepper
150 ml/¼ pint double cream
paprika

1. Slice carrots and onion thinly, chop giblets; place in the bottom of a well-buttered flameproof casserole. Heat gently for 5 minutes.

2. Place chicken, brushed with 100 g/4 oz melted butter, on top of this bed of vegetables and cook in a moderate oven (180°C, 350°F, Gas Mark 4) for 45 minutes, turning the chicken several times, as it cooks, basting well each time.

3. Fifteen minutes after putting in the chicken, add powdered thyme and bay leaf, a sprinkle of salt and coarsely chopped tomatoes.

4. Peel cucumber, cut into halves lengthwise, and remove seeds with a pointed teaspoon. Cut into 5-cm/2-inch segments and round off the edges to make prettier shapes. Blanch cucumber segments in boiling salted water for 3 minutes. Remove and drain. Season with salt and freshly ground black pepper and simmer gently in 100 g/4 oz butter and 150 ml/¼ pint double cream in a small pan with a tight-fitting lid. Season with salt and paprika, to taste.

5. When the chicken is tender, transfer it, with vegetables, to a warm serving dish. Pour remaining sauce from cucumbers into the casserole in which the chicken has been cooked, bring to the boil and simmer for 2 minutes. Check seasoning and strain over chicken. Arrange the cucumber segments around chicken and serve immediately.

Poulet aux Poivrons

1 roasting chicken (about 1.5 kg/3½ lb when
   cleaned)
2 level tablespoons butter
2 tablespoons olive oil
½ level teaspoon paprika
salt and freshly ground black pepper
cayenne
2 Spanish onions, finely chopped
4 cloves garlic, finely chopped
1 kg/2 lb ripe tomatoes, peeled, seeded and
   chopped
1 kg/2 lb red and/or green peppers, seeded
   and thinly sliced
2 bay leaves
2 sprigs thyme
4 sprigs parsley
boiled or steamed rice to serve

1. Clean chicken and cut into 8 serving pieces. Melt butter and olive oil in a large flameproof casserole and sauté chicken pieces in amalgamation of fats until golden. Season with paprika, salt and freshly ground black pepper and cayenne, to taste.

2. Add finely chopped onions and garlic, chopped tomatoes, thinly sliced peppers, bay leaves, thyme and parsley. Cook, covered, over a gentle heat, or in a cool oven (150°C, 300°F, Gas Mark 2) for 1½ to 2 hours.

3. To serve: remove herbs and correct seasoning (the dish should be very highly spiced). Serve in casserole accompanied by boiled or steamed rice.

235

236

Braised Chicken Henri IV

1 tender chicken (about 1.5 kg/3½ lb)
3 level tablespoons butter
3 tablespoons olive oil
6 tablespoons chicken stock
6 tablespoons dry white wine

STUFFING
chicken liver
100 g/4 oz green bacon
225 g/8 oz sausagemeat
2 cloves garlic
100 g/4 oz dried breadcrumbs
milk to moisten
3 level tablespoons finely chopped parsley
½ level teaspoon dried thyme
½ level teaspoon dried tarragon or chervil
generous pinch of mixed spice
2 eggs
salt and freshly ground black pepper

GARNISH
(1) poached vegetables of your choice, or
(2) individual baked tart cases filled with
    cooked peas, glazed carrots or button
    onions

1. **To make stuffing:** put chicken liver, green bacon, sausagemeat and garlic through the finest blade of your mincer. Moisten breadcrumbs with milk, combine with minced meats and add finely chopped parsley, dried herbs, mixed spice, eggs, and salt and freshly ground black pepper, to taste. Mix well, adding more milk if necessary to make fairly loose mixture.

2. Stuff chicken with this mixture; sew up openings and truss bird. Sauté bird in butter and olive oil in a flameproof casserole until golden on all sides. Add stock and dry white wine. Cover casserole and simmer gently for approximately 1 hour, or until tender. If there is any stuffing left over, place it in a small soufflé dish, cover with foil and cook it in the oven.

3. **To serve for a family luncheon:** Serve braised chicken surrounded by freshly poached vegetables . . . your choice of carrots, turnips, onions, green beans and potatoes.

4. **To serve for a dinner party:** Place braised chicken on a heated serving dish and surround with individual pastry cases filled with cooked peas, glazed carrots or button onions.

Coq-au-vin à la Beaujolaise

young cock or roasting chicken (about
    1.5 kg/3 lb)
3 level tablespoons butter
2 tablespoons olive oil
100 g/4 oz salt pork or unsmoked bacon,
    diced
12 button onions
12 button mushrooms
seasoned flour
300 ml/½ pint chicken stock (made with a
    stock cube)
4 tablespoons cognac, warmed
1 sugar lump
1 level tablespoon flour
2 tablespoons finely chopped parsley

MARINADE
2 cloves garlic, chopped
1 large Spanish onion, chopped
1 sprig thyme
2 bay leaves
2 sprigs parsley
½ bottle good Beaujolais
salt and freshly ground black pepper

1. Cut the chicken into serving pieces. Combine marinade ingredients in a large bowl (not metal), add chicken pieces and marinate chicken in this mixture overnight.

2. The following day, melt 2 level tablespoons butter with the olive oil in a flameproof casserole. Add salt pork or bacon, diced, and sauté until golden. Add button onions and cook, stirring, for 3 or 4 minutes; then add mushrooms and sauté the mixture gently until onions begin to turn transparent and mushrooms become brown. Remove pork or bacon, onions and mushrooms from the casserole and keep warm.

3. Remove chicken pieces from the marinade. Pat dry, roll in seasoned flour and sauté them in

the same fat for about 5 minutes, or until they turn golden brown on one side. Then, without piercing, turn chicken pieces over to brown on the other side. As each piece begins to 'stiffen', remove it and put in a covered dish in a warm oven.

4. When all of the chicken pieces have been browned, return the onions, bacon, mushrooms, chicken segments and their juices to the casserole. Pour over marinade juices, add chicken stock and bring to the boil. Cover casserole and cook in a moderate oven (180°C, 350°F, Gas Mark 4) for 50 to 60 minutes, until almost tender.

5. Remove chicken pieces, bacon and vegetables from the casserole and keep warm. Skim off excess fat from the juices in casserole. Set casserole on a high heat, pour in cognac, warmed in a soup ladle, and ignite. Allow to burn for a minute or two and then add a lump of sugar. Bring to the boil and reduce the sauce over a high heat to half the original quantity. Thicken with *beurre manié* made of the remaining 1 level tablespoon butter and 1 level tablespoon flour.

6. Strain sauce into a clean casserole; return chicken pieces, bacon and vegetables to the casserole; cover and let simmer in a cool oven (140–150°C, 275–300°F, Gas Mark 1–2) until ready to serve. Garnish with finely chopped parsley.

Pollo alla Romana con Peperoni

2 small frying chickens (about 1.25 kg/ 2½ lb each)
salt and freshly ground black pepper
4–6 tablespoons olive oil
½ Spanish onion, finely chopped
300 ml/½ pint dry white wine
450 g/1 lb tomatoes, peeled, seeded and chopped
2 cloves garlic, mashed
2–4 green peppers, sliced

1. Cut chickens into serving pieces and season to taste with salt and freshly ground black pepper.

2. Sauté chicken pieces in olive oil until golden brown on all sides. Add finely chopped onion and dry white wine, and cook over a high heat until wine is reduced to half the original quantity.

3. Add chopped tomatoes and garlic, cover pan and simmer for 20 to 30 minutes, until chicken is tender.

4. In the meantime, sauté sliced green peppers in a little olive oil until tender. Serve with the chicken.

238

Hochepot de Poularde

1 tender chicken (about 1.5 kg/3½ lb)
4-6 tablespoons Calvados (apple brandy)
salt and freshly ground black pepper
4 level tablespoons butter
2 tablespoons olive oil
4 sticks celery, thinly sliced
1 large Spanish onion, thinly sliced
150 ml/¼ pint dry white wine
300 ml/½ pint chicken stock
4 egg yolks
150 ml/¼ pint double cream

GARNISH
4-6 croûtons fried in butter
2 level tablespoons finely chopped parsley

1. Cut chicken into serving pieces and place in a large bowl with Calvados. Season to taste with salt and freshly ground black pepper and allow chicken pieces to marinate in this mixture for at least 4 hours, turning pieces from time to time.

2. Melt butter in a thick-bottomed flameproof casserole; add olive oil and sauté thinly sliced celery and onion over a low heat until vegetables are soft, stirring constantly. Add dry white wine, cover casserole and simmer gently for 10 minutes. Add chicken pieces (reserving marinade juices) and pour over chicken stock. Cover casserole and simmer gently for 50 to 60 minutes, until chicken is tender. Remove chicken pieces from casserole and keep warm.

3. Whisk egg yolks and cream and add to marinade juices. Pour this mixture into casserole and cook over a low heat with juices and vegetables, stirring constantly, until mixture is thick (do not allow mixture to come to the boil, or egg yolks will curdle and sauce will separate).

4. Add chicken pieces to sauce and heat through. Transfer to a heated serving dish, garnish with *croûtons* and sprinkle with finely chopped parsley.

Poularde St. Honoré

1 roasting chicken (about 1.5 kg/3½ lb)

FILLING
225 g/8 oz cooked ham
2-3 level tablespoons tomato purée
4 level tablespoons double cream
paprika
salt and freshly ground black pepper
2-3 drops red food colouring
   (optional)

GARNISH
cooked carrot, truffle, and white
   of hard-boiled egg, cut in
   fancy shapes
Aspic Jelly (see page 410)

1. Roast or cook chicken in a casserole until golden and very tender. When cold, ease the legs away from the body without quite separating them, and carefully remove the flesh from the breast in one long piece on each side. Cut away the upper part of the breast bone with kitchen shears, leaving the chicken quite hollow in the centre, ready for the filling. Lay breast fillets on a board, skin side up, and cut them into slices lengthwise without quite separating the pieces.

2. To make filling: trim ham, removing all gristle and skin, and chop or mince it finely. Pound it well in a mortar with tomato purée. Add cream gradually, until mixture has a creamy consistency, without being too soft. Season to taste with paprika, salt and freshly ground black pepper. Tint lightly with red food colouring if desired.

3. To decorate: fill hollow of the chicken with ham mixture, reforming the whole bird. Lay the breast pieces on each side, separating the slices a little to show some of the white. Decorate the top, where the filling shows, with pieces of cooked carrot, truffle, and white of hard-boiled egg, or any other garnish preferred, covering the filling entirely. Brush over with slightly liquid aspic jelly and allow to set.

4. Serve chicken surrounded with chopped aspic.

Chicken Paprika

2 young chickens (about 1.25 kg/2½ lb each)
salt and freshly ground black pepper
100 g/4 oz butter
1 large Spanish onion, chopped
2 level tablespoons paprika
1 level tablespoon flour
450 ml/¾ pint well-flavoured chicken stock
2 level tablespoons tomato purée
150 ml/¼ pint double cream
juice of ½ lemon

1. Rinse chickens and pat dry. Cut into serving pieces and season with salt and freshly ground black pepper.

2. Heat butter in a flameproof casserole or large iron frying pan, add onion and cook until transparent. Stir in paprika. Add chicken and cook slowly until pieces are golden, then reduce heat, cover casserole and simmer gently for 20 minutes longer, or until chicken is almost tender. Sprinkle with flour, add stock and tomato purée, stir well and cover. Bring to the boil and simmer for 20 minutes.

3. Remove chicken to a warmed serving dish.

4. Add cream and lemon juice to casserole, stir well and cook for 5 minutes. Correct seasoning and pour sauce over chicken.

Italian Chicken with Sausages

2 tablespoons olive oil
1 Spanish onion, sliced
2 cloves garlic, sliced
50 g/2 oz mushrooms, sliced
4 negroni or 8 chipolata sausages
1 chicken (about 2.25 kg/5 lb)
1 425-g/15-oz) can Italian peeled tomatoes
2 tablespoons tomato purée
6 tablespoons red wine
salt and freshly ground black pepper

1. Heat olive oil in a thick-bottomed pan. Sauté onion and garlic until transparent. Add mushrooms and sauté until golden. Set aside.

2. Sauté sausages in fat remaining in pan until golden. Remove, allow to cool and slice in 5-cm/2-inch segments.

3. Cut chicken into serving pieces and brown in the fat. Return onion, garlic, mushrooms and sausages to the pan. Add tomatoes and tomato purée, and simmer gently for at least 45 minutes.

4. Add the wine and cook for 5 minutes longer. Season with salt and freshly ground black pepper.

Moroccan Chicken
Illustrated on page 220

1 chicken (1.75–2.25 kg/4–5 lb)
salt
¼ level teaspoon paprika
¼ level teaspoon powdered cumin
freshly ground black pepper
butter
350 g/12 oz Spanish onions, sliced
⅛–¼ level teaspoon powdered saffron
100 g/4 oz chick peas, soaked overnight
well-flavoured chicken stock
4 tablespoons finely chopped parsley
1 sprig fresh coriander or lemon thyme
225 g/8 oz rice
lemon juice

1. Cut chicken into serving pieces and season to taste with salt, paprika, powdered cumin and freshly ground black pepper. Sauté chicken pieces with sliced onions in 75 g/3 oz butter in a casserole until golden.

2. Sprinkle with powdered saffron; add chick peas and enough well-flavoured chicken stock to cover, and simmer gently for 1 to 1½ hours, until chicken is tender. Just before serving, add chopped parsley and coriander or lemon thyme.

3. Cook the rice in salted water with 2 tablespoons butter.

4. To serve: spoon half the rice into a heated serving dish, place chicken pieces on it and pour over saffron sauce. Add remaining rice and sprinkle with lemon juice.

240

Poularde au Porto

1 plump chicken (about 1.5 kg/3½ lb)
4-6 level tablespoons butter
225 g/8 oz mushroom caps
4 tablespoons cognac
400 ml/14 fl oz double cream
4-6 tablespoons port
1 level tablespoon cornflour
salt and freshly ground black pepper

1. Cut chicken into 4 serving pieces and simmer gently in butter for 10 minutes, turning pieces from time to time so that chicken does not brown. Add mushroom caps, cover pan and continue cooking until tender, turning chicken pieces from time to time.

2. Place chicken and mushrooms on a hot serving dish and keep warm.

3. Add cognac to pan, stirring well to scrape all crusty bits from sides of the pan. Stir in cream and port, mixed with cornflour, and continue cooking over a high heat until sauce is reduced to half the original quantity. Correct seasoning and pour sauce over chicken and mushrooms. Serve immediately.

Poulet du Marquis

2 small chickens (about 1 kg/2 lb each)
2 rashers bacon, cut in half
salt and freshly ground black pepper
4 tablespoons cognac
300 ml/½ pint double cream
1 egg yolk
2 level tablespoons butter

1. Truss birds, cover breasts with rashers of bacon and place in a thick-bottomed flameproof casserole. Season to taste with salt and freshly ground black pepper. Roast in a moderately hot oven (190°C, 375°F, Gas Mark 5) for 30 to 40 minutes, until breasts are tender when pierced with a fork.

2. Remove birds from casserole and slice off breast meat in single pieces. Keep warm.

3. Remove remaining meat from carcasses and chop finely. Chop bones coarsely. Add chopped meat and bones to casserole and simmer gently for 5 to 10 minutes, stirring from time to time. Skim off fat and add 2 tablespoons cognac and flame.

4. Whisk cream and egg yolk together and pour into casserole. Cook sauce gently, stirring continuously, until slightly thickened. Do not allow sauce to come to the boil or it will curdle.

5. Finish sauce by whisking in remaining cognac and butter. Correct seasoning and strain sauce through a colander (to remove bones) on to chicken breasts. Serve immediately.

Egyptian Lemon Chicken

2 small chickens (about 1.25 kg/2½ lb each)
4 tablespoons olive oil
1 clove garlic, finely chopped
grated rind and juice of 1 lemon
¼ level teaspoon dried thyme
salt and freshly ground black pepper
100 g/4 oz butter
2 level tablespoons finely chopped parsley

1. Cut chickens into serving pieces and place in a shallow bowl.

2. Sprinkle with olive oil, finely chopped garlic, grated rind and juice of 1 lemon, and thyme, and season to taste with salt and freshly ground black pepper. Marinate chicken pieces in this mixture for at least 2 hours, turning pieces from time to time.

3. When ready to cook, butter a rectangular ovenproof baking dish generously. Place chicken pieces and juices in dish and dot with butter. Cook in a moderate oven (190°C, 350°F, Gas Mark 4) for 50 to 60 minutes, until tender, basting frequently. When tender, remove from oven, sprinkle with finely chopped parsley, and serve immediately.

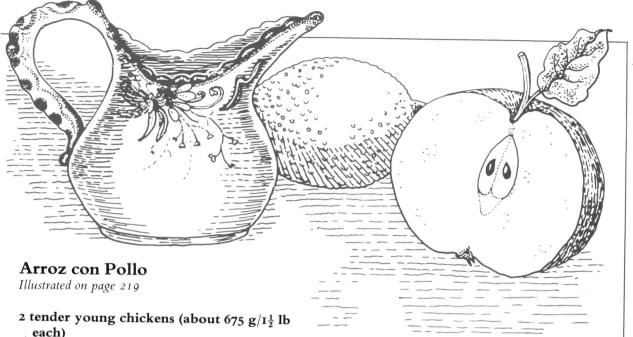

Arroz con Pollo
Illustrated on page 219

2 tender young chickens (about 675 g/1½ lb each)
salt and freshly ground black pepper
8 tablespoons olive oil
½ Spanish onion, finely chopped
1 clove garlic, finely chopped
6 tablespoons well-flavoured Italian Tomato Sauce (see page 415)
⅛ level teaspoon powdered saffron
2 canned pimientos, sliced
600 ml/1 pint well-flavoured chicken stock
175 g/6 oz rice
grated rind of ½ lemon
2 tablespoons freshly chopped parsley

1. Cut each chicken into serving portions, season, and sauté in olive oil until golden on all sides. Stir in finely chopped onion and garlic, and continue to cook until onion is soft. **Note:** do not let onion go brown.

2. Add Italian Tomato Sauce, saffron, sliced pimientos and chicken stock; cover saucepan and simmer for 15 minutes.

3. Stir rice into chicken and vegetable mixture and season with salt and freshly ground black pepper. Cover saucepan again and simmer for 30 minutes, or until all the liquids have been absorbed and the chicken is tender.

4. Sprinkle with grated lemon rind and chopped parsley, and serve immediately.

Curried Chicken

2 level tablespoons butter
2 tablespoons olive oil
1 Spanish onion, finely chopped
2 sticks celery, thinly sliced
2 cloves garlic, finely chopped
1–2 level tablespoons curry powder
2 level tablespoons flour
300 ml/½ pint chicken stock
150 ml/¼ pint dry white wine
675 g/1½ lb cooked chicken, diced
1–2 cooking apples (according to size), peeled, cored and diced
3 level tablespoons finely chopped parsley
cooked rice

1. Melt butter and oil and sauté finely chopped Spanish onion and sliced celery until onion is transparent. Add finely chopped garlic and curry powder mixed with flour and continue to cook, stirring constantly, until mixture begins to turn golden.

2. Stir in stock and white wine, and cook the sauce, stirring, until it is smooth and thick.

3. Add diced chicken, apple and finely chopped parsley, and simmer until heated through. Serve curried chicken in a ring of cooked rice.

242

Duck with Garlic

2 large cloves garlic, crushed
2 level teaspoons salt
1 level teaspoon freshly ground black pepper
1 level teaspoon paprika
1 tender duckling, cut into serving pieces
4 tablespoons olive oil
2 Spanish onions, finely chopped
2 bay leaves
1 strip dried orange peel

1. Mash garlic with salt to a paste; add freshly ground black pepper and paprika. Rub duck pieces on all sides with this aromatic paste.

2. Heat oil in the bottom of a flameproof casserole. Sauté onions in it until transparent. Remove onions from casserole with a slotted spoon and sauté duck pieces in remaining fat until golden on all sides.

3. Return onions to casserole; add 2 bay leaves and a strip of dried orange peel and simmer duck, covered, in a cool oven (150°C, 300°F, Gas Mark 2) for 40 to 50 minutes, until tender.

Duck en Daube
Illustrated on page 217

1 tender duck
salt and freshly ground black pepper
1 stick celery, chopped
2 carrots, sliced
2 large onions, sliced
8 tablespoons cognac
450 ml/¾ pint dry red wine
100 g/4 oz fat bacon, diced
1 tablespoon olive oil
1 bouquet garni (marjoram, 1 stick celery, 2 sprigs parsley)
1 clove garlic
225 g/8 oz mushrooms, sliced

1. Cut duck into serving pieces and place in a porcelain or earthenware bowl. Add salt and freshly ground black pepper, celery, carrots, sliced onions, cognac and red wine; marinate the duck in this mixture for at least 2 hours.

2. Remove duck pieces from the marinade; drain and dry with a clean cloth.

3. Sauté diced bacon in olive oil until golden. Remove bacon bits, and brown duck pieces in fat. Place bacon bits and duck pieces with pan juices in a large ovenproof casserole, cover, and simmer gently for 20 minutes.

4. Add the marinade, *bouquet garni*, garlic and mushrooms. Simmer over a very low heat for 1½ hours, or until duck is tender. Remove *bouquet garni*, skim fat and correct seasoning.

5. Serve from the casserole.

Duck with Turnips

1 tender duck (1.75 kg/4 lb)
salt
2 level tablespoons flour
freshly ground black pepper
4 level tablespoons butter
4-8 young turnips, quartered
1 level tablespoon castor sugar
900 ml/1½ pints well-flavoured stock
1 bouquet garni (marjoram, sage, 2 sprigs parsley)
1 Spanish onion, quartered

1. To prepare duck: singe and draw the duck, making a slit lengthwise above the vent to facilitate pulling out the inside. Then wash the bird quickly in warm water and dry it in a cloth. Cut off the feet and wings at the first joint, and rub the bird with salt inside and out.

2. To truss duck: lay the bird on its back and turn the wings under. Bring the legs close to the body and pass a metal or wooden skewer first through flesh of the wing, the middle of the leg and the body, then out the other side through the other leg and the wing. Pass a piece of string over each end of the skewer, bring it round the vent, fasten the legs tightly and tie securely.

3. Dust duck with 1 tablespoon flour and season inside and out with freshly ground black pepper.

4. Melt butter in a flameproof casserole and sauté duck on all sides until it is nicely browned.

5. Remove the duck and add quartered turnips to juices in the casserole. Sprinkle with sugar and simmer turnips until lightly coloured. Remove and keep warm.

6. Stir remaining flour into the fat left in the casserole until smooth, and pour in the stock. Bring to the boil and skim. Add *bouquet garni* and quartered onion, and season to taste.

7. Return duck to casserole, cover and cook gently for 1½ hours. Add turnips and continue cooking about 30 to 40 minutes longer, until the duck and turnips are tender, turning duck occasionally during cooking time.

8. When ready to serve: transfer duck to a hot serving dish, remove strings, and arrange turnips around duck. Skim fat from pan juices, reduce over a high heat, and strain over and round the duck.

Pineapple Duck

Illustrated on page 219

1 duck, cut into serving pieces
olive oil
1 (425-g/15-oz) can pineapple slices with juice
1 glass red wine
1 clove garlic, finely chopped
salt and freshly ground black pepper

PINEAPPLE AND ORANGE SAUCE
15 g/½ oz cornflour
juice and grated rind of 1 orange
juices from the duck, made up to 300 ml/ ½ pint with water
50 g/2 oz seedless raisins

1. Place the duck, cut into serving pieces, in a roasting tin and brush well with olive oil. Pour the juices from the can of pineapple into the tin

with the red wine, finely chopped garlic, and salt and freshly ground black pepper, to taste. Cook in a moderately hot oven (190°C, 375°F, Gas Mark 5) for 40 minutes, or until thoroughly cooked. Baste frequently with the juices.

2. To make Pineapple and Orange Sauce: mix cornflour to a smooth paste with orange juice. Heat pan juices, skimmed of fat and made up to 300 ml/½ pint with water, and pour over the cornflour mixture. Return to the roasting tin and cook until thick. Add chopped pineapple slices, raisins and grated orange rind, and heat through.

3. Serve duck with Pineapple and Orange Sauce.

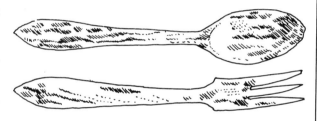

Malay Duck

2 level tablespoons coriander seeds, roasted in a dry pan
1 level teaspoon black peppercorns
2 level tablespoons honey
2 tablespoons soy sauce
salt
1 tender duckling, prepared
1 Spanish onion, finely chopped
4 tablespoons peanut oil
450 ml/¾ pint hot chicken stock
cinnamon and cloves

1. Pound 'roasted' coriander and black peppercorns in a mortar until powdered. Add honey, soy sauce, and salt, to taste, and rub mixture into duck, inside and out.

2. Sauté finely chopped onion in peanut oil until soft and transparent in a flameproof casserole. Add the duck and sauté it until golden on all sides. Then add chicken stock, and cinnamon and cloves, to taste. Simmer for 1½ hours, or until duckling is tender and there is little sauce left.

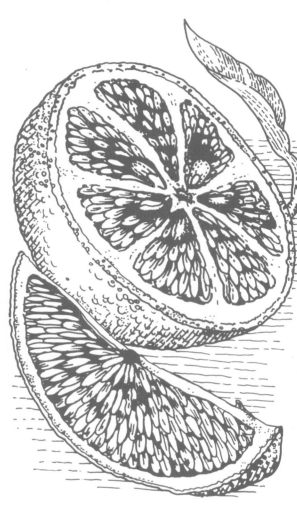

Canard Braisé à l'Orange

1 tender duck (2.25-2.75 kg/5-6 lb)
salt and freshly ground black pepper
6-8 level tablespoons butter
150 ml/¼ pint Cointreau
4 oranges
1 level tablespoon sugar
1 tablespoon vinegar
150 ml/¼ pint beef stock
watercress

1. Trim wingtips and cut off the neck of duck. Wipe the bird with a damp clean cloth inside and out, and sprinkle the cavity with salt and freshly ground black pepper.

2. Melt butter in a deep flameproof casserole just large enough to contain duck, and sauté duck until golden on all sides. Reduce heat, cover and simmer gently for 45 minutes, turning duck from time to time. Add two-thirds of the Cointreau and allow to simmer for a few more minutes.

3. In the meantime, peel 1 orange thinly. Then cut the rind into thin slivers. Reserve rind for later use. Peel remaining 3 oranges and cut into segments. Reserve segments for garnish.

4. Remove duck and keep warm. Add sugar, vinegar, juice of remaining peeled orange and beef stock to pan juices. Place casserole over a high heat and bring to the boil, stirring constantly, scraping all the crusty bits from sides of casserole into sauce. Add slivered orange rind, reduce heat to lowest possible, and simmer sauce gently for 10 minutes.

5. Skim fat from surface and pass sauce through a fine sieve. Season generously with salt and freshly ground black pepper, and add remaining Cointreau. (Sauce may be thickened if desired.)

6. Place half the orange segments in a saucepan, strain sauce over them and bring to the boil. Remove from heat.

7. To serve: place duck on heated serving dish, pour a little sauce around it and garnish with remaining fresh orange segments and sprigs of watercress. Serve orange sauce separately.

Cold Jellied Duck en Casserole

1 tender duckling, prepared
salt and freshly ground black pepper
butter
150 ml/¼ pint dry white wine
600 ml/1 pint chicken stock
1 bouquet garni (2 sprigs parsley,
   2 sprigs thyme, 1 stick celery,
   2 bay leaves)
100 g/4 oz fat bacon, cut into cubes
12 young turnips
12 button mushrooms
12 button onions
4 level tablespoons minced raw beef
2 egg shells, crushed
2 egg whites, beaten
2 level tablespoons gelatine

1. Wipe the duckling with a damp clean cloth inside and out and season generously with salt and freshly ground black pepper, both the cavity and the outside of the duckling. Sauté in 4 level tablespoons butter in a flameproof casserole until bird is golden on all sides. Moisten with dry white wine, bring to the boil and add chicken stock. Add salt, freshly ground black pepper and a *bouquet garni*.

2. Sauté bacon cubes in 2 level tablespoons butter until golden. Remove and sauté turnips in resulting fat until golden.

3. Combine sautéed bacon and turnips with button mushrooms and onions and add to duckling. Simmer, covered, for about 1½ hours, until duckling is tender and vegetables are cooked through, basting duckling from time to time.

4. Remove duckling, cut it into serving pieces and place pieces in a small oval casserole (or terrine) just large enough to hold it. Surround with bacon cubes, turnips, mushrooms and onions.

5. Strain stock through a sieve into a bowl; cool and remove fat from surface.

6. Clarify the stock by bringing it to the boil with minced raw beef, crushed egg shells and beaten egg whites. Strain, while hot, through a sieve lined with a wet flannel cloth. Soften gelatine in a little cold water, stir into the hot stock and pour over duckling, which should be covered. If not, add a little more water, stock and wine. Allow to set for 12 hours before serving. Serve with a tossed green salad.

Hungarian Duck

1 Spanish onion, finely chopped
100 g/4 oz cooked ham, chopped
2 rashers bacon, chopped
olive oil
8 level tablespoons cooked rice
4 level tablespoons finely chopped parsley
1 egg, well beaten
6 level tablespoons soured cream
salt and freshly ground black pepper
1 tender duckling, prepared
2 level tablespoons butter
450 g/1 lb tomatoes, peeled and quartered
2 small aubergines, quartered
2 small green peppers, seeded and quartered
2 Spanish onions, quartered
6 tablespoons dry white wine

1. Sauté finely chopped onion, ham and bacon in a little olive oil until onion is transparent. Combine with cooked rice, finely chopped parsley, well-beaten egg and soured cream and season generously with salt and freshly ground black pepper.

2. Stuff duckling loosely with this mixture and brown bird on all sides in 2 tablespoons each olive oil and butter in a flameproof casserole. Add quartered tomatoes, aubergines, green peppers and onions, moisten with 6 tablespoons each dry white wine and olive oil and season with salt and freshly ground black pepper, to taste. Cover casserole and cook in a moderate oven (160°C, 325°F, Gas Mark 3) for about 2 hours. Serve from the casserole.

246

Turkey à la King

butter
2 level tablespoons flour
½ chicken stock cube
300 ml/½ pint double cream
salt and freshly ground black pepper
675 g/1½ lb cooked turkey, cut into cubes
2 canned pimientos, cut into cubes
1 green pepper, cut into cubes
6 black olives
2 level tablespoons finely chopped parsley

1. Melt 2 level tablespoons butter in the top of a double saucepan over direct heat. Add flour and cook, stirring constantly, until the *roux* is well blended. Then stir in ½ chicken stock cube and double cream and cook over simmering water, stirring from time to time, until sauce is smooth and thick. Season with salt and freshly ground black pepper.

2. Butter an ovenproof casserole generously. Spread cubed turkey in the bottom of casserole. Add cubed pimientos and green pepper to cream sauce and pour over turkey.

3. Cook in a moderate oven (180°C, 350°F, Gas Mark 4) for 25 to 30 minutes. Garnish with a ring of black olives and a sprinkle of finely chopped parsley and serve immediately.

Guinea Fowl en Cocotte

1 large cooking apple, coarsely grated
1 Spanish onion, coarsely grated
1 (85-g/3-oz) packet Philadelphia cream
  cheese, mashed
6 juniper berries, crushed
lemon juice
salt and freshly ground black pepper
2 guinea fowl
butter
olive oil
150 ml/¼ pint dry white wine

1. Combine apple and onion with mashed cream cheese, crushed juniper berries, and lemon juice, salt and freshly ground black pepper, to taste.

2. Stuff birds with this mixture. Skewer openings and truss birds; spread with well-seasoned softened butter.

3. Place birds in a flameproof casserole and sauté in a little butter and olive oil until golden on all sides. Lower heat and add dry white wine. Cover casserole and simmer birds gently, turning them from time to time, until tender – about 45 to 60 minutes.

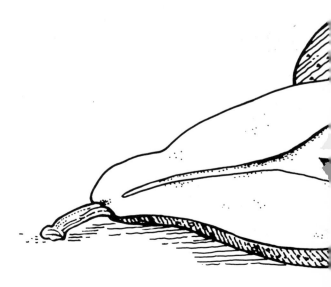

Pintade Roti aux Poires

2 Spanish onions, finely chopped
100 g/4 oz butter
2 small guinea fowl
salt and freshly ground black pepper
8 pears, peeled, cored and halved
100 g/4 oz sugar
300 ml/½ pint water
juice of 1 lemon
1 strip of lemon peel
150 ml/¼ pint dry white wine
150 ml/¼ pint port
boiled rice to serve

1. Sauté finely chopped onions in butter in a flameproof casserole until transparent. Remove onions from casserole with a slotted spoon and reserve. Sauté dressed guinea fowl in the butter until golden on all sides.

2. Return onions to casserole, season generously with salt and freshly ground black pepper and cook at medium heat, covered, turning guinea fowl from time to time.

3. Poach halved pears in a syrup of sugar, water, half the lemon juice and strip of lemon peel, until just tender. When the birds are half cooked (15 to 20 minutes), add halved pears, 8 tablespoons of the syrup, dry white wine and port to the casserole. Simmer for a further 15 to 20 minutes at the same heat, until guinea fowl are tender. Add salt, freshly ground black pepper and a little lemon juice, to taste.

4. To serve: cut guinea fowl into quarters, cover each quarter with a halved pear and coat with the strained reduced sauce. Serve with rice.

Game

Pheasant Soubise *Serves 4 to 8, according to size of birds*
Faisan aux Fruits *Serves 4 to 6*
Casseroled Pheasant in Red Wine *Serves 4 to 6*

248

Pheasant Soubise

2 plump pheasants
4 rashers streaky bacon, or thinly pounded
  pork fat
225 g/8 oz green bacon, in 1 piece
4 level tablespoons butter
2 tablespoons olive oil
2 Spanish onions, finely chopped
600 ml/1 pint single cream
salt and freshly ground black pepper

1. Clean and truss pheasants and cover breasts with bacon rashers or thinly pounded pork fat.

2. Dice green bacon and sauté in butter and olive oil in a flameproof casserole until golden. Remove and sauté finely chopped onions in resulting fats until transparent. Remove and sauté pheasants gently until they are golden on all sides. Return onions and bacon to casserole with pheasants, add cream and season generously with salt and freshly ground black pepper. Cover casserole and simmer gently for about 1 hour, until pheasants are tender.

3. To serve: transfer pheasants and bacon bits to a hot serving dish. Purée cream sauce in an electric blender (or force through a fine sieve) and pour over pheasants.

Faisan aux Fruits

2 fat pheasants
4 level tablespoons butter
salt and freshly ground black pepper
4 tablespoons cognac
2 tablespoons game fumet (see method,
  Step 2)
2 tablespoons lemon juice
2 tablespoons pineapple juice
4 slices fresh pineapple, halved
1 orange, peeled and cut in segments

1. To prepare birds: cut each bird into 8 serving pieces and sauté the wings, breasts and thighs in butter until golden. (Keep the drumsticks for another use; they are excellent devilled.) Season well with salt and freshly ground black pepper,

and continue to cook until pheasant is tender. Remove pieces and keep warm.

2. To make fruit sauce: remove half the fat in the pan, add cognac and set alight. Then bring to the boil, stirring briskly to dissolve crusty bits on side of pan. Add a little *fumet* of game (made by boiling neck, carcass and giblets of birds for a minute or two in a very little water with finely chopped onion, salt and pepper), then add lemon juice and pineapple juice.

3. Arrange pieces of pheasant on a warm serving dish, garnish with pineapple and orange segments and pour over sauce.

Casseroled Pheasant in Red Wine
Illustrated on page 256

2 young pheasants
olive oil
salt and freshly ground black pepper
8 level tablespoons finely chopped Spanish
  onion
3 level tablespoons butter
600 ml/1 pint red Burgundy
1 level tablespoon flour

SAUTÉED MUSHROOM CAPS
12-16 button mushrooms
2 level tablespoons butter
2 tablespoons lemon juice
$\frac{1}{4}$ level teaspoon thyme
salt and freshly ground black pepper

1. Clean birds; brush with olive oil and season generously inside and out with salt and freshly ground black pepper. Put 2 level tablespoons finely chopped onion and the pheasant liver into the cavity of each bird.

2. Heat 2 tablespoons olive oil and 2 level tablespoons butter in a large thick pan and sauté pheasants gently until they are a golden brown colour on all sides and almost tender. Transfer pheasants to a large ovenproof casserole and keep warm.

3. Pour red wine into pan in which you have

cooked birds and cook over a high heat, amalgamating wine with the pan juices. Add remaining finely chopped onion and continue to cook, stirring, until the liquid is reduced by half. Thicken the sauce with the remaining butter and flour. Simmer for a few minutes, strain through a fine sieve into a bowl and allow to cool slightly so that fat can be skimmed off the surface.

4. To cook mushroom caps: sauté button mushrooms in butter and lemon juice with thyme. Season to taste with salt and freshly ground black pepper. Keep warm.

5. Pour wine sauce over the pheasants, correct seasoning and add sautéed mushrooms. Cover casserole and cook in a moderately hot oven (190°C, 375°F, Gas Mark 5) for about 45 minutes, until pheasants are tender.

Grouse en Cocotte

2 tender grouse
fat bacon
salt and freshly ground black pepper
2 level tablespoons butter
2 tablespoons olive oil
4 shallots, coarsely chopped
2 carrots, coarsely chopped
2 tablespoons cognac
1 bouquet garni (2 sprigs parsley, 2 sprigs thyme, 1 bay leaf)
150 ml/¼ pint red wine
150 ml/¼ pint well-flavoured stock

1. Ask your poulterer to prepare birds for roasting.

2. Place a layer of fat bacon over breasts. Season birds with salt and freshly ground black pepper, to taste.

3. Heat butter and oil in an iron *cocotte* or a heavy flameproof casserole, and sauté 100 g/4 oz diced fat bacon until golden.

4. Remove bacon pieces and reserve. Add chopped shallots and carrots to the casserole and cook, stirring constantly, until vegetables soften. Then add grouse and brown well on all sides.

5. Return bacon pieces to the casserole, pour over cognac, and flame. Then add *bouquet garni*, red wine and well-flavoured stock. Cover the casserole and let the birds simmer over a low heat for 30 minutes, or until tender. Add more wine or stock if the sauce reduces too quickly while cooking.

Salmis of Grouse

3 grouse
6 tablespoons red or dry white wine
6 tablespoons rich beef stock
2 lemons
salt and freshly ground black pepper
freshly grated nutmeg
1–2 level tablespoons dry mustard
65 g/2½ oz mushrooms, sliced
1 level tablespoon butter
1 level tablespoon flour
2 level tablespoons finely chopped parsley

1. Roast grouse slightly in a moderately hot oven (200°C, 400°F, Gas Mark 6) for 15 to 20 minutes, until about half cooked. Cut them into serving pieces. Be sure to cut birds on a carving dish to catch blood and juices. Arrange pieces in a large shallow flameproof casserole.

2. Crush livers and giblets into a bowl with juices. Add red or dry white wine, beef stock and juice of 2 lemons; stir in the finely grated peel of 1 lemon and season to taste with salt, freshly ground black pepper, nutmeg and mustard.

3. Add sliced mushrooms and pour this mixture over the birds in the casserole. Cook until heated through, stirring so that each piece of meat is thoroughly moistened and is kept from sticking to the dish. Do not let the *salmis* come to the boil.

4. Just before serving, stir in a *beurre manié* made of equal quantities of butter and flour. Sprinkle with finely chopped parsley.

250

Pigeons with Green Peas

2 young pigeons
4 level tablespoons butter
8-10 small white onions, peeled
100 g/4 oz bacon, diced
1 level tablespoon flour
300 ml/½ pint chicken stock
225 g/8 oz peas, fresh or frozen
1 bouquet garni (2 sprigs parsley, 2 sprigs
thyme, 1 bay leaf)
salt and freshly ground black pepper

1. Clean and truss pigeons as for roasting.

2. Melt butter in a flameproof casserole and sauté pigeons, turning them over and over until browned on all sides.

3. Remove pigeons, add onions and diced bacon to the casserole, and sauté until golden. Sprinkle with flour and when flour has combined with the butter, add stock and stir until mixture boils.

4. Skim well and return pigeons to the sauce. Add green peas and *bouquet garni*. Season to taste with salt and freshly ground black pepper, cover and simmer gently until the pigeons are tender.

5. Transfer pigeons to the centre of a hot serving dish and surround with peas and onions.

Pigeons with Green Olives

2 young pigeons
4 level tablespoons butter
4 shallots, finely chopped
½ Spanish onion, finely chopped
100 g/4 oz unsmoked bacon, diced
1 level tablespoon flour
300 ml/½ pint chicken stock
2 level tablespoons finely chopped parsley
salt and freshly ground black pepper
thyme and marjoram
16 green olives, stoned, blanched and soaked
overnight in cold water and cognac
4 tablespoons cognac

1. Clean and truss the pigeons as for roasting.

2. Melt the butter in a flameproof casserole and sauté the pigeons, turning them over and over until browned on all sides.

3. Remove pigeons, add finely chopped shallots and onion with diced unsmoked bacon to casserole, and sauté until golden. Sprinkle with flour and when flour has combined with the butter, add stock and stir until mixture comes to the boil.

4. Skim well and return pigeons to the sauce. Add finely chopped parsley, and salt, freshly ground black pepper, thyme and marjoram, to taste. Cover casserole and simmer gently for about 2 hours, or until pigeons are tender.

5. Twenty minutes before pigeons are done, add blanched and soaked green olives. Remove cover and continue cooking.

6. To serve: arrange pigeons on a hot serving dish, surround with olives, and strain sauce over.

Pigeons in Red Wine

2 young pigeons
4 level tablespoons butter
1 Spanish onion, finely chopped
1 level tablespoon flour
300 ml/½ pint red wine
1 level teaspoon sugar
1 bouquet garni (2 sprigs thyme, 2 sprigs
parsley, 1 bay leaf)
salt and freshly ground black pepper
12 button mushrooms, sautéed in lemon
juice and butter
12 small white onions, simmered in red
wine and a little sugar
2 level tablespoons finely chopped parsley

1. Clean pigeons and cut them in half.

2. Melt butter in a large, thick-bottomed, flameproof casserole and sauté pigeons until well browned.

3. Remove pigeons from casserole and sauté finely chopped Spanish onion until golden brown. Return pigeons to casserole and sprinkle lightly with flour. When the flour is thoroughly mixed with the butter, add red wine, sugar and *bouquet garni*, and salt and freshly ground black pepper, to taste. Cover casserole and cook in a moderate oven (160°C, 325°F, Gas Mark 3) for 2 hours.

4. Fifteen minutes before serving, add cooked button mushrooms and onions to casserole.

5. When ready to serve, correct seasoning and sprinkle with finely chopped parsley. Serve from the casserole.

Salmis of Wild Duck

2 wild ducks
salt and freshly ground black pepper
dried thyme
8 rashers bacon
300 ml/½ pint port
1 Spanish onion, finely chopped
4 shallots, finely chopped
2 cloves
bouquet garni (4 sprigs parsley, 2 sprigs thyme, bay leaf)
300 ml/½ pint red Bordeaux
450 ml/¾ pint Brown Sauce (see page 411)
8 triangular croûtons, sautéed in butter

1. Clean, pluck and singe wild ducks. Rub cavities with salt, freshly ground black pepper and dried thyme. Place ducks, breast sides up, on rack in roasting tins. Cover breasts with bacon and pour port into tins. Roast ducks in a hot oven (230°C, 450°F, Gas Mark 8) for 20 minutes, basting several times with port.

2. Remove bacon, baste well with pan juices and continue roasting until ducks are cooked rare.

3. Cut breasts, wings and legs from ducks; remove skin and place pieces in a flameproof shallow casserole or chafing dish.

4. In a saucepan combine finely chopped onion and shallots, cloves, *bouquet garni*, bones, skins and trimmings from ducks, and red wine. Cook over a high heat until wine is reduced to half the original quantity. Add Brown Sauce, and salt and freshly ground black pepper, to taste; simmer gently for 20 minutes.

5. Strain sauce over duck pieces and simmer on top of the cooker or in a chafing dish at the table until duck is heated through. Garnish with *croûtons* and serve immediately.

Casseroled Partridge

2 small partridges
4 tablespoons melted butter
2 tablespoons olive oil
salt and freshly ground black pepper
2 slices of white bread, trimmed of crusts
4 level tablespoons finely chopped ham
4-6 juniper berries, crushed
grated rind of ½ lemon
marjoram
fat salt pork
6 tablespoons dry white wine
150 ml/¼ pint rich chicken stock
1 carrot, finely chopped
1 small onion, finely chopped

1. Clean partridges inside and out. Brush cavities with half the melted butter, and the olive oil and season liberally with salt and freshly ground black pepper.

2. Shred bread and combine with remaining melted butter, chopped ham, crushed juniper berries and grated lemon rind. Season to taste with salt, freshly ground black pepper and marjoram, and stuff birds loosely with this mixture.

3. Truss birds, wrap a thin piece of fat salt pork around each one and sauté birds in a flameproof casserole until golden on all sides. Add dry white wine, chicken stock, and finely chopped carrot and onion. Transfer casserole to a moderately hot oven (190°C, 375°F, Gas Mark 5) and roast, uncovered, basting birds from time to time, for 45 to 60 minutes, until tender.

251

252

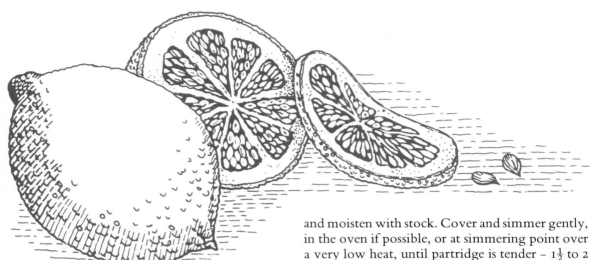

Partridge with Cabbage

2 small cabbages
salt
100 g/4 oz ham or lean bacon
2 level tablespoons butter or dripping
1 partridge (over 1 year old), trussed
2 large carrots, coarsely chopped
1 Spanish onion
1-2 cloves
1 bouquet garni (2 sprigs parsley, 2 sprigs
    thyme, 1 bay leaf)
2 small smoked sausages
freshly ground black pepper
well-flavoured stock

1. Trim the cabbages, cut in pieces and wash well. Cook cabbage in boiling salted water for 10 to 12 minutes. Then strain and press out the water.

2. Blanch ham or bacon for a few minutes to remove some of the salt.

3. Melt butter or dripping in a flameproof casserole, put in the partridge, trussed as for roasting, and brown it on all sides.

4. Remove partridge, add half the cabbage with the chopped carrots, the onion stuck with the cloves, and a *bouquet garni*. Lay the partridge, ham and sausages on top, and cover with remaining cabbage. Season with freshly ground black pepper

and moisten with stock. Cover and simmer gently, in the oven if possible, or at simmering point over a very low heat, until partridge is tender – 1½ to 2 hours.

5. To serve: remove the partridge, ham and sausages from the saucepan. Cut the partridge into neat joints, and slice the ham and sausages. Remove the carrot, onion and *bouquet garni*. Arrange cabbage on a hot serving dish; place the partridge pieces on top, and garnish with sliced ham and sausages.

Venison en Casserole

1.25 kg/2½ lb venison
100 g/4 oz bacon, in 1 piece
2 level tablespoons flour
450 ml/¾ pint stock or water
1 Spanish onion, finely chopped
2-4 level tablespoons redcurrant jelly
1 bouquet garni (2 sprigs parsley, 2 sprigs
    thyme, 1 bay leaf)
2 tablespoons lemon juice
salt and freshly ground black pepper

FORCEMEAT BALLS
225 g/8 oz sausagemeat
1 egg, beaten
dried herbs

1. Choose a nice fleshy piece of venison; wipe it and trim it carefully and cut it into 2.5-cm/1-inch cubes.

Guinea Fowl and Pheasants

Table of Raw Game and Fruits in Robert Carrier's Kitchen

Casseroled Pheasant in Red Wine (see page 248)

2. Trim rind from bacon and cut it into rectangles. Sauté bacon gently for a few minutes in a frying pan without allowing them to become too brown and crisp. Transfer bacon to a flameproof casserole, leaving the liquid fat in the pan.

3. Coat the pieces of venison with flour and sauté in bacon fat until well browned. Transfer venison to the casserole with bacon.

4. Add stock or water to the frying pan and cook over a high heat, stirring all the brown crusty bits from the sides of the pan into the stock. Skim if necessary and strain over the venison.

5. Add chopped onion, redcurrant jelly, *bouquet garni* and lemon juice, and season to taste with salt and freshly ground black pepper. Cover casserole and simmer venison gently for 2 to 2½ hours, until tender.

6. About 20 minutes before serving, add some small forcemeat balls made of sausagemeat mixed with egg and seasoned with dried herbs.

Stuffed Game Casserole

2 partridges or pheasants
100 g/4 oz lean veal, finely chopped
100 g/4 oz lean ham, finely chopped
6 tablespoons cognac
salt and freshly ground black pepper
¼ level teaspoon each thyme, nutmeg and
    crushed juniper berries
fat salt pork or fat bacon
4 level tablespoons butter
2 tablespoons olive oil
2 shallots, finely chopped
450 g/1 lb button mushrooms
1-2 cloves garlic, finely chopped
juice of ½ lemon

1. Clean partridges and stuff with the following mixture: finely chopped livers and hearts of the birds combined with finely chopped veal and ham, moistened with cognac and flavoured with salt, freshly ground black pepper, thyme, nutmeg and crushed juniper berries.

2. Truss birds firmly and wrap each one in fat salt pork or a slice of fat bacon. Place in a flameproof casserole with 2 tablespoons butter, the olive oil and finely chopped shallots. Cover casserole and simmer partridges for 1 to 1½ hours, until tender.

3. Sauté mushrooms in remaining butter with finely chopped garlic cloves. Season well and pour over partridges. Cover casserole and keep warm on an asbestos mat on top of the cooker or in a cool oven (150°C, 300°F, Gas Mark 2).

Hunter's Venison Stew

1.5 kg/3 lb venison
flour
3 Spanish onions, finely chopped
butter
225 g/8 oz unsmoked bacon, in 1 piece
6 cloves garlic
3 bay leaves
3 cloves
1 level teaspoon mixed dried herbs
    (marjoram, rosemary, thyme)
½ bottle red wine
3 large carrots, quartered
3 medium-sized potatoes, quartered

1. Trim sinews and bones from venison, and cut the meat into 5-cm/2-inch cubes. Roll them in flour.

2. Sauté onions in butter in a large flameproof casserole until soft. Remove from pan and reserve.

3. Dice unsmoked bacon, and sauté in remaining fat until golden. Remove and reserve.

4. Sauté venison in resulting fat until golden, then returned sautéed onions and bacon to casserole. Add garlic, bay leaves, cloves and dried herbs, and simmer, covered, in a cool oven (150°C, 300°F, Gas Mark 2) for 2 hours.

5. Reduce wine over a high heat to half the original quantity. Add to stew with quartered carrots and potatoes, and simmer for another hour.

258

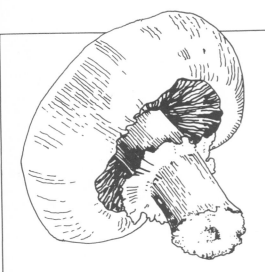

Jugged Hare

1 hare
18 small white onions
225 g/8 oz fat bacon, in 1 piece
2 level tablespoons butter or dripping
2 tablespoons olive oil
2 level tablespoons flour
1 bouquet garni (2 sprigs parsley, marjoram,
   1 bay leaf)
300 ml/½ pint red Burgundy
salt and freshly ground black pepper
2 level tablespoons tomato purée
100 g/4 oz mushrooms, quartered
vinegar

1. Ask your butcher to prepare hare, reserving the blood, which is a very necessary ingredient of this dish. Keep the saddle to serve roasted and cut remaining parts in serving pieces, chopping through the bones.

2. Peel onions and cut bacon into small thick strips. (If the bacon is very salty, the pieces should be blanched beforehand.)

3. Melt butter or dripping with oil in a thick-bottomed flameproof casserole and sauté onions and bacon until lightly browned. Remove onions and bacon, and reserve.

4. Put in the pieces of hare and brown them in the same fat. When coloured on all sides, sprinkle with flour and brown that also. Now add *bouquet garni* and wine, and enough water to cover. Season

to taste with salt, freshly ground black pepper and tomato purée. Simmer gently, covered, for 2½ to 3 hours, until hare is almost tender.

5. When ready, remove pieces of hare to a bowl and strain the sauce over them.

6. Return to a clean casserole; add onions, bacon and quartered mushrooms, and continue to simmer for 20 minutes, or until both the hare and vegetables are cooked through.

7. Then add the blood, mixed first with a little vinegar and some of the sauce. Strain it in beside the hare, mix well and bring to the boil. Be careful not to overboil it, or it will curdle.

Ragoût de Lapin

1 tender rabbit
18 button onions
12 shallots
3 level tablespoons butter
3 tablespoons olive oil
salt and freshly ground black pepper
2 level tablespoons flour
150 ml/¼ pint chicken stock
150 ml/¼ pint dry white wine
1 bouquet garni (2 sprigs parsley, 2 sprigs
   thyme, 1 stick celery, 2 bay leaves)
chopped fresh tarragon or parsley

1. Cut rabbit into serving pieces.

2. Sauté button onions and shallots in butter and olive oil until golden. Add rabbit pieces, season with salt and freshly ground black pepper, and sauté until well coloured. Transfer rabbit and vegetables to a flameproof casserole.

2. Add 2 level tablespoons flour to pan juices and stir until well blended. Add chicken stock and dry white wine and simmer, stirring continuously, until sauce has thickened. Add *bouquet garni*.
Note: If sauce is too thick, add a little more stock.

3. Pour sauce over rabbit pieces and vegetables, and simmer gently until rabbit is tender. Sprinkle with chopped fresh tarragon or parsley.

Blanquette de Lapin

1 tender rabbit
½ lemon
1.15 litres/2 pints chicken or veal stock
1 Spanish onion, stuck with 2 cloves
4 carrots
1 bouquet garni (2 sprigs parsley, 2 sprigs
   thyme, 1 bay leaf)
rice
powdered saffron
2 level tablespoons butter
2 level tablespoons flour
2 egg yolks
150 ml/¼ pint double cream
juice of ½ lemon

1. Cut rabbit into serving pieces. Leave overnight in cold water with half a lemon.

2. Rinse well. Blanch meat by putting it in cold water and bringing it slowly to the boil. Skim carefully and drain.

3. Place blanched rabbit pieces in a deep flame-proof casserole with enough chicken or veal stock (or stock and water) to cover. Add a Spanish onion stuck with 2 cloves, 4 carrots cut into quarters lengthwise, and the *bouquet garni*, and bring to the boil. Skim, lower heat and simmer gently for 30 minutes. Add a handful of rice and a pinch of powdered saffron, and simmer until rabbit is tender.

4. Make a white *roux* by combining 2 level tablespoons butter and 2 level tablespoons flour in a saucepan. Add 600 ml/1 pint of stock from the rabbit and stir well over a high heat until the sauce is smooth and creamy. Lower heat and simmer for 15 minutes, stirring from time to time. Remove saucepan from heat and 'finish' sauce by stirring in egg yolks, cream and the juice of ½ lemon.

5. Drain the rabbit pieces from the remaining stock. Clean the casserole, return rabbit pieces to it and strain sauce over meat through a fine sieve. Keep warm in the oven with the casserole covered until ready to serve. A little more fresh cream and a squeeze of lemon may be added just before serving.

Lapin aux Pruneaux

1 tender rabbit
300 ml/½ pint red wine
4 carrots, sliced
1 Spanish onion, sliced
2 bay leaves
salt and freshly ground black pepper
2 level tablespoons butter
2 tablespoons olive oil
350 g/12 oz dried prunes, soaked in water
   overnight
2 level tablespoons redcurrant jelly

1. Cut rabbit into serving pieces.

2. Marinate pieces in red wine for 24 hours with sliced carrots and onion, bay leaves, and salt and freshly ground black pepper, to taste. Drain and pat dry with absorbent paper or a clean cloth.

3. Sauté pieces in butter and olive oil until they are well coloured.

4. Add marinade juices and enough water to cover. Add soaked prunes and bring to the boil. Skim carefully, lower heat and simmer gently for 1 hour, or until rabbit is tender.

5. Arrange rabbit pieces and prunes on a serving dish. Reduce the sauce over a high heat, correct seasoning, blend redcurrant jelly into sauce and pour over rabbit pieces.

Salads and Vegetables

Are we slated to be the last generation to savour the new, fresh tastes of spring? Is modern science, in giving us year-round bounty, robbing us of the taste sensations of the first tender asparagus, the delicate flavour and texture of fresh garden peas and tomatoes sun-ripened on the vine? Are we to forgo the crisp raw delights of tiny radishes, baby cucumbers and little new carrots?

Today, the season of everything has been stretched, so that if we were to prepare a calendar of when the majority of salads and vegetables were available in the markets, our list would undoubtedly extend from end to end of the year. Gas-stored fruit from all over the world is on sale the year round, vegetables are frozen as soon as they are picked, even game is popped into deep-freeze by amateurs, so that what were delights of a few weeks of the year now rumble on, half unnoticed, from January to December.

Of course, the convenience of this year-round bounty is enormous. Today, we could not do without our perennially present tomatoes, lettuce, celery and green peppers. These year-round stand-bys, together with our frozen and canned foods from all over the world, all help in the daily planning of our menus. But must we – in the first flush of excitement over the immense potential of accelerated freeze-drying – forget the subtle, wistful pleasures of seasonal foods?

I am afraid that when it comes to eating, I am a traditionalist; I want my tastes seasonally inspired. I like to feel the months rolling by. I want to make the most of the tender new spring vegetables: tiny new potatoes of the season's first digging, each one a fragile melting mouthful, served with mint or dill, and lemon butter; fresh garden peas, twice as sweet as the later, full-blown ones, simmered in butter with bacon, tiny white onions and shredded lettuce; carrots and mushrooms so young that a few minutes of gentle cooking in butter, or butter and cream, brings them to the peak of perfection.

To Prepare Salads

Cos lettuce, endive, chicory, young and tender spinach leaves, watercress and French *mâche* (Lamb's lettuce) all make wonderful additives to a green salad. For a little variation in texture, add sliced or chopped celery, green pepper or fennel; or flavour with finely chopped shallots and chives, especially good with diced or finely sliced avocado pear. Epicures like to eat the avocado pear *au naturel* with just a touch of simple French dressing to fill the cavity. Try scoring the meat of the avocado into cubes with a knife before adding the dressing; this allows all the flavour of your dressing to permeate the avocado rather than remaining just on top. The cut squares look attractive too. In Britain, where we often get our avocados unripe, I like to dice the delicate buttery meat of the fruit: remove it entirely from the shell, and marinate it in French dressing with a hint of finely chopped chives. Then just before serving, refill the crisp green shells with the diced cubes which have been 'tenderised' and flavoured by the French dressing marinade.

I like salads, too, as a complete meal in themselves . . . the perfect answer for summer luncheons in the country when served with hot garlic bread and followed by a mammoth tray of cheeses and a cooling sweet. **Duck and orange salad** is a delicious example – tender nuggets of duck and orange segments and celery set in a bed of lettuce with spheres of jewel-bright black olives; or **Italian cauliflower salad** with a tangy anchovy dressing. Such salads are a boon to the host or hostess, for much of the preliminary preparation of meats, vegetables or poultry can be done the day before. Of course, tired lettuce or an indiscriminate sprinkling of left-over meat and vegetables is guaranteed to take the heart out of any salad. So make your salads with the best and freshest ingredients only . . . and with a watchful eye for colour, taste and texture contrast.

Asparagus, that most delicate of spring vegetables, I like thoroughly washed or scraped (they can be gritty), then simply steamed with the smallest amount of water and served hot with melted butter or Hollandaise sauce, or *à la polonaise*. I think asparagus is important in its own right and should be served separately as a hot or cold *hors-d'oeuvre*, or as a separate vegetable course.

And who can deny that a fresh, green salad is the very essence of spring? I like mine made of baby lettuces straight from the garden with the added peppery piquancy of watercress or *roquette*, bathed in an olive oil and wine vinegar dressing, with a hint of shallot and the merest breath of garlic to accent its delicate flavour. Later in the year, a little basil or *eau-de-Cologne* mint will add its touch to the harmony of the dish.

To Prepare Vegetables

Remove coarse or damaged leaves and decayed or discoloured parts from all vegetables before cooking. When freshly gathered, they should be washed just before cooking, but when bought commercially, it is often necessary to soak them in water for a short time in order to restore some of their original freshness.

Always soak close-leaved green vegetables such as cabbage, cauliflower and Brussels sprouts in water with a little lemon juice or vinegar for about 30 minutes before cooking to remove insects.

Select vegetables that are crisp, fresh-looking and colourful. No amount of cooking and attention will revive a limp, tired vegetable. It has lost its texture, a great deal of its flavour, and most of its goodness.

Do not peel vegetables unless absolutely necessary; most of the goodness is right under the skin or in the skin itself. Wash vegetables with a stiff vegetable brush or, in the case of mushrooms, tomatoes and very new potatoes, just wipe clean with a damp cloth.

Store cleaned vegetables in plastic bags or boxes in the refrigerator to keep them crisp and fresh until ready to be used. Parsley and other herbs will keep green and fresh in this way for weeks.

To Cook Vegetables

Both French and Chinese cuisines treat vegetables with the reverence they deserve, cooking them in a little butter or oil, with just enough water, stock, wine or even steam to bring out their delicate flavours and textures.

The Chinese, particularly, are masters of the art of vegetable cookery. Serve your vegetables slightly crisp as they do, and not reduced to a pulpy, colourless mass. And follow their method of cutting vegetables across the grain into small uniform pieces, so that they will cook evenly and quickly when simmered in liquid or 'stir-fried' in vegetable oil.

Steaming

The old-fashioned method of boiling vegetables in a pot full of water and then throwing the water away has much to condemn it; so many of the valuable vitamins and trace elements are lost in the water. I far prefer to steam vegetables to obtain the utmost flavour. The younger and more delicately flavoured vegetables can be cooked in this way in 15 minutes; older vegetables and more heartily flavoured vegetables can also be steamed if they are first blanched.

'Waterless' Cooking

I like to use heavy, shallow pans with tight-fitting lids for almost waterless cooking, with just a little chicken stock or water, and a little butter or olive oil to add lustre and savour. When served hot with fresh butter, freshly ground black pepper and salt, or with a lemon- or mustard-flavoured sauce, you have a dish fit for the gods.

Braising

Another very good way of cooking vegetables to preserve maximum flavour is to braise them in a shallow ovenproof casserole.

To Serve Vegetables

I have never been interested in the vegetable primarily as an accompaniment to meat or fish. Except in rare instances, potatoes or rice or noodles can do that with great ease. So take a page from the notebooks of the best French chefs, and serve vegetables as a separate course after the main course. This will allow guests to savour the flavour of meat, game or fish more fully, and permit you to add another texture and flavour surprise in your separate vegetable course.

One of the best vegetable salads in the world is chilled *haricots verts à la vinaigrette*: beans cooked in very little water with a little butter or olive oil until just tender, not mushy and overcooked, then drained and dressed with a vinaigrette dressing to which you have added finely chopped garlic and parsley. Try this, too, with broccoli or small Brussels sprouts. Delicious.

For interesting vegetable accompaniments to meat, try leeks or endive braised in oil and butter with a clove or two of garlic and a sprig of thyme; tomatoes or mushroom caps stuffed with a Provençal mixture of fresh breadcrumbs, finely chopped garlic and parsley; sliced mushrooms simmered for a moment only in butter and lemon juice with a hint of rosemary or thyme; or a noble **gratin dauphinois**, thinly sliced new potatoes cooked in cream with freshly grated Parmesan and Gruyère cheese.

Always serve vegetables as soon as possible after cooking; many lose flavour and texture if kept warm over any period of time.

Keep a vegetable juice jar for any liquid left over after cooking your vegetables. Strain the liquid into a special jar kept covered in the refrigerator for this purpose. Vegetable juices preserved in this way make wonderful flavour additives for soups, sauces and stews.

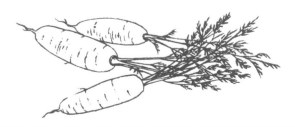

Salads

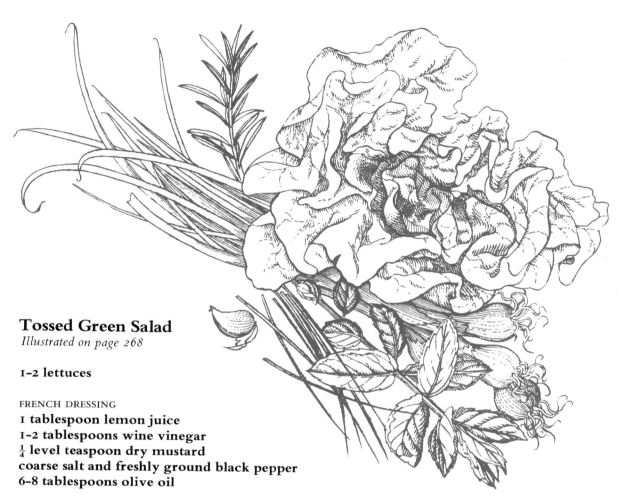

Tossed Green Salad

Illustrated on page 268

1–2 lettuces

FRENCH DRESSING
1 tablespoon lemon juice
1–2 tablespoons wine vinegar
$\frac{1}{4}$ level teaspoon dry mustard
coarse salt and freshly ground black pepper
6–8 tablespoons olive oil

1. Wash lettuce leaves well in a large quantity of water. They should be left whole, never cut. Drain well and dry thoroughly in a cloth or a salad basket so that there is no water on them to dilute the dressing.

2. To make French Dressing: mix together lemon juice, wine vinegar and dry mustard, and season to taste with coarse salt and freshly ground black pepper. Add olive oil, and beat with a fork until the mixture emulsifies.

3. To serve: pour French dressing into salad bowl, arrange prepared lettuce leaves on top. Then at the table, give a final toss to the ingredients to ensure that every leaf is glistening with dressing. Check seasoning and serve.

Green Salad Variations

1. Add other salad greens in season – Cos lettuce, endive, chicory, batavia, young spinach leaves, watercress and French *mâche* (Lamb's lettuce).

2. Add finely chopped garlic or shallots, or a combination of the two, to salad dressing.

3. Add fresh green herbs – finely chopped chervil, basil, tarragon, chives or *eau-de-Cologne* mint – to the dressing.

4. For crunch appeal, add diced celery, green pepper or fennel.

Tossed Green Salad with Avocado and Bacon
Tossed Green Salad with 'Turned' Potatoes
Tossed Green Salad with Poached Carrot and Turnip
    Sticks

264

Tossed Green Salad with Avocado and Bacon

1-2 lettuces
1 bunch watercress
1 clove garlic
4 level tablespoons chopped chives or green
    onions
olive oil
wine vinegar
salt and freshly ground black pepper
1 avocado pear, peeled and sliced
lemon juice
2 rashers cooked bacon, chopped

1. Wash and prepare lettuce and watercress. Shake dry in a salad basket, or dry each leaf carefully in a clean tea towel. Wrap in tea towel and allow to crisp in refrigerator until ready to use.

2. Rub wooden salad bowl with cut clove of garlic. Arrange lettuce and watercress in bowl. Chop garlic and chives finely; sprinkle over the salad and dress with an olive oil and wine vinegar dressing (3 to 4 parts oil to 1 part vinegar), and season to taste with salt and freshly ground black pepper.

3. Garnish with wedges of avocado, which you have marinated in lemon juice to prevent it from going brown, and chopped bacon. Just before serving, toss salad until each leaf is glistening.

Tossed Green Salad with 'Turned' Potatoes

1-2 lettuces
1 bunch watercress
1-2 cloves garlic
4 level tablespoons chopped chives or green
    onions
olive oil
wine vinegar
salt and freshly ground black pepper
450 g/1 lb potatoes
French Dressing (see Tossed Green Salad,
    page 263)

1. Wash and prepare lettuce and watercress.

Shake dry in a salad basket, or dry carefully in a clean tea towel. Wrap in tea towel and allow to crisp in refrigerator until ready to use.

2. Rub wooden salad bowl with cut clove of garlic. Arrange lettuce and watercress in bowl. Chop garlic and chives finely; sprinkle over the salad and dress with an olive oil and wine vinegar dressing (3 to 4 parts oil to 1 part vinegar), and season to taste with salt and freshly ground black pepper.

3. **To prepare 'turned' potatoes:** peel potatoes and cut into small 'olive' shapes with a cutter or a sharp knife. Boil 'turned' potatoes in salted boiling water until just tender. Drain and cool.

4. Toss potatoes in a well-flavoured French dressing. Add to salad and toss well.

Tossed Green Salad with Poached Carrot and Turnip Sticks

1-2 lettuces
1 bunch watercress
1-2 cloves garlic
4 level tablespoons chopped chives or
    green onions
olive oil
wine vinegar
salt and freshly ground black pepper
225 g/8 oz carrots
100 g/4 oz turnips
French Dressing (see Tossed Green Salad,
    page 263)

Prepare the green salad as in Steps 1. and 2. of Tossed Green Salad with 'Turned' Potatoes (above).

3. Peel carrots and turnips and cut into 5-mm/¼-inch slices, lengthwise. Cut each slice into 'sticks' 5 mm/¼ inch thick.

4. Poach carrot and turnip sticks in boiling salted water until just tender. Drain and cool.

5. Toss in a mustard-flavoured French dressing. Add to salad and toss well.

Vinaigrette Sauce with variations

Garden Vegetables

Caesar's Salad with Mushrooms (see page 272)
Salade Niçoise (see page 269)
Tossed Green Salad (see page 263)

Tossed Green Salad with Soured Cream Dressing

1–2 lettuces
choice of salad greens:
    endive, young spinach, watercress,
    chicory, dandelion, mâche (Lamb's
    lettuce), etc.
1 clove garlic, finely chopped
1 level teaspoon each finely chopped fresh
    basil, marjoram, chervil and chives

SOURED CREAM DRESSING
150 ml/¼ pint soured cream
2 tablespoons tarragon vinegar
¼ level teaspoon dry mustard
¼ level teaspoon sugar
salt and freshly ground black pepper

1. Wash and prepare lettuce and salad greens of your choice. Shake dry in a salad basket, or dry each leaf carefully in a clean tea towel. Wrap in tea towel and allow to crisp in refrigerator until ready to use.

2. To make Soured Cream Dressing: whip soured cream until smooth with tarragon vinegar, dry mustard, sugar and salt and freshly ground black pepper.

3. Arrange lettuce and salad greens in bowl. Sprinkle finely chopped garlic and herbs over salad and dress with soured cream dressing.

Tossed Green Salad with Mushrooms and Chives

2 lettuces
6 mushrooms
juice of ½ lemon
olive oil
wine vinegar
coarse salt and freshly ground black pepper
1 clove garlic, finely chopped
2–3 level tablespoons chopped chives

1. Wash and prepare lettuce. Shake dry in a salad basket, or dry each leaf carefully in a clean tea towel. Wrap in tea towel and allow to crisp in the refrigerator until ready to use.

2. Arrange lettuce leaves in bowl.

3. Wash mushrooms; trim stems and slice thinly. Toss in equal quantities of lemon juice and olive oil, to preserve colour.

4. Make a well-flavoured French dressing (using 3 to 4 parts olive oil to 1 part wine vinegar) and season to taste with coarse salt and freshly ground black pepper. Stir in chopped garlic and chives and pour over salad.

5. Add sliced mushrooms and toss salad until each leaf is glistening.

Salade Niçoise I
Illustrated opposite

4 tomatoes, seeded and quartered
½ Spanish onion, sliced
1 sweet green pepper, sliced
8 radishes
2 hearts of lettuce, cut into segments
4 sticks celery, sliced
1 (198-g/7-oz) can tuna fish, drained
8 anchovy fillets
2–3 hard-boiled eggs, quartered
black olives

SALAD DRESSING
2 tablespoons wine vinegar or lemon juice
6 tablespoons pure olive oil
salt and freshly ground black pepper
12 leaves fresh basil, coarsely chopped

1. Combine prepared vegetables in a salad bowl, placing neatly on top the tuna fish, anchovy fillets and quartered eggs. Garnish with black olives.

2. Mix salad dressing of wine vinegar, olive oil, seasoning and coarsely chopped fresh basil, and sprinkle over the salad.

270

Salade Niçoise II

1 lettuce
225 g/8 oz crisply-cooked green beans
150 ml/$\frac{1}{4}$ pint well-flavoured French
    Dressing (see Tossed Green Salad, page
    263)
3 medium-sized potatoes, cooked, peeled
    and sliced
1 (198-g/7-oz) can tuna fish, drained
3 hard-boiled eggs, shelled and quartered
3 large tomatoes, cut into quarters
6 black olives
6 anchovy fillets, drained and cut into small
    pieces
juice of 1 lemon
salt and freshly ground black pepper
150 ml/$\frac{1}{4}$ pint Mayonnaise (see page 417)

1. Wash lettuce and shake dry.

2. Arrange lettuce leaves in the centre of a large round platter or shallow salad bowl.

3. Cut cooked green beans into 2.5-cm/1-inch segments and toss in well-flavoured French dressing. Drain. Then toss sliced cooked potatoes in French dressing.

4. Arrange cooked green beans and sliced potatoes in alternate mounds around lettuce-lined dish. Break tuna fish into bite-sized pieces and pile in middle of salad. Garnish salad with egg and tomato slices. Sprinkle with black olives and anchovy fillets.

5. Mix lemon juice with mayonnaise and season generously with salt and freshly ground black pepper. Serve dressing separately.

Lettuce Hearts 'La Napoule'

2 small tight lettuces

'LA NAPOULE' DRESSING
6-8 tablespoons olive oil
2-3 tablespoons wine vinegar
$\frac{1}{2}$ level teaspoon paprika
150 ml/$\frac{1}{4}$ pint double cream
salt and freshly ground black pepper

GARNISH
2 hard-boiled eggs
2 level tablespoons finely chopped parsley

1. Wash and trim lettuce and cut hearts into quarters. Drain well, wrap in a clean tea towel and pat dry. Gather up the edges and corners of the

towel, and shake out any remaining moisture. Chill in the refrigerator until crisp.

2. To make 'La Napoule' Dressing: combine olive oil, wine vinegar, paprika and double cream, season to taste with salt and freshly ground black pepper, and whisk until creamy and thick.

3. To prepare garnish: separate yolks from whites of hard-boiled eggs and rub yolks and whites separately through a wire sieve. Chop parsley.

4. To serve: place 2 quarters of lettuce on each salad plate. Mask each quarter of lettuce with dressing and garnish a third of each portion with sieved egg white, a third with sieved egg yolks, and the remaining third with finely chopped parsley.

Chilled Watercress Salad

2 bunches watercress
2 oranges

CURRY DRESSING
6–8 tablespoons olive oil
2 tablespoons wine vinegar
1 tablespoon lemon juice
1 level tablespoon curry powder
salt and freshly ground black pepper
1 level teaspoon finely chopped shallots

1. Prepare watercress; chill in a damp tea towel. Peel oranges, cut into thin segments, and chill.

2. To make Curry Dressing: combine olive oil, wine vinegar, lemon juice and curry powder. Season to taste with salt and freshly ground black pepper. Chill.

3. Just before serving, place watercress in a salad bowl, arrange orange segments on top, add finely chopped shallots to Curry Dressing and pour over salad. Toss at table so that each leaf is glistening.

Watercress and Tomato Salad

271

2 bunches watercress
4–6 ripe tomatoes, peeled, seeded and diced
½ cucumber, peeled, seeded and diced
4 sticks celery, sliced
salt and freshly ground black pepper
French Dressing (see Tossed Green Salad, page 263)
1 clove garlic, finely chopped (optional)

1. Wash and pick over the watercress, drain well and wrap in a tea towel. Chill.

2. Make French dressing and flavour with a finely chopped clove of garlic if desired.

3. When ready to serve, turn out into a large salad bowl. Arrange prepared tomatoes, cucumber and celery in centre, season to taste with salt and freshly ground black pepper, and toss with French dressing.

Raw Spinach Salad

450 g/1 lb raw spinach leaves
6–8 tablespoons olive oil
2–3 tablespoons wine vinegar
1 clove garlic, finely chopped
1–2 level tablespoons finely chopped parsley
salt and freshly ground black pepper
dry mustard
2 hard-boiled eggs, cut in quarters
1 ripe avocado pear, peeled and sliced
1 small onion, thinly sliced

1. Wash spinach several times in cold water (spinach should be young and tender). Cut off stems, drain and chill until ready to use.

2. Make a dressing with olive oil, wine vinegar and finely chopped garlic and parsley, and add salt, freshly ground black pepper and dry mustard, to taste.

3. Arrange spinach leaves in a salad bowl. Pour dressing over them; toss salad well and garnish with quartered hard-boiled eggs, sliced avocado and onion rings.

Wilted Lettuce and Bacon Salad *Serves 4 to 6*
Caesar's Salad with Mushrooms *Serves 4 to 6*
Danish Cucumber Salad *Serves 6*
Cucumber and Nasturtium Leaf Salad *Serves 4 to 6*

272

Wilted Lettuce and Bacon Salad

1-2 lettuces
4 rashers bacon
2 tablespoons olive oil
2 tablespoons wine vinegar
salt and freshly ground black pepper
1 level teaspoon sugar
2 level tablespoons chopped green onions

1. Prepare lettuce.

2. Cook the bacon in olive oil in a frying pan until crisp and brown. Remove bacon and chop finely.

3. Stir wine vinegar into the hot fat. Add salt, freshly ground black pepper and sugar. Mix well.

4. Place lettuce leaves in salad bowl. Pour over warm bacon fat and vinegar dressing. Toss well. Sprinkle with crumbled bacon and chopped green onions.

Caesar's Salad with Mushrooms
Illustrated on page 268

1 Cos lettuce
6-8 tablespoons olive oil
2 tablespoons wine vinegar
6 level tablespoons finely grated Parmesan
   cheese
1-2 fat cloves garlic, mashed
salt and freshly ground black pepper
lemon juice
6 button mushrooms, sliced
2 slices bread, diced
2 level tablespoons butter
2 raw egg yolks
6 anchovy fillets

1. Prepare Cos lettuce; wash and drain.

2. Combine olive oil, wine vinegar, grated cheese and garlic in a large salad bowl and season to taste with salt, freshly ground black pepper and lemon juice. Add sliced mushrooms and toss.

3. Sauté diced bread in butter with a little garlic.

4. Add torn lettuce to salad bowl, and toss lightly. Then add egg yolks and toss salad until every leaf glistens. Top off with garlic-flavoured fried bread *croûtons* and anchovy fillets.

Danish Cucumber Salad

2 cucumbers
1 level tablespoon salt
water and wine vinegar
2 level tablespoons sugar
white pepper
2 level tablespoons finely chopped parsley

1. Peel and slice cucumbers very finely. Sprinkle with salt and place under a weight in a glass bowl for at least 1 hour. Wash well. Drain and dry thoroughly with a clean tea towel.

2. Combine water and wine vinegar, to taste; add sugar and white pepper and pour over cucumber slices. Leave salad in the refrigerator for 1 hour.

3. Just before serving, sprinkle with finely chopped parsley. Serve with grilled or fried meat, fish or chicken.

Cucumber and Nasturtium Leaf Salad

1 cucumber
36 small nasturtium leaves
1 level teaspoon Dijon mustard
2 tablespoons wine vinegar
6 tablespoons olive oil
salt and freshly ground black pepper
2 level tablespoons finely chopped fresh
   tarragon
6 nasturtium flowers (optional)

1. Peel and slice cucumber thinly. Wash nasturtium leaves, remove stems and drain.

2. Combine mustard and vinegar in a bowl and stir until well blended. Add olive oil, salt and freshly ground black pepper to taste, and blend well. Stir in tarragon.

3. When ready to serve, combine cucumber and nasturtium leaves in a salad bowl. Add dressing and toss well. Garnish with nasturtium flowers, if desired.

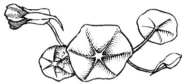

Raw Vegetable Salad with Green Dressing

12 **baby carrots**
12 **baby turnips**
12 **baby beets**
6 **tablespoons well-flavoured French Dressing (see Tossed Green Salad, page 263)**
lettuce leaves (1 lettuce)
12 **radishes**

GREEN DRESSING
150 **ml/¼ pint soured cream**
4 **level tablespoons sliced green onions**
lemon juice
salt and freshly ground black pepper
green food colouring

1. Wash fresh new vegetables from your garden: carrots, turnips and beets. Do not peel. Put them through the finest blade of your *mouli-légumes* to make long thin threads. Do beets last as they tend to stain other vegetables. Toss each vegetable separately in 2 tablespoons French dressing.

2. Wash and dry lettuce leaves. Arrange them around a large, shallow bowl. Pile each vegetable separately in centre of bowl, according to colour. Place washed and sliced radishes in centre. Serve with Green Dressing.

3. To make Green Dressing: combine soured cream with sliced green onions and a little lemon juice, salt and freshly ground black pepper, to taste. Whisk until smooth. Add a few drops green food colouring.

French Celery Appetiser Salad

2 **heads celery**
1 **chicken stock cube**
1 **level tablespoon salt**

VINAIGRETTE SAUCE
coarse salt and freshly ground black pepper
2 **tablespoons wine vinegar**
6–8 **tablespoons olive oil**
½ **level teaspoon paprika**
cayenne
150 **ml/¼ pint double cream**

GARNISH
4 **hard-boiled eggs**
4 **level tablespoons finely chopped parsley**

1. Trim heads of celery, cutting off top third and outside sticks. Cut each head in half and put in a saucepan with trimmings, chicken stock cube and salt. Cover with cold water and bring slowly to the boil. Simmer for 10 minutes. Remove from heat and leave in stock for 5 minutes. Drain and cool.

2. To make Vinaigrette Sauce: add coarse salt and freshly ground black pepper to wine vinegar, to taste. Stir the mixture well. Add olive oil and beat with a fork until the mixture thickens.

3. Arrange blanched celery halves in a flat dish. Spoon over half the vinaigrette sauce and allow celery to marinate in this mixture for at least 1 hour.

4. Combine remaining vinaigrette sauce with paprika, a pinch of cayenne and double cream. Mix well.

5. To prepare the garnish: separate yolks from whites of eggs, and rub each separately through a wire sieve.

6. To serve: place celery halves on a serving dish and cover with Vinaigrette Sauce. Garnish one-third of each celery half with sieved egg white, one-third with sieved egg yolk, and remaining third with finely chopped parsley. Serve immediately.

274

Tomato Salad with Basil

4 large tomatoes
salt and freshly ground black pepper
8 level tablespoons finely chopped echalote
rose, or finely chopped onion or spring
onions
4 level tablespoons finely chopped basil
leaves
4 level tablespoons finely chopped tarragon
leaves
4 level tablespoons finely chopped parsley
olive oil
wine vinegar
Dijon mustard

1. Wash tomatoes and cut in half horizontally. Arrange tomato halves, cut side up, on a serving dish and season generously with salt and freshly ground black pepper.

2. Sprinkle each tomato half with finely chopped *echalote rose* (or finely chopped onion or spring onions). Mix fresh herbs together and sprinkle each tomato half with a thick green layer of chopped herbs.

3. Make a well-flavoured French dressing (3 parts olive oil to 1 part wine vinegar, Dijon mustard and salt and freshly ground black pepper, to taste). Dribble 2 to 3 tablespoons dressing over each tomato half.

Tomato Salad with Mustard and Herb Dressing

4-6 large tomatoes
lemon juice
salt and freshly ground black pepper
1 bunch watercress

MUSTARD AND HERB DRESSING
2 tablespoons wine vinegar
1 level teaspoon dry mustard
1 small clove garlic, finely chopped
2 level tablespoons chopped chives
2 level tablespoons chopped parsley
2 level tablespoons chopped tarragon
6-8 tablespoons olive oil
salt and freshly ground black pepper

1. Wash tomatoes and cut into quarters. Place them in a bowl with lemon juice, salt and freshly ground black pepper, to taste. Wash and trim watercress.

2. To make Mustard and Herb Dressing: combine wine vinegar and mustard in a small bowl. Add finely chopped garlic and fresh herbs. Beat in olive oil and season to taste with salt and freshly ground black pepper. At the last moment, whisk an ice cube in dressing for a second or two to thicken emulsion. Remove cube.

3. To assemble salad: drain tomatoes and arrange in a shallow salad bowl. Garnish with watercress and pour over Mustard and Herb Dressing.

Celeriac Salad with Mustard Dressing

2 celery roots (celeriac)
salt

MUSTARD DRESSING
6–8 level tablespoons double cream
2 tablespoons olive oil
2–3 tablespoons lemon juice
1 level tablespoon finely chopped onion
dry mustard
salt and freshly ground black pepper

1. Cook celeriac in boiling salted water until tender. Cool. Peel and cut into thin strips.

2. To make Mustard Dressing: combine cream, olive oil, lemon juice and finely chopped onion, and dry mustard, salt and freshly ground black pepper, to taste. Blend well.

3. Marinate celeriac in Mustard Dressing overnight in the refrigerator.

Fresh Asparagus Salad

24 sticks fresh asparagus, cooked
150 ml/¼ pint well-flavoured French
    Dressing (see Tossed Green Salad, page
    263)
salt and freshly ground black pepper
1 lettuce
1 bunch watercress, or 6 Cos or escarole
    leaves
6–12 thin strips canned pimento
3 hard-boiled eggs, sliced in half

1. Cut cooked asparagus into 5-cm/2-inch lengths. Toss in half the French dressing; season generously with salt and freshly ground black pepper and chill until ready to serve.

2. When ready to serve: arrange lettuce leaves around the edges of a large flat serving dish or shallow salad bowl. Garnish with sprigs of watercress, or Cos or *escarole* leaves. Place marinated asparagus segments in the centre of the dish and garnish dish with thin strips of pimento and hard-boiled egg halves. Sprinkle salad with remaining French dressing and serve immediately.

Italian Cauliflower Salad

1 cauliflower
salt

ITALIAN DRESSING
4 anchovy fillets, finely chopped
150 ml/¼ pint olive oil
juice of 1 lemon
salt and freshly ground black pepper

1. Remove green leaves from cauliflower, trim stem and cut out any bruised spots. Break or cut into flowerets and poach in lightly salted water for about 5 minutes. Drain and place in a bowl of cold salted water until ready to use. Drain well.

2. To make Italian Dressing: mix finely chopped anchovy fillets with olive oil and lemon juice and season to taste with salt and freshly ground black pepper.

3. When ready to serve, mix flowerets thoroughly with Italian Dressing.

Courgette Salad

12 courgettes
salt
French Dressing (see Tossed Green Salad,
    page 263)
finely chopped parsley, chervil or tarragon

1. Cut unpeeled courgettes into thick slices or quarters and blanch in boiling salted water for 6 to 8 minutes. Drain well and chill.

2. Just before serving, place courgettes in a salad bowl, add a well-flavoured French dressing and sprinkle lightly with finely chopped parsley, chervil or tarragon.

St Tropez Salad 'Aux Frottes d'Ail' *Serves 4 to 6*
Austrian Potato Salad *Serves 4*
Potato Salad with Bacon and Frankfurters
Serves 4 to 6

276

St. Tropez Salad 'Aux Frottes d'Ail'

8 thin slices French bread
2-4 cloves garlic
coarse salt
olive oil
8 anchovy fillets
wine vinegar
Dijon mustard
salt and freshly ground black pepper
I curly endive
4 hard-boiled eggs, cut in halves
black olives

1. Slice French bread into thin rounds. Dry in oven and then rub each with garlic. Sprinkle with coarse salt and olive oil, using about 4 tablespoons olive oil. Place I anchovy fillet· on each round.

2. Make a mustard-flavoured French dressing (6 to 8 tablespoons olive oil, 2 to 3 tablespoons wine vinegar, ½ to 1 level teaspoon Dijon mustard, finely chopped garlic and salt and freshly ground black pepper, to taste). Add prepared curly endive and toss until each leaf glistens with dressing.

3. Garnish salad with garlic rubbed bread and halved hard-boiled eggs. Sprinkle with black olives.

Austrian Potato Salad

1-1½ kg/2-3 lb new potatoes
salt
4-6 slices ham, diced
chopped gherkins
150 ml/¼ pint double cream
4 level tablespoons Mayonnaise (see
    page 417)

1. Scrub new potatoes. Cook in boiling salted water until just tender – 15 to 20 minutes. Drain, peel and slice. Place potatoes in a bowl, add diced ham and chopped gherkins.

2. Combine double cream and mayonnaise. Pour over potatoes and toss gently.

Potato Salad with Bacon and Frankfurters

1-1½ kg/2-3 lb new potatoes
salt
I level tablespoon sugar
2 tablespoons wine vinegar
4-6 rashers bacon
olive oil
4 cooked frankfurters, thinly sliced
lemon juice
2-4 level tablespoons finely chopped onion
2-4 level tablespoons finely chopped parsley
salt and cayenne

1. Scrub new potatoes. Cook in boiling salted water until just tender – 15 to 20 minutes. Drain, peel and slice.

2. Place potatoes in a bowl and sprinkle with sugar and wine vinegar. Toss gently.

3. Sauté bacon in a little oil until crisp. Drain well, pouring bacon fat over potatoes. Crumble or chop bacon finely and add to potatoes. Add sliced frankfurters and toss gently.

4. Combine 6 tablespoons olive oil with lemon juice, to taste, and finely chopped onion and parsley. Season to taste with salt and cayenne. Pour over salad. Toss well. Correct seasoning, adding more olive oil, lemon juice, salt or cayenne, if desired.

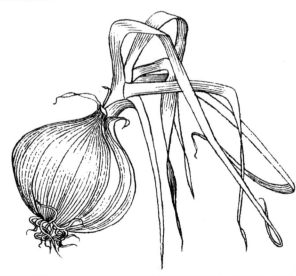

Hot Cauliflower Mousse (see page 29)

Salades Composées

Prawn and Corn Chowder (see page 92)

Minestre Verde (see page 91)

Vegetable Antipasto (see page 23)

Cooked Vegetable Salad I

6 medium-sized carrots, cooked
4 new potatoes, cooked
225 g/8 oz green beans, cooked
1 (113-g/4-oz) packet frozen peas, cooked
salt and freshly ground black pepper
2 level tablespoons finely chopped onion
2 level tablespoons finely chopped parsley
150 ml/¼ pint French Dressing (see Tossed
   Green Salad, page 263)
lettuce leaves (1 lettuce)
1 bunch watercress, or 6 Cos leaves
   (optional)
2 tomatoes, cut into wedges

1. Slice carrots. Peel and slice new potatoes. Cut cooked green beans into 2½-cm/1-inch segments. Combine these vegetables in a bowl with peas.

2. Season generously with salt and freshly ground black pepper. Add finely chopped onion and parsley and half the French dressing and toss well. Refrigerate until ready to serve.

3. **When ready to serve:** arrange lettuce leaves around the edges of a large flat serving dish or shallow salad bowl. Garnish with sprigs of watercress or dark Cos leaves. Mound vegetable salad in the centre of leaves and garnish with tomato wedges. Sprinkle salad with remaining French dressing and serve immediately.

Cooked Vegetable Salad II

281

6 large carrots
3 young turnips
3 large new potatoes
salt
225 g/8 oz string beans
½ cauliflower
6 tablespoons cooked peas
2 level tablespoons finely chopped parsley
150 ml/¼ pint French Dressing (see Tossed
   Green Salad, page 263)

1. Scoop balls from raw carrots, turnips and potatoes with a potato scoop (or cut into cubes), and cook them in boiling salted water until tender but still firm – about 5 or 6 minutes. Drain and cool.

2. Cut string beans into 2.5-cm/1-inch lengths and cook as above until tender but still firm. Drain and cool.

3. Break cauliflower into flowerets and cook as above until tender but still firm. Drain and cool.

4. Combine cooked vegetables and toss with French dressing. Sprinkle with finely chopped parsley.

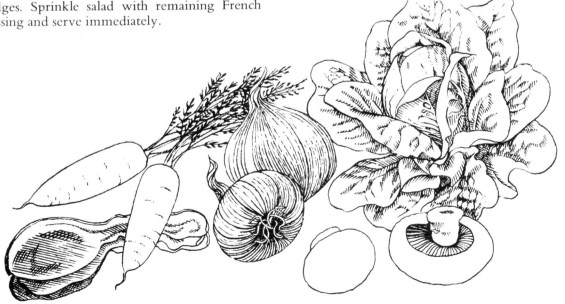

Main Course or Luncheon Salads

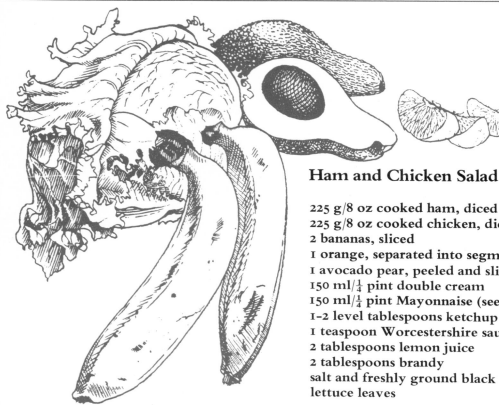

Julienne Salad

1-2 lettuces
225 g/8 oz smoked ox tongue
225 g/8 oz cooked ham
225 g/8 oz Swiss cheese
3 hard-boiled eggs, cut in quarters
6 tomatoes, cut in wedges
1 bunch watercress
French Dressing (see Tossed Green Salad,
    page 263)

1. Wash and dry lettuces carefully, leaf by leaf. Chop coarsely and arrange in the bottom of a large salad bowl.

2. Cut tongue, ham and cheese into thin strips and arrange according to colour on bed of lettuce with hard-boiled eggs and raw tomatoes.

3. Place a cluster of prepared watercress in centre of salad and serve with a well-flavoured French dressing.

Ham and Chicken Salad

225 g/8 oz cooked ham, diced
225 g/8 oz cooked chicken, diced
2 bananas, sliced
1 orange, separated into segments
1 avocado pear, peeled and sliced
150 ml/$\frac{1}{4}$ pint double cream
150 ml/$\frac{1}{4}$ pint Mayonnaise (see page 417)
1-2 level tablespoons ketchup
1 teaspoon Worcestershire sauce
2 tablespoons lemon juice
2 tablespoons brandy
salt and freshly ground black pepper
lettuce leaves

1. Combine diced cooked ham and chicken with sliced bananas, orange and avocado segments in a mixing bowl.

2. Whip the cream and blend in mayonnaise. Add ketchup, Worcestershire sauce, lemon juice and brandy, and pour over meat and fruit mixture. Season to taste with salt and freshly ground black pepper, and mix carefully. Serve on lettuce leaves.

Ham and Apple Salad

1 slice ham, 1 cm/$\frac{1}{2}$ inch thick
175 g/6 oz Danish Blue cheese
3 red eating apples
juice of 1 lemon
French Dressing (see Tossed Green Salad,
    page 263)
lettuce
chopped green pepper and parsley

1. Cut ham into 1-cm/$\frac{1}{2}$-inch squares. Roll cheese into small balls. Dice apples, leaving peel on, and dip in lemon juice to preserve their colour. Toss apples and ham in a well-flavoured French dressing.

2. Line a dish with lettuce leaves, and fill with cheese balls, ham and apple. Sprinkle with chopped green pepper and garnish with parsley. Serve with additional French dressing.

Cheese Salad

225 g/8 oz Gruyère cheese, diced
1 small green pepper, finely chopped
12 black olives, sliced
4 level tablespoons double cream
salt and freshly ground black pepper
2 bunches watercress
olive oil
lemon juice or wine vinegar

1. Combine diced Gruyère, finely chopped pepper, sliced olives and cream. Season to taste with salt and freshly ground black pepper. Toss well and allow to marinate for at least 1 hour.

2. To serve: toss prepared watercress in a dressing of 3 parts olive oil to 1 part lemon juice or wine vinegar. Place cheese salad mixture in centre. Serve immediately.

Autumn Salad

150 ml/¼ pint Mayonnaise (see page 417)
150 ml/¼ pint soured cream
1 level teaspoon Dijon mustard
salt and freshly ground black pepper
100 g/4 oz Swiss cheese, cut into thin strips
100 g/4 oz cooked ham, cut into thin strips
2 tart apples, cored and thinly sliced
lemon juice
lettuce leaves

1. Blend mayonnaise, soured cream and Dijon mustard and season with salt and freshly ground black pepper, to taste.

2. Combine cheese, ham and apple in a bowl. Pour over lemon juice and toss. Then add Soured

Cream Mayonnaise dressing and mix all together gently.

283

3. Serve on a bed of fresh lettuce.

Cucumber Salad Ring Mould

CUCUMBER RING MOULD
3 cucumbers
½ medium-sized onion
juice of 2 lemons
2 level teaspoons salt
freshly ground black pepper
2 level tablespoons gelatine
150 ml/¼ pint cold water
450 ml/¾ pint chicken stock
2 level teaspoons parsley
1 level teaspoon chopped tarragon
curly endive
well-flavoured French Dressing (see Tossed Green Salad, page 263)

GARNISH
12 black olives
3 ripe tomatoes, quartered
2 tablespoons finely chopped parsley or chervil

1. Remove peel from cucumbers and grate cucumber finely. Grate onion, strain lemon juice and mix together. Season with salt and freshly ground black pepper.

2. Soften gelatine in cold water. After about 5 minutes, pour in boiling stock and stir until dissolved. Cool; mix with cucumber mixture, and add finely chopped parsley and tarragon. Pour into a large ring mould or two smaller moulds. Chill until firm.

3. When ready to serve: turn out cucumber ring on a serving dish and fill centre with curly endive. Pour well-flavoured French dressing over salad. Garnish dish with olives and tomatoes and sprinkle with finely chopped parsley or chervil.

Note: The centre of the cucumber ring may also be filled with Mayonnaise of Chicken (see page 284) or Tuna Waldorf Salad (see page 289).

284

Mayonnaise of Chicken

6 level tablespoons stiff Mayonnaise
   (see page 417)
lemon juice
salt, celery salt and freshly ground black
   pepper
1 lettuce, finely shredded
3 hard-boiled eggs, finely chopped
350 g/12 oz cooked chicken, diced
4 sticks celery, diced
100 g/4 oz tuna fish, diced

1. Thin mayonnaise with lemon juice and season
to taste with salt, celery salt and freshly ground
black pepper.

2. Combine mayonnaise with shredded lettuce,
finely chopped hard-boiled eggs, diced chicken,
celery and tuna fish. Mix well. Add more lemon
juice, mayonnaise and seasoning if desired.

Truffled Turkey Salad

8-10 level tablespoons stiff Mayonnaise (see
   page 417)
lemon juice
1 small can black truffles
salt, celery salt and freshly ground black
   pepper
1 lettuce, finely shredded
4 hard-boiled eggs, finely chopped
675 g/1½ lb cooked turkey, diced
4 sticks celery, thinly sliced
4 tablespoons olive oil

1. Thin mayonnaise with lemon juice and the
juice from a small can of black truffles and season
to taste with salt, celery salt and freshly ground
black pepper.

2. Add 2 tablespoons finely sliced black truffles to
mayonnaise, then combine with shredded lettuce,
finely chopped eggs, diced turkey and sliced
celery. Add olive oil and mix well. Add more
lemon juice, mayonnaise and seasoning if desired.

Duck and Fresh Fruit Salad

675 g/1½ lb cold roast duck, cut into 'fingers'
2 oranges, peeled and cut into segments
2 thick slices fresh pineapple, peeled and cut
   into segments
8 peeled segments grapefruit
Soured Cream Mayonnaise (see Autumn
   Salad, page 283)
salt and freshly ground black pepper
crisp lettuce leaves
12 black olives
2 level tablespoons finely chopped chives,
   parsley or tarragon

1. Combine diced duck with segments of orange,
pineapple and grapefruit. Add enough Soured
Cream Mayonnaise to coat pieces lightly. Season
with salt and freshly ground black pepper.

2. Arrange lettuce leaves around a shallow salad
bowl. Pile duck and fruit mixture in centre of
dish. Garnish with black olives and a sprinkling of
finely chopped fresh herbs.

Duck and Orange Salad

diced meat of 1 roasted duck
4 shallots, finely chopped
2 sticks celery, sliced
olive oil and wine vinegar
salt and freshly ground black pepper
rosemary
4 small oranges, peeled and segmented
lettuce
8-10 black olives

1. Combine diced duck, finely chopped shallots
and sliced celery with a dressing made of 3 parts
olive oil to 1 part wine vinegar. Season to taste
with salt, freshly ground black pepper and rosemary. Toss well. Allow duck to marinate in this
mixture for at least 2 hours.

2. Just before serving, add orange segments, toss
again, adding more dressing if required.

3. Line a glass salad bowl with lettuce leaves. Fill
with salad and garnish with black olives.

Swedish Buffet Salad

1 kg/2 lb cold poached halibut
4 tart eating apples
2 level tablespoons butter
2 tablespoons cider
150 ml/¼ pint soured cream
2 level tablespoons grated horseradish
1 level tablespoon prepared mustard
2 tablespoons lemon juice
salt and freshly ground black pepper
2 hard-boiled eggs, finely chopped
sprigs of fresh watercress

1. Carefully flake poached halibut.

2. Peel, core and slice apples thinly.

3. Combine butter and cider in a frying pan and sauté apple slices until soft, stirring constantly.

4. Force apples and pan juices through a fine sieve and add soured cream, grated horseradish, prepared mustard and lemon juice.

5. Beat mixture until light and foamy, adding a little more cider if necessary, and toss flaked fish gently in this dressing. Season to taste with salt and freshly ground black pepper, and arrange salad in a glass serving bowl. Decorate with finely chopped hard-boiled egg and sprigs of fresh watercress.

Cold Lamb Salad

about 450 g/1 lb cold roast lamb
¼ Spanish onion, finely chopped
2 sticks celery, sliced
olive oil
tarragon vinegar
salt and freshly ground black pepper
1 level teaspoon finely chopped fresh
  tarragon
finely chopped parsley

1. Slice lamb thinly and then cut into thin strips.

2. Combine lamb with finely chopped onion and sliced celery in a salad bowl. Pour over a well-flavoured dressing made with olive oil and tarra-

gon vinegar and season to taste with salt and freshly ground black pepper.

3. Just before serving, sprinkle with finely chopped tarragon and parsley.

French Bean and Prawn Salad

450 g/1 lb haricots verts
well-flavoured French Dressing (see Tossed
  Green Salad, page 263)
225 g/8 oz Norwegian prawns
2 level tablespoons finely chopped onion
lemon juice
cayenne
lettuce leaves
olive oil
salt and freshly ground black pepper
2 level tablespoons chopped parsley
2 level tablespoons chopped chives
1 small clove garlic, finely chopped

1. Top and tail young green beans and cook them in boiling salted water until they are barely tender. Drain and toss immediately while still warm in a well-flavoured French dressing. Chill.

2. Defrost prawns in a small bowl. Drain, add finely chopped onion, lemon juice and cayenne, to taste, and toss well. Chill.

3. When ready to serve: drain prawns and beans from their respective marinades. Combine in a shallow salad bowl, garnish with lettuce leaves and add olive oil, lemon juice and salt and freshly ground black pepper, to taste. Sprinkle with chopped parsley and chives and finely chopped garlic.

286

Champagne Prawn Bowl

450 g/1 lb cooked small new potatoes
225 g/8 oz cooked prawns, shelled
French Dressing (see Tossed Green Salad,
  page 263)
2 hard-boiled eggs, sliced
lettuce leaves
2 level tablespoons finely chopped fennel or
  tarragon

MARINADE
8 black olives, stoned and sliced
¼ bottle dry champagne
2 shallots, finely chopped
2 level tablespoons finely chopped parsley
1 clove garlic, finely chopped
salt and freshly ground black pepper

1. Peel and slice new potatoes. Add shelled cooked prawns with first 5 marinade ingredients and season with salt and freshly ground black pepper. Chill and marinate overnight.

2. **One hour before serving:** drain off juices and dress salad with a well-flavoured French dressing.

3. Line a salad bowl with lettuce leaves. Arrange tossed salad ingredients in the centre; top with sliced hard-boiled eggs and chopped fennel or tarragon and serve immediately.

Salade Emile

4 tomatoes
1 large green pepper
4 sticks celery, thinly sliced
2 hard-boiled eggs, quartered
16 anchovy fillets
1 (198-g/7-oz) can tuna fish
green and black olives
mustard-flavoured French Dressing (see
  Tossed Green Salad, page 263)
1 level tablespoon each finely chopped
  chives, chervil, parsley and tarragon

1. Peel tomatoes and cut into quarters. Seed pepper and slice very thinly. Combine tomatoes and pepper with sliced celery and quartered hard-boiled eggs.

2. Garnish salad with anchovies, tuna fish and green and black olives and pour over a mustard-flavoured French dressing to which you have added finely chopped chives, chervil, parsley and tarragon.

Fruit Salads

Roquefort Pear Salad *Serves 4*
Fruit Salad with Mint Dressing *Serves 4*
Pear Waldorf Salad *Serves 4 to 6*
Greek Orange and Olive Salad *Serves 4*

Roquefort Pear Salad

4 ripe pears
juice of 1 lemon
100 g/4 oz Roquefort cheese
150 ml/¼ pint double cream
1 tablespoon cognac
paprika
Cos lettuce leaves
French Dressing (see Tossed Green Salad,
  page 263)
halved walnuts

1. Peel and core pears. Cut into 5-mm/¼-inch slices. Marinate in lemon juice to keep from browning.

2. Combine Roquefort cheese, cream and cognac and mash to a smooth paste. Add lemon juice (from pears) and paprika, to taste.

3. Sandwich cheese mixture between pear slices. Place on a bed of Cos lettuce leaves and dress with French dressing. Garnish with halved walnuts.

Fruit Salad with Mint Dressing

1 grapefruit
2 oranges
2 apples
2 pears
1 small bunch grapes

MINT DRESSING
2 level tablespoons finely chopped mint
  leaves
1 level tablespoon finely chopped chives
150 ml/¼ pint well-flavoured French
  Dressing (see Tossed Green Salad,
  page 263)
sugar

1. Peel and dice grapefruit and oranges.

2. Core and dice apples and pears, but do not peel.

3. Halve and seed grapes.

4. To make Mint Dressing: add finely chopped mint and chives to well-flavoured French dressing. Sweeten to taste with a little sugar. Chill in refrigerator for at least 1 hour before using.

5. Combine fruits and toss with Mint Dressing.

Pear Waldorf Salad

6 ripe pears
juice of 1 lemon
6 sticks celery, sliced
50 g/2 oz halved walnuts
Mayonnaise (see page 417) or French
  Dressing (see Tossed Green Salad,
  page 263)
1 lettuce

1. Halve and core pears. Cut into cubes and sprinkle with lemon juice.

2. Add sliced celery and walnut halves.

3. Toss together in mayonnaise or French dressing according to taste, and pile into a salad bowl lined with lettuce leaves.

Greek Orange and Olive Salad

3-4 ripe oranges
10-12 large black olives
1-2 level tablespoons finely chopped onion
150 ml/¼ pint well-flavoured French
  Dressing (see Tossed Green Salad,
  page 263)
salt and freshly ground black pepper

1. Peel and thinly slice oranges crosswise. Cut slices into quarters.

2. Stone and slice olives.

3. Combine orange quarters and olives in a salad bowl with finely chopped onion and French dressing. Season with salt and freshly ground black pepper, and toss before serving.

288

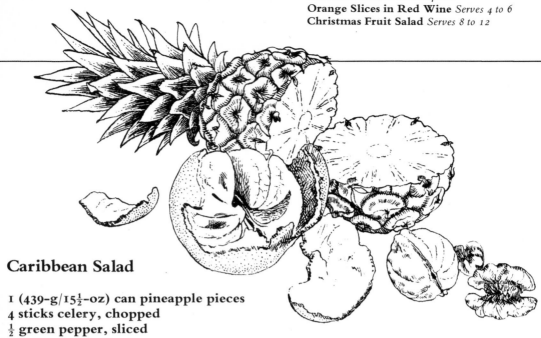

Caribbean Salad

1 (439-g/15½-oz) can pineapple pieces
4 sticks celery, chopped
½ green pepper, sliced
½ red pepper, sliced
4-6 level tablespoons coarsely chopped
   walnuts
4-6 level tablespoons well-flavoured
   Mayonnaise (see page 417)
lemon juice
lettuce

I. Drain pineapple pieces, reserving juice, and combine with celery, peppers, walnuts and mayonnaise.

2. Moisten salad with lemon juice and reserved pineapple juice, to taste.

3. Arrange some lettuce leaves on individual salad plates and mound Caribbean Salad in the centre.

Orange Slices in Red Wine

225 g/8 oz sugar
150 ml/¼ pint water
red Burgundy
1 clove
cinnamon
orange peel
lemon peel
4 large navel oranges

I. Make a syrup of sugar and water. Combine with 150 ml/¼ pint red Burgundy, clove, cinnamon and 2 strips each of orange and lemon peel. Boil until syrupy and reduced. Add another 2 tablespoons red Burgundy.

2. Peel oranges. Divide into segments and remove all membrane and pith.

3. Place orange segments in warm syrup and chill in refrigerator. Serve with slivers of fresh orange peel.

Christmas Fruit Salad

1-2 lettuces
1 bunch watercress
1-2 cloves garlic, finely chopped
2 level tablespoons finely chopped chives (or
   parsley)
olive oil
wine vinegar
coarse salt and freshly ground black pepper
4 slices pineapple, cut in thin wedges
2 oranges, peeled and cut in thin segments

I. Wash and prepare lettuce and watercress. Shake dry in a salad basket, or dry carefully in a clean tea towel.

2. Arrange lettuces and watercress in bowl. Combine finely chopped garlic and chives (or parsley). Sprinkle over the salad and dress with an olive oil and wine vinegar dressing (3 to 4 parts oil to 1 part vinegar). Season to taste with coarse salt and freshly ground black pepper.

3. Just before serving, toss salad until each leaf is glistening and garnish with pineapple wedges and orange segments.

Apple Coleslaw

350 g/12 oz crisp white cabbage, shredded
1 (226-g/8-oz) can pineapple cubes
2 tart eating apples, cored and sliced
2 sticks celery, finely sliced
150 ml/¼ pint Mayonnaise (see page 417)
lettuce

GARNISH
8 black olives, stoned
8 walnuts, coarsely chopped
parsley
1 tart eating apple, cored, sliced and dipped
  in lemon juice to preserve colour

1. Crisp cabbage in cold water for 30 minutes. Dry.

2. Combine crisped cabbage, drained pineapple chunks, sliced apples and celery with mayonnaise, tossing well until mayonnaise coats all ingredients.

3. Line salad bowl with lettuce leaves, pile salad in the centre and serve garnished with black olives, walnuts, parsley and sliced apple.

My Coleslaw

350 g/12 oz white cabbage, finely shredded
1 Spanish onion
2 red apples
1-2 tablespoons capers
1 dill-pickled cucumber, sliced thinly
well-flavoured French Dressing (see Tossed
  Green Salad, page 263)

1. Crisp cabbage in cold water for at least 30 minutes. Drain well and roll in a clean tea towel to dry.

2. Slice onion finely and separate into rings; core apples and cut into thin wedges.

3. Combine onion rings, apple wedges, drained cabbage, capers and pickled cucumber and toss with well-flavoured French dressing.

Waldorf Salad

2 eating apples, diced
lemon juice
4 sticks celery, sliced
6 level tablespoons broken walnuts
salt and freshly ground black pepper
Mayonnaise (see page 417)
soured cream
watercress

1. Sprinkle diced apples with lemon juice to preserve colour. Add sliced celery and broken walnuts. Season with salt and freshly ground black pepper, to taste.

2. Toss together in 4 to 6 level tablespoons each of mayonnaise and soured cream and pile into a salad bowl lined with watercress.

Tuna Waldorf Salad

2 (198-g/7-oz) cans tuna fish, drained
4-6 sticks celery, sliced
6-8 level tablespoons broken walnuts
Mayonnaise (see page 417)
lemon juice
salt and freshly ground black pepper
cayenne
3 tart apples, cored but unpeeled
crisp lettuce leaves

1. Break tuna into bite-sized pieces. Combine with celery, walnuts and enough mayonnaise to hold ingredients together. Season with lemon juice, salt, freshly ground black pepper and cayenne, to taste.

2. Cut apples into small cubes; toss them in lemon juice to preserve colour and stir into tuna mixture. Serve in crisp lettuce leaves to form cups.

Cooked Vegetables

290

Basic Boiled Green Beans

450 g/1 lb green beans
salt and freshly ground black pepper
butter
2 level tablespoons finely chopped parsley

1. Cook beans in boiling salted water until tender – about 20 minutes.

2. Drain. Place in a heated serving dish. Season to taste with salt and freshly ground black pepper. Toss, sprinkle with lemon juice, to taste, and top with a piece of butter and finely chopped parsley.

Basic Steamed Green Beans

450 g/1 lb green beans
2 level tablespoons finely chopped shallots
   or spring onions
butter
lemon juice
salt and freshly ground black pepper

1. Place whole beans in a shallow *gratin* dish or bowl with finely chopped shallots or spring onions and 2 level tablespoons butter, and steam over boiling water in a tightly closed saucepan or double steamer until tender – 15 to 20 minutes.

2. Season to taste with lemon juice, salt and freshly ground black pepper. Toss, and top with a piece of butter.

Haricots Verts au Gratin

675 g/1½ lb thin haricots verts
salt
butter
450 ml/¾ pint double cream
freshly ground black pepper
4-6 level tablespoons freshly grated Gruyère
   cheese
2-4 level tablespoons freshly grated
   Parmesan cheese

1. Poach beans in salted water for 20 minutes, or until almost tender. Drain.

2. Place in a well-buttered *gratin* dish and cover with cream. Season to taste with salt and freshly ground black pepper, and place in a hot oven (230°C, 450°F, Gas Mark 8) for 20 minutes.

3. Sprinkle with freshly grated cheeses, dot with butter and return to the oven until the cheese is golden brown and bubbling.

Italian Green Beans

6 tablespoons chicken stock
2 tablespoons olive oil
4 canned Italian peeled tomatoes, diced
450 g/1 lb fresh green beans
salt and freshly ground black pepper
pinch of dried oregano (optional)
2 level tablespoons finely chopped parsley

1. Combine chicken stock, olive oil and diced tomatoes in a saucepan, and bring to the boil.

2. Add prepared green beans, season to taste with salt and freshly ground black pepper, and a pinch of oregano if desired. Cover saucepan and simmer gently for 1 hour.

3. Remove cover and continue to simmer until excess moisture has evaporated and beans are tender. Sprinkle with finely chopped parsley and serve.

Italian Green Beans with Ham

1 kg/2 lb green beans
salt
100 g/4 oz prosciutto (Parma ham)
2-4 level tablespoons butter
freshly ground black pepper
2 level tablespoons finely chopped parsley
1-2 cloves garlic, finely chopped

1. Top and tail beans and cook in boiling salted water until tender. The beans should remain firm. Drain.

2. Cut ham into thin strips. Melt butter in a frying pan and sauté ham for 2 to 3 minutes.

Add the drained beans and salt and freshly ground black pepper. Heat through.

3. Garnish with a sprinkling of finely chopped parsley and garlic and serve immediately.

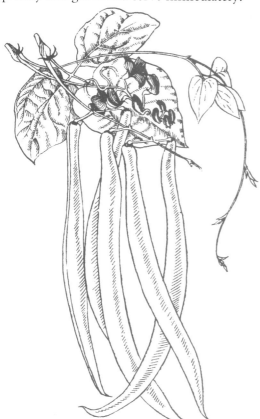

Green Beans à la Grecque

450 g/1 lb green beans
1 (64-g/2¼-oz) can tomato purée
600 ml/1 pint water
4-6 tablespoons olive oil
½ Spanish onion, finely chopped
½ clove garlic, finely chopped
salt and freshly ground black pepper

1. Top and tail green beans, and slice them in half lengthwise.

2. Mix tomato purée with water, olive oil, and finely chopped onion and garlic.

3. Put beans in a saucepan; pour over tomato-

onion mixture, and season to taste with salt and freshly ground black pepper. Bring to the boil. Lower heat and simmer gently, stirring from time to time, for 45 minutes or until sauce has reduced and beans are tender.

French Green Beans with Almonds

1 kg/2 lb green beans
salt
2-4 level tablespoons butter
50 g/2 oz almonds, blanched and shredded
1 clove garlic, finely chopped
freshly ground black pepper

1. Top and tail beans and cook in boiling salted water until tender but still firm. Drain.

2. Melt butter in a frying pan and sauté almonds until golden. Add finely chopped garlic and cook for a second or two more.

3. Toss cooked beans with almonds and garlic until heated through. Season with salt and freshly ground black pepper, to taste; serve immediately.

Creole Green Beans

1 kg/2 lb green beans
salt
2 level tablespoons finely chopped onion
2 level tablespoons finely chopped green pepper
4 level tablespoons butter
4 level tablespoons tomato ketchup
4 tablespoons vinegar
1 level tablespoon prepared mustard
1 level tablespoon curry powder
freshly ground black pepper

1. Top and tail beans and cook in boiling salted water until tender but still firm. Drain.

2. Sauté finely chopped onion and green pepper in butter until onion is transparent. Add all the remaining ingredients except cooked beans and simmer for 5 minutes. Add beans and cook over a low heat until beans are well flavoured.

292

Chinese Green Beans

450 g/1 lb green beans
2 tablespoons peanut oil or lard
1 level teaspoon salt
150 ml/¼ pint water
1 tablespoon soy sauce, sake or dry sherry

1. Wash and trim beans. Break them into sections about 2.5 cm/1 inch long.

2. Heat oil or lard in a *wok* or frying pan. Add beans and cook over medium heat for 1 minute, stirring constantly.

3. Add salt and water, cover pan and cook beans for 3 minutes. Remove cover and simmer, stirring from time to time, until all the water has evaporated – about 5 minutes. Add soy sauce, *sake* or dry sherry, to taste, and serve.

Purée of Green Beans

450 g/1 lb green beans
salt
4 level tablespoons double cream
freshly ground black pepper
freshly grated nutmeg

Use an electric blender for a particularly smooth purée. You can bind the purée with a little butter instead of cream, or it is excellent cold, mixed with a little well-flavoured mayonnaise.

1. Trim beans, wash them and drain well.

2. Bring a pan of water to the boil. When it

begins to bubble, add a generous pinch of salt and the beans. Boil briskly for 30 minutes, or until very tender. Drain thoroughly.

3. Purée beans through a fine sieve and return to the pan. Reheat over a moderate heat, beating vigorously with a wooden spoon to evaporate excess moisture.

4. Add cream, mix well and season to taste with salt, freshly ground black pepper and a pinch of freshly grated nutmeg.

5. Spoon into a heated serving dish and serve immediately.

Soufflé of Green Beans

450 g/1 lb green beans
salt
butter
2 level tablespoons flour
300 ml/½ pint hot milk
freshly ground black pepper
4–6 level tablespoons grated Parmesan
    cheese
2 eggs, separated

1. Cook beans in boiling salted water until tender – about 20 minutes. Drain.

2. Place 2 level tablespoons butter in the top of a double saucepan and melt it over water. Stir in flour until smooth, add hot milk and cook over a low heat, stirring constantly, for 10 minutes. Season to taste with salt and freshly ground black pepper. Remove from heat and stir in cheese and egg yolks.

3. Sauté drained beans in frying pan with 2 tablespoons butter for about 3 minutes. Put through fine sieve, or blend in electric blender, and stir purée into sauce. Beat egg whites with a little salt until stiff. Fold into mixture.

4. Spoon into a well-buttered baking dish (or soufflé dish) and bake in a moderate oven (180°C, 350°F, Gas Mark 4) for 30 to 35 minutes. Serve immediately as a vegetable.

Frijoles – Mexican Fried Beans

450 g/1 lb red beans
salt
6 level tablespoons lard

1. Soak beans overnight.

2. Drain. Add water to cover, season to taste with salt, and cook slowly until very tender.

3. Drain the beans and mash them. Add very hot lard, and continue cooking, stirring from time to time, until fat is absorbed by the beans. Do not let fried beans scorch.

Note: the famous *frijoles refritos*, Mexican refried beans, are made by heating fat in frying pan, adding mashed fried beans, and cooking, stirring continuously, until beans are completely dry.

Kidney Beans in Red Wine

293

450 g/1 lb red kidney beans
1 Spanish onion
salt
butter
1 level tablespoon flour
1 bouquet garni (2 sprigs parsley, 2 sprigs thyme, 1 stalk celery, 1 bay leaf)
freshly ground black pepper
225 g/8 oz fat bacon, diced
150–300 ml/$\frac{1}{4}$–$\frac{1}{2}$ pint red wine

1. Place kidney beans in a large saucepan. Fill pan with water and bring gently to the boil. Then let beans soak off the heat for 1 hour.

2. Drain. Simmer with onion in salted water in a large casserole until beans are almost cooked through – 45 to 60 minutes. Beans should remain fairly firm, otherwise they will break in subsequent cooking. Drain beans, reserving liquid, and remove onion.

3. Mix 1 tablespoon butter and flour to a smooth paste. Combine drained beans with butter and flour in a saucepan. Add 150 ml/$\frac{1}{4}$ pint bean liquor, *bouquet garni*, and salt and freshly ground black pepper, to taste. Simmer, stirring gently from time to time, for about 10 minutes, or until beans have absorbed flavour, adding more liquor if necessary.

4. Sauté diced bacon until golden. Add to beans with red wine, and simmer gently until sauce is smooth and rich – about 30 minutes. Remove *bouquet garni*. Serve immediately.

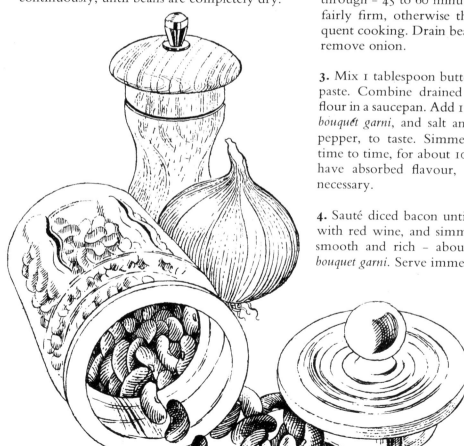

Sautéed Bean Sprouts with Green Pepper *Serves 4*
Sautéed Bean Sprouts and Green Pepper with
  Chinese Pork or Duck *Serves 2 to 3 as a main dish*
Harvard Beets *Serves 4 to 6*
Orange Beetroot *Serves 4*

294

Bean Sprouts

Bean Sprouts – *tou ya ts'ai* in Chinese, *moyashi* in Japanese – grown from mung or soy beans, are sold fresh or canned in Chinese supermarkets. Fresh bean sprouts should be rinsed in a large bowl of cold water and carefully picked over to remove any sprouts that are discoloured or bruised. Chinese cooks always remove heads and tails of sprouts before using. Use bean sprouts the day they are bought for best results or keep for two or three days in the refrigerator in a plastic bag. Canned bean sprouts should be drained and rinsed before using.

Sautéed Bean Sprouts with Green Pepper

450 g/1 lb bean sprouts
1 green pepper
4 tablespoons peanut oil
$\frac{1}{2}$ level teaspoon sugar
2 tablespoons sake, dry white wine or dry
  sherry
1 tablespoon light soy sauce

1. Remove heads and tails of bean sprouts and soak sprouts in cold water. Drain.

2. Wash green pepper; remove stem and seeds and cut into threadlike lengths the same size as bean sprouts.

3. Heat oil in a Chinese *wok,* or frying pan, and sauté shredded green pepper for 2 minutes. Add sugar and drained bean sprouts and continue to cook, tossing vegetables continuously, for a minute or two more. Then add *sake* (or dry white wine or dry sherry) and soy sauce.

Sautéed Bean Sprouts and Green Pepper with Chinese Pork or Duck

Cut 175 g/6 oz cooked pork or duck into thin strips the size of the bean sprouts. Sauté meat in a little peanut oil until golden. Flavour with a hint of *sake* and light soy sauce and toss with bean sprouts and green pepper cooked as above.

Harvard Beets

1 (361-g/12$\frac{3}{4}$-oz) jar baby beetroot
1 level tablespoon cornflour
3 tablespoons vinegar or lemon juice
2 level tablespoons sugar
salt and freshly ground black pepper
2 level tablespoons softened butter

1. Drain beetroot, reserving juice, and cut into even slices.

2. Mix cornflour with 150 ml/$\frac{1}{4}$ pint reserved beet juice. Add vinegar (or lemon juice), sugar, and salt and freshly ground black pepper, to taste. Cook until thickened, stirring constantly.

3. Add sliced beetroot. Warm through.

4. Just before serving, add softened butter and simmer until it has melted. Correct seasoning, adding more vinegar (or lemon juice), sugar or salt, as needed.

Orange Beetroot

1 large cooked beetroot
1 level teaspoon grated orange rind
150 ml/$\frac{1}{4}$ pint orange juice
2 tablespoons lemon juice
2 level tablespoons sugar
1 level tablespoon cornflour
2 level tablespoons butter
salt

1. Peel and dice beetroot.

2. Heat orange rind with orange and lemon juice.

3. Mix sugar and cornflour, and stir into hot liquid. Cook, stirring constantly, until thickened. Add diced beetroot and butter. Season to taste with salt, and heat through.

Basic Boiled Broccoli *Serves 4 to 6*
Broccoli Towers *Serves 6*
Broccoli with Cheese Sauce and Slivered Almonds
Serves 4 to 6

295

Basic Boiled Broccoli

675–900 g/1½–2 lb fresh broccoli
salt
4 tablespoons olive oil or melted butter
lemon juice
freshly ground black pepper

1. Wash broccoli in cold water. Discard coarse leaves and tough lower parts of the stems. Soak prepared broccoli in salted water for 30 minutes. Drain.

2. Half fill a saucepan with water, add salt, to taste, and bring to the boil. Lower broccoli gently into boiling water, keeping flowerets out of the water. Cover saucepan and cook broccoli for about 15 minutes, or until barely tender.

3. Drain the broccoli, transfer to a heated serving dish, sprinkle with olive oil (or melted butter) and lemon juice. Season with salt and freshly ground black pepper and serve immediately.

Broccoli Towers

1 (283-g/10-oz) packet frozen broccoli
4–6 level tablespoons butter
150 ml/¼ pint chicken stock
salt
2 eggs
butter
6–8 level tablespoons grated cheese
freshly ground black pepper

1. Defrost broccoli. Slice thickly and place in a saucepan. Cover with cold water and cook over a high heat until water boils. Drain.

2. Simmer blanched broccoli in butter, chicken stock and salt, to taste, until broccoli has absorbed the liquid without burning and is quite tender.

3. Mash broccoli mixture and mix well with 2 eggs, 4 tablespoons softened butter, cheese, and salt and freshly ground black pepper, to taste. Press into 6 well-buttered dariole moulds. Place moulds in a roasting tin and add enough boiling water to come half-way up moulds. Heat in a moderate oven (180°C, 350°F, Gas Mark 4) for 20 minutes.

4. When ready to serve, turn broccoli moulds out on a heated serving dish. (If desired, surround with sautéed button mushrooms.)

Broccoli with Cheese Sauce and Slivered Almonds

Illustrated on page 319

450–675 g/1–1½ lb fresh or frozen broccoli
spears
salt

CHEESE SAUCE
75 g/3 oz butter
2 level teaspoons Dijon mustard
75 g/3 oz flour
900 ml/1½ pints milk
225 g/8 oz grated Emmenthal cheese
salt and white pepper

GARNISH
50 g/2 oz almonds, blanched, slivered, fried
in oil and seasoned

1. Cook the broccoli spears in boiling salted water until tender. Drain.

2. To make cheese sauce: melt the butter in a saucepan over a high heat, then stir in the mustard and flour. Add the milk gradually, stirring continuously. Lower the heat and cook, stirring, until the sauce comes to the boil. Boil the sauce for 2 minutes, then remove from the heat, stir in the grated cheese, and season to taste with salt and white pepper. Return to heat and let sauce simmer until thick and smooth.

3. Pour the cheese sauce over the broccoli spears. Sprinkle with slivered almonds. The dish may be lightly browned under the grill if desired.

296

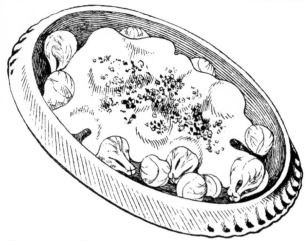

Brussels Sprouts au Gratin

450 g/1 lb small Brussels sprouts
salt
freshly ground black pepper
butter
600 ml/1 pint well-flavoured Cheese Sauce
(see Broccoli with Cheese Sauce and
Slivered Almonds, page 295)
4 walnuts, finely chopped
2 level tablespoons fresh breadcrumbs

1. To prepare Brussels sprouts: cut off stem
ends and remove any wilted or damaged outside
leaves. (If Brussels sprouts are older, remove
tough outside leaves entirely.) Soak sprouts in
cold water with a little salt or lemon juice for 15
minutes.

2. To cook Brussels sprouts: add to boiling
salted water and simmer uncovered for 5 minutes.
Cover pan and continue to cook for 7 (if very
young) to 15 minutes, or until just tender. Drain
well and season generously with salt and freshly
ground black pepper.

3. Place hot, seasoned sprouts in a well-buttered
ovenproof dish. Pour over well-flavoured cheese
sauce.

4. Melt 5 tablespoons butter in a small saucepan,
add finely chopped nuts and freshly grated breadcrumbs, simmer for a minute or two, then spoon
over cheese sauce. Bake in a moderately hot oven
(200°C, 400°F, Gas Mark 6) for 10 minutes.

Brussels Sprouts à la Provençale

450–675 g/1–1½ lb Brussels sprouts
salt
1 Spanish onion, finely chopped
2 small cloves garlic, finely chopped
3 tablespoons olive oil
½ level teaspoon chopped thyme
6 tomatoes, peeled and diced
2 level tablespoons finely chopped parsley
freshly ground black pepper
2 level tablespoons fresh breadcrumbs

1. Prepare and cook Brussels sprouts as in recipe
above (Brussels Sprouts in Beer Batter), but for
5 minutes only.

2. Sauté onion and garlic in olive oil with chopped
thyme until vegetables are transparent.

3. Add diced, peeled tomatoes and finely chopped
parsley; season with salt and freshly ground black
pepper.

4. Add cooked Brussels sprouts and breadcrumbs
and simmer for a further 10 minutes, or until
Brussels sprouts are tender.

Still Life of Winter Vegetables

Carrot Ring Mould with Peas and Onions
(see page 303)
Brussels Sprouts à la Polonaise (see page 301)

Leeks Béchamel (see page 310)

Oven-baked Potatoes with Soured Cream and Chive Dressing (see page 324)

Brussels Sprouts à la Polonaise

Illustrated on page 298

450 g/1 lb small Brussels sprouts
salt
freshly ground black pepper
4-6 tablespoons browned butter
grated rind and juice of 1 lemon
4 level tablespoons finely chopped parsley
whites of 2 hard-boiled eggs, finely chopped

1. To prepare Brussels sprouts: cut off stem ends and remove any wilted or damaged outside leaves. (If Brussels sprouts are older, remove tough outside leaves entirely.) Soak sprouts in cold water with a little salt or lemon juice for 15 minutes.

2. To cook Brussels sprouts: add sprouts to boiling salted water and simmer uncovered for 5 minutes. Cover pan and continue to cook for 7 (if very young) to 15 minutes, or until just tender. Drain well and season generously with salt and freshly ground black pepper.

3. Place hot, seasoned sprouts in a heated serving dish, pour browned butter over them, sprinkle to taste with grated lemon rind, finely chopped parsley and egg white, and lemon juice.

Brussels Sprouts with Buttered Breadcrumbs

450 g/1 lb small Brussels sprouts
salt
freshly ground black pepper
4-6 level tablespoons toasted breadcrumbs
½ clove garlic, finely chopped
4 level tablespoons butter
lemon juice

1. To prepare Brussels sprouts: cut off stem ends and remove any wilted or damaged outside leaves. (If Brussels sprouts are older, remove tough outside leaves entirely.) Soak sprouts in cold water with a little salt juice for 15 minutes.

2. To cook Brussels sprouts: add sprouts to boiling salted water and simmer uncovered for 5 minutes. Cover pan and continue to cook for 7 (if very young) to 15 minutes, or until just tender. Drain well and season generously with salt and freshly ground black pepper.

3. Combine hot, seasoned sprouts in a frying pan with toasted breadcrumbs and finely chopped garlic, and sauté in butter until breadcrumbs are golden. Sprinkle with lemon juice, to taste.

Brussels Sprouts in Beer Batter

450-675 g/1-1½ lb Brussels sprouts
salt or lemon juice
oil for deep-frying
1 egg
150 ml/¼ pint beer
100 g/4 oz flour
freshly ground black pepper
French Tomato Sauce (see page 416)

1. To prepare Brussels sprouts: cut off stem ends and remove any wilted or damaged outside leaves. (If Brussels sprouts are older, remove tough outside leaves entirely.) Soak sprouts in cold water with a little salt or lemon juice for 15 minutes.

2. To cook Brussels sprouts: add to boiling salted water and simmer, uncovered, for 7 (if very young) to 15 minutes, or until just tender. Drain.

3. To make Beer Batter: beat egg in a bowl, add beer and beat until smooth. Add flour and 1 level teaspoon salt, and freshly ground black pepper, to taste, and beat until smooth. Allow batter to rest for at least 30 minutes.

4. Heat oil to 190°C/375°F. Dip prepared Brussels sprouts into batter and deep-fry until golden. Drain and serve immediately with French Tomato Sauce.

Red Cabbage *Serves 6 to 8*
Carrots à la Béchamel *Serves 4*
Carrots à l'Orientale *Serves 4*
Carrots aux Fines Herbes *Serves 4*

302

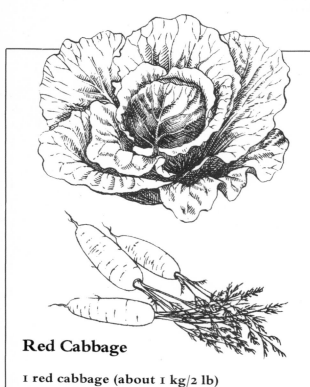

Red Cabbage

1 red cabbage (about 1 kg/2 lb)
2 level tablespoons bacon fat
3 tart red apples, cored and sliced
½ Spanish onion, finely chopped
1 clove garlic, finely chopped
2-4 tablespoons wine vinegar
1 level tablespoon flour
2 level tablespoons brown sugar
1 level teaspoon grated orange rind
salt and freshly ground black pepper
freshly grated nutmeg

1. Wash and shred cabbage, removing central core, ribs and outer leaves. Toss in bacon fat, in a covered saucepan, over a moderate heat for 5 minutes.

2. Add sliced apples and finely chopped onion and garlic, and bring to the boil with just enough water to cover. Cover, reduce heat, and simmer until tender but still crisp – about 15 minutes. Drain, reserving liquid.

3. Combine wine vinegar with flour and brown sugar, and stir in the reserved liquid. Cook, stirring, until thickened.

4. Stir into cabbage, add grated orange rind, and season to taste with salt, freshly ground black pepper and nutmeg.

Carrots à la Béchamel

450 g/1 lb carrots
4 level tablespoons butter
4 tablespoons chicken stock
sugar
salt and freshly ground black pepper
6 level tablespoons Béchamel Sauce (see
   page 412)

1. Wash carrots, slice thickly and place in a saucepan of cold water. Bring to the boil and drain.

2. Simmer carrots for 15 to 20 minutes in butter and chicken stock, with sugar, salt and freshly ground black pepper, to taste.

3. Just before serving, add Béchamel Sauce.

Carrots à l'Orientale

450 g/1 lb carrots
4 level tablespoons butter
4 tablespoons chicken stock
2 level tablespoons pre-soaked raisins
sugar
salt and freshly ground black pepper

1. Wash carrots, slice thickly and place in a saucepan of cold water. Bring to the boil and drain.

2. Simmer carrots for 15 to 20 minutes in butter and chicken stock, with pre-soaked raisins, sugar, salt and freshly ground black pepper, to taste.

Carrots aux Fines Herbes

450 g/1 lb carrots
4 level tablespoons butter
4 tablespoons chicken stock
sugar
salt and freshly ground black pepper
2 level tablespoons each chopped parsley
   and chervil

1. Wash carrots, slice thickly and place in a saucepan of cold water. Bring to the boil and drain.

2. Simmer carrots for 15 to 20 minutes in butter and chicken stock, with sugar, salt and freshly ground black pepper, to taste.

3. Just before serving, sprinkle with chopped parsley and chervil.

Pan-fried Carrots

8 small carrots
1 tablespoon olive oil
2 level tablespoons butter
salt and freshly ground black pepper
2 level tablespoons finely chopped parsley

1. Wash and scrape carrots, trim off ends and shred coarsely.

2. Sauté carrot strips in oil and butter, stirring constantly, until almost tender. Season generously with salt and freshly ground black pepper. Cover pan and cook over a low heat until tender (5 to 8 minutes in all).

3. Sprinkle with finely chopped parsley.

Carrot Ring Mould with Peas and Onions

Illustrated on page 298

1-1½ kg/2-3 lb new carrots
4-6 level tablespoons butter
150 ml/¼ pint chicken stock
1 level tablespoon sugar
salt
2 eggs
butter
6-8 level tablespoons grated cheese
freshly ground black pepper
cooked peas and button onions

1. Wash carrots, slice thickly and place in a saucepan. Cover with cold water and cook over a high heat until water boils. Drain.

2. Simmer blanched carrots in butter, chicken stock and sugar, with salt, to taste, until carrots have absorbed the liquid and are tender.

3. Mash carrot mixture and mix well with eggs, 4 tablespoons softened butter, cheese, and salt and freshly ground black pepper, to taste. Press into a well-buttered ring mould and heat through in a moderate oven (180°C, 350°F, Gas Mark 4) for 15 minutes.

4. Turn carrot ring out on a heated serving dish and fill centre with cooked peas and button onions. Surround with remaining peas and onions.

Carrot Towers

1 kg/2 lb new carrots
4-6 level tablespoons butter
150 ml/¼ pint chicken stock
1 level tablespoon sugar
salt
2 eggs
butter
6-8 level tablespoons grated cheese
freshly ground black pepper

GARNISH
button mushrooms (optional)

1. Wash carrots, slice thickly and place in a saucepan. Cover with cold water and cook over a high heat until water boils. Drain.

2. Simmer blanched carrots in butter, chicken stock and sugar, with salt, to taste, until carrots have absorbed the liquid without burning and are tender.

3. Mash carrot mixture and mix well with 2 eggs, 4 tablespoons softened butter, cheese, and salt and freshly ground black pepper, to taste. Press into 6 well-buttered dariole moulds.

4. Place moulds in a roasting tin and add enough boiling water to come half-way up moulds. Heat in a moderate oven (180°C, 350°F, Gas Mark 4) for 20 minutes.

5. When ready to serve, turn carrot moulds out on to heated serving dish and surround with sautéed button mushrooms (if desired).

304

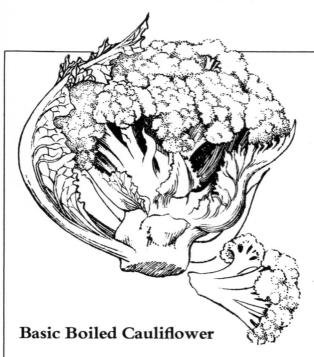

Basic Boiled Cauliflower

1 cauliflower
salt
melted butter
freshly ground black pepper

1. Trim off the base of a cauliflower, taking the remains of the outer leaves with it. Leave the fine, light green leaves intact. Using a potato peeler, hollow out the stem about 5 cm/2 inches deep.

2. Immerse cauliflower, head down, in a bowl of cold salted water.

3. Select a saucepan one size larger than the cauliflower. Pour in 5 cm/2 inches salted water and bring to the boil.

4. Lower cauliflower stem end down into boiling water. Bring back to the boil again before covering pan with a tight fitting lid. An average-sized cauliflower (about 700 g/1½ lb) will be cooked to perfection – tender but with a slight crispness still in evidence – in 15 minutes, but you may prefer it a little softer.

5. Remove cauliflower from pan and drain.

6. To serve: place it on a heated serving dish and pour over melted butter which you have generously seasoned with salt and freshly ground black pepper.

Cauliflower Amandine

1 cauliflower
salt
lemon juice
4 level tablespoons blanched slivered
   almonds
6 level tablespoons butter
freshly ground black pepper

1. To prepare cauliflower: trim stem and remove outer green leaves, wash and leave for 30 minutes in cold salted water to which you have added a little lemon juice.

2. To cook cauliflower: measure enough water to cover cauliflower into a deep saucepan. Add salt, to taste, and bring to the boil. Put cauliflower in the boiling water, bring to the boil again, then lower heat, cover saucepan and simmer gently for about 20 minutes, or until the cauliflower is just tender when pierced at the stem end with a fork. Do not overcook. Drain well.

3. Sauté blanched slivered almonds in butter, pour sauce over hot cauliflower, and season to taste with salt and freshly ground black pepper.

Cauliflower Sauté

1 cauliflower
salt
lemon juice
4 level tablespoons butter
2 level tablespoons finely chopped fresh
   herbs (chives, chervil, parsley)

1. To prepare cauliflower: trim stem and remove outer green leaves, cut into flowerets, wash and leave for 30 minutes in cold salted water to which you have added a little lemon juice.

2. To cook flowerets: measure enough water to cover cauliflowerets into a deep saucepan. Add salt, to taste, and bring to the boil. Put cauliflowerets in the boiling water, bring to the boil again, then lower heat, cover saucepan and simmer gently for about 10 minutes, or until the cauliflowerets are almost tender when pierced at the stem end with a fork. Drain well.

3. Sauté cauliflowerets in butter and lemon juice until tender. Sprinkle with finely chopped fresh herbs and serve immediately.

Cauliflower à la Niçoise

1 cauliflower
salt
1 Spanish onion, finely chopped
1 clove garlic, finely chopped
2 tablespoons olive oil
2 level tablespoons butter
4 tomatoes, peeled and diced
2 level tablespoons finely chopped parsley
freshly ground black pepper
2 level tablespoons breadcrumbs

1. Prepare and cook cauliflower in salted boiling water as in Steps **1.** and **2.** of Cauliflower Sauté (see page 304).

2. Sauté finely chopped onion and garlic until transparent in olive oil and butter. Add diced, peeled tomatoes and finely chopped parsley. Season with salt and freshly ground black pepper. Add cooked cauliflowerets and breadcrumbs and simmer for a further 10 minutes, or until tender.

French Fried Cauliflower

1 cauliflower
1 egg
150 ml/¼ pint milk
100 g/4 oz flour
salt
oil for deep-frying
French Tomato Sauce (see page 416)

1. To make batter: beat egg in a bowl, add milk and beat. Add flour and 1 teaspoon salt and beat until smooth.

2. Prepare and cook cauliflower in salted boiling water as in Steps **1.** and **2.** of Cauliflower Sauté (see page 304).

3. Heat oil to 190°C/375°F.

4. Dip flowerets into batter. Deep fry until golden. Drain and serve immediately with French Tomato Sauce.

Pain de Chou-Fleur

1 whole cauliflower
salt
lemon juice
3 egg yolks, well beaten
softened butter
freshly ground black pepper
freshly grated nutmeg
300 ml/½ pint Hollandaise Sauce (see page 412)

1. To prepare cauliflower: trim stem and remove outer green leaves, wash and leave for 30 minutes in cold salted water to which you have added a little lemon juice.

2. To cook cauliflower: measure enough water to cover cauliflower into a deep saucepan. Add salt to taste, and bring to the boil. Put cauliflower in the boiling water, bring to the boil again, then lower heat, cover saucepan and simmer gently for about 20 minutes, or until the cauliflower is just tender when pierced at the stem end with a fork. Do not overcook. Drain well.

3. Force cauliflower through a fine sieve. Beat in well-beaten egg yolks and 4 tablespoons softened butter, and season to taste with salt, freshly ground black pepper and freshly grated nutmeg.

4. Pour mixture into a well-buttered soufflé dish or charlotte mould, and cook in a pan of hot water in a moderately hot oven (190°C, 375°F, Gas Mark 5) for 25 minutes.

5. Turn out on to a heated serving dish and mask with Hollandaise Sauce.

306

Basic Boiled Chicory

8 heads chicory
300 ml/½ pint salted water
4 level tablespoons butter
juice of ½ lemon
2 level tablespoons finely chopped parsley

1. Trim root ends of chicory and wash well in cold water. Drain.

2. Place chicory in a saucepan with boiling salted water, 2 tablespoons butter and lemon juice, and cook for 20 to 30 minutes, or until tender. Drain thoroughly, reserving juices.

3. To serve chicory: boil reserved pan juices until reduced a little, pour over cooked chicory, sprinkle with finely chopped parsley and top with remaining butter.

Chicory au Gratin

8 heads chicory
salt
juice of 1 lemon
4 thin slices cooked ham
butter
8 level tablespoons freshly grated Parmesan
   cheese
300–450 ml/½–¾ pint well-flavoured
   Béchamel Sauce (see page 412)
4 level tablespoons fresh breadcrumbs

1. Trim root ends of chicory and wash well in cold water. Drain. Place chicory in a saucepan of boiling salted water with lemon juice, and simmer for 30 minutes. Drain well. Press in a clean cloth to remove excess moisture.

2. Roll each head in half a slice of ham and arrange in a well-buttered shallow ovenproof casserole.

3. Mix freshly grated Parmesan into Béchamel Sauce and pour over chicory. Sprinkle with fresh breadcrumbs and 2 tablespoons melted butter, and cook in a moderately hot oven (200°C, 400°F, Gas Mark 6) for 10 to 15 minutes, until golden.

Chicory Soufflé

225 g/8 oz braised chicory
butter
freshly grated Parmesan cheese
2 tablespoons lemon juice
5 egg yolks
2 level tablespoons grated onion
salt and freshly ground black pepper
6 egg whites

1. Pass braised chicory through a sieve and dry it out over a low heat in 1 tablespoon butter, stirring all the time with a wooden spoon to keep it from
   Stir in 50 g/2 oz freshly grated Parmesan and 2 tablespoons lemon juice.

2. Remove from the heat and stir in egg yolks one at a time. Season rather strongly with grated onion, salt and freshly ground black pepper. Beat egg whites until stiff but not dry and fold into soufflé mixture.

3. Butter a soufflé dish, dust with a little grated Parmesan cheese and fill with the mixture. Place in a preheated moderate oven (180°C, 350°F, Gas Mark 4) and bake for 25 to 35 minutes.

Chicory à la Béchamel

8 heads chicory
300 ml/½ pint salted water
4 level tablespoons butter
juice of ½ lemon
300–450 ml/½–¾ pint well-flavoured
   Béchamel Sauce (see page 412)

1. Trim root ends of chicory and wash well in cold water. Drain.

2. Place chicory in a saucepan with boiling salted water, butter and lemon juice, and cook for 20 to 30 minutes, or until tender. Drain thoroughly, reserving juices.

3. Place chicory in a shallow ovenproof baking dish. Add drained pan juices to hot Béchamel Sauce. Pour sauce over chicory and serve immediately.

Chinese Mushrooms *Serves 4*
Chinese Peas with Ham *Serves 4*
Chinese Braised Vegetables *Serves 4*
Chinese Spinach *Serves 4*

307

Chinese Mushrooms

2 tablespoons peanut oil or lard
225 g/8 oz mushrooms
$\frac{1}{2}$ tablespoon salt
150 ml/$\frac{1}{4}$ pint water
1 level teaspoon cornflour

1. Heat oil or lard in a *wok* or frying pan. Add mushrooms and salt and stir over medium heat for 1 minute. Add water, cover pan and simmer for 3 minutes.

2. Remove cover, add cornflour and simmer until thickened. Serve immediately.

Chinese Peas with Ham

450 g/1 lb frozen peas, defrosted
2 level tablespoons finely chopped spring
   onions
4 level tablespoons butter
1 slice of cooked ham, 5 mm/$\frac{1}{4}$ inch thick
soy sauce or lemon juice
salt and freshly ground black pepper

1. Place peas in a shallow *gratin* dish or bowl with finely chopped spring onions and 2 level tablespoons butter, and steam over boiling water in a tightly closed saucepan or double steamer for 15 minutes, or until tender.

2. Cut cooked ham into thin strips and sauté gently in remaining butter.

3. Combine with steamed peas and flavour to taste with soy sauce (or lemon juice), salt and freshly ground black pepper.

Chinese Braised Vegetables
Illustrated on page 318

1 head celery
225 g/8 oz button mushrooms
3 tablespoons peanut oil
$\frac{1}{2}$ level teaspoon salt
$\frac{1}{4}$ level teaspoon monosodium glutamate
   (optional)
1–2 tablespoons soy sauce
1 level teaspoon sugar

1. Cut the celery sticks diagonally into 2.5-cm/1-inch lengths. Wash the mushrooms and trim their stems.

2. Heat the oil in a thick-bottomed frying pan and sauté the celery and mushrooms, stirring frequently. Add the remaining ingredients to the pan and mix well. Continue cooking until the celery is just tender. Serve hot, with the pan juices poured over the top.

Chinese Spinach
Illustrated on page 318

1 kg/2 lb fresh spinach leaves
3 tablespoons peanut oil or lard
1 level teaspoon salt
1 tablespoon soy sauce, sake or dry sherry

1. Wash spinach leaves in several changes of water. Drain and dry thoroughly.

2. Heat oil or lard in a *wok* or frying pan. Add spinach and salt and cook over a medium heat for 3 minutes, stirring constantly. Add soy sauce, *sake* or dry sherry, to taste. Serve immediately.

308

Chinese Courgettes

450 g/1 lb courgettes
2 tablespoons peanut oil or lard
1 level teaspoon salt
150 ml/¼ pint water
1 tablespoon soy sauce
1 tablespoon sake or dry sherry

1. Wash courgettes, cut off ends and slice thinly.

2. Heat oil or lard in a *wok* or frying pan; add courgettes and salt and cook over medium heat for 3 minutes, stirring continuously. Add water, stir in and heat through. Add soy sauce and *sake* or dry sherry, to taste. Serve immediately.

Courgettes with Walnuts

8 walnuts
8 small courgettes
1 tablespoon olive oil
2 level tablespoons butter
salt and freshly ground black pepper

1. Shell walnuts and chop coarsely.

2. Cut unpeeled courgettes in 3-mm/⅛-inch slices. Sauté in oil and butter, stirring constantly, until courgettes are almost tender.

3. Add chopped walnuts and salt and freshly ground black pepper, to taste, and continue to cook over a low heat until done.

New Courgettes Hollandaise

450 g/1 lb courgettes
2 tablespoons peanut oil or lard
salt and freshly ground black pepper
150 ml/¼ pint water
1 tablespoon soy sauce
1 tablespoon dry sherry
300 ml/½ pint Hollandaise Sauce (see page 412)

1. Wash courgettes, cut off ends and slice very thinly.

2. Heat oil or lard in a large, thick-bottomed frying pan; add thinly sliced courgettes, and salt and freshly ground black pepper, to taste, and cook over medium heat for 3 minutes, stirring continuously. Add water and soy sauce and dry sherry, and cook for a few minutes more. Drain.

3. Transfer cooked courgettes to 4 individual flameproof *gratin* dishes. Top with Hollandaise Sauce and place under a preheated grill for a few seconds, watching carefully, until sauce begins to turn golden brown. Serve immediately.

Glazed Sliced Courgettes

12 courgettes
4 level tablespoons butter
4 level tablespoons chicken stock
salt and freshly ground black pepper
sugar
finely chopped parsley

Cut unpeeled courgettes into thin slices. Combine in a shallow saucepan with butter, chicken stock, salt and freshly ground black pepper and sugar, to taste. Simmer gently, covered, until liquid has almost disappeared and courgettes are glazed and tender. Sprinkle with finely chopped parsley and serve immediately.

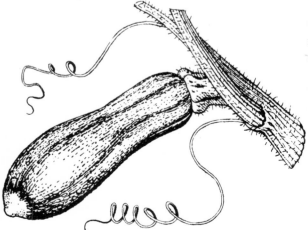

Courgettes in Red Wine *Serves 4*
Stuffed Courgettes à la Provençale *Serves 4*
Courgettes Soufflées *Serves 4*
Mrs Glasse's Stew'd Cucumbers

Courgettes in Red Wine

12 courgettes
100 g/4 oz finely chopped Spanish onion
4 tablespoons olive oil
2 level tablespoons butter
150 ml/¼ pint red wine
salt and freshly ground black pepper
lemon juice and olive oil
finely chopped parsley

1. Cut courgettes into slices 1 cm/½ inch thick and sauté with finely chopped onion in olive oil and butter for 5 minutes, stirring frequently.

2. Add wine, and season to taste with salt and freshly ground black pepper. Simmer for 5 minutes.

3. Just before serving, sprinkle with a little lemon juice, olive oil and finely chopped parsley.

Stuffed Courgettes à la Provençale

12 courgettes (for cases)
salt
olive oil
butter

PROVENÇAL STUFFING
175 g/6 oz minced veal
25 g/1 oz fat salt pork, diced
1 onion, finely chopped
olive oil
1 clove garlic, crushed
minced fresh tarragon
minced fresh parsley
1 egg, beaten
1 tablespoon grated Parmesan cheese
4 tablespoons boiled rice
courgette pulp
salt and freshly ground black pepper

1. Simmer courgettes whole in salted water for about 5 minutes. Cut tops off courgettes, scoop out interiors and keep pulp for stuffing.

2. To make stuffing: sauté meats and onion in olive oil. Mix remaining ingredients in a bowl and add them to the meat and onion mixture, adding salt and freshly ground black pepper, to taste. Sauté for a few minutes, stirring continuously, and then stuff courgettes with the mixture.

3. Place stuffed courgettes in an ovenproof baking dish to which you have added a little olive oil. Place a knob of butter on each courgette and bake in a moderate oven (190°C, 375°F, Gas Mark 5) for 30 minutes.

Courgettes Soufflées

6 courgettes
2–4 level tablespoons butter
salt and freshly ground black pepper
150 ml/¼ pint Béchamel Sauce (see page 412)
2 egg yolks
freshly grated Parmesan cheese
2 egg whites

1. Wash the courgettes and cut them in two lengthwise. Scoop out the flesh, being careful not to pierce the skin. Cook the pulp in butter until it becomes a thick purée. Season generously with salt and freshly ground black pepper.

2. Make a Béchamel Sauce. Remove the sauce from the heat and beat in the egg yolks, one by one. Add the cooked courgette pulp and freshly grated Parmesan. Check seasoning. Beat the egg whites until stiff and fold gently into the mixture.

3. Place the courgette shells in a buttered baking dish. Fill with the soufflé mixture and bake for 25 minutes in a moderate oven (160°C, 325°F, Gas Mark 3). Serve immediately.

Mrs. Glasse's Stew'd Cucumbers

'Pare twelve Cucumbers, and slice them as thick as a Crown piece, and put them to drain, and then lay them in a coarse Cloth till they are dry, flour them and fry them Brown in Butter; pour out the Fat, then put to them some Gravy, a little Claret, some Pepper, Cloves, and Mace, and let them stew a little; then roll a Bit of Butter in Flour, and toss them up seasoned with Salt.'

310

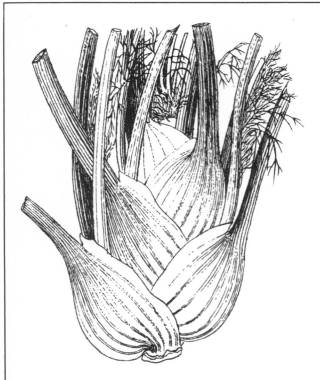

Braised Fennel

4 fennel roots
juice of $\frac{1}{2}$ lemon
2 tablespoons olive oil or butter
150 ml/$\frac{1}{4}$ pint chicken stock
salt and freshly ground black pepper
2 level teaspoons butter
2 level teaspoons flour
finely chopped parsley

1. Wash and trim fennel roots, and cut in half lengthwise.

2. Put fennel roots in an ovenproof dish with lemon juice, olive oil or butter, and stock. Season to taste with salt and freshly ground black pepper, then cover pan and cook slowly until tender – 30 to 40 minutes.

3. Five minutes before you remove vegetables from heat, stir in butter and flour, mixed to a smooth paste.

4. Just before serving, sprinkle with finely chopped parsley.

Basic Boiled Leeks

12 small or 8 large leeks
salted water
2–3 level tablespoons finely chopped parsley
melted butter

1. Trim roots and cut off the tops of leeks, leaving 2.5 cm/1 inch to 7.5 cm/3 inches of the green portion. Halve the leeks, leaving the halves attached at the root end. Wash thoroughly.

2. Simmer leeks in boiling salted water for 20 minutes, or until tender. Drain thoroughly. Sprinkle with finely chopped parsley and serve with melted butter.

Leeks in Butter

12 small or 8 large leeks
100 g/4 oz butter
salt and freshly ground black pepper

1. Trim roots and cut off the tops of leeks, leaving 2.5 cm/1 inch to 7.5 cm/3 inches of the green portion. Halve the leeks, leaving the halves attached at the root end. Wash thoroughly.

2. Simmer leeks in boiling water for 5 minutes. Drain thoroughly.

3. Place leeks in a shallow ovenproof baking dish; add butter, and salt and freshly ground black pepper, to taste, and cook in a moderately hot oven (190°C, 375°F, Gas Mark 5) for 35 to 40 minutes, or until tender.

Leeks Béchamel
Illustrated on page 299

12 small or 8 large leeks
100 g/4 oz butter
salt and freshly ground black pepper
300–450 ml/$\frac{1}{2}$–$\frac{3}{4}$ pint well-flavoured
    Béchamel Sauce (see page 412)

1. Trim roots and cut off the tops of leeks, leaving 2.5 cm/1 inch to 7.5 cm/3 inches of the green portion. Halve the leeks, leaving the halves attached at the root end. Wash thoroughly.

2. Simmer leeks in boiling water for 5 minutes. Drain thoroughly.

3. Place leeks in a shallow ovenproof baking dish; add butter, and salt and freshly ground black pepper, to taste, and cook in a moderately hot oven (190°C, 375°F, Gas Mark 5) for 35 to 40 minutes, or until tender.

4. Drain pan juices and add to well-flavoured Béchamel Sauce. Pour over leeks and serve immediately.

2. Drain lentils and cook with onion in salted water until tender. The length of time for cooking lentils depends on their type and their age. In any case, after 30 minutes look at them from time to time to see if they are cooked. When ready, drain.

3. Heat olive oil in a saucepan, add finely chopped garlic and lentils, and continue to cook, shaking pan from time to time, until lentils are heated through.

4. Pound anchovy fillets and butter to a smooth paste, and add to lentils, stirring in well. Season to taste with salt and freshly ground black pepper. Place in serving dish and serve very hot.

Lentils Provençale

450 g/1 lb lentils
1 Spanish onion
salt
4-6 tablespoons olive oil
1 clove garlic, finely chopped
1 (56-g/2-oz) can anchovy fillets
100 g/4 oz butter
freshly ground black pepper

1. Place lentils in a large saucepan. Fill pan with water and bring gently to the boil. Remove saucepan from heat and let lentils soak in hot water for 1 hour.

312

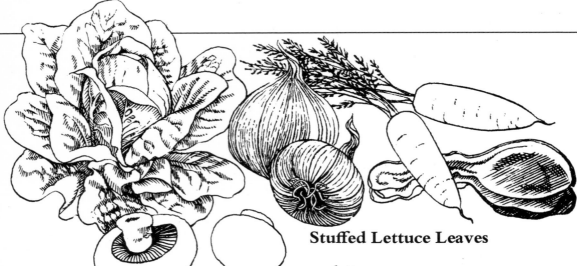

Braised Lettuce

4-6 small Cos lettuces
butter
1 rasher bacon, diced
½ Spanish onion, thinly sliced
2 small carrots, thinly sliced
150 ml/¼ pint chicken stock
salt and freshly ground black pepper
2 level teaspoons flour
finely chopped parsley

1. Clean lettuces, leaving them whole. Pare the base of each lettuce to a point. Drop lettuces into a large saucepan filled with boiling water, and boil for 5 minutes.

2. Pour off water and plunge lettuces into a bowl of cold water for a few minutes. Drain lettuces and press out excess moisture.

3. Butter an ovenproof dish. Place lettuces, diced bacon, and thinly sliced onion and carrots in dish, and add chicken stock. Season to taste with salt and freshly ground black pepper, then cover and cook slowly until tender – about 45 minutes.

4. About 5 minutes before you remove vegetables from heat, stir in 2 teaspoons butter which you have mixed to a smooth paste with 2 level teaspoons flour.

5. Just before serving, sprinkle with parsley.

Stuffed Lettuce Leaves

1-2 lettuces
2 level tablespoons butter
100 g/4 oz uncooked rice
600 ml/1 pint hot beef stock
½ Spanish onion, finely chopped
50 g/2 oz chopped mushrooms
2 tablespoons olive oil
100 g/4 oz ham, finely chopped
salt and freshly ground black pepper
2 level tablespoons tomato purée
2 level tablespoons finely chopped parsley

1. Separate lettuce leaves and wash well. Drain.

2. Melt butter in a thick-bottomed frying pan. Add rice, and sauté until golden. Cover with 300 ml/½ pint hot beef stock, adding a little water if necessary, and cook, stirring constantly, until the mixture comes to the boil. Reduce heat, cover pan, and cook slowly for about 15 minutes, adding a little more beef stock if necessary.

3. Sauté chopped onion and mushrooms in oil, and add to rice mixture. Mix in the finely chopped ham and season well.

4. Place equal quantities of the mixture on each lettuce leaf, and roll up, tucking ends in, to form neat 'packages'. Arrange them in a flat ovenproof dish.

5. Blend tomato purée with remaining 300 ml/½ pint hot beef stock, pour over stuffed lettuce leaves and bake in a moderately hot oven (190°C, 375°F, Gas Mark 5) for 30 minutes, or until done, basting frequently. Sprinkle with finely chopped parsley.

Mushrooms en Brochette *Serves 6*
Sautéed Mushrooms Hong Kong *Serves 4*
Spinach Stuffed Mushrooms *Serves 4*

313

Mushrooms en Brochette

Illustrated on page 320

36 button mushrooms (about 1 kg/2 lb)
6 tablespoons melted butter
2 tablespoons olive oil
lemon juice
salt and freshly ground black pepper
finely chopped garlic
crushed rosemary

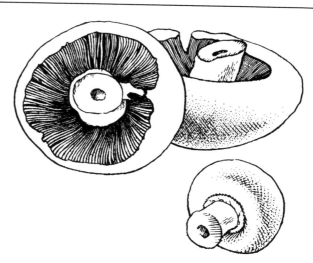

1. Clean mushrooms, remove stems (saving them for another use) and place 6 mushroom caps on each of 6 metal skewers.

2. Combine melted butter and olive oil, and flavour to taste with lemon juice, salt, freshly ground black pepper, garlic and rosemary.

3. Brush mushrooms with this mixture. Grill over charcoal or under the grill, turning mushrooms to brown them on all sides, and basting from time to time with sauce. Serve with grilled beef steak or lamb chops.

Sautéed Mushrooms Hong Kong

450 g/1 lb button mushrooms
100 g/4 oz cooked chicken breast
4 tablespoons peanut oil or lard
2 tablespoons sake, or dry white wine or
  dry sherry
1 tablespoon light soy sauce
$\frac{1}{2}$ level teaspoon sugar
$\frac{1}{2}$ level teaspoon cornflour

1. Wipe mushrooms and trim stems. Cut chicken into short thin matchsticks. Heat oil or lard in a Chinese *wok* or frying pan, add chicken and sauté until golden.

2. Add mushrooms and stir over medium heat for 1 minute. Add *sake* (or dry white wine or dry sherry) and soy sauce and sugar; cover pan and simmer for 3 minutes.

3. Remove cover. Add cornflour, mixed with a tablespoon or two of water, and simmer until sauce is slightly thickened. Serve immediately.

Spinach Stuffed Mushrooms

16–24 open button mushrooms, according
  to size
4 shallots, finely chopped
1 clove garlic, finely chopped
225 g/8 oz cooked spinach, chopped
$\frac{1}{4}$ level teaspoon dried thyme
2 bay leaves, crumbled
1 egg, beaten
olive oil
salt and freshly ground black pepper
breadcrumbs
2 tablespoons finely chopped parsley
4 tablespoons dry white wine

1. Wipe mushrooms and trim stem ends. Remove stems from caps and chop finely. Combine chopped stems, shallots and garlic with chopped spinach, herbs and beaten egg. Moisten with a little olive oil. Season with salt and freshly ground black pepper, to taste, and sauté mixture in a little olive oil.

2. Fill mushroom caps with spinach mixture. Sprinkle lightly with breadcrumbs and finely chopped parsley.

3. Pour 4 tablespoons olive oil and dry white wine into a flameproof *gratin* dish and heat through on top of the cooker. Arrange stuffed mushroom caps in the dish and cook in a preheated moderate oven (190°C, 375°F, Gas Mark 5) for 15 to 20 minutes.

314

and bake in a moderately hot oven (190°C, 375°F, Gas Mark 5) for 15 to 20 minutes.

Onions and Carrots

350 g/12 oz small white onions
350 g/12 oz small carrots
4 level tablespoons butter
4 tablespoons chicken stock
salt
1 level tablespoon sugar

1. Peel onions.

2. Scrape carrots and slice them thickly.

3. Place vegetables in a saucepan, cover with cold water and cook over a high heat until water boils. Remove from heat and drain.

4. Replace vegetables in the saucepan, add butter and chicken stock, season to taste with salt and sugar, and simmer over a low heat until vegetables have absorbed all the liquid without burning, and have taken on a little colour.

Onion and Potato Gratinée

1 kg/2 lb Spanish onions, peeled
1 kg/2 lb large potatoes
300 ml/½ pint milk
6 level tablespoons freshly grated Parmesan cheese
4 eggs, well beaten
freshly grated nutmeg
salt and freshly ground black pepper
4 level tablespoons fresh breadcrumbs
2 tablespoons melted butter

1. Put peeled whole onions in a large saucepan, cover with cold water and bring slowly to the boil. Drain. Cover with fresh hot water and cook until tender. Drain.

2. Peel potatoes and boil them.

3. Put onions and potatoes through a *mouli-légumes*, or 'rice' them. Add milk, grated cheese

Creamed Onions with Cloves

48 small white onions
salt
4 level tablespoons butter
8 whole cloves
1 level teaspoon sugar
freshly ground black pepper
1 level tablespoon flour
300 ml/½ pint cream
freshly grated Parmesan cheese

1. Peel onions and cook in boiling salted water, uncovered, until almost tender. Drain, and rinse in cold water.

2. Melt 3 level tablespoons butter in a large frying pan or casserole.

3. Stick 8 onions with cloves. Add all the onions to the melted butter, sprinkle with sugar and cook over a low heat, shaking pan frequently, until onions are golden brown on all sides.

4. Transfer onions and pan juices to a shallow baking dish. Season to taste with salt and freshly ground black pepper.

5. Melt remaining butter in a small saucepan, add flour and stir until smooth. Add cream and cook, stirring constantly, until sauce is thick. Pour sauce over onions, sprinkle with freshly grated Parmesan

and well-beaten eggs. Beat mixture until soft and creamy, season to taste with freshly grated nutmeg, salt and freshly ground black pepper. Place in an ovenproof dish and sprinkle with breadcrumbs and melted butter. Bake in a moderate oven (160°C, 325°F, Gas Mark 3) for 40 to 45 minutes.

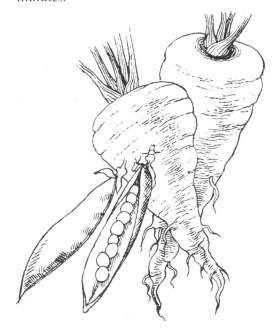

Cider-glazed Parsnips

12-18 small parsnips
salt
3 level tablespoons brown sugar
6-8 tablespoons cider
3 level tablespoons butter
freshly ground black pepper

1. Preheat oven to moderately hot (200°C, 400°F, Gas Mark 6).

2. Scrape parsnips and cut into quarters lengthwise. Cook in boiling water which has been salted until just tender. Drain.

3. Put parsnips in a shallow baking dish, sprinkle with sugar and cider, dot with butter, season with salt and freshly ground black pepper to taste and bake for 20 minutes, basting parsnips occasionally with glaze.

Garden Peas in Cream

675 g/1½ lb fresh peas in the pod
3 level tablespoons butter
150 ml/¼ pint water
¼ chicken stock cube
6 lettuce leaves, coarsely shredded
2 level tablespoons chopped onion
2 level tablespoons chopped parsley
1 level teaspoon sugar
salt and freshly ground black pepper
4-6 level tablespoons double cream

1. Shell peas.

2. Heat butter, water and stock cube to boiling point. Add peas, lettuce, chopped onion, parsley, and sugar, salt and freshly ground black pepper, to taste.

3. Cover pan and simmer over a low heat until peas are tender – 8 to 15 minutes. Remove pan from heat, stir in double cream and serve.

Hasty Peas and Onions

350 g/12 oz frozen peas
350 g/12 oz small button onions
6 level tablespoons butter
6 tablespoons chicken stock
2 level tablespoons sugar
salt and freshly ground black pepper

1. Place peas in a small saucepan, cover with cold water and cook over a high flame until the water boils. Remove from the heat and drain.

2. Place button onions in a saucepan, cover with cold water and bring to the boil. Lower heat and simmer for 10 minutes. Remove from the heat and drain.

3. Combine peas and onions in a large saucepan, add butter and chicken stock. Season with sugar and salt and freshly ground black pepper, to taste.

4. Simmer over a low flame until the vegetables have absorbed the liquid and are tender.

315

316

Roman Peas

4 level tablespoons finely chopped
    Parma ham
½ Spanish onion, finely chopped
butter
450 g/1 lb shelled peas, fresh or frozen
150 ml/¼ pint well-flavoured beef stock
sugar
salt and freshly ground black pepper
2 level tablespoons finely chopped parsley

1. Sauté finely chopped ham and onion in 4 tablespoons butter until onion begins to take on colour.

2. Add peas and beef stock, and season to taste with sugar, salt and freshly ground black pepper. Simmer peas, covered, for 10 to 15 minutes.

3. Just before serving, top with finely chopped parsley and a knob of butter.

Purée Saint-Germain

1 kg/2 lb frozen peas
1 lettuce heart, shredded
12 tiny spring onions, or ½ Spanish onion,
    sliced
3 sprigs parsley
100 g/4 oz butter
4 tablespoons chicken stock or water
sugar
salt
2 boiled potatoes, puréed (optional)

1. Put peas in a saucepan with the shredded heart of a lettuce, spring onions, parsley, half the butter, chicken stock or water, and sugar and salt, to taste. Bring to the boil and cook slowly until peas are tender.

2. When cooked, remove parsley and drain, reserving juices.

3. Blend to a fine purée in an electric blender (or press through a fine sieve) and reheat in the top of a double saucepan, adding a little of the strained juices and the remaining butter. If purée is too thin, add puréed potatoes to lend body.

Buttered Peas Elysées

450 g/1 lb frozen peas
4 level tablespoons butter
4 tablespoons chicken stock
salt and freshly ground black pepper
1 level tablespoon sugar
4 lettuce leaves, cut into thin strips
1 egg yolk
4 level tablespoons double cream

1. Place peas in a small saucepan, add enough cold water to just cover peas and cook over a high heat until the water boils. Remove from the heat and drain.

2. Replace peas in the saucepan, add butter and chicken stock, season to taste with salt and freshly ground black pepper and sugar. Cover with lettuce strips and simmer over a low heat until the peas have absorbed the liquid and are tender.

3. Combine egg yolk and double cream and stir into hot peas and lettuce. Serve immediately.

Note: Frozen peas cooked in this manner may also be puréed to serve as a vegetable or fold into a soufflé; or thinned with cream and well-flavoured chicken stock, to serve as a delicious soup.

Stuffed Green Peppers (see page 321)

Chinese Braised Vegetables (see page 307)

Chinese Spinach (see page 307)

Broccoli with Cheese Sauce and Slivered Almonds (see page 295)

Mushrooms en Brochette (see page 313)

Peas au Gratin

100 g/4 oz diced cooked ham
½ Spanish onion, finely chopped
butter
450 g/1 lb cooked peas, fresh or frozen
300 ml/½ pint cream, warmed
salt and freshly ground black pepper
2-4 level tablespoons freshly grated
    Parmesan cheese
2-4 level tablespoons freshly grated
    Gruyère cheese

1. Sauté diced ham and finely chopped onion in 2 tablespoons butter until onion begins to take on colour.

2. Combine ham and onion with cooked peas and warmed cream, and season to taste with salt and freshly ground black pepper. Pour mixture into a well-buttered casserole, sprinkle with freshly grated cheeses, dot with butter and cook under grill until top is golden.

Green Pea Pudding

450 g/1 lb split peas
1 (226-g/8-oz) packet frozen peas
50 g/2 oz butter
salt and freshly ground black pepper
3 eggs
flour

1. Soak split peas in water overnight. Drain. Defrost frozen peas.

2. Combine split peas and frozen peas and tie them in a thick pudding cloth, allowing enough room to swell. Cover them with cold water, bring to the boil and cook gently for 2 hours.

3. Lift pudding into a colander; drain well then untie cloth.

4. Rub peas through a sieve. Add butter and salt and freshly ground black pepper and mix well. Beat eggs until foamy and blend into the pudding gradually. Tie the mixture tightly in a well-floured pudding cloth and boil it again for 1 hour.

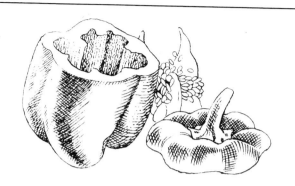

Stuffed Green Peppers

Illustrated on page 317

4-6 green peppers
olive oil
butter
salt and freshly ground black pepper
1 Spanish onion, finely chopped
450 g/1 lb pork sausagemeat
freshly grated nutmeg
2 level tablespoons grated Parmesan cheese
2 level tablespoons chopped chives
2 level tablespoons chopped parsley
300 ml/½ pint chicken stock (made with
    a cube)
strips of canned pimento

1. Remove the tops of the peppers. Remove pith and seeds. Place peppers in boiling water, to cover. Add 2 tablespoons olive oil and leave for 5 minutes. Drain well and dry.

2. Place a small piece of butter in the bottom of each pepper and season well. Sauté finely chopped onion in 4 tablespoons olive oil until onion is soft. Add crumbled sausagemeat and continue to cook, stirring constantly, until meat just begins to brown. Add salt, freshly ground black pepper, freshly grated nutmeg, grated Parmesan cheese, chopped chives and parsley and mix well.

3. Stuff peppers with this mixture and place in a flat, ovenproof dish. Pour chicken stock over peppers and bake in a preheated moderately hot oven (190°C, 375°F, Gas Mark 5) for 30 to 40 minutes, or until done, basting frequently. Just before serving, garnish each pepper with narrow strips of canned pimento.

322

Basic Boiled Potatoes

675-900 g/1½-2 lb new potatoes
coarse salt
butter
freshly ground black pepper

1. Wash potatoes and either scrape them or, if they peel easily, simply rub off a neat band of skin round the middle of each potato with your finger.

2. Put the potatoes in a pan. Cover with cold water, add a small handful of coarse salt and bring to the boil.

3. Simmer potatoes until they feel soft when pierced with a fork. Small ones will take about 18 minutes.

4. Drain well and serve with plenty of butter and coarse salt and freshly ground black pepper, to taste.

Mrs. Beeton's German Potatoes

75 g/3 oz butter
2 level tablespoons flour
300 ml/½ pint broth
2 tablespoons vinegar
8-10 medium-sized potatoes
1 bay leaf (optional)

'Put the butter and flour into a stew pan; stir over the fire until the butter is of a nice brown colour, and add the broth and vinegar; peel and cut the potatoes into long thin slices, lay them in the gravy, and let them simmer gently until tender, which will be from 10 to 15 minutes, and serve very hot. A laurel-leaf (bay leaf) simmered with the potatoes is an improvement.'

Scalloped Potatoes with Cheese

4 large baking potatoes
butter
225 g/8 oz Cheddar cheese, grated
1 Spanish onion, finely chopped
4 level tablespoons finely chopped parsley
salt and freshly ground black pepper
½ level teaspoon paprika
450 ml/¾ pint milk
150 ml/¼ pint double cream

1. Peel potatoes and slice them thinly. Soak sliced potatoes in cold water for 10 minutes. Drain and dry carefully.

2. Butter a shallow baking dish generously and cover bottom of dish with a layer of potatoes. Season to taste with grated cheese (reserving 4 tablespoons for later use), onion, parsley, salt, freshly ground black pepper and paprika. Cover with another layer of potatoes and season as above. Cover with remaining potatoes, pour in milk and cream to cover, and bake in a hot oven (230°C, 450°F, Gas Mark 8) for 10 minutes.

3. Reduce oven heat to (180°C, 350°F, Gas Mark 4), sprinkle with remaining cheese and bake until the potatoes are tender – about 2 hours.

Buttered New Potatoes with Chicken or Goose Fat

675-900 g/1½-2 lb tiny new potatoes
salt
4 level tablespoons chicken or goose fat
4 level tablespoons butter
4 level tablespoons finely chopped parsley
freshly ground black pepper

1. Scrub the skin from potatoes, place them in a large casserole, add enough salted water to just cover and parboil them for 3 minutes. Drain.

2. Heat chicken or goose fat in a large frying pan, add potatoes and cook, shaking pan frequently, until potatoes are tender and golden brown on all sides.

3. Remove potatoes from pan with a slotted spoon and pour off fat from the pan. Return potatoes to the pan, add butter and continue to cook for a few minutes, rolling potatoes in the butter as it melts.

4. Just before serving, sprinkle with finely chopped parsley and season with salt and freshly ground black pepper, to taste.

Gratin Dauphinois

450 g/1 lb new potatoes
2 level tablespoons butter
1 egg
150 ml/¼ pint double cream
8 level tablespoons freshly grated Gruyère cheese
4 level tablespoons freshly grated Parmesan cheese
salt and freshly ground black pepper

1. Peel or scrape potatoes and slice them very thinly (about 1 mm/1/16 inch thick). Rinse thoroughly and leave to soak in a bowl of cold water for 15 minutes. Select a shallow ovenproof dish about 23 cm/9 inches by 13 cm/5 inches. Grease with 2 level teaspoons of the butter.

2. Preheat oven to cool (150°C, 300°F, Gas Mark 2).

3. Drain potato slices and dry them thoroughly with a cloth or absorbent paper.

4. Whisk egg and cream together until well blended.

5. Arrange a quarter of the potato slices in the dish in overlapping rows; pour over 2 level tablespoons egg and cream mixture; sprinkle with 2 level tablespoons Gruyère and 1 level tablespoon Parmesan; dot with 1 level teaspoon butter; and finally, season to taste with salt and freshly ground black pepper.

6. Repeat layers exactly as above, making four in all, and ending with grated cheese and butter.

7. Bake *gratin* for 1 hour 20 minutes, or until potatoes feel tender when pierced with a sharp skewer and are golden and bubbling on top.

8. Allow to 'settle' for a few minutes before serving.

Note: If top browns too quickly, cover with a sheet of foil. If you use old potatoes, the cooking time will be slightly shorter.

Pommes de Terre Soufflées

900 ml/1½ pints peanut oil
675 g/1½ lb new potatoes, peeled, dried and thinly sliced
salt
deep fryer, with frying basket

1. Heat the oil. Place sliced potatoes in a frying basket and plunge them into the hot oil. They should begin to colour in a few minutes. Remove basket from oil and allow potatoes to cool.

2. When ready to serve: heat the oil again, this time a little hotter than before (this is the magic trick that makes the twice-fried potatoes swell up into feather-light 'balloons', but you'll have to practise to make perfect), and plunge the basket of sliced potatoes into it again. Continue to cook until potatoes are puffed and golden. Drain, season with salt, and serve immediately.

323

Pommes de Terre Duchesse *Serves 4 to 6*
Pommes de Terre en Daube *Serves 4 to 6*
Oven- baked Potatoes with Soured Cream and Chive
     Dressing *Serves 4*

324

Pommes de Terre Duchesse

1 kg/2 lb potatoes
salt
butter
2 eggs
2 egg yolks
freshly ground black pepper
freshly ground nutmeg

1. Peel potatoes and slice them thickly. Cook them, covered, in simmering salted water until soft but not mushy. Drain well. Return potatoes to pan and remove all moisture by shaking pan over heat until they are dry.

2. Rub potatoes through a fine sieve, add 2 to 4 tablespoons butter, beating with a wooden spoon until mixture is very smooth.

-3. Combine eggs and egg yolks, and beat gradually into potato mixture. Season to taste with salt, freshly ground black pepper and freshly grated nutmeg, and beat until mixture is very fluffy.

If potatoes are to be used to garnish a meat, fish or vegetable dish, pipe mixture through a pastry tube to make a border, brush with butter and brown under the grill. Or pipe individual shapes with a pastry tube, brush with butter and brown under the grill.

Pommes de Terre en Daube

1 kg/2 lb small new potatoes
100 g/4 oz green bacon, in 1 piece
1 Spanish onion
4-6 tomatoes
4 tablespoons olive oil
4 level tablespoons tomato purée
1 piece dried orange peel
1 bouquet garni (2 sprigs parsley, 2 sprigs
   thyme, 1 bay leaf)
300 ml/½ pint water or light chicken stock
salt and freshly ground black pepper
finely chopped parsley

1. Peel small new potatoes. If larger ones are used, peel and slice them thickly. Slice bacon thickly

(about 5 mm/¼ inch) and then cut slices into 5-mm/ ¼-inch thick 'fingers'. Chop Spanish onion. Seed and chop tomatoes.

2. Sauté bacon pieces in olive oil until golden; remove bacon and reserve for later use. Sauté chopped onion in remaining fat until transparent. Stir in chopped and seeded tomatoes and tomato purée and cook for a few minutes more. Then add peeled potatoes, bacon bits, orange peel and *bouquet garni* to pan. Add water or chicken stock and salt and freshly ground black pepper, to taste, and simmer until potatoes are tender.

3. Serve garnished with finely chopped parsley.

Oven-baked Potatoes with Soured Cream and Chive Dressing
Illustrated on page 300

4 large baking potatoes
softened butter or olive oil
coarse salt

SOURED CREAM AND CHIVE DRESSING
300 ml/½ pint soured cream
coarsely chopped chives
salt and freshly ground black pepper

1. Scrub the potatoes thoroughly and dry them. Rub with softened butter or olive oil. Sprinkle with coarse salt. Place on a baking tray and bake in a moderately hot oven (190°C, 375°F, Gas Mark 5) for 1½ hours.

2. To make Soured Cream and Chive Dressing: combine 300 ml/½ pint commercial soured cream with 2 to 4 level tablespoons coarsely chopped chives, and season to taste with salt and freshly ground black pepper.

3. Make two deep incisions crossing on top of each cooked potato and then squeeze the base of the potato gently to force the cooked potato inside to emerge.

4. Top with Soured Cream and Chive Dressing, add a sprinkling of chopped chives and serve hot.

Rosti (Swiss Potato Cake)

1 kg/2 lb large potatoes
salt and freshly ground black pepper
4 tablespoons butter
2 tablespoons olive oil

1. Scrub potatoes clean under running water. Place in a large saucepan, cover with water and add salt. Bring to the boil then simmer for 15 minutes, or until potatoes are three-quarters cooked.

2. Drain then cool under running water. Peel off the skins and coarsely grate potatoes into a large bowl. Season well with salt and freshly ground black pepper.

3. Heat butter and olive oil in a large thick-bottomed frying pan. Place grated potatoes in the pan and press lightly into a smooth cake. Season generously with salt and freshly ground black pepper. Cover pan and cook over a medium heat for 8 to 10 minutes.

4. Remove cover and continue cooking for 5 minutes or until bottom of potato cake is crusty and brown, shaking pan from time to time so potatoes do not stick to the pan. Add a little more olive oil or butter if necessary.

5. To serve: turn potato cake out on to a heated serving dish with crusty side up, and cut into thin wedges. Serve immediately.

Pommes Sarladaise

450 g/1 lb new potatoes
4 level tablespoons goose fat, lard or
   softened butter
salt and freshly ground black pepper
black truffles, thinly sliced

1. Rub a frying pan generously with goose fat, lard or softened butter.

2. Peel and slice potatoes thinly and soak in cold water for a few minutes. Drain and dry thoroughly with a clean tea towel.

3. Place a layer of sliced potatoes on bottom of frying pan in overlapping rows. Sprinkle with salt and freshly ground black pepper, to taste, and add a few thin slices of black truffle. Repeat until pan is filled, or potatoes are used up, finishing with a layer of potatoes.

3. Cover potatoes with a plate to weight them and to keep moisture in, and sauté them over a gentle heat until bottom layer is crisp and golden, adding a little more fat or butter from time to time, if necessary.

4. Turn potatoes like a pancake and cook again (without the plate) until potatoes are cooked through and nicely browned on both sides. Turn out potato cake and serve immediately.

Buttered Spinach with Ham

1 kg/2 lb fresh spinach leaves
butter
salt and freshly ground black pepper
4-6 level tablespoons diced cooked ham
4-6 level tablespoons diced white bread

1. Wash spinach leaves in several changes of water. Drain.

2. Put spinach in a thick-bottomed saucepan with 225 g/8 oz butter, season to taste with salt and freshly ground black pepper, and cook, stirring constantly, over a fairly high heat until spinach is soft and melted. Transfer to a serving dish and keep warm.

3. Melt 2 tablespoons butter in a frying pan and toss diced ham and diced bread in butter until golden.

4. Fold ham and *croûtons* into spinach, and serve at once as a separate vegetable course.

325

326

Italian Baked Tomatoes and Leeks

4-8 tomatoes, according to size, peeled
4 leeks
4 level tablespoons butter
6 tablespoons dry white wine
$\frac{1}{2}$ chicken stock cube
**4 level tablespoons finely chopped fresh
  basil or chives**
salt and freshly ground black pepper
olive oil
1 egg yolk
150 ml/$\frac{1}{4}$ pint double cream
**4 level tablespoons freshly grated Parmesan
  cheese**

1. Preheat oven to moderate (190°C, 375°F, Gas
Mark 5).

2. Cut tomatoes in half and gently press out seeds
and water. Trim and wash leeks and cut into
2.5-cm/1-inch pieces.

3. Place leeks with butter and dry white wine
and $\frac{1}{2}$ chicken stock cube, crumbled, in a large
shallow flameproof *gratin* dish. Sprinkle leeks
with finely chopped fresh basil or chives and
season with salt and freshly ground black pepper.
Bake in a preheated oven for 10 minutes.

4. Season peeled tomatoes with salt and freshly
ground black pepper and arrange them, cut-side

Grilled Italian Tomatoes

6 large ripe tomatoes
butter
salt and freshly ground black pepper
dried oregano
2 level tablespoons breadcrumbs
**2 level teaspoons finely chopped chives
  or onion**
**2 level tablespoons freshly grated Parmesan
  cheese**

1. Cut tomatoes in half.

2. Place tomato halves in a buttered baking dish.
Season to taste with salt, freshly ground black
pepper and dried oregano. Sprinkle with breadcrumbs, finely chopped chives or onion and
freshly grated Parmesan. Dot tomatoes with
butter and grill them 7.5 cm/3 inches from the
heat until tender.

down, on top of the leeks. Brush with olive oil; return dish to oven and cook for 10 more minutes.

5. Beat egg yolk and double cream together and spoon over vegetables. Sprinkle with freshly grated Parmesan and continue to cook until sauce is bubbling and lightly browned.

Green Souffléd Tomatoes

8 medium-sized tomatoes, or 4 very large
  tomatoes
salt and freshly ground black pepper
100 g/4 oz frozen spinach, defrosted
butter
1 (85-g/3-oz) packet Philadelphia cream
  cheese, diced
6 level tablespoons double cream
2 egg yolks, beaten
4-5 level tablespoons freshly grated
  Parmesan cheese
cayenne
olive oil
4 egg whites
dry white wine

1. Preheat oven to moderately hot (200°C, 400°F, Gas Mark 6).

2. Slice tops off tomatoes, scoop out interiors carefully and discard. Season insides of tomatoes generously with salt and freshly ground black pepper. Drain tomato cases upside down in refrigerator for at least 30 minutes.

3. Heat spinach with a little butter and purée in an electric blender. Drain.

4. Beat cream cheese with double cream until smooth. Add beaten egg yolks and puréed spinach and season with freshly grated Parmesan and salt, freshly ground black pepper and cayenne, to taste.

5. Brush tomato cases, inside and out, with olive oil and heat through in oven.

6. Beat egg whites until stiff. Gently fold into spinach and cheese mixture.

7. Pile mixture into tomato cases and place in a flameproof *gratin* dish. Add a little olive oil and dry white wine to moisten bottom of dish. Bring liquid to the boil on top of the cooker, then cook tomato soufflés in preheated oven for 5 minutes. Reduce heat to moderate (160°C, 325°F, Gas Mark 3) and continue to cook for 10 to 15 minutes, until well risen and cooked through.

Tomatoes Stuffed with Mussels

8-12 firm tomatoes
salt and freshly ground black pepper
1 Spanish onion, finely chopped
1 clove garlic, finely chopped
4 level tablespoons finely chopped parsley
6 button mushrooms, finely chopped
4-6 anchovy fillets, finely chopped
olive oil
6 level tablespoons fresh breadcrumbs
8-12 mussels
dry white wine
butter

1. Cut a slice from the stem end of each tomato and scoop out the seeds with a spoon. Season insides of tomatoes generously with salt and freshly ground black pepper and turn them upside down to drain.

2. Sauté finely chopped onion, garlic, parsley, mushrooms and anchovies in 4 tablespoons olive oil until vegetables are brown. Stir in half the fresh breadcrumbs, season with salt and freshly ground black pepper and simmer mixture for 5 more minutes.

3. Scrub mussels, remove beards and stem in a little dry white wine until mussels open. Remove mussels from shells, discarding any that have not opened. Strain mussel liquor into sauce. Chop mussels finely and stir into sauce.

4. Arrange the prepared tomatoes in a buttered baking dish and stuff them with the mussel and breadcrumb mixture. Sprinkle with remaining breadcrumbs and a few drops of olive oil. Brown the topping in a moderately hot oven (200°C, 400°F, Gas Mark 6).

Desserts and Pastries

My first arrival in England was not auspicious. On my twenty-first birthday I disembarked at Plymouth – an involuntary pilgrim – en route to the front. The invasion of Normandy had just taken place; the first casualties were beginning to be listed; flying bombs were roaring over London; and the English were tired. They seemed to have ceased to feel – the food was appalling and the war was welcomed as a God-given excuse for all the pent-up puritanism of the people to come to the fore. To serve unimaginative food was looked on almost as a virtue; to enjoy a meal, a sin.

How different it was when I reached France. Here the nightmare was over, and feasting – with that skilful logic the French apply to their own comfort – was considered a patriotic gesture. So it was in France I stayed. For six years I lived in St. Germain des Près, the most exciting quarter of what was then the most exciting city in the world: creative, young, experimental – ready for every new experience, whether philosophical or physical. But when I returned to England in 1953 for the Coronation, I might never have been here before, so different was it. Here was the Mrs. Miniver-land I had imagined in my childhood. London was en fête, buildings garlanded, crowds jubilant, pageantry to the fore.

One meal summed up the change for me – and led me to stretch my three weeks' visit to twelve years. I was asked to tea by Sir Stephen Tallents, well known for his evocations of the country life. The very name of his house was almost parody – St. John's Jerusalem. On my arrival, my host greeted me from the moat – knee-deep in water, rubber waders to the thighs, raking for the monastic relics that he discovered every now and then.

Then tea itself. No bread and jam and cakes, but mounds of fresh strawberries and cream – strawberries such as I had never tasted before – and when we had eaten our way through an absolute mountain of them, Sir Stephen rose from the table to return a few minutes later with another great bowl of the fruit, still hot from the sun, brushed clean, not washed. Perfection!

Featherlight Puddings

Most households in England had at least one recipe for a delicate pudding or a satin smooth cream which was truly their own speciality. These featherlight confections were not reserved for occasions – birthdays and anniversaries – but were served with pomp and pride at dinner parties throughout the year. Creamy baked custards made with fresh cream and eight egg yolks were deliciously flavoured with sugar, cinnamon and orange flower water; sharp gooseberries were whipped with cream and egg whites into frothy astringent fools and chocolate mousses vied with fresh fruit tanseys, burnt creams and extravagant rice moulds for top of the popularity poll.

To be memorable, autumn and winter sweets need not be elaborate or difficult. After a well-planned dinner the finest dessert imaginable is a plate of glistening ripe fruit: fresh golden peaches, fragrant grapes and apricots, crisp red and green apples, ripe, succulent pears. My grandmother used to spice peeled whole peaches and then bottle them in brandy-flavoured syrup. They were wonderful served chilled with lashings of whipped cream. Her fresh fruit pies were worth remembering, too, for she used to make, in place of a pastry cover, a sauce of double cream, brown sugar and a little flour; or dot the fruit slices with a crumble of flour, butter and sugar, that browned appetisingly during baking. Perhaps the most delicious memory of my childhood was the home-made vanilla and praline ice creams we used to eat in her snug country kitchen. My grandmother's version of this recipe – hand-turned in those days – was rich with her own farm eggs and double cream. Today I plump for the nursery sweets of those bygone days – and, judging from the menus at London's better restaurants, I am not alone.

Pears in Burgundy (see page 333)

Summer Fruit Harvest

Fresh Fruit Salad
Figs with Brandy (see page 333)
Caramel Cream (see page 346)

Easy Fruit Desserts

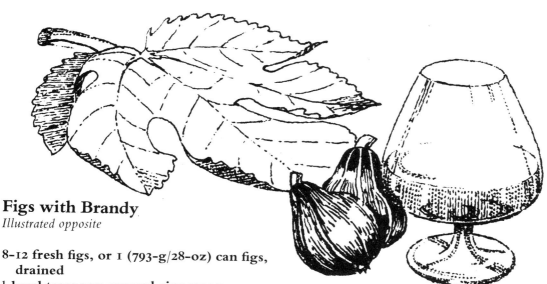

Figs with Brandy
Illustrated opposite

8–12 fresh figs, or 1 (793-g/28-oz) can figs,
    drained
$\frac{1}{4}$ level teaspoon ground cinnamon
1 level tablespoon grated orange rind
2–4 tablespoons brandy
4 tablespoons sherry
icing sugar (optional)
150 ml/$\frac{1}{4}$ pint double cream, whipped
2 level tablespoons toasted almonds

1. Heat cinnamon, grated orange rind, brandy
and sherry, and sprinkle over figs. If figs are fresh,
add a little icing sugar, if required. Allow figs to
marinate in this flavouring for at least 1 hour
before serving.

2. Spoon whipped cream on to figs and garnish
with toasted almonds.

Pears in Chablis
Illustrated on page 386

12 small or 6 medium-sized pears
225 g/8 oz sugar
150 ml/$\frac{1}{4}$ pint water
1–2 cinnamon sticks
150 ml/$\frac{1}{4}$ pint Chablis, or other dry white
    wine
whipped cream

1. Peel pears but do not core them. Put them in a
saucepan with the sugar, water and cinnamon
sticks. Simmer, covered, for about 15 minutes.

Add Chablis and continue to cook over a low
heat, uncovered, for 15 minutes. Remove cinnamon sticks.

2. Put pears in a deep serving dish. Reduce liquid
to the consistency of a light syrup. Pour syrup
over the pears and chill. Serve very cold with
whipped cream.

Pears in Burgundy
Illustrated on page 329

12 small or 6 medium-sized pears
225 g/8 oz sugar
150 ml/$\frac{1}{4}$ pint water
1–2 cinnamon sticks
150 ml/$\frac{1}{4}$ pint red Burgundy
whipped cream

1. Peel pears but do not core them. Put them in a
saucepan with the sugar, water and cinnamon
sticks. Simmer, covered, for about 15 minutes.
Add Burgundy and continue to cook over a low
heat, uncovered, for 15 minutes. Remove cinnamon sticks.

2. Put pears in a deep serving dish. Reduce liquid
to the consistency of a light syrup. Pour syrup over
the pears and chill. Serve very cold with whipped
cream.

334

Transparent Apple Slices

4 Bramley seedlings
50 g/2 oz butter
4 tablespoons water
100-175 g/4-6 oz sugar
cinnamon

1. Peel, core and cut Bramley seedlings in thick slices.

2. Melt butter, add apple slices and water. Cover and allow to steam gently over a low heat until apple slices are almost tender – about 4 or 5 minutes.

3. Add sugar and sprinkle generously with cinnamon to taste. Cook, stirring gently, until apple slices are transparent and glazed with thick syrup.

4. Allow apple slices to cool, then serve.

Apple Hedgehog

6 medium-sized eating apples
225 g/8 oz granulated sugar
300 ml/½ pint water
grated rind of 1 lemon
1 kg/2 lb cooking apples
3 egg whites
castor sugar
icing sugar (optional)
24 almonds

1. Peel and core the eating apples, leaving them whole.

2. Combine granulated sugar with water and grated lemon rind in a saucepan. Bring to the boil and simmer apples in it gently until they are tender but not broken. Lift out and drain.

3. Peel, core and slice the cooking apples and cook them in the same syrup until reduced to a thick pulp.

4. Arrange the whole apples in a pyramid shape on a serving dish, spreading the apple pulp over them to make a smooth mound.

5. Whisk egg whites stiffly and fold in 2 tablespoons castor sugar.

6. Spread this meringue over the surface of the apples, covering them entirely, and sprinkle with a little more castor or icing sugar.

7. Blanch and split the almonds, and stick them here and there over the top. Brown meringue lightly in a moderately hot oven (190°C, 375°F, Gas Mark 5) for 5 to 10 minutes.

Blackberry Fool

675 g/1½ lb blackberries
150 ml/¼ pint water
100-225 g/4-8 oz sugar
150 ml/¼ pint Vanilla Custard Sauce (see page 419)
150 ml/¼ pint double cream, whipped

1. Wash blackberries and reserve 12 to 18 of the best. Put remainder in a saucepan with water and sugar. Cook until they are soft and then rub them through a fine sieve.

2. Mix vanilla custard and whipped cream (reserving a little cream for garnish) with the blackberry purée, and serve in a glass bowl or in individual glasses. Garnish with reserved blackberries and a swirl of whipped cream.

Rhubarb Fool

675 g/1½ lb young rhubarb
225 g/8 oz sugar
2 tablespoons lemon juice
4 level tablespoons butter
450 ml/¾ pint double cream, whipped
sugar or lemon juice

1. Wash and trim young rhubarb stalks and cut into 2.5-cm/1-inch segments.

Apple and Blackberry Fool *Serves 6 to 8*
Pineapple and Strawberries Romanov in the Shell
Serves 4
Oranges Flambées *Serves 4*

2. Combine rhubarb, sugar, lemon juice and butter in a thick-bottomed saucepan and bring gently to the boil, stirring continuously. Lower heat and simmer, stirring all the time, for 5 to 8 minutes, until rhubarb is soft but still keeps its identity.

3. Whisk in an electric blender until smooth, or press through a fine sieve. Allow to cool, then chill in refrigerator until ready to use.

4. Just before serving, combine purée with whipped cream, and flavour to taste with sugar or lemon juice.

Apple and Blackberry Fool

1 kg/2 lb cooking apples
450 g/1 lb blackberries
100 g/4 oz granulated sugar
150 ml/¼ pint double cream, whipped
150 ml/¼ pint Vanilla Custard Sauce (see
  page 419)

1. Peel, core and slice apples. Wash blackberries and cook fruits with sugar to taste, in a little water until thoroughly softened.

2. Remove from the heat and sieve. Add more sugar if necessary and fold in whipped cream and vanilla custard. Turn into a glass bowl and decorate as desired.

Pineapple and Strawberries Romanov in the Shell

2 small pineapples
6 level tablespoons icing sugar
3 tablespoons Cointreau
3 tablespoons rum
300 ml/½ pint double cream
3 tablespoons Kirsch
8–12 strawberries
grated rind of 1 orange

1. Slice the pineapples in half lengthwise. With a sharp knife remove pineapple flesh, leaving a shell about 5 mm/¼ inch thick. Refrigerate shells

until ready to use. Slice pineapple, removing the hard central core, and cut into segments.

2. Toss segments with 4 level tablespoons icing sugar. Arrange segments in a bowl suitable for serving at the table, and pour over them a mixture of Cointreau and rum. Chill in the refrigerator until ready to use.

3. One hour before serving, whip cream, add remaining icing sugar and flavour with Kirsch. Spoon whipped cream into marinated pineapple pieces, tossing until every piece is coated with creamy liqueur mixture.

4. Pile prepared pineapple pieces into reserved shells, garnish with strawberries, top with finely grated orange rind and serve immediately.

Oranges Flambées

4 large oranges
350 g/12 oz sugar
4 tablespoons Grand Marnier

1. Remove bright outer peel carefully from oranges with a fruit parer. Cut into matchstick-sized pieces and reserve. Remove remaining pith from oranges and separate each orange into 8 segments.

2. Melt sugar in a small thick-bottomed saucepan, and stir over a low heat until it is a good caramel colour.

3. Spear each orange segment with a fork and dip into caramel mixture. Place caramel-glazed orange segments thin sides up in a metal serving dish.

4. Stir *julienne* of orange matchsticks into caramel sauce and cook over a very low heat, stirring constantly.

5. Drain and garnish each glazed orange section with caramelised matchsticks of orange.

6. When ready to serve, heat metal serving dish and flame with Grand Marnier. Serve immediately.

Summer Fruit Cup *Serves 6 to 8*
Summer Pudding under a Blanket *Serves 6 to 8*
Quick Fruit Compote in Wine *Serves 4 to 6*

336

Summer Fruit Cup

225-350 g/8-12 oz strawberries
225-350 g/8-12 oz raspberries
2 bananas, sliced
225 g/8 oz redcurrants or whitecurrants
100 g/4 oz loaf sugar
150 ml/¼ pint water
6 tablespoons claret or Burgundy
1 tablespoon brandy
2 level tablespoons chopped pistachio nuts
 or shredded coconut
whipped cream and biscuits (optional)

1. Prepare fruits and mix lightly in a glass bowl.

2. Boil the sugar and water together until they form a syrup; skim if necessary.

3. Allow the syrup to cool, then add wine and brandy, and pour over fruit. Stand in a cool place for several hours.

4. Just before serving, sprinkle nuts or coconut over the top. Whipped cream and biscuits may be served separately.

Summer Pudding under a Blanket

225 g/8 oz redcurrants or blackcurrants
350 g/12 oz cherries
225 g/8 oz raspberries
150 ml/¼ pint water
100-175 g/4-6 oz sugar
7-8 thin slices white bread
double cream, whipped
ripe cherries or raspberries to decorate

1. Strip all stalks from currants, stone cherries, combine with raspberries and wash if necessary.

2. Place fruits with water and sugar in a saucepan, and simmer gently until sugar melts.

3. Trim crusts from bread, cut each slice in half lengthwise and line sides of a 1-litre/1½-pint pudding basin or soufflé dish with bread. Cover bottom of dish with triangles of bread, and trim off bread slices at top edge of dish.

4. Fill dish with fruit mixture. Cut additional bread triangles to cover pudding. Place a flat plate on pudding, weight it and chill in refrigerator overnight.

5. When ready to serve, turn out pudding on to a moistened serving dish and pipe top and sides of pudding with whipped cream. Decorate with ripe cherries or raspberries.

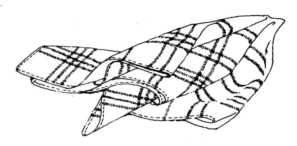

Quick Fruit Compote in Wine

4 canned pineapple rings
4 canned whole peaches
4 canned whole mirabelles or golden plums
1 (213-g/7½-oz) can apricots
1 (225-g/8-oz) can green figs
1 (312-g/11-oz) can lychees (optional)
fresh strawberries (optional)
finely grated orange peel

SAUCE
4 level tablespoons brown sugar
2 level tablespoons butter
300 ml/½ pint rosé wine
2 cloves
½ cinnamon stick

1. Drain canned fruits from syrup with a slotted spoon, reserving syrup for another use. Cut pineapple rings into halves or quarters and combine in a serving bowl with whole peaches, mirabelles, apricots and green figs. Garnish with a few canned lychees and fresh strawberries, if desired. Chill.

2. Combine sugar, butter and rosé wine in a small saucepan and add cloves and cinnamon. Bring to the boil and cook until reduced and slightly thickened. Pour over fruits, sprinkle with finely grated orange peel and return to refrigerator until required.

Macedoine of Fruit

1 stale Madeira or sponge cake
175 g/6 oz butter
675 g/1½ lb pears
1 (339-g/12-oz) can pineapple pieces
12 canned or glacé cherries
25 g/1 oz granulated sugar
little rum or Kirsch

1. Cut the sponge cake into 2 layers. Cut each layer into thin strips.

2. Melt 100 g/4 oz of the butter in a shallow pan and lightly fry the cake strips, remove and arrange some decoratively round a shallow dish. Dice remainder and pile in centre of dish.

3. Peel, slice and core the pears and lightly fry in the remainder of the butter together with the drained pineapple pieces. Mix with the cherries and spoon fruits into the centre of the dish.

4. Add granulated sugar to the pineapple juice with a little rum or Kirsch and cook until thick. Pour over the fruit and serve.

Port Wine or Claret Jellies

300 ml/½ pint water
100 g/4 oz sugar
2 level tablespoons redcurrant jelly
2.5-cm/1-inch stick cinnamon
3 cloves
rind and juice of 1 lemon
25 g/1 oz gelatine
300 ml/½ pint port or claret
2-3 drops of red food colouring (optional)
whipped cream (optional)

1. Combine water, sugar, redcurrant jelly, cinnamon stick and cloves in a saucepan. Add very thinly peeled lemon rind, strained lemon juice,

and gelatine which you have dissolved in a little water. Stir over heat until gelatine is dissolved. Simmer very gently for a few minutes, then add port or claret. Do not allow to boil again.

2. Strain through a piece of muslin and, if necessary, add a few drops of red food colouring to improve colour. Cool.

3. When almost cold, pour into small individual moulds that have been rinsed out with cold water. Chill until firm. Turn out when ready to serve, and decorate with whipped cream if desired.

Orange Jelly Quarters

5 thin-skinned oranges
150 ml/¼ pint port
15 g/½ oz powdered gelatine
150 ml/¼ pint water
1 lemon
100 g/4 oz sugar
sponge fingers and cream (optional)

1. Wash oranges well, pare 1 orange very thinly and infuse peel in port for 1 hour.

2. Soak gelatine in half the water, stir over a low heat until dissolved.

3. Slice remaining oranges in half, and scoop out pulp and juices, reserving orange shells. Discard pips. Combine juice and pulp of all oranges and the lemon with sugar and remaining water.

4. Strain dissolved gelatine and port into orange mixture.

5. Fill emptied orange shells with mixture, cool and chill. When set, cut into halves again. Serve alone, or with sponge fingers and cream.

337

338

Poached Pear Zabaglione

**6 small pears poached in white wine (see
    Pears in Chablis, page 333)**
syrup from pears
3 egg yolks
40 g/1½ oz castor sugar
a little grated lemon rind peel
6-8 tablespoons Marsala, Madeira or sherry

1. Place cold poached pears in individual sorbet glasses with a little of the syrup.

2. **To make zabaglione sauce:** beat egg yolks and castor sugar together in a mixing bowl. Add a little grated lemon rind and pour mixture into the top of a double saucepan. Place over simmering water and beat mixture until frothy.

3. Add Marsala, Madeira or sherry, a little at a time, and beat until the sauce is thick and smooth.

4. Pour sauce over cold poached pears and serve.

Brandied Pears

1 kg/2 lb sugar
1 teaspoon vanilla essence
1 long strip lemon peel
2 cloves
1.15 litres/2 pints water
2.75 kg/6 lb ripe pears
600 ml/1 pint brandy

1. Combine sugar, vanilla essence, lemon peel, cloves and water in large saucepan, and bring to the boil, stirring constantly. Lower heat and simmer, uncovered for 15 minutes.

2. Peel, halve and core pears. Add them to syrup and simmer gently, uncovered, for 30 to 40 minutes, until pears are translucent and soft. Remove from syrup with a slotted spoon.

3. Sterilise 4 600-ml/1-pint jars and leave in hot water until ready to fill.

4. Place 4 tablespoons brandy in each hot jar. Half-fill jars with drained pears, add 2 tablespoons

brandy to each jar. Fill jars with remaining pears, add 2 final tablespoons brandy, and fill with strained syrup to within 1 cm/½ inch of top. Seal jars and store.

Orange Slices Ambrosia

4-6 oranges
4 tablespoons Curaçao
4 tablespoons lemon juice
6 level tablespoons freshly grated coconut

1. Peel oranges, removing all white pith, and separate into segments. Marinate orange segments overnight in Curaçao and lemon juice.

2. Arrange orange segments in a shallow glass serving dish. Pour marinade juices over them and sprinkle with freshly grated coconut.

Sherried Prunes

1–1.5 kg/2–3 lb dried prunes
1 kg/2 lb sugar
1 teaspoon vanilla essence
4 lemon slices
2 cloves
1.15 litres/2 pints water
1 bottle sherry
whipped cream
Vanilla Custard Sauce (see page 419)

1. Soak prunes overnight in cold water. Drain.

2. Combine sugar, vanilla essence, lemon slices, cloves and water in a large saucepan, and bring to the boil, stirring constantly. Lower heat and simmer, uncovered, for 15 minutes.

3. Add prunes to sugar syrup and simmer gently, uncovered, adding more water if necessary, for 30 to 40 minutes, or until prunes are almost cooked through. Remove prunes from syrup with a slotted spoon.

4. Sterilise 4 600-ml/1-pint jars, leave in hot water until ready to fill. Fill jars almost to the top with drained prunes. Half-fill each jar with sherry and add strained syrup to cover. Seal jars and store.

To serve sherried prunes as a dessert: chill prunes in their liqueur. Serve with accompanying sauce boats of whipped cream and vanilla custard.

Baked Pear Compote

1 kg/2 lb firm pears
butter
rind and juice of 1 lemon
175 g/6 oz brown sugar
double cream

1. Peel, slice and core pears, and place in a buttered ovenproof baking dish. Sprinkle the slices with lemon juice, grated lemon rind, brown sugar and dot with butter.

2. Bake uncovered in a moderately hot oven (190°C, 375°F, Gas Mark 5) for 30 minutes, or until tender. Serve with double cream.

Rum Baked Pears in Cream

6 pears
butter
3 tablespoons rum
3 tablespoons water
175 g/6 oz sugar
½ level teaspoon cinnamon
¼ level teaspoon freshly ground nutmeg
150 ml/¼ pint double cream

1. Wash, peel, core and thinly slice the pears and arrange them in a well-buttered ovenproof baking dish. Dot with butter.

2. Combine remaining ingredients, pour over apples and bake in a moderately hot oven (190°C, 375°F, Gas Mark 5) for 30 minutes, or until tender. Serve hot.

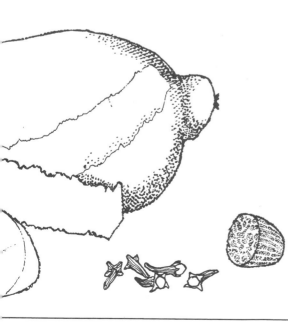

Water Ices, Sorbets and Ice Creams

Syrup for Water Ices *Makes 750 ml/1¼ pints*
Strawberry Water Ice *Serves 4*
Pineapple Water Ice *Serves 4*

Syrup for Water Ices

225 g/8 oz sugar
600 ml/1 pint water
juice of ½ lemon

Combine sugar and water in a saucepan, bring to the boil and boil for 10 minutes, removing any scum that rises. Cool to lukewarm, add lemon juice and strain through a muslin-lined sieve.

Strawberry Water Ice

300 ml/½ pint strawberry purée (see step 2)
300 ml/½ pint syrup for water ices
   (see above)
juice of 1 lemon, strained
red food colouring
2 egg whites

1. Turn refrigerator to its lowest temperature (i.e. highest setting).

2. Rub enough ripe strawberries through a hair sieve to make 300 ml/½ pint of puréed fruit.

3. Combine fruit purée, syrup, strained lemon juice, and enough red food colouring to make a pink ice.

4. When quite cold, pour mixture into freezing tray or loaf tin and freeze, stirring the mixture vigorously with a fork every 30 minutes, until half-frozen.

5. Whisk egg whites until stiff and stir into the half-frozen mixture.

6. Continue freezing until the ice is sufficiently stiff for serving.

Pineapple Water Ice
Illustrated on page 366

1 (376-g/13¼-oz) can pineapple slices
300 ml/½ pint syrup for water ices
   (see above)
juice of 1 lemon, strained
vanilla essence or Kirsch
yellow food colouring

1. Turn refrigerator to its lowest temperature (i.e. highest setting).

2. Chop the pineapple and pound it in a mortar with a little juice from the can. Rub it through a fine sieve. To 300 ml/½ pint of this purée add 300 ml/½ pint syrup, the strained lemon juice and vanilla essence or a little Kirsch. Tint with a little yellow food colouring.

3. When cold, pour mixture into a freezing tray

or loaf tin and freeze, stirring the mixture vigorously with a fork every 30 minutes, until half-frozen, then leaving it for a further 2 or 3 hours until frozen solid. Transfer water ice to main cabinet of refrigerator about 1 hour before serving. Serve water ice piled up in individual iced serving dishes, or in a scooped out pineapple shell.

Grape Water Ice

450 g/1 lb muscat grapes
300 ml/½ pint syrup for water ices (see
  page 340)
juice of 2 lemons
1 tablespoon orange flower water
3 tablespoons Marsala

1. Turn refrigerator to its lowest temperature (i.e. highest setting).

2. Wash grapes, crush them and rub them through a hair sieve.

3. Strain syrup and lemon juice over the grape purée, add orange flower water and Marsala and allow to cool.

4. Pour mixture into freezing tray and freeze, stirring the mixture vigorously with a fork every 30 minutes, until half-frozen, then leaving it for a further 2 or 3 hours until frozen hard. Transfer water ice to main cabinet of refrigerator about 1 hour before serving.

5. Serve water ice piled up in small cups.

Blackcurrant Sorbet

600 ml/1 pint blackcurrants, topped and
  tailed
juice of 2 lemons, strained
75-100 g/3-4 oz granulated sugar

1. Turn refrigerator to its lowest temperature (i.e. highest setting).

2. Place half the blackcurrants in an electric blender and blend for a few seconds until puréed.

Repeat the process with the remaining currants, and add them to the first purée.

341

3. Add the strained lemon juice to the sugar and stir well. Add to the fruit purée.

4. Pour mixture into freezing tray and freeze until almost stiff, about 1 hour.

5. Put half the blackcurrant ice in the blender and blend until softened to sorbet consistency. Repeat with second half. Spoon into chilled glasses and serve at once.

Tangerine Sorbet with Lychees
Illustrated on page 368

175 g/6 oz castor sugar
300 ml/½ pint water
finely grated rind and juice of 8 tangerines
finely grated rind and juice of 1 large lemon
1 egg white, stiffly beaten
lychees
mandarin orange segments
toasted almond spikes

1. Turn refrigerator to its lowest temperature (i.e. highest setting).

2. To make sorbet: dissolve the sugar in the water and then boil rapidly for 5 minutes. Add the rind and juice of the tangerines and lemon and leave to cool. When cold, strain into a deep freezing tray (I often use a loaf tin) and place in the ice-making compartment of the refrigerator. Freeze for 1 hour.

3. Remove from the tray, beat well and then return to the freezer for 1 hour, then fold in the stiffly beaten egg white and beat well. Freeze until firm and set.

4. To serve: spoon sorbet into individual dishes and top with lychees and orange segments. Spike with almonds.

342

Vanilla Ice Cream

4 egg yolks
100 g/4 oz sugar
pinch of salt
450 ml/¾ pint single cream
1-2 teaspoons vanilla essence

1. Turn refrigerator to its lowest temperature (i.e. highest setting) about 1 hour before you make ice cream.

2. Beat egg yolks, sugar and salt until light and lemon-coloured.

3. Scald single cream, and add to egg and sugar mixture, whisking until mixture is well blended.

4. Pour mixture into top of a double saucepan and cook over water, stirring continuously, until custard coats spoon.

5. Strain mixture through a fine sieve and stir in vanilla essence.

6. Pour mixture into containers of your choice and put in freezing compartment. Stir mixture every 30 minutes until it is semi-frozen, then leave for 2 or 3 hours, until it is frozen.

Apricot Ice Cream

300 ml/½ pint apricot purée (see step 2)
300 ml/½ pint double cream, lightly whipped
lemon juice
2-3 tablespoons apricot liqueur
2-3 drops of red food colouring
castor sugar

1. Turn refrigerator to its lowest temperature (i.e. highest setting) about 1 hour before you make ice cream.

2. Make the apricot purée by rubbing canned apricots through a hair sieve, using some of the syrup. The purée must not be too thick.

3. Mix the lightly whipped cream into the purée, then add lemon juice, apricot liqueur and enough red food colouring to give the mixture a good apricot colour. Sweeten to taste.

4. Pour mixture into containers of your choice and put in freezing compartment. Stir mixture every 30 minutes until it is semi-frozen, then leave for 2 or 3 hours, until it is frozen.

Note: Fresh apricots may be used, but they must be stewed until soft in a syrup of sugar and water, before serving.

Liqueur Ice Cream

600 ml/1 pint double cream
100 g/4 oz castor sugar
Maraschino or other liqueur

1. Turn refrigerator to its lowest temperature (i.e. highest setting) about 1 hour before you make ice cream.

2. Whip cream and add sugar. Flavour to taste with Maraschino or liqueur of your choice. Mix well.

3. Pour mixture into containers of your choice and put in freezing compartment. Stir mixture every 30 minutes until it is semi-frozen, then leave for 2 or 3 hours, until it is frozen.

Banana Ice Cream

5 bananas, peeled and sliced
4 egg yolks
100 g/4 oz sugar
pinch of salt
450 ml/¾ pint single cream
1-2 teaspoons vanilla essence
grated rind and juice of 1 orange
150 ml/¼ pint double cream, whipped
castor sugar
1-2 tablespoons Maraschino or other liqueur
yellow food colouring (optional)

1. Turn refrigerator to its lowest temperature (i.e. highest setting) about 1 hour before you make ice cream.

2. Beat egg yolks, sugar and salt until light and lemon-coloured.

3. Scald single cream, and add to egg and sugar mixture, whisking until mixture is well blended.

4. Pour mixture into top of a double saucepan and cook over water, stirring continuously, until custard coats spoon.

5. Strain mixture through a fine sieve and stir in vanilla essence. Flavour custard with grated orange rind.

6. Rub ripe bananas through a sieve to make 150 ml/$\frac{1}{4}$ pint banana purée. Add strained orange juice, chilled custard and whipped double cream to banana purée, and flavour to taste with castor sugar and 1 or 2 tablespoons Maraschino or other liqueur. Colour slightly if desired with yellow food colouring.

7. Pour mixture into containers of your choice and put in freezing compartment. Stir mixture every 30 minutes until it is semi-frozen, then leave for 2 or 3 hours, until it is frozen.

344

Tangerine Ice Cream

6 tangerines
100 g/4 oz castor sugar
600 ml/1 pint double cream

1. Turn refrigerator to its lowest temperature (i.e. highest setting) about 1 hour before you make ice cream.

2. Grate the rind of 3 tangerines very lightly and rub rind into the sugar. Put this flavoured sugar in the top of a double saucepan with half the cream, and scald until sugar is quite dissolved. Remove from the heat and cool.

3. Strain the juice of the 6 tangerines into the mixture.

4. Whip remaining cream and fold into mixture.

5. Pour mixture into containers of your choice and put in freezing compartment. Stir every 30 minutes until it is semi-frozen, then leave for 2 or 3 hours, until it is frozen.

Biscuit Tortoni
Illustrated on page 368

300 ml/½ pint double cream
2 egg whites
castor sugar
salt
100 g/4 oz chopped toasted almonds
sherry, Marsala or cognac

1. Turn refrigerator to its lowest temperature (i.e. highest setting) about 1 hour before you make ice cream.

2. Whip cream.

3. Whisk egg whites, add sugar and salt to taste, and continue whisking until mixture is stiff and glossy.

4. Fold chopped almonds (reserving 2 tablespoons for garnish) into egg mixture with whipped cream.

5. Stir in sherry, Marsala or cognac, to taste, and spoon mixture into 6 to 8 individual soufflé dishes or custard cups. Sprinkle with reserved almonds and put in freezing compartment; leave for 2 or 3 hours, until it is frozen.

Ice Cream with Summer Fruits

225 g/8 oz fresh raspberries
225 g/8 oz redcurrants
225 g/8 oz blackberries
4-6 scoops Vanilla Ice Cream (see page 342)
4-6 tablespoons Poire liqueur or Kirsch

1. Clean and prepare fruits. Chill in refrigerator.

2. Place 1 scoop of ice cream in each individual *coupe* or champagne glass. Sprinkle with 1 tablespoon *Poire* liqueur or Kirsch.

3. Cover ice cream with chilled fruits and serve immediately.

Praline Ice Cream

100 g/4 oz almonds
225 g/8 oz sugar
few drops of lemon juice
oil
4 egg yolks
pinch of salt
450 ml/¾ pint single cream
1-2 teaspoons vanilla essence
300 ml/½ pint double cream
liqueur or cognac

1. Turn refrigerator to its lowest temperature (i.e. highest setting) about 1 hour before you make ice cream.

2. Blanch almonds, chop them roughly and dry well.

3. Combine half the sugar in a small saucepan with

lemon juice and melt it carefully over a medium heat until it takes on a good caramel colour. Add chopped almonds and stir constantly until they are golden brown.

4. Pour the mixture on to a flat tin that has been greased with olive oil, and let it cool.

5. Beat egg yolks, remaining sugar and salt until light and lemon-coloured.

6. Scald single cream, and add to egg and sugar mixture, whisking until mixture is well blended.

7. Pour mixture into top of a double saucepan and cook over water, stirring continuously, until custard coats spoon.

8. Strain mixture through a fine sieve and stir in vanilla essence.

9. When praline mixture is cold and hard, reduce it to a powder by pounding it in a mortar. Add this powder to the warm custard.

10. Pour mixture into containers of your choice and put in freezing compartment. Stir mixture every 30 minutes until it is semi-frozen.

11. Whip double cream, fold into custard with a little liqueur or cognac, and freeze for 2 or 3 hours, until it is frozen.

Christmas Snowball Bombe

345

4 level tablespoons diced candied cherries
4 level tablespoons diced candied pineapple
4 level tablespoons diced candied citron
3 level tablespoons dried sultanas
2 level tablespoons dried currants
Kirsch
900 ml/1½ pints Vanilla Ice Cream (see page 342)
600 ml/1 pint double cream
½ teaspoon vanilla essence
sugar
crystallised violets
small holly leaves

1. Soak all fruits in 6 tablespoons Kirsch for 2 hours, stirring from time to time.

2. Combine fruits and liqueur with softened vanilla ice cream and mix well. Pack mixture into a round *bombe* mould (or fill 2 small pudding basins and press together to form sphere) and freeze until solid.

3. Just before serving, unmould 'snowball' on to a chilled serving dish. Whip cream and flavour with vanilla essence, sugar and Kirsch, to taste. Place in a piping bag fitted with a 'rosette' nozzle. Mask ice cream completely with rosettes of whipped cream and decorate with crystallised violets and small holly leaves.

Creams, Custards and Baked Puddings

Caramel Cream

Illustrated on page 332

4 egg yolks
castor sugar
600 ml/1 pint double cream

1. Beat egg yolks with 4 tablespoons castor sugar until light and frothy.

2. Bring cream to the boil and boil for 1 minute, then pour over the egg yolks. Pour this custard into the dish in which it is to be served. Allow it to cool, then chill in refrigerator.

3. Just before serving, sprinkle a layer of castor sugar 3 mm/⅛ inch thick on top, and brown it quickly under a preheated grill. The grill must be very hot to caramelise the surface.

Baked Custard Pudding à l'Orange

4 egg yolks
2 egg whites
4 tablespoons castor sugar
pinch of salt
½ teaspoon vanilla essence
600 ml/1 pint milk
grated rind and juice of ½ orange
1-2 tablespoons Grand Marnier
butter

1. Beat the egg yolks and whites in a bowl with castor sugar, salt and vanilla essence.

2. Heat the milk and freshly grated orange rind, without allowing it to boil, and pour slowly over the beaten eggs, stirring constantly. Beat in orange juice and Grand Marnier and strain the mixture

into a well-buttered 1-litre/1½-pint soufflé dish, or into individual buttered ramekins.

3. Place the dish, or ramekins, in a baking tin two-thirds full of hot water, and cook in a moderately hot oven (190°C, 375°F, Gas Mark 5) for about 1 hour, or until the custard sets and the top is golden brown. Sprinkle custard with a little castor sugar.

Baked Bread and Butter Pudding

Illustrated on page 388

2-4 slices bread
softened butter
2 eggs
600 ml/1 pint milk
castor sugar
vanilla essence
4 level tablespoons currants or sultanas

1. Remove crusts from bread, butter slices, and cut into thin strips. Lay bread strips in a well-buttered oblong ovenproof dish. The dish should be about half full.

2. Whisk eggs in a mixing bowl, add the milk, and sugar and vanilla essence to taste. Mix well together and strain over bread strips. Allow pudding to stand until bread is well soaked.

3. Sprinkle with currants or sultanas. Bake in a moderately hot oven (190°C, 375°F, Gas Mark 5) for 20 to 30 minutes until golden brown and firm to the touch. Sprinkle with sugar and serve hot.

Brown Betty

675 g/1½ lb apples, peeled, cored and sliced
butter
175 g/6 oz browned breadcrumbs
3 level tablespoons golden syrup
150 ml/¼ pint water
½ level teaspoon ground cinnamon
sugar
cream

1. Place a layer of sliced apples in a buttered pie dish. Sprinkle some of the breadcrumbs over them, and dot with butter. Put in some more apples and repeat these alternate layers until all the apples and breadcrumbs are used up, finishing with a top layer of breadcrumbs.

2. Mix syrup with water and cinnamon, and pour this over the top of the apples. Sprinkle with sugar and dot with butter.

3. Place the pie dish in a baking tin two-thirds full of hot water, and bake in a moderately hot oven (190°C, 375°F, Gas Mark 5) for 1 hour, or until the apples are soft. Serve with cream.

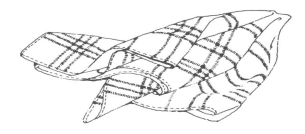

Apple Amber Pudding

675 g/1½ lb apples, peeled, cored and sliced
2-4 level tablespoons granulated sugar
4 level tablespoons butter
grated rind of 1 lemon
2 egg yolks, beaten
1 quantity shortcrust pastry (see page 378)
2 egg whites
1 level tablespoon castor sugar
vanilla essence
glacé cherries
angelica

1. Combine apples, sugar, butter and grated lemon rind in a saucepan, and simmer gently, stirring from time to time, until mixture is reduced to pulp. Beat mixture with a wooden spoon until perfectly smooth, or rub it through a sieve, then add beaten egg yolks.

2. Line a large deep pie dish with shortcrust pastry and pour apple mixture into it. Bake in a moderately hot oven (190°C, 375°F, Gas Mark 5) for 30 to 40 minutes, until the pastry is cooked and the apple mixture set.

3. Whisk egg whites until stiff and flavour with 1 tablespoon castor sugar and a few drops of vanilla.

4. Pile meringue on top of the pudding and decorate with a few pieces of glacé cherry and angelica. Return to a cool oven (150°C, 300°F, Gas Mark 2) for 10 to 15 minutes until lightly browned.

Queen of Puddings

50 g/2 oz fresh breadcrumbs
3 tablespoons butter
3-4 level tablespoons sugar
grated lemon rind
vanilla essence
600 ml/1 pint milk
3 egg yolks
3-4 level tablespoons apricot or strawberry jam
lemon juice

MERINGUE
4 egg whites
castor sugar

1. Combine breadcrumbs with butter and sugar. Flavour to taste with grated lemon rind and vanilla essence.

2. Bring the milk almost to the boil in a small saucepan. Pour it over the crumb mixture and let it soak for 10 minutes.

3. Stir in egg yolks, pour the mixture into a well-buttered large deep pie dish and bake in a moderately hot oven (190°C, 375°F, Gas Mark 5) for 20 to 25 minutes, until set. Remove from oven and allow to cool.

4. When cool, spread with apricot or strawberry jam flavoured to taste with lemon juice.

5. Beat egg whites until stiff but not dry, fold in castor sugar to taste.

6. Pile meringue on pudding in high peaks and bake in a moderate oven (180°C, 350°F, Gas Mark 4) until meringue is lightly browned.

347

348

Baked Sultana Pudding

225 g/8 oz plain flour
salt
1 level teaspoon baking powder
6 tablespoons butter or lard
75 g/3 oz sultanas
3 level tablespoons sugar
little candied peel, finely shredded
1 teaspoon vanilla essence
2 eggs, well beaten
175 ml/6 fl oz milk
cream

1. Sift the flour, salt and baking powder into a bowl, and rub in butter or lard until free from lumps.

2. Pick and clean the sultanas, and add them with the sugar, candied peel and vanilla essence. Make a well in the centre, add the beaten eggs, and then gradually mix in the milk. Mix together thoroughly.

3. Put the mixture in a well-buttered deep oven-proof dish about 38 by 23 cm/15 by 9 inches, and bake in a moderately hot oven (190°C, 375°F, Gas Mark 5) for 30 minutes, or until well risen and firm to the touch.

3. To serve: cut into squares, sprinkle with additional sugar and serve hot with cream.

Baked Apricot Roll

225 g/8 oz plain flour
1 level teaspoon baking powder
1 level teaspoon salt
1-2 level tablespoons castor sugar
100 g/4 oz shredded suet
6-8 tablespoons water
350 g/12 oz apricot jam
butter
Vanilla Custard Sauce (see page 419) or
**   whipped cream**

1. Combine flour, baking powder, salt, sugar and suet in a large mixing bowl. Work suet into dry ingredients with fingertips. Mix in enough water

(6 to 8 tablespoons) with a fork to make dough leave sides of the bowl.

2. Roll dough into an oblong about 30 by 45 cm/12 by 18 inches. Spread with apricot jam and roll lengthwise into a large sausage shape. Seal edge with water and fold ends like an envelope.

3. Place roll in a large buttered baking tin and bake in a hot oven (220°C, 425°F, Gas Mark 7) for 20 to 30 minutes, until golden.

4. Serve warm with Vanilla Custard Sauce or whipped cream.

Cottage Pudding

275 g/10 oz plain flour
2 level teaspoons baking powder
½ level teaspoon salt
6 level tablespoons softened butter
½ teaspoon vanilla essence
150 g/5 oz sugar
2 eggs
250 ml/8 fl oz milk
Lemon or Strawberry Hard Sauce (see
**   page 419)**

1. Sift flour, baking powder and salt into a mixing bowl.

2. Work softened butter and vanilla essence together until soft, add sugar gradually and continue beating until mixture is creamy.

3. Separate eggs and beat yolks thoroughly into creamed mixture. Stir in a third of the flour mixture and add a third of the milk. Repeat these ingredients alternately, ending with flour, until all ingredients are used.

4. Beat egg whites until stiff and fold gently into batter.

5. Pour batter into a greased 1.25-litre/2-pint pudding basin and bake in a moderate oven (180°C, 350°F, Gas Mark 4) for 30 to 40 minutes. Cool slightly and serve topped with Lemon or Strawberry Hard Sauce.

Gâteau de Pommes à la Crème

1½ quantity shortcrust pastry (see page 378)
butter
finely chopped almonds
melted apricot jam

APPLE FILLING
2 sheets leaf gelatine or 7 g/¼ oz powdered
    gelatine
300 ml/½ pint lemon or wine jelly
150 ml/¼ pint double cream, whipped
300 ml/½ pint thick apple purée
1 tablespoon liqueur

TO DECORATE
300 ml/½ pint double cream, whipped,
    sweetened and flavoured
diced preserved fruits

1. Make shortcrust pastry as directed.

2. Butter a 1-litre/1½-pint soufflé mould and line
it with shortcrust pastry, rolled out very thinly.
Prick dough with a fork; chill in the refrigerator
for 2 hours. Then line the mould with foil, fill
with rice or dried haricot beans and bake 'blind'
in a moderately hot oven (200°C, 400°F, Gas
Mark 4) for about 15 minutes, or until pastry is
thoroughly cooked. Reduce heat to moderate
(180°C, 350°F, Gas Mark 4); then remove foil
and rice or beans, and return the pastry case to
the oven for 5 to 10 minutes to dry and brown
inside. **Note:** if pastry begins to brown at edges,
cover edges with a little foil. When cooked, turn
it out carefully and cool on a wire tray.

3. Brown finely chopped almonds in the oven.

4. Brush outside of the pastry case with melted
apricot jam, and coat it with finely chopped
almonds.

5. To make apple filling: soak gelatine (see
Rice à la Royale, page 355, step 3) and then dissolve
in lemon or wine jelly to make it extra stiff.
Strain mixture into a mixing bowl and whisk
until white and frothy. Stir whipped cream into
jelly and fold into thick apple purée. Add liqueur
or other flavouring, to taste, and when mixture

is on the point of setting, pour it into the pastry
case. Set aside to cool for at least 30 minutes.

6. To finish: have whipped cream, sweetened
and flavoured, ready in a piping bag fitted with a
rose pipe. Pipe whipped cream 'rosettes' into top
of *gâteau* and decorate with diced preserved fruits.

Coeur à la Crème

175 g/6 oz cream cheese
1 egg yolk
2 level tablespoons sugar
grated rind of 1 orange
1 teaspoon vanilla essence
salt
200 ml/7 fl oz double cream
fresh berries of your choice: strawberries,
    blueberries, raspberries, etc.

1. Beat the cream cheese until very light and fluffy.
Then beat in egg yolk, sugar, grated orange rind,
vanilla essence and a generous pinch of salt.

2. Whip the cream with a large whisk until the
cream holds its shape. Fold the cream into the
cream cheese mixture with a spatula.

3. Cut squares of cheesecloth (double thickness)
large enough to come about 3.5 cm/1½ inches outside each heart-shaped mould when used as a
lining. Moisten with cold water, wring out, then
carefully line each heart-shaped dish.

4. Fill the cheesecloth-lined dishes with the cheese
mixture, piling mixture into a slight dome in each
dish. Fold over ends of cheesecloth to cover cheese.
Place the moulds on a wire tray placed over a
baking tin to drain in the refrigerator overnight.

5. To serve: unmould 1 delicate cheese 'heart' on
to each dessert plate. Fill each heart-shaped mould
(which you have first washed and dried) with
chilled fresh berries, and place on each plate beside
the moulded *coeur à la crème*. If desired, serve
with fresh cream, or a sauce made by heating
4 tablespoons redcurrant jelly and 4 tablespoons
water until jelly melts, and stirring in 2 to 4 tablespoons Kirsch or cognac.

349

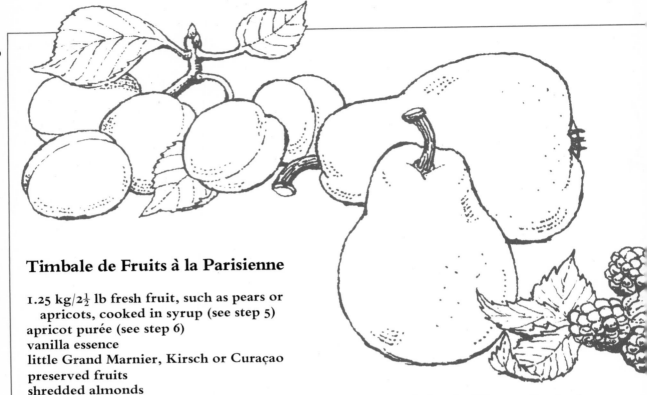

Timbale de Fruits à la Parisienne

1.25 kg/2½ lb fresh fruit, such as pears or
   apricots, cooked in syrup (see step 5)
apricot purée (see step 6)
vanilla essence
little Grand Marnier, Kirsch or Curaçao
preserved fruits
shredded almonds

BRIOCHE
450 g/1 lb plain flour
15 g/½ oz dried yeast
salt
lukewarm water
4 eggs
2–4 level tablespoons sugar
butter

1. To make a yeast sponge: sift 100 g/4 oz flour
into a small mixing bowl and make a well in the
centre. Sprinkle yeast and a pinch of salt into 4
tablespoons lukewarm water; after a few minutes,
stir well. Strain yeast mixture into the centre of
the flour. Make into a soft dough. Roll this in a
little flour to make a ball and cut it across the top
with a sharp knife. Place 'sponge' in just enough
warm water to cover it while you are preparing
the dough – about 15 minutes. Keep the water
warm but not hot over a saucepan, and the
'sponge' will swell to two or three times its
original volume.

2. To make the dough: sift 350 g/12 oz flour
into a mixing bowl and make a well in the centre.
Add eggs to well, and mix in the flour gradually
to make a soft dough. When well mixed, turn
dough out on a lightly floured board and knead
it until the dough becomes smooth and elastic
and no longer sticks to your fingers. Then mix in
the sugar, a pinch of salt and 100-175 g/4-6 oz
slightly softened butter. When these are well
incorporated, drain the 'sponge', place it in the
centre of the other dough, and mix the two
doughs lightly. Place the dough in a floured
bowl, cover it and let it stand in the natural heat
of the kitchen for about 3 hours, by which time
it should have doubled its original volume.
Knock the dough back to its original size, and
set it in a cool place until the next day, knocking
it down again if it rises too much. It may be
kept for 24 hours in this way so long as it is not
allowed to rise too much.

3. To make a large brioche: butter a soufflé
mould 20 to 25 cm/8 to 10 inches in diameter and
tie a strong band of buttered greaseproof paper
round the outside to make a high mould. Half-fill
the mould with *brioche* dough and set it in a warm
place to rise. When the dough has risen to the
top of the mould, put it in a moderately hot oven
(190°C, 375°F, Gas Mark 5) to bake for 30 to 40
minutes, until brown.

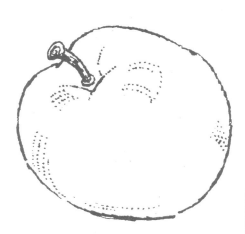

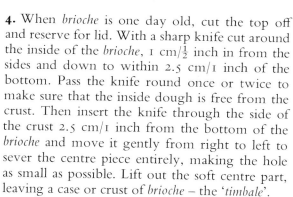

8. Add a little Grand Marnier, Kirsch, or Curaçao, and remaining apricot glaze to fruits. Fill *timbale* with glazed fruits, using as little syrup as possible. Put on lid, and serve remaining syrup and fruit separately.

Blackberry and Apple Sponge

1 kg/2 lb apples
225 g/8 oz blackberries, hulled and washed
4-6 level tablespoons castor sugar
cream or Vanilla Custard Sauce (see page 419)

SPONGE
75 g/3 oz butter
75 g/3 oz castor sugar
2 eggs, beaten
100 g/4 oz self-raising flour
25 g/1 oz cornflour

1. Peel, core and slice the apples into a pie dish, and add hulled and washed blackberries and sugar.

2. To make sponge: cream butter and sugar until light and fluffy. Add eggs one at a time, adding a little flour with the second egg. Fold in the remaining flour and cornflour.

3. Spread sponge mixture over the fruit. Bake in a moderately hot oven (190°C, 375°F, Gas Mark 5) for 30 to 40 minutes. Sprinkle with a little castor sugar, and serve hot with cream or Vanilla Custard Sauce.

4. When *brioche* is one day old, cut the top off and reserve for lid. With a sharp knife cut around the inside of the *brioche*, 1 cm/½ inch in from the sides and down to within 2.5 cm/1 inch of the bottom. Pass the knife round once or twice to make sure that the inside dough is free from the crust. Then insert the knife through the side of the crust 2.5 cm/1 inch from the bottom of the *brioche* and move it gently from right to left to sever the centre piece entirely, making the hole as small as possible. Lift out the soft centre part, leaving a case or crust of *brioche* – the '*timbale*'.

5. To prepare fruit for filling: peel and dice fresh fruit and cook until tender in a syrup of 2 tablespoons sugar and 150 ml/¼ pint water flavoured with vanilla essence.

6. To make apricot glaze: Sieve or liquidise 6–8 canned apricot halves (or 150 ml/¼ pint apricot jam). Mix purée in a small saucepan with some of the fruit syrup (see step 5), flavour with vanilla essence and/or a little liqueur (Grand Marnier, Kirsch or Curaçao), and boil quickly until reduced to a thick syrup or jelly.

7. Brush this hot syrup over *timbale*, glazing well both inside and out. Decorate top edge with preserved fruits and shredded almonds, while syrup is still sticky.

352

Apple Bread Pudding

about 14 slices fresh bread, cut medium
   thick
100 g/4 oz butter, softened
675 g/1½ lb tart apples
finely grated rind and juice of 1 lemon
finely grated rind and juice of ½ orange
50 g/2 oz Demerara sugar
2 level tablespoons raisins
generous pinch of ground cloves
¼ level teaspoon ground cinnamon
450 ml/¾ pint Vanilla Custard Sauce (see
   page 419)

1. Remove crusts from the bread and butter each slice generously on one side. Cut 3 or 4 small rounds from each slice with a cutter. Cut bread trimmings (not crusts) into small dice.

2. Butter a 1.25-litre/2-pint rectangular baking dish generously and line base and sides completely with some of the bread rounds, buttered sides inwards.

3. Peel, core and cut apples into small chunks. Toss them thoroughly with lemon and orange juice and finely grated lemon and orange rind, sugar, raisins and spices.

4. Pack half the apple mixture into the bread-lined baking dish and dot with a level tablespoon of butter.

5. Scatter surface with diced bread and fill to the top with remaining apple mixture. Press down slightly and dot with another tablespoon of butter. Cover surface entirely with overlapping bread rounds, buttered sides uppermost.

6. Cover pudding loosely with a sheet of foil and bake in a moderately hot oven (190°C, 375°F, Gas Mark 5) for 30 to 40 minutes, removing foil for last 10 minutes of cooking time.

7. Serve warm with Vanilla Custard Sauce (or whipped cream flavoured with a little rum).

Zuppa Inglese

900 ml/1½ pints milk
½ teaspoon vanilla essence
¼ level teaspoon ground cinnamon
1 strip lemon rind
pinch of salt
4-6 tablespoons sugar
1 level tablespoon cornflour
8 egg yolks
6-8 tablespoons rum
grated rind and juice of ½ orange
4 tablespoons Kirsch
finely grated chocolate

SPONGE CAKE
6 egg yolks
225 g/8 oz sugar
2 tablespoons lemon juice or water
grated rind of ½ lemon
generous pinch of salt
75 g/3 oz plain flour, sifted 4 times
25 g/1 oz cornflour
6 egg whites

1. To make sponge cake: beat egg yolks, sugar, lemon juice or water, lemon rind and salt until light and fluffy (5 minutes at high mixer speed). Sift flour and cornflour, and mix into egg yolk mixture a little at a time. Whisk egg whites until soft peaks form, and fold gently into egg yolk mixture. Divide mixture into two unbuttered 21-cm/8½-inch cake tins. Cut through mixture gently several times to break up any larger air bubbles. Bake in a moderate oven (180°C, 350°F, Gas Mark 4) for 25 to 30 minutes. Test by denting with finger; if the cake is done, the dent will spring back. Invert cakes on wire trays. When cool, loosen edges and remove from tins.

2. Combine milk, vanilla essence, cinnamon, lemon rind and salt in a saucepan, and bring just to boiling point. Remove from heat.

3. Mix sugar and cornflour together in the top of a double saucepan. Add egg yolks and blend well. Gradually stir in the scalded milk, and cook over hot water, stirring constantly, until mixture is smooth and thick. Remove from heat. Cool. Remove lemon peel.

4. At least 2 hours before serving: place 1 layer of cake in a serving dish, sprinkle with rum and orange juice, and cover with about two-thirds of the cooled custard mixture. Top with second cake, sprinkle with Kirsch and pour over remaining sauce. Chill.

5. Just before serving, remove from refrigerator and sprinkle with finely grated chocolate and orange rind.

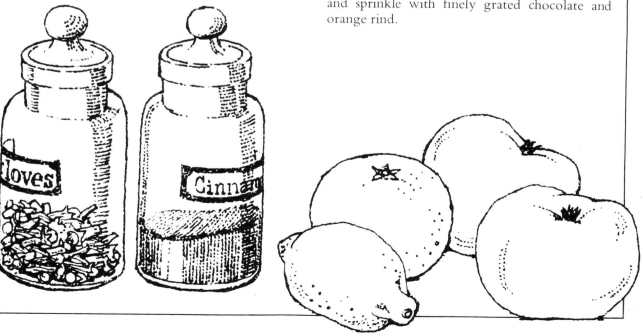

354

Simple Rice Pudding

8 level tablespoons rice
butter
2-4 level tablespoons sugar
salt
nutmeg or other flavouring
750 ml/1¼ pints milk
150 ml/¼ pint double cream
2 level tablespoons finely shredded or
    chopped suet or butter
sultanas (optional)

1. Wash the rice, and put it in a well-buttered pie dish with the sugar, salt, and a little grated nutmeg or other flavouring. Pour in milk and double cream, and sprinkle the finely shredded or chopped suet over the top.

2. Bake the pudding in a moderate oven (180°C, 350°F, Gas Mark 4) for 2 to 3 hours, until the rice is quite soft. The slower it is cooked, the softer and creamier it will be. Sultanas may also be added if desired.

Old English Rice Pudding

6 level tablespoons rice
150 ml/¼ pint water
900 ml/1½ pints milk
pinch of salt
grated lemon rind
150 ml/¼ pint double cream
sugar
2 eggs, separated
butter

1. Wash the rice and put it in a saucepan with the water. Bring to the boil and cook until water is absorbed.

2. Add the milk, salt and a little grated lemon rind. Reduce heat and simmer slowly for about 15 minutes, until the rice is thoroughly cooked, stirring occasionally with a wooden spoon.

3. When ready, remove the saucepan from the heat, and when slightly cooled, stir in cream, 2 tablespoons sugar and egg yolks.

4. Whisk egg whites until stiff and fold them lightly into mixture. Pour the mixture into a well-buttered pie dish, and bake in a moderate oven (180°C, 350°F, Gas Mark 4) until nicely browned. Sprinkle with sugar.

Rice à la Royale

75 g/3 oz rice
300 ml/½ pint milk
4-6 tablespoons sugar
pears poached in syrup
chopped pistachio nuts or shredded almonds

CUSTARD
300 ml/½ pint milk
½ level teaspoon cornflour
4-6 level tablespoons sugar
4 egg yolks
vanilla essence
2 sheets leaf gelatine, or 7 g/¼ oz powdered
   gelatine
150 ml/¼ pint double cream
2-3 tablespoons Kirsch

I. Place rice, milk and sugar in a saucepan, bring to the boil and simmer until rice is tender. Cool.

2. To make custard: Scald milk and remove from heat. Mix cornflour and sugar together in top of a double saucepan. Add egg yolks and blend well. Gradually stir in scalded milk and cook over hot water, stirring constantly, until mixture is smooth and thick. Flavour to taste with vanilla essence, strain and divide into two equal parts.

3. If using leaf gelatine, soak in water for 10 minutes. Drain and dissolve in any water clinging to the gelatine, over a gentle heat. If using powdered gelatine, sprinkle over 2 tablespoons water and allow to soften. Stir gelatine over hot water until completely dissolved and clear. Add to one part of the custard, reserving remainder to use as a sauce.

4. When the rice is cool, add custard containing gelatine along with 2 or 3 tablespoons double cream, and additional sugar if desired. Mix lightly and spoon into a china or glass serving dish.

5. Drain poached pears, pat them dry of syrup and arrange on top of rice. Add remaining cream to remaining custard, flavour with Kirsch and pour it around pears and over pudding. Sprinkle pears with chopped pistachio nuts or shredded almonds. Serve very cold.

Cold Soufflés

356

4. Stir custard mixture over ice, and when it begins to set, fold in whipped cream, followed by egg whites, beaten until stiff but not dry.

5. Tie a band of double greaseproof paper around the outside of a 14.5-cm/5¾-inch soufflé dish to stand 7.5 cm/3 inches above the rim of the dish. Pour in the mixture and allow to set in refrigerator. Remove paper carefully before serving.

Basic Cold Soufflé

300 ml/½ pint milk
2.5-cm/1-inch vanilla pod
3 egg yolks
3 level tablespoons sugar
1 level tablespoon powdered gelatine
3 tablespoons water
150 ml/¼ pint double cream, whipped
4 egg whites

1. Heat milk with vanilla pod. Remove pod and keep milk hot.

2. Whisk egg yolks and sugar until thick and lemon-coloured. Add hot milk and cook over hot water without allowing mixture to boil.

3. Dissolve gelatine in water and add to custard, strain and cool.

Cold Lemon Soufflé

6 egg yolks
175 g/6 oz castor sugar
juice of 2 large lemons
grated rind of 1 lemon
6 egg whites, stiffly beaten
25 g/1 oz powdered gelatine
150 ml/¼ pint water
½ jar redcurrant jelly
2 tablespoons Kirsch or lemon juice
1 tablespoon water

1. Beat egg yolks thoroughly with sugar, lemon juice and grated lemon rind. Transfer mixture to the top of a double saucepan and whisk over hot water, until mixture thickens.

2. Remove from the heat and allow to cool

slightly. Then fold in the stiffly beaten egg whites.

3. Dissolve gelatine in water and fold into egg mixture. Pour the mixture into a serving bowl and chill.

4. Whisk redcurrant jelly with a little Kirsch, or lemon juice, and water, and serve separately.

Chocolate Soufflé Glacé
Illustrated on page 368

1 medium-sized orange
1 level tablespoon instant coffee
150 g/5 oz bitter chocolate
15 g/½ oz powdered gelatine
6 eggs
100 g/4 oz castor sugar
300 ml/½ pint double cream
1–2 tablespoons brandy, rum or liqueur
   (optional)
coarsely grated dark bitter chocolate and
   whipped cream, to decorate

1. Tie a band of double greaseproof paper around the outside of a 14.5-cm/5¾-inch soufflé dish (measured across the top), to stand 7.5 cm/3 inches above the rim of the dish. Select two bowls, a large one for beating the eggs and a smaller one for melting chocolate. Find a saucepan over which both bowls will fit securely. Fill saucepan half full with water. Fit each bowl in position over the pan and check that base does not touch water. Put water on to heat gently.

2. Scrub the orange clean and dry it thoroughly with a cloth. Finely grate rind into the smaller bowl. Squeeze juice and strain it into the same bowl. Add instant coffee, dissolved in 3 tablespoons boiling water, and chocolate broken into small pieces. Put aside.

3. In a small bowl or cup, sprinkle gelatine over 4 tablespoons cold water and put aside to soften until needed. Break eggs into the large bowl and add sugar.

4. When water in saucepan comes to the boil, reduce heat to a bare simmer. Fit bowl containing

eggs and sugar over pan, and whisk vigorously until mixture is light and bulky, and leaves a trail on the surface when beaters are lifted.

5. Remove bowl and in its place put the smaller bowl containing chocolate mixture. Heat gently until chocolate has completely melted. Meanwhile, continue to whisk egg mixture until barely lukewarm.

6. When chocolate has melted, remove from heat. Remove saucepan of water from heat as well. Stand bowl (or cup) containing softened gelatine in the hot water and stir until completely dissolved. Remove. Whisk chocolate mixture lightly to ensure it is quite free of lumps.

7. When chocolate mixture and dissolved gelatine are both just warm, blend them together thoroughly.

8. Pour cream into a bowl and whisk carefully until it is just thick enough to leave a barely perceptible trail on the surface. (If you have been using an electric mixer so far, this operation may be safer done with a hand whisk to avoid overwhipping cream.)

9. Quickly and lightly fold chocolate gelatine mixture into cream. Then, before mixture has had a chance to start setting, fold it into the cooled whisked egg mixture, together with brandy, rum or liqueur, if used. Stop folding as soon as you have got rid of chocolate 'streaks' in mixture.

10. Stand prepared soufflé dish on a plate. Pour in soufflé mixture, taking care not to dislodge or crumple paper collar. Leave it to firm slightly for 15 to 20 minutes before transferring dish to the refrigerator. Chill soufflé for 2 to 3 hours until firmly set.

11. Just before serving, peel off paper collar. Press coarsely grated bitter chocolate around exposed sides of soufflé and decorate top with grated chocolate and piped whipped cream.

358

Amaretti Soufflé Glacé

½ **level teaspoon powdered gelatine**
4 egg yolks
100 g/4 oz granulated sugar
300 ml/½ pint milk
3-4 tablespoons Amaretti liqueur
few drops of vanilla essence
300 ml/½ pint double cream
6 small Italian macaroons (amaretti),
    crushed

1. Turn refrigerator down to lowest temperature, (i.e. highest setting).

2. Select 6 individual soufflé dishes about 6 cm/ 2½ inches in diameter and tie double-thickness collars of greaseproof paper around them to come 2.5 cm/1 inch above the rim.

3. In a small cup, sprinkle gelatine over 1 tablespoon cold water and leave to soften.

4. In a bowl, beat egg yolks with sugar until thick and light.

5. Pour milk into the top of a double saucepan and bring to the boil over direct heat. Then whisk into egg mixture in a thin stream.

6. Return mixture to double saucepan and stir over gently simmering water until it coats back of spoon, taking care not to let custard boil, or egg yolks will curdle. Cool slightly.

7. Dissolve softened gelatine by standing cup in hot water and stirring until liquid is clear. Blend into the cool custard, together with *Amaretti* liqueur and a few drops of vanilla essence, to taste.

8. Whip double cream until soft peaks form and fold into custard.

9. Divide mixture between prepared soufflé dishes. It should come well above the rim of each dish.

10. Freeze for about 5 hours, or until very firm. Then transfer to the main compartment of the refrigerator for about 1 hour before serving.

11. To serve: sprinkle top of each iced soufflé with finely crushed macaroons, patting the crumbs in lightly to make them stick. Carefully peel off paper collars and serve immediately.

Soufflé Glacé Praliné 'East Arms'

90 g/3½ oz sugar
4 egg yolks, well beaten
100 g/4 oz loaf sugar
100 g/4 oz chopped almonds
350 ml/12 fl oz double cream, whipped
6 egg whites, stiffly beaten
crystallised violets (optional)

1. Boil 4 tablespoons water and the sugar in the top of a double saucepan until sugar is dissolved. Allow to cool and add beaten egg yolks. Whisk over simmering water until mixture is thick and light. Allow to cool.

2. Boil loaf sugar and 4 tablespoons water until sugar is caramel-coloured. Stir in almonds and pour into an oiled baking tin. When cool, crush with a rolling pin.

3. Mix custard mixture, whipped cream and crushed almond mixture until smooth, and then carefully fold in stiffly beaten egg whites. Pour soufflé mixture into 2 0.75-litre/1-pint soufflé dishes with a band of double greaseproof paper tied around the outside. Allow to set in refrigerator for 5 to 6 hours. Remove the bands of paper and decorate with crystallised violets if desired.

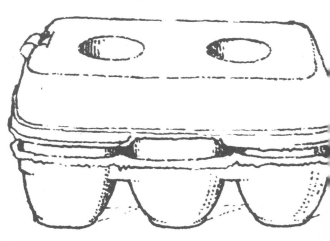

Soufflé Glacé au Cointreau

400 ml/14 fl oz whipped cream
4-6 level tablespoons chopped crystallised
  fruits
Cointreau

CRÈME PÂTISSIÈRE
8 egg yolks
225 g/8 oz castor sugar
400 ml/14 fl oz milk
1 vanilla pod

MERINGUE ITALIENNE
8 egg whites
450 g/1 lb sugar
6-8 tablespoons water

1. To make Crème Pâtissière: beat egg yolks
and sugar together until mixture is lemon-
coloured. Then add milk and vanilla pod, and
mix thoroughly. Place mixture in the top of a
double saucepan and cook over water, stirring
constantly, until smooth and thick. Remove from
heat and discard vanilla pod. Sieve and allow to
cool.

2. To make Meringue Italienne: beat egg
whites until stiff but not dry. Then melt the sugar
and water and cook until you can pull it to a fine
thread with a spoon. Allow to cool. Pour syrup
over egg whites gradually, beating well as you
pour.

3. Add Crème Pâtissière to the cold meringue,
together with whipped cream, some crystallised
fruits, and Cointreau, to taste.

4. Tie a band of double greaseproof paper around
the outside of a 15 to 18-cm/6 to 7-inch porcelain
soufflé dish to stand 7.5 cm/3 inches above the rim
of the dish. Pour the mixture into the soufflé dish,
allowing it to come above the rim of the dish (it
will be held in place by the paper). Chill in the
refrigerator, and just before serving, remove the
band of paper. The *soufflé glacé*, higher than the
dish, will give the appearance of a raised soufflé.

Mocha Bavarois

360

40 g/1½ oz bitter chocolate
450 ml/¾ pint milk
6 egg yolks
175 g/6 oz castor sugar
2 level tablespoons instant coffee
2 tablespoons orange liqueur
15 g/½ oz powdered gelatine
4 tablespoons very cold milk
300 ml/½ pint double cream
flavourless cooking oil for brushing

TO DECORATE
2 level tablespoons freshly roasted coffee
 beans
1 tablespoon orange liqueur
whipped cream

1. Break chocolate into small pieces. Pour milk into the top of a double saucepan, scald over direct heat. Add chocolate and stir until dissolved.

2. Beat egg yolks with sugar until fluffy and lemon-coloured. Gradually add scalded chocolate milk mixture, beating constantly.

3. Dissolve instant coffee in 3 tablespoons boiling water. Stir into milk mixture. Pour back into top of double saucepan and cook over lightly simmering water, stirring constantly for about 20 minutes until mixture coats back of spoon. Take care not to let it boil, or egg yolks will curdle.

4. As soon as custard has thickened, plunge pan into cold water to arrest cooking process and cool custard slightly. Stir in liqueur.

5. Soften gelatine in 3 tablespoons cold water. Then put basin in a pan of hot water (the bottom half of the double saucepan is the most convenient), and stir until gelatine has completely dissolved and liquid is clear. Stir into the cooling custard. Leave until cold and just on the point of setting.

6. Add cold milk to double cream and whisk until floppy. Ideally, it should have the same consistency as the cold custard, so that the two can be combined with the minimum of folding. Fold cream into cold custard.

7. Brush a 1.25-litre/2-pint mould with oil. Pour in *bavarois* mixture and chill until set; allow 2 hours at least.

8. To unmould bavarois: dip mould in hot water **for 2 to 3 seconds only** to loosen cream – not too long, or cream will begin to melt. Turn out carefully on to a serving dish, and return to the bottom of the refrigerator until an hour before serving.

9. To decorate bavarois: soak coffee beans in orange liqueur for at least 30 minutes, longer if possible. Drain them and chop coarsely.

10. Just before serving, decorate *bavarois* with whipped cream and sprinkle with chopped coffee beans.

Chocolate Rum Mousse

175 g/6 oz milk chocolate
5 eggs, separated
1 teaspoon vanilla essence
1–2 level teaspoons instant coffee
1 tablespoon hot water
300 ml/½ pint double cream
2 tablespoons rum

1. Melt chocolate in the top of a double saucepan over hot but not boiling water. Remove from heat and allow to cool.

2. Beat egg yolks lightly and then beat them gradually into the melted chocolate. Flavour to taste with vanilla essence and instant coffee dissolved in hot water.

3. Whip cream until thick, stir in rum and fold into the chocolate mixture.

4. Beat egg whites until stiff and fold into the mixture.

5. Pour mixture into a serving dish. Chill for at least 2 hours.

Soufflé Glacé aux Fraises
Illustrated on page 367

225 g/8 oz granulated sugar
6 egg whites
450 ml/¾ pint strawberry purée
300 ml/½ pint double cream, whipped
juice of lemon or lime
icing sugar

1. Boil the sugar with 450 ml/¾ pint water until it reaches the soft ball stage (115°C/240°F).

Note: Test sugar syrup from time to time while cooking by dropping a little syrup into a small bowl of iced water. When you can pick it out and roll it into a tiny ball the syrup is ready to use.

2. Beat egg whites very stiff and carefully fold in the slightly sugar cooled syrup. Chill in the freezer compartment of your refrigerator or in the

freezer, until it reaches the mushy stage. (**Note:** You'll find it necessary to stir egg white and syrup mixture from time to time to keep it from separating.) Then remove from the freezer and gently fold in the strawberry purée and the stiffly whipped cream. Add lemon or lime juice and mix well.

3. Tie a band of double greaseproof paper around the outside of a 0.75-litre/1-pint soufflé dish, to stand 5 cm/2 inches above the rim of the dish. Pour the soufflé mixture into the dish and freeze for about 2 hours.

4. Just before serving, remove the band of paper and dust soufflé liberally with icing sugar.

Chocolate Mould

50 g/2 oz plain chocolate
450 ml/¾ pint milk
7 g/¼ oz powdered gelatine
25–50 g/1–2 oz sugar
2 egg yolks
¼ teaspoon vanilla essence
whipped cream

1. Break the chocolate into small pieces and put it in a saucepan with 150 ml/¼ pint milk. Dissolve chocolate slowly, until smooth.

2. Then remove saucepan from heat, and add the remaining milk, gelatine, sugar and egg yolks. Stir again over heat until the mixture is hot, and the gelatine has dissolved. **Do not allow the mixture to boil.**

3. Strain mixture into a bowl and add vanilla essence. Allow to cool slightly, then pour mixture into a wet mould and set aside until firm.

4. When ready to serve, invert mould on to a serving dish. Serve with whipped cream.

Hot Soufflés

362

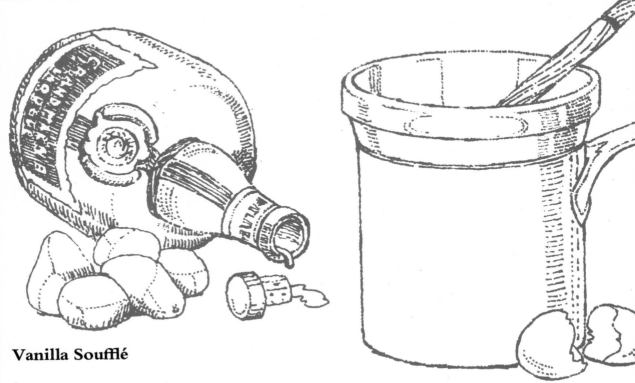

Vanilla Soufflé

butter
3 level tablespoons flour
300 ml/$\frac{1}{2}$ pint hot milk
pinch of salt
5 egg yolks
sugar
$\frac{1}{2}$ teaspoon vanilla essence
6 egg whites

1. Melt 4 level tablespoons butter in the top of a
double saucepan. Stir in the flour and cook until
well blended. Add hot milk and salt, stirring
constantly, and cook until smooth and thick.
Continue cooking and stirring for a few more
minutes. Let sauce cool slightly.

2. Beat egg yolks well with 4 tablespoons sugar
and vanilla essence, and mix well with sauce.
Beat egg whites until they are stiff but not dry,
and fold gently into the sauce mixture.

3. Pour the mixture into a buttered and lightly
sugared 1.5-litre/2$\frac{1}{2}$-pint soufflé dish, and bake in
a moderate oven (180°C, 350°F, Gas Mark 4) for
35 to 45 minutes, until the soufflé is puffed and
golden. Serve at once.

Soufflé aux Fruits Confits

6 level tablespoons crystallised fruits,
   coarsely chopped
2 tablespoons cognac
4 egg yolks
2 level tablespoons flour
4 level tablespoons sugar
300 ml/$\frac{1}{2}$ pint double cream
$\frac{1}{2}$ teaspoon vanilla essence
4 tablespoons Grand Marnier
5 egg whites
pinch of salt
butter
whipped cream

1. Soak coarsely chopped crystallised fruits in
cognac for at least 2 hours.

2. Beat egg yolks, flour and sugar together in the
top of a double saucepan. Add the cream. Place
over hot water and cook, stirring constantly, until
thick and smooth. Do not allow to come to the
boil. Stir in vanilla essence and Grand Marnier.
Allow to cool, stirring occasionally.

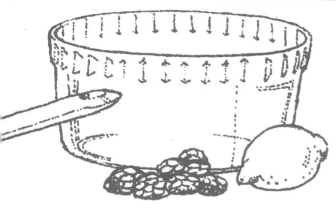

3. Beat the egg whites and salt until stiff but not dry, and fold into the cooled mixture. Pour half the mixture into a buttered 1.25-litre/2-pint soufflé dish. Scatter cognac-soaked fruits over soufflé mixture and then cover with remaining mixture. Bake in a moderate oven (180°C, 350°F, Gas Mark 4) for 35 minutes, or until soufflé is well puffed and golden. Serve immediately with whipped cream.

Raspberry Lemon Soufflé

350 g/12 oz frozen raspberries
6 tablespoons Kirsch or Framboise liqueur
50 g/2 oz castor sugar
5 egg yolks
100 g/4 oz icing sugar, sifted
3 level tablespoons flour, sifted
450 ml/$\frac{3}{4}$ pint milk
$\frac{1}{2}$ level teaspoon finely grated lemon rind
3 tablespoons lemon juice
1 level tablespoon butter
50 g/2 oz stale sponge cake
6 egg whites
pinch of salt

1. Place frozen raspberries in a wide dish. Sprinkle with Kirsch or Framboise liqueur and castor sugar, and leave to defrost completely, about 2 hours, turning occasionally.

2. Grease a 1.5-litre/2½-pint soufflé dish with butter, paying particular attention to the top rim, and dust with granulated sugar, shaking out excess. Set soufflé dish in a deep baking tin and put aside until needed.

3. Preheat oven to moderately hot (200°C, 400°F, Gas Mark 6).

4. Put egg yolks in the top of a double saucepan, add sifted icing sugar and beat with a wire whisk until light and well blended. Add sifted flour, beating constantly until mixture is smooth.

5. In another pan, bring milk to the boil. Remove from heat and add to egg yolk mixture in a thin stream, beating vigorously.

6. Place the egg mixture over a pan of simmering water and cook, stirring constantly, for 7 to 10 minutes, until custard is thick and smooth. Then remove from heat and beat in finely grated lemon rind, lemon juice and butter. Pour custard into a large bowl and allow to cool to lukewarm, stirring occasionally to prevent a skin forming on top.

7. Drain raspberries thoroughly in a sieve, reserving juices.

8. Cut sponge cake into neat, 5-mm/¼-inch dice. Toss lightly with raspberry juices until thoroughly saturated but not crumbly. Any juice which has not been absorbed by the sponge cake may be beaten into the cooling custard.

9. Place egg whites in a large, spotlessly clean, dry bowl. Add a pinch of salt and whisk until stiff but not dry.

10. Fold egg whites into lukewarm custard, using a spatula or a large metal spoon, folding in as quickly and as lightly as possible. Finally, fold in the raspberries and soaked sponge, taking care not to knock any air out of the mixture.

11. Spoon mixture into prepared soufflé dish. Pour 2.5 cm/1 inch of boiling water into the baking tin and gently bring back to the boil over a low heat.

12. As soon as water bubbles, transfer to the oven. Immediately reduce oven temperature to moderate (180°C, 350°F, Gas Mark 4) and bake soufflé for 45 to 50 minutes until well puffed and just set in the centre – this is a very creamy, moist soufflé. Serve immediately.

364

Chocolate Soufflé

65 g/2½ oz chocolate
150 ml/¼ pint milk
4–6 level tablespoons castor sugar
3 egg yolks
vanilla essence
1 level tablespoon cornflour
4 level tablespoons double cream
4 egg whites

1. Break chocolate into small pieces and place in a saucepan with half the milk. Cook gently, stirring occasionally until chocolate is melted.

2. Combine sugar, egg yolks and vanilla essence, to taste, in a mixing bowl, and work them together with a wooden spoon until they are of a creamy consistency. Mix remaining milk with cornflour and add it gradually to the egg mixture, together with the chocolate. Pour into a saucepan and cook until almost boiling. Remove from heat, add cream and cook for a few minutes, stirring occasionally.

3. Beat egg whites until stiff and fold them into chocolate mixture. Pour into a well-buttered 1-litre/1½-pint soufflé dish and bake in a moderate oven (180°C, 350°F, Gas Mark 4) for 30 to 40 minutes, until well risen and firm to the touch. Should the soufflé become too brown, put a piece of paper over the top. Sprinkle with a little sugar just before serving.

Chocolate Rum Soufflé

50 g/2 oz plain chocolate, cut in small pieces
300 ml/½ pint hot milk
4 level tablespoons butter
3 level tablespoons flour
100 g/4 oz sugar
4 egg yolks
pinch of salt
1–2 tablespoons Jamaica rum
5 egg whites, stiffly beaten
whipped cream

1. Melt chocolate in the milk in the top of a double saucepan and beat until smooth and hot. Do not allow it to come to the boil. Melt butter in a saucepan and blend in flour and sugar. Add chocolate mixture and stir over a low heat until the mixture starts to boil. Remove from heat.

2. Beat egg yolks and stir in 2 tablespoons of the hot chocolate mixture. Then pour the egg yolks into the chocolate mixture. Add salt and Jamaica rum, and beat over a low heat until mixture thickens slightly.

3. Remove from heat, and when cool, fold in stiffly beaten egg whites. Pour mixture into a 20-cm/8-inch soufflé dish. Place dish in a baking tin two-thirds full of boiling water and cook in moderate oven (160°C, 325°F, Gas Mark 3) for 45 minutes, or until soufflé is puffed and golden. Serve immediately with whipped cream.

Apricot Soufflé

4 level tablespoons butter
3 level tablespoons flour
300 ml/½ pint hot milk
pinch of salt
3 egg yolks
100 g/4 oz sugar
4 tablespoons Kirsch
300 ml/½ pint puréed apricots, cooked in
   syrup
4 egg whites

1. Melt butter in the top of a double saucepan. Stir in the flour and cook until well blended. Add hot milk and salt stirring constantly and cook the sauce until smooth and thick. Continue cooking and stirring a little longer, then cool slightly.

2. Beat egg yolks well with sugar and combine with the sauce. Flavour with 2 tablespoons Kirsch and add puréed apricots, to which you have added remaining Kirsch. Let the mixture get cold, then fold in egg whites, beaten until they are stiff but not dry.

3. Place mixture into a lightly buttered and sugared 14.5-cm/5¾-inch soufflé dish. Cook in a moderate oven (180°C, 350°F, Gas Mark 4) for 30 to 35 minutes, until cooked.

Fresh Fruit Sorbets

Pineapple Water Ice (see page 340)

Soufflé Glacé aux Fraises (see page 361)

Biscuit Tortoni (see page 344)

Chocolate Soufflé Glacé (see page 357)

Tangerine Sorbet with Lychees (see page 341)

Normandy Soufflé

2 ripe apples
butter
2 level tablespoons sugar
2 ripe pears
lemon juice
2 tablespoons Calvados or cognac
5 egg whites

CRÈME PÂTISSIÈRE
4 egg yolks
100 g/4 oz sugar
2 level tablespoons sifted flour
300 ml/½ pint milk
½ teaspoon vanilla essence

1. To make Crème Pâtissière: beat egg yolks and sugar together until mixture is lemon-coloured. Stir in flour, then add milk and vanilla essence, and mix thoroughly. Place mixture in top of a double saucepan and cook over water, stirring constantly, until smooth and thick. Remove from heat and sieve. Allow to cool.

2. Peel, core and slice apples. Add 1 tablespoon butter and sugar, and simmer over a gentle heat until soft. Peel and core pears. Mash pears and cooked apples, drain off excess liquid if necessary, and flavour to taste with sugar, lemon juice and Calvados or cognac.

3. Whisk egg whites until stiff and fold into Crème Pâtissière. Place half the custard in a well-buttered 1.25-litre/2-pint soufflé dish. Cover with a layer of fruit purée and top with remaining custard mixture. Bake in a moderate oven (180°C, 350°F, Gas Mark 4) for 40 minutes. Serve at once.

Soufflé Puddings

8 tablespoons softened butter
100 g/4 oz icing sugar
100 g/4 oz plain flour, sifted
400 ml/14 fl oz milk, boiled
½-1 teaspoon vanilla essence
5 egg yolks
6 egg whites

SABAYON SAUCE
4 egg yolks
100 g/4 oz sugar
175 ml/6 fl oz Marsala
1 tablespoon cognac

1. Work butter into a *pommade* in a mixing bowl. Add icing sugar and sifted flour, beating well between each addition. Dilute with hot milk flavoured with vanilla essence.

2. Cook over a high heat, stirring continuously, until mixture dries out and leaves the side of the pan (like a *pâte à choux*).

3. Remove from heat; thicken with egg yolks, one by one, then carefully fold in the beaten egg whites. Pour into well-buttered individual soufflé dishes and place in a baking tin half filled with hot water. Cook in a moderate oven (180°C, 350°F, Gas Mark 4) for 40 to 45 minutes, until puddings are cooked. Serve with Sabayon Sauce.

4. To make Sabayon Sauce: whisk egg yolks and sugar until yellow and frothy in the top of a double saucepan. Add the Marsala; place over hot water and cook until thick and foamy, stirring constantly. Stir in cognac and chill.

Variations

Orange Curaçao Soufflé Puddings
Kümmel Soufflé Puddings
Benedictine Soufflé Puddings

Make puddings as above, but flavour with the liqueur of your choice. Serve with Sabayon Sauce flavoured with the same liqueur used for the puddings instead of Marsala and cognac as in above recipe.

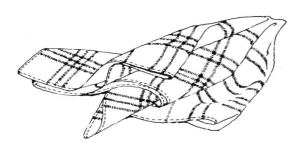

Batters, Crêpes and Fritters

370

Basic French Crêpes (for Sweet Filling)

100 g/4 oz plain flour
½ level teaspoon salt
2 level tablespoons sugar
2 eggs
450 ml/¾ pint milk
butter or oil

1. Sift flour, salt and sugar into a mixing bowl. Beat eggs and add them to dry ingredients. Mix in milk and 2 tablespoons melted butter or oil and beat until smooth. Strain through a fine sieve and leave batter to stand for at least 2 hours before cooking the *crêpes*. Batter should be as thin as cream. Add a little water if too thick.

2. Place about 2 tablespoons batter into a heated and buttered pan, swirling pan to allow batter to cover entire surface thinly. Brush a piece of butter around edge of hot pan with the point of a knife and cook over a medium heat until just golden but not brown (about 1 minute each side). Repeat until all *crêpes* are cooked, stacking them on a plate as they are ready.

Batter I

(To use for fritters, croquettes or batter-fried meats, fish or poultry)

100 g/4 oz plain flour
pinch of salt
150 ml/¼ pint warm water or milk
1 tablespoon oil or melted butter
2–3 egg whites

Sift flour and salt into a mixing bowl, and make a well in the centre. Gradually pour water or milk into the well, beating with a wooden spoon to make batter smooth and free from lumps. Add oil or melted butter and beat again for a few minutes. Whisk egg whites to a stiff froth and fold them lightly into the batter. Use immediately and cook as for Basic French Crêpes (see above).

Batter II

(**Beer Batter:** excellent for prawns, shrimps and other seafood)

225 g/8 oz plain flour
pinch of salt
2 eggs, well beaten
2 tablespoons oil or melted butter
1 tablespoon brandy
300 ml/½ pint pale ale

Sift flour and salt into a mixing bowl, and make a well in the centre. Stir beaten eggs into the well and then gradually beat in the other ingredients until batter is perfectly smooth. Cover the bowl and let batter stand for at least 6 hours in a very cool place before using. Cook as for Basic French Crêpes (see above).

Swedish Pancakes

100 g/4 oz plain flour
1 level tablespoon sugar
½ level teaspoon salt
2 egg yolks
450 ml/¾ pint warm milk
2 tablespoons melted butter
2 egg whites, stiffly beaten
preserved lingonberries or cranberries
beaten butter (see step 3)

1. Sift flour, sugar and salt into mixing bowl. Beat egg yolks and add them to dry ingredients. Combine warm milk and melted butter and gradually beat in avoiding any lumps. Strain through a fine sieve and leave batter to stand for at least 2 hours.

2. Before cooking beat again, and fold in stiffly beaten egg whites. Bake on either a greased griddle, a large iron frying pan, or a special Swedish *plattar* pan with indentations for pancakes. Pour in enough batter to make pancakes about 7.5 cm/3 inches in diameter. Cook as for Basic French Crêpes (see above).

3. Serve with preserved lingonberries and beaten butter. (Soften fresh butter and beat it in electric mixer on low speed until smooth. Then beat on highest speed until butter is fluffy and a delicate light yellow colour – 8 to 10 minutes. If you store it in refrigerator, allow to soften again at room temperature before using.)

Pfannkuchen (German Pancakes)

3 eggs, beaten
300 ml/½ pint milk
generous pinch of salt
1 level tablespoon sugar
75 g/3 oz plain flour
butter
strawberry jam, cooked apples or Chocolate
  Sauce (see page 418)
cinnamon-flavoured sugar

1. Beat eggs, milk, salt, sugar and flour together and stand for 30 minutes.

2. Brush thick-bottomed 25-cm/10-inch frying pan with butter. Pour in 5 to 6 tablespoons batter at a time tilting pan to make batter spread to form large, flat pancake. Cook over medium heat until batter bubbles. Turn and cook other side. Stack on plate in heated oven.

3. Coat each pancake with butter and strawberry jam, cooked apples or Chocolate Sauce, and roll up. Cut each pancake in half. Sprinkle with cinnamon sugar.

Crêpes des Oliviers

150 g/5 oz plain flour
100 g/4 oz sugar
200 ml/7 fl oz warm milk
4 eggs, beaten
100 g/4 oz butter
grated rind and juice of 2 oranges
Grand Marnier

1. Combine flour and 2 tablespoons sugar in a mixing bowl, and gradually beat in warm milk, beaten eggs and melted butter. Add finely grated rind of 1 orange to flavour the *crêpes* batter and allow to stand for 2 hours before using.

2. Make a syrup with remaining sugar, grated rind of remaining orange and juice of 2 oranges. Flavour to taste with Grand Marnier.

3. Make pancakes in usual way and fold in four. Place on a well-buttered ovenproof dish and heat through in the syrup.

Crêpes aux Marrons Glacés

½ quantity Basic French Crêpes (see page 370)
150 ml/¼ pint double cream
vanilla essence
icing sugar
8 marrons glacés, chopped

1. Make about 12 *crêpes*, transferring them to a warm plate as you cook them.

2. Whip cream, flavoured to taste with vanilla essence and icing sugar, adding a little iced water to make mixture lighter. Fold in chopped *marrons glacés* with syrup. Fill *crêpes* with this mixture and roll up. Dust with icing sugar.

372

Crêpes aux Fruits

½ quantity Basic French Crêpes (see page 370)
3 eating apples, peeled, cored and diced
butter
juice of ½ lemon
4 level tablespoons apricot jam
4 level tablespoons chopped almonds
150 ml/¼ pint whipped cream
2-3 tablespoons Calvados
crushed macaroons
sugar

1. Make about 12 *crêpes*, transferring them to a warm plate as you cook them.

2. Cook diced apples in 3 tablespoons butter and lemon juice until tender. Stir in apricot jam and chopped almonds. Then fold in whipped cream flavoured with Calvados.

3. Cover *crêpes* with apple mixture, fold in four and place them in a buttered flameproof dish. Sprinkle with crushed macaroons and sugar, and place under a preheated grill for a minute or two to glaze.

Crêpes au Kümmel

225 g/8 oz plain flour
75 g/3 oz icing sugar
4 eggs
3 egg yolks
vanilla essence
600 ml/1 pint milk
8 level tablespoons double cream
2 level tablespoons butter
3 tablespoons Kümmel
finely crushed macaroons

1. Sift flour and icing sugar into a mixing bowl, then beat in eggs and egg yolks one at a time until mixture is thick and lemon-coloured.

2. Add vanilla essence to milk, and heat. Combine with double cream and beat gradually into batter mixture. Add butter, which you have cooked until it is light brown in colour and Kümmel (cognac or rum may be substituted). Strain through a fine sieve and let stand for 1 to 2 hours.

3. Cook as for Basic French Crêpes (see page 370). Place *crêpes* one on top of the other as they are cooked, sprinkling each with icing sugar and finely crushed macaroons.

Crêpes aux Mandarines

½ quantity Basic French Crêpes (see page 370)
grated rind of 1 mandarin orange
2-4 tablespoons Curaçao

BEATEN MANDARIN BUTTER
225 g/8 oz fresh butter
juice of 1 mandarin orange
little grated mandarin orange rind
2-4 tablespoons Curaçao

1. Make *crêpes* adding grated mandarin rind and Curaçao, to taste. Place in an ovenproof dish and keep hot in the oven. At the table, place a spoonful of Beaten Mandarin Butter on each *crêpe*, fold in four and serve immediately.

2. To make beaten Mandarin Butter: soften fresh butter and beat it at low speed in electric mixer until smooth. Then add mandarin juice, a little grated mandarin rind and Curaçao. Beat at high speed until butter is fluffy and a delicate light yellow in colour – 8 to 10 minutes.

Apple Fritters

4 ripe apples
sugar
lemon or orange juice
rum or cognac
1 quantity Batter I or II (see page 370)
fat or oil for deep-frying

1. Peel, core and chop the apples. Sprinkle them with sugar and a little lemon or orange juice, and rum or cognac, to taste. Let them stand for a few minutes, and then mix them with Batter I or II.

2. Place a spoonful of the mixture at a time in hot fat or oil and fry until puffed and golden brown in colour. Do not make fritters too large or they will not cook through. Test the first one before lifting the others from the fat. Sprinkle with sugar and serve immediately.

American Apple Fritters

2 level tablespoons butter
2 level tablespoons sugar
2 eggs, separated
175 g/6 oz plain flour, sifted
1-2 tablespoons milk
1 level teaspoon baking powder
pinch of salt
3 ripe apples, peeled, cored and finely
    chopped
fat or oil for deep-frying
icing sugar

1. Cream butter and sugar until smooth. Beat egg yolks into mixture, then gradually add the sifted flour and milk, beating well. Add baking powder and salt, then fold in finely chopped apple. Beat egg whites until stiff and fold them gently into the mixture.

2. Form the mixture into small balls the size of a walnut. Drop them into hot fat or oil, and fry until golden. Drain, sprinkle with icing sugar and serve immediately.

Fresh Peach Fritters

4 ripe peaches
sugar
Maraschino or Kirsch
macaroon crumbs
1 quantity Batter I or II (see page 370)
fat for frying
lemon wedges

1. Peel and stone peaches, and cut into quarters. Sprinkle the pieces with sugar and a few drops of

Maraschino or Kirsch, and toss in macaroon crumbs. Allow to stand for a few minutes.

2. Dip the coated peaches in Batter I or II, lifting each one out with a skewer and dropping it into a saucepan of hot fat.

3. Fry fritters, turning them from time to time, until golden brown on all sides. Lift fritters out of fat with a skewer or perforated spoon and dry on sugared paper in a moderate oven (160°C, 325°F, Gas Mark 3). Continue until all are cooked. Serve with additional sugar and lemon wedges.

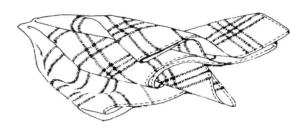

Pear Fritters

4 ripe pears
sugar
white wine
Kirsch
macaroon or cake crumbs
1 quantity Batter I or II (see page 370)
fat or oil for deep-frying
lemon wedges

1. Peel and core pears, and cut into quarters or eighths. Sprinkle slices with sugar and marinate in dry white wine with a little Kirsch for at least 15 minutes.

2. Toss slices in macaroon or cake crumbs, and dip in batter, lifting each piece out with a skewer.

3. Fry fritters in hot fat or oil, turning them from time to time, until golden brown on all sides. Lift fritters out of fat with a skewer or perforated spoon and dry on sugared paper in a moderate oven (160°C, 325°F, Gas Mark 3). Continue until all are cooked. Serve with additional sugar and lemon wedges.

Steamed Puddings

374

Basic Steamed or Boiled Sponge Pudding

butter
3 level tablespoons jam
3 level tablespoons castor sugar
1 egg, well beaten
75 g/3 oz plain flour
150 ml/¼ pint milk
1 level teaspoon baking powder
pinch of salt
Vanilla Custard Sauce or Ginger Sauce
    (see page 419)

1. Butter a 1.25-litre/2-pint pudding basin and coat bottom with jam.

2. Cream 2 tablespoons butter with sugar in a mixing bowl, add beaten egg and half the flour. Beat well and then add the milk and remaining flour. The mixture should have the consistency of a thick batter that will just drop from the spoon. Beat again, and finally add baking powder and salt, to taste.

3. Pour the mixture into the prepared basin, cover with buttered paper then secure tightly with a double thickness of foil. Steam for 45 to 60 minutes, until well risen and firm to the touch. When ready, turn out and serve quickly. Serve with Vanilla Custard Sauce or Ginger Sauce.

Baroness Pudding

225 g/8 oz plain flour
½ level teaspoon salt
1 level teaspoon baking powder
25 g/1 oz castor sugar
100 g/4 oz suet, chopped
100 g/4 oz sultanas
150 ml/¼ pint milk
butter
Apricot Sauce or Vanilla Custard Sauce
    (see page 419)

1. Sift flour, salt and baking powder into a mixing bowl, add sugar, finely chopped suet and sultanas.

2. Mix dry ingredients together thoroughly, make a well in the centre and gradually pour in enough milk to make a soft dough.

3. Pour the mixture into a well-buttered 1.25-litre/2-pint basin which you have decorated with a few sultanas. Cover with buttered paper then secure tightly with a double thickness of foil. Steam steadily for 3 hours. Serve with Apricot Sauce or Vanilla Custard Sauce.

Rich Steamed or Boiled Sponge Pudding

butter
4-6 level tablespoons tart jam or warm
    syrup, honey or treacle
225 g/8 oz plain flour
2 level teaspoons baking powder
100 g/4 oz butter
100 g/4 oz castor sugar
2 eggs
about 150 ml/¼ pint milk

FLAVOURINGS
vanilla essence
grated lemon rind
mixed ground spice, cinnamon or ginger
50 g/2 oz sultanas or raisins
Vanilla Custard Sauce (see page 419)

1. Butter a 1.25-litre/2-pint pudding basin and spread jam, syrup, honey or treacle over the bottom and about a quarter of the way up sides.

2. Sift flour and baking powder into a mixing bowl.

3. Rub in butter with your fingertips until mixture resembles fine breadcrumbs. Stir in sugar and make a well in the centre.

4. Beat eggs lightly. Pour them into the well, together with enough milk to make a batter with a good dropping consistency. Beat vigorously with a wooden spoon until smoothly blended.

5. Beat in chosen flavouring.

6. Pour batter into prepared basin. Cover surface with a disc of buttered greaseproof paper, then cover basin tightly with a double thickness of foil, or tie on a pudding cloth.

7. Steam or boil pudding for 1½ to 2 hours until well risen and firm to the touch.

8. To serve: turn pudding out on to a hot serving dish and serve immediately with a Vanilla Custard Sauce.

Chelsea Pudding

100 g/4 oz suet
100 g/4 oz breadcrumbs
100 g/4 oz plain flour
salt
1 level teaspoon baking powder
100 g/4 oz currants
100 g/4 oz raisins
250 ml/8 fl oz treacle or molasses, slightly
   warmed
250 ml/8 fl oz milk
butter
Vanilla Custard Sauce (see page 419)

1. Chop suet finely and mix with breadcrumbs, flour, salt and baking powder. Mix well together with the tips of the fingers, then add the currants and raisins.

2. Make a well in the centre, stir in slightly warmed treacle, then gradually add milk, beating all together. Pour mixture into a well-buttered 1.25-litre/2-pint pudding basin, or copper mould, cover with buttered paper, then secure tightly with a double thickness of foil. Steam steadily for 3 hours. When ready, turn out and serve with Vanilla Custard Sauce.

Steamed Gingerbread Pudding

100 g/4 oz suet
100 g/4 oz plain flour, sifted
1 level teaspoon ground ginger
½ level teaspoon ground cinnamon
1 level teaspoon baking powder
pinch of salt
250 ml/8 fl oz treacle or molasses
1 egg, well beaten
250 ml/8 fl oz milk
butter
Vanilla Custard Sauce (see page 419)

1. Chop suet finely and mix it in a bowl with sifted flour, ground ginger and cinnamon, and baking powder, adding salt to taste.

2. Make a well in the centre, pour in the treacle and well-beaten egg, and gradually mix in the dry ingredients, adding the milk slowly as you mix. Beat for a minute and pour the mixture into a well-buttered 1.25-litre/2-pint pudding basin, or copper mould. Cover with buttered paper and secure tightly with a double thickness of foil. Steam steadily for 2 to 3 hours, until well risen and firm to the touch. When ready, turn out and serve with Vanilla Custard Sauce.

376

Chocolate Bread Pudding

75 g/3 oz semi-sweet chocolate
50 g/2 oz butter
150 ml/¼ pint milk
50 g/2 oz castor sugar
2 eggs, separated
150 g/5 oz fresh white breadcrumbs
pinch of ground cinnamon
vanilla essence
Chocolate Sauce or Vanilla Custard Sauce
  (see pages 418, 419)

1. Dissolve chocolate with butter in the top of a double saucepan. Add milk and simmer gently. Sprinkle sugar over the top, add egg yolks and half the breadcrumbs, and mix well. Stir in remaining breadcrumbs, cinnamon and vanilla essence, to taste.

2. Whisk egg whites to a stiff froth. Fold them into mixture at the last moment, and then pour mixture into a well-buttered 1.25-litre/2-pint pudding basin. Cover with buttered paper and secure tightly with a double thickness of foil. Steam for 1 to 1½ hours, until the pudding is well risen and feels firm to the touch. Serve with Chocolate Sauce or Vanilla Custard Sauce.

Steamed Apricot Pudding

50 g/2 oz butter
50 g/2 oz castor sugar
50 g/2 oz plain flour
2 eggs
4-6 canned apricot halves
pinch of ground cinnamon
grated rind and juice of ½ lemon
¼ level teaspoon baking powder
300 ml/½ pint Apricot Sauce (see page 419)

1. Cream butter and sugar in a bowl until light and fluffy. Gradually add the flour and eggs. Beat well until light and frothy.

2. Drain the apricot halves and cut them in small pieces. Add them to the mixture with the cinnamon, lemon rind and lemon juice, and last of all the baking powder. Mix well and pour into a well-buttered pudding basin. Cover with buttered paper and secure tightly with a double thickness of foil.

3. Steam for 1 to 1½ hours, until the pudding is well risen and firm to the touch.

4. When ready, turn out and strain the Apricot Sauce over pudding.

Steamed Cherry Pudding

225 g/8 oz fresh cherries
75 g/3 oz brown breadcrumbs
65 g/2½ oz castor sugar
grated rind of ½ lemon
150 ml/¼ pint double cream
2 egg yolks, beaten
2 egg whites
butter
juice of ½ lemon
100 ml/4 fl oz water
red food colouring (optional)

1. Combine breadcrumbs, 40 g/1½ oz castor sugar and grated lemon rind in a mixing bowl.

2. Wash, pick and stone the cherries, and add three-quarters of them to breadcrumb mixture.

3. Scald cream and pour over the crumbs and fruit. Stir in beaten egg yolks.

4. Beat whites until stiff and fold into mixture.

5. Pour the mixture into a well-buttered 1.25-litre/2-pint mould or basin. Cover with a piece of buttered paper then secure tightly with a double thickness of foil. Steam slowly and steadily for about 1½ hours, or until pudding is well risen and firm to the touch.

6. Combine remaining cherries, lemon juice, water and 25 g/1 oz sugar in a saucepan. Bring to the boil, reduce heat and simmer gently for 15 minutes. Tint sauce with red food colouring if necessary. Invert the pudding carefully on a hot dish, pour the sauce around it and serve immediately.

Traditional English Christmas Pudding

A home-made Christmas pudding can never be a last-minute preparation. First of all, the raw mixture has to stand overnight before being cooked, and then the pudding must be left to mature in a cool, dry place for 3 to 4 months, preferably longer.

350 g/12 oz sultanas
350 g/12 oz raisins
350 g/12 oz currants
350 g/12 oz shredded suet
225 g/8 oz fresh white breadcrumbs
225 g/8 oz soft dark brown sugar
100 g/4 oz self-raising flour, sifted
100 g/4 oz chopped mixed peel
1 level teaspoon mixed spice
$\frac{1}{2}$ level teaspoon freshly grated nutmeg
$\frac{1}{4}$ level teaspoon salt
2 level tablespoons treacle or golden syrup
1 level teaspoon finely grated orange rind
1 level teaspoon finely grated lemon rind
4 tablespoons fresh orange juice
4 tablespoons lemon juice
4 large eggs, lightly beaten
150 ml/$\frac{1}{4}$ pint stout
8 tablespoons brandy

TO SERVE
sprig of holly
sifted icing sugar
brandy
Brandy Sauce or Brandy Butter
 (see page 418)

1. Pick over dried fruit and if necessary, wash and dry thoroughly on a cloth.

2. In a large porcelain or earthenware bowl, assemble first eleven ingredients and toss together until thoroughly mixed. Make a large well in the centre.

3. In another, smaller bowl, blend treacle or syrup thoroughly with grated orange and lemon rinds. Blend in orange and lemon juice gradually, and when mixture is smooth again, beat in lightly beaten eggs, stout and brandy.

4. Pour this mixture into dry ingredients and stir vigorously with a large wooden spoon until well blended.

5. Cover bowl with a damp cloth and leave overnight in a cool place to allow flavours to develop.

6. The following day, start by preparing your pudding basins. Grease two 1.4-litre/2$\frac{1}{2}$-pint pudding basins with butter and line bottoms with circles of buttered greaseproof paper.

7. Divide pudding mixture evenly between prepared basins, levelling off tops.

8. Cover top of each pudding with another circle of buttered greaseproof paper, then cover basins with pudding cloths and tie down with string.

9. Steam puddings for 3 hours, taking care not to let water underneath evaporate. Allow to cool before storing in a cool, dry cupboard.

10. On the day you wish to serve a pudding, steam it slowly for 2 hours until thoroughly reheated.

11. To serve: turn pudding out on to a heated serving dish. Decorate with holly and a sifting of icing sugar, and flame with brandy at the table. (To avoid an anti-climax it is best to heat the brandy in a large metal ladle or spoon and set it alight *before* pouring it over the pudding.) Serve with Brandy Sauce, Brandy Butter or whatever accompaniment is traditional in your family.

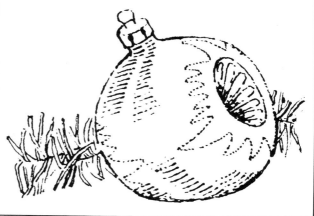

Tarts, Flans and Pastry

378

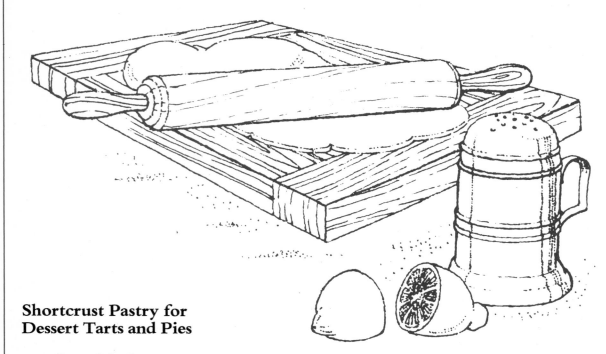

Shortcrust Pastry for Dessert Tarts and Pies

225 g/8 oz plain flour
1 tablespoon icing sugar
squeeze of lemon juice
pinch of salt
100 g/4 oz butter, diced
½ teaspoon vanilla essence
iced water

1. Sift flour and sugar into a mixing bowl. Add lemon juice, salt, butter and vanilla essence, cover well with the flour and rub together lightly with the tips of the fingers until the mixture resembles fine breadcrumbs. Whilst rubbing in, keep lifting the flour well up in the bowl, so that air may mix with it and the butter is not made too soft.

2. When pastry is thoroughly mixed, make a well in the centre and gradually add 1-2 tablespoons cold water, mixing with one hand or a knife. Do not add too much water, or pastry will be tough instead of short.

3. Sprinkle the pastry board with flour, turn the dough on it and knead lightly with the hands until dough is smooth. Flour a rolling pin, press down pastry and then with sharp quick strokes roll pastry on one side only to the thickness required. Roll pastry lightly and try to press equally with both hands. Never allow pastry to stick to the board, but lift occasionally on the rolling pin and dust some flour underneath. If dough has stuck to the board, scrape it off carefully with a knife before beginning to roll again. Always sprinkle flour over board and pastry using a flour sifter to make it finer and lighter, using as little flour as possible for this, as too much tends to make the pastry hard. If the rolling pin sticks to the pastry, dust with a little flour and brush it off again lightly with a small brush kept for this purpose.

4. To bake pastry: a fairly hot oven is required for pastry. If it is not hot enough the butter will melt and run out before the starch grains in the flour have had time to burst and absorb it. If the oven is too hot, however, the pastry will burn before it has risen properly. When baking pastry, open and close the door as gently as possible and never more often than is absolutely necessary. If pastry becomes too brown before it has cooked sufficiently, cover it over with a piece of foil or a double sheet of greaseproof paper that has been lightly sprinkled with water. If pastry is not to be used at once when taken from the oven, allow it to cool slowly in the warm kitchen. Light pastry tends to become heavy when cooled too quickly.

To bake 'blind'

Line a 20 or 23-cm/8 or 9-inch flan ring or tin with pastry, fluting the edges if necessary and chill. Prick bottom with a fork, cover bottom of pastry with a piece of waxed paper or foil and cover with dried beans. Bake in a hot oven (230°C, 450°F, Gas Mark 8) for about 15 minutes, just long enough to set the crust without browning it. Remove beans, paper or foil and allow to cool. Fill with desired filling and bake in a moderately hot oven (190°C, 375°F, Gas Mark 5) until cooked. The beans can be reserved in a storage jar and used again.

To bake pastry case only

Bake 'blind' as above for 15 minutes, remove beans and foil. Reduce oven temperature to moderately hot (190°C, 375°F, Gas Mark 5) and bake for 10 to 15 minutes. If crust becomes too brown at edges, cover rim with a little crumpled foil.

Rich Biscuit Crust

A richer pastry for dessert tarts and pies can be made in the same way, using 150–175 g/5–6 oz butter and adding 1 egg yolk, beaten with a little water for mixing.

Rich Shortcrust Pastry

225 g/8 oz plain flour
½ level teaspoon salt
1 level tablespoon icing sugar
150 g/5 oz butter
1 teaspoon lemon juice
1 egg yolk, beaten with 1 tablespoon water
1–2 tablespoons water

1. Sift flour, salt and icing sugar into a mixing bowl. Dice slightly softened butter and add to flour mixture. Using pastry blender or two knives scissor fashion, cut in butter until blend begins to crumble. Then rub in butter with the tips of fingers until mixture resembles fine breadcrumbs. Do this very gently and lightly or the mixture will become greasy and heavy. Add lemon juice, beaten egg yolk and water mixture gradually, all the time tossing gently from bottom of bowl with a fork. Add water and mix into a soft dough.

2. Shape dough lightly into 2 flattened rounds, place in a polythene bag and put in refrigerator for at least an hour, or overnight, to ripen and become firm.

3. If chilled dough is too firm to handle, leave it at room temperature until it softens slightly. Pat one ball of dough on a floured board with a lightly floured rolling pin to flatten and shape it. Then roll from the centre to edges until pastry is 3 mm/⅛ inch thick and 5 cm/2 inches larger in diameter than pie dish. Fold in half and lift into position over dish. To prevent shrinkage, ease pastry gently into dish without stretching.

Use in the following ways:

Two-crust Pie: Fill with fruit, moisten edge, cover with remaining pastry and press edges together to seal. Trim off excess pastry, press edge with fork or crimp with fingers. Cut slits in top for the steam to escape. Bake in a moderately hot oven (200°C, 400°F, Gas Mark 6) for 30 minutes, or until crust is brown and fruit is tender.

One-crust Pie: Using scissors, trim pastry 1 cm/ ½ inch beyond edge of dish. Fold edge under and crimp with fingers. Prick the base with a fork and cover bottom of pastry with a piece of waxed paper or foil. Fill with dried beans and bake in a hot oven (220°C, 450°F, Gas Mark 7) for about 15 minutes, just long enough to set the crust without browning it. Remove beans, paper or foil and allow to cool. Fill with uncooked filling and bake in a moderately hot oven (190°C, 375°F, Gas Mark 5) until cooked.

Flan case: Line flan ring or dish with pastry and prick bottom and sides well with fork. Bake 'blind' (see above) in a hot oven (230°C, 450°F, Gas Mark 8) for 15 minutes. Remove beans and foil then reduce oven temperature to moderately hot (190°C, 375°F, Gas Mark 5) and bake for a further 10 to 15 minutes.

380

Fingertip Pastry for Tarts and Flans

225 g/8 oz plain flour
pinch of salt
2 level tablespoons icing sugar
150 g/5 oz butter, finely diced
1 egg yolk
4 tablespoons cold water

1. Sift flour, salt and sugar into a mixing bowl. Rub in butter with the tips of fingers until mixture resembles fine breadcrumbs. Do this very gently and lightly, or mixture will become greasy and heavy.

2. Beat egg yolk and cold water and sprinkle over dough working in lightly with your fingers. Shape moist dough lightly into a flattened round. Place in a polythene bag and leave in refrigerator for at least 1 hour to 'ripen'.

3. If chilled dough is too firm for handling, allow to stand at room temperature until it softens slightly. Then, turn it on to a floured board and roll out as required. Press into a 20 to 23-cm/8 to 9-inch flan ring, pie dish or individual patty tins with your fingers and prick with a fork. Cover bottom of pastry with a piece of waxed paper or foil. Fill with dried beans and bake in a hot oven (230°C, 450°F, Gas Mark 8) for about 15 minutes. Reduce oven temperature to moderate (180°C, 350°F, Gas Mark 4) and bake for 30 minutes. If crust becomes too brown at edges, cover with a little crumpled foil.

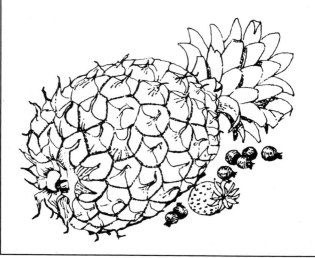

Pineapple Tart
Illustrated on page 385

1 (23-cm/9-inch) shortcrust pastry case, unbaked (see page 378)
fresh pineapple sliced into thin rings
glacé cherries

FRENCH PASTRY CREAM
100 g/4 oz sugar
3 level tablespoons cornflour
450 ml/¾ pint milk
5 egg yolks
½–1 teaspoon vanilla essence
2 teaspoons Kirsch

APRICOT GLAZE
6–8 level tablespoons apricot jam
3 tablespoons water
1–2 tablespoons rum, brandy or Kirsch (optional)

1. To bake prepared pastry case: bake 'blind' in a hot oven (230°C, 450°F, Gas Mark 8) for 15 minutes. Reduce oven temperature to moderate (180°C, 350°F, Gas Mark 4) and bake for 30 minutes. If crust becomes too brown at edges, cover with a little crumpled foil.

2. To make French pastry cream: combine sugar and cornflour in the top of a double saucepan. Stir in milk and cook over direct heat, stirring all the time, until mixture comes to the boil. Boil for 1 minute. Beat yolks slightly, add a little hot milk mixture and pour back into milk and sugar mixture, stirring. Cook over hot but not boiling water, stirring until thickened – 5 to 10 minutes. Strain and cool. Add vanilla essence and Kirsch. Cover with waxed paper and chill thoroughly.

3. To make apricot glaze: heat apricot jam and water in a small saucepan, stirring constantly, until mixture melts. Strain, and stir in rum, brandy or Kirsch if desired. Keep warm over hot water.

4. To assemble tart: half fill baked pastry case with French Pastry Cream and arrange thin slices of fresh pineapple in overlapping rows on top. Coat with golden-coloured apricot glaze. Decorate tart with glacé cherries. Serve chilled.

Individual Apple Tarts
Illustrated on page 385

4 individual pastry cases, baked
675 g/1½ lb eating apples, peeled, cored and
thinly sliced
melted butter

CRÈME PÂTISSIÈRE
450 ml/¾ pint milk
5-cm/2-inch piece vanilla pod, split
5 egg yolks
100 g/4 oz castor sugar
2 level tablespoons plain flour
1 level tablespoon cornflour
1 level tablespoon butter
few drops of vanilla essence

APRICOT GLAZE
6 level tablespoons apricot jam
3 tablespoons water
1 tablespoon rum, brandy or Kirsch

1. To make crème pâtissière: pour milk into a medium-sized pan and add vanilla pod, split to give out maximum flavour. Bring to boiling point over a low heat. Cover pan and put aside to infuse until needed. In a bowl, whisk egg yolks with sugar until thick and light. Gradually whisk in flour and cornflour. Take out vanilla pod. Gradually pour milk into egg yolk mixture, beating with the whisk until well blended. Pour mixture back into pan. Bring to the boil over a moderate heat, stirring constantly. Then simmer for 3 minutes longer, beating vigorously with a wooden spoon to disperse lumps. (These lumps invariably form, but you will find that they are easy to beat out as the cream thickens.) Remove pan from heat. Beat in butter and continue to beat for a minute or two longer to cool the pastry cream slightly before adding vanilla essence. Pass cream through a sieve if necessary. Put it in a bowl and cover with a sheet of lightly buttered greaseproof paper to prevent a skin forming on top. Allow the *crème pâtissière* to become quite cool.

2. To make apricot glaze: heat apricot jam and water in a small saucepan, stirring constantly, until mixture melts. Strain. Stir in rum, brandy or Kirsch. Keep warm over hot water.

3. Half fill baked pastry cases with *crème pâtissière*. Cover with overlapping rings of thinly sliced eating apples. Brush with melted butter and bake in a hot oven (230°C, 450°F, Gas Mark 8) for 5 minutes. If apples do not brown sufficiently at edges to be attractive, put under grill for a minute or two. Cool tarts then brush with apricot glaze.

382

French Raspberry Tart

1 (23-cm/9-inch) shortcrust pastry case,
 unbaked (see page 378)
fresh raspberries, to cover

FRENCH PASTRY CREAM
100 g/4 oz sugar
3 level tablespoons cornflour
450 ml/¾ pint milk
5 egg yolks
½–1 teaspoon vanilla essence
2 teaspoons Kirsch

RASPBERRY GLAZE
6–8 level tablespoons raspberry jam
3 tablespoons water
1–2 tablespoons Kirsch

1. To bake prepared pastry case: bake 'blind'
in a hot oven (230°C, 450°F, Gas Mark 8) for 15
minutes. Reduce oven temperature to moderate
(180°C, 350°F, Gas Mark 4) and bake for 30
minutes. If crust becomes too brown at edges,
cover with a little crumpled foil.

2. To make French pastry cream: combine
sugar and cornflour in the top of a double saucepan. Stir in milk and cook over direct heat, stirring all the time, until mixture comes to the boil.
Boil for 1 minute. Beat yolks slightly, add a little
hot milk mixture and pour back into milk and
sugar mixture, stirring. Cook over hot but not
boiling water, stirring until thickened – 5 to 10
minutes. Strain and cool. Add vanilla essence and
Kirsch. Cover with waxed paper and refrigerate
until well chilled.

3. To make raspberry glaze: heat raspberry
jam and water in a small saucepan, stirring
constantly, until mixture melts. Strain and stir in
Kirsch. Keep warm.

4. To assemble tart: half-fill baked pastry case
with French pastry cream and arrange raspberries
in circles on top. Coat with glaze. Serve chilled.

Apple Pie with Cheese Apples

8 tart eating apples
225 g/8 oz rich shortcrust pastry (see
 page 379)
50 g/2 oz granulated sugar
50 g/2 oz dark brown sugar
1 level tablespoon flour
¼ teaspoon grated nutmeg
grated rind of 1 orange
grated rind of 1 lemon
75 g/3 oz chopped raisins and sultanas
2 tablespoons orange juice

CHEESE APPLES
225 g/8 oz processed cheese
angelica or clove 'stalks'
paprika

1. Peel and core apples. Cut each into 8 to 10
slices, depending on size.

2. Line a deep 23-cm/9-inch pie dish with two-
thirds of the shortcrust pastry.

3. Combine granulated sugar, dark brown sugar,
flour and nutmeg. Sprinkle a little into pastry case.
Add grated rinds to remaining sugar mixture.

4. Arrange sliced apples, sultanas and raisins in
pastry case, sprinkling each layer with some of the
sugar mixture. Pour over the orange juice. Fit
remaining pastry over apple layers, pressing the
edges together or fluting them. Cut several slits in
the top of the pastry crust to release steam. Bake in
a hot oven (220°C, 425°F, Gas Mark 7) for 40 to
45 minutes until tender.

5. To make cheese apples: roll processed cheese
into little balls approximately 2.5 cm/1 inch in
diameter. Press thumb in top to form indentation
for angelica or clove 'stalk'. Dust cheek of 'apple'
with paprika for 'blush'.

6. Serve pie warm with tiny cheese 'apples' placed
around outside of pie crust.

Little Christmas Tarts

Illustrated on page 388

**individual shortcrust pastry cases, baked
(see page 378)**

VANILLA CREAM
175 g/6 oz sugar
3 tablespoons flour
2½ level tablespoons cornflour
450 ml/¾ pint milk
6 egg yolks
6 level tablespoons butter
vanilla essence
Grand Marnier

APRICOT GLAZE
6-8 level tablespoons apricot jam
3 tablespoons water
**1 tablespoon rum, brandy or Kirsch
(optional)**

FRUITS
**whole strawberries, grapes, mandarin
segments, pear slices, pineapple slices,
peach slices, banana slices, whole cherries,
apricot halves, etc.**

1. To make vanilla cream: combine sugar,
flour and cornflour in the top of a double saucepan. Stir in milk and cook over direct heat, stirring
all the time, until the mixture comes to the boil.
Boil for 1 minute. Beat egg yolks lightly and add
a little hot milk mixture, then pour into saucepan
with milk and sugar mixture, stirring constantly.
Cook over hot but not boiling water stirring for
5 minutes. Strain and allow to cool slightly. Mix
with butter and flavour to taste with vanilla
essence and Grand Marnier.

2. To make apricot glaze: heat apricot jam and
water in a small saucepan, stirring constantly,
until mixture melts. Strain and stir in rum, brandy
or Kirsch if desired. Keep warm over hot water
until ready to use.

3. Place a spoonful of vanilla cream in the bottom
of each individual pastry case. Arrange fruits of
your choice on top of vanilla cream and glaze with
golden coloured apricot glaze.

Easy Fruit Bande

**canned pear halves, sliced into 6 or 8,
according to size**
canned sliced peaches
small canned pineapple rings, halved
canned orange segments
canned mandarin segments
fresh black grapes
crisp dessert apples
lemon juice

WHIPPED HONEY CREAM
2 level tablespoons clear honey
1 tablespoon orange juice
1-2 teaspoons lemon juice
150 ml/¼ pint double cream
¼ level teaspoon ground cinnamon

1. Drain canned fruits thoroughly, reserving
syrup, and slice or halve as directed. Wash and
halve grapes.

2. Peel and core some of the apples and slice into
rings 8 mm/⅓ inch thick. Toss rings in lemon
juice until thoroughly coated to prevent discoloration. As a contrast, use apples with bright red
skins, and prepare as before.

3. Arrange prepared fruits in closely overlapping
rows on a long shallow serving dish, taking colour
and texture into account when deciding on the
order. Sprinkle with some of the syrup from
canned fruit or a little castor sugar, or spoon over
a glaze made with syrup from cans thickened
with arrowroot (2 level teaspoons arrowroot to
150 ml/¼ pint syrup). Serve with whipped honey
cream.

4. To make whipped honey cream: put honey
in a small bowl or jug and gradually stir in orange
and lemon juice with a teaspoon. Whip cream
until slightly thickened. Gradually whisk in honey
mixture, and continue to whisk until cream is of a
soft floppy consistency. Whisk in cinnamon to
taste.

384

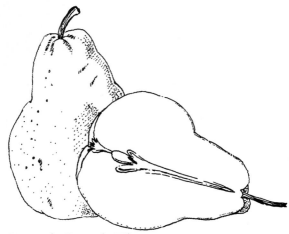

French Peach Flan
Illustrated opposite

1 (20–23-cm/8–9-inch) fingertip pastry case,
    baked (see page 380)
fresh peaches

FRENCH PASTRY CREAM
100 g/4 oz sugar
3 level tablespoons cornflour
450 ml/¾ pint milk
5 egg yolks
½–1 teaspoon vanilla essence
2 teaspoons Kirsch

APRICOT GLAZE
6–8 level tablespoons apricot jam
3 tablespoons water
1 tablespoon rum, brandy or Kirsch
    (optional)

1. To make French pastry cream: combine
sugar and cornflour in the top of a double saucepan. Stir in milk and cook over direct heat,
stirring all the time, until mixture comes to the
boil. Boil for 1 minute. Beat yolks slightly, add a
little hot milk mixture and pour back into milk
and sugar mixture, stirring. Cook over hot but
not boiling water, stirring until thickened – 5 to
10 minutes. Strain and cool. Add vanilla essence
and Kirsch. Cover with waxed paper and refrigerate until well chilled.

2. To make apricot glaze: heat apricot jam and
water in a small saucepan, stirring constantly, until

mixture melts. Strain and stir in rum, brandy or
Kirsch if desired. Keep warm over hot water.

3. To assemble flan: half fill baked pastry case
with French pastry cream and arrange halved
fresh peaches on top. Coat with golden-coloured
apricot glaze.

Grape Tart Pâtissière
Illustrated on page 387

1 (23-cm/9-inch) shortcrust pastry case,
    unbaked (see page 378)
225 g/8 oz green grapes
225 g/8 oz black grapes
French Pastry Cream (see above)

APRICOT GLAZE
6–8 level tablespoons apricot jam
3 tablespoons water
1–2 tablespoons Kirsch

DECORATION (optional)
1 egg white
1 small bunch black grapes
castor sugar

1. To bake prepared pastry case: bake 'blind'
in a hot oven (230°C, 450°F, Gas Mark 8) for 15
minutes. Reduce oven temperature to moderate
(180°C, 350°F, Gas Mark 4) and bake for 30
minutes. If crust becomes too brown at edges,
cover with a little crumpled foil.

2. Peel and deseed grapes.

3. To assemble tart: half fill baked pastry case
with French pastry cream. Arrange grapes decoratively on top. Coat with apricot glaze.

4. To make apricot glaze: add 3 tablespoons
water to apricot jam and heat, stirring constantly,
until melted. Flavour to taste with Kirsch.

5. To decorate: lightly beat the egg white. Dip
bunch of black grapes into the egg white, holding
it by the stalk. Drain slightly and then roll gently
in castor sugar. Leave to dry and then place in
centre of flan.

Pineapple Tart (see page 380); Chocolate Pear Flan (see page 389);
Individual Apple Tarts (see page 381); French Peach Flan (see page 384); Orange and Almond Flan (see page 389)

The Sweets of Summer – Pears in Chablis (see page 333); Grape Tart Pâtissière (see page 384)

Little Christmas Tarts (see page 383)

Banana Cream Pie (see page 395)

Peach Cobbler (see page 394)

Baked Bread and Butter Pudding (see page 346)

Chocolate Pear Flan
Illustrated on page 385

1 deep (20–25-cm/8–9-inch) shortcrust pastry
  case, baked (see page 378)
1 level tablespoon powdered gelatine
1 level tablespoon cornflour
75 g/3 oz castor sugar
4 egg yolks
450 ml/¾ pint milk
75 g/3 oz bitter chocolate
vanilla essence
5–6 canned pear halves
apple jelly, sieved
whipped cream and chopped bitter
  chocolate, to decorate

1. Sprinkle powdered gelatine over 2 tablespoons cold water in a cup and put aside to soften.

2. In the top of a double saucepan, stir cornflour into castor sugar.

3. Beat egg yolks lightly, pour them over cornflour mixture, stirring vigorously with a wooden spoon until smoothly blended.

4. Bring milk to the boil, pour in a thin stream into egg mixture, stirring vigorously.

5. Cook over simmering water, for 15 to 20 minutes, stirring until custard coats back of spoon, taking great care not to let it boil, or egg yolks may curdle. Remove from heat.

6. Stand cup of softened gelatine in hot water (use the water in the bottom of the double saucepan) and stir until gelatine has dissolved and liquid is clear. Blend thoroughly with custard.

7. Melt chocolate on a plate over simmering water – yes, use the water left in the bottom of the double saucepan.

8. Blend chocolate smoothly with hot custard and flavour to taste with vanilla essence. Pour into pastry case and chill until set on top.

9. Arrange 5 to 6 canned pear halves on chocolate filling, cut sides uppermost. Brush pears with

sieved apple jelly to give them an attractive glaze, and just before serving, pipe a little whipped cream into each pear half and sprinkle with chopped bitter chocolate.

Orange and Almond Flan
Illustrated on page 385

1 23-cm/9-inch shortcrust pastry case, baked
  (see page 378)

ALMOND FILLING
2 eggs
5 level tablespoons castor sugar
6 level tablespoons double cream
100 g/4 oz ground almonds
finely grated rind and juice of 1 large lemon
1–2 drops almond essence

ORANGE AND ALMOND TOPPING
4 small oranges
slivered almonds
apple jelly or greengage conserve, sieved

1. To prepare almond filling: whisk eggs with sugar until thick and creamy. Add remaining ingredients and beat vigorously with a wooden spoon until smoothly blended.

2. Fill pastry case with almond mixture and bake in a moderate oven (180°C, 350°F, Gas Mark 4) for 15 to 20 minutes until puffed and golden, and firm to the touch.

3. Peel 4 small oranges, removing all pith and slice thinly. Arrange orange slices on top of the flan in an overlapping circle. Fill centre with slivered almonds. Brush orange slices with a little sieved apple jelly or greengage conserve.

390

Sour Cream – Sultana Pie

225 g/8 oz sugar
½ level teaspoon powdered cinnamon
½ level teaspoon ground nutmeg or allspice
salt
2 eggs, beaten
300 ml/½ pint soured cream
2 tablespoons lemon juice
100 g/4 oz sultanas
1 (20–23-cm/8–9-inch) shortcrust pastry case,
    unbaked (see page 378)

1. Combine sugar, spices, salt, eggs, cream, lemon juice and sultanas. Mix until well blended.

2. Pour into pastry case and bake in a moderate oven (180°C, 350°F, Gas Mark 4) for 1 hour, or until filling has set. Cool.

American Custard Pie

1 level tablespoon cornflour
450 ml/¾ pint milk
grated rind of ½ lemon or orange
4–6 level tablespoons sugar
½ teaspoon vanilla essence
salt
3 eggs
1 (20–23-cm/8–9-inch) shortcrust pastry case,
    unbaked (see page 378)

1. Mix cornflour smoothly with a little milk. Combine remaining milk with lemon or orange rind in the top of a double saucepan and simmer gently over hot water for 15 minutes.

2. Strain hot milk into cornflour and return to double saucepan, cook over water, stirring constantly, until thickened. Add sugar, vanilla essence and salt, to taste. Cool.

3. Beat eggs and add to custard mixture. Mix well.

4. Prick base of unbaked pastry case with a fork. Cover with a piece of foil or waxed paper, weight this with dried beans and bake 'blind' in a hot oven (230°C, 450°F, Gas Mark 8) for 15 minutes. Remove foil and beans. Allow pastry case to cool.

5. Pour custard mixture into pastry case, sprinkle with ground nutmeg and bake in a moderately hot oven (190°C, 375°F, Gas Mark 5) for 25 to 30 minutes, until the pastry is cooked and the custard has set. Serve cooled but not chilled.

Variations

Cherry Custard Pie: Add to mixture 225 g/8 oz stoned unsweetened cherries soaked in 4 tablespoons cherry brandy (add the brandy, too) and bake as above.

Pear Custard Pie: Add to mixture 2 ripe pears (peeled, cored and thinly sliced) soaked in 4 to 6 tablespoons Kirsch (add Kirsch, too) and bake as above.

Apple Cream Pie

175 g/6 oz shortcrust pastry (see page 378),
    made with addition of 75 g/3 oz grated
    cheese
75 g/3 oz castor sugar
75 g/3 oz soft brown sugar
25 g/1 oz cornflour
½ level teaspoon ground cinnamon
¼ level teaspoon grated nutmeg
pinch of salt
40 g/1½ oz butter
8 tart cooking apples
2 teaspoons lemon juice
6 level tablespoons double cream

1. Make up shortcrust pastry, adding the cheese after the butter has been rubbed in. Roll out pastry and line a 20-cm/8-inch pie plate.

2. Mix together sugar, brown sugar, cornflour, cinnamon, nutmeg and salt in a bowl. Rub in the butter.

3. Peel, core and slice the apples and sprinkle with the lemon juice in a bowl. Add three-quarters of the sugar mixture and toss apples, coating them evenly.

4. Arrange coated apple slices in pastry case, piling them high in a dome, and sprinkle with remaining sugar mixture. Bake in a hot oven (230°C, 450°F, Gas Mark 8) for 10 minutes, then reduce oven temperature to moderately hot (190°C, 375°F, Gas Mark 5) and continue baking for 25 minutes, until the apples are tender. Pour cream over the pie, and bake for 10 minutes longer. Serve immediately.

Chocolate Cream Pie

50 g/2 oz bitter chocolate
225 g/8 oz sugar
2 level tablespoons cornflour
¼ level teaspoon salt
450 ml/¾ pint milk
2 eggs, well beaten
2 level tablespoons butter
½ teaspoon vanilla essence
1 (23-cm/9-inch) shortcrust pastry case, baked (see page 378)

GARNISH
300 ml/½ pint double cream
50 g/2 oz sugar
½ teaspoon vanilla essence
15 g/½ oz bitter chocolate, coarsely grated

1. Melt chocolate over hot water in the top of a double saucepan.

2. Combine sugar, cornflour and salt in a bowl. Gradually stir in milk, then stir mixture into melted chocolate. Cook over boiling water for 10 minutes, stirring constantly until thick.

3. Pour hot mixture into well-beaten eggs a little at a time, stirring after each addition. Return to top of double saucepan and cook, stirring occasionally, for 5 minutes. Remove from heat, add butter and vanilla essence. Cool.

4. Pour mixture into baked pastry case.

5. To serve: whip cream and blend in the sugar and vanilla essence. Decorate pie with piped cream and sprinkle grated chocolate on top of the cream. Chill and serve.

Tartes aux Pêches

6 small peaches
225 g/8 oz sugar
150 ml/¼ pint water
ground cinnamon
150 ml/¼ pint red Burgundy
1 strip orange peel
2 tablespoons Grand Marnier or Curaçao
12 individual shortcrust pastry cases (see page 378)
whipped cream

1. Pour boiling water over peaches in a bowl, remove and peel. Slice in half and remove stones.

2. Poach peaches, uncovered, in syrup made of sugar, water, and cinnamon, to taste, for about 15 minutes. Add Burgundy and orange peel and continue to cook, uncovered, over a low heat until fruit is tender – about 15 minutes.

3. Put peaches in a deep bowl. Reduce liquid over high heat to the consistency of a thick syrup. Add Grand Marnier or Curaçao and pour syrup over the halved peaches. Put in the refrigerator to chill thoroughly.

4. Place a halved peach inside each pastry case. Glaze with the reduced syrup and garnish with rosettes of whipped cream.

392

Lemon Sponge Tart

3 level tablespoons butter
175 g/6 oz sugar
3 eggs, separated
3 level tablespoons plain flour
450 ml/¾ pint milk
juice of 3 lemons
grated rind of 1 lemon
1 (20–23-cm/8–9-inch) shortcrust pastry case,
  unbaked (see page 378)

1. Cream butter and blend with sugar and egg yolks until light and creamy.

2. Sprinkle with flour, then mix in milk, lemon juice and rind.

3. Whisk egg whites until stiff, fold into lemon mixture.

4. Pour lemon mixture into unbaked pastry case and bake in a moderate oven (180°C, 350°F, Gas Mark 4) for approximately 45 minutes.

Eggnog Pie

150 ml/¼ pint single cream
3 egg yolks
75 g/3 oz granulated sugar
salt and freshly grated nutmeg
1½ level teaspoons powdered gelatine
2 tablespoons cold water
2 tablespoons rum
1 tablespoon brandy
½ teaspoon vanilla essence
3 egg whites
150 ml/¼ pint double cream
1 (20–23-cm/8–9-inch) shortcrust pastry case,
  baked (see page 378)

1. Scald cream in the top of a double saucepan.

2. Combine egg yolks, sugar, salt and freshly grated nutmeg, and stir into the scalded cream. Cook over hot water until the mixture coats a spoon, stirring constantly.

3. Soften gelatine in water, add to custard mixture and stir until dissolved. Add rum, brandy and vanilla essence and strain custard into a glass bowl. Chill until mixture begins to set.

4. Whisk egg whites until stiff and whip cream. Fold egg white and cream into custard mixture and pour into the baked pastry case. Chill.

5. Just before serving, sprinkle with a little freshly grated nutmeg.

Lemon Soufflé Pie

4 egg yolks, well beaten
175 g/6 oz sugar
4 tablespoons lemon juice
¼–½ level teaspoon ground nutmeg
1–2 level teaspoons grated lemon rind
1 teaspoon vanilla essence
salt
4 egg whites
1 (23-cm/9-inch) shortcrust pastry case,
  baked (see page 378)

1. Combine egg yolks, a third of the sugar, and lemon juice. Flavour to taste with nutmeg and cook over water, stirring constantly, until mixture thickens. Remove from heat. Mix in grated lemon rind and vanilla essence. Cool.

2. Add salt to egg whites and whisk until soft peaks form. Gradually add remaining sugar and whisk until stiff. Fold into warm lemon mixture.

3. Spoon mixture into baked pastry case and bake in a moderate oven (160°C, 325°F, Gas Mark 3) for about 30 minutes, or until golden brown.

Pears in Pastry Sabayon

6 pears
150 ml/¼ pint syrup (100 g/4 oz sugar,
 8 tablespoons water)
150 ml/¼ pint apricot jam
cream (optional)

PASTRY
250 g/9 oz plain flour
1 level teaspoon salt
4 level tablespoons lard
100 g/4 oz softened butter
water, to mix

SABAYON SAUCE
4 egg yolks
100 g/4 oz sugar
175 ml/6 fl oz Marsala
1–2 tablespoons cognac

1. To make pastry: sift flour and salt together, rub in lard and half the butter until mixture resembles fine breadcrumbs. Add sufficient water to form into a ball which will just hold together, and knead firmly but quickly until smooth. Allow to rest in a cool place for 15 minutes. Roll out into an oblong and spread remaining butter over surface. Fold in half, seal edges, rest for 5 minutes and roll out to 3-mm/⅛-inch thickness. Cut 6 pastry rounds large enough for pears to sit upon and cut remainder of pastry into strips about 1 cm/ ½ inch wide.

2. Peel pears and poach them whole in syrup and apricot jam for 10 to 15 minutes. Remove pears and cool. Reserve apricot syrup. Place one pear on each pastry round.

3. To make cage of pastry strips for each pear: cross two strips at right angles, seal well with water and place cross at top of each pear. Snip strips at base and seal well with water.

4. Place pears in pastry on baking tray and bake in a moderately hot oven (200°C, 400°F, Gas Mark 6) for 20 to 30 minutes, until pastry is set. Remove and brush with apricot syrup glaze.

5. To make Sabayon sauce: beat egg yolks and sugar in the top of a double saucepan until yellow and frothy. Add Marsala, place over hot water and cook, stirring constantly, until thick and foamy. Stir in cognac and chill.

6. Serve pears with cream or Sabayon sauce.

Coffee Chiffon Flan

1 (23-cm/9-inch) rich shortcrust flan case,
 baked (see page 379)
1 level tablespoon powdered gelatine
4 tablespoons cold water
450 ml/¾ pint milk
4 eggs, separated
100 g/4 oz castor sugar
2 level tablespoons powdered coffee
150 ml/¼ pint double cream, whipped
¼ teaspoon salt
coarsely grated chocolate

1. Soak gelatine in cold water.

2. Warm the milk in a small saucepan.

3. Cream together egg yolks, half the sugar, and coffee. Pour on warm milk, stirring constantly. Return to heat and cook gently until custard just coats the spoon. Cool.

4. Dissolve softened gelatine over gentle heat and stir into cooled coffee custard. Fold in whipped cream.

5. Whisk egg whites with salt until stiff but not dry, then whisk in remaining sugar a little at a time.

6. Whisk coffee custard and fold gradually into beaten egg whites. Turn into baked flan case and decorate with coarsely grated chocolate.

394

Peach Cobbler

Illustrated on page 388

PASTRY
225 g/8 oz plain flour, sifted
25 g/1 oz cornflour
1 level teaspoon salt
175 g/6 oz butter
4 tablespoons water

FILLING
225 g/8 oz sugar
2 level tablespoons cornflour
2 tablespoons butter
450 ml/¾ pint peach juice
6 peaches, sliced
1 tablespoon lemon juice

1. To make pastry: combine sifted flour, corn-flour, salt, butter and water in a bowl. Mix well into a dough. Line a large deep dish with the pastry, reserving enough for lattice topping.

2. To make filling: combine sugar, cornflour and butter with peach juice. Cook until thick – about 5 minutes. Add lemon juice and pour over peaches.

3. Pour filling into pastry case. Dot with butter. Top with strips of pastry and bake in a moderate oven (160°C, 325°F, Gas Mark 3) for 30 minutes.

Peach Pie with Streusel Topping

6 peaches
juice of 1 lemon
1 (20–23-cm/8–9-inch) shortcrust pastry case,
unbaked (see page 378)
50 g/2 oz sugar
½ level teaspoon powdered cinnamon
¼ level teaspoon ground nutmeg or allspice

STREUSEL TOPPING
75 g/3 oz brown sugar
75 g/3 oz plain flour, sifted
grated rind of 1 lemon
6 tablespoons softened butter

1. Peel and slice peaches discarding stones and toss in lemon juice.

2. Arrange prepared peaches in unbaked pastry case. Combine sugar and spices, and sprinkle over peaches.

3. To make streusel topping: combine brown sugar, flour and grated lemon rind, and cut soft-ened butter into mixture until crumbly, with a pastry blender or 2 knives.

4. Sprinkle mixture over peaches and bake in a hot oven (230°C, 450°F, Gas Mark 8) for 15 minutes. Reduce oven temperature to moderate (180°C, 350°F, Gas Mark 4) and bake for a further 30 minutes.

Autumn Pear Flan

I (23-cm/9-inch) rich shortcrust flan case,
  baked (see page 379)
6-8 pears

PASTRY CREAM
100 g/4 oz sugar
4 level tablespoons cornflour
450 ml/$\frac{3}{4}$ pint milk
5 egg yolks
$\frac{1}{2}$-I teaspoon vanilla essence
2 teaspoons Kirsch

WINE SYRUP
175 g/6 oz sugar
300 ml/$\frac{1}{2}$ pint red wine
grated rind of I lemon
4 cloves
2.5-cm/I-inch piece of root ginger
I-I$\frac{1}{2}$ teaspoons red food colouring
I level teaspoon gelatine
4 tablespoons cold water
juice of I lemon
150 ml/$\frac{1}{4}$ pint thick unsweetened apple purée

I. To make pastry cream: combine sugar and
cornflour in the top of a double saucepan. Stir in
milk and cook over direct heat, stirring all the
time, until mixture comes to the boil. Boil for I
minute. Beat yolks slightly, add a little hot milk
mixture and pour back into milk and sugar mixture. Cook over hot but not boiling water, until
thickened – 5 to 10 minutes, stirring continuously.
Strain and cool. Add vanilla essence and Kirsch.
Cover with waxed paper and refrigerate until
well chilled.

2. Peel and core pears.

3. Dissolve sugar in wine with lemon rind, cloves
and ginger. Bring to the boil and cook for 3
minutes. Reduce heat to simmering point, stir in
red food colouring and poach pears very gently,
turning occasionally, until tender but not mushy.
Remove from syrup and cool.

4. Soak gelatine in cold water and add with
lemon juice and apple purée to the hot syrup. Mix
thoroughly until smooth, cool.

5. Half fill flan case with pastry cream. Arrange
pears on top and cover with red apple-wine sauce.

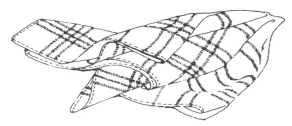

Banana Cream Pie
Illustrated on page 388

I (20-23-cm/8-9-inch) shortcrust or rich
  biscuit crust pastry case, baked (see
  pages 378, 379)
3 bananas, sliced
juice of I lemon
150 ml/$\frac{1}{4}$ pint double cream, whipped

VANILLA ICE CREAM
100 g/4 oz sugar
3 level tablespoons cornflour
450 ml/$\frac{3}{4}$ pint milk
5 egg yolks
$\frac{1}{2}$-I teaspoon vanilla essence
2 teaspoons Kirsch

I. To make vanilla ice cream: combine sugar
and cornflour in the top of a double saucepan. Stir
in milk and cook over direct heat, stirring constantly, until mixture comes to the boil. Boil for I
minute. Beat egg yolks slightly and pan in a little
hot milk mixture. Return to the milk and sugar
mixture and cook over hot but not boiling water
until thickened – 5 to 10 minutes, stirring continuously. Strain and cool, then add vanilla
essence and Kirsch.

2. Combine sliced bananas and lemon juice in a
shallow bowl and toss.

3. Place a third of drained banana slices in a layer
in the bottom of baked pastry case. Cover with
half the vanilla ice cream and arrange another
third of banana slices on top. Cover with remaining vanilla ice cream. Top pie decoratively with
remaining banana slices and decorate with
whipped cream. Serve cold but not chilled.

Cakes

396

Basic Sponge Cake

100 g/4 oz slightly softened butter
100 g/4 oz castor sugar
¼ teaspoon vanilla essence
¼ level teaspoon finely grated lemon rind
2 eggs
100 g/4 oz plain flour
1 level teaspoon baking powder
redcurrant jam or a flavoured butter icing
icing sugar

1. Lightly butter two 18-cm/7-inch sandwich tins and line bases with circles of *very* lightly buttered greaseproof paper.

2. Combine butter with the castor sugar, vanilla essence and finely grated lemon rind in a large bowl. Cream together with a wooden spoon until light and fluffy.

3. In another bowl whisk eggs until light and frothy. Beat whisked eggs, a few tablespoons at a time into creamed butter and sugar mixture.

4. Sift flour and baking powder into creamed mixture. Fold in lightly but thoroughly with a metal spoon or spatula.

5. Divide batter evenly between prepared sandwich tins and level off tops with your spatula.

6. Bake in a moderate oven (180°C, 350°F, Gas Mark 4) for 25 minutes or until a good golden brown. The cakes are cooked when they shrink away slightly from the sides of the tin and spring back when pressed lightly with a finger.

Note: Always place baking tins in the centre of the oven. And if you are using 2 rungs, it is a good idea to switch the two tins over two-thirds of the way through cooking time to allow them to brown evenly.

7. When cakes are done, turn out on to a folded cloth and carefully peel off base papers. Then turn right side up again and allow to cool on a wire tray.

8. When layers are cold, sandwich with warm redcurrant jam or a rich chocolate- or butterscotch-flavoured butter icing and top with a sprinkling of icing sugar.

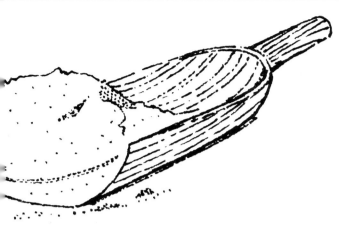

Basic Genoese Sponge Cake

(Excellent for layer cakes, iced cakes and *petits fours*.)

75 g/3 oz plain flour
25 g/1 oz cornflour
about 150 g/5 oz unsalted butter
4 eggs
100 g/4 oz castor sugar
1 teaspoon vanilla essence or finely grated
   rind of $\frac{1}{2}$ lemon

1. Sift flour with cornflour three times.

2. Take the mixing bowl in which you intend to whisk up the cake and select a large saucepan over which it will fit firmly. Pour 5 cm/2 inches water into the saucepan and bring to the boil.

3. Place unsalted butter in another, smaller saucepan and lower into the heating water, so that the butter melts without sizzling or bubbling. Remove saucepan from water.

4. Brush two 19- or 20-cm/7$\frac{1}{2}$- or 8-inch sandwich tins with a little of the melted butter. Line bases with greaseproof paper and brush with melted butter as well.

5. Combine eggs, castor sugar and vanilla essence or grated lemon rind in a mixing bowl. Set it over the barely simmering water and whisk vigorously until very thick, light and lukewarm.

6. Remove bowl from heat. Stand bowl on a cool surface and continue to whisk until mixture leaves a distinct trail on the surface when beaters

are lifted (3 to 5 minutes if beating with an electric mixer at high speed).

7. Gradually resift flour and cornflour mixture over surface, at the same time folding it in lightly but thoroughly with a large metal spoon or spatula.

8. Add 8 tablespoons melted butter and continue with the folding motion until it has been completely absorbed. This may take slightly longer than you expect, so work as lightly as you can to avoid knocking the air out of the mixture.

9. Divide batter evenly between prepared tins.

10. Bake in a moderate oven (180°C, 350°F, Gas Mark 4) for 15 to 20 minutes, until cakes are well risen, golden brown on top and springy to the touch.

11. Turn out on to wire trays. Peel off lining paper and allow cakes to cool completely before using.

American Refrigerator Cake

2 (18-cm/7-inch) sponge cakes (see preceding
   recipes)
600 ml/1 pint double cream
4-6 level tablespoons cocoa
4 tablespoons hot water
2-4 tablespoons crème de cacao
icing sugar

1. Split each sponge layer in half to make two layers each.

2. Whip double cream until thickened. Dissolve cocoa in hot water and cool. Then beat into whipped cream. Add *crème de cacao* and icing sugar, to taste.

3. Spread cocoa cream between layers and on top and sides of cake. Chill cake for at least 1 hour in the refrigerator.

398

Baked Almond Apples

4 large apples
lemon juice
cornflour
50 g/2 oz blanched almonds
100 g/4 oz sugar
50 g/2 oz butter
1 egg
40 g/1½ oz cakecrumbs

1. Peel and core apples, brush with lemon juice and roll in cornflour.

2. Chop almonds and mix with half the sugar.

3. Melt butter in an ovenproof dish, put in apples and fill centres with almond and sugar mixture.

4. Beat egg and rest of sugar together and stir in 25 g/1 oz cakecrumbs.

5. Mix any left-over almond and sugar mixture (Step 3) with egg, sugar and cakecrumbs and pour over the apples.

6. Sprinkle remaining 15 g/½ oz breadcrumbs on top and bake in a moderately hot oven (190°C, 375°F, Gas Mark 5) until tender, approximately 45 minutes.

Pear Clafouti

50 g/2 oz flour
pinch of salt
2 eggs, beaten
300 ml/½ pint milk
4 ripe pears
50 g/2 oz castor sugar
juice of ½ lemon
1 level teaspoon powdered cinnamon
melted butter
icing sugar

1. Sift flour and salt into a mixing bowl, make a well in the centre and pour in the eggs. Stir thoroughly, gradually adding the milk, and beat well.

2. Peel, core and slice the pears and mix with sugar, lemon juice and cinnamon.

3. Grease a 20-cm/8-inch baking dish or cake tin. Stir three-quarters of the pears into the batter and pour into the tin, arrange remaining pears over top, and brush these with melted butter. Bake in a moderate oven (180°C, 350°F, Gas Mark 4) for 40 minutes. Serve dredged with icing sugar.

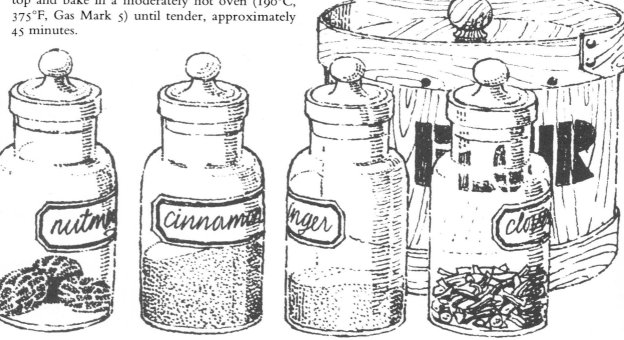

Christmas Spice Cookies

Illustrated on page 408

225 g/8 oz flour, sifted
½ level teaspoon salt
½ level teaspoon bicarbonate of soda
½ level teaspoon baking powder
½ level teaspoon ground ginger
½ level teaspoon cloves
1½ level teaspoons powdered cinnamon
¼ level teaspoon freshly ground nutmeg
4-6 level tablespoons softened butter
100 g/4 oz granulated sugar
250 ml/8 fl oz golden syrup
1 egg yolk

SUGAR ICING
175 g/6 oz icing sugar
⅛ level teaspoon cream of tartar
1 egg white
¼ teaspoon vanilla essence
food colouring

DECORATION
coloured sugar
candies
silver balls
chocolate chips
nuts
raisins

1. Sift flour with salt, bicarbonate of soda, baking powder and spices into a bowl.

2. Beat butter, sugar and syrup until creamy. Add egg yolk and beat well. Blend in flour mixture.

3. Roll out dough 3-5 mm/⅛-¼ inch thick on a lightly floured board. With floured biscuit cutters, cut into different shapes. Place cookies on an ungreased baking sheet, 2.5 cm/1 inch apart. Bake in a moderate oven (180°C, 350°F, Gas Mark 4) for 8 to 10 minutes, until cooked. Beat sugar icing ingredients together, and when cookies are cold decorate with piped icing. Trim with coloured sugar, candies, silver balls, chocolate chips, nuts, raisins, etc.

4. To make sugar icing for cookies: sift icing sugar with cream of tartar. Add egg white and vanilla essence. Then with a rotary beater or electric mixer, beat mixture until icing holds its shape.

Note: To prevent icing from setting while you are decorating cookies, cover bowl with a damp cloth. Colour icing, as desired.

400

Sicilian Cassata Cake

100 g/4 oz glacé fruit, chopped
4 tablespoons Strega liqueur or brandy
350 g/12 oz Ricotta cream cheese or cottage cheese
100 g/4 oz vanilla-flavoured sugar
100 g/4 oz plain eating chocolate (slightly bitter if possible), chopped
butter
sponge fingers, halved

ICING
350 g/12 oz bitter chocolate
2 level tablespoons softened butter
3 tablespoons milk

DECORATION
candied cherries
whipped cream
angelica leaves (optional)

1. Place chopped glacé fruit in a small bowl; add *Strega* liqueur or brandy, and allow fruits to marinate in the liqueur for at least 1 hour.

2. Sieve the cheese into a large earthenware mixing bowl. Add the vanilla-flavoured sugar, working the mixture with a wooden spoon until you have a smooth, fluffy cream. Drain the chopped fruits, reserving liqueur, then stir the fruits and chocolate into cream.

3. Line a long narrow loaf (or pâté) tin with waxed paper. Spread lightly with softened butter. Line the tin, sides and bottom, with halved sponge fingers cut to fit (round sides of fingers facing outside of tin), saving enough halved sponge fingers to cover the top of the cake. Spoon in the mixture until just under half-full. Add trimmings and ends of sponge fingers, diced and soaked in remaining liqueur (adding a little extra liqueur if necessary). Then top with remaining cream mixture. Cover with reserved halved sponge fingers and chill in refrigerator for at least 2 hours.

4. When ready to serve, turn the sweet out and carefully remove waxed paper.

5. To make icing: melt the chocolate and butter in a small saucepan over water, stirring until smooth. Add enough milk to make it of coating consistency, then coat each sponge finger.

6. To decorate: place half a candied cherry between each sponge finger all around the top of the rectangular cake, then decorate with whipped cream and 'leaves' of angelica.

Poire Vefour

4-6 ripe fresh pears

VANILLA SYRUP
450 ml/$\frac{3}{4}$ pint water
225 g/8 oz sugar
few drops of vanilla essence

PASTRY CREAM
175 g/6 oz sugar
3 level tablespoons flour
2$\frac{1}{2}$ level tablespoons cornflour
450 ml/$\frac{3}{4}$ pint milk
6 egg yolks
6 level tablespoons butter
vanilla essence
Grand Marnier

GARNISH
macaroon halves
Grand Marnier
150 ml/$\frac{1}{4}$ pint double cream, whipped
sugar
crystallised violets

1. To prepare pears: peel, core and cut in half. Poach in vanilla syrup. Allow to cool.

2. To make vanilla syrup: dissolve water, sugar and vanilla essence over a low heat. Simmer until of a syrupy consistency.

3. To make pastry cream: combine sugar, flour and cornflour in the top of a double saucepan. Stir in milk and cook over direct heat, stirring all the time, until mixture comes to the boil. Boil for 1 minute. Beat egg yolks lightly and add a little hot milk mixture. Return to the saucepan with milk and sugar mixture, stirring constantly. Cook over

Walnut Butter Cookies

225 g/8 oz plain flour, sifted
100 g/4 oz granulated sugar
$\frac{1}{4}$–$\frac{1}{2}$ level teaspoon salt
$\frac{1}{4}$ level teaspoon powdered cinnamon
2 level teaspoons instant coffee
225 g/8 oz butter, diced
225 g/8 oz walnuts, chopped

1. Place flour, granulated sugar, salt, cinnamon and instant coffee into a medium-sized mixing bowl.

2. Add diced butter to a bowl and cut in with a pastry blender or knife until butter is the size of very small peas.

3. Press dough together and knead once or twice. Divide dough into small balls and then roll each ball in chopped walnuts.

4. Place balls on an ungreased baking tray about 2.5 cm/1 inch apart. Flatten each ball using the bottom of a tablespoon dipped in granulated sugar. Put a few more chopped nuts on to each side. Bake in a moderate oven (160°C, 325°F, Gas Mark 3) for 20 minutes, or until the edges are crisp and lightly browned. Cool and remove to wire tray.

hot but not boiling water, for 5 minutes, stirring constantly. Strain and allow to cool slightly. Stir in the butter and flavour to taste with vanilla essence and Grand Marnier.

4. To assemble dish: spread the bottom of a serving dish with half of the pastry cream. Allow to cool. Garnish with macaroon halves which you have sprinkled lightly with Grand Marnier. Cover lightly with remaining pastry cream and arrange poached pear halves on top.

5. Sweeten whipped cream with a little sugar and Grand Marnier, to taste. Decorate dish with cream and crystallised violets.

Cherry Cheesecake

Illustrated on page 405

Canned cherries may be used to make this cheese-cake when fresh ones are out of season, but if you do use them, you may have to use less sugar (or more lemon) in the cheese filling, and sharpen the flavour of the glaze with a little lemon juice as well.

BISCUIT BASE
175 g/6 oz digestive biscuits
50 g/2 oz softened butter

FILLING
350 g/12 oz ripe fresh cherries, halved and stoned
175 g/6 oz cream cheese
225 g/8 oz cottage cheese
4 level tablespoons castor sugar
1 teaspoon vanilla essence
finely grated rind and juice of 1 lemon
2 egg yolks, beaten
1 level tablespoon powdered gelatine
300 ml/½ pint double cream
2 egg whites

TOPPING
50 g/2 oz sugar
450 g/1 lb fresh cherries, halved and stoned
2 level tablespoons cherry jam, sieved
1 level tablespoon toasted flaked almonds

1. To make biscuit crust: crush biscuits finely and blend with softened butter. Press mixture evenly into a 20-cm/8-inch, loose-bottomed cake tin. Bake in a moderate oven (160°C, 325°F, Gas Mark 3) for 10 minutes. Remove from oven and allow to cool.

2. To make filling: put halved, stoned cherries in a saucepan with 150 ml/¼ pint water. Bring to the boil and simmer, mashing occasionally with a wooden spoon, until cherries are reduced to a pulp. Cool and drain off excess liquid.

3. Combine cheeses, sugar and vanilla essence in a large bowl. Add lemon juice, grated lemon rind and beaten egg yolks, and whisk until smooth.

4. Soften gelatine in 2 tablespoons cold water in a small cup. Place cup in a bowl of hot water and stir until gelatine has completely dissolved. Add to cheese mixture and blend thoroughly.

5. Whip cream lightly and fold into mixture, together with cherry pulp.

6. Whisk egg whites until stiff but not dry and fold gently into cheese mixture.

7. Spoon cheese mixture over biscuit base, and chill in the refrigerator until set.

8. To make topping: dissolve sugar in 300 ml/½ pint water over a low heat. Poach cherries in this syrup until just cooked, 10 to 15 minutes, depending on ripeness. Drain fruit, reserving syrup. Remove skins carefully, pat cherry halves dry and arrange them on top of chilled cheesecake, close together.

9. Add sieved cherry jam to syrup and spoon over top of cheesecake. Sprinkle with toasted flaked almonds. Serve very cold.

German Cheesecake

PASTRY BASE
175 g/6 oz plain flour
100 g/4 oz softened butter
50 g/2 oz castor sugar
1 egg yolk
¼ level teaspoon finely grated lemon rind

CHEESE FILLING
50 g/2 oz sultanas
1–2 tablespoons dark rum
225 g/8 oz cottage cheese
150 ml/¼ pint soured cream
4 eggs, separated
1 level teaspoon finely grated lemon rind
100 g/4 oz castor sugar
1 level tablespoon plain flour, sifted

1. To make pastry case: sift flour into a large bowl and make a well in the centre.

2. In another bowl, cream butter and sugar together, until light and fluffy.

3. Blend in the egg yolk and finely grated lemon rind.

4. Finally, work in flour to make a smooth, soft dough.

5. Press dough evenly over the base of a deep, loose-bottomed 18-cm/7-inch cake tin.

6. Bake in a moderate oven (160°C, 325°F, Gas Mark 3) for 20 minutes or until firm but not coloured.

7. Remove pastry base from oven and allow to cool in the tin. At the same time, reduce oven temperature to cool (140°C, 275°F, Gas Mark 1).

8. To make cheese filling: toss sultanas in rum in a small bowl and leave to infuse until required.

9. Rub cottage cheese through a fine sieve into a large bowl.

10. Beat in soured cream, egg yolks and finely grated lemon rind until smoothly blended.

11. Whisk egg whites until stiff but not dry. Then gradually whisk in castor sugar and sifted flour, and continue to whisk until meringue is stiff and glossy.

12. With a large metal spoon or spatula, carefully fold meringue into cheese mixture.

13. Spoon mixture over baked pastry case. Sprinkle surface with rum-soaked sultanas.

14. Bake cheesecake in the cool oven for 40 to 50 minutes until firm to the touch.

15. Cool, remove from tin and chill lightly before serving.

404

Summer Orange Cake
Illustrated on page 407

CAKE
6 eggs, separated
175 g/6 oz sugar
2 tablespoons water
grated rind of 1 orange
generous pinch of salt
75 g/3 oz flour
25 g/1 oz cornflour

ORANGE TOPPING
1 egg
150 g/5 oz sugar
grated rind and juice of 1 orange made up
   to 150 ml/¼ pint with water
25 g/1 oz flour
300 ml/½ pint double cream, whipped
100 g/4 oz chopped toasted almonds
candied orange slices

1. To make cake: beat egg yolks, sugar, water, orange rind and salt until light and fluffy (5 minutes in mixer at high speed). Sift flour and cornflour, and gradually blend into egg yolk mixture. Whisk egg whites until stiff but not dry and fold gently into yolk mixture. Place equal quantities of mixture into three round 20-cm/8-inch cake tins which have been buttered and lightly dusted with flour. Bake in a moderate oven (180°C, 350°F, Gas Mark 4) for 45 minutes, or until golden brown. Invert layers on wire racks. When cool, loosen edges and remove from pans.

2. To make topping: beat egg, sugar and orange rind together until foamy; add sifted flour and orange juice, and cook in the top of a double saucepan, stirring all the time, until smooth and thick. Cool. Fold in whipped cream. Spread 2 cake layers with orange topping and put together. Cover top and sides of cake with topping and pat chopped almonds firmly around the sides. Decorate with candied orange slices.

Note: Alternatively the cake may be baked in a single cake tin and the almonds omitted in the decoration.

Chocolate Pear Meringues

3 large pears
150 ml/¼ pint lemon juice
40 g/1½ oz granulated sugar
2 level tablespoons redcurrant jelly
2 egg whites
100 g/4 oz castor sugar

SAUCE
75 g/3 oz unsweetened chocolate
50 g/2 oz sugar
1–2 level teaspoons cocoa
300 ml/½ pint water
vanilla essence
2 egg yolks

1. Peel and core the pears, cut them in half and simmer gently in water with a squeeze of lemon juice. Do not allow them to break. Drain and place in a buttered ovenproof dish.

2. Put the rest of the lemon juice, granulated sugar and redcurrant jelly into saucepan and bring to the boil. Pour over the pears.

3. Whisk egg whites stiffly and fold in the castor sugar. Pipe in circles around the top of each pear, leaving cavity of each pear visible. Bake meringued pears in a cool oven (150°C, 300°F, Gas Mark 2) for 15 to 20 minutes, until lightly browned.

4. To make chocolate sauce: break up chocolate and reserve 1 small piece. Put the rest into a small pan with sugar, cocoa and water. Stir until boiling, and the chocolate has dissolved. Simmer for about 15 minutes, until syrupy. Add vanilla essence and stir in egg yolks, off the heat. Fill centres of pears with this sauce, and grate the reserved chocolate on top. Serve remaining sauce separately.

Cherry Cheesecake (see page 402)

Summer Orange Cake (see page 404)

Christmas Spice Cookies (see page 399)

Summer Almond Cake

409

CAKE
6 eggs, separated
175 g/6 oz sugar
2 tablespoons water
grated rind of 1 lemon
generous pinch of salt
75 g/3 oz flour
25 g/1 oz cornflour

LEMON TOPPING
1 egg
150 g/5 oz sugar
grated rind and juice of 1 lemon made up to 150 ml/¼ pint with water
25 g/1 oz flour
300 ml/½ pint double cream, whipped
100 g/4 oz chopped toasted almonds

1. To make cake: beat egg yolks, sugar, water, lemon rind and salt until light and fluffy (5 minutes in mixer at high speed). Sift flour and cornflour, and gradually blend into egg yolk mixture. Whisk egg whites until stiff but not dry and fold gently into yolk mixture. Place equal quantities of mixture into three 20-cm/8-inch round cake tins which have been buttered and lightly dusted with flour. Bake in a moderate oven (180°C, 350°F, Gas Mark 4) for 45 minutes, or until golden brown. Invert layers on wire racks. When cool, loosen edges and remove from pans.

2. To make topping: beat egg, sugar and lemon rind together until foamy; add sifted flour and lemon juice, and cook in the top of a double saucepan, stirring all the time, until smooth and thick. Cool. Fold in whipped cream. Spread 2 cake layers with lemon topping and put together. Cover top and sides of cake with topping and pat chopped almonds firmly around sides.

American Devil's Foodcake

3 tablespoons cocoa
3 level tablespoons sugar
3 tablespoons water
150 ml/¼ pint milk
1 teaspoon vanilla essence
100 g/4 oz butter
225 g/8 oz brown sugar
3 egg yolks
75 g/3 oz plain flour
25 g/1 oz cornflour
1 level teaspoon bicarbonate of soda
pinch of salt
3 egg whites, stiffly beaten

CHOCOLATE FILLING AND ICING
175 g/6 oz plain chocolate
8 tablespoons double cream
50 g/2 oz butter
450 g/1 lb icing sugar, sifted

1. Combine cocoa, sugar and water in the top of a double saucepan, and cook over water, stirring, until smooth and thick. Stir in milk and vanilla essence, blend well and set aside to cool.

2. Cream butter and sugar. Beat in egg yolks one at a time, then beat in chocolate mixture.

3. Sift flour and cornflour three times with bicarbonate of soda and salt, and beat into cake mixture. Fold in egg whites. Butter and lightly dust with flour three 20-cm/8-inch sandwich tins. Pour cake mixture into prepared tins and bake in a moderate oven (180°C, 350°F, Gas Mark 4) for 30 to 35 minutes.

4. To make chocolate filling and icing: melt chocolate with cream and butter in a double saucepan over hot water. When smooth, add sifted icing sugar. Mix well. Cool slightly and spread between cake layers and over top and sides of cake.

410

Basic Meat Aspic

225 g/8 oz beef bones
duck or chicken carcass, if available
1 calf's foot or 4 cleaned chicken feet
1 Spanish onion, sliced
1 large leek, sliced
2 large carrots, sliced
2 sticks celery, chopped
1.15 litres/2 pints water
salt and freshly ground black pepper
1 bouquet garni (parsley, 1 sprig thyme,
    1 bay leaf)
1 egg white
100 g/4 oz raw lean beef, chopped
1 teaspoon finely chopped chervil and
    tarragon

1. Combine first ten ingredients in a large stock-pot, bring slowly to the boil and simmer gently for about 4 hours, removing scum from time to time. Strain and cool before skimming off the fat.

2. **To clarify stock:** beat egg white lightly, and combine with chopped lean beef and herbs in the bottom of a large saucepan. Add the cooled stock and mix well, bring stock to the boil, stirring constantly. Lower heat and simmer the stock very gently for about 15 minutes. Strain through a flannel cloth while still hot. Allow to cool and then stir in one of the following:

Sherry Aspic
Stir in 4 tablespoons dry sherry.

Madeira Aspic
Stir in 4 tablespoons Madeira.

Port Aspic
Stir in 4 tablespoons port wine.

Tarragon Aspic
When clarifying aspic, add 6 additional sprigs of tarragon.

This recipe will make 1.15 litres/2 pints of jelly and will keep for several days in the refrigerator.

Basic Game Aspic
Prepare game aspic in the same way as basic meat aspic. Reinforce its flavour with 100 g/4 oz lean chopped beef and 100 g/4 oz lean dark meat from the particular game the aspic is to be served with – partridge, pheasant, grouse, etc. – when you add egg white and fresh herbs to clarify the stock. I always add a tablespoon or two of *fine champagne* to game aspic after it has been clarified to improve the flavour further.

English Bread Sauce

300 ml/½ pint milk
½ onion stuck with 1-2 cloves
50 g/2 oz fresh breadcrumbs
2-3 tablespoons butter or double cream
salt and white pepper
pinch of cayenne

1. Simmer milk and onion stuck with cloves until the milk is well flavoured.

2. Remove onion and cloves and add the bread-crumbs, which you have made fine by rubbing them through a wire sieve. Simmer sauce gently, stirring continuously, until the breadcrumbs swell and thicken the sauce.

3. Add the butter or cream, and season to taste with salt, white pepper and a pinch of cayenne.

Velouté Sauce (Chicken Velouté)

2 tablespoons butter
2 tablespoons flour
600 ml/1 pint chicken stock
salt
white peppercorns
mushroom peelings or stems
lemon juice

1. Melt butter in the top of a double saucepan, add flour and cook for a few minutes to form pale *roux*. Add boiling stock, salt and peppercorns, and cook, whisking vigorously until well blended.

2. Add mushroom peelings or stems, reduce heat and simmer gently. Stir occasionally and skim from time to time, until the sauce is reduced to

two-thirds of the original quantity and is thick but light and creamy. Flavour with lemon juice and strain through a fine sieve.

Note: This sauce forms the foundation of a number of the best white sauces, which take their distinctive names from the different ingredients added. It can be used by itself, but in that case it is much improved by the addition of a little double cream and egg yolk.

Basic Brown Sauce

2 tablespoons butter
1 small onion, thinly sliced
2 tablespoons flour
750 ml/1¼ pints well-flavoured brown stock
1 small carrot
1 small turnip
1 stick celery or ¼ teaspoon celery seed
4 mushrooms
2-4 tomatoes or 1-2 tablespoons tomato purée
1 bouquet garni (3 sprigs parsley, 1 sprig thyme, 1 bay leaf)
2 cloves
12 black peppercorns
salt

1. Heat butter in a thick-bottomed saucepan until it browns. Add thinly sliced onion and simmer stirring constantly, until golden. Stir in flour and cook, stirring constantly, for a minute longer.

2. The good colour of your sauce depends upon the thorough browning of these ingredients without allowing them to burn. When this is accomplished, remove saucepan from the heat and pour in the stock. Return to heat and stir until it comes to the boil. Allow to boil for 5 minutes, skimming all scum from the top with a perforated spoon.

3. Wash and slice carrot, turnip, celery, mushrooms and tomatoes, and add them with the *bouquet garni*, cloves and peppercorns, and salt, to taste. Simmer the sauce gently for at least 30 minutes, stirring occasionally and skimming when necessary. Strain through a fine sieve, remove fat and reheat before serving.

Brown Chaudfroid Sauce

1 tablespoon gelatine
8 tablespoons cold water
450 ml/¾ pint Basic Brown Sauce (see above)
300 ml/½ pint stock
4-6 tablespoons Madeira or dry sherry

1. Soften gelatine in cold water.

2. Combine Brown Sauce with stock and bring to the boil. Skim well, remove sauce from heat and dissolve gelatine in it. Add Madeira or dry sherry, to taste, and strain sauce through a fine sieve.

Sauce Demi-Glace

600 ml/1 pint Basic Brown Sauce (see above)
chopped stems and peelings of 6 mushrooms
6 tablespoons dry sherry or Madeira
1-2 tablespoons meat glaze

1. Simmer chopped mushroom stems and peelings in dry sherry or Madeira until liquid is reduced by half.

2. Reduce Brown Sauce to half of the original quantity. Then add meat glaze, mushrooms and juices to this mixture, and simmer over a low heat for 15 minutes. Strain before serving.

Basic Court-Bouillon

4.5 litres/8 pints water
150 ml/¼ pint wine vinegar
100 g/4 oz carrots, sliced
100 g/4 oz onions, sliced
1 handful parsley stalks
1 bay leaf
1 sprig thyme
coarse salt
12 peppercorns

1. Combine *Court-Bouillon* ingredients in a large saucepan or fish kettle and bring to the boil; skim and boil for 45 minutes.

2. Strain and cool.

412

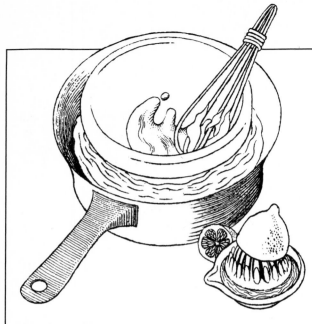

Hollandaise Sauce

1 teaspoon lemon juice
1 tablespoon cold water
salt and white pepper
100 g/4 oz soft butter
4 egg yolks
lemon juice

1. Combine lemon juice, water, salt and white pepper in the top of a double saucepan or *bain-marie*.

2. Divide butter into four equal pieces.

3. Add the egg yolks and a quarter of the butter to the liquid in the saucepan, and stir the mixture rapidly and constantly with a wire whisk over hot, but not boiling, water until the butter is melted and the mixture begins to thicken. Add the second piece of butter and continue whisking. As the mixture thickens and the second piece of butter melts, add the third piece of butter, stirring from the bottom of the pan until it is melted. Be careful not to allow the water over which the sauce is cooking to boil at any time. Add rest of butter, beating until it melts and is incorporated in the sauce.

4. Remove top part of saucepan from heat and continue to beat for 2 to 3 minutes. Replace saucepan over hot, but not boiling, water for 2 minutes more, beating constantly. By this time

the emulsion should have formed and your sauce will be rich and creamy. 'Finish' sauce with a few drops of lemon juice. Strain and serve.

Note: If at any time in the operation the mixture should curdle, beat in 1 or 2 tablespoons cold water to rebind the emulsion.

Béchamel Sauce

butter
½ onion, minced
2 tablespoons flour
600 ml/1 pint hot milk
2 tablespoons lean veal or ham, chopped
1 small sprig thyme
½ bay leaf
white peppercorns
freshly grated nutmeg

1. In a thick-bottomed saucepan, or in the top of a double saucepan, melt 2 tablespoons butter and cook onion in it over a low heat until transparent. Stir in flour and cook for a few minutes, stirring constantly, until mixture cooks through but does not take on colour.

2. Gradually add hot milk and cook, stirring constantly, until the mixture is thick and smooth.

3. In another saucepan, simmer finely chopped lean veal or ham in 1 tablespoon butter over a very low heat. Season with thyme, bay leaf, white peppercorns and grated nutmeg. Cook for 5 minutes, stirring to keep veal from browning.

4. Add veal to the sauce and cook over hot water for 45 minutes to 1 hour, stirring occasionally. When reduced to the proper consistency (two-thirds of the original quantity), strain sauce through a fine sieve into a bowl, pressing meat and onion well to extract all the liquid. Cover surface of sauce with tiny pieces of butter to keep film from forming.

Note: For a richer Béchamel, remove the sauce-pan from the heat, add 1 or 2 egg yolks, and heat through. Do not let sauce come to the boil after adding eggs or it will curdle.

Sauce Suprême

3 tablespoons butter
2 tablespoons flour
600 ml/1 pint boiling chicken stock
2 button mushrooms, finely chopped
150 ml/$\frac{1}{4}$ pint cream
lemon juice
salt
cayenne

1. Melt 2 tablespoons butter in the top of a double saucepan and blend in the flour thoroughly, being very careful not to let it colour.

2. Remove saucepan from heat and pour in the boiling stock. Cook over water, stirring constantly until it thickens slightly. Add finely chopped mushrooms and simmer for 10 to 15 minutes, stirring from time to time.

3. Strain sauce, reheat and add cream and a little lemon juice. Season to taste with salt and a little cayenne.

4. Remove sauce from the heat and whisk in the remaining butter, adding it in small pieces.
Note: If the sauce is not to be used immediately, put several dabs of butter on top to prevent a skin forming.

Celery Sauce

6 sticks celery, finely sliced
450 ml/$\frac{3}{4}$ pint well-flavoured chicken stock
2 level tablespoons butter
2 level tablespoons flour
150 ml/$\frac{1}{4}$ pint double cream
2 level tablespoons finely chopped parsley
celery salt
freshly ground black pepper
lemon juice

1. Combine finely sliced celery and chicken stock in a saucepan and cook until celery is soft. Keep warm.

2. In the top of a double saucepan, melt butter.

Add flour and cook gently over a low heat, stirring, until *roux* turns a pale golden colour.

3. Add hot celery stock (including celery) and cook over simmering water, stirring occasionally and skimming surface, until sauce has reduced to two-thirds of the original quantity.

4. Stir in double cream; add finely chopped parsley and correct seasoning, adding a little celery salt, freshly ground black pepper and lemon juice, to taste.

Extra-thick White Sauce

butter
$\frac{1}{2}$ onion, minced
2 tablespoons flour
300 ml/$\frac{1}{2}$ pint hot milk
2 tablespoons lean veal or ham, chopped
1 small sprig thyme
$\frac{1}{2}$ bay leaf
white peppercorns
freshly grated nutmeg

1. In a thick-bottomed saucepan, or in the top of a double saucepan, melt 2 tablespoons butter and cook onion in it over a low heat until transparent. Stir in flour and cook for a few minutes, stirring constantly, until mixture cooks through but does not take on colour.

2. Add hot milk and cook, stirring constantly, until the mixture is thick and smooth.

3. In another saucepan, simmer finely chopped lean veal or ham in 1 tablespoon butter over a very low heat. Season with thyme, bay leaf, white peppercorns and grated nutmeg. Cook for 5 minutes, stirring to keep veal from browning.

4. Add veal to the sauce and cook over hot water for 45 minutes to 1 hour, stirring occasionally. When reduced to the proper consistency (two-thirds of the original quantity), strain sauce through a fine sieve into a bowl, pressing meat and onion well to extract all the liquid. Cover surface of sauce with tiny pieces of butter to keep film from forming.

413

Cream Sauce

3 tablespoons butter
½ onion, minced
2 tablespoons flour
600 ml/1 pint hot milk
2 tablespoons lean veal or ham, chopped
1 small sprig thyme
½ bay leaf
white peppercorns
freshly grated nutmeg
150 ml/¼ pint fresh cream
lemon juice

1. In a thick-bottomed saucepan, or in the top of a double saucepan, melt 2 tablespoons butter and cook onion in it over a low heat until transparent. Stir in flour and cook for a few minutes, stirring constantly, until mixture cooks through but does not take on colour.

2. Add hot milk and cook, stirring constantly, until the mixture is thick and smooth.

3. In another saucepan, simmer finely chopped lean veal or ham in 1 tablespoon butter over a very low heat. Season with thyme, bay leaf, white peppercorns and grated nutmeg. Cook for 5 minutes, stirring to keep veal from browning.

4. Add veal to the sauce and cook over hot water for 45 minutes to 1 hour, stirring occasionally. When reduced to two-thirds of the original quantity, strain sauce through a fine sieve into a bowl, pressing meat and onion well to extract all the liquid. Add fresh cream and a few drops lemon juice. Cover surface of sauce with tiny pieces of butter to keep film from forming.

English Parsley Sauce

1 tablespoon butter
1 tablespoon flour
300 ml/½ pint milk
2 tablespoons finely chopped parsley
salt and white pepper
lemon juice

1. Melt butter in the top of a double saucepan;

stir in the flour and mix with a wooden spoon until smooth. Cook for a few minutes over water but do not allow *roux* to colour.

2. Add milk, heated to boiling point, and cook, stirring constantly, until boiling. Add finely chopped parsley, season to taste with salt and white pepper, and simmer for 2 to 3 minutes longer. Just before serving, add lemon juice, to taste.

Note: A richer sauce can be made by using Béchamel or Velouté Sauce as a foundation.

Béarnaise Sauce

4 sprigs tarragon, chopped
4 sprigs parsley, chopped
1 level tablespoon chopped shallots
2-3 crushed peppercorns
2 tablespoons tarragon vinegar
150 ml/¼ pint dry white wine
3 egg yolks
1 tablespoon water
soft butter, diced
salt
lemon juice
cayenne

1. Reserve 1 level tablespoon each chopped tarragon and parsley, and combine remainder with chopped shallots, crushed peppercorns, vinegar and white wine in the top of a double saucepan. Cook over a high heat until liquid is reduced to approximately 2 tablespoons (practically a glaze). Cool to lukewarm.

2. Beat egg yolks with water and add to the juices in the top of the double saucepan. Stir briskly over hot, but not boiling, water with a wire whisk until light and fluffy. Never let water in bottom of saucepan begin to boil, or sauce will not 'take'.

3. Gradually add butter to egg mixture, whisking briskly as sauce begins to thicken. Continue adding butter and stirring until sauce is thick. Season to taste with salt, lemon juice and cayenne.

4. Strain · through a fine sieve, add reserved chopped tarragon leaves and parsley, and serve.

Mushroom Sauce Suprême

5 level tablespoons butter
2 level tablespoons flour
600 ml/1 pint boiling chicken stock
100 g/4 oz button mushrooms, finely
   chopped
100 g/4 oz button mushrooms, thinly sliced
150 ml/¼ pint double cream
Madeira
salt and cayenne

1. Melt 4 level tablespoons butter in the top of a double saucepan and blend in the flour thoroughly, being very careful not to let it colour.

2. Remove saucepan from heat and pour in the boiling stock. Cook over water, stirring constantly, until it thickens slightly. Add finely chopped mushrooms and simmer for 10 to 15 minutes, stirring from time to time.

3. Strain sauce, forcing mushrooms and onion through a fine sieve. Add sliced mushrooms, double cream and Madeira, to taste, and cook over a low heat until mushrooms are tender. Season to taste with salt and a little cayenne.

4. Remove sauce from the heat and whisk in the remaining butter, adding it in small pieces.

If the sauce is not to be used immediately, put several dabs of butter on top to prevent a skin forming.

Vinaigrette Sauce

1 tablespoon lemon juice
1-2 tablespoons wine vinegar
¼-½ level teaspoon dry mustard
coarse salt and freshly ground black pepper
6-8 tablespoons olive oil

1. Mix together lemon juice, wine vinegar and dry mustard, and season to taste with coarse salt and freshly ground black pepper.

2. Add olive oil, and beat with a fork until the mixture emulsifies.

Italian Tomato Sauce

2 Spanish onions, finely chopped
2 cloves garlic, finely chopped
4 tablespoons olive oil
6 tablespoons Italian tomato purée
1 (793-g/1 lb 12-oz) can Italian peeled
   tomatoes
2 bay leaves
4 tablespoons finely chopped parsley
¼ teaspoon oregano
1 small strip lemon peel
6 tablespoons dry white wine
salt and freshly ground black pepper
1-2 tablespoons Worcestershire sauce

1. Sauté finely chopped onions and garlic in olive oil in a large, thick-bottomed frying pan until transparent and soft but not coloured.

2. Stir in tomato purée and continue to cook for a minute or two, stirring constantly. Pour in Italian peeled tomatoes with their juice and add bay leaves, parsley, oregano and lemon peel. Add dry white wine, an equal quantity of water, and salt and freshly ground black pepper, to taste. Simmer gently, stirring from time to time, for 1 to 2 hours.

3. Just before serving, stir in Worcestershire sauce, to taste.

416

Raw Tomato Sauce

(Excellent for pasta and fish dishes.)

1.25 kg/2½ lb ripe tomatoes
1 large Spanish onion
1 clove garlic
3 tablespoons olive oil
**3 level tablespoons finely chopped fresh
   basil**
**3 level tablespoons finely chopped fresh
   chives**
salt and freshly ground black pepper

1. Quarter tomatoes. Peel and quarter onion. Peel garlic and cut in half.

2. Place onion and garlic pieces in an electric blender with olive oil and blend until finely chopped. Add quartered tomatoes and finely chopped herbs and blend until sauce is smooth. Season with salt and freshly ground black pepper, to taste. Chill until ready to use.

French Tomato Sauce

2 level tablespoons butter
4 level tablespoons finely chopped ham
1 small carrot, finely chopped
1 small turnip, finely chopped
1 onion, finely chopped
1 stick celery, finely chopped
6-8 ripe tomatoes, sliced
2 level tablespoons tomato purée
1 level tablespoon flour
**1 bouquet garni (1 sprig each thyme,
   marjoram and parsley)**
300 ml/½ pint well-flavoured beef stock
salt and freshly ground black pepper
lemon juice
sugar

1. Melt butter in a thick-bottomed saucepan; add finely chopped ham and vegetables, and sauté mixture until onion is transparent and soft.

2. Stir in sliced tomatoes and tomato purée and simmer for a minute or two. Sprinkle with flour and mix well. Then add *bouquet garni* and beef stock, and simmer gently, stirring continuously,

until sauce comes to the boil. Skim sauce; season to taste with salt and freshly ground black pepper, and simmer gently for 30 minutes, stirring from time to time. If the sauce becomes too thick, add a little more stock.

3. Strain sauce through a fine sieve. Reheat and add lemon juice and sugar, to taste.

English Onion Sauce

2 Spanish onions, quartered
4 level tablespoons butter
2 tablespoons flour
½ chicken stock cube, crumbled
150 ml/¼ pint milk or single cream
salt and freshly ground black pepper
pinch of nutmeg

1. Boil onions until tender and drain well, reserving onion liquor. Chop onions finely. Reserve.

2. Melt butter in the top of a double saucepan. Remove pan from heat, stir in flour and ½ chicken stock cube, crumbled; return to heat and cook gently for 3 to 5 minutes, stirring constantly, until the flour is cooked through. Add milk (or single cream), heated to boiling point, and cook over water, stirring constantly, until sauce starts to thicken.

3. Add chopped onions, 150 ml/¼ pint reserved onion liquor, and salt, freshly ground black pepper and nutmeg, to taste. Heat through.

Mayonnaise

2 egg yolks
salt and freshly ground black pepper
½ teaspoon Dijon mustard
lemon juice
300 ml/½ pint olive oil

1. Place egg yolks (make sure gelatinous thread of the egg is removed), salt, freshly ground black pepper and mustard in a bowl. Twist a cloth wrung out in very cold water round the bottom of the bowl to keep it steady and cool. Using a wire whisk, fork or wooden spoon, beat the yolks to a smooth paste.

2. Add a few drops of lemon juice (the acid helps the emulsion), and beat in about a quarter of the oil, drop by drop. Add a little more lemon juice to the mixture and then, a little more quickly now, add more oil, beating all the while. Continue adding oil and beating until the sauce is of a good thick consistency. Correct seasoning (more salt, freshly ground black pepper and lemon juice) as desired. If you are making the mayonnaise a day before using it, stir in 1 tablespoon boiling water when it is of the desired consistency. This will keep it from turning or separating.

Note: If the mayonnaise should curdle, break another egg yolk into a clean bowl and gradually beat the curdled mayonnaise into it. Your mayonnaise will begin to 'take' immediately.

If mayonnaise is to be used for a salad, thin it down considerably with dry white wine, vinegar or lemon juice. If it is to be used for coating meat, poultry or fish, add a little liquid aspic to stiffen it.

If sauce is to be kept for several hours before serving, cover the bowl with a cloth wrung out in very cold water to prevent a skin from forming on the top.

Aïoli Sauce

4 fat cloves of garlic per person
1 egg yolk for each 2 persons
salt
olive oil
freshly ground black pepper
lemon juice

1. Take 4 fat cloves of garlic per person and 1 egg yolk for each 2 persons. Crush garlic to a smooth paste in a mortar with a little salt; blend in egg yolks until mixture is a smooth, homogeneous mass.

2. Now add olive oil, drop by drop at first, a thin, fine trickle later, whisking the mixture as you would for a mayonnaise. The *aïoli* will thicken gradually until it reaches a stiff, firm consistency. The exact quantity of oil is, of course, determined by the number of egg yolks used.

3. Season to taste with additional salt, a little pepper and lemon juice. This sauce is served chilled, in a bowl. Guests help themselves.

Aïoli Sauce Without Eggs

4–6 cloves garlic
1 boiled potato, chilled
lemon juice
salt and freshly ground black pepper
olive oil

1. Peel garlic and boiled potato.

2. Pound garlic in a mortar until smooth; add potato and pound until it is well mixed with garlic. Add a little lemon juice, salt and freshly ground black pepper, to taste.

3. Then, drop by drop, whisk in olive oil as you would for mayonnaise, until *aïoli* is thick and smooth. Correct seasoning and serve.

Brandy Sauce *Makes 300 ml/½ pint*
Brandy Butter *Makes 225 g/8 oz*
Hot Chocolate Sauce *Makes 450 ml/¾ pint*

418

Brandy Sauce

4 egg yolks
4 level tablespoons double cream
4 tablespoons brandy
2 level tablespoons castor sugar

1. Combine all the ingredients in the top of a double saucepan. Add 4 tablespoons water.

2. Place pan over lightly simmering water and whisk for 6 to 8 minutes to make a thick, frothy sauce. Do not allow sauce to boil or it will curdle.

3. Serve warm or cold.

Brandy Butter

100 g/4 oz butter
100 g/4 oz castor sugar
2 tablespoons brandy

1. Soften butter with a wooden spoon, then beat until smooth and fluffy.

2. Put aside 1 level tablespoon castor sugar and gradually add remainder to creamed butter, beating vigorously until mixture is very fluffy and almost white.

3. Soak remaining sugar in brandy. Incorporate into butter cream a little at a time, and beat until smooth again. Chill until firm.

Hot Chocolate Sauce

50 g/2 oz bitter chocolate
300 ml/½ pint water
225 g/8 oz sugar
1 tablespoon cornflour
salt
2 tablespoons butter
2 tablespoons cognac
½ teaspoon very finely grated orange rind

1. Combine chocolate with water and melt over a gentle heat. When smooth add sugar, cornflour and salt. Cook, stirring continually, until sugar is dissolved and sauce is thick. Allow to boil for 3 minutes, then add butter and cognac and stir until smooth.

2. Remove from heat and add finely grated orange rind.

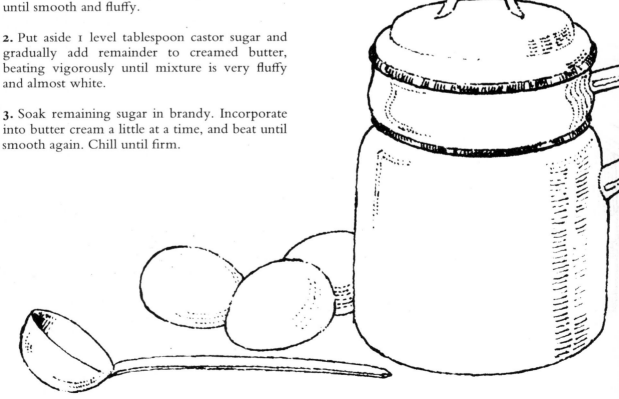

Apricot Sauce *Makes 300 ml/½ pint*
Vanilla Custard Sauce *Makes 450 ml/¾ pint*
Lemon or Strawberry Hard Sauce *Makes 450 g/1 lb*

Apricot Sauce

6-8 canned apricot halves
sugar
1 teaspoon cornflour
150 ml/¼ pint water
1-2 tablespoons Grand Marnier
2-3 drops of red food colouring

1. Make apricot purée by sieving canned apricots through a fine sieve or by liquidising in an electric blender, and add sugar to taste.

2. Combine purée with cornflour which you have dissolved in cold water, and heat in the top of a double saucepan until it boils and thickens. Add Grand Marnier and a few drops of red food colouring, and simmer for 2 to 3 minutes longer.

Vanilla Custard Sauce

450 ml/¾ pint milk
½ teaspoon vanilla essence
4 tablespoons sugar
4 egg yolks
¼ teaspoon salt

1. Simmer milk for 5 minutes then stir in vanilla essence.

2. Combine sugar, egg yolks and salt in a mixing bowl, and beat until fluffy and lemon-coloured.

3. Pour a little of the hot milk into the egg and sugar mixture, blend well, and then stir into the hot milk. Heat slowly in the top of a double saucepan, stirring constantly, until the mixture coats the back of a spoon. Serve warm.

To make Ginger Sauce: add 4 level tablespoons of finely chopped preserved ginger, and ginger syrup, to taste.

Lemon or Strawberry Hard Sauce

100 g/4 oz butter
350 g/12 oz icing sugar
grated rind and juice of 1 lemon or
    100 g/4 oz mashed strawberries

1. Work butter until soft, stir in icing sugar gradually and beat until smooth.

2. Stir in grated rind and juice of lemon, or mashed strawberries, and mix until smooth. Add more sugar if desired. Should sauce separate after standing, beat until well blended.

420

Shortcrust Pastry for Savoury Tarts and Pies

225 g/8 oz plain flour
1 teaspoon castor sugar
squeeze of lemon juice
pinch of salt
100 g/4 oz butter, diced
1-3 tablespoons iced water

1. Sift flour and sugar into a mixing bowl. Add lemon juice, salt and butter. Cover well with the flour and rub together lightly with the tips of the fingers until the mixture resembles fine bread-crumbs. While rubbing, keep lifting the flour well up in the bowl, so that air may mix with it and the butter is not made too soft.

2. When pastry is thoroughly mixed, make a well in the centre and add cold water very gradually, mixing with one hand or a knife. Add very little water or pastry will be tough instead of short.

3. Sprinkle the pastry board with flour. Lay the dough on it and work lightly with the hands until free from cracks. Flour a rolling pin. Press down the pastry and then with sharp quick strokes roll pastry on one side only to the thickness required. Roll pastry lightly and try to press equally with both hands. Never allow pastry to stick on the board, but lift occasionally on the rolling pin and dust some flour underneath. If anything has stuck to the board, scrape it off carefully with a knife before beginning to roll again. Always sprinkle flour over board and pastry through a flour sifter to make it finer and lighter, using as little flour as possible for this, as too much tends to make the pastry hard. If the rolling pin sticks to the pastry, dust with a little flour and brush it off again lightly with a small brush kept for this purpose.

4. To bake pastry: a fairly hot oven is required for pastry, for if it is not hot enough the butter will melt and run out before the starch grains in the flour have had time to burst and absorb it. If the oven is too hot, however, the pastry will burn before it has risen properly. When baking pastry, open and close the door as gently as possible and never more often than is absolutely necessary. If pastry becomes too brown before it has cooked sufficiently, cover it over with a piece of aluminium foil or a double sheet of paper that has been lightly sprinkled with water. If the pastry is not to be used at once when taken from the oven, allow it to cool slowly in the warm kitchen. Light pastry becomes heavy if cooled too quickly.

TO BAKE 'BLIND'
Line a pie tin with pastry, fluting the edges. Chill. Prick bottom with a fork and cover bottom of pastry with a piece of waxed paper or aluminium foil. Cover with dried beans and bake in a hot oven (230°C, 450°F, Gas Mark 8) for about 15 minutes, just long enough to set the crust without browning it. Remove beans and paper or foil and allow to cool. Fill with desired filling and bake in a moderately hot oven (190°C, 375°F, Gas Mark 5) until done. The beans can be reserved in a storage jar and used again.

TO BAKE PASTRY CASE ONLY
Bake 'blind' as above for 15 minutes. Remove beans and foil, lower heat to 190°C, 375°F, Gas Mark 5 and bake for 10 to 15 minutes. If crust becomes too brown at edges, cover rim with a little crumpled foil.

RICH BISCUIT CRUST
A richer pastry can be made in the same way, using 150-175 g/5-6 oz butter and adding the yolk of 1 egg beaten with a little water for mixing.

Puff Pastry (Pâte Feuilletée)

225 g/8 oz plain flour
generous pinch of salt
squeeze of lemon juice
225 g/8 oz butter, finely diced
1-3 tablespoons iced water

1. Sift flour and salt into a clean, dry mixing bowl, and add lemon juice and a quarter of the diced butter. Rub together lightly with the tips of your fingers until the mixture resembles fine bread-crumbs. Then mix with just enough iced water to make a rather stiff dough. Turn this out on to a floured board and work it well with the hands until it no longer sticks to the fingers and is perfectly smooth.

2. Roll it rather thinly into a square or round shape.

3. The remaining butter to be used should be as nearly as possible of the same consistency as the dough, so work it with your hands into a neat thin cake and place it in the centre of the dough. Fold dough up rather loosely, and flatten the folds with a rolling pin. Then roll the pastry out into a long, narrow strip, being careful not to allow the butter to break through.

4. Fold dough exactly in three. Press down the folds and lay the pastry aside in a cool place for at least 15 minutes. This is called giving the pastry one 'turn'; seven of these operations are usually required for puff pastry.

5. The next time the pastry is rolled, place it with the joins at your right-hand side and the open end towards you. Give it two turns this time, and again put it in the refrigerator for at least 15 minutes. Repeat this until the pastry has had seven rolls in all, one roll or turn the first time, and after that two each time with an interval between. The object of cooling the pastry between rolls is to keep the butter and flour in the distinct and separate layers (in which the rolling and folding has arranged them), and on which the lightness of your pastry depends. When rolling, keep the pressure of your hands on the rolling pin as even as possible.

6. After you have given the pastry its last roll, put it in the refrigerator for 30 minutes before using it, then roll to the required thickness.

Note: This pastry will keep for several days in the refrigerator if wrapped in a piece of waxed paper or in a damp cloth.

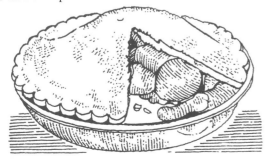

Flaky Pastry

275 g/10 oz plain flour
generous pinch of salt
squeeze of lemon juice
200 g/7 oz butter
1–3 tablespoons iced water

1. Sift the flour and salt into a clean, dry bowl and add lemon juice.

2. Divide butter into 4 equal parts. Take one of these pieces and rub it into the flour with the tips of the fingers until mixture is quite free from lumps. Then add just enough iced water to form dough into one lump. Mix with hands as lightly as possible and turn out on to a floured board. Knead lightly until free from cracks, and then roll out into a long narrow strip, rather less than 5 mm/¼ inch in thickness.

3. Take one of the remaining portions of butter, and with the point of a knife put it in even rows of small pieces all over the pastry, leaving a 2.5-cm/1-inch margin without butter round the edges. (If butter is too hard, work it on a plate with a knife before commencing.)

4. Now flour the surface lightly and fold the pastry exactly in three. Turn the pastry half round, bringing the joins to the right-hand side, and press the folds down sharply with the rolling pin so as to enclose some air.

5. Roll the pastry out again into a long narrow strip, and proceed as before until the two remaining portions of butter have been used. If the butter becomes too soft during the rolling, refrigerate the pastry for a short time before completing the process.

6. The last time, roll the pastry out to the desired thickness, and if it requires widening, turn it across the board and roll across. Never roll in a slanting direction, or the lightness of the pastry will suffer.

Note: This pastry is not quite as rich as puff pastry. It may be kept for several days in the refrigerator if wrapped in waxed paper or in a damp cloth.

Index

430